ELIZABETH I AND HER CIRCLE

Elizabeth I
and Her Circle

SUSAN DORAN

OXFORD
UNIVERSITY PRESS

UNIVERSITY PRESS

Great Clarendon Street, Oxford, OX2 6DP,
United Kingdom

Oxford University Press is a department of the University of Oxford.
It furthers the University's objective of excellence in research, scholarship,
and education by publishing worldwide. Oxford is a registered trade mark of
Oxford University Press in the UK and in certain other countries

First Edition published in 2015

Impression: 1

Published in the United States of America by Oxford University Press
198 Madison Avenue, New York, NY 10016, United States of America

British Library Cataloguing in Publication Data
Data available

Library of Congress Control Number: 2014946127

ISBN 978-0-19-957495-7

Printed in Italy by
L.E.G.O. S.p.A.

For Hugo when he is older

ACKNOWLEDGEMENTS

I owe a great debt to friends and colleagues who have read and commented most helpfully on part or all of this book: Joanna Coates, Alan Doran, Alexandra Gajda, Paulina Kewes, Judith Richards, and Corinna Streckfuss. Additionally, Paulina has my deep gratitude for her encouragement, advice, and generosity in sending me essays and articles that I would otherwise have missed, while I cannot thank Corinna enough for checking the text and the many footnotes, and recommending amendments. All remaining mistakes are of course mine. I am also very grateful to Natalie Mears and Charlotte Merton, who kindly sent me copies of their important unpublished theses, which I have cited frequently, and Caroline McManus, who emailed me her article in the Ben Jonson Journal. Caroline Warman translated a difficult French passage, for which I also offer thanks.

I am immensely grateful to Jesus College Oxford for the award of a Major Research Grant that enabled me to spend a month at the Huntington Library, San Marino, California. At the library, the then archivist Mary Robinson was particularly helpful, as was Edward Rinderle in arranging the photographic reproduction of HM 68350. The kind offer of accommodation by Carole Levin near the Folger Shakespeare Library allowed me to consult their collection.

Finally, I must thank Luciana O' Flaherty and Matthew Cotton at Oxford University Press for commissioning the book, accepting the changes to my original proposal, and allowing me more time than originally agreed. Their support has been very much appreciated. I would also like express my thanks to everyone in the production team at OUP.

CONTENTS

List of Plates   xi
Genealogical Chart   xiii
Chronology   xv
Conventions   xix

Introduction   1

PART 1 KIN

1 Parents and Siblings   13
2 The Suffolk Cousins   43
3 Mary Queen of Scots   65
4 James VI of Scotland   90

PART 2 COURTIERS

5 'Eyes': Robert Dudley, Earl of Leicester   117
6 'Lids': Sir Christopher Hatton   143
7 Her 'moste humble vassall': Robert Devereux,
     Second Earl of Essex   165
8 The Women who Served   193

PART 3 COUNCILLORS

9 'Sir Spirit': Sir William Cecil, Lord Burghley   219
10 The 'Moor': Sir Francis Walsingham   247
11 The 'Pygmy': Sir Robert Cecil   276

     Epilogue   303

Abbreviations   309
Notes   311
Select Bibliography   360
Picture Acknowledgements   380
Index   381

LIST OF PLATES

1. Portrait of Anne Boleyn, late sixteenth century
2. The family of Henry VIII, *c.* 1544
3. Elizabeth as a princess, aged about 13, *c.* 1546
4. Lady Katherine Grey holding her son, Edward, by Lievine Teerlink
5. Double portrait of Mary Queen of Scots and James VI, dated 1583
6. 'The most ancient and famouse pedygrye' of the earl of Leicester
7. Robert Dudley, earl of Leicester
8. Elizabeth I, 1575
9. Preparatory sketches of Elizabeth and Leicester by Federigo Zuccaro
10. The 'Sieve Portrait' of Elizabeth
11. Sir Christopher Hatton
12. 'Young Man among Roses', a miniature by Nicholas Hilliard
13. Sir Walter Raleigh attributed to 'H', 1588
14. The second earl of Essex before Cadiz by Marcus Gheeraerts the younger
15. A lady called 'Countess of Nottingham' by John de Critz the elder
16. William Cecil, Lord Burghley, on his mule
17. 'The Family of Henry VIII' attributed to Lucas de Heere
18. Sir Robert Cecil by John de Critz
19. 'The Rainbow Portrait' attributed to Isaac Oliver

GENEALOGICAL CHART

Genealogical Chart

d. = died
ex. = executed
m = murdered
Only characters relevant to the book are shown.

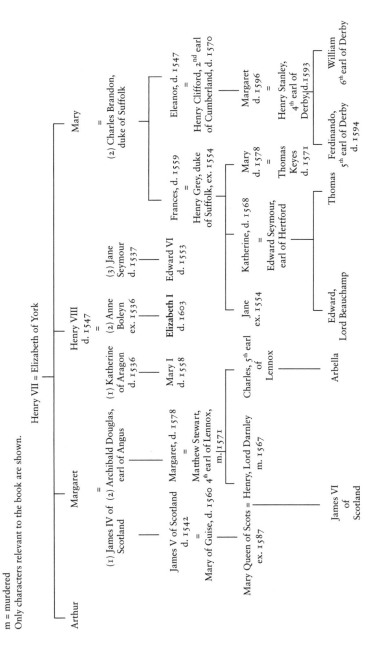

Henry VII = Elizabeth of York

Arthur   Margaret   Henry VIII   Mary
                      d. 1547

(1) James IV of   (2) Archibald Douglas,   (1) Katherine   (2) Anne   (3) Jane   (2) Charles Brandon,
Scotland   earl of Angus   of Aragon   Boleyn   Seymour   duke of Suffolk
                                             d. 1536   ex. 1536   d. 1537

James V of Scotland   Margaret, d. 1578   Mary I   Elizabeth I   Edward VI   Frances, d. 1559   Eleanor, d. 1547
d. 1542   =   d. 1558   d. 1603   d. 1553   =   =
=   Matthew Stewart,   Henry Grey, duke   Henry Clifford, 2nd earl
Mary of Guise, d. 1560 4th earl of Lennox,   of Suffolk, ex. 1554 of Cumberland, d. 1570
                       m. 1571

Mary Queen of Scots = Henry, Lord Darnley   Charles, 5th earl   Jane   Katherine, d. 1568   Mary   Margaret
ex. 1587   m. 1567   of   ex. 1554   =   d. 1578   d. 1596
                                             Lennox   Edward Seymour,   =   =
                                                                              earl of Hertford   Thomas   Henry Stanley,
                                                                                                    Keyes   4th earl of
                                                                                                    d. 1571   Derby, d. 1593

James VI   Arbella   Edward,   Thomas   Ferdinando,   William
of   Lord Beauchamp   5th earl of Derby 6th earl of Derby
Scotland   d. 1594

CHRONOLOGY

1558   (17 Nov.) Accession of Elizabeth I.

1559   (Jan.) Coronation of queen. (Apr.) Treaty of Cateau-Cambrésis ending war with France. Re-establishment of Protestant Church in England. (May) Protestant rebellion in Scotland. (July) Accession of Francis II to French throne.

1560   (Feb.) Treaty of Berwick. (July) Treaty of Edinburgh ending war in Scotland. (Aug.) Protestantism established in Scotland. (Dec.) Death of Francis II of France.

1561   (Aug.) Mary Queen of Scots' return to Scotland.

1562   (July) Massacre of Vassy. First French civil war. (Sept.) Treaty of Hampton Court with French protestants. (Oct.) Elizabeth ill with smallpox. English occupation of Le Havre.

1563   (Jan.–Apr.) Succession debates in parliament. (July) Surrender of Le Havre.

1564   (Apr.) Treaty of Troyes with France. Resumption of archduke marriage negotiations.

1565   (July) Mary's marriage to Lord Darnley.

1566   (Summer) Unrest in the Netherlands. (Oct.–Dec.) Succession debates in parliament.

1567   (Feb.) Darnley's murder. (July) Mary's imprisonment and deposition. (Aug.) Alva's arrival in the Netherlands. (Sept.) Outbreak of second war of religion in France.

1568   (May) Mary's flight to England. (Dec.) Breach with Spain.

1569   (Jan.) Suspension of Anglo-Spanish trade. (July) Outbreak of first Desmond rebellion. (Oct.) Rising of the northern earls.

1570   (Jan.) Assassination of Regent Moray. (Feb.) Papal bull of excommunication. (May) Restart of negotiations for Mary's restoration. (Aug.) Peace of St-Germain between Charles IX and Huguenots.

1571   Marriage negotiations with Henry, duke of Anjou. Ridolfi plot.

1572   (Apr.) Anglo-French treaty of Blois. Reopening of revolt against Spain in Holland and Zeeland. (Aug.) St Bartholomew massacre of protestants in France. (Nov.) Election of Morton as Scottish regent.

1573   (Apr.) Capture of Edinburgh Castle for regent.

1574   (May) Accession of Henry III of France. (Aug.) Treaty of Bristol ending trade dispute with Spain. (During year) Arrival of first Catholic priests from Douai.

1575   (July) Edmund Grindal's translation to see of Canterbury.

1576   (Feb.) Offer of sovereignty of Holland and Zeeland to Elizabeth. (May) Establishment of Catholic League in France. (June) Queen's ban on prophesyings. (Nov.) Sack of Antwerp by Spanish troops. Pacification of Ghent.

1577   (Feb.) Perpetual edict. (May) Suspension of Grindal. (July) Truce broken in the Netherlands. (Dec.) Drake's departure on voyage resulting in circumnavigation of the globe.

1578   (Jan.) Don John's victory at Gembloux. (Mar.) End of Morton's regency. (July) Suggestion of Anjou match.

1579   (Jan.) Arrival of Jean de Simier to negotiate Anjou marriage. Division of Netherlands into two unions (Arras and Utrecht). (July) Rebellion in Ireland. (Oct.) Death of Don John.

1580   (June) Arrival in England of first Jesuits, Robert Persons and Edmund Campion. (Aug.) Spanish conquest of Portugal. (Sept.) Drake's return to Plymouth. (Nov.) Massacre of Spanish and papal troops at Smerwick, Ireland. (Dec.) Morton's arrest.

1581   (Apr.) French embassy to England. (June) Morton's execution. (July) Dutch declaration of independence from Spain. (July–Aug.) Negotiations for French alliance. (Oct.) The 'association' initiative.

1582   (Feb.) Anjou's arrival in the Netherlands as duke of Brabant. (Aug.) Ruthven raid

1583   (June) James's escape from Ruthven raiders. (Aug.) Appointment of John Whitgift as archbishop of Canterbury. Beginning of crackdown on nonconforming clergy. (Oct.) Revelation of Throckmorton plot.

1584   (Apr.) Ruthvenite lords' failed attempt to capture James VI and oust Arran. (June) Death of Anjou. (July) Murder of William of Orange. (Oct.) Bond of association. Presbyterian campaign in parliament. (Dec.) Treaty of Joinville allying Spain to French Catholic League.

1585   (Feb.) William Parry's arrest. (Mar.) Act for the Queen's Surety. (Aug.) Treaties of Nonsuch. (Nov.) Successful coup against Arran. (Dec.) Leicester's arrival in the Netherlands.

1586   (July) Treaty of Berwick. Babington plot. (Sept.) Battle of Zutphen. (Oct.) Mary's trial.

1587   (Feb.) Mary's execution.

1588   (May) Peace talks at Bourbourg. (July) Defeat of the Spanish Armada. (Oct.) Publication of first four 'Marprelate' tracts.

1589   (Apr.) Embarkation of Portugal expedition. (Nov.) Henry III's assassination. Disputed succession of Henry IV.

1590   Fighting in France and Netherlands.

1591   (May) Presbyterian leaders brought before Star Chamber. (Nov.) Start of siege of Rouen. Proclamation against Catholics.

1592   (Apr.) Relief of Rouen.

1593   (Jan.) Investigation of 'Spanish blanks'. (July) Henry IV's conversion to Catholicism.

1594   (Feb.) Henry IV's coronation.

1595   Tyrone's rebellion in Ulster.

1596   (Apr.) Fall of Calais. (June) Attack on Cadiz. (Oct.) Triple Alliance of England, France, and the Dutch.

1597   (Summer) The Islands' voyage.

1598   (May) Treaty of Vervins. Philip II's cession of Netherlands to his daughter Isabella and Archduke Albert. (Aug.) Anglo-Dutch treaty. Rout of English army in battle of Yellow Ford in Ulster. (Sept.) Philip III's accession.

1599   (Mar.) Essex campaign in Ireland. (May) Peace talks at Boulogne. (Aug.) Armada scare.

1601   (Feb.) Essex rising.

1602   (Jan.) Defeat of Spanish troops and Tyrone at Kinsale.

1603   (24 Mar.) Elizabeth's death.

CONVENTIONS

In quotations, I have kept the spellings as they appear in manuscripts and printed sources with only a few changes. For easier reading, I have converted the u to v, j to i, and i to j where appropriate. Double fs are made singular, also where appropriate. Punctuation and capitalization, however, have been modernized, following the conventions of the text. Words abbreviated or compressed in the original texts are given in full.

Foreign names and places are anglicized. The Netherlands refers to the geographical area of present-day Belgium and Holland; the United Provinces is the name used for the northern Netherlands after 1581, when it broke away from Spanish rule. The south continued to be called the Netherlands.

Many sources used here are now online. I have used the 'state papers online' and 'Cecil Papers online', and cite the folio numbers provided there, unless they seem to me a definite error. I have also given the document number and dates of online calendars to facilitate searches.

Old Style dating (following the Julian calendar) is used throughout, but the year is assumed to start on 1 January not 25 March—Lady Day—as was customary in this period.

Introduction

This book is about relationships: the personal and political relationships of Queen Elizabeth I with the men and women in her circle: her 'near' family, some of her most favoured courtiers, and leading privy councillors. Embedded in the interactions between the queen and these individuals lie some riveting stories that have fired the imagination of later novelists, dramatists, and film-makers, and have been largely responsible for the manifold popular images of the queen, whether the frustrated virgin, ruthless politician, brilliant ruler, or vain queen bee. Equally important, Elizabeth's relationships were pivotal to the substance and style of national political life in her reign. Sixteenth-century monarchical government operated through the interplay of individual personalities rather than through bureaucratic institutions and structures.[1] Therefore, only by studying the nature, contexts, and contemporary representations of Elizabeth's relationships can we begin to understand the high politics and culture of her reign; and high politics impacts upon popular politics and, indeed, on everyday life.

Other books purporting to be about Elizabeth's relationships offer a biographical and chronological history of her life and reign.[2] Here, I choose a thematic structure, devoting each chapter to the queen's communications and interactions with an individual or a group of men and women who were key figures within her circle. This approach produces new and multiple perspectives on the reign: we learn not only about how the queen related to her kin, courtiers, and councillors but also how they viewed and dealt with her. Each chapter tells its own story, but to avoid repetition there is cross-referencing in the notes from one story to another. I have also produced a timeline of key political and international events for easy reference.

Elizabeth's kin is the subject of Part 1. As will be seen in Chapter 1, her parents and siblings were significant in affecting the course of her early life, moulding her character, and influencing her policies and self-image as queen. Additionally, after Elizabeth's accession to the throne in November 1558, her Boleyn cousins—the many descendants of Anne Boleyn's sister Mary—clustered in the court, serving the queen in a variety of roles. Although Mary Boleyn (later Carey) was the mother of only two, her daughter Katherine—married to Sir Francis Knollys—had thirteen children who survived childhood, while Mary's son Henry and his wife Anne had twelve offspring.[3] The place of all these Boleyn cousins in Elizabeth's affections (with the later exception of Lettice Knollys) is evident from the honours they received and the way the queen addressed them: her 'well-beloved' cousin, Henry Carey, Lord Hunsdon, for example, she called 'Harry', and his son Robert was affectionately dubbed 'Robin'.[4] The influence of these Boleyn kin will be seen throughout the book.

Elizabeth's paternal line was less prolific, but, because they were of royal blood, the progeny of her aunts Margaret and Mary (see the 'Genealogical Chart') created political problems that dominated the queen's reign and take up three chapters of Part 1. The Suffolk cousins of Chapter 2 were the grandchildren of Mary, the younger sister of Henry VIII. Mary Queen of Scots and James VI of Scotland—the subjects of the next two chapters—descended from Margaret, Henry's elder sister and her first husband, James IV. Besides these close kin, Elizabeth had more distant cousins that stretched into the many aristocratic and gentry families of England. Although most of them did not share an intimacy with the queen based on their familial relationship, their kinship ties helped create cohesiveness within the ruling elite.[5] Their stories need to be told, but are outside the scope of this book.

The second group in Elizabeth's circle—discussed in Part 2—are courtiers. Historians generally define 'courtiers' as those people in attendance at the royal court. The vast majority of them—perhaps some 2,000 in number—attended court sporadically, either summoned on specific occasions—such as the arrival of visiting foreign dignitaries—or else coming on their own initiative to attend parliament or present a suit (a petition) to a patron or the queen. They had no rooms in the royal palaces and flocked to see the queen in the public space of the ceremonial rooms, especially the presence chamber. A number would be granted her hand to kiss; far fewer would be given an audience. Although part of Elizabeth's circle, no one in this group has a place in Part 2 of my book.

The focus here is on Elizabeth's intimates, the minority of courtiers who were allocated rooms in the palaces and invited to enter the privy chamber (the queen's private day room) or even royal bed-chamber. Contemporaries understood that regular and near access to the queen outside public spaces signified political intimacy. The rise of an individual to a place of influence, therefore, could be gauged by his or her entry into the queen's privy chamber. Likewise, setbacks to an individual's political career were apparent from his or her temporary exclusion from the queen's presence. Permanent exclusion meant political death.

Regular and near access to the queen was highly prized as a mark of royal favour, and many of those with this access were among the elite few who held offices in the royal household. Because of shortage of space, this book has to concentrate on only a selection of them. Nonetheless, readers will, I hope, get a sense of the important roles played in political life by other important intimates—courtiers such as Sir Thomas Heneage and Sir Walter Ralegh—who are referred to, but not discussed fully, in the text.[6]

The male courtiers I have chosen as my subjects are those well known from films, novels, and 'popular histories': Robert Dudley, earl of Leicester; Christopher Hatton; and Robert Devereux, second earl of Essex. Retelling the stories of their relationships with the queen allows me to correct some common misconceptions. To take a few examples, these men's intimacy with Elizabeth was not sexual; indeed, it is highly unlikely that she had a sexual relationship with anyone. Furthermore, although these three courtiers were considered good-looking with a fine physique, their physical attractiveness does not explain their influence with the queen. As will be seen, they all had considerable abilities and important connections; each of them served a political apprenticeship before acquiring political office; and each gave the queen loyal and valuable service. Finally, although some contemporaries and later commentators accused them of being favourites who monopolized the queen's affections and counsels, such allegations were biased and unfounded. Complaints of this kind were voiced at the time either by Catholic propagandists abroad seeking to discredit the Elizabethan regime or by disaffected courtiers at home who were denied the favours, they believed, they deserved.[7] In reality, Leicester, Hatton, and Essex had to share honours, influence, and material rewards with other individuals at court.

The court was the setting and environment in which the queen and these courtiers operated, and it had a variety of functions that influenced their roles and interactions. First and fundamentally, it was Elizabeth's place of residence, where courtiers were obliged to serve and entertain her. As in all Renaissance courts, both female and male courtiers amused their monarch with dancing, playing cards, and witty conversations, sometimes in the public space of the presence chamber, which was open to anyone allowed at court, more often in the privy chamber, where Elizabeth spent most of her day. Additionally, when she was touring the country on royal progress, her male and female hosts were expected to entertain her and the huge train of courtiers in accompaniment, by staging plays, masques, fireworks, and sports.[8]

Within the privy chamber, Elizabeth's courtiers were required to anticipate and satisfy their mistress's everyday needs and desires. Her women—the subject of Chapter 8—attended to her personal requirements—washing, dressing, toiletries, mending clothes, and serving her meals. All these domestic duties were carried out in a highly ritualized way; so, for example, when the queen dined in private—as was her usual custom—the table in her presence chamber was set with 'as much awe as if the queen had been present' and, 'at the end of all this ceremonial', a number of her unmarried ladies conveyed the dishes to the queen in the privy chamber.[9] The men who entered the privy chamber did so to transact governmental business, offer her counsel, and attend when she met foreign guests or regular ambassadors. In the evenings, they were usually there for play.

The court also functioned as 'a theatre of display', an arena where monarchical power and magnificence were put on show for subjects, ambassadors, and foreign visitors.[10] On those occasions that Elizabeth gave audience at Hampton Court to envoys from abroad, 'excessively rich tapestries', normally kept in the hall, were exhibited on the walls of the presence chamber.[11] Even the queen's private apartments had this function. Foreign envoys and special guests were received there as a special mark of honour, and visitors from abroad were sometimes taken on tours around the rooms when the queen was absent.[12] Everything, therefore, had to be sumptuous: at Whitehall Palace, Elizabeth's bedchamber was decorated with strikingly rich tapestries, while her bed was 'ingeniously composed of woods of different colours with quilts of silk, velvet, gold, silver, and embroidery'; and, as one sixteenth-century 'tourist' noted, in the adjoining bathroom 'the water pours from oyster shells and different kinds of rock'.[13] Also designed to awe and impress visitors were the tournaments, balls, feasts, 'shows', and many ceremonials at the centre of court life.

Courtiers, as well as their sovereign, were on display. The court was a magnet for ambitious men and women seeking individual advancement, the satisfaction of personal suits, and the promotion of a particular political cause. As contemporaries noted, it was 'the only mart of preferment and honour' and 'full of those who shall have this and that office'.[14] The court, therefore, could become the focal point of rivalries and intense competition among elite men and women seeking patronage. Virtually no important honour, benefit, or privilege could be granted without the queen's acquiescence, but relatively few suitors directly petitioned her. To procure the patronage she dispensed, they required a good court connection who could speak in favour of their suit to the queen. Even when someone did petition her in person or by letter, he or she relied upon one or more leading courtier to reinforce the suit. The number of suits a courtier was petitioned to raise was, therefore, a mark of his or her perceived intimacy with the queen.

Bombarded as Elizabeth was with both important and trivial requests for favour, she had to be constantly prodded about individual demands. As shown in Chapter 8, it was in this context that the women of the privy chamber, with their constant access to the queen and knowledge of her moods, could make the difference between success and failure. Elizabeth tried to distribute patronage broadly to prevent disaffection, eliminate factionalism, and ensure that no member of the court became too powerful or could be considered a 'favourite'. On the whole—at least until towards the end of the reign—she used patronage wisely; nonetheless, accusations that favourites dominated her ear to the exclusion of able men remained common.

Elizabeth's court is sometimes portrayed as a den of flatterers and sycophants. This is understandable. After all, male courtiers wore cameos or miniature portraits of the queen to signify adoration, or possibly loyalty; masques and pageants at court celebrated the queen as a goddess or Gloriana; and numerous gentlemen wrote verses, poems, or letters to Elizabeth, expressing adulation in an amorous language, which to the modern reader seems at best extraordinary and at worst nauseating. Yet, these outpourings of love, loyalty, and devotion should not be viewed as the obsequious language of ambitious men simply pandering to a queen thirsty for compliments and praise. Nor should the avowals of adoration be understood as the spontaneous and sincere outbursts of deep emotions or sexual desire. Rather, they were integral to the language and code of behaviour called 'courtly love' that was a central feature of the chivalric values permeating Elizabethan court culture. Highly stylized and artificial, 'courtly love' went back to twelfth-century romance literature that narrated the adventures that young knights carried out on behalf of noble women whom they loved and served. In these stories, the knight wooed his lady by offering her songs, poems, tokens, favours, and ceremonial gestures of devotion. She, meanwhile, maintained a disdainful distance from her socially inferior admirer, thereby causing him acute torment, but she nonetheless inspired him to perform great deeds and undergo heroic journeys. These medieval romances were widely read in Elizabethan England, and courtiers adapted the genre for their own purposes. Its attractiveness to a court presided over by a female ruler is obvious. Some who used the language of courtly love were aspiring intimates suing for favour; others were already close to the queen but seeking greater rewards or hoping to see off rivals. Whichever case applied, by following the conventions of the genre, aristocratic men could serve beneath a female monarch, accept her commands, and sue for her favour without impugning their masculinity or subverting gender norms.[15] Who initiated this practice at Elizabeth's court, we cannot tell, but queen and courtiers exploited it in equal measure.

While enjoying the benefits of 'courtly love', Elizabeth preferred to exploit the language and coded behaviour associated with intimacy rather than disdainful distance in order to create and strengthen bonds of loyalty. She and close members of her courtly circle would exchange personal gifts and share private jokes; she would allow them, or their representatives, easy access to her person and sometimes address them affectionately, often by particular nicknames. It was only when courtiers had incurred her anger that Elizabeth employed distance as a political tool. She would then withdraw all signs of intimacy, often temporarily but on some notable occasions permanently.

Elizabeth's courtiers were not just decorative ornaments or amusing companions. The most important of them held some form of office and carried out vital tasks of governance. Between a dozen and twenty were promoted to sit on the privy council, which was the main permanent institution of government. Part 3 of the book focuses on three privy councillors who also spent part of their careers as the queen's principal secretary: William Cecil, later Lord Burghley, Francis Walsingham, and Robert Cecil. The secretary was, actually, not one of the great officers of state: at court functions he would sit with the controller of the queen's household, away from the lord treasurer, lord admiral, and lord chamberlain.[16] But, under Elizabeth, he could be one of the most powerful and influential figures in government: the office was very much what its holder made of it, and all three secretaries discussed here utilized the open-ended responsibilities to the full.[17] Until December 1573, the queen relied upon only one principal secretary, but, after the work proved too onerous for Sir Thomas Smith, Walsingham was brought in as his junior.

As a body, the privy council discussed matters of state and had the function of advising the monarch.[18] The queen very rarely attended its meetings, but learned of the proceedings through her principal secretary, who met her daily. She also regularly consulted the privy council's inner core—some half a dozen of her most trusted men— on important matters in more informal settings, sometimes even allowing one of its members' personal secretaries rather than a clerk of the council to take notes.

Privy councillors also had collective responsibility for administering the realm. As Thomas Norton (one of the Elizabethan agents used by the council) declared, they were 'the wheels that hold the chariot of England upright'.[19] English monarchs had not the time— nor probably the inclination—to deal with the various routine, or relatively trivial, matters that came within the privy council's compass on a day-to-day basis. On one day alone, for example, its registers record that the council dealt with prisoners in the Tower and Fleet, the jurisdiction of the Welsh council, 'lewd wordes' uttered in Chichester, reinforcements for Ireland, a wreck in Devon, maritime insurance, reprisals against Spain, and the examination of various people concerning 'a religion's case'.[20] So, like her father and siblings before her, Elizabeth delegated her royal authority to the council when it came to managing the realm.

The functions of privy councillors did not stop there. Every Wednesday and Friday they joined with the chief justices of the common law courts (the queen's bench and common pleas) to sit as the court of Star Chamber hearing judicial cases that could range from treason and breaches of the public order to matrimonial disputes and jail deliveries. Its sessions usually took place in the *camera stellata* in Westminster Palace, a room whose ceiling of azure blue was decorated with stars of gold leaf, hence the name of the court. The chamber could also be the venue for privy council meetings, and, to mark the change in its function, the tablecloth was changed; it was red when a court and green when a council.[21]

Privy council meetings could, in fact, take place in any state room at court or even in the private chambers (or houses) of individual members such as Sir William Cecil. At their sessions, members would give instructions for drafting letters or approve their final form, which would then be signed. These would subsequently be sent to local nobles, gentlemen, or bishops, who would put the orders and directives into operation. Letters went out in the privy council's name, signed by its members, not the queen. Nonetheless, the privy council had no bureaucratic existence outside the monarchy. When a monarch died, the council was immediately dissolved, and the new monarch would then appoint his or her own privy councillors.

On her accession, Elizabeth appointed twenty privy councillors, but the death of Sir Thomas Cheney and resignation of Archbishop Nicholas Heath of York swiftly reduced the total number to eighteen. The queen continued to keep the council small: in 1568 the number declined to fifteen; it rose again to twenty in September 1586 but plummeted to eleven in 1597; at the time of her death in March 1603, fourteen men sat on the council.[22] Meetings, however, never contained the full complement of men, and for most of the reign an inner core carried through the business. Over the whole reign, only three men were dismissed: Essex and Thomas Howard, fourth duke of Norfolk, both executed for treason; and William Davison, who became the scapegoat after the execution of Mary Queen of Scots.

Elizabeth's privy councillors came from similar backgrounds. Before 1586—when Archbishop John Whitgift of Canterbury took his seat—all of them were lay people. Fewer than half were noblemen until 1578, when the proportion increased to exactly half. Privy councillors were also a cohesive group in terms of kinship ties. Between 1568 and 1582, no fewer than eighteen of them (out of twenty-five) were related to each other and the queen.[23] The most extreme example was Robert Dudley, earl of Leicester, who was brother to Ambrose Dudley, earl of Warwick, and brother-in-law to Sir Henry Sidney and Thomas Radcliffe, third earl of Sussex. Leicester also became son-in-law to Sir Francis Knollys in 1578 and had marriage ties to Sir Francis Walsingham, when his nephew Philip Sidney married the secretary's daughter Frances in 1583.

The three parts of my book are far from hermetically sealed compartments. Some of the figures who appear in Part 1 as Elizabeth's kin—for example, Katherine Grey, Margaret Lady Strange, and Henry Carey, Lord Hunsdon—were equally courtiers. The distinction between courtiers and councillors is also rather artificial in that they all operated within the court, relied for their power and influence on access to the queen, and participated in the prevailing court culture. All three of the male courtiers discussed in Part 2 came to be privy councillors. Furthermore, both councillors and courtiers sat in the Elizabethan parliaments, a forum where the governing class of the realm could discuss problems and propose solutions. Nonetheless, I think the divisions within this book remain useful. In Part 1, the key element in the queen's relationships was the tie of kinship, while the courtiers I have placed in Part 2 began their political life in the court and played a central role in entertaining the queen and fulfilling household tasks, functions that were not expected of the men in Part 3. Although, as the years rolled by, most men in Elizabeth's circle employed the language of courtly love, the courtiers in the second section experienced a flirtatious dimension with the queen that was generally lacking in her relationships with the men placed in the final section. Visually too there is a distinction: the portraits of William Cecil, Francis Walsingham, and Robert Cecil depict men in sober black rather than the colourful garb on display in those of Hatton and the earls of Leicester and Essex. This was how these men chose to be portrayed, so they presumably saw a distinction between the style of a courtier and that of the ministerial office-holders—especially the principal secretary—who carried the heaviest administrative responsibilities.[24]

In 1586 Elizabeth declared to her MPs and lords that 'we princes, I tell you, are set on stages in the sight and view of all the world duly observed'.[25] Unfortunately for historians, many of those observations went unrecorded or have been lost over time. As a result, our knowledge about the queen's relationships is patchy, based on the survival of sources, many of which are unsubstantiated rumours, ill-informed gossip, or later anecdotes. Elizabeth exchanged few letters with her closest courtiers and councillors, because they were usually accessible to her in person or through messengers. But, even more problematic, the inner feelings of the queen and her intimates were rarely on view at all, and remain a mystery. As a result of these difficulties, the reader will encounter the words 'perhaps', 'possibly', and 'very likely' more often than I would like. However, by presenting a wide range of sources—official records, private correspondence, commissioned masques, poetry, and portraits—I hope the narratives and interpretations offered here will provide a fresh set of insights into the queen's character and policies, the characters of leading figures in the regime, and the politics of the reign.

Part 1

Kin

I

....

Parents and Siblings

The birth of Elizabeth on 7 September 1533 was a dreadful disappointment to her father King Henry VIII and a catastrophe for her mother, Queen Anne. They had fervently hoped that their first child would be a male; and indeed astrologers, doctors, and midwives had all assured them that Anne was carrying a boy. A son was so important to them because a male child would settle Henry's long-standing anxieties about the succession and, no less important, be a sign of God's approval of their controversial marriage and Henry's recent policy towards the papacy.

In the full expectation of Anne bearing him a son, Henry had severed the ties of the English Church to Rome, so that his marriage to his first wife, Katherine of Aragon, could end without interference from the pope. Katherine's first husband had been Henry's elder brother, Arthur, and the king came to believe that her failure to deliver a male heir was divine punishment for their ignoring the verse in scripture that prohibited a man from taking his sister-in-law to bed. The pope, however, disagreed and, under pressure from Katherine's nephew, Emperor Charles V, refused to grant Henry's request for an annulment. After four years of soul-searching, Henry decided that popes had no authority in England, broke all ties with Rome, divorced Katherine, and wed Anne. Had his new wife delivered a healthy son on 7 September 1533, Henry would have been assured that God blessed his marriage and schism, but it was not to be.

Despite his dismay at Elizabeth's sex, Henry was determined that she and not Mary (his older daughter by Katherine), would be recognized as heir until a son was born to him. Consequently, for the first two and a half years of her life, Elizabeth was Henry's favoured child. At her baptism she was declared 'the high and mightie princes of England', and the following year parliament formally bastardized Mary.[1] To spread the message, preachers were ordered to name the Princess Elizabeth (but not Mary) alongside her parents in prayers.[2] Elizabeth's household was spared no expense. Until March 1535 it was costing the king at least £2,000 per annum, a sum roughly twice the outlay of Mary's household before she had been demoted.[3] Anne also ensured that her young daughter was expensively dressed, and the queen's final set of accounts included sums paid out for several satin caps embroidered in gold for the child, velvet and satin ruffs, and kirtles (a sleeveless gown) of yellow satin, green satin, and orange velvet.[4]

As was customary for royal children, Elizabeth did not live at court and saw her parents only intermittently. Once she was three months old, the princess had a peripatetic existence, residing in several country houses and palaces. Visits from her mother, or father, or both, were relatively infrequent and short, although there were times when Elizabeth stayed with the court at the royal palaces. On these special occasions she would often be displayed to foreign ambassadors as a good marriage prospect.

Elizabeth was with her parents at Eltham on Friday 7 January 1536 when the news of Queen Katherine's death came through. The following Sunday, the 2-year-old was conducted to mass 'with trumpets and other great triumphs'; and after dinner Henry sent for his daughter and, 'carrying her in his arms, he showed her first to one and then to another'.[5] On a far less cheerful occasion, Elizabeth was also with the court at Greenwich Palace when her mother was arrested; according to a later—supposedly eye-witness—account, the queen took her daughter in her arms and unsuccessfully pleaded with the king 'from the open window of which he was looking into the courtyard'.[6]

Historians disagree strongly about the reasons for Anne's arrest on Mayday 1536 on charges of adultery and incest. For some, the queen was the victim of faction; for at least one, she was guilty as charged; while yet another sees Anne as playing a dangerous game of flirting with her courtiers and gossiping about the king's impotency, a foolhardiness that her many enemies could exploit ruthlessly. But, whatever the immediate reasons for her downfall, it was the birth of a daughter and miscarriage of a son in early 1536 that turned Henry irrevocably against Anne and made her vulnerable to her enemies.[7]

Anne's trial and execution transformed her daughter's legal status. On 17 May 1536, Thomas Cranmer, the archbishop of Canterbury, pronounced his sentence that Henry's marriage to Anne was invalid, though on what grounds he left unsaid. The same day, a hastily summoned parliament passed a new Act of Succession confirming Elizabeth's bastardy and consequent ineligibility to inherit the throne.

Elizabeth's title was no longer 'princess'; she was now simply the Lady Elizabeth, and her elder sister Mary enjoyed precedence over her. With this diminution in status, there came a reduction in the size of her household, although a substantial sum was still directed towards its maintenance. Otherwise, little changed in the child's circumstances. She continued to live in one of the minor royal palaces, and her main servants remained the same. It was only with the birth of her half-brother Edward in October 1537 that she lost the care of her governess, Lady Margaret Bryan, and indeed this may have proved a greater emotional upheaval than the loss of a semi-absent mother. If so, the void was soon filled by Katherine Champernowne (better known by her nickname 'Kat' and married name 'Astley' or 'Ashley'). On Lady Bryan's departure, Kat took over the responsibilities for the child's care, training, and education.[8]

Anne's condemnation on charges of adultery gave opportunity for her enemies to deny that Elizabeth was the king's daughter: some named Sir Henry Norris as her father; others the musician Mark Smeaton.[9] Henry, though, never doubted that Elizabeth was his child, and insisted that she be treated as such. In court, both she and her sister Mary were given precedence over his nieces, and at particular times of celebration they were accorded places of honour. At Prince Edward's baptism, the 4-year-old Elizabeth held the chrism cloth, wrapped around the baby's head, and on the return to the royal apartments she and Mary carried his train. Two years later, Elizabeth was a member of the royal party that received the king's new bride, Anne of Cleves. In July 1543, Elizabeth was also one of the few witnesses at the more private wedding of her father to his last wife, Katherine Parr, at Hampton Court. Both daughters were regularly the recipients of presents from the king and his many queens. From surviving accounts, it appears that over Christmas, on Palm Sunday, and at other times when they were at court, Henry would provide rich materials or fine apparel for 'his dearest children the prince, Lady Mary, and Lady Elizabeth'.[10] Henry's queens tended to give the girls jewellery, although not always items of great value, for it was noted in one set of accounts that Queen Katherine Howard's gift to Elizabeth was a brooch of 'little thing worth' and a pair of beads.[11]

Legitimate or not, as a king's daughter Elizabeth could be useful diplomatic bait. Consequently, discussions about her marriage to a foreign prince did not cease after Anne's execution. When Henry was seeking an alliance with Charles V in February 1538, Elizabeth's name was raised as a possible bride for a Habsburg prince or ally.

When seeking a French alliance in March 1542, Henry promoted a marriage between Elizabeth and the duke of Orléans. Then in April 1543, as part of his diplomacy in Scotland, Henry offered her hand to the son of Scotland's governor James Hamilton, second earl of Arran: 'The king has a daughter called the Lady Elizabeth, endowed with virtues and qualities agreeable with her estate,' the English ambassador was instructed to tell Arran.[12] The matrimonial negotiations, however, came to nothing after the governor refused to meet the king's political conditions. Over the next four years Henry solicited other marriage proposals, but few foreign princes manifested interest in a marriage to either of his bastard daughters.

In 1544, Elizabeth's fortunes again turned when she and her half-sister were restored to the line of succession by act of parliament. Henry initiated the measure because he wanted to leave his dynasty secure before setting off with his army to fight in France, and he commemorated the event in a magnificent painting depicting him with all three of his children (Plate 2). However, as the wording of the statute confirmed Elizabeth's (and Mary's) status as bastards, Henry was running roughshod over an established principle of English common law—namely, that a bastard was *nullius filius* and hence could not be heir to a father's property, in this case the throne. Henry's refusal to legitimize his daughters at this opportune time did them ill service, for in later years opponents of their accessions used this legal point to challenge their right to sit on the throne.[13] In his will, dated just before his death in January 1547, Henry confirmed his daughters' places in the succession and bequeathed them each an income of £3,000 a year until they married, at which point they would receive a dowry of £10,000. By the standards of the day, the yearly sum was not that great. Consequently, in the 1550s, Elizabeth had to learn the pattern of parsimony that was to mark her running of the royal household when queen.

Despite her improved status, growing maturity, and a good relationship with her last stepmother, Elizabeth rarely stayed at court during the 1540s. In fact, it is often difficult to track her movements, since she is seldom visible in the public record because of her perceived political insignificance. Nonetheless, it is apparent that her interactions with her father were few and formal. A passing reference made in a letter, dated 16 December 1543, suggests that Henry and his children spent time 'in one howshold' over the Christmas period of that year. A household ordinance tells us that, on 26 June 1544, the children attended a formal dinner and reception (called a 'void') with the king at Whitehall, an event probably organized to mark the princesses' reinstatement in the succession.[14] However, it is quite likely that these visits to court were short, since, on 31 July 1544, Elizabeth wrote a formal note in Italian to Queen Katherine expressing sadness that a whole year had passed without the two meeting together.[15] While Henry was fighting in France during the summer of 1544, Elizabeth was to join her siblings in the queen's household at Hampton Court, but no sooner did the king return to England than Elizabeth and Edward departed for Ashridge in Hertfordshire.[16] Towards the end of 1545 and again in 1546, Elizabeth spent time at court; but unfortunately surviving documents do not allow us to piece together exactly when or for how long.

It is very difficult to uncover Elizabeth's private feelings towards her father. Certainly, she paraded her filial descent with pride. A decade after Henry's death, the Venetian ambassador noted that she 'prides herself on her father and glories in him'.[17] Later still, during her own coronation procession in January 1559, Elizabeth smiled on hearing one of the spectators refer to King Henry, and she claimed it was because 'she rejoysed at his name whom this realme doth hold of so woorthy memorie: so in all her doinges she will resemble the same'.[18] On the strength of such observations, biographers have commented on Elizabeth's adulation of the king.[19] However, given the allegations that she was not Henry's daughter, Elizabeth had every motive for flaunting her affection and admiration for her royal father. Moreover, in view of Henry's treatment of his wives and daughters, she had every reason to fear—rather than to love—the irascible, volatile, and merciless monarch. And, indeed, her calm reaction to the news of his death suggests that she experienced no great grief at his passing. Furthermore, her New Year's gifts for both him and Queen Katherine in 1544 betray an unsettling ambivalence in her inward feelings towards the king.

On New Year's Eve 1544, Elizabeth probably gave her father a handwritten French translation of Erasmus' *Dialogus fidei*, though we cannot be certain, as the work is no longer extant.[20] A matching gift to her stepmother has survived in the form of a handwritten twenty-seven-page English translation of a volume of meditations that had been composed by Margaret of Navarre, sister of King Francis I of France. Every aspect of this gift to Katherine was carefully thought out and redolent in meaning.[21] Its title, *The glasse of the synnefull soule*, drew attention to Elizabeth's royal lineage, as it alluded to her paternal great-grandmother Margaret Beaufort's volume of translations entitled *Miroure of golde for the sinful soul*. The pages were bound together within a blue cover on which Elizabeth had embroidered pansies in each corner and a knotwork pattern in silver thread surrounding Katherine's initials in the centre. Pansies both punned with the French word for meditations, *pensées*, and, in the language of flowers, sent out the message 'think of me' to Katherine, from whom she had just parted. The embroidered forget-me-nots on the spine of the book signified the 'love' or 'affection' she held for her stepmother. This was a gift, then, that not only displayed the young girl's intellectual precociousness and feminine skills but also drew attention to her royal ancestry and signalled her devotion to the queen-consort and, by extension, the king. It can be read as a bid to retain their affections and receive in return a more permanent place at court.

Possibly too, although this is necessarily more speculative, Elizabeth's gift reveals a deeper and darker psychological side to her feelings towards her father. Margaret's original poem was a set of meditations on family relationships through which humans may understand God's love. In fact, the work touched on adultery, bastardy, and incest, all sensitive subjects for the 11-year-old daughter of Anne Boleyn to handle. What is more, its presentation of God as a great king and judge who is kind to daughters and merciful to adulterous wives might have touched a raw nerve in Elizabeth. For this reason, some scholars have argued that her mistranslations and departures from the original text stem, not from a young girl's carelessness, but from a deep-rooted, perhaps subconscious, anxiety and anger about her own father's lack of mercy towards his adulterous wife. These scholars also point out that Elizabeth's level of anxiety may have been all the greater if she was working from a copy of the meditations originally owned by her mother.[22]

Elizabeth's gifts to her father and stepmother the following New Year are equally suggestive. Her present to Katherine was an English translation of the first chapter in John Calvin's *Institution de la religion chrestienne*. Though a daring choice given the religious orthodoxy demanded in the 1539 Act of Six Articles, Elizabeth neutralized its impact by selecting (or being given) for translation a chapter that did not touch on the theologian's more controversial doctrines concerning predestination or the eucharist but instead focused on the authority of scriptures and their importance in understanding God's purpose.[23] Elizabeth's epistolary prologue emphasized the primacy of the written Word as the way to bring Christians to knowledge of

God, sentiments that reflected the reformist religious education she was then receiving.[24] Since this reformist position was one she shared with Queen Katherine, her gift was evidently designed to reveal and reinforce the religious bond between them.

For Henry, Elizabeth translated into Latin, French, and Italian a collection of prayers and meditations that Katherine had originally composed in English. The painstaking work of writing out 117 pages in her neatest hand was meant to be seen as a mark of respect towards the king, a compliment to his wife, and of course a testimony to her own industry, accomplishments, and piety. The words of the epistolary prologue were likewise calculated to please her father: they referred to him as 'a God on earth' and claimed his virtues were a model for his subjects. At the same time, the gift again drew attention to Elizabeth's royal lineage: in the short preface she referred six times to their familial relationship; and on the elaborately embroidered cover she included the eglantine rose that had been the symbol of her paternal grandmother and namesake, Elizabeth of York.[25] This constant reference to her royal bloodline is indicative, perhaps, that Elizabeth still did not feel confident of her place in her father's affections and had some anxiety that in the future she might again be ousted from the succession.

Another possible clue to Elizabeth's feelings about her father is her treatment of his trusted servant, William Baron Paget, on her accession. To his surprise and chagrin, Paget was excluded from Elizabeth's first privy council in 1558.[26] When pleading for a rethink, he reminded her (through an intermediary) that Henry had seen his worth and appreciated his good service.[27] Elizabeth, however, was unmoved, and the very able and experienced Paget remained in the political cold until his death in 1563.

This sidelining of Paget can be contrasted with the favours and rewards that Elizabeth offered to the kin and close associates of her mother. Anne's uncle, William Baron Howard of Effingham, who like Paget had served—and been Elizabeth's protector—under Mary, was sworn into the new queen's privy council and appointed head of her household as lord chamberlain. A Boleyn cousin, Thomas Radcliffe, third earl of Sussex, who had likewise served under Mary, retained his important office as lord deputy of Ireland in November 1558. Other Boleyn relations were advanced to positions that were well beyond what they might have expected, were it not for their kinship ties to Elizabeth's mother.[28] Anne's first cousin, Sir Richard Sackville, became a privy councillor in 1558, even though previously he had only held the relatively minor administrative office of under-treasurer of the exchequer. Still more unexpectedly, on 6 January 1567, about a year after Sackville's death, his son Thomas was elevated to the peerage as baron of Buckhurst, a major promotion achieved only because of the Boleyn connection. Henry Carey, the son of Anne's sister Mary, similarly owed his political and social prominence to his Boleyn blood. One of Elizabeth's gentlemen while she was a princess, Carey was created baron of Hunsdon on 13 January 1559, granted Hunsdon House in Hertfordshire, and soon afterwards received lands worth £4,000 per annum. Over the next decade, he held household offices and entered the elite chivalric order of the garter; and, in August 1568, the queen appointed him governor of Berwick, a senior military post that led to his entry into the privy council in 1577. His 'propinquyte in blood doothe somewhat preveyle', murmured another privy councillor disapprovingly, whenever Hunsdon gave advice to the queen.[29] John Astley, a more distant Boleyn relation, was also given trusted positions within the royal household. Admittedly his marriage to Katherine Champernowne helps explain his appointments as master of the jewel house and treasurer of the queen's jewels and plate in December 1558, but he retained his offices after his wife's death and his remarriage. Boleyn women too were honoured with preferment at the hands of Elizabeth.[30] Finally, the choice of Matthew Parker as the queen's first archbishop of Canterbury had much to do with his previous role as one of Anne's chaplains. Parker, moreover, agreed to accept only on account of his close relationship with Anne. As he explained later: 'if I had not been so much bound to the mother, I would not so soon have granted to serve the daughter.'[31]

This promotion of Boleyn relatives indicates that Elizabeth had no wish to distance herself from the memory of her mother. Recognizing this, several men called her attention to their connection with Anne in the hope of securing favour and patronage. In the dedication to a manuscript translation of an Italian book, William Bercher explained that he was a scholar who had benefited from Anne's 'bountyfull benevolence' while studying at Cambridge and now hoped to serve her daughter 'to shewe my selffe myndefull of the renomyd memorye of your hyghnes' mother'. In a blatant request for patronage, Bercher wrote: 'And so deryvynge the course of my days, from a renomyd quene, the mother, to a moste exelent quene the daughter, I maye in the one, honour the memory of the other.'[32] William Latimer was another man on the make who hoped to benefit from his connection with Elizabeth's mother, but in his case he chose to pen a manuscript life of the late queen that lauded her modesty, piety, and philanthropy.[33] Others showed their loyalty to Elizabeth by hanging Anne's portrait on their walls: whereas no portrait of Anne survives from her lifetime, many of the best known can be dated to the later sixteenth century (Plate 1).[34]

It is impossible to figure out Elizabeth's deepest feelings towards Anne. We do not know when and how she was told of her mother's 'crime', trial, and execution, or how she reacted to the information. We do know that she kept Anne's memory alive by adopting her motto *Semper eadem* ('Always the same') and appropriating her badge of the crowned falcon holding a sceptre and perched on a tree stump from which Tudor roses sprang. However, Elizabeth rarely spoke of her mother and made no attempt to make reparation for past injustices. Unlike her predecessor Mary, she introduced no act of parliament that declared the 'most just and lawfull matrimonie' of her mother's marriage, nor repealed the statutes pronouncing the contrary.[35] Unlike her successor James I, she did not disinter her mother's bones and rebury them in the family chapel in Westminster Abbey; indeed, Anne's grave remained unmarked without any inscription.[36] But this does not mean that Elizabeth was ashamed of Anne or so traumatized by her death that she could not bear to think of her. Quite simply it was not in Elizabeth's interests to open up the question of her legitimacy by making statements or introducing laws that asserted the legality of her parents' marriage. With a Catholic claimant—Mary Queen of Scots—waiting in the wings, it was politically wiser to stay silent and simply assume her own legitimacy. The 'Act of Recognition of the Quene's Highness Title', passed in Elizabeth's first parliament, therefore just accepted implicitly that Elizabeth was born in wedlock in its bald statement that the new queen was 'rightlye lynyallye and lawfully discended and come of this bloodd royal of this realme of Englande'. Furthermore, by declaring that she owed her throne to both the 'lawes of God' and the laws and statutes of the realm, the act implied that her title depended upon not only the 1544 Act of Succession but also hereditary right.[37] Another statute passed in 1559 also revealed Elizabeth's low-key determination to rehabilitate her mother, for it declared that 'every acte, recorde, sentence, matter, or writing whatsoever' that was 'contrary or repugnant' towards Anne would be 'clerely and utterly voyde and of none effecte', words that presumably encompassed her attainder and the annulment of her marriage.[38]

The time was therefore right for Anne's public rehabilitation in England. During Elizabeth's coronation procession through London, the first pageant to greet the new queen depicted King Henry and

> the right worthy ladie quene Anne, wife to the said king Henry th'eight, & mother to our most soveraign ladie quene Elizabeth that now is, both apparelled with sceptours & diademes, and other furniture due to the state of a king & queene.[39]

Here and elsewhere, Elizabeth's genealogy was not treated with shame, but celebrated. Throughout the reign, English protestants made public reference—if only in passing—to the legal marriage and 'sacred wedlock' of Henry and Anne.[40] With the advantage of an English mother, Elizabeth could also present herself as fully English in contrast to her half-Spanish sister, Mary.

In other respects, too, Elizabeth's mother was not hidden from history. Rather than treating Anne as 'the elephant in the room', protestants chose to refashion her as a virtuous and godly queen. John Aylmer's 1559 polemical work justifying female rule set the tone. Without Anne, he wrote, there would have been no break with Rome and restoration of true faith in England: 'Was not Quene Anne, the mother of this blessed woman, the chief, first, and only cause of banyshing the beast of Rome, with all his beggarly baggage?' As an instrument of God's providence, went on Aylmer, Anne could be compared to the biblical Queen Esther, a woman who was generally viewed as the paragon of wifely virtue as well as an intercessor for God's people: 'if God had not gyven Quene Anne favour in the sight of the kynge, as he gave to Hester in the sight of Nabucadnezar [sic]: Haman and his company' (meaning the papists) would have won. 'Wherfore though many deserved muche praise for the helping forwarde of it: yet the croppe and roote was the quene, whiche God had endewed with wisdome that she coulde, and gyven hir the minde that she would do it.'[41] A godly Anne likewise emerged from the pages of John Foxe's *Acts and Monuments*. In his first edition of 1563, Foxe—like Aylmer—gave Anne credit for the abolition of papal power, and claimed it was she 'who wythoute all controversye was the privye and open comforter and aider of al the professors of Christe's gospel, as well of the learned as the unlearned'. Foxe's Anne was far removed from the wanton whore condemned for adultery and incest; instead, she represented the ideal of Christian womanhood. Modest and pious, she gave alms to widows and the poor, while her women occupied themselves with sewing shirts and smocks for the needy.[42]

Later on in Elizabeth's reign, the godly theme re-emerged in the poetic commemoration of Anne in Ulpan Fulwell's *The Flower of Fame*:

> Her vertuous mynde and godly harte
> God's worde doth so embrace:
> As well deserves in Bibel's tome
> her noble name to place.

Furthermore, Fulwell did not just laud Anne as a biblical figure; she was also a model of courtly queenship, embodying the grace, beauty, and wisdom of classical goddesses. As a compliment to the present queen, the genealogical connection was stressed: Anne was the phoenix 'Whose ashes yeldes another byrde'. She

> hath of her sinders sent
> A noble Impe, a worthie queene
> ere shee from worlde went.[43]

Unsurprisingly perhaps, Fulwell's epitaph on the passing of Anne omitted entirely the story of her trial and execution. Elizabethan chroniclers, however, could hardly ignore the event, but had to find ways of shaping the historical narrative to exonerate the queen's mother without impugning her father. They found different solutions to this dilemma. The anonymous compiler of 'the progenie of the monarchs of the English men' simply stated that Anne had been 'malitiously slandered', falsely arrested, and wrongfully condemned.[44] The English translator of John Sleidan's *Chronicle* declared Henry had condemned Anne 'unjustly as it is supposed and proved synce', thereby implying that the king did not know the truth way back in 1536.[45] By contrast, in John Stow's chronicles, Anne's innocence appeared obvious at her trial in that she provided 'so wise and discrete answeres that she seemed fully to cleere hirselfe of all matters layd to hir charge'. But, in his account, it was the peers of the realm who condemned her to die, not the king who had no role in the proceedings.[46] Foxe laid the blame squarely at the feet of a Catholic faction, unequivocally asserting in his 1570 edition that 'Queene Anne was falsely condemned, and Queene Elizabeth her daughter as falsely dishereted'. Papists who realized 'what a myghtye stoppe' Anne was to 'their purposes and procedynges' trumped up the charges against her, and Henry was only at fault in listening to them.[47]

Such representations of Anne were multi-purpose: they provided a means of complimenting Elizabeth, of offering her a worthy precedent to follow, and of saving her from the defamatory jibes of Catholics. Roman Catholics, especially those living in exile abroad, were having a field day in blackening Anne's name in order to discredit her daughter. They tapped into Anne's reputation as 'a goggyll eyed hoore', while libelling Elizabeth by drawing on the popular belief that children could imbibe a mother's characteristics through her milk.[48] Stories about Anne's lustful disposition had long circulated orally and in manuscript. Under Elizabeth, they came to be printed. In August 1561, the English ambassador in Paris was shown a French book printed in Lyons, which contained 'odious' clauses referring to Anne 'unreverently'.[49] In 1585, the worst libels were set down in Edward Rishton's enormously influential revision of Nicholas Sander's manuscript text *De origine ac progressu scismatis Anglicani liber*. In this dramatic and excoriating account of Henry VIII's schism, Anne was given the physical characteristics of a witch (a projecting tooth, a large wen under her chin, and six fingers on one hand), and she behaved like the stereotype in her sexual promiscuity. Most scandalous of all, Sander/Rishton maintained that Anne's daughter, Elizabeth, was not only illegitimate but also the product of an incestuous relationship. Anne, they claimed, was the daughter as well as the lover of Henry VIII, and heresy was all that could be expected of such a monster.[50] The English cardinal William Allen repeated this absurd allegation in 1588. When calling upon the people of England to rise up against Elizabeth, he declared that, as the child of Henry's 'incestuous copulation with Anne Bullen', she could not sit legitimately on the throne.[51] Although most of the Catholic libels (including *De origine*) were not published in English, protestants nonetheless felt the need to rescue Anne's reputation. The narrative of her life and death therefore became something of a battleground between the rival confessions during the reign of her daughter.

Elizabeth's relationship with her parents was dysfunctional even by sixteenth-century standards. It was not so much the early decease of her mother and long absences of her father; those occurrences were far from unusual in a society where mothers often died in childbirth and fathers took little care of their children. What was extraordinary, and potentially damaging, were the nature of her mother's death and the changes to the girl's status that resulted from it. The problem for historians is that the extent of their impact is impossible to assess. A bright child, Elizabeth apparently noticed something was amiss when a year or so later she allegedly asked her governess: 'how happs it yesterday Lady Princess and today but Lady Elisabeth?'[52]

Later on, her gifts to her father and stepmother hint at insecurities. Nonetheless, Elizabeth's childhood was relatively secure; she was not rejected by her father; she had a mother surrogate in first Lady Bryan and then Mistress Astley; and she enjoyed the experience of studying a wide range of subjects under her personal tutors. It was during her siblings' reigns that Elizabeth's life became more difficult, even dangerous, and taught her the tough lessons that stayed with her through adulthood. To this I shall now turn.

For most of her childhood, Elizabeth had little to do with her siblings. She was usually based in her own separate household establishment, well away from her half-sister and half-brother. Family reunions were few and far between. The summer of 1544 that the siblings spent in Queen Katherine's household was exceptional, and even then the yawning age gap between Elizabeth and Mary and the difference in gender between Elizabeth and Edward kept Henry VIII's children physically apart.

Sibling separation was not atypical for royal children. However, the physical and tense proximity that Elizabeth and Mary had been forced to endure during the former's earliest years was abnormal. It was harder for Mary than her baby sister. In December 1533, the 17-year-old princess was wrenched from her own household and ordered to attend upon the child who had usurped her royal title and status, creating a 'strange and dishonorable' situation that Mary found intolerable.[53] Despite her father's threats, Mary refused to recognize Henry's second marriage and avoided, whenever she could, the obligation of paying court to her 'bastard' younger sister.[54] Mary's sullen presence at meals and her battles with the women of their joint household were a regular feature of their life together, but whether or not Elizabeth later remembered the experience is questionable.

Normality returned with Anne's fall in May 1536 and Mary's reconciliation with her father the following July; she was then allowed her own household servants and given precedence over her younger sibling.[55] With her honour restored, Mary's anger and resentment apparently evaporated; at the very least, she seemed protective of the toddler, speaking well of her to the king. Elizabeth, she told him shortly after Anne's execution, was 'such a child toward, as I doubt not but your highness shall have cause to rejoice of in time coming'.[56] From then on, the sisters saw considerably less of each other. Mary attended court for longer periods, while Elizabeth remained for the most part in the country. They ritually exchanged gifts and formal letters, but their relationship was distant.

Edward probably saw more of Elizabeth as he was growing up. The siblings lived together at court in August 1543 and during the summer of 1544, and they resided in the same manor houses in Hertfordshire for short periods.[57] But, since they had separate households and schoolrooms, it is not clear how frequent was their actual contact.

When the 55-year-old king died on 28 January 1547, Mary was at court, Edward at Hertford, and Elizabeth at Enfield. The boy was hurriedly brought to Elizabeth in order that they could be told the news together, but he was immediately taken to London while she stayed behind. Presumably, the thinking behind this arrangement was that the 13-year-old Elizabeth could comfort her grieving 9-year-old brother before he set off on his royal entry into the City. After initial tears, both children were in fact stoical in the face of their father's death, as a letter from Edward to Elizabeth reveals:

> There is very little need of my consoling you, most dear sister, because from your learning you know what you ought to do, and from your prudence and pity you perform what your learning causes you to know…I perceive you think of our father's death with a calm mind.[58]

Elizabeth did not stay at court upon her father's death; she did not even attend her brother's coronation. From Enfield she went to live with her stepmother, who had moved into houses at Chelsea and Hanworth. Perhaps Katherine sought her company, or more likely the king's advisers placed the young princess there while the provisions of Henry's will were being sorted out. Elizabeth kept in touch with Edward through formal letters in Latin or French, which expressed her affection to him as a brother and respect for him as a sovereign, yet she did not write to him as often as was expected.[59] In her first letter to him as king, dated 14 February 1547, she apologized for not taking up her pen sooner and hoped 'that your highness will be inclined to accept my feelings towards you as a substitute for my letters'. When she wrote in September the same year, she similarly expressed regret that she had sent him so few letters over so long a space of time but assured Edward of her affection and reverence.[60] Perhaps to make amends for her inadequacies as a correspondent, she sent him her own translation from Italian into Latin of a sermon by the evangelical reformer Bernardo Ochino, a thoughtful gift that would remind the young king of their shared interests and religious beliefs. Yet here too Elizabeth managed her time badly and had to offer excuses for not finishing the work punctually. Intended as a

New Year's gift (probably for January 1548), she sent it off a month late.[61]

Elizabeth's strong relationship with her brother was soon put to the test as a consequence of the scandal that linked her to Edward's maternal uncle, Thomas Baron Seymour of Sudeley. Barely four months after Henry's death, Seymour married the dowager queen, to the dismay and disapproval of both Mary and Elizabeth.[62] The marriage was short lived, for Katherine died in September 1548 from complications following childbirth. On the prowl to find another wife who would satisfy his political and personal ambitions, Seymour had private talks with two of Elizabeth's household servants about a possible future marriage with the young princess. Because he was also plotting against his elder brother, Lord Protector Somerset, the *éminence grise* behind Edward's throne, Seymour came under investigation in January 1549.[63] Rumours and interrogations brought to light the disreputable story that he had been flirting outrageously with Elizabeth while his wife was alive and planned to marry her after Katherine's death. Elizabeth's reputation as a chaste, obedient, and pious princess was shattered. Gossip and innuendo now portrayed her as a shameless hussy, no better than her mother, and as a disobedient daughter by going against her father's command that she should not marry without the privy council's consent. Rumours were circulating, Elizabeth complained ruefully, 'wiche be greatly bothe agenste my honor, and honestie'.[64]

Under intense interrogation, Elizabeth showed her mettle. She denied all the charges that could not be proved against her and, as a good patron, defended her household servants. Knowing the importance of appearances, the princess upheld her reputation in letters to the lord protector and requested permission to come to court so that all could see the spuriousness of the rumours that she was pregnant. Whatever her feelings for Seymour, Elizabeth entirely dissociated herself from him and displayed no outward emotion when he was executed on 20 March 1549.

Exactly what the young king was told about the Seymour scandal is unknown. In his journal Edward referred briefly to his uncle's condemnation and execution, but made no mention of Elizabeth's role in his treasons. Since Seymour was condemned without a trial, it is possible that Edward did not learn all the damaging details gleaned from the depositions of Elizabeth's servants, though it is unlikely that he was entirely insulated from the gossip circulating the court. In any case, after the affair had died down, Elizabeth set about repairing any possible harm to their relationship. Absent from court, she sent Edward a portrait of herself on 15 May 1549 in the hope that her likeness would remind him of her existence and their former friendship. In the accompanying letter, her first to him written in English, she both expressed her affection for her brother and hinted that she would like to be welcomed again at his court: he should, she wrote, 'think that as you have but the outward shadow of the body afore you, so my inward mind wisheth that the body itself were oftener in your presence'.[65] The painting has not survived, but it probably depicted her as the pious, scholarly princess that we can see in the portrait painted late in Henry's reign (Plate 3). In other letters to Edward, all written in English, Elizabeth tried to display her scholarship and piety by inserting quotations from, or references to, Pindar, Horace, Homer, and Isaiah. And when she did attend court, Elizabeth, similarly, presented herself as a serious-minded, godly princess, by dressing as simply and modestly as possible. Following the precepts of court preachers who declaimed against 'gold, jewels, and braidings of the hair', she went 'clad in every respect as becomes a young maiden', setting 'a virtuous example' to the 'painted peacocks' of court ladies, commented one approving observer.[66]

Elizabeth's tactics seemed to work. If her first historian William Camden is correct, Edward came to call her 'his sweet sister temperance', a sign that he had forgotten, forgiven, or chosen to disbelieve the scurrilous stories surrounding her relationship with Seymour.[67] Elizabeth was no doubt helped in her rehabilitation by the conflict over religion that was developing between Edward and his other half-sister. At loggerheads with Mary over her refusal to cease hearing the mass, Edward was inclined to show favour to Elizabeth, who accepted, even welcomed, the protestant religious practices introduced by his government. Elizabeth, therefore, was invited to spend Christmas at court in December 1549, while Mary stayed at home. The princess was 'received with great pomp and triumph', spent time privately with the king, and afterwards dined with him in the presence chamber: 'it was seyd that afterwards dyvers great ladyes coming from the courte by the duces of Somersett (the lord protector's wife) went yn and vysyted hur.'[68] It seemed, wrote the imperial ambassador disapprovingly, 'that they have a higher opinion of her for conforming with the others and observing the new decrees, than of the Lady Mary, who remains constant in the Catholic faith'.[69]

The following year, Elizabeth was again received at court over Christmas. Escorted by 100 of the king's cavalrymen, she arrived with similar ceremony in order 'to show the people how much glory belongs to her who has embraced the new religion and is become a very great lady'. On the feast of epiphany, she dined with Edward and immediately afterwards joined him to see some bear-baiting and other sports.[70] Unusually, Elizabeth spent the Christmas of 1551–2 in the country. Her letter, penned on 2 January from Hatfield, explains this unusual absence from court during the winter festivities, for she made reference there to the 'long duration of my sickness'. The letter also stated that 'the infirm state' of her health had prevented her from finishing her customary New Year's gift for the king, a translation copied out from her 'literary store-house'. It was therefore a relief, she declared, that her brother had just abolished the practice of exchanging New Year's gifts on religious grounds.[71] To compensate for her absence at Christmas, Elizabeth was invited to court in mid-March 1552 as a guest at the king's expense. Her ride through London created quite a splash; a London diarist noted that she came 'with a grett compeny of lord[s] and knight[s] and gentlemen and after her a grett nombur of lades and gentyllwomen to the nombur of 200 on horssebake, and yomen'.[72] As far as we know, this was the last time that Elizabeth saw her brother. She had intended to visit him again at the feast of Candlemas (on 2 February 1553), but to her distress was turned away because of his illness.[73]

Despite their surface good relations, the dying Edward was prepared to override the 1544 Act of Succession, overturn his father's will, and exclude Elizabeth (as well as Mary) from the throne. He wanted to bypass Mary because she had emerged as a committed Catholic, defiantly hearing mass in her own household in contempt of the law, but why did he seek to exclude the protestant Elizabeth as well? According to his own explanation, he believed that both his sisters were bastards, as his father had ruled, and therefore had no rights of inheritance. Additionally, he may have decided that the daughter of Anne Boleyn was unworthy to take the throne. According to one contemporary account, he told his judges that Elizabeth was to be disinherited because her mother 'was more inclined to couple with a number of courtiers rather than reverencing her husband, so mighty a king'.[74] Furthermore, the Seymour episode possibly led him to doubt her judgement and bolstered his fear that she might take an unsuitable husband. Certainly, as part of his stated justification for the decision, he argued that his unmarried sisters might marry a foreigner, thereby putting the independence and religion of the realm at risk. To avoid this calamity, he insisted upon bequeathing the crown to his cousin, the protestant Lady Jane Grey, who was already married to a protestant Englishman, the son of his closest adviser John Dudley, duke of Northumberland.[75]

Publicly at least Elizabeth bore no bitterness towards her brother for disinheriting her. During the next reign and beyond, she made a strong statement of her lasting love and affection towards him by wearing at her waist a small gold miniature book that contained the prayer that he had supposedly made three hours before his death.[76] It was Northumberland and the Greys whom Elizabeth held responsible for the attempt at trampling over her rights, but in this judgement she was mistaken.[77]

During the short succession crisis between Edward's death on 6 July 1553 and Mary's successful accession thirteen days later, Elizabeth and her sister operated independently. While Mary raised her standard in East Anglia and made preparations to fight for the throne, the 19-year-old Elizabeth pleaded illness and stayed quietly at Hatfield. By keeping her head down, Elizabeth no doubt hoped to safeguard her future position, were Jane to be successful in taking the throne. Only when it became obvious that Mary had won the day did Elizabeth come out in open support of her sister's title. She then left Hatfield for London. 'Well accompanyed with gentlemen and others', wearing the green and white Tudor livery, she stayed in her own London home, Somerset House, before riding through the City to join Mary, who was progressing down to London from her base at Framlingham in Suffolk. Their meeting was cordial: she had come, said Elizabeth, 'to wish the queen joy as well as to offer her fealty', but Mary may reasonably have wondered why she had left it so late to do so. The two sisters then rode down to London together, making a formal entry on 3 August.[78]

Despite the outward show of sisterly solidarity, cracks soon appeared in their relationship. The main reason was religion. Interpreting her triumph in providential terms, Mary was resolved to restore the Roman Catholic Church as quickly as possible, whereas Elizabeth remained a convinced protestant. Even before parliament had repealed the Edwardian legislation authorizing protestant worship, Mary expected the court to follow her example and attend mass in the royal chapel, but Elizabeth baulked at the change in religious practice and even stayed away from the private requiem mass that Mary had arranged for their brother. In early September 1553, aware that Mary was becoming annoyed at her frequent absences from mass, Elizabeth requested a private audience with the queen to explain her reasons. However, Mary signalled her displeasure and disdain by making her sister wait in suspense for several days before agreeing to see her. By then Elizabeth appeared distraught, although how far this was an affectation to gain sympathy we can only guess. Weeping, she 'threw herself on her knees' before Mary and 'entreated the queen to let her have books controverting the religion which she has always been taught' so that she might 'overcome her scruples' and attend mass. A few days afterwards, on the Feast of the Nativity of the Virgin (8 September), Elizabeth went to mass for the first time, but she complained loudly all the way to church 'that her stomach ached, wearing a suffering air'. No wonder then that 'everyone believes that she is acting rather from fear of danger and peril from those around her than from real devotion'.[79] Nevertheless, Mary seemed initially inclined to give her sister the benefit of the doubt. Throughout September, she showed great courtesy towards Elizabeth, assigning her precedence at court, and sitting next to her during dinner and supper. During the coronation celebrations on 1 October, Elizabeth was given pride of place as heiress to the throne: in the royal procession to Westminster on the preceding day, she sat in the first closed carriage immediately after the queen; during the coronation itself, she carried Mary's train; and at the post-coronation banquet she sat at the central table on one side of the newly crowned monarch.[80]

Soon afterwards, Mary's attitude to her sister noticeably changed. In her first parliament, summoned in October, the queen introduced a statute that reinforced Elizabeth's bastardy by confirming the legality of Henry VIII's marriage to Katherine of Aragon. The same parliament repealed all the religious innovations of Edward VI's reign and reinstated the mass as the focal point of religious worship. Once these laws had been enacted, Mary made it obvious that she held her heretical half-sister 'in small account'.[81] As a public sign that she no longer considered Elizabeth to be her heir, she several times ordered Elizabeth to yield precedence to their first cousins Frances, duchess of Suffolk (the mother of the disgraced Lady Jane Grey, now a prisoner in the Tower), and Margaret, countess of Lennox. Privately, on 25 November, Mary admitted to Simon Renard (the imperial ambassador) and William Lord Paget that she wanted Elizabeth to be excluded from the succession because 'of her heretical opinions, illegitimacy, and characteristics in which she resembled her mother'.[82]

Impatient with Elizabeth's intermittent attendance at mass, Mary now suspected that her sister was insincere in her promises to open her heart and mind to Catholic teachings. The queen also began paying heed to Renard's warnings that Elizabeth was politically subversive, involved in 'heretic intrigues', and plotting with the French. Consequently, Elizabeth found herself 'in so much disfavour that there is not one lady in this court who dares to visit her in her chamber, or even to speak to her without the permission of the queen', or so claimed Antoine de Noailles, the French ambassador. There was even talk of putting her in the Tower.[83] However, Paget warned Mary that parliament would not endorse Elizabeth's disinheritance and that unrest might follow her imprisonment. Bearing this in mind, Mary could only hope that the succession problem would ultimately be solved by her own marriage and delivery of a healthy baby.

By early December, Elizabeth was so humiliated and isolated at court that she requested permission to withdraw. For two days Mary left her in suspense (another sign of disdain) but then agreed to Elizabeth's departure. Anxious that the tales of her disloyalty might grow during her absence, Elizabeth tried to clear her name before leaving and also begged Mary 'not to put faith in bad reports of her without hearing her defence'. At their parting on 6 December 1553, the sisters made a public show of friendship. Mary presented Elizabeth with a gift of a 'very beautiful sable wrap'; en route to Hertfordshire, Elizabeth sent back a messenger to ask for vestments, chalices, and other Catholic ornaments so that she could hear mass in her household. According to Noailles, 'the two sisters were completely reconciled'; according to Renard, Mary 'dissembled very well' and had arranged a close watch on her sister's movements.[84] The latter was the more perceptive and better-informed witness.

Whether or not Elizabeth was caught up in plots with the French, English heretics, or disaffected members of the court is unknown. It is very unlikely that she engaged directly in dangerous political conspiracy, if only out of fear of discovery, but a plot was afoot in late 1553 that surrounded her person. Alarmed by Mary's decision to marry her Habsburg cousin, Prince Philip of Spain, a group of courtiers was scheming to raise the country in arms to depose Mary and crown Elizabeth. According to their plan, Elizabeth would marry Edward Courtenay, earl of Devon, an Englishman of Yorkist descent, who would rule in her name. If Elizabeth did know about the plot—which seems likely—she decided to follow a 'wait-and-see' strategy, just as she had done during the succession crisis the previous July.[85]

The projected risings in the Welsh borders, south-west, and Midlands proved abortive, but some 3,000 gentlemen from Kent came out in rebellion in late January 1554 under the leadership of Sir Thomas Wyatt. Suspecting Elizabeth of involvement, Mary immediately summoned her to London. The queen's letter of 26 January contained no open threats but merely stated that the princess should move to court for her own protection in case the rising spread to Hertfordshire. But Elizabeth feared the worst and 'excused herself from obeying the queen's summons because she was ill, and begged the queen to send her own doctor to see whether it was feigned or not'.[86] The royal physicians were hurriedly sent to Elizabeth's residence at Ashridge and confirmed that she was indeed on her sickbed. Mary therefore left Elizabeth alone and concentrated on stopping Wyatt, who was on the march to London.

Thanks to Mary's leadership and the loyalty of Londoners, Wyatt's rebellion was stopped in its tracks just outside the gates of the City on 7 February 1554. The danger over, Mary's next task was to dig out details of the conspiracy and punish the participants. Certain now of Elizabeth's involvement, she sent three councillors accompanied by 250 horsemen to Ashridge on 10 February to escort her sister to court. Although not formally under arrest, Elizabeth had no choice but to obey the summons, especially as the queen's doctors advised that she was well enough to travel, 'without danger to her person', provided that the journey was undertaken slowly with many stops on the way. Taking advantage of this dispensation, Elizabeth took ten days to cover the thirty-three miles to Westminster. As she came into London, she opened the litter's curtains, possibly in a symbolic gesture to demonstrate that she had nothing to hide, but more likely to advertise her whereabouts so that she could not be quietly imprisoned or even murdered.[87]

Mounting evidence disclosed that the princess and members of her household had been in communication with Wyatt and the French. Renard, therefore, urged that she and Courtenay be executed on the grounds that 'they would be justly punished, as it is publicly known that they are guilty and so are worthy of death'.[88] Nonetheless, as heir to the throne, Elizabeth had influential protectors, notably Paget and Howard of Effingham. So, to validate a charge of treason, Mary needed to find conclusive proof of her sister's complicity in the plot. Testimonies were gathered from the main conspirators, and interrogators 'travailed with Sir Thomas Wyot touching the Lady Elizabeth'. In the meantime, she was left a virtual prisoner in Whitehall Palace, without access to the queen, and allowed no visitors.[89] Under intense questioning, Elizabeth denied any prior knowledge of the plot.

On 17 March 1554, William Paulet, second marquess of Winchester, and Henry Radcliffe, second earl of Sussex, came to Elizabeth's lodgings with an order to take her to the Tower.[90] Terrified that she would be summarily condemned and executed, Elizabeth begged the noblemen to permit her to write to the queen, requesting an audience. After they reluctantly agreed, Elizabeth set to work to craft a letter that would play upon Mary's sisterly feelings: 'I pray God,' she wrote, 'evil persuasions persuade not one sister again [against] the other'. Reminding the queen of 'your last promise and my last demand [request]' of the previous December that she 'be not condemned without answer and due proof', she begged 'to let me answer afore yourself'. The letter was signed 'Your highness' most faithful subject that hath been from the beginning and will be to my end'. Then Elizabeth scored across the remainder of the last page to prevent enemies from inserting a forged confession.[91]

Mary's only response to this desperate plea was anger that her sister had been granted the concession of petitioning her, for this special treatment was yet another indication of Elizabeth's privileged position in the eyes of her subjects.[92] She ignored the request. The next morning (Palm Sunday) Elizabeth was conveyed to the Tower by barge. Again Elizabeth's privileged position was evident when Sussex protested 'with weeping eyes', as the doors to her apartments in the Tower were about to be locked: 'What will ye doe, my lords?', he was heard to say 'What means ye therin? She was a king's daughter, and is the queen's syster'.[93]

During her time in the Tower the 20-year-old Elizabeth had good reason to fear that she would follow the innocent Lady Jane Grey and the guilty Sir Thomas Wyatt, both brought to the block after the rebellion. Mary continued to demand ongoing investigations that would bring forth an airtight case against the princess so that she could be put on trial, while privy councillors tried to wring a confession out of her during interrogations. However, Mary eventually had to accept that no irrefutable proof could be found against her sister, especially as Elizabeth continued to protest her innocence and Wyatt publicly declared on the scaffold that she 'never knewe of the conspiracy, nether of mye first risinge'.[94] As Renard complained in disgust, 'the judges can find no matter for her condemnation'.[95] To undercut Elizabeth's protectors who were calling for her immediate release, Renard advised Mary that her husband-to-be could not possibly come to England with the princess at liberty, since another conspiracy could easily develop around her person and put Philip's life in danger.

Caught between these conflicting viewpoints, Mary decided to free Elizabeth from the Tower but to place her under house arrest. The location chosen for her custody was the royal hunting lodge at Woodstock. Still hoping that continued pressure might induce Elizabeth to make a confession, Mary issued instructions that she should remain there 'untill suche tyme as certain matters towchyng hir case which bee not yet clered maye be thoroughlye tried and examined'.[96] On Saturday 19 May 1554, after two months of incarceration, Elizabeth left the Tower, and an armed guard of some 300 horsemen conveyed her by barge to Richmond Palace on the first leg of her journey by carriage to Oxfordshire.

Sir Henry Bedingfield, one of Mary's privy councillors and constable of the Tower, had charge of guarding Elizabeth and supervising her activities at Woodstock. His task was not easy, for he needed to find the right balance that would allow her to be treated as both a princess and a prisoner. According to Mary's instructions, Elizabeth—as the queen's sister—had to be used 'in such goode and honourable sorte as maye be agreeable to our honor and hir estate and degree', but—as a suspect—she was also to be under close and constant surveillance. Elizabeth could take a walk in the gardens only if accompanied by Bedingfield; she was prohibited 'conference with anye suspected person oute of hys heryng', and refused communication with the outside world by 'message, letter, or token'.[97] Determined to carry out these instructions to the letter, Bedingfield asked for guidance whenever he was required to take a decision that might be thought to lean to the side either of too great leniency or of dishonouring his charge. In her responses and specific orders, Mary tried to keep a similar fine balance herself. So, when she demanded the dismissal from Elizabeth's service of Elizabeth Sandes—'a person off an evyll opinion'—Mary let Bedingfield know 'our wyll and pleasure ys, ye shall traveyle with our sayde syster, and by the beste meanes ye can *perswade* hir to be contented to have the sayde Sands removed from hyr' (emphasis added). Yet, if Elizabeth was not content, continued Mary, 'we require yow...to gyve order' for Sandes's discharge.[98] As Mary had predicted, Elizabeth was not 'contented', and her parting from Sandes took place 'not without grette mournyng'.[99]

Mary had reluctantly agreed that Elizabeth could write to her from Woodstock, perhaps expecting words of submission or better still a confession. When Elizabeth's letters contained, instead, the usual protestations of innocence, Mary grew even angrier at what she saw as her sister's obstinate defiance in face of the truth. On 25 June 1554, the queen asserted that, like King Solomon, she could judge between truth and lies, and knew that Elizabeth's 'menying and purpose to be farre otherwise then hir letters purporteth'. From then on, Mary refused direct contact with her sister. She was not to be 'enye moore molested with suche her [Elizabeth's] disguise and colourable [deceitful] letters', nor would she communicate with Elizabeth except through Bedingfield, who was to read out even this message to the prisoner.[100]

Mary's message failed to have the desired effect. Elizabeth showed no remorse but, on the contrary, swore to Bedingfield that her words to the queen were 'the playn troth, even as I desire to be saved afore godde all myghtye'. Furthermore, she insisted that her gaoler should now let her petition the whole privy council.[101] Without waiting for his consent, Elizabeth composed her letter on 30 July 1554, formally requesting that she be put on trial or permitted access to the queen. Failing that, she asked for some councillors to come to Woodstock to listen to her suit in person. It was not until September that Mary allowed the letter to be delivered to the privy council, and even then it had no perceptible effect.[102]

Mary granted this concession only on receiving Bedingfield's report that Elizabeth had affirmed her innocence and loyalty after going to Catholic confession and before taking the eurcharist. Less impressed with Elizabeth's words (which were hardly new) than with her conformity to Catholic practice, Mary was rewarding what she hoped was Elizabeth's sincere religious conversion. She had offered prayers for this outcome and had done her best to isolate Elizabeth from the 'evil' influence of heretics, such as Elizabeth Sandes. Mary now declared herself 'verrye gladde that the Lady Elizabethe's grace doth so well conforme hir self in the receyviyng off the most blessed sacramente off the alter'.[103]

During the autumn of 1554, the queen demanded further signs of her sister's conversion. On 6 October she insisted that the princess should cease to hear any part of the divine service in English, as was her custom at least twice a week. Although Elizabeth promised to obey Mary 'with all my harte', she raised an objection. Given that the lord chamberlain and captain of the guard had let her hear the litany and suffrages in English when she was in the Tower (because it had been so used in Henry VIII's day), why was this form of prayer now unacceptable?[104] The outcome of her protest is unknown, but almost certainly Mary's will was followed in this matter, as in all others.

At last, on 17 April 1555, eleven months after Elizabeth's arrival at Woodstock, the order was given for her release and presence at Hampton Court. The reason was political. It was believed that Mary was in the last stages of pregnancy, and Philip was worried about what might happen if his wife and baby were to die during the dangers of childbirth. All things considered, Elizabeth's smooth accession would be less detrimental to Habsburg interests, he judged, than a succession dispute or civil war that might end in a victory for the next strongest claimant, Mary Stewart—Mary Queen of Scots. As the Scottish queen was betrothed to the dauphin, her accession would ultimately unite the British Isles to France, a nightmare scenario for a prospective Spanish king. Consequently, Philip wanted Elizabeth to be brought back to court as the potential successor waiting in the wings.[105]

Elizabeth arrived at Hampton Court during the last week of April 1555, and remained for two weeks in partial isolation, a pattern that was by now familiar to her. Eventually, at 10.00 p.m. on 21 May, she was brought before the queen for an interview that proved chilly and difficult, given that Elizabeth's continuing refusal to admit to any treasonable offence was an implicit accusation of her wrongful imprisonment. The sisters consequently parted unreconciled. Nonetheless, Mary had little choice but to remove the guard around Elizabeth and allow her some freedom, for the princess now had not only powerful friends on the council but also an ally in Philip. By this time, the king had realized that his wife was not pregnant at all. Instead, she may have been suffering from prolactinoma (a tumour on the pituitary gland) that produced the symptoms of pregnancy.[106] Of course Philip did not know of this illness, but he did recognize that something was wrong and suspected that Mary was unlikely to conceive in the future. Consequently, it was in his interests that his sister-in-law be treated as heir presumptive and married off as soon as possible to a Catholic ally of the Habsburgs. But this had to be left for Mary to arrange, since Philip was to leave England for the Netherlands, where his father demanded his presence.

After Philip's departure from London in late August 1555, Elizabeth resided with the queen at Greenwich. At a time when her co-religionists were being burnt for refusing to recant their beliefs, Elizabeth found herself forced to participate publicly in a wide range of Catholic ceremonies, such as a papal jubilee fast, in order to avoid prosecution for heresy.[107] It came as a great relief when Mary gave her licence to retire to Hertfordshire in mid-October 1555.[108]

The following year, some members of Elizabeth's household were implicated in a new conspiracy against the queen, but, in contrast to the situation two years previously, Mary affected to trust her sister. Following her husband's wishes, the queen publicly took the line that Elizabeth's servants had acted treacherously without their mistress's knowledge. In early June 1556, Mary sent Elizabeth 'a message of goodwill' along with a diamond ring, said to be worth 400 ducats, 'to show her that she is neither neglected nor hated, but loved and esteemed by her majesty'.[109] Nonetheless, for security's sake, Mary dispatched a trusted privy councillor, Sir Thomas Pope, to Hatfield to keep watch on the princess. According to the Venetian ambassador, Giovanni Michiel, a new governess was also appointed at this time, 'so that at present having none but the queen's dependents about her person, she [Elizabeth] herself likewise may be also said to be in ward and custody, though in such decorous and honourable form as becoming'.[110] This was an exaggeration. No one replaced Kat Astley, who had been dismissed from Elizabeth's service, and Pope was an unobtrusive guardian who reported nothing of significance to the queen or council during his four-month stay at Hatfield.

Only one letter between Elizabeth and Mary survives for this period. Elizabeth penned it on 2 August 1556 in reaction to the news that a pretender, impersonating Courtenay, had proclaimed himself and his 'beloved bedfellow' (Elizabeth) as king and queen of England. The conspiracy was crazed and easily suppressed, but Elizabeth took the opportunity to write effusively to Mary of her revulsion at all 'rebellious hearts and devilish intents' towards their anointed monarch. If only, declared Elizabeth, 'there were as good surgeons for making anatomies of hearts that might show my thought to your majesty', then Mary could see that, 'whatsoever other should suggest by malice, yet your majesty should be sure by knowledge, so that the more such misty clouds obfuscates the clear light of my truth, the more my tried thoughts should glister to the dimming of their hidden malice'. Peppering her extravagant prose with quotations from the Vulgate Bible (the version approved by Catholics), Elizabeth constructed her letter to convince Mary of her sincerity as a Catholic as well as a loyal subject.[111] As events were to prove, if the latter were true, the former was not.

That Christmas, Elizabeth was invited to enjoy the festivities at court. She arrived in London on 28 November 1556 'with a handsome retinue' of more than 200 horsemen clad in her own livery, and she resided several days in her own house in Somerset Place. After demonstrating her power, status, and independence by this means, she visited the queen, where she 'according to report was received very graciously and familiarly'. Afterwards she met the archbishop of Canterbury, Cardinal Pole, in his own chamber. This was the first time Pole had deigned to grant the princess an audience, and it marked her new political importance. The Venetian ambassador was impressed: 'now that she seems to be in good favour with her majesty, [I] will not fail to visit her before her departure, not having done so hitherto.'[112] Out of all danger and with Mary childless, Elizabeth was widely considered the next queen of England.

During this visit Mary probably raised the subject of Elizabeth's marriage, for Philip had made known his wish that she wed his cousin, Emmanuel Philibert, prince of Piedmont and duke of Savoy. Elizabeth's reply can only be guessed at; all we know for certain is that she returned to Hatfield on 3 December well before Christmas, so suddenly that Michiel was taken by surprise and 'had not time to pay her my visit'.[113] Pressure on Elizabeth to marry Savoy was resumed when Philip returned to England in April 1557. This time, both Mary and Elizabeth proved implacably opposed to the scheme. Mary refused to acknowledge Elizabeth's legitimacy and status as heir, a prerequisite of the match; Elizabeth objected because the marriage would commit her to a religion that she fundamentally opposed and to a pro-Spanish foreign policy. Neither sister would budge.[114] At the same time, Elizabeth had no wish to take a protestant husband who might act as her protector. When Mary grew suspicious that a clandestine plan was underway for a Swedish marriage alliance, Elizabeth protested: 'I so well lyke of this [single] estate as I perswade unto my self there is not any kynde of lyfe comparable unto it.'[115]

Elizabeth saw Mary for the last time on 28 February 1558 at Whitehall. The princess had ridden into London three days earlier 'with a gret compene of lord[s] & nobull men and nobull women' to display her status as heir and power as a major landowner, so that no challenge to her accession would be mounted on Mary's death.[116] The rest of the year she remained in Hertfordshire, where her household had been noticeably increasing: 'there is not a lord or gentleman in the kingdom' who did not endeavour 'to enter her [Elizabeth's] service himself or to place one of his sons or brothers in it', wrote the Venetian ambassador.[117] For her part, Elizabeth had good reason to employ these men in case she needed to fight for the throne against a Catholic contender. At last, Elizabeth learned in mid-October 1558 that Mary was seriously ill, probably dying. The princess then stepped up her preparations to take the crown, if necessary by force.

Mary had long resisted naming her sister as heir.[118] But, on the evening of 6 November, her privy council eventually persuaded her to send two councillors to Elizabeth. They were 'to inform her that the queen is willing that she succeed in the event of her own death, but that she asks two things of her: one, that she will maintain the old religion as the queen has restored it; and the other that she will pay the queen's debts'.[119] Elizabeth's actual response is not recorded, but two contemporaries—one a Catholic and the other a protestant—gave entirely different accounts of it. The Catholic Jane Dormer, Mary's lady in waiting, claimed in her later memoirs that Elizabeth then 'did swear and vow that she was a Catholic', and promised 'to uphold and continue Catholic religion' when Dormer handed over to her the queen's 'rich and precious jewels', a gift signifying her nomination of Elizabeth as heir.[120] By contrast, according to a protestant (who admittedly was not in England at the time), Elizabeth told the councillors that her right to the crown was hereditary and therefore not dependent on Mary's goodwill; as for religion, she promised: 'I will not change it, provided only it can be proved by the word of God, which shall be the only foundation and rule of my religion.'[121] As the 'word of God' was so often code for protestant teachings, this response indicated that Elizabeth would change the religion of England. Most Catholics also assumed that this would be the case. The count of Feria, an envoy from Philip, who was later to become Dormer's husband, came away from a meeting with Elizabeth, shortly before Mary's death, with the strong impression that the prospective queen would 'not be well-disposed in matters of religion' and would rule with the help of her protestant friends.[122]

The reigns of her siblings were perilous years when Elizabeth learned important political lessons. Personal experience taught her to distrust malign gossip and unsubstantiated rumours, yet at the same time to be wary and suspicious of competitors for the throne. After all, whatever the truth of the accusations against her, Elizabeth had had to dissimulate, hide her emotions, and be economical with the truth, when under investigation. As she later admitted, her future relationships—especially those with potential heirs—were affected by recollections of her own predicament in 1549 and 1554. It is, therefore, no wonder that she attempted to combine caution and circumspection with a degree of fairness in her later dealings with Mary Queen of Scots. Elizabeth's consistent decision not to name her successor arose from similar memories. First, the 1553 crisis had showed her that a sovereign's decision concerning the succession was not necessarily paramount and could be overturned after his or her death. Second, Wyatt's rebellion and the later Marian conspiracies convinced her that, if disaffected subjects 'knew a certain successor of our crown, they would have recourse thither'.[123] Third, she believed that any named heir would be as unhappy as she had been under Mary, as monarchs could not possibly see them as anything other than a danger to their own person.

Elizabeth also took more positive lessons from the reigns of her siblings. From both monarchs she learned much about the art of self-representation. Like Edward, she presented herself as a learned, godly, protestant monarch, who was well versed in the classics and scriptures. From Mary, she learned how to project authority and power while 'circumventing masculine stance and military symbols'.[124] So, for example, Elizabeth appropriated the images of the biblical women Deborah, Judith, and Esther, who had previously been associated with her immediate predecessor.[125] Furthermore, Elizabeth carried out royal rituals that had fallen into abeyance under the protestant Edward but had been restored by the Catholic Mary: the exchange of gifts on New Year's Day; the touching for the king's evil to cure scrofula; the royal washing of paupers' feet on Maundy Thursday; and the celebration of the Feast of St George.[126] Even though some protestants criticized these rituals as superstitious, Elizabeth continued them because they added to the charisma of monarchy.

Protestant propagandists, however, would not admit to any borrowing from Mary. Instead, they worked hard to distance and dissociate the new queen from her half-sister. According to their binary approach, Elizabeth was legitimate, Mary a bastard; Elizabeth embraced true religion, Mary superstition and error; Mary was attached to Spain while Elizabeth was born and bred an Englishwoman; Mary was a warmonger, Elizabeth a prince of peace; Mary allowed the cruel burnings of protestants, while Elizabeth refused to open a window into people's souls. When Elizabeth deliberately took over Mary's motto 'Truth the daughter of time', her purpose was to show that time had exposed the false religion of the Catholic queen.

At the same time, Elizabeth and her supporters exploited the facts of her short imprisonment in the Tower and Woodstock to relate a tale of her providential deliverance from danger and death. Such a fashioning was popular throughout Elizabeth's reign, not least because it gave legitimacy to her exercise of political power as both a woman and a protestant. Many of Elizabeth's subjects encountered the story, whether in Foxe's *Acts and Monuments*, in a variety of English chronicles, or in sermons preached on 17 November, the anniversary of Elizabeth's accession. Some subjects and foreign visitors visited the lodge at Woodstock to see for themselves the poem that she had scratched in charcoal on a shutter frame and the couple of lines inscribed (it was said) with a diamond on a windowpane:

> Much suspected by me
> Nothing proved can be.[127]

When Elizabeth herself visited Woodstock on her 1592 progress, the poet Thomas Churchyard celebrated the place as:

> This seat nay sure this shrine
> That thousands now doth praise:
> That did preserve, by power divine,
> The phoenix of our daies.[128]

That Churchyard needed simply to allude to Elizabeth's imprisonment without spelling out any details is testimony to the familiarity of the story within England. The perils of the princess under Mary had become central to the Elizabethan myth, while her difficulties under Edward were all but forgotten.

2

....

The Suffolk Cousins

The presence at court of her Boleyn cousins brought Queen Elizabeth comfort and support. By contrast, her relationships with the English cousins on her father's side of the family were often tense and troubled. Since they were of royal blood, this was to be expected, for English history contained several worrying examples of ambitious members of a royal family emerging as rivals to their sovereign. But, an even more important issue affected their relationship with Elizabeth: the unsettled succession. With a childless queen on the throne and no person designated her heir presumptive, all the descendants of Henry VIII's two sisters were politically significant figures, being potential claimants on Elizabeth's death (see the 'Genealogical Chart').

Elizabeth's Suffolk cousins were the descendants of Henry VIII's younger sister Mary, who had married Charles Brandon, duke of Suffolk, immediately after her first husband, Louis XII of France, had died in 1515. Close to death in December 1546, Henry had bequeathed the English crown to Mary's progeny in the event of his own children dying without issue.[1] In so doing, he was overturning the common law principle of primogeniture, which, if applied, would have left the succession in the line of his older sister Margaret. Mary had been Henry's favourite sister, and her husband his good friend, but the reasons behind the king's decision had less to do with affection or sentiment than prejudice and politics. Margaret had married two Scots; her children were born in Scotland; and her eldest grandchild—the infant Mary Stewart—had inherited the Scottish throne in 1542. For several years afterwards Henry had attempted to arrange—or force through—a marriage between Mary and his son Edward, only to be thwarted by the Scots, who resisted what they understandably saw as a dynastic union that would end their independence. By effectively disinheriting Margaret's descendants, Henry was punishing the Scots for their intransigence and forestalling the possibility of a Scottish monarch ever ruling England in his or her own right.[2]

Mary, duchess of Suffolk, had two daughters: Frances born in 1517, and Eleanor, whose year of birth was either 1519 or 1520 and who died in November 1547. Both girls married young and had surviving female offspring. Aged just 15, Frances wed Henry Grey, marquess of Dorset, who later became duke of Suffolk. She gave birth to a son, who died in infancy, and three healthy daughters, who were named Jane, Katherine, and Mary. Eleanor married before she was 15, her nuptials to Henry Clifford (the future earl of Cumberland) taking place in 1533. The couple had two sons, who similarly died very young, as well as a daughter Margaret, born in either 1538 or 1540.[3] For two generations, therefore, the Suffolk line was monopolized by women, and Henry's will privileging his great-nieces was to dominate and, in some cases, damage or destroy their lives.

Before her accession Elizabeth had no recorded contact with any of the daughters of Frances, duchess of Suffolk. It seems likely that she knew Jane when both girls were briefly residing in the household of the dowager queen, Katherine, after Henry VIII's death, but, since Elizabeth was 4 years older than her 10-year-old cousin, they spent little, if any, time together. The two probably met again at Edward VI's court, for Jane certainly knew about—and approved of—her cousin's rejection of rich clothes and jewels as a statement of her protestant piety.[4] Nonetheless, they were not in the least intimate, and Elizabeth did not attend the private wedding ceremony in May 1553, when the 15-year-old Jane married Guildford Dudley (a son of the powerful duke of Northumberland) and Katherine (nearly three years younger) wed Lord Herbert (heir to the first earl of Pembroke). For this reason, Jane felt no personal disloyalty to her protestant cousin when she abided by the terms of Edward VI's will and took the throne. Her proclamation of July 1553 declared the legality of her accession on the grounds that Elizabeth and Mary were 'but of the halfe bloud' and therefore 'be not inheritable unto our sayd late cosin, although [even if] borne in laweful matrimony as in deed they were not'.[5] From Elizabeth's viewpoint, these justifications were spurious; Jane's accession was illegal and a sign of the overweening political ambitions of the Grey family. The only tears to be shed over Jane's execution on 9 February 1554, just after the failure of Wyatt's rebellion, arose from the fear that Queen Mary and her advisers might likewise show Elizabeth no mercy.

Jane was not the only Grey to die on the scaffold. For their part in Wyatt's rebellion, her father and uncle (Lord Thomas Grey) also went to their deaths. Queen Mary, though, listened to Frances's personal plea for pardon, and in July 1554 the duchess joined the queen's privy chamber and brought her daughters to court.[6] Indeed, for a short while, Mary showed great favour to Frances, who conformed to Catholicism, and gave her first cousin precedence over her half-sister so as to ram home Elizabeth's bastardy. However, on Frances's marriage in 1555 to Adrian Stokes, a commoner who had previously served as her master of the stables, the duchess effectively lost her royal status and withdrew from court, leaving her elder daughter behind, possibly as a maid of honour to the queen.[7] Katherine was now single, since her father-in-law had arranged for the annulment of her unconsummated marriage, but a poor marriage prospect, as her family name was dishonoured and she had no fortune of her own. As for her sister Mary, some five years younger, her chances of marriage were still worse, as she did not share her sister's good looks and was described as 'crook-backed'.

During Queen Mary's reign, Margaret Clifford—the daughter of Eleanor, late duchess of Cumberland—was also treated as a close member of the royal family. She had been betrothed to Andrew Dudley (a brother of the duke of Northumberland), whom she had very probably never met, but his attainder for treason in supporting Lady Jane Grey put an end to their engagement. Margaret was in consequence left free to marry Henry Stanley, Lord Strange, the heir to the wealthy third earl of Derby. Since Derby was a strong supporter of Mary and Philip, his son's wedding to Margaret on 7 February 1555 took place in the chapel royal at Whitehall Palace and was celebrated with jousts, a grand feast, a masque, and the new Spanish game, the *juego de cañas*. Although the queen was unable to attend, because of her supposed pregnancy, she gave the bride a brooch of thirteen diamonds, household linen, and robes of gold and silver tinsel.[8] After the marriage, Strange bore the sword of state before King Philip, an honour usually reserved for a near relative of the monarch. Indeed, Margaret believed she had a 'just claim' to be the queen's successor, because, 'treason being upon the house of her cousin', Katherine Grey, she was 'the nearest in blood (and legitimately of English birth)'. The Venetian ambassador Giovanni Michiel was inclined to agree that 'to her the succession belongs', but Queen Mary thought otherwise and would have named the countess of Lennox (the daughter of Henry VIII's sister Margaret) as her heir, had not her half-sister Elizabeth commanded so much support that her title could not be ignored.[9]

Although—once queen—Elizabeth is often accused of acting unfairly, even vindictively, towards all her royal cousins, Margaret was accorded great honour and kindness during the first twenty-two years of the reign.[10] Elizabeth chose to have her cousin regularly in attendance upon her at court, 'being nere in blood to us', and Lady Strange usually bore the queen's train during processions, while 'all the other ladies followed in their degrees'.[11] After Margaret had separated from her husband and was financially embarrassed, Elizabeth tried several times to help her out. In January 1567, the queen entered into a financial arrangement with the Stranges that would provide them with an annual income.[12] Later that year, the queen 'commanded she [Margaret] shold have a lodging in the courte to lessen her charges lyving in the towne'.[13] Then in 1570, when the earl of Cumberland died and Margaret lost his vital financial support, Elizabeth 'ernestly' urged her impoverished cousin's estranged husband to take on some responsibility 'towards the maytenance of hir resonable and ordinary charge'.[14] As for herself, the usually parsimonious Elizabeth agreed to give Margaret 'our interest in some portions of such lands as she ought to have in reversion' so that they could be sold in order to offset her outstanding debts.[15] Despite her financial difficulties (or perhaps contributing to them), Margaret gave expensive New Year's gifts to the queen: in January 1573, now the countess of Derby, she presented Elizabeth with two pieces of jewellery made of gold and precious stones. Less extravagantly, in 1578, her gift was a personal item of clothing—an embroidered petticoat made of satin—and in 1579 it was a gown of tawny velvet.[16] Until the countess began dabbling with politics and magic in the late 1570s, Elizabeth did not appear threatened by her cousin's nearness to the throne, nor by the fact that she was the mother of several sons. On the contrary, there is every reason to suppose that their relationship was cordial, possibly even close.

Lady Katherine Grey was never close to Elizabeth. Nonetheless, at her accession, Elizabeth took on the 18-year-old as a maid of honour. But, apparently, Katherine was not content with her position, for she complained to the Spanish ambassador, the count of Feria, that Elizabeth did not accord her the status of heir presumptive. Feria suspected that Elizabeth was mistrustful of her cousin, and—if true—she had good cause. As had occurred when Elizabeth was Queen Mary's heir, plots and conspiracies began to gel around Katherine, who was considerably less circumspect in dealing with them. According to Feria, she was 'very friendly' towards him, grumbled to him about Elizabeth, and promised that she would remain a Catholic and not marry without his approval.[17] The English ambassador at King Philip's

court in the Netherlands, meanwhile, heard that 'there ys practysing
for a mariage to be made betwyxt the prince of Spayne and the Lady
Kateryn'; and there was also talk of plans to kidnap and wed her to
Philip's heir. Elizabeth may well have heard of Katherine's disaffection and Spanish contacts, and consequently for safety's sake she was
'straytely loked to' (closely watched) in the privy chamber.[18]

Katherine, though, had matters other than politics on her mind.
Since the summer of 1558 she had been romantically attached to
Edward Seymour, the son of the attainted Lord Protector Somerset.
The couple first met in early 1558 when Katherine went to stay at his
mother's house at Hanworth in Middlesex to attend upon her friend,
his sister Lady Jane Seymour, who was then sick. They were immediately attracted to each other, and Seymour even spoke to her of marriage at that time, although he kept his feelings from their respective
families.[19] At Elizabeth's accession, the young man was elevated to
the peerage as earl of Hertford and Katherine returned to court. Separated from his pretty companion, he seemingly cooled in his affections until the queen and her entourage visited Hanworth in the
spring of 1559, when the 'love did againe renewe betwixt them'.
Their families and friends then noticed the change in their behaviour
towards each other, and several grew concerned about their relationship in the knowledge that Elizabeth would almost certainly oppose
a match between a potential heir and a powerful and ambitious
nobleman. Such a union might establish a strong power base against
a queen ruling alone, especially before she had had time to consoli-
date her position. Furthermore, Katherine's marriage to a protestant
nobleman would strengthen her claim to the succession against the
Catholic Mary Queen of Scots, an outcome Elizabeth simply did not
want. Hertford's mother, therefore, told the young earl to cease
spending time with Katherine, but his response was that 'he trusted
he might use her company being not forbidden by the queen's highnes's expresse commaundment'.

Sometime around October 1559, Katherine's stepfather talked to
Hertford about a possible betrothal and advised him 'to make suite to
such of the queene's majesty's counsaile as he thought weare most
his freindes to be a meane to the queene's highnes for him for
th'accomplishment of the saied marriadge'. Once Hertford had
spoken to the councillors, continued Stokes, Katherine's mother would
seek the queen's permission for the match. In preparation, Frances
asked her husband to draft a letter to the queen. However, shortly
afterwards Hertford backed out of the commitment. He returned

to their house and declared that 'he wolde noe further medle in the matter'. His reason was that the queen's principal secretary, Sir William Cecil, and his mother were again warning him that the affair was unwise, as Elizabeth would be certain to forbid the match.

Meanwhile, the death of her mother on 20 November 1559 put Katherine's thoughts of marriage on hold. In early December, she and her sister participated in the formal obsequies for the duchess and officially mourned their loss. In death Elizabeth gave Frances the honours she deserved as a granddaughter of King Henry VII. She paid for the funeral in Westminster Abbey and issued a warrant granting 'unto her and her posteryte' a royal quartering of her arms, 'wich shal be an apparent declaration of here consanguynyte unto us'. The herald (the Clarencieux king of arms) called out loudly Frances's title of duchess of Suffolk and her royal pedigree as the daughter of a French queen and the granddaughter of a king of England.[20]

No sooner was Katherine's period of mourning over than she and Hertford became secretly betrothed, and together with his sister Jane they made arrangements for a clandestine wedding. All were certain that the queen would refuse permission for the marriage, but it did not seem to occur to them that to wed without her consent might be considered an act of treason.[21] The exact date of the wedding was not planned in advance, since it had to depend on the queen going 'abroad' without her two maids. It actually occurred sometime between Allhallowtide (the season around All Saints' Day on 1 November) and Christmas 1560, when Katherine and Jane took the opportunity to slip away from court while Elizabeth went off to hunt at Eltham. Katherine had pleaded 'a swelling in her face', and Jane offered to stay behind to look after her. The next morning, the two women hurried to Hertford's house in Cannon Row, Westminster, for the ceremony. The resourceful Jane pulled in a 'priest or minister' from the street, and he solemnized the marriage using the Book of Common Prayer. The marriage was consummated immediately afterwards.

Returning to court that evening, Katherine resumed her duties in the privy chamber, telling no one of her new married status. Over the next few months, the couple met secretly at Cannon Row or in Katherine's chamber at one of the royal palaces. Whether or not the queen suspected anything is unknown, but it seems very likely. Certainly, others noticed the couple's 'familiaritie' and spoke to Katherine about it. Cecil advised her 'to take good heede how she proceeded in familiaritie with the said earle withowt makeinge the queene's majestie pryvie thereunto'. Similarly, Elizabeth, marchioness of Northampton, and Elizabeth Lady Clinton—both intimates of the queen—'did seriouslie advertise her to beware the companie and familiaritie with the saied earle'. They may all have been acting independently, but it is equally possible that the queen was using her secretary and her women as intermediaries to warn off Katherine from pursuing a relationship with Hertford.[22] All this time, the maid of honour consistently and fraudulently denied any liaison with the earl.

To separate the couple, Cecil recommended at the end of May 1561 that Hertford be sent to France on an extended educational tour. By that time, Katherine suspected she was pregnant but could not confirm it, and so Hertford decided to leave the country anyway. If she were pregnant, he told her complaisantly, they must 'trust to the queene's mercy'. To safeguard her position in case Hertford died while abroad (according to their later testimony), he gave her a deed that bequeathed her a widow's jointure of £1,000 a year, which she put in a coffer for safety.

In July that year, Katherine accompanied the queen on her summer progress. By then, she was in no doubt about her condition and wrote to Hertford, begging him to return home as she was 'quick with childe'. She received no reply. Now seven months pregnant, Katherine began to be the subject of gossip at court. Realizing that she could no longer keep the marriage and pregnancy a secret, she confessed all to Mistress St Loe (the mother of the maids in the privy chamber) on Saturday 9 August, but she received no help from that quarter. St Loe simply wept and 'declared she was sorrie therefore because that shee [Katherine] had not made the queene's majestie pryvie thereunto'. The next night, Katherine went to the room of Lord Robert Dudley, and 'by his bedd's side' she appealed for him to 'be a meane to the queene's highness for her'. Elizabeth learned of 'this mishapp'—as Cecil euphemistically put it—the next day.[23]

Elizabeth had been in a bad mood for much of the summer. At a personal level she had been forced to lay aside thoughts of marrying Dudley and was being pressured against her will to consider King Eric XIV of Sweden as a suitable husband. Politically, she was preoccupied with the many problems associated with Mary Queen of Scots.[24] While on progress, her ill humour manifested itself in a number of trivial ways but caused considerable unease when she displayed 'daily offence' at the 'undiscreet behaviour' of the clergy in Suffolk and Essex, who were publicly parading their wives and children in colleges and cathedrals. It had been a 'troublesome progress', bemoaned Cecil to Archbishop Parker, and it had been all he could do to stop the queen from banning clerical marriage altogether.[25] Yet, even had the timing been better, it is very unlikely that Elizabeth would have been sympathetic to Katherine and Hertford. Not only had her maid been deceptive and disobedient, but also the queen understandably—if mistakenly—strongly suspected 'some greater drift was in this' and that a plot was afoot.[26] So did others. The Spanish ambassador reported—wrongly—that 'the marriage was effected with the connivance and countenance' of Cecil and the nobles who were enemies of Dudley. Their aim, thought Alvaro de la Quadra, was to marry Elizabeth's heir to a protestant as an insurance policy in case Elizabeth married Dudley with assistance from the king of Spain and returned England to the Catholic fold.[27]

Certain that there had been 'great practisees and purposees', Elizabeth commanded Sir Edward Warner the lieutenant of the Tower to examine Lady Katherine 'very streightly' even though she was in the last month of pregnancy. What Elizabeth required him to discover was who exactly had been 'privy' to the love affair right from the beginning. Katherine should be made to understand, went on the queen 'that she shall have no manner of favour, except she will shew the truth…for it doth now appere that sondry personagees have delt herin'. Elizabeth also wanted Mistress St Loe to be questioned in the Tower over two or three nights so that she might confess all she knew about the matter.[28] Hertford was summoned back from France and likewise ordered to the Tower, where he too was interrogated.

Katherine's first interrogation took place on 22 August 1561 before Hertford had returned from France. As she later explained:

> shee was then in such troble of minde for feare of the queene's majes-tie's displeasure and for absence of her husbande and her imprison-ment and being great with child that was she not then soe well advised in her saied answeares as shee hath sithence considered the same.[29]

Indeed, her initial testimony seemed to Warner 'so unlykly' that he used all means he could to persuade her to be 'more playne' with the queen, but Katherine insisted that 'all that she hathe sayd ys trewe'. Warner spent 'moche tyme with hyr the rather to se yf any thynge wold fall owt unadvyssydly', but he proved unsuccessful.[30] Katherine's evasions and untruths intensified Elizabeth's belief that either a conspiracy lay behind the marriage or else no marriage had in fact occurred.

On 24 September 1561, Katherine gave birth to a son, who was baptized Edward after his father and paternal grandfather. Elizabeth's immediate reactions to the birth are nowhere recorded, but it soon became evident that her intention was for the baby to be declared a bastard and excluded from the succession. To achieve this purpose, she appointed a commission—led by Matthew Parker (the archbishop of Canterbury), Edmund Grindal (bishop of London), and Sir William Petre (a respected privy councillor)—to inquire into the validity of the marriage. As she explained to Warner, its remit was 'to examyn, inquire, and judge of the infamose conversacion, and pretended mariage', a choice of words demonstrating that the queen had already determined its outcome.[31]

Appearing before the commission separately, Katherine and Hertford were subjected to the same questions on oath over several days in February 1562.[32] Their answers did not help their case. First—and of least importance—even if a marriage had taken place, the wedding ceremony they described was irregular, since no banns had been read or communion celebrated beforehand. Second, the answers they gave to their interrogators were often suspiciously vague: neither of them, for example, remembered the date of the marriage ceremony; Hertford did not recall how much money he had assigned to Katherine on his departure to France; for her part, Katherine frequently responded to questions with words like 'shee cannott call to her remembrance'. Third, their accounts did not always tally. In an attempt to protect Stokes and other kin, Hertford declared that he 'did not reveale nor disclose' his marriage proposal to Frances or anyone else, whereas Katherine admitted freely that her mother had been told of their intention. In an attempt to protect herself, Katherine claimed she 'had companie and carnall copulation' with Hertford in Cannon Row 'but not elsewheare to her remembrance', but Hertford confessed that he 'laie' with her 'in the queene's howses both at Westminster and Greenwich'. Katherine maintained that 'shee received noe letteres to her remembrance' from Hertford after he had gone abroad, whereas he (and his servant) testified that he sent her two or three letters from France.[33] Fourth, and crucially important, there were no witnesses or documents to support their statements: Lady Jane Seymour had died in early 1561; the minister who married them had disappeared, and they had failed to take his name or address; and Hertford's gentleman usher and the grooms of his chamber had not stayed home on the day of the ceremony and therefore could not testify to the cleric's arrival. The other servants noticed nothing amiss and especially not the arrival of a stranger who could be a priest. The written evidence for the marriage was also missing.[34] The documents drawn up by Hertford and handed over to Katherine had been lost during the preparations for the royal progress, and the earl had kept no copy in his possession. Furthermore, the executors of his estate during Hertford's absence abroad had received no instructions or written documents concerning Katherine. Consequently, the couple's claim that Hertford had made provision for a widow's jointure could not be substantiated.

The lovers' carelessness was truly astounding and left the commission with no legal grounds for overriding the queen's predetermined political decision. Its verdict—announced on 12 May 1562—predictably found that no marriage had taken place and that Hertford was guilty of carnal copulation with a princess of royal blood. His punishment was a hefty fine of £1,500.[35] Opinion in the country was divided about the ruling: 'some saied they were married, som that they were not.' The former thought the couple was 'sharply handled', but the latter judged their treatment to be fair, given that 'they agre not in the circumstances' nor could find the priest.[36] Apparently two of the guards in the Tower were among the former group. In sympathy with their prisoners, as well as tempted by bribes, they disobeyed royal orders and allowed Hertford 'secrett accesse by night to the Ladye Katherine', with the upshot that she 'brought a boye childe to the worlde'.[37] Conceived in late May, the baby—baptized Thomas—was born on 10 February 1563. For this offence Hertford was summoned before Star Chamber, fined a crippling £15,000, and ordered to remain in prison during the queen's pleasure.[38] This time, word on the street was that the couple were indeed married, and the question was raised 'whye sholde men and wief be lett from coming together?'[39] Katherine's uncle, Lord John Grey, even suggested that the queen's conduct was unchristian: if he were a preacher, Grey later wrote to Cecil, he would 'tell her highnes that God will not forgeve her, unleast she freely forgeve all the worlde'.[40]

The birth of this second child created a serious dilemma for Elizabeth. Conceived after his parents had publicly avowed their marriage before the commission of inquiry, Thomas could be considered legitimate according to canon law, which merely demanded witnessed consent and 'carnal copulation' for a 'perfect marriage'. Elizabeth, however, refused to acknowledge this possibility. Instead, she insisted that the child was a bastard and Hertford guilty of fornication in siring him. Why? One possible explanation is that the queen wanted to place every obstacle in the way of a Suffolk succession on her own death, partly because she disliked Katherine for flouting her authority and partly because she had not forgiven the whole Grey family for their attempted coup in July 1553. While there may be some truth in this interpretation, it needs to be remembered that Elizabeth had not yet decided upon perpetual virginity; still under 30 years old, she might still marry and produce an heir of her own body. But, even if she remained childless, Elizabeth knew from her own experience that illegitimacy was not a total bar to the succession.

A more convincing explanation for Elizabeth's severity towards Katherine and her children was her own delicate relationship with Mary Queen of Scots. It was not simply that Elizabeth favoured Mary's claim to the succession—which she almost certainly did; far more important was Elizabeth's need to have Mary believe that she favoured her succession. With her French relations and Catholic connections, Mary was a far greater threat to Elizabeth's throne than was Katherine. Elizabeth had already assured a Scottish envoy that she considered Mary's hereditary right to the succession to be superior to Katherine's, despite the evident proof that the latter was 'not barren but able to have children'.[41] Had Katherine's second child been recognized as legitimate, Mary would have viewed the decision as a direct challenge to her own claim and deeply hostile to her interests. One possible consequence might be her rejection of the anglophile policies she was then pursuing in the hope of being named Elizabeth's heir. Even worse, she might marry a foreign prince who would choose to back her immediate claim to the throne. This Elizabeth wanted to prevent at all costs. Elizabeth, moreover, was hoping to tempt Mary into a marriage with Robert Dudley by hinting that this would assist her title to the succession.[42] In these circumstances, Katherine's imprisonment was necessary for her own security and that of the realm.

Despite her callous punishment of her Suffolk cousin, Elizabeth did not want any harm to come to Katherine or her sons. When plague hit London and threatened the Tower in the summer of 1563, the queen readily agreed to Katherine's transfer with her baby to the safer environment of Lord John Grey's home in Essex. Hertford's release from the Tower was more difficult to secure, and it was only 'uppon muche humble suyte' that he and his older son were permitted to move to the dowager duchess of Somerset's house in Middlesex.[43] Still under house arrest, the prisoners were forbidden to leave their immediate environment 'under payne of our indignation'. Nonetheless hope was offered that they might be liberated in the near future. If Katherine behaved well and learned to be obedient to her superiors while in her uncle's household, promised Cecil, 'she shuld not long lack hir majesty's favor, but recover it by all good meanes'.[44] Katherine therefore did her best to convince Elizabeth of her submission. In a petition to the queen, vetted by Cecil, she called herself an 'unworthye creature' for having forgotten her duty in rashly wedding without royal consent.[45] The couple's friends and supporters also tried to intercede with the queen.[46] According to Dudley, his representation on Hertford's behalf 'was not myslyked', but Elizabeth would still not be pressurized into giving a 'comfortable answour' to his suit. Hertford would just have to wait, he explained: 'Your lordship can consider princes must be obeyed and ther wylles fulfilled yf God have not yet stirred her hart hereunto'. All that the earl could do now, he concluded, was offer prayers to God, as men had done all they might. A week later Dudley was more optimistic: Hertford had cause to be hopeful of an early release, given the queen's clemency already 'shewyd to many'.[47]

It is highly unlikely that Elizabeth would ever have permitted Katherine and Hertford to live together as man and wife. The most they could realistically hope for was a royal pardon and freedom from house arrest. But that outcome was not enough for Hertford and some of his supporters; they wanted the marriage to be declared valid and Katherine's title as heir presumptive enacted in statute. And their misguided campaign to achieve these ends sabotaged the earlier efforts by Cecil and Dudley to have the couple set at liberty.

During 1563, Lord John Grey and his friend John Hales sent the 'scholar' Robert Beale abroad to consult 'lerned men' on the Continent about the marriage, with the intention of obtaining arguments that contradicted the findings of the commission of inquiry.[48] This Beale did successfully, and Hertford planned to use the learned judgments as evidence in an appeal against the original verdict.[49] Hales, meanwhile, criticized the original commission's findings as 'unjust' and pronounced publicly that the marriage was valid according to 'the lawe of nature, Godd's lawe, and the common lawe'. Unsurprisingly, this outspoken challenge to a royal commission was condemned as malicious, arrogant, scandalous, seditious, and 'an offence in law'.[50]

At the same time, Hales got into further trouble because he was the author of a pamphlet that promoted Katherine's title to be Elizabeth's heir. She was the legitimate successor, he declared, first because Henry VIII's will privileging the Suffolk line was authentic and legal, and second because common law barred foreigners (and hence the Stewarts) from inheriting the English throne.[51] These arguments had already been raised in the parliament of January 1563 when the claims of individual candidates had been discussed and a Commons' petition had been introduced that was designed to exclude Mary Queen of Scots from the succession. Elizabeth had naturally rejected the petition and hoped the matter would die down. She was therefore outraged at the appearance of Hales's pamphlet. As late as November 1564, she was still angry. 'The queen's majesty contynueth her displeasur towardes John Hales, for his foolish attempt in wrytyng the book so precisely agaynst the queen of Scotland's title,' wrote Cecil to his friend Sir Thomas Smith.[52] By this time, Elizabeth was convinced that Hales had not acted alone and that a wider, dangerous conspiracy was involved. Here her fears were exaggerated. It is true that Lord Keeper Nicholas Bacon helped Hales gather information and seek legal opinions (and as a result fell into deep disgrace).[53] However, the others most directly implicated in Hales's initiative—Hertford's stepfather Francis Newdigate and Katherine's uncle Lord John Grey—were politically insignificant; while the other men who came under investigation—Thomas Dannett, John Foster, and David Whitehead—were minor figures without the political influence to cause Elizabeth serious problems.[54] As for Katherine herself, she had no knowledge of Hales's activities; under interrogations he denied any contact with the 'poore woman'.[55] Nonetheless, all these men were working together to overturn a royal policy that lay outside their competences and, as far as the queen was concerned, such action was subversive and potentially seditious. Consequently, Hales spent a year in the Tower after his examination in the Fleet prison, and on his release was put under house arrest until his death in 1571. Bacon escaped jail, but was banished from court from the last months of 1563 until the spring of 1565. The others got off more lightly: Newdigate was confined to his own house; Grey spent a short period in the Tower and was then released.[56]

As Elizabeth had feared, Hales's pamphlet reopened the succession debate. Supporters of Mary Queen of Scots' title read it, were dismayed by its conclusions, and wrote their own responses. These were, in turn, answered by those who favoured Katherine's claim. During 1565 and 1566, several succession tracts came to be distributed in England, while protestant MPs in the parliament of October 1566 called upon Elizabeth to name her heir and clearly favoured Katherine.[57] Furthermore, Cecil and other privy councillors urged

Elizabeth 'to shew some remission of hir displeasur' towards Katherine and Hertford, so that 'the Queen of Scottes thereby may find some change and hir friends putt in doubt of further proceeding' in her favour.[58] The succession debate, which Elizabeth had hoped to keep under wraps, had entered the public arena. In those circumstances, Katherine and Hertford could not expect release from house arrest. Not only was Elizabeth furious with Hertford for instigating an appeal; she also did not want to signal in any way that she favoured a Suffolk-line succession on her death.[59]

The embers of Elizabeth's rage against Katherine were stoked again in August 1565 when a secret marriage was discovered between the youngest of the Grey sisters, the 19-year-old Mary, and the middle-aged Thomas Keyes, who was the sergeant porter responsible for the security of the court.[60] Pretty much everyone found this union to be monstrous, because the married couple were not just unequal in status but also physically ill matched. Mary was not only crook-backed but also extremely short (described as 'the lest of all the court'), while her new husband was 'the biggest gentillman in this court'.[61] The main problem for the newly married couple, though, was their failure to seek the permission of their mistress and sovereign, an insubordination that required punishment. As William Lord Howard of Effingham explained, Elizabeth needed to make an example of them. Too many people

> be in so litle feare of the prince that they dare think to enterprise so great a matter. I dowt not hit wilbe so ponished as hit maie geve suche a terror to all her majestie's subjectes they maie ever hereafter beware howe to enter in any kynde of matter that maye in any case sounde against their bounde for safety, dutye of allegiance.[62]

And punish them Elizabeth did. Although she suspected no political motive behind the secret marriage, she came down very hard on both Mary and Keyes. He was imprisoned in the Fleet; she was placed in the custody of William Hawtrey at his house at Chequers in Buckinghamshire and ordered to be 'straightly used from enjoyeng of any liberty, as a meane to correct hir'.[63]

Over the next few years, the Grey sisters were to stay in the houses of several different custodians. At the time of her uncle's arrest, Katherine was relocated to the home of Sir William Petre at Ingatestone in Essex, and she resided there until her host's sickness necessitated her removal in May 1566 to Gosford Hall in Essex, the house of Sir John Wentworth. After Wentworth's death in September 1567, she was placed in the charge of Sir Owen Hopton and his wife at Cockfield Hall, Yoxford, in Suffolk. Since the succession question was raised again in the 1566 parliament and further pamphlets circulated, Elizabeth remained apprehensive about Katherine having any contact with friends or kin, so Hopton was ordered to keep her 'secluded' and 'away from conference or sight of strangers'.[64] In fact, Katherine lived at Cockfield for only fourteen weeks. Her mental and physical health had been poor throughout her long detention, but she seemed to have lost the will to live once she despaired of ever seeing her husband and elder son again. After a short illness, the 27-year-old died on 27 January 1568. Elizabeth publicly 'expressed sorrow' at her death, but the Spanish ambassador was right to think 'it is not believed that she feels it'.[65] Nonetheless the queen could not ignore Katherine's royal lineage, and she paid for the embalming of the body and an elaborate funeral. The interior of the unprepossessing parish church at Yoxford was decorated with 'a great banner of armes', four 'bannerolls' (banners displayed at a funeral procession and set over the tomb), six great escutcheons on paste paper, twenty-four escutcheons on 'buckeram' (coarse linen), and twenty-four 'eschutcheons of paper in metal' for 'garnisshing' the house and church. Seventy-seven official mourners, plus a herald and two pursuivants of arms (junior heraldic officers), were sent down from the court to participate.[66]

Protestants mourned Katherine's loss, 'as they had fixed their eyes on her for the succession in any eventuality'.[67] Some still hoped, though, that Elizabeth would relent and overturn the commission of inquiry's original decision so that Katherine's sons could be next in line for the throne, but all Hertford's attempts to reopen the case came to nothing, as he was unable to obtain the necessary documentation.[68] Nonetheless, as late as March 1574, Archbishop Parker—who had headed the original inquiry—privately admitted that he had thought to himself, 'but uttered it to no body lyving', that 'som man might worke' to have the case opened again so that the earl's children could be pronounced legitimate and 'heritable'.[69] Other protestants, however, by now despaired of a Suffolk succession, and began to look to the Stewart line for their salvation. After Mary's deposition in 1567 and flight to England in May 1568, her infant son James was brought up a protestant, and seemed to be the most satisfactory claimant to the succession during the early and mid-1570s.[70]

Although politically unimportant, Mary Grey (as she still called herself) remained in custody for several years after her sister's death.

Like Katherine before her, she addressed individual letters to Cecil and Dudley (now earl of Leicester), admitting her folly, expressing her grief at displeasing the queen, and begging for their intercession to secure 'remysion of that whiche is past'.[71] However, Elizabeth was not ready to issue a pardon and, besides, did not know what to do with her cousin were she to be allowed freedom. Mary could not live with Keyes without dishonouring the crown, and she had insufficient income to establish her own household, since most of her mother's property had been left to Stokes until his death. As a result, Elizabeth continued to place her in the houses of trustworthy men and women. In August 1567, she was lodged in the London house of her stepgrandmother Katherine, dowager duchess of Suffolk. Two years later, Sir Thomas Gresham became her guardian, much to the annoyance of his wife, who deeply resented the cost, burden, and disturbance to her household.[72] Yet, despite the Greshams' pleas for Mary to go elsewhere, she stayed with them for over three years.

With Katherine's death, Elizabeth's anger at the Grey marriages gradually ebbed away. Hertford was the first to benefit. In June 1568, arrangements were made for his fine to be paid in manageable instalments, and the queen then released him from the custody of Sir John Spencer, permitting him to live at his country home in Wiltshire, albeit under some restrictions.[73] Admittedly the earl continued to feel the ill effects of his loss of favour, and in June 1571 urged Cecil (now Lord Burghley) to 'release me of the heavy yoke of her majestye's continued displeasure', arguing that it disadvantaged him in a legal dispute over land.[74] The following month, the queen lifted all limits on his movements, and gradually received him back at court; in 1575, he hunted with the queen at Kenilworth.[75] Never entirely trusted by the queen, he profited from his close relationship with Burghley, Leicester, and (later) Lady Frances Howard, a favoured lady of the privy chamber who eventually became his second wife. In 1582, the queen was ready to admit that Hertford had deserved 'favour better of me than those I have done much for'.[76]

Keyes was the next to benefit, but in his case too late. Discharged from the Fleet in 1568 and given a post at Sandgate Castle in Kent in 1571, he was broken in health by his experiences in prison and died in late August or early September that year. Mary Grey was the last to be pardoned. With her husband's death, she took the opportunity to renew her petitions to Burghley: 'seing God hathe taken awaye the occacyon of her majeste's justly conceved displeassuer towardes me itt myghte therfor please her hyghenes of her wonttede marcyfullnes to pardonn this my greatt faulte.'[77] A few months later, Elizabeth finally relented and allowed her 'free liberty' to go wherever she wanted. But Mary had nowhere to go. As she explained to Burghley, she was 'voyd' and 'destetud' of all friends, and with an income of only £20 a year lacked sufficient resources to set up her own independent establishment. Mary was, therefore, obliged to live with her stepfather and his new wife, but no one was pleased with this arrangement, and she did not stay there long.[78] Within a few years, she took on the lease of a house in London.[79] How she paid for it is unrecorded, but it seems likely that the queen made a contribution by continuing to pay the £80 a year that had been assigned for Mary's upkeep while in custody. Over the next few years, Mary recovered royal favour. She occasionally attended court and in 1578 she exchanged New Year's gifts with the queen—Mary's gift being two pairs of perfumed gloves embellished with four-dozen pearl buttons.[80] After she died in April 1578, she was laid to rest in Westminster Abbey alongside her mother.[81]

After the deaths of the Grey sisters, Margaret, countess of Derby, may have considered herself Elizabeth's heir, though few others shared this view because of suspicions that she was a crypto-Catholic. Then suddenly, in August 1579, she was accused of consulting a 'conjurer' to discover 'whether the queen would live long' (an act of treason) and suspected of planning to hasten the event through poison.[82] Her physician and astrologer William Randell was implicated and put to death the following year. Margaret pleaded innocence of any malevolence towards the queen, and Elizabeth may well have believed her, for she was treated remarkably well given the severity of the accusations. She was not dispatched to the Tower but confined in the Clerkenwell home of her kinsman Thomas Seckford, master of the court of requests, 'a place where is wholsome and good ayre, without the which I had perished'.[83] Furthermore, Elizabeth took steps to protect the countess from her creditors; after her house arrest, the privy council repeatedly ordered the lord mayor of London to persuade them 'to forbeare for a time' to call in her debts: 'until with her majestie's good favor the lady may be inlarged.'[84]

Shamed by her banishment from court and house arrest, the countess begged a return to the queen's favour. She wrote at least once to Elizabeth and several times to Sir Christopher Hatton, 'the sole person in court that hath taken compassione on me, and hath geeven comforte unto my carfull hart'.[85] No letter from Elizabeth to her cousin is extant, but the queen evidently listened to Hatton's intercession. Margaret was permitted to take up residence in Isleworth House at some unspecified date, and she returned to Clerkenwell after purchasing Seckford's house, sometime before his death in 1587. She never returned to court, however, and remained at Clerkenwell until her own death in 1596, apparently in some comfort.[86] How the impecunious countess found the purchase price is unknown, but the queen probably helped her out again.

Despite their closeness to the throne, Katherine Grey's two sons were not persecuted by the queen. It is true that she never acknowledged their legitimacy and indeed foiled their every attempt to appeal against the original verdict that their parents had never married. After all, such a decision would have brought into disrepute a royal commission and would also have bolstered their claim to the succession, which Elizabeth wanted quashed. Yet, she otherwise treated them fairly. They were permitted to live with Hertford and his family, and the older son was able to use the courtesy title of Lord Beauchamp, which was associated with the Seymour family. Even when the young men actively sought to have their legitimacy acknowledged in law, she made no move to deprive them of their freedom, but simply warned them off.[87] Only when Hertford tried to do the same in 1595 did Elizabeth dole out a severe punishment. He had to spend two months in the Tower for what she called 'an act of lewde and proude contempt against our owen direct prohibition'.[88] Nonetheless, the earl was never in any danger of a longer stay, as she realized he was not making a bid for the royal succession but simply seeking to find a way for his sons to inherit his estates.

By this time, anyway, the queen had virtually nothing to fear from the elder son. Beauchamp's marriage to Honora Rogers, a kinswoman of gentle but not noble birth, took him out of the running as a potential successor to Elizabeth and was sufficient evidence that he had no ambition for the crown. The relationship between Beauchamp and his future wife had begun in 1581, much to the chagrin of Hertford, who uncharitably called Honora 'Onus blowse', loosely translated as 'that burdensome whore'. At the end of the year, the couple secretly exchanged vows and a ring. But when their relationship was discovered, the terrified young man declared to family members that he 'wold make no bones to mary her' and was free to enter into a match arranged by his father. He was lying. Even while he was denying the seriousness of the relationship, he was swearing his devotion to Honora. The following year, Beauchamp admitted to the marriage, but Hertford would not accept it as valid and kept his son in close custody.[89] The dispute rumbled on until 1584. Asked to intervene, Elizabeth initially took Hertford's part and commanded that Beauchamp be temporarily held 'in a kind of custody in respect of his disordered mariadg without the consent or knolledg of the erle'. But in 1586 she 'remitted her displeasur' and ordered Beauchamp's release.[90] Hertford had to comply, and his son's marriage to Honora was recognized. Their first child, Edward, was born early the next year, and two further sons and three daughters followed.

We can suspect that the queen was secretly pleased that the marriage revealed Beauchamp's unsuitability to be a future king. Nor would the irony of Hertford's refusal to recognize the clandestine marriage have escaped her. We know very little about the second son, Thomas, but he evidently kept his head down and himself out of the public eye. When 'conspiracies' were uncovered that seemed to implicate him in meddling with the succession, the queen initiated inquiries but took the matter no further.[91] Thomas died before the queen, leaving no heirs.

Beauchamp's son Edward unexpectedly came to the queen's attention during the last months of her life. Out of the blue, in December 1602, Hertford received an extraordinary message from Arbella Stuart, another member of the extended royal family (see the 'Genealogical Chart'). In it she said that she was ready to take up his suggestion that she marry his grandson. But, there had been no such suggestion, and such a match would have been political dynamite. The 27-year-old Arbella was the English-born great-granddaughter of Margaret Tudor, and had been many times spoken of as a possible heir to Elizabeth's throne. The fusion of two English claimants to the succession would mount a serious challenge to the title of James VI of Scotland, who was by then the favourite in the succession stakes. Well aware of this, Hertford instantly informed the queen's privy council of the letter, while denying that he had put forward any proposal of marriage. Elizabeth took the matter seriously and immediately sent someone to interrogate Arbella at her home at Hardwick Hall in Derbyshire. Only because her agent—Sir Henry Brouncker—decided that the girl's wits were disturbed did the affair die down.[92]

Just as Elizabeth affected to trust all the descendants of Katherine Grey, so she appeared to trust the elder son of the countess of Derby.

In 1573, the queen brought Ferdinando Stanley, Lord Strange, into her household to serve as a squire during his teenage years. Luckily for her, Ferdinando was more interested in poetry and drama than politics. Not only did he write poetry himself but from the late 1570s onwards he was the patron of a troupe of actors, known as Lord Strange's Men, which soon developed into a large, innovative, and successful theatrical company playing at court and in London. At Christmas 1591, it performed six plays before the queen, whereas other companies played only one each.[93]

Strange, however, could not avoid politics altogether. After Mary Queen of Scots' execution in February 1587, some Catholics started to focus upon him as a potential heir to Elizabeth, despite his outward conformity to the Protestant Church. In the spring of 1591, the government learned that Strange's cousin, the renegade William Stanley, had instructed two missionary priests to 'cause Catholiques to caste theyre eyes' upon Strange as a potential successor to Elizabeth and 'to make tryall of my Lord Strange, and see how he was affected to that pretence of the crowne, after her majestie's deathe'. A little later, the confessions of a captured priest revealed that Stanley had considered sending another missionary to Strange, this time 'to induce him to the Catholike religion'.[94] Despite Strange's kinship with Stanley and royal blood, he was not brought in for questioning, although he was probably kept under surveillance.

In the autumn of 1593, Catholics communicated with Ferdinando directly. Immediately upon the death of the earl of Derby, Richard Hesketh—an exiled Lancashire recusant—contacted his son, the new earl, in the hope of persuading him to claim the crown on Elizabeth's death. This bid (said Hesketh) would have the backing of the Catholic leadership abroad, provided that 'he be a Catholike and that he will binde him selfe to restore and advance and perpetually maintaine the Catholic religion in our countrie'. Ferdinando would have none of it. After holding two secret meetings with Hesketh in Lancashire, the earl accompanied him to London and 'dyd presentlye apprehend the party, and made yt knowen to her majestie'.[95] Notwithstanding this evident loyalty, Derby may have come under suspicion; he and his wife believed so and that as a result 'he shall be crossed in court and crossed in his country'.[96] Unusually, therefore, he remained at home in Lancashire that year during the period of Christmas festivities at court.

The story did not end there. In April 1594, the previously healthy earl was suddenly struck down with a mysterious sickness from which he died. The symptoms—vomiting, diarrhoea, and blood in the urine—made it seem a case of poisoning, and the government gave out that the Jesuits had murdered him in revenge for Hesketh. Others believed the young earl had been 'beweeched' rather than poisoned.[97] As Derby had fathered daughters not sons, the earldom passed to his brother William, who was safely married to Lord Burghley's granddaughter Elizabeth, and consequently no target for Catholic conspiracy. The upshot was that by the time of Elizabeth's last illness and death nobody from the Suffolk line either could—or chose to—contend for the throne. Beauchamp and Derby were kept under watch, but they and their sons had no desire to found their own royal dynasty and were content to stay out of national political life. Their lack of ambition kept them safe from the conspiracies of contemporaries who might have wanted to challenge the Stewart claim.

Historians have generally attributed the sad fates of so many of Elizabeth's Suffolk relatives—especially Katherine and Mary Grey—to the queen's anxiety about their place in the succession.[98] Elizabeth's own words have misled them. During an interview in 1561 with the Scottish ambassador William Maitland, laird of Lethington, she declared that princes could not love their heirs and spoke of the dangers that could arise from known successors.[99] However, members of the Suffolk line did not pose this kind of political threat to Elizabeth. Even when ardent protestants became disillusioned with the queen's religious conservatism and refusal to introduce further reform, they did not plot against her. A flawed protestant she might be, but she was still a protestant; and, besides, there was also no guarantee that Katherine might be any better. Although Katherine's sibling relationship with the pious Jane was used as propaganda to bolster her case to be Elizabeth's named heir, her true religious sensibilities were unknown but hardly ardent enough to warrant protestants rallying around her as an alternative to Elizabeth. As explained above, the political threat from Katherine's marriage stemmed from her influence on the succession debate and from the dangerous possibility that recognition of her sons' legitimacy might sabotage the entente Elizabeth was attempting to develop with Mary Queen of Scots. As for Mary Grey, her punishment was all to be expected, given her affront to the conventions of sixteenth-century society. She had proved wilful, disobedient, and guilty of a misalliance of mammoth proportions. Similarly, the countess of Derby's disgrace was almost certainly her own doing; she probably had been dabbling in magic, a pursuit that left her vulnerable—especially as a suspected Catholic—to accusations of treason. Elizabeth may have been wary of her Suffolk cousins, but she did not tyrannize them; and in this she showed herself very different from her father, who destroyed so many of his Yorkist kin.

3

Mary Queen of Scots

Except in plays, opera, and film, Queen Elizabeth famously never met her cousin Mary Queen of Scots. Yet, from Elizabeth's accession on 17 November 1558 until Mary's execution on 6 February 1587, their problematic relationship dominated English political life, ultimately giving rise to the popular reputation of Mary as a romantic victim and Elizabeth as her cruel captor. Conflicting interests and needs overshadowed and scarred their interactions, yet it would be a mistake to portray their relationship simply as a duel.[1] Yes, Mary desperately wanted to be named Elizabeth's heir, and Elizabeth equally desperately wanted Mary to offer assurances that she would not plot against her. Nonetheless, except for short periods (while she was in France and towards the end of her captivity in England), Mary did not make a bid for Elizabeth's throne; and, right until the last months of Mary's life, Elizabeth did not seek the Scottish queen's destruction. Indeed, for long periods, Elizabeth acted as Mary's protector against those in England who were baying for her blood.

The initial source of the distrust and hostility between the two queens was the 'pretended title' of the Catholic Mary to the crown of the protestant Elizabeth. No sooner had Elizabeth inherited the throne than Mary quartered the arms of England on her heraldic devices and added 'queen of England and Ireland' to her other titles of queen of Scotland and *reine dauphine* of France. This she continued to do after her father-in-law's death in July 1559 when she became queen consort of France.[2] The implication was, of course, that, as a bastard, Elizabeth could not be the legitimate sovereign; the fear was that Catholics in England and abroad would rally around Mary and support her as the rightful monarch. From Elizabeth's ambassador in France came intelligence that the French king was eager to 'prosecute the Frenche quene's title to England'.[3] Mary was later to profess that she had not taken the initiative in this matter, but had simply followed the directions of her father-in-law (Henry II of France), her husband (Francis II of France), and her maternal uncles (Francis, duke of Guise, and Charles, cardinal of Lorraine). But, whether true or not, Mary's actions alarmed Elizabeth and sowed seeds of distrust that were never to be eradicated.

Indeed, the distrust grew when Mary refused to ratify the treaty of Edinburgh, negotiated in July 1560 between the English, French, and Scots. This treaty was signed at the end of a short war in Scotland, which had begun when Elizabeth gave military aid to the Scottish protestant lords who had taken up arms against Mary's mother, the French-born Catholic regent Mary of Guise.[4] The French had supported the regent, and Elizabeth had intervened on behalf of her co-religionists. Although the fighting did not go well for the English army, the treaty of Edinburgh secured Elizabeth's most important war aims, including Mary's renunciation of her immediate claim to Elizabeth's crown and promise that she would never 'from hence-furth' use 'the stile, title, and armes of Englande and Irelande'.[5] But Mary baulked at this. The wording, she protested, was prejudicial to any future claim that she might have to be queen of England and would debar her from the succession, were Elizabeth to die childless. She therefore wanted this article revised.[6]

Elizabeth was unsympathetic and unbending. As far as she was concerned, the treaty needed no renegotiation, and its ratification was essential for her security and the peace of her realm. For Mary to sign it, she believed, would be a mark of Mary's goodwill and provide the basis for a 'knot of frendshipp' between the two monarchs and their realms, and reinforce 'the knott of nature and blood'.[7] Conversely, a refusal to ratify it would signify Mary's unwillingness to cease her challenge to Elizabeth's royal title and reveal her inclination to renew Scotland's traditional alliance with France. Elizabeth was consequently insistent that Mary accept the 1560 treaty as it stood. If Mary did so, she was ready 'to have all former unkindness and occasions of unkindness buried'; but, if not, then 'the quene your good syster will be very sorie and shall be compelled (to her greate greife) to alter her friendship and love to some other affection'.[8]

This implied threat had no perceptible effect on Mary, however. Despite professing friendship and goodwill, she continued to with-hold her signature. Moreover, after the death of her husband King Francis in December 1560, the 18-year-old widow found a ready excuse: she needed to return to Scotland and consult her council there before reaching a decision.[9] Elizabeth remained unimpressed. Mary, she believed, was simply prevaricating; after all, she had already been given plenty of opportunity to consult her councillors through the Scottish envoys who had visited her in France.

Mary's return to Scotland without ratifying the treaty presented a scary prospect for Elizabeth and her advisers: a French base could be re-established in Scotland; the newly recognized Scottish protestant Church would be put in jeopardy; England might well face a hostile Catholic power on its northern border; and the highland Scots would probably provide aid to rebel chieftains in Ireland. All the advantages recently gained from military intervention in Scotland would be lost.[10] So, in retaliation for Mary's refusal to sign the treaty, Elizabeth denied her passage through England on her way home to Edinburgh, as Mary had wished. Sometimes portrayed as an act of petty spite, Elizabeth's snub was designed to exert diplomatic pressure on the Scottish queen. Mary would learn, she hoped, just how important ratification of the treaty was to both their interests. But another consideration lay behind Elizabeth's denial of a passport: her unspoken worry that Mary might be offered a rapturous reception when travelling though the Catholic north of England. Such a welcome would expose Elizabeth's unpopularity with her Catholic subjects, underline her precarious hold on power, and consequently encourage Mary to renew her claim to the English throne.

Elizabeth's fears that Mary's homecoming would destabilize Scotland proved unfounded. Mary made no radical changes to the political and religious status quo, and she kept in power the anglophile protestant lords, notably her half-brother James Stewart (later ennobled as the earl of Moray) and William Maitland of Lethington, who both had a good working relationship with Elizabeth's principal secretary Sir William Cecil. In small but significant ways, Mary displayed her good 'disposicion' to Elizabeth by responding positively to English requests to curb piracy and maintain order and justice on the borders.[11] Furthermore, Mary repeatedly expressed her desire 'to unite the two realms in a perfect amity' and bind the two queens together in a strong personal relationship. For this purpose, she requested an exchange of portraits, desired Elizabeth to write her letters in her own hand (not just through a clerk or secretary), and asked for a face-to-face meeting. At that interview, thought Mary, Elizabeth would 'mair clarlie persave the synceritie of our meaning, than we can expres be writing', and consequently understand her qualms about ratifying the treaty of Edinburgh as it then stood.[12] Elizabeth responded in kind by calling Mary her 'derest sister and coosyn', writing some holograph letters, exchanging gifts of verses, agreeing to send her portrait, suggesting a league between the two realms, and finally granting Mary's request that they meet 'personallie together' in England.[13] All looked set for a rapprochement. On 6 July 1562, the final arrangements were made for Elizabeth to entertain Mary at York during August and September that year.[14] Protestants in Scotland had high expectations for a successful outcome of their interview; with a close entente in prospect, they suggested, Elizabeth might even persuade Mary to 'give over her mass'.[15]

So what went wrong? Well, first, to the great annoyance of Mary, the planned meeting never took place. Cecil had always disliked the idea, and the international crisis looming that summer enabled him to convince Elizabeth that an interview was untenable at that time.[16] In March 1562, French protestants (known as Huguenots) had been massacred on the estates of Mary's uncle, the duke of Guise, and soon afterwards France had descended into civil war, with the Catholic Guises pitted against the protestants led by the prince of Condé. For a variety of reasons, Elizabeth was considering supporting Condé, and in these circumstances she needed to extricate herself from a potentially difficult and embarrassing diplomatic meeting with a member of the Guise family. Mary was consequently told that their interview was to be deferred until the spring or summer of 1563, 'utterly against our [Elizabeth's] will and determination', because the religious war in France threatened to escalate into a wider confessional conflict. The Guise party, explained Elizabeth, was intending the 'wilful subversion and destruction of all manner of nations that consent not with them in the rites of Christian religion', and it was therefore far too dangerous for the royal party to leave London.[17] Mary's immediate reaction to these excuses was 'a passionate grief', but she soon declared herself 'well satysfied', accepted the delay as 'just and reasonable', and 'showyth great joy' at the prospect of a future meeting.[18] However, England remained at war in France throughout 1563, so again the interview had to be postponed. When Elizabeth proposed it the next year, it was the Scots who prevaricated.[19] By that time, the moment for an entente had passed. The reason was that the two queens had fallen out badly over two other issues: the English succession and Mary's marriage.

As the basis of a settlement between the two queens, Mary's councillors proposed that she would renounce her claim to Elizabeth's throne and receive in recompense a formal recognition of her place in the English succession after any children whom Elizabeth might bear.[20] Given that Elizabeth was expected to marry and have children, the Scots argued, they were offering a very good deal for England: 'it will be easily espyed who shall have the better by the bargayne…Yowr gayne shalbe assured and in your hand; ours onely in possibility,' wrote Maitland.[21]

However, Elizabeth did not see it that way and rejected 'amity' on those terms. Naturally, she could not admit that the Scottish queen had any immediate claim to renounce, but, equally important, she refused to recognize Mary formally as her heir. This was not because she favoured another candidate. On the contrary, all the evidence suggests that Elizabeth believed that Mary had the best right to the succession: she consistently referred to the Scottish queen as her 'next kinswoman' and 'nerest in blood'; and she even announced before Mary's special envoy that 'I (for my part) know none better, nor that myself would prefer to her'.[22] Nonetheless, Elizabeth believed that she had good reasons for not making her choice public. First, the succession was a divisive issue. Because of her Catholic faith, Mary was unacceptable to many protestants, including Cecil, even though the Scottish queen showed herself to be tolerant in matters of religion and was allowing the protestant Church (the Kirk) to flourish. Second, drawing on her own experiences during her half-sister's reign, Elizabeth feared that English Catholics might engage in plots to hasten her own demise and Mary's accession in anticipation of a change in religion. Also based on her earlier experience, Elizabeth could hardly believe the two queens would become closer were Mary to be her indisputable heir. And, finally, Elizabeth was unconvinced that the succession question would be settled by a statement from her, or even a statute in parliament. Quite the reverse; in her opinion, any intervention would open up, rather than close down, debate and in the long run would prove unsuccessful, just as had Edward VI's attempt in 1553 to promote Lady Jane Grey. All things considered, decided Elizabeth, it was far better to leave the succession to God's will. Ultimately, 'when I am dead, they shall succeed that has most right', she declared confidently.[23]

This response dismayed and angered Mary. Not only was it a slight to her honour not to be recognized as Elizabeth's heir, but moreover she did not share Elizabeth's confidence that her claim would be respected if the English queen died childless. When Elizabeth was taken sick with smallpox and thought to be on the point of death in October 1562, only one privy councillor (Mary was told) spoke up for her dynastic right. Additionally, in early 1563, some English MPs tried to exclude Mary by statute from the succession. Growing anxious that her just claim might be set aside, Mary began to question the value of her pro-English stance, which, as yet, had delivered nothing tangible.[24]

Badly needing Mary's goodwill, Elizabeth did what she could to keep her on board. Her refusal to accept Katherine Grey's marriage as valid and acknowledge her sons as legitimate was intended in large part to reassure Mary that she would indeed do nothing to prejudice her rights. Learning in mid-1563 that foreign Catholic princes were courting the Scottish queen, Elizabeth even held out the possibility that she would 'treat further' in the matter of the succession provided that her cousin married an English protestant nobleman. Were Mary to marry an Austrian, French, or Spanish prince, warned Elizabeth, it would threaten 'our private amity' and 'dissolve the concord' current between the two realms. But were Mary to marry 'some noble person of good birth within this our realm', Elizabeth would show her goodwill by allowing an 'inquisition' to investigate the legality of Mary's place in the succession.[25] Not knowing which particular English noblemen Elizabeth had in mind, Mary prevaricated, claiming that 'the remembrance of her late howsbonde is yet so freshe in her mynde that she cane not thynke of anye other' and asking why Elizabeth had not yet chosen a husband herself.[26]

At last, in March 1564, Elizabeth ceased to be coy and named Lord Robert Dudley as her preferred candidate for Mary's hand, a strange choice in many ways since Dudley had been romantically attached to the English queen for several years. Elizabeth's resident ambassador to Scotland, Thomas Randolph, reported home that Mary had listened to this proposal 'with meetly good patience', promising to give it due consideration. Writing privately to Cecil, he was more frank, explaining that Mary had firmly—if politely—raised strong objections and had to be persuaded to take the offer seriously. Unspoken was Dudley's scandalous liaison with Elizabeth, but Mary did point out that it would be demeaning and dishonourable for her to marry her cousin's subject.[27] In no hurry to discuss the matter further, the 22-year-old Scottish queen put thoughts of marriage on hold while she spent the summer on royal progress.

During these months, relations between the two queens cooled noticeably. Their personal correspondence grew infrequent, and what letters were exchanged were written in the hand of secretaries. The new *froideur* began when Mary took offence at a letter written to her by Elizabeth (on another subject altogether) and dashed off a response in 'a gret choler' that in turn offended the English queen.[28] Keen to 'renew ther outwart frendschip', Mary made the first move at reconciliation and sent Sir James Melville as her envoy to London in late September 1564. The morning after his arrival, Melville was given a royal audience in which Elizabeth immediately demanded an explanation for his mistress', letter, which had contained such 'dispyt-full langage unto her' that she could only believe 'all frendschip and famyliarite had bene geven up'.[29] Easily pacified by Melville's splut-tered excuses, Elizabeth then tore up in his presence a sharply worded letter she had drafted in reply. Her honour restored, Elizabeth got down to business and opened up discussions about a Dudley mar-riage. As instructed by Mary, Melville answered evasively, suggesting a meeting between Scottish and English commissioners where *all* matters of importance to the queens might be discussed.

Throughout Melville's nine-day visit, Elizabeth took every oppor-tunity to press Dudley's suit. In addition to regularly praising her favourite's worth, she ennobled him as earl of Leicester before Melville in order to make him an appropriate groom for a royal bride. Elizabeth also laid out plainly the importance she placed on the match and its vital role in reinforcing the amity between the two realms. To demonstrate her offer was not intended as an insult but tendered out of love and goodwill for her cousin, she showed great familiarity towards Melville, making it clear that her intimacy towards him should be understood as a measure of her affection for his mistress. Since she could not meet 'to confer familiarly' with Mary, Melville was told, Elizabeth would instead 'open a gud part of her inwart mynd' unto him so that he 'mycht schaw [show] it again unto the quen'. She saw the ambassador every day and even brought him into the private space of her bedchamber, where she took out a set of miniatures kept wrapped up in a drawer. Revealing the one of his queen, she kissed it; as she had explained earlier to Melville, she 'delyted to luk upon hir [Mary's] picture' as a substitute for seeing her cousin in person. Yet, according to Melville, Elizabeth also expressed a rivalry with her cousin by asking: who was the fairer in looks? Which one performed better on the virginals? Was she or Mary the finer dancer? But the tone was always light-hearted, even though Elizabeth displayed pleasure or relief when Melville admitted her superiority at the virginals and in dancing.[30]

Melville was not fooled by Elizabeth's demonstrations of love towards the Scottish queen. Reporting back his meeting to Mary, he declared that, in his judgement, 'ther was nather plain dealing nor uprychyt meanyng, bot gret dissimulation, emulation, and fear' on Elizabeth's side.[31] Melville's opinion confirmed Mary's own suspicions that Elizabeth was insincere in her expressions of goodwill and even in her offer of Leicester. If Mary accepted his hand, she wondered, would Elizabeth then declare that, if the earl was good enough for the queen of Scotland, he should be considered a suitable match for her? Yet, despite these doubts, Mary came to see that a marriage to Leicester might well be tolerable if, in return, she could be promised a parliamentary statute affirming her place in the English succession. For this purpose, she sent commissioners to meet Elizabeth's representatives at Berwick on 18 November 1564.

Unfortunately for their future relations, Elizabeth would or could not meet Mary's conditions. Whether or not she was prepared to name an heir was immaterial, for—as she well knew—there was very little likelihood that the English parliament would approve the Scottish queen's title. Elizabeth's response, therefore, was that Mary would have to rely solely on her goodwill for the fulfilment of her claim. This was utterly unacceptable to the Scots; as Mary's advisers warned Cecil, unless their queen received statutory provision of her place in the succession, she would marry whomsoever she wished, whether an Englishman or a foreigner, a friend to England or an enemy.[32]

And Mary did exactly that. To Elizabeth's surprise and intense disapproval, on 29 July 1565, Mary wed her first cousin Henry Stewart, Lord Darnley, the elder son of the earl and countess of Lennox. Since his mother was the daughter of Henry VIII's elder sister Margaret by her second husband, Darnley had English royal blood in his veins and also a claim to the succession (see 'Genealogical Chart'). It could even be argued that he had the better claim, as he was not a foreigner but born in England. Mary had informed Elizabeth of her intention to marry Darnley the previous April and asked for the English queen's 'good will and assent'. After all, Mary explained disingenuously, she was taking her cousin's advice in forbearing to marry a foreigner and choosing one of Elizabeth's own subjects. To prevent the projected marriage, Elizabeth immediately sent off Sir Nicholas Throckmorton to Scotland to convey her 'disliking and disallowance' of such a match. Apart from all other considerations, she pointed out that Darnley had shown disloyalty to his sovereign in pursuing it without her permission or knowledge. But Mary did not listen; she simply affected surprise that Elizabeth should take offence at her choice, and it was evident to Throckmorton that her decision was irrevocable.[33]

A little later, when Elizabeth ordered Darnley back to England, Mary encouraged him not to go.

Did Mary intend a breach with Elizabeth when deciding upon this marriage? She claimed not, yet her sudden disdainful treatment of Randolph as if 'he was a man newe and fyrste come into her presence, whome she had never seen' led the ambassador to fear the worst.[34] 'With England this queen meaneth to make a divorce, although she will make fair weather; but with France she will join,' he reported home.[35] Cecil and other privy councillors agreed with Randolph; to their mind, Mary's choice of husband indicated that her ambitions went beyond the succession and that she again intended to challenge Elizabeth's right to the throne. Apart from Darnley's nearness in blood to Elizabeth, and his gender, a further reason for concern was his religion: although a conforming protestant under Elizabeth, he had been brought up a Catholic and was considered to be at best 'indifferente to both the religions'.[36] So, the consideration that Mary might be persuaded to abandon the mass through the influence of an English protestant husband did not apply to this match. A far more likely prospect was that his wife would draw Darnley first into the Roman Catholic Church and then into an international Catholic league headed by the pope, the Guises, and Philip II of Spain.[37] Paranoid about the supposed militancy of the continental Counter-Reformation, Elizabeth's advisers were convinced that the Darnley marriage played into the hands of the Catholic powers, who (they wrongly believed) had recently forged a holy league to extirpate heresy throughout Europe.

These fears were further enflamed when Mary and her husband drew up a list of their terms for a future good relationship with England. If Elizabeth showed 'amytie and frendshipp towards them' by establishing the succession in Mary's and Darnley's favour through an act of parliament, then they would neither directly or indirectly 'attempte anye thinge prejudiciall' to Elizabeth's title or 'disturb the comen quitnes of the realme of Englande'.[38] The implication of this offer was, of course, that they would be free to meddle in English politics or align themselves with foreign powers against the queen if no statute was passed securing their rights. It was to protect themselves against such forces and take the sting out of the succession question that Cecil and the queen reignited negotiations for a marriage alliance with the Catholic Archduke Charles of Austria. However, irreconcilable differences over religion put an end to these talks at the beginning of 1567.

By then, Mary had troubles of her own. The English queen had consistently warned her that marriage to Darnley could well destabilize political life in Scotland, since his father had many enemies within the Scottish nobility. And over the next few years Elizabeth could take some comfort from the fact that her warnings proved prescient. Admittedly, the English did what they could to encourage factionalism in Scotland by supporting dissident lords in undercover operations against their monarch.[39] It was also true that much of the political unrest did not work to England's interests. The anglophile earl of Moray was forced into exile after an abortive rebellion, and Mary came to rely on men who were no friends of Elizabeth.

Marriage did not bring Mary personal happiness. Within a few months of conjugal life, the couple had quarrelled; the following March, Darnley was implicated in the brutal murder of Mary's secretary David Riccio; and by the time their son was born on 19 June 1566, husband and wife were barely on speaking terms. After Riccio's murder, Elizabeth and Mary began to repair their differences. Elizabeth was clearly shocked that subjects had burst into their queen's private chambers and assassinated a trusted royal servant. To display publicly her sympathy for Mary, she wore her cousin's portrait on a golden chain hanging from her waist and told the Spanish ambassador that she was horrified by the behaviour of both the Scottish lords and Mary's husband. Elizabeth also wrote her a holograph letter, offering the queen aid in her troubles.[40]

The birth of a Scottish prince provided further possibilities for a rapprochement between the two queens. Just before Mary's confinement, Elizabeth accepted her invitation to be the child's godmother; and, although she could not personally attend the baptism, Elizabeth told her proxy (the countess of Argyle) to express to Mary on her behalf 'as much good will and affection as your hart can conceave'.[41] Elizabeth also instructed her diplomatic representative at the ceremony—Francis Russell, second earl of Bedford—to begin the process of rebuilding 'amity' between the two monarchs. Declaring his queen's love, affection, and friendship, the earl was to put Mary's mind at rest about the succession by assuring her that Elizabeth 'never intended to doe or suffer anie thinge to be done that might be anie wise prejudiciall to her interest' and would 'to the uttermost of our power' suppress any attempts to do so.[42]

By the time that Bedford delivered this message, Elizabeth's sincerity had been tested and proved, for during the October and November session of parliament she angrily silenced MPs who called

for Mary's exclusion from the succession. Through Bedford, Elizabeth also made more concrete offers to Mary. First she granted Mary's request that a judicial inquiry be held into the 'manner of' Henry VIII's will disinheriting the Stewart line in order to determine whether or not it had actually been signed by the king. If it had been dry stamped, not signed in the king's own hand, it would have no validity as far as the succession was concerned, and Mary's claim to be Elizabeth's heir on grounds of primogeniture would, therefore, be stronger.[43] Second, Elizabeth agreed to renegotiate the 1560 treaty of Edinburgh in a new 'reciprocal contract' that would protect her own security as well as Mary's rights.[44] Elizabeth was ready to make these compromises now, because she disliked the alternative strategy (favoured by Cecil) of working with dissident Scottish nobles against their queen. Not only had this radical path been tried unsuccessfully in the past but it was also beginning to look ideologically dangerous, for in 1566 subjects were rebelling against their rulers in France and the Netherlands, putting the theory of divine right monarchy at risk.

Mary was delighted with Elizabeth's proposals, seeing them as a first step towards a public recognition of her right and a future of amicable relations between the two monarchs and realms.[45] However, on the night of 10 February 1567, Darnley was murdered. Mary's failure to arrest the assassins and her remarriage on 19 May 1567 to James Hepburn, fourth earl of Bothwell, who was said to be 'the principall author' of the crime, transformed the relationship between the two queens. Two weeks after the king consort's death, instead of writing Mary a letter of condolence, Elizabeth sent her a message of counsel and rebuke. Addressing her fellow queen simply as 'Madame', she warned Mary that her honour was then on the line. As Darnley's cousin, wrote Elizabeth:

> my nature compels me to take his death in the extreme, he being so close in blood...O madame, I would not do the office of faithful cousin or affectionate friend if I studied rather to please your ears than employed myself in preserving your honor...I exhort you, I counsel you, and I beseech you to take this thing as much to heart that you will not fear to touch even him whom you have nearest to you [Bothwell].[46]

Soon afterwards, when Elizabeth was told of Mary's intimate relationship with Bothwell, she demanded the truth from her cousin: should Elizabeth believe the slanderous rumours and 'enter into some doutfullnes of the quene's integrite, which of all other thynges she most mislyketh to conceave'?[47] News of Mary's marriage to Bothwell Elizabeth received with disgust: 'for how could a worse choice be made for your honor than in such haste to marry such a subject, who besides other and notorious lacks, public fame hath charged with the murder of your late husband?'[48]

More appalling intelligence soon followed. In July 1567, Elizabeth learned with much 'greef and displeasure' of the noble rebellion that ended in Mary's defeat at Carberry Hill and imprisonment at Lochleven Castle.[49] Angry with both Mary, whom she blamed for causing the trouble, and the Scottish lords for treating their sovereign with such dangerous disrespect, Elizabeth tried to tread a middle path: she distanced herself from her cousin by refusing to write as formerly 'with our own hand', yet at the same time she promised to act as 'a good neighbour, a dear sister, and a faithful friend' in protecting her honour.[50] To resolve the crisis and secure Mary's liberty, Elizabeth offered to mediate between the Scottish queen and her subjects. If this could be managed successfully, her intercession, she hoped, might also work to England's interest in 'that the queen of Scotland would be obliged to be guided by her, and the lords also if possible'.[51]

However, the Scottish lords were in no mood to take advice from Elizabeth. Her envoy, Sir Nicholas Throckmorton, was refused access to the prisoner, and the lords arranged Mary's deposition on 24 July, although it was dressed up as an abdication.[52] Elizabeth was deeply disturbed. It might be permissible in certain circumstances for lords to take up arms against a ruler in defence of their lives and rights, but it transgressed civil law and scripture for a monarch to be deposed. Whatever wrongs Mary had committed, she was not answerable to her subjects, for 'we doe not think it conformeth in nature the head should be subject to the foote'.[53] Elizabeth felt so strongly about this principle that she instructed Throckmorton to threaten that

> we will mak our selfe a playne party against them to the revenge of their soverayne...we doubt not but God will assist us and confound them and their devises, considering they have no warrant nor authorite by the law of God or man to be as superiors, judges, or vindecators over their prince and soverayne, how so ever disorders they do gather or conceyve mater of disordre against her.[54]

When she heard that the deposition had occurred and Mary's infant son had been crowned James VI under the regency of Moray, Elizabeth was so incensed that she threatened the lords with war. She backed down only when advised that such threats would put

Mary's life at risk. The best way to 'amend her [Mary's] fortune' was for Elizabeth to speak to the lords 'more calmly', counselled Throckmorton.[55]

Mary's escape from Lochleven, her unsuccessful battle against the Scottish lords at Langside, and subsequent flight into England on 17 May 1568 all put Elizabeth into a new quandary: what to do with her sister-queen who was now an unexpected guest in England. Despite her sorry plight, Mary still faced charges of adultery and the murder of her husband, accusations that could not be ignored. Furthermore, Mary's enemies in Scotland (the protestant nobility) were England's friends, while her friends (mainly Catholics and francophiles) were potentially England's enemies. Elizabeth's welcome to Mary was therefore muted: in her first letter to the fugitive, she congratulated her on her escape from captivity but continued to censure her for marrying Bothwell.[56] Over the next few months the cousins exchanged letters regularly, but Elizabeth explained that there could be no interview between them until Mary was cleared of the allegations against her.[57] So, instead of allowing Mary to come down to London, Elizabeth placed the Scottish queen under the guardianship of Sir Francis Knollys and Lord Henry Scrope, first at Carlisle Castle in Westmorland and then at Bolton Castle in North Yorkshire.

Nonetheless, Elizabeth was unwilling to put Mary on trial, as it would offend the principle of divine right monarchy. As an alternative, she elected to examine the allegations against Mary by another route: a tribunal would be established to decide whether or not the Scottish lords had been justified in their rebellion and could prove their accusations against their queen. Unsurprisingly, Mary objected strongly to such a process. She demanded to come into Elizabeth's presence 'and to be by her restored' or else to be permitted to leave for France 'without tryall first had'. Elizabeth could not possibly agree to either of these courses of action. Letting Mary go to her powerful Catholic kinfolk in France was far too dangerous; restoring her to the Scottish throne was impossible without using military force against the protestant lords there. Besides, there was the matter of Elizabeth's honour: if she tried to restore Mary, it would imply that 'she doth acquite hir of the murder of hir husband or ells doth beare with the crymes'.[58] So, despite Mary's protests, Elizabeth decided to go ahead with the tribunal. Her hope was that Mary would be found innocent and then allowed back to Scotland as titular queen alongside her crowned son. Cecil, though, hoped and believed that Mary's guilt would be proved.[59]

Mary was not permitted to attend the legal proceedings, which were held initially at York and afterwards in London, but she did send representatives to put her case. During the period while the tribunal was in session (October till December 1568), she received no letters from her cousin. As Elizabeth explained, she could not compromise herself by writing to a woman whose reputation was under investigation. Equally important, Elizabeth would have difficulty in claiming impartiality if she appeared to be on intimate terms with her kinswoman.

During the course of the 'trial', Mary's adversaries brought forth the so-called casket letters that appeared to incriminate her in adultery with Bothwell and the murder of her husband. Although she denied ever penning the letters, she did not otherwise put up any defence. It was, she explained, beneath her honour as a queen to answer the charges in writing, and Elizabeth refused her request to appear in person before the judges. An impasse was therefore reached. With no defence provided, Elizabeth and her judges could deliver no verdict, and consequently the legal proceedings had to be suspended.[60] As a result, the political status quo in Scotland was confirmed. Regent Moray returned to rule in the name of the king, confident of English support, since he had a loan of £5,000 in his pocket.[61] Mary, her reputation now in tatters, remained a virtual captive in England far away from Elizabeth's court. To ensure that she did not escape, she was moved to strongholds distant from possible sympathizers in the Catholic north, and placed in the custody of the powerful magnate George Talbot, sixth earl of Shrewsbury. However, both queens viewed this situation as undesirable and temporary. While Mary understandably chafed at her detention, Elizabeth too wanted a settlement that would send her 'prisoner' home. Not only was it unsafe to have a potential rival lodged in England, but also there was the danger that the French might intervene on Mary's behalf.

In April 1569, Mary gave her representative John Leslie, bishop of Ross, the authority to negotiate her restoration. According to Leslie, Elizabeth talked with him for nearly two hours, expressed warm sympathy for his mistress, and promised to do anything she could that 'may stand with her honor and seurty' to help Mary.[62] Leslie was then referred to the privy council to discuss particulars, and talks took place over the next few months. However, in secret, Leslie held simultaneous talks with some English nobles (including the earls of Pembroke, Leicester, and Arundel, and Lord Lumley) about a proposal for a marriage between Mary and the recently widowed duke of Norfolk that would take place after her marriage to Bothwell had been annulled.[63]

The Norfolk–Mary marriage scheme would, its proponents believed, work in the interests of both England and Scotland. Under the control of a husband who was personally loyal to Elizabeth and protestant in his faith, Mary could be safely restored to her throne and trusted to maintain the religious status quo in Scotland and the Anglo-Scottish league of friendship. Once she proved herself a good friend to England, moreover, she could be named Elizabeth's heir; and the succession problem that had blighted the politics of the previous decade would be over. Seeing the marriage as her route to freedom, Mary was cautiously supportive of the scheme. She evidently believed that Elizabeth would approve it, since four years previously the English queen had pressed on her the matrimonial suit of Leicester.[64]

Unaware of these discussions, Elizabeth was becoming increasingly irritated at the steadfast opposition of the Scottish regent to any settlement encompassing Mary's return. But when the secret communications concerning the Norfolk–Mary marriage came fully to light in September 1569, Elizabeth's anger was redirected towards the duke, the Scottish queen, and Leslie. They had all behaved duplicitously by initiating a political project behind her back, and Elizabeth distrusted their motives. All those implicated were interrogated; Mary was placed under greater restraint and her rooms searched for incriminating documents; Leslie was imprisoned; and Norfolk ended up in the Tower after fleeing the court.[65]

Although historians now consider the marriage scheme to have been harmless, it exploded in Elizabeth's face by triggering off a major Catholic rebellion in the north of England during the autumn and winter of 1569. The noble rebels claimed they were simply trying to secure Mary's release and nomination as Elizabeth's heir. But, had they been militarily successful, they would surely have deposed Elizabeth and replaced her with Mary. At any rate, that was what Elizabeth, Cecil, and many other protestants believed. Their suspicions seemed substantiated in February 1570 when Pope Pius V issued a bull that excommunicated Elizabeth, called her the 'pretended queen of England', and released all her subjects from their allegiance to her.[66]

While Mary was the focus of the northern rising, she was not its instigator, so, once the danger was over, Elizabeth resolved again to reinstate her in Scotland.[67] A settlement seemed even more urgent at this point. Elizabeth's concerns that Mary's presence might stimulate a Catholic revolt had proved correct, but even worse Scotland was suddenly plunged into political chaos. In January 1570, Regent Moray was assassinated, and Mary's adherents—exploiting the political vacuum—raised an army against her opponents, the 'king's party'. Given that the French king now threatened to intervene on the Marian side, Elizabeth thought the best solution would be to arrange Mary's restoration under the most stringent of conditions. However, a number of her privy councillors disagreed. As Cecil wrote despairingly to Sir Henry Norris in France: 'your opinion was for the queen's majesty to be delivered of the Scotish queen. But surely, few here amongst us conceive it feasible, with surety.'[68] Their preference was for Elizabeth to keep Mary in captivity in England and send financial and military aid to the king's party in Scotland.

Elizabeth initially had her way, and negotiations with Mary restarted in May 1570, with Leslie acting as an intermediary between the two queens.[69] Although the negotiations stalled for a short time with the untimely publication of two pamphlets—one defending Mary's probity and the other her claim to the succession—Elizabeth was ready by late September to lay before her cousin a list of tightly worded articles that would form the basis for an accord.[70] Two trusted privy councillors, Cecil and Sir Walter Mildmay, were ordered to discuss them with Mary in person, even though—or perhaps because—neither of them liked this way of proceeding. 'God be our guide, for neither of us like the message,' Cecil told his friend Norris.[71] In fact Elizabeth's message, including the articles for a peace treaty, was very tough indeed. Her envoys were to put to Mary all the 'unkindness and injuryes' she had committed against Elizabeth and to request how she intended to 'make recompence to us for them'. Only then were they to open talks on the conditions drawn up for her release and restoration.[72]

Elizabeth's message reveals how she constructed her relationship with Mary: she was the injured party, yet had remained at all times her cousin's long-suffering friend and protector. Within the list of injuries were the familiar charges that Mary had attacked Elizabeth's title while in France and married Darnley against the queen's will. Added to these were two new accusations: since coming to her realm, the Scottish queen had had 'intelligence and practises' with English nobles and rebels; and she was now encouraging her supporters in Scotland to despoil the borders. Elizabeth's many kindnesses to Mary were also listed: she had saved Mary's life at Lochleven; she had 'taken no avenge upon her person' as other princes would have done; she kept her in 'honorable estate' with a sumptuous 'table'; she had refused to publish the evidence against the maligned queen concerning the murder of her husband; and finally she had protected the title of King James.[73]

Mary constructed their relationship in quite different terms: she was the one who had suffered unkindness at the hands of her fellow queen and nearest kinswoman. So Cecil and Mildmay found Mary 'most trowbled and amazed' at the charges levelled against her, and also inclined to weep whenever she tried to defend herself. Nonetheless, when it came to negotiating the terms for a treaty, Mary acquiesced in most of the English demands. She had expressed problems with the wording of several articles. She disliked, for example, the one that implied that her 'demission' (abdication in favour of her son) was beneficial to her realm. She also insisted that she should be allowed to visit her son, who, according to the projected treaty, would live in England until he was 15 years old. Overall, though, Mary followed the advice of Leslie, who counselled her to give way on disputed points. Consequently, after eleven days, the envoys returned home with an agreement ready to present to the Scots ruling in King James's name. Its terms seemed to protect Elizabeth, England, and the protestant Church from hostile acts from Scotland. As far as the English succession was concerned, it was agreed that Mary and her children would not be excluded from any 'right or tytle' to the crown if Elizabeth died without issue, unless she attempted 'any thing derogatory to the queene's majestie's right and title to the crown of England'.[74] From the English point of view, the main problem was whether Mary could be trusted to keep her word; after all, she had signed and sealed her abdication only to forswear it afterwards.[75]

In the event, Mary's word was not to be tested. Evidence soon came into Cecil's possession that she had resumed her secret correspondence with Norfolk about their marriage and had, through Leslie, embarked upon communications with the Spanish ambassador and a Florentine merchant named Roberto di Ridolfi. Frustrated and suspicious at the lack of progress in her negotiations with Elizabeth (even though the delays were largely the responsibility of the king's party, who thoroughly opposed the return of their disgraced and deposed queen), Mary had decided to put her trust in Elizabeth's enemies abroad.[76] Her primary objective was not to foment rebellion in England but to escape and assist her allies in Scotland.

The full extent of the Ridolfi plot was revealed in the summer of 1571. The confessions of Leslie, blurted out under fear of the rack, and the documentary evidence intercepted by Cecil convinced Elizabeth of Mary's complicity in intrigues that were intended to go way beyond foreign intervention in Scotland. It was clear that Philip II, with papal support, had been planning an invasion of England, the deposition of Elizabeth, and the restoration of Catholicism.[77] Elizabeth therefore announced that she 'hathe cause to alter her curteous dealings' with her cousin, and would keep her in closer confinement.[78] Mary, however, denied any wrongdoing. Her conduct, she declared defiantly, had been exemplary and very different from the behaviour of Elizabeth towards her: whereas she had not 'gone about to styrre up a rebellion in this realme', Elizabeth 'hath maintained my rebels against me, to the taking away of my crowne from my head'.[79]

Only the intervention of Elizabeth saved both Mary and Leslie from the same fate as Norfolk: execution for high treason. Elizabeth resisted demands from two successive Scottish regents that Leslie should be handed over to them as a rebel, as well as calls from her own bishops, councillors, and MPs that Mary should be executed.[80] At the same time, Elizabeth was still not ready to exclude Mary from the succession, and she withheld her assent from a parliamentary bill to that effect. Yet, in her poem, 'The doubt of future foes' composed around 1570, the final stanzas had articulated the English queen's readiness to use the sword of justice against her Catholic enemies, and even to behead her royal cousin, the 'daughter of discord' (as referred to in an earlier line):

> No foreign banished wight [the exiled Mary]
> Shall anchor in this port:
> Our realm brooks no seditious sects
> Let them elsewhere resort.
> My rusty sword through rest
> Shall first his edge employ
> To poll their tops [behead] who seek such change
> Or gape [long] for future joy.[81]

But, notwithstanding this private resolve, a mixture of principle and pragmatism restrained Elizabeth from 'polling' Mary's 'top' in 1571 and 1572. Putting the Scottish queen on trial would violate the sacred quality of monarchy, a step too far for Elizabeth at that time. Furthermore, it would set her on a collision course with the king of France, with whom she was negotiating a defensive alliance. Cecil, now Lord Burghley, just prayed that his mistress could be persuaded to hand Mary over to the king's party in Scotland, who could then 'proceed with hir by wey of justice'—in other words put her on trial for Darnley's murder.[82] However, since the Scots would not relieve Elizabeth of her prisoner, Elizabeth was not under any strong pressure to deliver Mary up to certain death.

Although saved from the block, Mary was held under much closer guard after the Ridolfi plot. For a time, she was confined within the 'foure walls' of Sheffield Castle and not allowed to ride or hunt in adjoining parks, although these restrictions were eventually eased. Even then, since Elizabeth wanted her to remain isolated, Mary was banned from seeing any of her custodian's visitors or showing herself to neighbours passing through the parks and gardens.[83] Inevitably, her letters were subjected to inspection, while English agents were entrusted with intercepting secret messages passing between her and the outside world. During these years, Elizabeth preferred to make contact with Mary through intermediaries and tried to keep her own letters to a minimum. As one historian has commented, the English queen used silence as a 'passive–aggressive weapon' whenever she felt aggrieved by the prisoner's litany of complaints.[84] On her side, Mary tried to sustain the personal relationship by keeping up a constant flow of holograph letters and sending 'tokens' to her cousin. When she received no reply, she badgered Leicester and Burghley to find out if her letters had gone astray or complained bitterly about the queen's refusal to reciprocate.[85]

Despite the severe curtailment to her liberty, Mary lived in considerable style, paid for largely out of her own income as dowager queen of France. Reduced to about sixteen servants in 1571, her household grew by the end of the decade to over forty, including several secretaries. Her clothes were made of expensive fabrics and fashionably cut, her meals elaborate and served according to royal ritual. Indeed, Elizabeth tried to treat Mary as a monarch in exile, permitting her to correspond with friends and foreign princes and to sit under a regal cloth of state in her privy and presence chamber to signify her royal status.[86]

In 1581, political negotiations began again for Mary's release. The initiative came from the Scottish queen, who told Elizabeth on 10 October that the French had proposed an 'association' or arrangement whereby mother and son would have joint rule of Scotland. In fact Mary was being economical with the truth, as it was *she* who had kick-started this particular scheme several months previously.[87]

To her, the time seemed opportune for the Scots to agree to her return, since the 15-year-old James VI had thrown off the tutelage of his anglophile protestant regent and come under the influence of a French Catholic cousin, Esmé Stuart, created first the earl and later the duke of Lennox.

Apprehensive about the genesis and implications of the French approach, Elizabeth sent envoys to both James in Scotland and Mary (then living at Sheffield Castle) to discover what each knew and thought about it. During her meetings with Robert Beale, Mary was wary about showing too much enthusiasm for the scheme, no doubt out of fear that her excitement would arouse Elizabeth's suspicions. She simply promised to deal plainly with Elizabeth and follow her advice in the matter, declaring 'her desyre was so to have this matter ordered as that she might by her humble service winne her majesty's favour, and procure her self more libertie to remayne in some of her houses, and be ready always to do any thing that she should be commanded'.[88]

Mary discussed Scottish affairs with Beale in general terms but used their time together to drive home the message that her health and life depended upon her being granted greater liberty. Their interview was held while she lay sick in bed, and Mary blamed her sorry condition on the lack of air and exercise she had to endure as a prisoner: 'the want wherof had brought her into such a weaknes and impotency of the lymmes [limbs] as that she could not goe six steppes,' she told him. Her plea was that Elizabeth would take 'some consideration and remorse of the state of her body and her longe emprisonment, and that she was her next kinsewoman' and so grant her 'some more liberty than hitherto she hath had'. Through these words, Mary was not just seeking to evoke Elizabeth's sympathy and guilt; she was trying to demonstrate that the English queen could have nothing to fear from the sick, old woman that she now was, were she to be restored to the Scottish throne alongside her son. There was certainly no danger of her marrying again, even if she aspired to, she assured Beale, as 'she was nowe olde, yf not in years yeat in health of body, all the heares of her head were gray'.[89] But, despite her efforts, Mary's drive for the 'association' lost momentum shortly afterwards. Turbulent events in Scotland together with Elizabeth's understandable and justified suspicions of both Mary and her son slowed everything down to a snail's pace.

Irritated and frustrated at the lack of progress in the negotiations and Elizabeth's failure to answer her letters of complaint, Mary appealed to the French; and in March 1583 their ambassador raised the matter again with the English queen. In response, Elizabeth 'at once began to abuse the queen of Scotland and the "association", which, she said, was only for the purpose of upsetting everything that had been done in Scotland'.[90] To silence Mary and satisfy the French, Elizabeth dispatched Beale again to Sheffield to tell the Scottish queen that her complaints 'grewe more of passion then truthe, as might appeare if all thinges were duelye examined'. Following his mistress's instructions, Beale then recited 'all thinges' at considerable length. However, Mary made her intentions clear:

> she answered us, that her meaninge was not anye wayes to charge your majestie in anye thinge; but beinge desirous of libertye, [she] thought to laye open before your majesty her grievances, to th'intent your majestie might be the rather moved to have compassion on her, and after so manye yeres emprisonment and requests made for libertie, to grante some favour unto her. The lacke wherof she imputed, not (as she said) unto your majestie, but unto some enemyes.[91]

Mary's main objective now was to have Elizabeth agree to a watered-down 'association'; she no longer sought co-rulership with her son but simply to be allowed to live in freedom. Nor did she demand formal acknowledgement of her title as Elizabeth's heir but only that nothing should be done to prejudice it. In return for her freedom, she promised to perform certain conditions that would guarantee Elizabeth's safety.[92]

Mary's improved offers were brought back to Elizabeth, who immediately sent Sir Walter Mildmay to Sheffield to make the negotiations more official and draw up articles for a draft treaty. These were agreed in June 1583. But, again, the question arose about whether or not the word of Mary could be trusted. Furthermore, at this point, a new issue arose: could her son, James VI, be trusted? As will be seen in the next chapter, Elizabeth found his current behaviour, at best, erratic and, at worst, double-dealing. Negotiations, therefore, did not proceed at the pace or in the form that Mary had anticipated. As a result, she kept her options open and continued to seek help from Catholics abroad, although she had promised Elizabeth not to do so.

What about Elizabeth? Did she ever intend to go ahead with the 'association'? It is impossible to tell, but it is most likely her thinking about it wavered in response to differing circumstances. During the brief periods when Scotland appeared stable and James loyal, she could see advantages in Mary's restoration, provided that it was secured under the most rigorous of conditions. However, the prospect of Mary's return could not be entertained when James looked unreliable or Scotland was politically unsettled or a pro-French faction seemed to be directing his government. And these were exactly the set of circumstances in Scotland after June 1583. For some twenty months, James excluded pro-English lords from his counsels, exchanged secret letters with his mother, and made overtures to the French. Consequently, the 'association' was pretty much dead in the water by April 1584, although Elizabeth dangled it as bait before Mary in an attempt to stop her plots and to enlist her aid in bringing James to heel.[93] By the autumn of 1584 Mary rightly despaired that the 'association' would ever go ahead.

Most of Elizabeth's leading advisers had never wished to see Mary freed. Convinced that the Scottish queen was already at the centre of an international conspiracy to kill or depose their monarch, they were equally certain that she would be still more dangerous if liberated. During the early 1580s Spain's growing power and hostility towards protestants in general, and Elizabeth in particular, were generating huge anxiety. Meanwhile, the Elizabethan spy network was rooting out conspiracies—some real, some imagined—that linked Mary to the Spanish threat. The most serious was a genuine plot, detected in November 1583, to bring about a Catholic invasion of England led by Henry, duke of Guise, and financially backed by Philip II of Spain and the pope. Under intense interrogation and the use of torture, one of the leading conspirators (Francis Throckmorton) implicated Mary and the Spanish ambassador in the enterprise. In January 1585, the more dubious Parry plot was uncovered. Its instigator, Sir William Parry—a double agent—first admitted but later denied that he had intended to assassinate the queen, claiming in his defence that he had been seeking to entrap other suspects. Whatever the truth, in the wake of the successful assassination of the protestant leader of the Dutch rebels (William of Orange) the previous year, it was all too easy for the English to believe that Elizabeth was next on the Catholic hit list.

To avert such a catastrophe, Elizabeth's privy councillors drew up a document in October 1584 that would bind its signatories in an oath to prosecute and kill anyone who claimed a title to the throne as a result of Elizabeth's murder, even if that person had not approved, or even known about, the 'detestable act'.[94] Copies of this 'bond of association' were circulated throughout the country, and many thousands of people (including Mary herself) attached their signatures and seals to it. The following March, the bond was converted into a statute—called the Act for the Queen's Surety—a parliamentary measure that eschewed lynch law in favour of proper judicial proceedings. If any 'wicked person' in the future was 'privy to' or assented to a conspiracy against the queen's life, he or (more likely) she would now be brought to trial by a special commission.[95]

Amid these security fears, Mary was transferred to the inhospitable Tutbury Castle in Staffordshire, where she was shortly subjected to an even stricter supervisory regime under Sir Amias Paulet, an uncompromising guard whom she came to dislike heartily. While there, any lingering hope she might have for a negotiated treaty to set her free was cruelly shattered when on 12 March 1585 she received a letter from her son, saying that he rejected outright the proposal of an 'association'.[96] With no prospect now of her release and bitterly aggrieved at Elizabeth's 'hard usage', Mary was in the right frame of mind to listen to, and endorse, any rash plan that promised her freedom. And this was exactly what Elizabeth's principal secretary Sir Francis Walsingham hoped would happen. On top of all Mary's correspondence, he confidently expected to find evidence that would condemn her under the recent parliamentary statute.[97]

Moved to Chartley Castle at the beginning of 1586, Mary used a beer keg to smuggle her correspondence in and out of the house. But, despite all her precautions, Walsingham had suborned Mary's new courier (Gilbert Gifford) to pass on the letters to Thomas Phelippes, the government's chief code-breaker. After Phelippes had deciphered and copied them, the originals continued on their way to their intended recipients. By this means, Walsingham soon uncovered a conspiracy, but he allowed it to develop for several months in order to incriminate Mary in treason. In July he struck lucky. On the 6th of the month, a young recusant gentleman Anthony Babington sent the prisoner a letter, giving details of his plan to carry out the 'dispatch of the usurper' and to 'undertake the deliverie of your royall person from the handes of your enemies'.[98] Eleven days later, Mary replied positively to Babington's proposal.[99] Naturally she agreed to her rescue, but did she endorse regicide? Her most recent biographer argues not, on the grounds that she would never have resorted to such a dishonourable act and that Phelippes added a forged postscript to the letter that condemned her.[100] However, even without his insertion, the wording of the letter implicated Mary in the Babington plot. The postscript, which requested the names of the six gentlemen who would assassinate Elizabeth, certainly nailed her completely, but its purpose was to elicit further information. Anyway, from other letters we can see that, at this stage in her imprisonment, Mary was discounting Elizabeth's claim to be a legitimate monarch. In May 1586, she had stated her desire that Philip II 'wold take revenge of the queen of Englande' and 'ridde him selfe altogether of this Queen of Englande's malice agaynst him', a move that would end in Elizabeth's deposition and death. She was also prepared to aid Philip's 'enterprise' against England by using whatever influence she had in Scotland.[101]

Although Elizabeth was convinced of Mary's treachery, she found it difficult to face the political consequences and constitutional implications of putting a monarch on trial and sentencing her to death. In October 1586, she reluctantly agreed to Mary's trial by a royal commission, on a charge of 'the privity and assent to that most horrible and unnatural attempt' on her life.[102] But she delayed imposing the death penalty after Mary was predictably found guilty. Parliament and her privy councillors assured their sovereign that there was no alternative remedy, but Elizabeth waited until 1 February before signing Mary's death warrant and handing the document over to William Davison, one of her secretaries. Even then, she was unhappy with her decision, and had a letter sent to Mary's gaoler requesting that he 'shorten the life of that queen' in accordance with the vow he had taken when signing the bond of association.[103] The following day, Elizabeth requested the warrant's return, but she did not demand its recall when told that it had already been sealed. Consequently, on 3 February, her privy councillors, led by Burghley, agreed to deliver the warrant to Fotheringhay Castle, where Mary was being held. Five days later the Scottish queen was executed.[104]

In the immediate aftermath, Elizabeth displayed a rage that lasted longer than her customary displays of fiery temper. Claiming Davison had exceeded his instructions by taking the warrant to the other privy councillors, she punished him severely.[105] She rebuked the other councillors for concealing from her their dispatch of the warrant. Presumably, her anger was in part a projection of guilt, but it also arose from the knowledge that she had been cornered into taking a line of action that she believed to be deeply damaging to her reputation: 'what will they [her enemies] not now say when it shall be spread that for the safety of her life, a maiden queen could be content to spill the blood even of her own kinswoman?', she had asked her parliament rhetorically on 24 November 1586.[106]

Mary's last letter to Elizabeth was written before the death warrant was signed. Far from being contrite, as Elizabeth had wanted,
Mary took the moral high ground, declaring that she had not committed any malevolent, cruel, or hostile act against her cousin. Her
tone was one of pious resignation to her hard fate, the malice of her
enemies, and injustice of the world. She was now ready to die and 'me
fortifier' (fortify myself) in Christ, who had helped her endure the
unjust calumnies and false accusations of the past. As a symbolic act,
Mary returned the jewel that Elizabeth had originally sent her as a
token of support while she was imprisoned at Lochleven. Finally,
Mary asked two favours from her cousin: permission to send a jewel
and her last blessing to her son; and licence to be buried in holy
ground in France, preferably in the Catholic convent at Rheims where
her mother lay: 'I beg you, in the name of Jesus Christ and in respect
of our consanguinity…and by the honour of the dignity we both
held and of our sex in common, that you grant these requests'.[107] But
the latter request Elizabeth did not grant. The last thing she wanted
was for Mary's burial place to become a site of pilgrimage. Instead,
Mary's body was quietly interred in a side chapel within Peterborough Cathedral, close to the burial place of another discarded queen,
Katherine of Aragon. There her body remained until her son arranged
for its reburial in the royal chapel at Westminster Abbey in 1612.

As with partners in a bad marriage, both Elizabeth and Mary had
legitimate reasons to feel aggrieved in their relationship, and each
could claim to be the victim of the other. Elizabeth was at the mercy
of plots to advance Mary to her throne; Mary was locked away in
cold, damp castles from the age of 25 until her death, aged 44, on the
scaffold. Elizabeth felt betrayed by Mary's duplicity and alarmed by
her threat to England's security; Mary felt betrayed by Elizabeth's
hypocrisy in keeping her captive after offering to protect her person
and uphold her status as a monarch. Also, as with a marriage, it is
difficult for observers to remain neutral, and, over the centuries,
writers and film-makers have taken sides when depicting the 'rival'
queens' relationship. As for me, Mary evokes my sympathy but Elizabeth earns my respect. After all, for eighteen years, the English queen
battled to resolve the problem of her cousin in some better way, but
was repeatedly foiled by the intransigence of Mary's enemies in Scotland, the hysteria surrounding Mary in England, and finally by Mary's
fatal naivety in encouraging unrealistic conspiracies to effect an
escape.

4

James VI of Scotland

One of Elizabeth I's most memorable comments was prompted by the birth in June 1566 of Prince James, later to be King James VI of Scotland. As recounted in the memoirs of Sir James Melville, when she heard the news, a visibly distressed Elizabeth laid aside all merriness, 'bursting out to some of her ladies that the queen of Scots was lighter of a fair son, while she was but a barren stock'.[1] The next day Melville's friends at court told the Scottish ambassador how despondent Elizabeth was, but that she had been told to disguise her feelings and put on a brave public face. Writing in old age, after the deaths of both queens, Melville may have fashioned his account in full knowledge of Elizabeth's later virginal status and the accession in 1603 of Mary's son as James I. Nonetheless, his words contained a political truth. The birth of a Scottish prince was a blow to Elizabeth: in the patriarchal world of the sixteenth century, it offered the Stewarts a better opportunity to challenge Elizabeth's title to the throne of England and lay their claim to the succession.

If Elizabeth was indeed sorrowful on hearing the news from Scotland, she soon recovered her spirits. Gratified by Mary's invitation to be the child's godmother, Elizabeth dispatched her representative, the earl of Bedford, to attend the baptismal celebrations on 17 December 1566 and deliver a magnificent and expensive gift. The elaborately carved golden font, studded with many precious stones, was (according to one observer) 'so designed that the whole effect combined elegance with value'.[2] Nonetheless, concerned that Mary might take offence at its small size—Elizabeth had ordered it immediately when notified of the baby's birth but the child was now six months old— she told Bedford to excuse its uselessness 'in a kind of mirth', saying that Mary 'maie reserve it for the next'.[3] In fact the font turned out to be 'of sufficient proportions to immerse the infant prince', and, as no doubt intended, it far outshone the other gifts, even the jewellery presented by the ambassador of Charles IX of France and the huge

90

jewel-encrusted fan sent by the duke of Savoy.[4] This significant mark of respect to her cousin was reciprocated when Mary gave her son the second baptismal name of James in accordance with Elizabeth's wishes. (His first name, 'Charles', was in honour of the French king, but was never used.)[5] The signs now looked auspicious for a new—more amicable—relationship between the two queens.[6]

Elizabeth affected to take her role as James's godmother very seriously, claiming over the years to have a responsibility for the boy's physical safety, spiritual health, and political development. Thanks to this special relationship, she was able to call herself James's protector and justify her intervention in Scottish politics during the tumultuous six years that followed his mother's deposition in July 1567. Both at the time and afterwards she was to declare that the much-needed financial and military support she channelled to the 'king's party' and the various Scottish regents was a selfless act taken on behalf of her godson and made at great cost to herself. Once James became an adult, Elizabeth was sure to remind him—no doubt to his intense irritation—that it was to her that he owed the preservation of his crown and the pacification of his realm.[7] In truth, as James must have known, Elizabeth's primary political motive in shoring up support for the 'king's party' was to maintain the anglophile protestant lords in power and keep the French out of Scotland, the postern gate to England.

For some five years after 1573 (the year when the staunchly protestant and anglophile James Douglas, fourth earl of Morton, was firmly established as regent and defeated Mary's remaining supporters), Scotland ceased to be a security danger to England, and Elizabeth could turn her attention elsewhere. She could also be reassured by the fact that Scotland's future ruler, though baptized according to the Roman Catholic rites, was now being brought up a Calvinist under the influence of his tutors: the humanist historian and playwright George Buchanan and the younger scholar Peter Young. Thus there was good reason to be confident that the young king of Scotland would eventually make a fine protestant king of England if, as seemed increasingly likely, Elizabeth failed to marry and give birth to her own child. Indeed, one Englishman proposed that an act of succession be introduced in which 'the childe should be preferred before the mother'.[8]

All changed, however, as James grew into adolescence and demonstrated that he had a mind of his own that did not always accord with English interests. In March 1578, three months before his twelfth birthday, the king ended the regency of Morton and assumed the government himself. Although the ex-regent initially retained some influence, James soon came under the sway of two other men who were thought to be a danger to England. The first was James's French cousin, the charming and sophisticated Esmé Stuart, the lord of Aubigny. Attracting the king's attention on his arrival from France in September 1579, he was created earl of Lennox in March 1580 and duke of Lennox the next year. The second important figure was the one-time mercenary Captain James Stewart, who was appointed a gentleman of the king's chamber during 1580 and elevated to the earldom of Arran in 1581. With the support of these two men, and possibly under their influence, James was prompted to take revenge on the Scottish nobles whom he held responsible for the murders of his kinsmen before his birth and during his minority—his father (Lord Darnley) in 1567, his uncle (the earl of Moray) in 1570, and his grandfather (the earl of Lennox) in 1571. Some of these lords had taken refuge in England, and James demanded in vain their return from Elizabeth.[9] Another guilty party was Morton, who on the last day of 1580 was accused of being an accessory to Darnley's murder.

With Morton out of the picture and Lennox the dominant figure in the Scottish government, Elizabeth could no longer have confidence in the goodwill of the Scottish king and the security of her northern border. Lennox was believed to be pro-French and an enemy of the gospel, and Elizabeth's privy councillors urgently warned that he would bring James into the orbit of his Catholic Guise relations, persuade him to marry a Frenchwoman, and—most serious of all—'when he shall be of more yeres, fyndyng hir majesty not assisted with some good frendshipps, attempt to mak present title as the queen his mother did when marryed to the dolphyn [dauphin] of France'.[10] The possibility also existed that the Spanish king would seek to make Scotland a base for an invasion of England and that James might agree to an alliance with Philip II in order to make a bid for the English crown.[11]

Although Elizabeth had realized that her ally Morton was in trouble during 1580 and in early 1581, she had decided against supporting him and his friends with an English army, not least because she was in the process of negotiating an alliance with the French king against the growing threat of Spain. As she well knew, Henry III would not countenance English armed intervention in Scotland.[12] Nonetheless, Elizabeth had tried to prevent the fall of Morton and ascendancy of Lennox by diplomatic means. Before Morton's arrest, she had presented herself to James as a potential mediator who could settle the disputes that were causing factional conflicts within his nobility. Professing neutrality, she claimed 'to inclyne to no partye' but only to favour those 'most careful for the safety of your [James's] person and the contynewaunce of quyet'.[13] In reality, of course, Elizabeth *was* partial. This can be seen when she instructed her diplomatic envoy to undermine Lennox's influence with the king so that James would 'remayne constant in depending still upon this crowne as he hath hitherto done and is bound in true gratuitye to do, considering the care we have always had of his well doeinge'.[14] In any event, her diplomatic efforts proved fruitless, as James remained determined to pursue an independent course. His letters to Elizabeth were courteous, acknowledging her as 'his mother and deerest cosin', and thanking her for her 'loving caire and freindship' towards him, but he stuck fast to his own policies and retained his close relationship with Lennox.[15] Consequently, to Elizabeth's dismay and chagrin, Morton was executed in June 1581.

The king's mother Mary, meanwhile, took advantage of the change of regime in Scotland to propose the 'association' that would allow her to be released from custody in England and returned to Scotland as co-ruler with her son.[16] While Elizabeth was prepared to listen to this proposal, she was initially unreceptive, fearing that the Scottish queen's homecoming would add to the factional conflicts over the border and increase French influence there. James's own thoughts on the matter are by no means clear. All we know for sure is that Lennox encouraged him to take the scheme seriously and that the king kept his negotiations with his mother secret from Elizabeth. The discovery of his murky dealings with Mary reinforced Elizabeth's sense that James could not be trusted while under the influence of Lennox. By the summer of 1582, some believed that the English queen 'hates him more than she ever did the queen of Scotland, his mother, and thinks that one day her ruin will come from that side'.[17]

Lennox was as unpopular in Scotland as in England. To remove the king from his influence, a group of prominent Scottish protestant lords—including former adherents of Morton—kidnapped James in August 1582, as he returned from a hunting trip, and took him under duress to Ruthven Castle in Perthshire, the seat of their leader, the first earl of Gowrie. Separated from Lennox and Arran, James was now in the hands of pro-English nobles and forced to follow their directives. Elizabeth was 'overjoyed', as well she might be, since the Ruthven raiders had received encouragement and financial inducements from her agents.[18] In a letter to James, written a week later, the queen could barely disguise a note of triumph. She had just cause, she wrote, to leave the king to his fate as a prisoner, since he had previously ignored her advice and 'loving and neighbourly care to preserve your state and person'. However, she went on:

> we do conceyve this error to have proceeded rather through the practise and indirect persuasions of some ill instruments about you then of your owne motion whom we would be loth to touch with so fowle a vice as ingratitude, which we could not well do, without some blemish to our selves, being so neere tied to us in degree of consanguinitie as you are.

Because of this, she concluded, she would continue her 'care and best indevour for the preservation of your person, and the quieting of your estat'.[19] In brief, she was telling James that he had been punished for failing to follow her disinterested advice and instead listening to evil counsel, and as a result he was now entirely dependent upon her goodwill.

During his time in captivity, James had no choice but to express his gratitude to his 'dearest' cousin for her 'motherly affection' and declare his readiness to adhere to her good counsel.[20] English observers found 'his former affectione and love to your majestie revived, which before was halfe buried thoroughe the perswations of the evell affected about him, and him self now well inclined to embrace your favoure and folowe your directions'.[21] Actions seemed to follow words when James acceded to Elizabeth's 'advice' that Lennox return to France, Arran be kept under guard, and her 'well-affected' friends be given positions in his government. But it soon became evident that James was far less amenable than he appeared. Elizabeth's agents in Scotland learned that he was holding secret talks with the French ambassador and keeping quiet about further underhand negotiations with his mother concerning the French-backed 'association'. In addition, they heard of his evident 'mislike' of his 'presente estate and companie' and his desire 'to be rydd therof'.[22]

James was indeed unwilling to be a puppet king of Scotland or allow his realm to be a satellite of England. With the help of friends, he escaped from his captors in late June 1583 and occupied St Andrew's Castle. Still uncertain of his strength, James tried to keep on the right side of Elizabeth by assuring her on 2 July that he intended 'always to conforme us to your gude advise and counsele', rise above faction, and rule all his subjects 'indifferentlie'. He would not, he promised, act against any of his nobility without first informing the queen.[23]

However, it soon became obvious that James would not keep his word. Expressly against Elizabeth's wishes, Arran was recalled to court and in May 1584 appointed James's chancellor. Had Lennox not died in France, he too would have returned. As it was, the duke's son, Ludovic Stuart, was summoned from France in July 1583 to be confirmed in his father's titles and to receive open signs of favour from the king. Meanwhile pro-English protestant lords—especially John Erskine, second earl of Mar (who had played a significant role in the Ruthven raid), and Archibald Douglas, eighth earl of Angus (Morton's nephew)—were removed from James's court and placed 'under ward'. When Elizabeth protested, James smoothly assured her of his goodwill and amity but asserted confidently that he was the best judge of his own security and would manage his nobility in his own way. He also warned her against dealing with his nobles behind his back: 'it [was] more convenient to deale now with himself than heretofore it was in his unperfyte age, with anie his subjects in his name.'[24]

Elizabeth had already realized that she needed to deal with the adult James directly. From July to September 1583, she sent high-profile diplomats to his court to place before him her grievances and requirements. She also gave thought to buying his loyalty, suggesting a yearly pension of 10,000 crowns (£2,500) soon after his escape from Ruthven. When the king's councillors advised that the amount was so derisory that 'they thought he myght nott with honor receve ytt', the cash-strapped queen even considered raising the amount.[25] At a time when the Guise party in France and the Spanish king were known to be plotting an 'enterprise' against England, it was vital that Scotland did not become a base for invasion. But, in return for the money, Elizabeth stipulated concrete concessions: that James grant clemency to the Ruthven raiders, return anglophile lords to favour, and allow her to oversee his relations with foreign powers, especially France.[26]

On the surface James responded positively to Elizabeth's requests. In a proclamation of 21 September 1583, he announced his intention to observe his promise to his 'dearest sister' the queen of England and pardon all the Ruthven raiders, 'who will humbly crave the same'.[27] On 31 October he issued another proclamation, in which he demanded that these lords should beg his mercy and prove their future good behaviour. Yet, despite these marks of goodwill towards

Elizabeth, James remained averse to freeing Angus, who was still 'under ward', and ordered Mar to leave the country, alleging he was guilty of a new offence. At the same time, Arran was building up his political power base, while in November James made the second duke of Lennox a gentleman of the bedchamber and great chamberlain for life. In these circumstances, Gowrie understandably felt his position was precarious and planned to leave the country.[28]

Because of James's mixed messages, Elizabeth received conflicting advice from observers and counsellors. The most 'godly' of them, such as her principal secretary, Sir Francis Walsingham, deeply distrusted the king and recommended that Elizabeth provide the 'well-affected' Scottish lords with aid to help them mount another coup against Arran.[29] On the other hand, her cousin Lord Hunsdon favoured a diplomatic solution, advocating that an accommodation be reached with James and Arran. For the time being, Elizabeth preferred to do nothing. Since James was still mouthing words of friendship towards her and making no moves to draw closer to his Guise kin, she could afford to leave him to his own devices. A more urgent problem for her, during the autumn and winter of 1583–4, was the military situation in the Netherlands, where the Spanish army looked set to defeat the protestant rebels who had held them at bay for over a decade. It looked increasingly likely that England would have to offer additional financial assistance and even military help to their co-religionists there. Furthermore, Elizabeth would not risk alienating the French king (whose support she wanted against Spain) by interfering directly in Scottish politics.

To Elizabeth's disquiet, during the spring of 1584, trouble flared up once more between James and the Ruthvenite lords. In a reckless attempt to overthrow Arran, a small force under Mar, Angus, and the master of Glamis seized the castle and town of Stirling in mid-April. They then appealed to Elizabeth for military and financial support.[30] Although a military entanglement in Scotland was out of the question, Elizabeth could hardly abandon her few Scottish friends and allow the northern kingdom to fall entirely into the hands of men thought hostile to English interests. With war looming against Spain, it was imperative for England's back door to be securely locked. Lord Treasurer Burghley, therefore, authorized the distribution of a significant sum of money to the lords holding Stirling, so that they might 'prevaile' against those who did 'abuse both the king's eare and authority'.[31] Concurrently, Elizabeth arranged to send a special envoy to Scotland who would inform the king of her readiness to mediate between him and his disaffected subjects. Again, the mediation offered was hardly neutral, but rather grounded in her previous advice that James should bring back to court the Scottish nobles 'well-affected' to England. As far as she was concerned, the Ruthvenite lords were not rebels against their king but ousted *good* councillors who were seeking to displace James's *evil* councillors for the well-being of their country.[32]

James naturally did not see it that way at all and was in no mood for mediation. Before her special envoy arrived, the 17-year-old king had raised an army and gone after the lords at Stirling. Failing to raise the country, Angus, Mar, Glamis, and their many followers fled across the border to England and requested asylum. Reprisals soon followed in Scotland, and English observers were soon (erroneously) predicting a bloodbath.[33] On 4 May 1584, Gowrie (who had been seized before the rising) was beheaded for treason, and some of Mar's servants were hanged. That same day, three presbyterian ministers who had approved the 1582 Ruthven raid also fled to England out of fear of arrest or worse.[34] Two days later, James demanded the extradition of his rebels.

James's letter to Elizabeth containing this demand was uncompromising. The nobles were his 'rebellious subjectes' and their assault on Stirling could not be defended. After all, he had pardoned them 'frelie thair former offenses, cheiflie at your earnest request' and had only sent some of them 'to be furth of our realme' for a short space of time 'until our estate had bene better setled'. Through their actions, these rebels had endangered 'his honour, persoun, croun, and estate' and were now attempting to stain Elizabeth's honour by seeking refuge in her realm. The king therefore insisted that she cease harbouring these men and immediately hand them over for punishment 'according to the treateis of peax standing betuix us and oure cuntreis'. If Elizabeth did not comply, he warned, their friendship would be over.[35] James's envoy was still more explicit, letting Elizabeth understand 'that in case of refusall he shalbe constrayned to crave the assistaunce and supporte of forein princes'.[36] Indeed, James did appeal to the French king for a two-year loan of his elite 'Scottish guard' as protection against Elizabeth.[37]

Taken by surprise at the speed of events and James's unexpected triumph, Elizabeth faltered. She was at a loss about how to proceed. Indeed, by now her stock in Scotland was so low that she was reduced to seeking the intercession of James's mother. Offering as bait the implementation of the 'association', Elizabeth's messengers asked

Mary to demonstrate the power she claimed to have over her son, and to confirm the goodwill she professed towards Elizabeth by persuading James to make peace with the refugee nobles and to reject his 'evil' councillors.[38] As to be expected, Mary was prepared to exert her influence over James only *after* the conclusion of a treaty that guaranteed her freedom, so no immediate progress was made on that front, although negotiations lingered on for months once Mary had agreed to a compromise. But rather than helping to ease relationships, Mary's claims that James was at her command worked to deepen suspicions of the Scottish king at the English court and made the crisis still worse.

Despite the extreme weakness of her position, Elizabeth held firm against James. Too much seemed to be at stake. Unless the Scottish king broadened the basis of his government to include protestant anglophile lords, she could not be sure of his support against her enemies at home and abroad. The absence of these lords from the Scottish government also put at risk the future of the Kirk. James's new advisers were believed to be crypto-Catholics, and his policies during 1584 raised questions about his own commitment to protestantism.

That year, the king had re-established episcopacy and declared a form of royal supremacy over the Kirk that aroused presbyterian opposition. Some twenty ministers chose to leave the country and take refuge in England, from where they lambasted Arran and their monarch in print and from the pulpit. Although at one level Elizabeth was unworried about James's oppression of presbyterians, at another she was concerned that it might signify his sympathy for popery. After all, James seemed to be concurrently in cahoots with Jesuits. Not only had he given protection to the English Jesuit William Holt, eventually allowing his escape to the Continent, but he had also been engaged in correspondence with the Scottish Jesuit William Crichton, who was fomenting conspiracies abroad.

For all these reasons, Elizabeth refused to extradite the fugitive Scots, justifying her position by denying that they were rebels at all. Had James accepted her advice, she told him, the recent upheavals in Scotland would not have occurred. Furthermore, because the king still chose to ignore her counsel and preferred to listen instead to evil councillors, he was putting at risk the amity between the two realms:

> Tyme, perhaps, with to deare experience, when the eyes of your owne
> judgement shall learne you to discerne howe perilouse yt is for princes
> to have such dangerous and wicked instrumentes abowt them, will

then leade you to see your owne error in neglecting the councell of those that have had more care of your well doing and safetie than others, perhaps, that pretend to beare most love and affection towards you.[39]

Notwithstanding Elizabeth's failure to cave in before his ultimatum, James held back from a total breach. Had Henry III or his Guise relations been ready to support him financially and militarily, he might have chosen to renew the 'auld alliance' with France and abandon friendship with England, but the French were beset with their own internal troubles and not free to pursue their traditional ambitions in Scotland.[40] Equally, James saw no advantage in an 'association' with his mother unless it came with a French alliance and money. By contrast, an agreement with Elizabeth—together with an English pension—seemed the best way forward, as long as it could be achieved honourably. So, despite his earlier tough stance, James—through Arran—told Elizabeth's ambassador of their 'desier of continuance of straight frendship and amitie', and proposed a high-level conference at which a prominent representative from each side could thrash out the issues in dispute.[41]

Elizabeth did not really expect a satisfactory outcome from such a conference. Hence, to avoid exposure to another public and humiliating rebuff, she turned down James's invitation for the meeting to take place in Scotland and demanded that it be convened near Berwick in order to give the appearance that the talks were to be merely about border matters. To keep up this pretence, she named Hunsdon as her representative, since he was the lord warden of the east marches and responsible for border security.[42] But Hunsdon was also a close cousin and privy councillor, and therefore had the authority and dignity to discuss important affairs of state with James's own representative, Arran.

As predicted, the conference held on 14 August 1584 failed to resolve the differences between the two sides. Arran and Hunsdon related to each other very well, but they could not reach agreement on the substantive points at issue. What is more, by the time of their meeting James had further cause of complaint against Elizabeth. The Scottish fugitives, now based in Newcastle, had conspired to seize Edinburgh Castle and overturn the Arran regime. Although they denied it vigorously, these lords—with English backing—had indeed been plotting a coup. Elizabeth also did not admit to their guilt and protested strongly when James's parliament forfeited their lands.[43]

At the August interview, Arran had disclosed to Hunsdon some of the manœuvres of French and Spanish envoys to win over his king. Afterwards, James and the earl decided to use their knowledge of foreign intrigues as a last bargaining counter with Elizabeth. Their plan was to dispatch to England an envoy who would offer to reveal to Elizabeth all the 'practices' that her enemies 'intended against her majesty and her state' provided that she pledged to expel the Scottish fugitives from England and Ireland. This proposition—sent in advance to the queen—had some appeal.[44] First, James was making a conciliatory gesture by agreeing to the banishment of the fugitive lords instead of insisting on their extradition to Scotland, where they might well be imprisoned or put to death. More importantly, in the aftermath of the discovery of the Throckmorton plot, the privileged information on offer could be very valuable. On the other hand, the proposal revealed that James knew far more than he had so far admitted about foreign schemes that put Elizabeth's life in danger. If he was such a good friend to his kinswoman, why had he not warned her about the 'practices' earlier? Additionally, Elizabeth was deeply suspicious about James's choice of envoy. He was Patrick, master of Gray, a man who was, 'as is certenelie knowen, a professed devoted servitor to the Scottishe quene, and, by common report, either a great papist or worse'.[45] Nonetheless, Elizabeth put these reservations aside and consented to receive Gray at her court, even though some of her privy councillors still advised her against it.

Elizabeth had one last card up her sleeve in her dealings with James: the succession. Although it was never mentioned directly in the exchanges between them, the queen several times hinted that James's position as her heir might well be compromised if he failed to take heed of her wishes. In a letter of 3 October 1584, she warned the king that, if he failed to keep his word (again), then she would have

> just cause to doubt that these late protestations you make are not accompanied with that sincerity that we could wish in one so neerely tyed unto us in blood, and neighborhood, and therefore cannot but plainely lett you understand, as our neerest kinsman and neighbor, that accordingly as we shall receave answeare from you, so are we hereafter to make accompt of your good will and frend shipp towardes us.[46]

By twice stating his position as her nearest blood relative, her coded message was pretty clear.

A month later, James received an even starker message. Elizabeth had decided 'to forbeare to have any further dealing with the king, but to wish him well'; and only if James changed his ways, would he 'be assured...to receave such frutes of her friendship as shalbe to the comfort of himself and his whole realme'.[47] These cautionary words were accompanied by one significant action: in October 1584 Elizabeth allowed James to be encompassed within the bond of association—the brainchild of Burghley, Walsingham, and Leicester—that was designed to protect her life. The king, as well as his mother, would be disinherited if Elizabeth became the object of an assassination attempt.[48] If James were not her friend, he would be treated as a potential enemy until he mended his ways.

Elizabeth's attitude towards James softened during Gray's embassy. Smooth-tongued diplomat that he was, Gray convinced the queen and some of his former critics that James had never signed an 'association' with Mary, nor would he do so in the future. Indeed Gray proposed an alliance between the two monarchs in which James would repudiate any interest in the 'association'. But this could only happen, Gray explained, once Elizabeth had ended her support for the fugitive Scottish lords and ministers. James's security, as well as his honour, depended upon it.[49]

To show his good faith, James issued a proclamation, late in 1584, banishing Jesuits and other Catholic priests from his kingdom. It may also have been then that he wrote a paraphrase of the Revelation of John the Divine, a manuscript copy of which seems to have been sent to Elizabeth, to demonstrate his endorsement of the standard protestant identification of the pope with the Antichrist.[50] After Gray's return to Scotland, James publicly denounced 'the association'. At his council meeting in January 1585, 'in one voice it was concludit, as a thing verie disa[d]vantageouse bothe for the estat of his majestie and countrie, that it should never be'.[51] Well satisfied, Elizabeth showed her appreciation by lifting the threat of the Scottish king's exclusion from the English crown if another assassination attempt was discovered. When in March 1585 parliament introduced a bill to incorporate the bond of association into a statute, Elizabeth ensured that the wording was changed so that James could not be held responsible for his mother's actions.

The groundwork was now laid for a bilateral treaty between James and Elizabeth. Learning in early 1585 that a treaty had just been signed between Philip II and the leaders of the Catholic league in France to provide for joint action against protestants, Elizabeth suggested to James an Anglo-Scottish league with its declared purpose to establish their mutual defence against Catholics who were seeking to overthrow 'the professours of the gospel'.[52] However, one obstacle still stood in the way of its conclusion: Elizabeth's steadfast refusal to expel the Scottish exiles. She had them banished from the borders so that they could not intervene in Scottish political life, but she would not desert them completely. Nevertheless, hopes were high that James would be enticed by thoughts of a regular English pension and drop that particular demand. To encourage James to enter a league, Elizabeth sent the experienced and adept diplomat Edward Wotton to Scotland with a gift of hounds and horses for the hunting-loving king. Wotton slipped in business effortlessly while at sport with him or attending entertainments, but James proved a determined negotiator, insisting upon a larger pension than the one offered, demanding an English peerage, and declining to discuss his marriage.

At the end of July 1585 the talks stalled, even though agreement could still have been reached. The cause was the murder of Sir Francis Russell, the eldest surviving son of the second earl of Bedford, in a violent affray on the border during a day of truce. Wotton 'cast the blame of the disorder' upon Arran, and Elizabeth demanded the earl's arrest: it was an affront that 'a Skot shuld dare violate his handes on any of our noble bloude, in a peacable concord, whan our frendship shuld have sent out his [its] hotest beames to the kindeling of the entier affection of bothe realmes', she protested to James.[53]

Shocked by the murder, James placed Arran under confinement, but to Elizabeth's annoyance released him after only three days. Convinced that the earl was pro-French, pro-Catholic, and opposed to the English league, Elizabeth was now ready to connive at a plot to overthrow his government. Although she denied it afterwards, she almost certainly approved the coup planned by the earls of Mar and Angus and the master of Glamis. In November 1585, these exiled lords left England and joined with other Scottish nobles to seize Stirling Castle. This time they were successful: the friendless Arran fled, and James restored the fugitives' lands and honours, and submitted himself—apparently willingly—to the new regime.[54]

With the anglophile lords now at the helm, peace talks were resumed, but Elizabeth and James still haggled over the terms of a treaty. The king not only rejected the size of the English pension on offer, but also wanted Elizabeth to sign and seal a formal guarantee that he would be her heir. Their disagreements on this latter point became personally heated, each accusing the other of behaving dishonourably. Fearing their bad feeling might be getting out of hand, James sent his cousin a sonnet to lower the temperature and play down the significance of their disagreements. Comparing their 'contentions' to 'sudden summer showers' and the 'sudden choler strife' between 'the husband and his loving wife', James affirmed that just as

> brethren, loving others as their life
> Will have debates at certain times and hours.
> ...
>
> Even so this coldness did betwixt us fall
> To kindle our love as sure I hope it shall.[55]

As far as we know, Elizabeth did not reciprocate with a verse of her own, nor did she acknowledge receipt of the sonnet so her reactions to it are unknown.

In July 1586, the differences between the two monarchs were resolved and the treaty of Berwick signed. According to its terms, Elizabeth and James would bind together to maintain the gospel, and neither of them would make an arrangement with another foreign power to the prejudice of the league. It was also agreed that all rebels who took refuge within either country were to be extradited or banished from the relevant realm.[56] James successfully secured his larger pension, but not the formal recognition of his place in the English succession (nor even the English title) that he had requested. All he received was a separate written guarantee from the queen that she would 'never directly or indirectly do or suffer to be don any thing' that might result in 'the diminution, emparing [impairing], or derogation of...any right or title that may be due to you in any sort or in any tyme present or future', unless James displayed some 'manifest ingratitude' towards her.[57] This conditionality of James's right was as far as Elizabeth would go; as it stood, she had a lever over him that could safeguard her interests.

In retrospect, the treaty of Berwick and the fall of the Arran regime marked a turning point in Elizabeth's relationship with James. But it did not seem that way at the time. There was no firm guarantee that the king would hold faith with the returning lords or cease his interactions with the European Catholic powers. Furthermore, James's affection for the Catholic George Gordon, sixth earl of Huntly, boded ill for the future. Huntly was appointed justice and lieutenant in the north in December 1586 and lord high chamberlain the following June. Other Catholic noblemen in Scotland were also becoming more prominent and assertive. Meanwhile Jesuits were frequenting Scotland, celebrating public masses, and reporting the conversion of three great nobles and many gentlemen.[58] Finally, faction was to continue for many more years in Scotland, resulting in a number of abortive plots aimed at capturing the king, the last taking place as late as 1600.

The first major test of the treaty of Berwick came with the trial and execution of Mary Queen of Scots. At first all seemed calm. On hearing the news of the 1586 Babington plot, James congratulated Elizabeth on her 'narrow escape from the chaws [jaws] of death' and offered 'all best wishes' for her safety.[59] He did not raise objections to his mother being put on trial, even though the jurisdictional claim of an English court to prosecute one of his subjects, let alone a Scottish queen, was a challenge to his kingship. According to the master of Gray, James was content that 'the law go fordwart' concerning his mother and would gladly wish for all foreign princes to know 'how evil she has usit hirself towardis the queen's majestie'.[60] In the late summer and autumn of 1586, the king was not too worried about Mary's fate, as he fully expected Elizabeth to show clemency at the trial and not impose the death penalty.[61] His immediate priority at that time was to protect his own place in the succession by dissociating himself from his mother's treason.

However, once the legal proceedings began in mid-October, James began to experience unease about its outcome and started the process of interceding for his mother's life. When the death sentence was pronounced, he became seriously alarmed and even threatened that 'he will in no ways keep friendship if his mother's life be touched'.[62] However, James went too far in his protest. He insulted both Elizabeth's parents by commenting that Henry VIII's reputation had been badly tarnished when he beheaded 'his bedfellow', Anne Boleyn, and maintained that 'that tragedy' would be 'farre inferior to this', presumably because his own mother was a queen whereas Elizabeth's was merely a commoner.[63] When relayed to the queen, she was so deeply offended that James had to apologize. She had 'misconstrued' his letter, he wrote. He was her 'most honest and steadfast friend' and was certain that she would treat him as such.[64]

In his final plea for Mary's life on 26 January 1587, James adopted a very different tone. Reversing their previous roles, he assumed the persona of the plain-speaking, 'honest friend' and counsellor, who was giving 'friendly and best advice' to his kinswoman on an important political matter. His aim, he wrote, was to appeal to Elizabeth's 'ripest judgment', and he did so by warning her calmly and rationally of the danger to their personal relationship and the challenge to divine right monarchy if she went ahead with the execution:

> What thing, madame, can greatlier touch me in honor that is a king and a son than that my nearest neighbor, being in straitest friendship with me, shall rigorously put to death a free sovereign prince and my natural mother, alike in estate and sex to her that so uses her, albeit subject (I grant) to a harder fortune, and touching her nearly in proximity of blood? What law of God can permit that justice shall strike upon them whom He has appointed supreme dispensators of the same under Him, whom He hath called gods and therefore subjected to the censure of none in earth.[65]

Elizabeth was therefore well aware of the depth of James's feeling when she signed the death warrant, and fully understood that she needed to appease his anger to save the treaty between them. Her tactic was to claim total innocence in the affair. In a personal letter to James written a week after the execution, she expressed 'the extreme dolor that overwhelms my mind for that miserable accident, which far contrary to my meaning hath befallen', and continued:

> I beseech you that—as God and many more know—how innocent I am in this case, so you will believe me that, if I had bid aught, I would have bid [abided] by it. I am not so base minded that fear of any living creature or prince should make me afraid to do that were just or, done, to deny the same. I am not of so base a lineage nor carry so vile a mind; but as not to disguise fits most a king, so will I never dissemble my actions but cause them show even as I meant them.

Elizabeth also tried to comfort James with thoughts of the succession, reminding him that, although he had lost his natural mother, 'you have not in the world a more loving kinswoman nor a more dear friend than myself, nor any that will watch more carefully to preserve you and your estate'.[66]

James was not easily consoled. Elizabeth's action hit him hard, not only because he had failed as a son to protect his mother but also because Elizabeth had treated him as a man of little account by ignoring his strong entreaties on Mary's behalf. Many of James's subjects were equally outraged at their deposed queen's death, demanding an end to the English alliance and calling for some form of military retaliation against Elizabeth. The result was an immediate diplomatic breach between the two realms, disturbances on the border, and international uncertainty about the future of the Anglo-Scottish league.[67]

A pragmatist to his fingertips, James soon realized that he had far more to lose than gain in seeking retribution. Elizabeth's privy councillors were issuing warnings that he would forfeit his right to the succession if he embarked on a war of revenge.[68] Besides, he began to appreciate that he might be able to profit from the situation by demanding 'satisfaction' for the 'accident'. As compensation, he would ideally have liked to be named the queen's heir; but, knowing this to be unobtainable, he was prepared to make do with the grant of an 'earldom' or 'dukedom' and the acquisition of his paternal family's English lands, which the queen had seized on his grandmother's death.[69] With a noble title and an extensive English estate, he would be in a stronger position to bid for the crown when the queen died. Elizabeth, as usual, would make no such concessions. She only offered James assurances that Mary's conviction for treason would in no way prejudice 'his pretended title' by 'corruption of blode'.[70]

James continued to ask for 'satisfaction' for well over a year with no greater success. However, during the Spanish invasion scare of July to August 1588, he grasped the opportunity for putting a squeeze on Elizabeth. As requested, the king pledged the queen his loyalty, promising her ambassador William Asheby, on the word of a prince, that he intended 'to joyne and concurr in all actions, preferring her good amitie and friendship before all other princes whatsoever, accompting her majestie's foes his foes, and willing to show a gratefull mynd for the favours receaved even from his cradell'.[71] Nevertheless, behind the scenes, James tried to do a deal. Making it clear that he expected some substantial return for his support, he demanded a dukedom, his family estates, a pension of £5,000 a year, and the maintenance of a royal guard and border force at Elizabeth's expense.[72] Not really knowing what to do, Asheby gave James 'fair promises' on his own authority, but Elizabeth disavowed them as soon as the invasion threat had passed.[73] James took the refusal surprisingly well; the annuity of £3,000 that he did receive no doubt helped mollify him.

Despite James's display of loyalty during the great Armada crisis, the Anglo-Scottish entente ran into rough waters soon afterwards. Beneath the two monarchs' affirmations of affection and friendship lay a deep seam of suspicion and discord. One immediate cause of friction between them related to the protection James gave to religious fugitives from England in contravention of the treaty of Berwick.

In 1589 and 1590, a couple of prominent English presbyterians fled over the border to avoid prosecution for their suspected involvement in writing or printing a series of clandestine pamphlets attacking the episcopacy, which were known as the Marprelate tracts.[74] One of the refugees, Robert Waldegrave, was even awarded a printing licence in Scotland and soon afterwards appointed the king's printer. At the same time, James allowed—perhaps even encouraged—ministers in Scotland to preach and print diatribes against the English bishops, who, they pronounced, were persecuting their godly brethren in the southern realm. James himself took up their case, urging Elizabeth in a personal letter 'for oure cause and intercessioun it may please [you] to lett thame [the presbyterians] be relevit of thair present strait'.[75] Possibly James was enjoying giving the queen a taste of her own medicine; after all, she had harboured Scottish presbyterians some five years earlier. But he was also seeking to mend his own relations with the Kirk and thereby strengthen monarchical power in his realm.

Elizabeth was predictably furious. She reminded James that they shared the same interests in suppressing religious radicals, members of 'a secte of perilous consequence, such as wold have no kings but a presbitrye'. She went on: 'I pray you stap the mouthes, or make shorter the toungz of suche ministars as dare presume to make oraison in ther pulpitz for the persecuted in Ingland for the gospel. Suppose you, my deare brother, that I can tollerat suche scandalz of my sincere gouvernement?'[76] Acknowledging he had gone too far, James immediately ordered a ban on the printing of books that insulted the English Church and the suspension of prayers for the 'afflicted' English presbyterians. He also had the English refugee—John Penry—declared an outlaw, although no attempt was made to oust him from Scotland.[77]

While baffled by James's support for the English presbyterians, Elizabeth was far more alarmed by his protection of Scottish Catholics. Both the Jesuits and Catholic lords had links to, and communications with, her enemies abroad and would, she thought, allow Scotland to become a base for the invasion of England. The defeat of the Armada extended, rather than ended, England's war against Spain, and consequently the neutrality of Scotland remained a vital security interest for the queen. At this time, the French connection was far less menacing, because that realm was embroiled in a devastating civil war of succession. But many of the Catholic nobility had pro-Spanish sympathies, and could provide havens in their regions for enemy ships carrying troops.

No sooner was the Armada crisis over than the English government received incontrovertible evidence that Huntly, John Maxwell,
earl of Morton, Francis Hay, ninth earl of Erroll, and David Lindsay,
eleventh earl of Crawford, were corresponding secretly with Philip II
and encouraging him to attempt another invasion of England, this
time through Scotland. James raised forces against Erroll, but he took
only mild measures against the others, and by 1590 all the hispano-
phile lords remained at large.[78] Elizabeth's advisers could not decide
whether James was colluding with pro-Spanish interest groups in his
realm or felt too weak to take action against them. Elizabeth herself
seemed to believe that James lacked the determination and courage
to take on the Catholic lords, and she gave general lectures to her
young cousin on the need for strong kingship. 'Your behaviour is
so exasperating', she reprimanded him in March 1589, 'that if I did
not love you better than you deserve, I should not mind to see you
ruined'.[79] But, even had James wanted to—and the jury is out on
that—he lacked the resources to raise an army that could challenge a
confederacy of the powerful Catholic nobles; and, despite her protests, Elizabeth refused to increase his pension or send him a lump
sum to finance a small standing force.

Over the next few years, rumours of papist conspiracies and Jesuit
activities continued to alarm the queen, who repeatedly urged James
to arrest the Catholic lords and expel the missionary priests. The king
did nothing. However, matters came to a head in early 1593. On
1 January, treasonable dealings were brought to light after suspicious-
looking papers were found in the possession of a Scottish courier
embarking for the Continent. Among them were eight clean sheets of
gilded paper (to be known as the 'Spanish blanks'), which had been
signed (either singly or collectively) by Huntly, Erroll, and William
Douglas, tenth earl of Angus. Under torture, the courier confessed
that these men were involved in a plot to help Spanish troops land in
Scotland as a preliminary to an invasion of England; the terms, which
they were to negotiate with Philip II, were allegedly to be inserted
onto the blank sheets of paper.[80] Called upon by Scottish protestants
as well as the English queen to arrest the conspirators, James could
not ignore the evidence and announced that the implicated earls
would be put on trial. However, when Huntly and Erroll fled to their
northern strongholds, James failed to apprehend them. His army
marched north, but 'little or nothing was done'.[81] Still more suspiciously, the arrested courier somehow escaped from Edinburgh Castle,
and without him there was no case against the suspects. Consequently,

when the three Scottish lords denied the charges, James let them go unpunished.

Elizabeth was infuriated by the courier's escape and outraged at the leniency shown towards 'thos wicked conspirators of the Spanische faction'. She dismissed James's excuses, and urged him to 'play the king, and let your subjects see you respect yourself'. Again she accused him of listening to evil counsel, calling him—most famously and insultingly—'a seduced king'.[82] By now, she feared, James's weakness was seriously endangering her own realm. If he did not take action against Huntly and the rest, they would plot again, and, if they were successful, Scotland would be turned into a Spanish base. More immediately, the Catholic lords were now free to send troops to aid the restless Ulster chieftains who were on the brink of serious revolt in Ireland.

For this reason, during 1593 and 1594, Elizabeth virtually turned her back on the treaty of Berwick and returned to the pre-1586 policy of intervening in Scotland's internal politics. On her orders, envoys and agents secretly encouraged the 'well-affected' protestant members of the Scottish nobility to form an association against the Catholic faction. Money was offered 'to make their party more strong then their adversaries'.[83] Elizabeth also decided to use Francis Stewart, earl of Bothwell, for this purpose, a man whom James had branded a rebel after he had led unsuccessful assaults on the king in December 1591 and June 1592. After each occasion the earl had fled over the frontier, where English borderers gave him refuge; and, in flagrant flouting of the treaty of Berwick, Elizabeth had not ordered his extradition. Now, towards the end of 1593, her agent was sent to offer active support to the earl if he would drive out the Scottish Catholic nobles.[84]

By the spring of 1594, the political and personal relationship between Elizabeth and James was at breaking point. Their letters grew angrier in tone, and doubts were expressed as to whether or not the league would survive. James was furious that 'his avowed traitor' received favourable treatment in England; Elizabeth was equally angry that James proffered favour to her enemies. Yet, in truth, both monarchs knew that cooperation was ultimately in their best interests and that neither could afford to provoke the other too far. Additionally, they each began to question the value of their relationship with their respective *protégés*, as both Bothwell and Huntly were proving unreliable friends as well as a major cause of conflict between the two realms. In June 1594, the monarchs drew back from the brink. James apologized for an offensive letter he had previously written and invited Elizabeth to act as godmother to his first-born son, Prince Henry. Seizing the opportunity to repair their relationship, she accepted his apology and invitation. At the end of August she sent a 'cupboard richly wrought' as a 'liberal' gift for the baby prince.[85] Once the baptism celebrations were over, James kept his word and sent armies against Huntly and his friends; meanwhile, Elizabeth deserted Bothwell.

After 1595, the Anglo-Scottish league was in better shape, although relations between the two monarchs grew difficult again in 1597, when Huntly, who had gone into exile, came back to Scotland, ostensibly converted to protestantism, and was made a marquess. Relations were also unsettled because James—in an attempt to rise above faction—was appointing other Catholics to important positions in his government. Joining with the Kirk, Elizabeth issued strong warnings to the king about the dangers of tolerating and giving power to papists in his territories, but again her 'counsel' was ignored.[86] Actually, her fears proved groundless. Huntly soon retired to his estates and played no further significant role in political life, while James made no attempt to undermine the protestant reformation in his realm.

Despite the continuing security concerns for Elizabeth, a decade on from the signing of the treaty of Berwick, it was James who had most cause for disappointment. The gains for him were considerably less than he had anticipated. The receipt of the English pension was vital for his crown's finances, but he was irritated that it arrived sporadically and sometimes in smaller amounts than, he felt, were his due. By his calculation, he was entitled to at least £4,000 a year, and consequently he objected when Elizabeth either reduced the amount or failed to pay up at the specified times. He also quite reasonably expected that the queen's gifts to him should be considered as extras and not be deducted from the annuity (as when Elizabeth had deducted from his pension £2,000 worth of plate sent to him as a wedding gift). He had no sympathy with her excuse that she was short of money because of the costly war against Spain. James's feelings about the pension had been summed up in a letter he sent to Elizabeth in December 1591: it was not only his need for the money that irked him, he explained, but also the dishonour of constantly having to request his dues:

> I wearie to be so long time sutire, as one who was not borne to be a beggar, but to be beggit at...Remember, that as I ame your kinsman,

so am I a true prince. The disdaining of me can be noe honor to you. The use of tempting your freinds so sore cane turne you to no advantage.[87]

However, from Elizabeth's perspective, the pension was intended as recognition and reward for James's friendship, and not a right in itself. Hence she declared herself unwilling to pay the sum whenever the king appeared to be pursuing policies that were not in the English interest.[88] Ultimately Elizabeth usually paid up, but only after humiliating petitioning from James.

Elizabeth's continuing refusal to name James her heir was his second disappointment, and he could not understand why she would not do so. As far as he was concerned, he had proved his loyalty during the war against Spain and was assisting her against Irish rebels. Increasingly he came to suspect that he had enemies at the English court who were poisoning the queen against him. His most regular correspondents there were Robert Devereux, second earl of Essex, and members of his circle, and they encouraged James to believe that Lord Burghley and his son Robert Cecil were his enemies, opposed to a Stewart succession and preferring that of Lord Beauchamp, Arbella Stuart, or even the infanta of Castile.[89]

That he might be excluded from the succession on the grounds of his mother's treason was the king's greatest fear, especially after the Jesuit polemicist Robert Doleman (aka Persons) had mistakenly referred to the 1585 Act for the Queen's Surety as a barrier to the Scottish king's accession.[90] James was, consequently, acutely sensitive to any disparaging reference in England to Mary. Edmund Spenser's representation of the Scottish queen through the figure of Duessa gave the king 'great offence' in 1596, when the extended version of *The Faerie Queene* was published. The work was immediately banned in Scotland, and James criticized Elizabeth for licensing it in England. The following year, James reacted angrily to reports that the queen and parliament had spoken disrespectfully about his mother.[91]

Anxieties about the implications of the Act for the Queen's Surety also led James in 1598 to pester Elizabeth about a relatively trivial issue, concerning the criminal Valentine Thomas. Thomas had accused the king of employing him in an assassination plot against the English queen, and James demanded that Elizabeth should publicly exonerate him. The accusation touched his honour, but of equal importance it might be used as a pretext for disinheriting him under the terms of the 1585 statute. Elizabeth tried to reassure James, charging him 'in

God's name to belyve, that I am not of so viperous a nature to suppose or have thereof a thought against you'.[92] But James carried on petitioning her about the matter until at last Elizabeth lost patience and accused him of 'preparing untymouslie' for her funeral.[93] Whether James was truly worried that he might suffer exclusion or just hoping to pressurize Elizabeth into formalizing his position as her heir is uncertain. He ceased harassing the queen only once he had entered into a secret correspondence with the queen's secretary Sir Robert Cecil and felt more secure about the succession.[94]

Elizabeth never gave her reasons for not naming James her heir. However, we can assume that they were similar to those she had expressed earlier in her reign with respect to Mary. In Elizabeth's view, James was almost as untrustworthy as his mother, and there was always the possibility that he would seek to anticipate her funeral if secure of his place in the succession. His uncertainty about the succession could also be—and indeed was—used as an inducement to encourage his good behaviour at moments when he was taking an independent line and appeared to be putting her realm in peril. Finally, at this later stage in Elizabeth's life, reference to the succession was a reminder of her own mortality and thus, as she explained, 'a matter of soo soure and distastefull nature to any prince'.[95] Notwithstanding her silence on this all-important matter, Elizabeth did everything she could to ensure James's smooth accession after her death by preventing any rivals from building up a power base or political support. Arbella Stuart was kept far away from court in Derbyshire, and, when Hertford attempted to have his sons made legitimate, he spent a spell in the Tower.

As near neighbours and cousins, Elizabeth and James used the rhetoric of intimacy in their epistolary conversations. Yet it was exactly because they were neighbours and close kin that mutual suspicion and coldness so often corroded their relationship. As neighbours, they had the incentives and opportunities to intervene in the internal affairs of each other's realms; as kin, the thorny question of the succession came between them. Given that it was historically rare for English and Scottish monarchs to live in peace and harmony, Elizabeth and James actually did pretty well. The international situation helped keep the peace, as the French king was rarely in a position to intervene in what was for France a traditional zone of interest. At the same time, it was in neither James's nor Elizabeth's interest to provoke a war: James might lose his place in the succession; Elizabeth could not afford to fight on another front. Then again, their diplomatic efforts played their part in preventing open rupture and warfare. Through sending special embassies to James's court, granting him the order of the garter, and plying him with expensive gifts at his wedding and the baptism of the first son, Elizabeth showed the king the respect he craved from a senior monarch and fed his sense of honour. Likewise, the mutual exchange of letters and lesser gifts played their role in easing tensions. However, for James perhaps the most important consideration of all after 1586 was the pension he received. On a yearly basis, the £3,000 he was due amounted to about one-sixth of his annual income, and, between 1586 and 1603, Elizabeth supplied the king with the considerable sum of £58,000; James could therefore ill afford to break with his 'dear cousin'; after all, she was also his paymaster.

Part 2

Courtiers

5

....

'Eyes': Robert Dudley,
Earl of Leicester

In late 1583, twenty-five years after Elizabeth's accession, a secret press on the Continent printed the first edition of a notorious libel that mounted an excoriating attack on Elizabeth's long-time intimate, Robert Dudley, earl of Leicester. The following year, this tract hit the streets of London. Entitled *The Copie of a Letter Written by a Master of Art of Cambridge*, it soon became known as 'Greencoate' but is remembered today as *Leicester's Commonwealth*.[1] Written in the form of a conversation between three men, it was highly readable but also defamatory. Leicester, the authors asserted, had treason in his blood: both his grandfather (Edmund Dudley) and father (John, duke of Northumberland) 'were found worthy to leese their heads for treason', and 'this man would not be found unworthy to make the third in kindred, whose treacheries do far surpass them both'. In his 'outrageous ambition and desire of reign', went on the authors, Leicester was 'not inferior to his father', but he was 'far more insolent, cruel, vindictive, expert, potent, subtile, fine, and fox-like' than ever Northumberland had been. Among the earl's many crimes, they alleged, were the murder of his first wife and the fatal poisoning of the husbands of his second and third wives, not to mention the destruction of his political rivals: 'Would God her majesty could see the continual fears that be in her faithful subjects' hearts whiles that man is about her noble person, so well able and likely (if the Lord avert it not) to be the calamity of her princely blood and name.'

Despite Elizabeth's attempts at suppression, the pamphlet was read widely within court circles as well as private homes. Although undoubtedly a malicious product of Catholic propaganda, the libel both reflected and helped reinforce popular hostility towards the earl, whose relationship with the queen was deeply resented or despised, not only among the English Catholic exiles who produced the pamphlet but also among some protestants in England.

Little is known about Leicester's early connections with Elizabeth: there are many probabilities and 'may haves', but few certainties. According to one of the earl's later asides, 'they had first become friends before she was eight years old', which would date their relationship back to 1540 or 1541. But it is more likely that their circles did not overlap until after 1542, when Elizabeth was at Henry VIII's court or sharing a household with her brother.[2] Any notion that they studied or played together as children should be scotched, since their gender would have kept them apart, even though they were about the same age.[3] During Elizabeth's brief visits to court during Edward VI's reign, the two very likely encountered each other again. As Northumberland was the pre-eminent figure in the privy council after 1549, his sons regularly attended court; indeed, in 1551, Robert was appointed a gentleman of the king's privy chamber. They had greater cause to communicate with each other during the first half of 1553, while Robert acted as keeper of Somerset House, Elizabeth's official London residence. By this time, though, Dudley was a married man, living in London with his young wife Amy, the daughter of a Norfolk gentleman Sir John Robsart.

Mary's accession in July 1553 was a difficult time for both of them. Dudley and his four brothers were incarcerated in the Tower for their role in their father's botched attempt to place Lady Jane Grey on the throne. Elizabeth was to follow him there in March 1554. But they would have been unable to converse, let alone begin a romance, as is sometimes suggested. Although their rooms were nearby, they were both strictly guarded. Nonetheless, 'their common condition of imprisonment' may have later created a bond between them, or so thought William Camden.[4]

Both prisoners were released well before the end of Mary's reign. After the Tower and nearly a year's house arrest at Woodstock, Elizabeth retired to Hertfordshire; after regaining his freedom, Dudley went off to fight in Mary's war against France. Once he returned to England, the two had plenty of opportunities to meet, for Amy Dudley was then based in Throcking, a manor close to Elizabeth's residence at Hatfield. During this period, Dudley may have helped out the financially strapped princess by selling 'a good peece of his land to ayde her' in the maintenance of her large establishment and retinue.[5] Whatever the case, he must have built up a close rapport with Elizabeth at this time, because in early November 1558 he was identified as one of the men with whom she was 'on very good terms' and who would be influential after she had inherited the throne.[6]

One of Elizabeth's first appointments as queen was to make Dudley master of the horse.[7] This was a prestigious household office, coming third in rank after the lord steward and lord chamberlain. With full responsibility for the royal stables, he was expected to ensure the supply of horses for transport, hunting, tournaments, and war. Shortly afterwards he was granted lands in Kew, property conveniently close to the royal palace of Richmond.[8] Yet, the appointment and grant did not actually signify any special favour towards him personally but was part of the rehabilitation of his whole family: his married sister Lady Mary Sidney was appointed a gentlewoman 'without wages' in Elizabeth's privy chamber; and his older and only surviving brother, Ambrose, was soon granted lands and the office of master of the ordnance, which gave him responsibility for supervising military equipment and supplies. Their elevation was part of Elizabeth's general policy of restoring offices and titles to loyal families who had lost out under Queen Mary, for Dudley's late brother John had been master of the horse briefly under Edward VI, while his father had taken charge of the ordnance early in his career.[9]

The master of the horse had daily access to the monarch, and Dudley was always at Elizabeth's side when hunting, an activity that she came to love. In lifting the queen on and off her horse, Dudley was also permitted a physical contact with her. A 'handsome' man of 'comely feature of body and limbes', he was unquestionably attractive to the queen.[10] She especially admired his athleticism, and enjoyed watching him perform at the tilts, practise running at the ring, and play tennis. She also praised his 'grace', an ease of movement and manner that was much esteemed in the sixteenth century. Furthermore, the two had much in common. Like Elizabeth, Dudley was an accomplished linguist, reading French and Latin, and speaking Italian fluently. They shared a love of dancing, musical entertainments, gambling, and plays. Dudley was one of the first courtiers to form his own troupe of players, and his men performed at his house at Kew in 1559 and at court during the Christmas celebrations between 1560 and 1563.[11] Dudley, therefore, had much to recommend him as a cultured and entertaining companion for the queen.

After five months in which they were constantly in each other's company, the first rumours of a love affair between them began to break. Courtiers whispered that the queen was in love with Dudley and would marry him 'if his wife, who has been ailing for some time, were perchance to die'. In mid-April 1559, the Spanish ambassador Feria was told that the queen visited Dudley's chamber 'day and night' and 'never lets him leave her'.[12] That same month, Elizabeth's favour towards him became very public, when she chose him—the younger son of a beheaded traitor—to be a knight of the elite, chivalric order of the garter alongside two earls of ancient lineage. Now recognized as a figure with great influence over the queen, Dudley became the recipient of a flood of letters, offering him loyalty, reminding him of kinship ties, and requesting favours.[13]

Nonetheless, during 1559, other men's names were also coupled with the queen's: in London, men were betting that the handsome Sir William Pickering would be chosen as her husband; others thought that the wealthy Henry FitzAlan, twelfth earl of Arundel, stood a good chance as a suitor, even though he was twenty years her senior and a Catholic to boot. Foreign ambassadors, meanwhile, flocked to England to woo the queen on behalf of their princely masters. 'Here is great resort of wowers [wooers] and controversy amongst lovers,' wrote Cecil in October 1559.[14] Elizabeth, however, rejected all advances. In late June she told the Emperor Ferdinand that she declined the suit of his son, the Archduke Charles, because 'we cannot discending into the bottom of our harte fynd any inclination to leave this solitary liffe'.[15] In November, she wrote in the same vein to the king of Sweden: his son Eric would be well advised to seek his wife elsewhere, as 'it pleaseth God to direct our mynd to remayne in this single estate without inclination to marriadg'.[16] Yet, because she had not ruled out marriage in the future, foreign princes persisted in their courtship of the queen, and London buzzed with talk about the candidates' relative merits and prospects.

All this was a distraction and cover for the true state of affairs: Elizabeth's developing romantic relationship with Dudley. However, it could not be hidden for long. In November 1559, Alvaro de la Quadra, the new Spanish ambassador, was dismayed to learn from one of his most trustworthy informants 'some extraordinary things about this intimacy, which I would never have believed'.[17] The ambassador from Austria heard similar tales and made his own enquiries, for the last thing he wanted was to arrange a marriage between the emperor's son and a 'notoriously loose woman'. To his relief the queen's women of the bedchamber all reassured him that Elizabeth's honour was intact and no improprieties had taken place, even though they did admit that their mistress had behaved unwisely in displaying her great liking for her master of the horse.[18]

But, if Elizabeth's honour was still intact, her reputation was not. During 1560, Elizabeth became the subject of salacious gossip in inns and taverns of southern England. A drunkard in Totnes, Devon, declared that 'the Lord Robert Dudley dyd swyve [copulate with] the quene'.[19] Another drunkard—this time a 68-year-old widow from Essex—spoke words that 'moche touched her majestie's honor' and 'not mette [suitable] to be divulged amongst the commen people'.[20] Also in Essex, a man relayed the gossip heard in London that a person had been sent to the Tower 'for saieng the queen's majestie was with childe'.[21] It did not stop there. Thanks to ambassadors' reports, shaming slanders and 'much lewde talke' were repeated in foreign courts. Thomas Challoner, the English ambassador in Brussels, warned that the queen needed to take care of her reputation: 'a yong princesse canne not be to ware [wary] what contenance or familiar demonstration she maketh, more to oon than an other.'[22]

Elizabeth, however, seemed untroubled about the damage to her international standing. Knowing that she was still a virgin, she would allow no criticism of her behaviour nor take any advice to cool her affection for Dudley and marry elsewhere.[23] Even worse, she provoked jealousies among her courtiers and councillors by allowing Dudley constant access to her person and bestowing prestigious honours and lucrative grants upon him. On 24 November 1559, she awarded him the office of lieutenant of the castle, forest, and great park of Windsor; on 23 January 1560, he received the lands of Watton priory in Yorkshire that had previously belonged to his father; and, on 12 April, he was given an export licence for wool that was worth a great deal of money.[24] Noblemen grumbled at his prominence; wool manufacturers and merchants 'muche grudged at' the lucrative export licence. Cecil even thought of resigning, or so he told the Spanish ambassador Quadra.[25] For once in her life, Elizabeth discarded her customary caution and shrewdness, choosing to ignore the growing disaffection and alarm developing at court. She was determined to keep up the same degree of intimacy with her 'favourite', failing to appreciate how much it was weakening her authority and confirming patriarchal beliefs about the dangers of female rule.

At this time, Elizabeth showed every sign of being passionately in love with Dudley. Cecil disapprovingly confided to Quadra that she 'meant to marry him', and he may well have been correct.[26] The same month, she told the duke of Norfolk that she would be married before six months were out, though she did not say to whom.[27] Since rumours had been flying around the court that Dudley's wife Amy was terminally ill, perhaps Elizabeth was just waiting for her to die so that she could marry the not-so-grieving widower. Then again, Elizabeth might have been thinking in terms of an annulment, as Dudley was said to be planning to divorce his wife.[28] Annulments were certainly not too difficult for people of power and influence to acquire. Elizabeth's aunt Margaret had divorced her second husband so that she could marry her third; Charles Brandon, duke of Suffolk, had two marriages dissolved before marrying Elizabeth's other aunt, Mary; and, of course, Elizabeth's father had his marriages to both Katherine of Aragon and Anne of Cleves annulled.

There was one other route for removing Amy, and that was by murder. Speculations that Dudley intended such a dastardly act were in circulation in late 1559.[29] Then, in early September 1560, Cecil told Quadra that 'Robert was thinking of killing his wife, who was publicly announced to be ill, although she was quite well, and [she] would take very good care they did not poison her'.[30] Shortly afterwards the news broke that Amy was dead, but not by poison nor from any natural disease. On the afternoon of 8 September 1560, she was found at the bottom of a stone spiral staircase with a broken neck. The coroner later noted that she had also sustained two deep cuts to her head, but otherwise there were no injuries to her body and her face was unmarked. At that time, she was living in the house of one of Dudley's associates, Sir Anthony Forster, at Cumnor Place near Oxford. Dudley himself had not seen his wife for more than a year.[31]

Dudley was undeniably shocked and distraught at hearing the news. He realized immediately that this 'misfortune' might do him great harm, if common talk linked him to his wife's death. Sending his chief household officer Thomas Blount to investigate, the widower could take no rest until he had heard 'how the matter standeth or how this evil should light upon me, considering what the malicious world will bruit [voice abroad]'.[32] He judged correctly: it did not take long for the word to spread that Amy had been murdered. The bishop of Coventry reported on 17 September of 'a grievous and dangerous suspicion and muttering' concerning her death and warned that, if there was a cover-up, 'the displeasure of God, the dishonour of the quene, and the danger of the whole realme is to be feared'.[33] Within Berkshire, it was said, 'the people' suspected the worst because Dudley's friends 'used before her death, to wyshe her death'.[34] Abroad, the news was 'malicisely reported'. The French especially took 'great joy' in the reports of Amy's 'strange deathe', hoping it would bring down Elizabeth's government. 'I am almost at wittes end and know not what to saye,' wrote Sir Nicholas Throckmorton, the queen's ambassador in France; 'one laugheth at us, an other threateneth, an other revileth her majestie, and some let not to say what religion is this that a subject shall kill his wife, and ye prince not onely beare withal but mary with him'.[35]

Amy's death did indeed have some strange features to it that would nourish gossip of this kind. Even today, historians chew over the possible cause, but with no agreement or certainty. The coroner's inquest reported that she came to her death 'by misfortune', breaking her neck in 'an accidental injury' resulting from a fall.[36] Many historians are unconvinced by this verdict, suspecting instead murder, but they finger different men as the culprit. Dudley was, of course, thought guilty at the time, while Cecil has more recently been accused of ordering the deed so as to defame Dudley and prevent his marriage to the queen. Lastly, some historians have suggested that the murderer can be found among Dudley's servants or dependants acting on their own initiative.[37] The evidence against all these men is deeply problematic, based mainly on hearsay and malevolent gossip; furthermore, the accusations sound unconvincing. Would Cecil really have carried out an action that exposed his queen to such scandal and benefited her Catholic enemies? Would Dudley have expressed such shock and alarm had he been guilty of the deed? Would his agents have risked disclosure and the damage to their master's reputation? Suicide, therefore, seems to me the more likely explanation for Amy's death, if misadventure is ruled out. Amy's odd behaviour on the day reinforces that suspicion, for she sent all her household away to attend a nearby fair at Abingdon and grew 'very angry' when her gentlewoman, Mrs Odingsells, chose to stay behind. Amy clearly wanted to be alone in the house. Her maid Mrs Picto, moreover, unwillingly admitted, under questioning, that Amy had been seen praying 'divers times' for God 'to deliver her from desperation'.[38] Isolated as she was in Oxfordshire and virtually abandoned by her husband, Amy had good reason to succumb to bouts of depression. Had she committed suicide, it would have greatly touched Dudley's honour, giving him strong cause to hush it up. Thought guilty of a heinous crime, suicides were not buried in holy ground but at crossroads with a stake through their bodies, and their possessions were forfeited to the crown. Fear that Amy had killed herself would explain another feature of the case: what seems like an attempt by Dudley to pack or nobble the coroner's jury. The foreman appointed was a man who had once been Elizabeth's servant and in 1564–5 was to become one of her gentleman ushers. Dudley knew another juror personally, and his servant Blount had dined with two more jurors before they reached their verdict.[39] Admittedly, suicide by a fall—especially down a short flight of stairs—is not a sure-fire method, but Amy may have been attempting simply to capture her husband's attention rather than seeking her own death; or possibly her body was moved.

Like Dudley, Elizabeth was dismayed and distressed when she learned of Amy's death, but she never openly wavered in her belief that Dudley was innocent of all wrongdoing. For form's sake, he retired to his house at Kew while the inquest sat, but he returned to court a week after the funeral and then resumed his intimacy with the queen. As a result, many predicted that the couple would soon marry; indeed, Quadra believed that a secret ceremony had already taken place.[40] Yet, in truth, Elizabeth could not make up her mind about what to do. While her attraction towards Dudley remained intense, Cecil and Throckmorton made sure that she heard all the arguments against such a marriage, and other councillors and court-iers probably spoke against it too. These men pointed to the further damage to her reputation, the factionalism that would result in England, and the lack of political advantage in such a match, espe-cially in contrast to one with a foreign prince. So Elizabeth was undecided; at one moment, she planned to raise Dudley into the nobility, a move that would have signalled her readiness to marry him; at another, she decided against it and cut up the 'bills' that had been prepared. The strain began to tell, and at the end of November 1560 she was said to be looking 'not so hearty and well as she did, by a great deal, and surely the matter of my Lord Robert doth much perplex her'.[41]

The matter rested in this state of uncertainty until the end of the year, when Elizabeth began to turn more decisively against the idea of marriage, leaving Dudley in 'more feare than hope'.[42] Aware of this change, the frustrated suitor decided to enlist the help of the Spanish king, and for a short while it looked as if his strategy might work. Quadra broached the subject with Elizabeth and told her that he was fairly sure that Philip II would approve of such a match. With Spanish support behind it, Elizabeth's marriage to Dudley might just be polit-ically viable, and so the queen's indecision returned.[43] During early spring, the 'great matter' of her marriage went through 'some fyttes bothe hote and colde'; one day it was 'a slepe', and another 'revy-ved'.[44] However, by May 1561 there seemed little chance of further revival. Elizabeth had to acknowledge that political opposition in England to the marriage had not sufficiently abated, while the price of Spanish support was far too high. In return for his backing, Philip expected to obtain toleration for English Catholics or, better still, a return to the Roman Church.

To compensate Dudley for his disappointment, Elizabeth found other ways to demonstrate her affection. She gave him manors in Kent, Leicestershire, and Yorkshire; and, on 26 December 1561, it pleased her to restore his 'house to the name of Warwick' by granting his brother Ambrose the earldom and other titles that had been held by their father before he was raised to a dukedom in 1552.[45] During the St George's Day festivities, the following year, Robert was 'preferred to a higher place, having his crest alterid from a blew libart [blue leopard] to a beare and the ragged staf', the heraldic device of the medieval Beauchamp earls of Warwick.[46] That year Robert also received new offices and grants: he was appointed the constable of both Windsor and Warwick Castles as well as steward of the town of Warwick; and he was awarded an annuity of £1,000 and various export licences that he sold to London merchants.[47] But, although some observers thought that these signs of royal favour were a prelude to a royal marriage, the moment had evidently passed. Elizabeth no longer displayed anguish about what decision to take, and could even laugh or tease the Spanish ambassador when the possibility of her marriage to Dudley came up in conversation.[48] Although she showed no inclination to accept anyone else's hand in marriage, Dudley's hopes were dashed at the end of 1561. According to court tittle-tattle, he had given her a 'notable' New Year's gift, and it was thought that she would have reciprocated with a grant of lands worth at least £4,000 a year and a dukedom to pave the way for his further elevation, yet all he received was land worth £400, and 'it ys not of the very best land'.[49]

Despite rejecting their marriage, Elizabeth's strong feelings for Dudley again became evident when she fell ill with smallpox in October 1562. Believing she was close to death, her thoughts turned to him. With one eye on the past, she declared that their relationship had not been dishonourable (that is sexual); with the other eye on the future, she called for Dudley to be named protector of the realm in the event of her death, until a new monarch was instated. This impractical proposal demonstrated the extent of her trust and love for the man. However, it proved to be a warning to her other advisers about the dangers of her dying without a known heir.

As soon as she had recovered her health, Elizabeth appointed Dudley to the privy council. His promotion was not unexpected, since he had for some time been offering advice on foreign policy and building up contacts with important figures abroad. Together with Cecil, he had persuaded a reluctant queen to sign a treaty of alliance with the leaders of the Huguenots (French protestants) and to intervene in the religious civil war then raging in France. By the treaty of Hampton Court of September 1562, Elizabeth pledged to assist her new allies with 6,000 soldiers and 140,000 crowns in loans; and in return they promised to hand over the port of Le Havre (known as Newhaven) in Normandy, which would later be exchanged for Calais. Elizabeth had grudgingly conceded the humiliating loss of Calais in the peace of Cateau-Cambrésis, signed at the beginning of her reign. Its recovery mattered hugely to her and was the bait that tempted her into continental war in 1562.

Once a privy councillor, Dudley worked closely with Cecil in organizing the expedition to France. About one-quarter of the soldiers who served as captains or held staff appointments on the campaign can be identified as his friends and/or followers. Ideally he would have liked the command of the English army himself, but he had to be satisfied with the appointment of his brother as its general. Elizabeth would not risk his injury or death—wisely as it turned out. During the siege of Le Havre, Warwick was very badly wounded in the thigh by a French musketeer, while many of his company succumbed to the plague. In fact the campaign was disastrous for England. Abandoned by their Huguenot allies and decimated by plague, Elizabeth's troops were withdrawn from France in July 1563; the French king retained Calais; and the protestant position in France remained precarious. However, Elizabeth did not blame Warwick, her soldiers, or her ministers for the military failure; she targeted her anger on her untrustworthy foreign allies.[50]

Even before the war's formal conclusion in April 1564, Elizabeth's marriage was again mooted. Most of her suitors had by now fallen by the wayside, but Dudley was still available and viewed as a possible and, for some English people, a preferable contender. In a poetic address delivered before the queen at Windsor in September 1563, one of the scholars from Eton school lavishly praised the lord's beauty and virtue, ending with the hope:

> May Heaven bring to pass that you may marry such a husband,
> O Queen, as is worthy of your love. For sure, the people hope that

this may happen, and that at some point you may be joined to such a man in a perpetual flame of love.[51]

The following summer, the new Spanish ambassador, Diego Guzman de Silva, was told that 'Robert still looks to marry the queen', but 'fears she will not decide'.[52] In fact, Elizabeth had other plans for both herself and Dudley. In 1563 she had mischievously recommended him as a mate for Mary Queen of Scots, but in 1564 she pursued the proposal in all seriousness. At the same time, she allowed her agents to reopen talks with the emperor in order to arrange her own marriage to Archduke Charles. It looks as if she was planning a double wedding.

To make Dudley worthy of a royal bride, the queen granted him the lordships of Kenilworth, Denbigh, and Chirk on 9 June 1563, and ennobled him as earl of Leicester and baron of Denbigh on 29 September 1564.[53] The noble title was of special significance because of its royal associations: four earlier holders had been sons of English kings. Although Leicester did not want to appear too keen on the Scottish match for fear of offending Elizabeth, he too was determined to appear a fitting husband for Mary. Aside from the circumstances of his wife's death, the major arguments against his marriage to Elizabeth had always been that he was not descended from an ancient noble lineage, that his father and grandfather had been traitors, and that he was her subject, not a prince. To counter such objections to a union with Mary, the new earl commissioned the herald of Chester in late 1564 or early 1565, to produce 'The most ancient and famouse pedygrye' of his family (Plate 6). Written on vellum, this richly decorated 'lyttyll booke' traced Leicester's lineage through the female line right back to the Anglo-Saxon King Edmund Ironside, whom Mary claimed as her ancestor. The book also purported to show that the Dudley family was 'lineallie descendyd' from the main ancient noble families and royal houses of England and Europe; in several places the herald noted that Leicester shared the same ancestor as Mary, Elizabeth, and Philip II of Spain, whose son had been suggested as a suitable consort for the Scottish queen. Unsurprisingly, no reference was made in the manuscript to the recent executions of family members; on the contrary, Leicester's brother Guildford was said to have 'dyed with' the Lady Jane, his wife, as if the beheading had never taken place.[54]

In March 1565, Mary rejected Leicester's hand and shortly afterwards wed her cousin Lord Darnley. But Elizabeth's negotiations for a marriage to the Archduke Charles continued apace. An Austrian ambassador arrived in London on 6 May and stayed until August 1565, trying to hammer out terms for a matrimonial contract. During this period, Elizabeth distanced herself somewhat from Leicester, perhaps as a sign of her serious intent to marry elsewhere. Silva noticed in late July that Leicester 'seems lately to be rather more alone than usual, and the queen appears to display a certain coolness towards him'.[55] The following month, Cecil reported that she had fallen 'into some misliking' of Leicester, and she let 'it appear in many overt speeches that she is sorry of her loss of tyme' at not marrying elsewhere.[56]

On the surface, Leicester showed no opposition to the Austrian match.[57] However, he privately admitted that 'he could not contemplate the queen's marriage to anyone else but himself without great repugnance'.[58] Behind the scenes, moreover, he was evidently working with the French to sabotage the Austrian courtship by backing an alternative—and unviable—suitor, the 14-year-old Charles IX of France. In the event, both princely matches fell by the wayside: the French king was too young, and the archduke too Catholic. It took over two years of negotiations, though, to reveal the archduke's intransigence in religion and insistence on obtaining regular access to the mass in England. These were two years during which Leicester felt unsettled: his future would be uncertain if Elizabeth married anyone else; his unpopularity would grow if the marriage fell through and 'everyone thought that he was the cause of her remaining unmarried'.[59]

Even while Elizabeth was discussing matrimonial plans with a princely suitor, Leicester was close by her side. He was rarely absent from court, and then only for short periods. This probably suited them both: Elizabeth depended upon him for emotional and political support, while he could not afford to leave a space for his rivals or enemies to fill. Yet, despite his constant presence and undoubted influence on the queen, Leicester never functioned in the role of a 'king figure' nor as a substitute for a royal consort.[60] Elizabeth took great care in both her words and deeds to prevent the earl acting, or being treated, as her unofficial or potential partner. One example of this can be found in her reaction to Charles IX's suggestion in October 1564 that she nominate Leicester for entry into the French chivalric order of St Michael. Elizabeth did not doubt that the earl was 'as mete to have the honor of that order as any whom we can name', but she expressed two reservations about the nomination. The first related to her understanding that, because she (as a woman) could not her-self enter the order, the king desired her to select a man 'whomsoever hereafter we would make our husband'. Her second reservation arose from a concern that such an honour would reignite envy and mis-liking of the earl.[61] Elizabeth evidently judged that her nobility could not tolerate Leicester taking on the role of a 'king figure'. Indeed, it was owing to her intervention that Leicester was not created a knight of the order until January 1566; and then he was installed jointly with Norfolk.

Elizabeth also made it clear to Leicester that he enjoyed no mon-opoly on her affections but had to share her favour and its rewards with other courtiers. An anecdote repeated by Sir Robert Naunton in the mid-seventeenth century tells of Elizabeth upbraiding the earl with the words: '(God's death) my Lord, I have wisht you well, but my favour is not so lockt up for you, that others shall not partake thereof...I will have here but one mistress, and no master.'[62] Whether true or not, Elizabeth's insistence on this principle could sometimes lead to angry scenes with Leicester, but she always stuck to her guns. In the summer of 1565 she had 'begun to smile on' Sir Thomas Heneage, a married gentleman of the privy chamber. When Leicester retaliated by quarrelling with Heneage and flirting with Elizabeth's cousin Lettice (who was then pregnant by her husband Walter Devereux, Viscount Hereford), Elizabeth lost her temper and spoke bitterly to the earl. According to the Spanish ambassador, the 'result of the tiff was that both the queen and Robert shed tears, and he has returned to his former favour'.[63] Nonetheless, Heneage also remained in Elizabeth's favour, regularly receiving lands and offices that cul-minated in 1570 with the major household post of treasurer of the queen's chamber.[64]

A similar tiff between monarch and courtier occurred in the spring of 1566, when Elizabeth developed a close personal relationship with Thomas Butler, tenth earl of Ormond. He was a kinsman of her mother and 'an Irishman, of good disposition, some 30 years of age'. For a time, Ormond acted as her chief male companion on state occasions, and she gave him the pet nicknames of 'Lucas' and 'black husband'.[65] This time, Leicester left court in a huff. Although he pleaded 'private business', he was obviously offended by his apparent displacement. It did not take very long before Elizabeth herself became offended. Leicester soon learned that the queen not only 'dothe muche marvell' that 'she hard [heard] nott' from him but had even remarked that he might not continue as her master of the horse if he pursued his absence.[66] On learning this, Leicester hastened back to court where Elizabeth greeted him graciously. But Ormond continued in high favour.[67]

When it came to political matters, Leicester was also not supreme. Here, he had to share power and influence with Cecil. Letters from ambassadors were sometimes addressed to both of them, and, when written to just one, the expectation was that it should be shown to the other. Many men and women soliciting favours also went through both men. To take two relatively trivial examples: in July 1565, William Drury, seeking an increase in his expense allowance, asked both 'your honors to be meanes to her majestie for me'; and, the following May, the earl of Pembroke asked both Leicester and Cecil to intercede on his behalf to secure a pardon for an offender.[68] On some occasions, moreover, Leicester had to use Cecil as his own intermediary with the queen.[69] In court ceremonials, the earl was not alone in taking a prominent role. When Elizabeth visited Cambridge in August 1564, Cecil, as the university's lord chancellor, received the same honours as Leicester, who was its lord high steward.[70] At tournaments Leicester shared centre stage with Hunsdon, Norfolk, and other skilled jousters. Elizabeth's visits to Kenilworth Castle in the summers of 1566, 1568, and 1572 were only for a few days and relatively low-key affairs; they were also somewhat impromptu and not the centrepiece of the royal progresses.

Nevertheless, after the collapse of the matrimonial negotiations with Archduke Charles, Leicester may well have retained a glimmer of hope that Elizabeth might at long last wed him. After all, he was now a territorial magnate of noble status; he had a good working relationship with Cecil and other privy councillors; and the scandal about his wife's death had subsided. No other candidate for the queen's hand stayed long in the running, and her biological clock was ticking away.[71] For this reason, Leicester remained single until September 1578. He was also careful to keep his sexual liaisons as quiet as he could. Indeed he might not have had very many. Despite a reputation as a roué, he is only known to have had one mistress before he took to bed his second wife, Lettice Devereux, the widow of Walter, earl of Essex.[72] This mistress was Douglas, the widow of Lord Sheffield and daughter of William Lord Howard of Effingham. She and her sister Frances (both unpaid women of the privy chamber) were said to be 'very farr in love' with Leicester in May 1573, but it was Douglas who gave birth to his son in August 1574.[73] Leicester admitted paternity and took responsibility for the child, but he consistently denied Douglas's unsubstantiated claim that they had been formally, if secretly, betrothed in 1571 and married in 1573;[74] and with good reason, for he had in fact rejected marriage explicitly in an undated 'Dear John' letter, trying to break off their affair. Marriage, he explained, would prove 'myne utter overthrow', and 'yf I shuld marry I am seuer never to have favor of them that I had' (meaning the queen).[75] However, Elizabeth's capacity for jealousy should not be exaggerated. There is some evidence that she knew about the relationship yet did not punish either Lady Sheffield or Leicester.

Leicester made his last bid to marry Elizabeth when she stayed at Kenilworth Castle for nineteen days during her 1575 summer progress. In preparation for a major royal visit, the earl had spent a number of years and a huge sum of money (said to be £60,000) remodelling and extending the castle, adding a vast artificial lake, and enlarging the chase where his guests would hunt. Together he and his designer William Spicer created a castle that looked like an ancient medieval fortress but incorporated the latest fashions in architecture, including a symmetrical layout and a vast expanse of windows. The total effect evoked the Arthurian romance literature so popular at court, embodied the traditional values of feudal lordship, and displayed Leicester's avant-garde tastes.[76] The newly laid-out ornamental garden was equally designed to display the earl's ancient lineage, wealth, wisdom, and sophistication. It was one of the first Italianate gardens in England, with a great grass terrace designed as a viewing platform for the whole estate. Amid the ornaments on the terrace were obelisks (symbolizing glory and immortality), white bears and ragged staffs (his own emblems), and spheres (denoting heavenly prudence and wisdom, and often an emblem used for the queen). An aviary, 'garnish'd with gold', decorated with painted gems, and filled with real and mechanical birds, was its centrepiece.[77]

This magical setting was the stage for Leicester's 'Princely Pleasures', a varied programme of events to entertain the court that included bear-baiting, tilting, dancing, sports, 'countrie shews', firework displays, acrobatics, allegorical masques, and scripted pageants. The spectacles were all devised to amuse and impress the royal party, while the dramatic interludes also gave voice to Leicester's personal and political ambitions. Because the theme of love and marriage dominated the proceedings, the whole occasion can, and probably should, be interpreted as an extended and elaborate marriage proposal. One of the scheduled masques was especially explicit in this respect, indeed too explicit for the queen's liking. It told the story of

Zabeta (obviously standing for Elizabeth) who for 'neere seventeen years past' (the number of years Elizabeth had been on the throne) had been a 'best-beloved' nymph of Diana (the goddess of chastity and hunting), and it ended with Iris (the goddess of marriage) addressing Elizabeth with the message:

> How necesserie were
> for worthy queenes to wed
> That know you wel, whose life always
> in learning hath been led.
> The country craves consent
> your virtues vaunt themselfe,
> And Jove in Heaven would smile to see
> Diana set on shelfe.

The masque was cancelled at short notice after the queen had vetted the script.[78] However, its author (perhaps instructed by the earl) was determined that Elizabeth should hear something of the nymph's story. So, on the last day of her visit, the playwright George Gascoigne ran alongside the queen, who was preparing to depart on horseback, and explained somewhat breathlessly how Zabeta had cruelly metamorphosed her lovers into trees. Then, from within a 'holly bush' came the voice of one of them, 'Deepe Desire', who sang a long lament of farewell to the queen and pleaded with her to remain at Kenilworth and

> command again
> This castle and the knight
> Which keeps the same for you.

Elizabeth, apparently not amused, rode off.

The four portraits Leicester commissioned to be hung in Kenilworth for the queen's visit likewise reveal his marital ambitions.[79] Two sets of companion pieces, they were clearly designed to be seen together. In the first pair, each of the full-length figures (they were later cut down) was placed against a similar dark background and flanked by a chair with identical knobs, tassels, and rivets (Plates 7 and 8). Leicester was clad from head to toe in red, a colour associated with both love and royalty, while Elizabeth was wearing the jewel-encrusted doublet that Leicester had given her as a New Year's gift in 1575.[80] The other set of portraits has not survived, but the preparatory sketches are extant, showing that they were also companion pieces, both painted by the Italian master Federigo Zuccaro (Plate 9).

Daringly, all four images were hung in the picture gallery alongside portraits of European rulers with their consorts. However, Leicester refrained from displaying them as if they too were marriage portraits, in case the queen took offence at his presumption. Consequently, he placed the queen's images behind one curtain and those of himself behind another. Given her reaction to the Zabeta masque, such prudence was wise.

Leicester probably did not expect Elizabeth to accept his marriage proposal after so many years of rejection. Nonetheless, at the very least, he knew that proffering it during the Kenilworth visit would advertise his unique relationship with the queen to all those present as well as to readers of the printed accounts. He may also have had a wish for a degree of closure: if the queen would only confirm that their marriage was impossible, then he would be free to offer his hand elsewhere or to pursue a military, rather than a predominantly courtly, role in the queen's service.

That Leicester desired military responsibilities was another message of the Kenilworth entertainments. For several years, he had been a keen advocate of an interventionist foreign policy on behalf of the protestants in the Netherlands who were in revolt against their ruler, Philip II of Spain. In the summer of 1575 he was urging the queen to take the Dutch provinces of Holland and Zeeland under her protection and to raise an army under his command to help them fight against Spain. One of the allegorical interludes of the entertainments was supposed to dramatize this ambition. The original script was meant to have an exciting 'skirmish by night' take place between the 'cruel knight' Sir Bruce sans Pity (representing Spain) and 'a captaine with twentie or thyrtie shotte' (played by Leicester). After Sir Bruce had been put to flight, the captain was to call upon the queen to rescue the distressed Lady of the Lake (representing the Netherlands) from the clutches of Sir Bruce. Again this allegory may have proved too much for the queen when she inspected the script beforehand; at any rate, the spectacle was severely curtailed when performed, and its meaning diluted.

The Kenilworth entertainments succeeded in at least one of Leicester's objectives. They were a dazzling display of his wealth, power, and inventiveness, and became the benchmark for future Elizabethan entertainments. However, Leicester did not achieve his other ends: Elizabeth accepted neither the sovereignty of the Netherlands nor the earl's hand in marriage. Indeed, Leicester may even have temporarily damaged his standing with the queen, who was evidently peeved by his pretentions and unwilling to hear his messages. As already mentioned, two of his scheduled pieces were either modified or cancelled. Additionally, one of her responses to the pageants was distinctly acerbic, demonstrating disapproval of the earl's arrogance: when the allegorical figure of the Lady of the Lake offered the lake to the queen in welcome, Elizabeth answered: 'we had thought indeed the lake had been oours, and doo you call it yourz noow?'[81] Elizabeth also left earlier than originally planned.

Despite her apparent irritation, Leicester's long-term relationship with the queen remained as affectionate and bantering after Kenilworth as it had ever been. As before, she needed his attention when she felt unwell, and enjoyed his company when in high spirits.[82] In letters, he continued to refer to himself by her nickname, her 'eyes', by signing off ŌŌ or addressing her as 'My mōōst gracious lady'.[83] Yet in some respects, the two did seem less close. The earl was permitted to be absent from court more frequently, whether to spend time at one of his houses or to take the spa waters at Buxton. As for assuming a military role in the Netherlands, he continued to be thwarted in his hope that the queen could be persuaded to send him at the head of an army to help the Dutch rebels. International developments kept the prospect alive, and he felt assured that, 'yf there be cause to send ayd, her majestie doth promys myself shuld have the chardge'.[84] But Elizabeth blew hot and cold, and it was not until 1585 that she accepted the arguments for direct military intervention in the Netherlands and the earl received the generalship he had so long desired.

Three years after the Kenilworth entertainments, Leicester married elsewhere. The decision was not taken lightly, because he knew it would threaten his relationship with the queen. The main incentive was his longing to sire an heir and keep alive the Dudley name, for his brother's marriage was childless. But undoubtedly Leicester was attracted to his choice of mate, the 35-year-old Lettice Devereux, dowager countess of Essex (previously the Viscountess Hereford, with whom he had flirted more than a decade earlier). Lettice was reputedly a great beauty, and her name had been linked to the earl even while her husband was alive. During Essex's absences serving the queen in Ireland, the London rumour-mill claimed that Leicester had seduced his wife, and in December 1575 the resident Spanish agent repeated unfounded gossip that she had given birth to two children by Leicester.[85] When Essex died in Ireland in September 1576, probably of dysentery, suspicions were voiced that he had

been poisoned. Even then Leicester may have been thought the instigator, but the allegation did not appear in print until *Leicester's
Commonwealth*.

Leicester and Lettice wed on Sunday, 21 September 1578, immediately after the bride had come out of the conventional two-year
period of mourning for her late husband. The ceremony was private,
taking place in Leicester's house at Wanstead in the presence of only
six witnesses, including the earl's chaplain, who presided over the
service. It has been suggested that Lettice may have been pregnant,
for she was noted as wearing 'a loose gowne', but this seems unlikely
given the secrecy surrounding the event.[86] Two days after the wedding, the court arrived at Wanstead for the last stage of the queen's
summer progress, and Leicester hosted a magnificent feast for Elizabeth that Lettice presumably attended. No one mentioned the marriage, not even the bride's father and brother who were in the know.
And when Lettice gave the queen a New Year's gift in 1579, it was
recorded as from the countess of Essex.[87]

Surprisingly, at this very time, the 45-year-old Elizabeth was also
contemplating marriage. Her new suitor was Francis, duke of Anjou,
the 22-year-old brother of Henry III of France. Unlike Leicester, Elizabeth was not motivated by any desire for an heir; on the contrary, a
pregnancy at her age would be unwelcome as too dangerous. The
spur in her case was the foreign policy crisis that had developed in the
Netherlands. The protestant rebellion, originally confined to Holland
and Zeeland, had spread to Catholic provinces in the south, and in
1578 Anjou was offering military support to its leaders. While
Leicester and most others on the privy council were pressing Elizabeth hard to send her own army to help their co-religionists and keep
out the French, Elizabeth had 'slacke determynation' for this course
of action. Instead, she fell back on dynastic politics as a way to resolve
the problem. With a French marriage alliance in hand, she hoped, her
international influence, would be stronger.[88] First mooted in the
summer of 1578, the Anjou match took off in January 1579, when
the duke's master of the wardrobe and personal ambassador, Jean
de Simier, arrived in England. The following August, Anjou himself
came to woo the queen, and she seemed much taken with 'her frog',
as she fondly dubbed him.

It was probably during Simier's visit that Elizabeth first learned
of Leicester's marriage. By then, it was an open secret at court, but
nobody had dared tell the queen. According to William Camden,
Simier broke the news in order 'to remove Leicester out of place and

grace' so that he could not influence Elizabeth against the Anjou match. Camden also claimed that the queen 'grew into such a chafe that she commanded Leicester to keepe himselfe within the Tower of Greenwich, and thought to have committed him to the Tower of London, which his enemies much desired'.[89] Although Camden's account embellished what actually happened, Leicester certainly found himself bereft of the queen's favour in November 1579. Distressed and disgruntled, he then wrote to Burghley:

> I perceive by my brother of Warwycke, your lordship hath found the lyke bytternesse in her majestie toward me that others (to many) have aquainted me lately withal. I must confes yt greveth me not a lytle, having so fathfully, carefully and chargeably served her majestie this twenty yeres as I have done...

For years, went on Leicester, he had been content to be 'a bond man' to the queen, and only when he was 'aquytted and delyvered' of hope of marriage, had he wed another. He therefore did not deserve 'so great displeasure'.[90] Royal displeasure hit him financially too. Elizabeth demanded early repayment of an outstanding loan of £5,000 and also stayed the suit for an exchange of some lands that she had previously agreed to.[91] Elizabeth left no record of her emotions on hearing the news, but we can easily surmise that she felt betrayed, as a woman, by his marriage and, as a sovereign, by his deceit. Reminding her principal courtier how much he owed to her favour, and of the consequences of losing it, was therefore both a private act of revenge and a political necessity.

Over the next year, Elizabeth's relations with Leicester were changeable and unpredictable. In February 1580, one of the earl's correspondents congratulated him on 'the bettering and good successe of your lordship's owne affayires and condicon'.[92] However, that very same month, his 'affairs' dipped again when Elizabeth was told (possibly by Simier) that Leicester had, some years before, contracted to marry Lady Sheffield. Such conduct, she may have judged, was shabby and untrustworthy. But, of course, had this union taken place, the earl's marriage to Lettice would be bigamous, an outcome far from unwelcome to the queen. In the end, no witnesses or documentary proof could be produced to show that Leicester was bound to Douglas, and so Elizabeth had to accept that the recent marriage to Lettice was legal.[93] By the spring of 1580, the storm of Elizabeth's anger seemed to have blown over. In May, she 'stayed' Leicester's journey to Wilton, the home of his niece Mary, and demanded that he remain at court; later that month, he accompanied the queen to Nonsuch, apparently on very good terms with her. In June, she granted him the office of keeper of the New Forest. Yet, towards the end of July 1580, Leicester bemoaned the fact that he had 'less of her majesty's wontyd favour than I take comfort to think of', and in exasperation exclaimed 'the hartes of princes are in the handes of god'.[94] Then, in late August, Elizabeth's good temper towards him returned. However, it was only with the death of his 3-year-old son on 19 July 1584 that Elizabeth fully forgave Leicester for his marriage. On hearing the news from Sir Christopher Hatton, she expressed her sorrow and wished the grief-stricken earl comfort, 'even from the bottom of her hart'. Afterwards she wrote him a personal letter of condolence that unfortunately has not survived.[95]

By this time, anyway, Leicester's role had subtly changed. He had long supported protestant causes at home and abroad: protecting non-conforming members of the English clergy in trouble with their bishops; and recommending military support for co-religionists in the Netherlands and France. But from the later 1570s onwards, the earl grew in confidence in his role as the key spokesperson for military intervention against Spain on the Continent. Kept well informed about events abroad by English and foreign politicians, divines, soldiers, and ambassadors, Leicester settled into the role of trusted privy councillor, while playing less frequently the part of the entertaining courtier.[96]

Leicester's advice was unwelcome to the queen only when it came to her own marriage. Otherwise, she sought him out and talked confidentially to him about important matters of state. In April 1580, for example, when the question of Philip II asserting his rights to the Portuguese throne was raised, Elizabeth 'desired that no one but himself [Leicester] and Cecil should hear of it'.[97] In 1583, she spoke with Leicester about whether or not to make a treaty or 'association' with Mary and her son, James VI of Scotland, and shortly afterwards the earl wrote down his opinion 'to your self only'.[98] His advice proved to be extraordinarily influential. Counselling Elizabeth against the 'association' because neither Mary nor James could be trusted, he went on to advocate the enactment of a parliamentary statute that would state that they should 'forfytt for ever what soever claym or title that they have or dow pretend to this crown', if they ever threatened the queen's person or realm. This recommendation was to be the genesis of the Act for the Queen's Surety.[99]

Much to Leicester's relief—though not as a result of his influence—Elizabeth did not marry Anjou. The weight of hostile public opinion forced her to rethink in late 1579, and in 1581 she decided to forgo a formal marriage alliance with the French and to sponsor instead Anjou's campaigns in the Netherlands. But the duke proved an unsatisfactory knight errant, and, by the time he died in June 1584, Spain had reasserted its control over the southern provinces and look set to besiege Antwerp, the largest and richest city in the Netherlands. With the assassination of their leader William of Orange the following month, the rebels desperately needed foreign military aid. Initially Elizabeth tried to negotiate a joint Anglo-French initiative, but Henry III would not cooperate. Elizabeth, therefore, had to act alone. Although she refused to accept sovereignty over the rebel provinces, in the 1585 treaties of Nonsuch with the states-general (their governing body) she pledged to defend them with an English army and to appoint an English lieutenant general with civic responsibilities.[100] The treaty, however, came too late to save Antwerp.

The next question was which nobleman should command the English army and liaise with the rebel leadership. Leicester was the obvious choice because of his great prestige and extensive contacts with the Dutch protestants, but Elizabeth was initially not 'dysposed to use' his service. She wanted to select in his stead the experienced soldier Lord Grey. Leicester was displeased. Although he conceded there might be 'meny more fit and able to serve her then my self', he nonetheless grumbled that the queen 'doth take every occasion by my mariage to withdraw any good from me'.[101] In the end, on 23 September 1585, Leicester got his way. Elizabeth reluctantly consented to his appointment, but even then she applied emotional pressure to prevent him from taking it up. She was 'very desirous to stay me', wrote Leicester to Walsingham, and 'used very pittyfull words to me', confessing her fear that she might die during his absence. All Leicester could do was 'comfort hir asmuch as I could' but also 'lett her know how farr I had gone in preperacion' so that she would not change her mind.[102]

Given how much Leicester had craved the honour and responsibility of commanding the royal army in the Netherlands, it is an irony that his eventual appointment brought him nothing but grief. His problems started in January 1586, when he accepted the title of governor general from the states-general and was publically installed in the office without consulting his sovereign and in contravention of her express orders. His excuse to the queen was that the offer had taken him by surprise and left him with little choice but to say yes.[103] However, that could scarcely be true, since the appointment had been discussed, and rejected by Elizabeth, before his departure from England. More likely, Leicester hoped to railroad the queen into accepting the fait accompli of his appointment. He and his soldier friends were convinced that the rebels needed a figure at the centre of the Netherlands' government to bring a degree of political unity to the fragmented and fractious provinces, and they may even have engineered the states-general's offer themselves.[104]

Naturally, Elizabeth was furious at her subject's disobedience and independence, but equally she was alarmed by the political implications of his action. Leicester's new title gave the lie to her public statements that she had no territorial ambitions in the Netherlands and was simply seeking to protect them against Spanish tyranny. Her rage was further stoked on hearing that Leicester's wife was due to join him in Holland with 'suche a trayne of ladies and gentylwomen, and such ryche coches, lytters, and syde-saddles, as hir majestie had none suche'. If true, it would appear that the earl and countess of Leicester were intending to set up their own quasi-royal court in the Netherlands, an action again implying that the queen had accepted sovereignty of the rebellious provinces. To her great relief, the report proved false, but, nevertheless, the queen remained incensed with Leicester for some time afterwards.[105]

The privy council warned Leicester, somewhat euphemistically, that Elizabeth was 'much offended' by his presumptuous acceptance of the appointment.[106] The depth of her anger was revealed to him only in a blistering letter of 10 February 1586 and the instructions she gave its bearer. 'Howe contemptuously we conceave ourselfe to have been used by you, you shall by this bearer understand,' began the letter. And the bearer was directed to tell Leicester and the states-general that his 'verie great and strange contempt' was all the more offensive as he was 'a creature of our owne'. Leicester was ordered 'uppon paine of his allegancie' to renounce his new title publicly 'in the place where he accepted the same absolute governement, as a thinge done without our privitie and consent'.[107] Despite her fury at his flagrant insubordination, Elizabeth's insistence on this public climb-down was not primarily to humiliate 'her creature': her main objective was to undo the political damage by signalling to Philip II and Henry III that she had no aspiration to rule the Netherlands as the appointment implied.

Elizabeth could not stay angry with Leicester for long. Six weeks after writing her contemptuous letter, he was again her 'sweet Robyn', as she tried to put the matter behind them:

> for that your grieved and wounded mind hath more need of comfort than reproof whom we are persuaded (though the act in respect of the contempt can no way be excused) had no other meaning and intent than to advance our service, we think meet to forbear to dwell upon a matter wherein we ourselves do find so little comfort...[108]

Elizabeth then agreed that Leicester might carry the authority of a governor general while holding the title of lieutenant general. But, ultimately, he kept both titles, for it was made clear to Elizabeth that his authority in the Netherlands would be seriously impaired by the retraction.[109]

Leicester served in the Netherlands against impossible odds: an underfunded army, major personality clashes with other military commanders, and destructive disputes with the states-general. Personal tragedy also touched him when in October 1586 he suffered the loss of his 'dearest nephew' and heir, the poet Sir Philip Sidney, who was mortally wounded at the battle of Zutphen.[110] The cost to his purse was great too: he claimed to have spent over £35,000 in 1586 alone, and he mortgaged several important estates to raise the sums.[111]

Worn down by a series of military failures, and upset by accusations of financial incompetence (or worse), Leicester asked in April 1587 to be permanently recalled, 'seing I find her majesty's hardnes contynew styll to me' and 'my hart ys more than half broken'.[112] Over the next months, still in the job, he grew dismayed by the direction of royal policy that was disregarding his advice: 'I have said if your majestie will continue the countenance of the war here, you must alsoe encrease your charge here,' he complained. But this Elizabeth would not do. Worse still, Leicester was disconcerted to learn from the Dutch that Elizabeth was close to signing a peace treaty with Spain and withdrawing from the war in the Netherlands, a matter of which he had no knowledge and thought unwise, for it was 'better for you to fight with your enemyes abroad then at home'.[113]

Eventually in December 1587 Elizabeth released the earl from service abroad. Before his departure, he was rewarded with the post of lord steward of the household, the most important office in the court. Notwithstanding this promotion, Leicester again found himself

the butt of the queen's 'indignacion' on his return home. Consequently, in January 1588 he penned an unusually formal letter to
'your sacred majestie' in which he complained of the 'wretched and
depressed estate of your poore, trewe, and faithefull servant' and
begged to be restored 'to some degree of your majestie's former grace
and favour', since no evidence of 'disloaltie or negligence' in him had
been found.[114]

Elizabeth's good favour did follow, and, during the Spanish invasion threat of 1588, Leicester was appointed lieutenant general of
England's land forces. In this role, he was by her side at Tilbury when
she reviewed her troops and delivered her much celebrated speech.
After the dispersion of the Spanish Armada, Leicester disbanded the
mustered army at Tilbury camp and then set out with his wife to take
the medicinal baths at Buxton. On 29 August, he wrote to Elizabeth,
asking about her health, thanking her for some medicine, and praying
for her continuing preservation from danger. It was his last communication with her. At Cornbury House in the forest of Wychwood,
Oxfordshire, he suddenly died on 4 September. Elizabeth was devastated by the news. A Spanish agent reported that her distress was so
great that she locked herself away for several days until Burghley and
other councillors 'had the doors broken open and entered to see
her'.[115] Responding to the earl of Shrewsbury's condolences, she tried
to be stoical: 'we can admitt no comfort otherwise than by submit-
ting our will to God's inevitable appointment.'[116] Leicester's final
communication to her, endorsed 'his last letter', remained by the
queen's bedside until her death. The earl received no state funeral
but was buried in his family chapel in St Mary Warwick, as he had
directed.

Leicester's political importance owed everything to his intimacy
with the queen. At a personal level, theirs was a unique relationship
based on mutual affection and probably love. But it was one that was
difficult for them both, because Elizabeth's royal status prevented the
norms of gender roles from operating properly; Leicester was always
subject to a woman's orders and dependent on her favour. In political
terms, their relationship brought Leicester huge rewards, including
the opportunity to exercise extensive patronage and, thereby, exert
widespread influence. Over his career Leicester built up a substantial
clientage in the Midlands, the universities, the Church, and the military; he also offered promotion and protection to a coterie of poets,
such as Philip Sidney and Edmund Spenser, and sponsored the successful theatrical company, Leicester's men, that performed all over

the realm. The numbers of his would-be clients was huge: hundreds of books were dedicated to him; hundreds of men and women petitioned him for favours. Kinsfolk and friends obviously benefited from his patronage, but so increasingly did men who shared his politico-religious agenda.

Throughout his lifetime Leicester remained a controversial figure. Defamed by Catholics and disliked by many protestants, he was frequently associated with sexual excess and Machiavellian politics. Men and women were arraigned and punished for declaring that he and the queen were lovers who had produced numerous bastards.[117] Although similar allegations continued over the centuries and are still the stuff of popular novels and drama, most serious historians today think it most unlikely that Elizabeth and Leicester had a full sexual relationship. The two certainly flirted, and may have gone further, but intercourse was far too dangerous for Elizabeth to contemplate. Similarly, Leicester's reputation as a self-interested, devious, and ruthless politician—the Machiavellian evil counsellor of *Leicester's Commonwealth*—lived on well beyond the earl's death, influencing seventeenth-century biographies of the queen and many political histories thereafter. But today a different Leicester has emerged. Now, historians focus on Leicester's ideological commitments, refined cultural tastes, and administrative talents.[118] Of course he was ambitious and sometimes deceitful, but few were not in the world of Elizabethan court politics.

The shift in Leicester's historical reputation reflects well on Elizabeth too. Undoubtedly, she was first attracted to Dudley's physical appearance and personal charm (especially in the early years of their relationship), but she was usually a good judge of a person's worth and soon came to recognize his abilities, respect his judgement, and admire his style, even while she was wary of his ambition and ready to cut him down to size. Leicester was always her 'creature', but one whose service and talents she valued, while their shared personal history brought her emotional comfort and strength.

6

'Lids': Sir Christopher Hatton

Contemporary commentators generally dismissed the Elizabethan courtier Sir Christopher Hatton as a political lightweight. His enemy Sir John Perrot was apparently 'wont to say' that Hatton had entered the court 'by the galliard' (a fashionable dance), a sneer designed to signify that he was unworthy of the many honours and offices he eventually won. Sir Robert Naunton, who reported Perrot's cutting comment, went on to deride Hatton as 'a meer vegetable of the court, that sprang up at night, and sunk again at his noon'.[1] William Camden also made light of the courtier's abilities. While making no mention of Hatton's skill as a dancer, the historian attributed the courtier's prominence to his 'comely talnesse of body and countenance' and 'his modest sweetnesse of manners'.[2]

This belittling of Hatton arose in part through snobbery, for he came from a modest gentry family of little wealth, influence, or connection. A second son, he was orphaned by the time he was 6, and his nearest kin had little political or social clout in their home county of Northamptonshire.[3] Then again, Naunton and Camden were also describing Hatton using the familiar tropes of the court favourite, stereotypically a social upstart and sycophant, who was handsome and skilled in dancing but lacked military expertise and political wisdom.[4] Yet, in truth, there was far more to Hatton than just his attractive looks and manners. With his strong interest in Italian culture, it comes as no surprise that he mastered the tastes and manners of the exemplary courtier who was the subject of Baldassare's Castiglione's *Il Cortegiano*, the popular book of manners that was translated into English in 1561.[5] But Hatton also served his sovereign effectively as a privy councillor and lord chancellor.

The training for the role Hatton was to play at court and in government began at St Mary's Hall, Oxford, which he briefly attended as a gentleman commoner during Queen Mary's reign, and it continued at the Inner Temple, where he was enrolled in May 1560, aged 20. His Oxford education gave him a sound knowledge of Latin and the classical world, an essential requisite for an Elizabethan courtier, as well as a solid grounding in classical rhetoric that was to prove invaluable during his parliamentary career.[6] Hatton's longer residence at the Inner Temple offered him instruction in the common law and, equally important, allowed him to become proficient in gentlemanly pursuits. The four Elizabethan Inns of Court were not just a training ground for lawyers but a kind of finishing school for young nobles and gentlemen, a place where they perfected their manners and took lessons in fencing, dancing, music, and singing.[7]

Hatton took advantage of all the opportunities offered at the Inner Temple. Like most fellow students, he probably attended lectures and may even have qualified as a barrister, although we cannot be sure, since the records of those called to the bar before 1567 have not survived. All we know for certain is that he never became a senior member of his Inn. Hatton also participated fully in the dinners, dances, and revels that were the lifeblood of the Inn's social and cultural life. 'To dance cumlie' was one of 'the pastimes that be fit for courtlie gentleman', wrote the English scholar Roger Ascham, and it was probably at the Inner Temple that Hatton learned the galliard, a difficult dance that consisted of five quick steps and a leap in the air with a beating of the feet.[8] Hatton was an officer of the Christmas revels of 1561–2, and, somewhat later, he penned one act of a play, which was performed by the gentlemen of the Inner Temple before the queen at Greenwich, possibly during Shrovetide 1566.[9] While at the Inn, Hatton also made some useful social and political connections: a close friendship with the courtier poet Edward Dyer; an acquaintanceship with Robert Wilmot, then a playwright and poet; and interactions with Thomas Norton, who later looked to Hatton as a patron.[10] In late 1561, the 20-year-old Hatton encountered the queen's favourite, Lord Robert Dudley, who was the elected 'Christmas prince' while Hatton was 'master of the game'.[11]

It was during the 1561–2 Christmas festivities that a play called *Gorboduc* was performed by the Inner Templars and brought to court, and it is generally assumed—although there is no definite proof—that it was then that the queen first spotted Hatton. If so, Hatton initially must have made little impression on her, since it was not until 1564 that he was admitted into the elite band of fifty gentlemen pensioners who acted as the queen's personal and ceremonial bodyguard. His entry was a significant promotion, seeing that the band was filled with gentlemen of high rank and sons of nobles. As a gentleman pensioner, Hatton received full board at court but had to pay for his own suit of armour.[12] His duties were to attend regularly upon the queen, accompany her to chapel and on royal progresses, and participate in tilts and martial exercises.[13] Hatton had the looks, athleticism, and skill to be a credit to his sovereign in this service. He was an especially fine horseman, and observers at court noted approvingly his performance in tournaments.[14] Yet the sources are very quiet about this period of his life, and there is no evidence at all that Elizabeth singled him out for special favour during the 1560s. His rise was not as meteoric as is often claimed.

Like most other gentlemen pensioners, Hatton became a recipient of the queen's bounty, obtaining modest grants of land, offices, and other benefits.[15] His first recorded land grant came in April 1568, when he received a forty-year lease on Holdenby in Northampton-shire. This was to be the location for the prodigy house he built a decade later. Grants of thirty-year leases on other parcels of land soon followed, including an inn called 'the Shippe' near Temple Bar in London in 1571.[16] A number of offices also came his way. In July 1568, he was appointed keeper of the royal parks and master of the game of wild beasts at Eltham and Horne; and, in February 1570, he received the reversion of the office of queen's remembrance of first fruits and tenths with an annuity of £80.[17] These offices and lands were not excessive for a gentleman pensioner, and the grants did not signify exceptional royal regard. Consequently, Hatton did not ini-tially arouse the jealousy of other courtiers or even excite gossip. Sir Thomas Heneage and the earl of Ormond, not Hatton, were Leices-ter's rivals, during the mid- and later 1560s. It took several more years before Hatton enjoyed any notable signs of royal favour.

The first surviving mention of Hatton enjoying a special relation-ship with the queen is found in 1571, when a traitor declared that 'one Mr Hatton' had 'more recourse unto her majestie in her pryvye chamber than reason would suffer, yf she weare so vertuouse and well inclined as some naysythe [noiseth] her'.[18] This sexual innuendo was soon succeeded by more scurrilous gossip. In September 1572, Archbishop Matthew Parker 'was credibly informed' that some man had uttered 'most shameful words' against the queen—namely, 'that the earl of Leicester and Mr Hatton should be such toward her, as the matter is so horrible, that they would not write down the words'.[19] Such scandalous talk about Elizabeth's sexual mores was far from unusual; what was novel was the linking of Hatton with Leicester as the two favourites, even lovers, of the queen.

This identification of Hatton as a favourite reflected the more prominent role he was playing at court in the early 1570s. Elizabeth was allowing him greater access to her private apartments and bestowing more substantial rewards upon him. His political apprenticeship was also underway. According to Hatton's somewhat elliptical testimony, the queen had in June 1572 'layd on my weke shoulders' some heavy responsibilities in 'thes late great causes that most displeased your nobles, as of the duke of Norfolk and queen of Scots, the acts of parlement for religion, and other strange courses in thos thyngs taken'.[20] Exactly what these responsibilities were, Hatton did not specify. But, he was likely referring to his interventions on the queen's behalf in the 1572 parliament. During one debate, he announced to the Commons that Elizabeth would not permit the discussion of an unauthorized bill to reform the rites and ceremonies of the Church. During another—to forestall a petition calling for Mary's execution—Hatton entered the House and whispered to the speaker. 'By the sequel, it was geassed [guessed] he brought a message from the quene', and it changed the whole course of the proceedings.[21] Hatton may have also tried, on Elizabeth's behalf, to protect Norfolk when the Commons drew up a petition against the duke.[22] If so, he was unsuccessful.

Why Hatton's relationship with the queen developed and improved in 1571 and 1572, some seven years after his arrival at court, is something of a mystery. One possibility is that, whereas Leicester had blotted his copybook in 1569 by keeping quiet about the underhand discussions concerning a marriage between Norfolk and Mary Queen of Scots, Hatton had demonstrated a much-appreciated support and loyalty during the years of crisis.[23] But, whatever the cause, Elizabeth's gifts to Hatton were certainly in a different order of magnitude after 1571. Between February and July 1572, he was granted woods in Herefordshire, the manor of Frampton in Dorset, the reversion of the house of the monastery de Pratis in Leicestershire, and the stewardship of the manor of Wendlingborough in Northamptonshire. All these lands and offices boosted his relatively meagre income significantly. That year, Hatton also participated for the first time in the courtly ritual of exchanging gifts with the queen on New Year's Day, and he never missed out thereafter. On the first occasion, he gave her a piece of golden jewellery, possibly a coin, set with rubies, diamonds, and two pearl pendants, while the queen's gift to him was silver-gilt plate weighing 400 ounces. Silver-gilt plate (typically in the form of cups, bowls, and spoons) was her normal gift to courtiers, but 400 ounces was a far greater amount than was customary. This preferential treatment continued throughout Hatton's life. For example, while Leicester received 100 ounces and Ormond 165 ounces in 1578, Hatton again received 400 ounces, a mark of special favour.

On 13 July 1572, Hatton succeeded Sir Francis Knollys as captain of the queen's yeomen guard, a position that gave him official entry into the privy chamber and even closer access to Elizabeth.[24] At the same time, he retained his place among the gentlemen pensioners, presumably because it gave him additional *cachet*. However, in October that year, Hatton unexpectedly incurred the queen's displeasure for having displayed 'unthankefulnes, covetoness [covetousness], and ambicon'. The precise nature of his offence is nowhere stated, but the language of his apology intimates that Elizabeth was irritated by the inordinate 'honor, or riches, place, callinge, or dignitey' that he continued to demand despite his recent promotion and other rewards.[25] Hatton's repeated requests for favours were in part owing to his financial embarrassments. The cost of living at court was high, and he was almost always in debt, needing a constant stream of royal bounty in order to survive. But, perhaps, too, he was also pestering the queen for signs of favour because he was unsettled by the attention she was then paying to the handsome and talented Edward de Vere, the seventeenth earl of Oxford, who had recently married the 15-year-old Anne Cecil, daughter of Sir William Cecil, now Baron Burghley.[26] Since a belief in the inconstancy of women was so common in the sixteenth century, it is unsurprising that Hatton fretted at the arrival of this new star at court and feared that he would soon be displaced in the affections of his 'mutable' queen and thereby lose all his newly-won advantages. Tempted at first to complain that Elizabeth was treating him unfairly, Hatton eventually took the advice of his close friend Dyer and was dissuaded from reproaching Elizabeth or displaying jealousy towards his rival. Instead, Hatton wisely played to his strengths by exerting his charm and showing Elizabeth his adulation.[27]

In consequence, all tensions between queen and courtier vanished. When Hatton fell ill with kidney trouble the following May, Elizabeth became so concerned that she visited him 'almost every day to see how he doth'.[28] To aid his recuperation she granted him permission to convalesce overseas, and in early June he left England for first Antwerp and then Spa in the Netherlands.[29] For Hatton this trip abroad was a mixed blessing. As he well knew, non-attendance at court could well work to his disadvantage, resulting in an immediate

loss of influence that would be readily exploited by aspiring courtiers. So, to prevent Elizabeth forgetting him, Hatton sent her frequent, passionate letters. Adopting the persona of a lover forced to
leave his mistress against his will, he wrote in almost poetic prose of
his pain at their separation and his devotion to her person. Berating
his absence on 'so lothsom [loathsome] a pilgrimage', he declared: 'to
serve you is a heven, but to lacke you is more then hell's torment unto
them.' And, using one of her nicknames for him (lids) to express his
distress, he pleaded: 'But, Madam, forgett not your Lidds that are soe
often bathyd with teares for your sake. A more wise man may seke
you, but a more faythful and worthy can never have you.' In another
letter, he obliquely warned Elizabeth against his rival Oxford, telling
her 'the boore's [Boar] tuske may bothe rayse and teere [tear]',
whereas the sheep 'hathe no touth too bite'; the boar was the earl's
heraldic device, and the sheep another pet name the queen used for
Hatton.[30] In many of his letters Hatton used the cipher of two tri-
angles to signify his nickname, 'lids', and he also signed off with
'EveR', where the capital letters stood for *Elizabetha Regina*. Both
devices were designed to signify the constancy of his adoration for
the queen. Although Elizabeth evidently responded to his letters,
none has survived, and so we have no way of knowing whether or
not she wrote to him in a similar vein. These letters of Hatton did
much to tarnish his reputation among nineteenth-century historians—
such as the editor of Hatton's letter-book—who found them overly
sycophantic and amorous, not fully understanding the courtly and
political context of the writing.

During his few months abroad, Hatton earned a reputation as a
Catholic sympathizer. Quite why, we do not know; it is unlikely that
he attended mass in the Netherlands, but it is possible that some in
his household did. At home, members of his family were drifting
towards recusancy. Whatever the reason, in June 1573, a Catholic
(who signed himself TG) sent Hatton a copy of a vicious polemical
tract (*A Treatise of Treasons*) that attacked the queen's ministers
from a Catholic perspective. The accompanying 'seditious letter'
addressed Hatton as one likely to return to the Catholic fold and
therefore 'the most fit instrument' to present the book to the queen.
Instead, Hatton loyally handed it over to Burghley, who had been
ferociously libelled in the work.[31]

Soon after his homecoming in the autumn of 1573, perhaps because
of his reputation as a papist, Hatton escaped an assassination attempt
by a 'crazed' puritan, Peter Burchet, who stabbed John Hawkins by

mistake.[32] According to witnesses, Burchet had never spoken ill of Hatton before that day, and indeed had praised his performance at the tilts. What had stirred Burchet into this uncharacteristic act, said his friends, was 'a song made against the Scottishe queen' and a lecture by a godly minister.[33] Although Hawkins survived, Elizabeth was so incensed by the attempted murder of her intimate that she wanted the would-be assassin condemned and executed by martial law without a proper trial, and it was only with difficulty that she was persuaded otherwise.[34]

Burchett and TG were both wrong. Hatton was no 'papist', although he was certainly conservative in his religious belief and practice.[35] Indeed, as will be seen later, Hatton's religious sensibilities were close to those of Elizabeth herself. Like her, too, he offered friendship to Catholics as well as to committed protestants, which helps explain the ongoing accusations that he was crypto-papist. Catholic polemicists abroad chose to see Hatton as one of their number, and they branded him as a hypocrite for working so closely with the protestant regime.[36]

Hatton continued to rise in royal favour after his return to England. Over the next few years, he remained in almost daily attendance upon the queen, with only a few breaks from service. Further lucrative royal gifts came his way, including an annuity of £400 for life in 1575, the ownership of Corfe and Branksea Castles in 1576, lands in his home county of Northamptonshire in 1576, and custody of Moulton Park in Northamptonshire with rights of herbage and pannage (dues received from grazing).[37] As a result of his growing landholdings, Hatton now became an important figure in several counties, even though he rarely ventured from court. A commissioner of the peace for Northamptonshire since 1569, Hatton afterwards sat on the bench for Dorset, Kent, Leicestershire, Middlesex, and Warwickshire.

Despite greatly improved revenues from rents, dues, and perks of office, Hatton continued to fall into debt. According to his own estimate, his liabilities were £10,000 in 1575, and on his death in 1591 they were said to be at least £42,000.[38] Emergency help from the queen sometimes baled him out, but his expenditure always exceeded his income, and there were also times when Elizabeth helped him less than he would have liked.[39] Although Hatton never married, his household was large and its upkeep costly, especially on those occasions when he entertained colleagues or foreign dignitaries.[40] Most of his wealth, though, came to be consumed on lavish building projects.

Like other rising men of the sixteenth century, Hatton yearned for the status of a landed gentleman with a coat of arms, county power base, and an ancestral home. To secure the former, he adopted the ancient arms of the Hattons of Cheshire, which he proudly emblazoned on his books. A county power base was built up through his lands, offices, and personal patronage. For an ancestral home, he obtained Kirby Hall in Northamptonshire (possibly in 1578) and defrayed considerable expenses on alterations to both the interior and the exterior façades.[41] Soon afterwards, he began work on the even more impressive mansion at Holdenby. Built in imitation of Burghley's magnificent 'howse and plott' of Theobalds, Holdenby was the largest private house in Elizabethan England, standing three storeys high with two state rooms, two great courtyards, a formal garden, deer park, and orchard.[42] Heneage called it 'the best house that hath been built in this age', and, judging from surviving plans and surveys, he was not exaggerating.[43] Why Elizabeth never visited Holdenby is unknown, but maybe she did not want to put the impecunious Hatton to extra expense, especially as she might afterwards be called upon to rescue him.

Palatial country homes were insufficient for Hatton's requirements. Because of his role at court, he also needed a permanent residence in central London, and so, with Elizabeth's help, he acquired the London house of the bishops of Ely, much against the will of its occupier, Bishop Richard Cox. The rent for the property was nominal, but Hatton spent £1,800 in repairing and rebuilding the site.[44] It was said that he tried to recoup some of the cost by letting out space under the chapel for the sale of drink and that 'revellings were frequently heard there during divine service overhead', but this may just have been malicious gossip.[45]

It was not until November 1577 that Hatton was appointed to the privy council, but, for several years prior to that, he served a useful political apprenticeship. In addition to performing his household duties as captain of the guard, the queen trusted him with the responsibilities of acting regularly as a parliamentary manager, as her official mouthpiece in the Commons, and also an informal channel of communication to foreign ambassadors. In the first capacity, Hatton sat on at least fourteen committees during the 1576 parliament, working alongside privy councillors in steering the debates on bills. Additionally, he rose to his feet in the Commons alongside two privy councillors to defend Elizabeth when Peter Wentworth called for liberty of speech for MPs and uttered that 'none is without fault, no, not our noble queen', words that most found 'scandalous'.[46] Wentworth was immediately arrested and put in the Tower. When the queen decided to pardon the MP, it was Hatton she chose to relay her decision to the House on 12 March.[47]

At around the same time, Hatton played the role of the queen's un-official conduit during the visit of a special envoy sent by the Spanish government in Brussels. This ambassador, Frédéric Perrenot, baron de Champigny—the governor of Antwerp—arrived in February 1576 at a very sensitive moment in Anglo-Spanish relations. His appear-ance deliberately coincided with the arrival of an embassy from the provinces of Holland and Zeeland, which was offering Elizabeth sovereignty in place of their legitimate ruler Philip II.[48] If she accepted—a policy recommended by most privy councillors—Spain would undoubtedly take severe reprisals against England, and war might well ensue. However, refusal would also be dangerous. Holland and Zeeland would then either stand pitifully alone against the over-whelming might of Spain or else call upon the king of France to aid them. To avoid all these dangers, Elizabeth needed to persuade Philip to reach a peaceful settlement with his rebellious subjects. But, because the Dutch might interpret amicable parleying with Spanish representatives as an outright rejection of their offer, she used Hatton from outside the council to discuss the matter with Champigny, seemingly in an unofficial capacity.

This task Hatton fulfilled admirably. While entertaining the am-bassador royally at Eltham (presumably on the queen's instructions), Hatton gave him constant and convincing assurances that Elizabeth was keen to keep Spain's friendship, had no desire to see Philip's rule overturned in the Netherlands, and 'was very willing to be a faithful intercessor in order to bring about a peaceful settlement' there—all of which was true.[49] Champigny was impressed. Hatton, he believed, was a powerful figure who could overcome the anti-Spanish element on the council: 'The entire court was stirred up by this, because of the high credit they know him to have with the queen, and that she defers as much and more to him than to any of her council, even though he is not on it.'[50]

While exaggerating Hatton's influence, Champigny correctly detected Elizabeth's readiness to listen to her courtier's advice. Although not appointed a privy councillor until late 1577, Hatton was consulted on a range of political issues during the mid-1570s. In each case we know about, his opinions chimed with Elizabeth's own instincts. On the question of whether or not she should accept the sovereignty of Holland and Zeeland in early 1576, he backed her policy of seeking a peaceful settlement rather than intervening directly on the rebels' side.[51] Hatton was similarly at one with Elizabeth on religious matters. Whereas many of her bishops and councillors protected those 'godly' ministers who refused to conform to all the rituals in the 1559 prayer book or wear clerical dress that they considered 'popish', Hatton and the queen saw such men (called 'puritans' by their enemies) as dangerous dissidents. Likewise, they judged presbyterians (who wanted to remove bishops and remodel church government) to be a seditious sect, posing a major threat to Church and State.

For this reason, Elizabeth and Hatton disliked 'prophesyings' (gatherings of godly ministers who preached before zealous laypeople and other clerics). In their opinion, these meetings were a breeding ground for puritans and presbyterians, even though many privy councillors and divines viewed them as an excellent training ground for a preaching ministry. As the queen was to tell her bishops, at these assemblies, the 'vulgar sort' (common people) would be 'schismatically divided among themselves into variety of dangerous opinions, not only in towns and parishes, but even in some families, and manifestly thereby encouraged to the violation of our laws, and to the breach of common order'.[52] It was for this reason that, in June 1576, the queen was 'moved by Hatton and some other' to ban prophesyings, an order that was so controversial that Archbishop Edmund Grindal of Canterbury refused to implement it.[53] Furious at his presumption, Elizabeth suspended him from office. Around the same time, she also appointed, on Hatton's recommendation, two anti-puritans to fill vacant sees in the archdiocese: Hatton's conservatively minded chaplain John Aylmer as bishop of London in March 1577, and John Whitgift as bishop of Worcester the following May. Grindal, though, had many supporters on the privy council who were anxious to secure the archbishop's full reinstatement. Recognizing Hatton's close relationship with the queen (and possibly his role in Grindal's downfall), they sought out his help. But either Hatton was less influential with Elizabeth than they imagined or else he did not work terribly hard on the archbishop's behalf. At any rate, in December 1577 and again in May 1578, Grindal thanked Hatton for his 'long and instant travail to her majesty for my benefit', but bemoaned his lack of success.[54]

By this time, Hatton had already moved into the inner circle of Elizabeth's policy-makers, for, on 12 November 1577, he was sworn in as vice-chamberlain of the household and a privy councillor. To give him a title appropriate to his more elevated status, Elizabeth soon afterwards knighted him at Windsor Castle.[55] As vice-chamberlain, Hatton retained his place in the royal household, where he now worked with the lord chamberlain to fulfil the duties of allocating lodgings at court, organizing royal progresses, arranging audiences with the queen, and receiving foreign ambassadors. As a privy councillor, Hatton shared in the official responsibility of governing the realm and advising the queen on matters of state. He soon joined Leicester, the principal secretary Sir Francis Walsingham, and Lord Treasurer Burghley as Elizabeth's foremost councillors, deliberating upon difficult and sometimes contentious issues concerning religion, foreign policy, and the queen's marriage. It is very likely that his promotion came because the queen needed an ally in her determination to discipline Grindal and clamp down on puritan activity. Up to that point she had been, in the words of her previous archbishop of Canterbury (Matthew Parker), 'almost alone to be offended with the puritans'.[56]

Some modern historians have accused Hatton of continuing to be the queen's yes-man after his promotion.[57] This is misleading. As far as religion was concerned, he and Elizabeth remained in total agreement. But, on foreign policy, Hatton was now ready to assist Walsingham and Leicester in their attempts to chivvy the queen into taking a more proactive course in supporting the protestant rebels in the Netherlands and building up a pro-English party in Scotland. Also like them, he also opposed the Anjou marriage scheme upon which Elizabeth had set her heart. However, Hatton generally put his case in ways calculated to avoid causing offence, using suave words of gentle persuasion that kept him out of trouble.

Hatton and Elizabeth were in complete accord on matters concerning religion. They were each determined to discipline 'the papist and the purytaine' and 'correcte offendours on boeth sides which swerve from the righte pathe of obedyence'. The queen told Bishop Aylmer, who was charged with enforcing this policy, that he would 'understande her mynde' via Hatton 'in those thinges'.[58] In the event, both Elizabeth and Hatton showed a certain tolerance towards Catholics that was missing from their dealings with puritans. They counted Catholics among their friends and were protective of those who did not flagrantly break the law. Consequently, Aylmer was soon in trouble with both his patron and queen for ordering 'the rifling' of the house of one of Hatton's friends, and generally coming down hard on relatively minor offences, such as possessing 'popish' orna-ments and books.[59] Nonetheless, Hatton, like Elizabeth, was far from lenient towards Catholics thought to be disloyal or dangerous. Hat-ton added his signature to letters from the privy council, demanding the apprehension of 'popish and massing prestes' and requiring the names of recusants who should be monitored and fined.[60] Several times, he was given individual responsibility for interrogating men suspected of being Catholic traitors, or seminary priests, or Jesuits. Indeed, in May 1585, Hatton was examining so many at his home in Ely Place that 'her highness thinketh your house will shortlie be lyke Graves end barge, never without a knave, a preiste, or a theefe'.[61]

When it came to disciplining 'puritans', Hatton—like the queen—gave no quarter to non-conformists of any colour. Aylmer was allowed full rein in his drive to impose ritual conformity on the prot-estant clergy within his jurisdiction, and, once Whitgift succeeded to the see of Canterbury in 1583, the archbishop came to rely upon Hatton and the queen to support his policy of suppressing all clerical non-conformity. 'Her majestie must be my refuge; and I beseeche you that I may use you as a meane, when occasyone shall serve,' pleaded Whitgift to Hatton in 1583, when some 'puritans' planned to appeal to other members of the privy council for protection.[62] And Hatton did proffer reliable and vital support. According to George Paule, Whitgift's servant and biographer, the archbishop 'linked himself in a firm league of friendship' with Hatton, who kept the queen informed about 'the crosses offered him [Whitgift] at the council-table, as also sundry impediments, whereby he was hindred from the performance of many good services towards her majesty and the state'.[63]

Hatton not only defended Whitgift; he also passed on to him infor-mation about puritan petitions and parliamentary bills so that the archbishop could prepare responses to them in good time. During the early 1580s, Hatton was pretty much Whitgift's sole ally at the heart of government, although others councillors later joined the anti-puritan cause, notably Lord Buckhurst and Lord Cobham (both of whom entered the council around February 1586) and the lawyer Sir John Puckering (in 1592). In virtually all of Elizabeth's parliaments Hatton spoke out against puritans, presbyterians, and separatists, staunchly defending the Elizabethan prayer book, and championing the royal supremacy over the Church. In December 1584, he led the charge against a bill proposed by Dr Peter Turner and 'framed by certain godly and learned ministers'. In fact, the bill was not well received, since it was far too radical in its scope, calling for a Genevan form of prayers to replace the 1559 prayer book and a system of ministers and lay elders, but it was Hatton who 'pressed and moved the House so far therein that it was at length resolved that the said book and bill should not be read'.[64] In the next parliament, Hatton was one of those selected by Elizabeth to oppose a similar 'bill and book', this time proposed by Sir Anthony Cope.[65] At the opening of the 1589 parliament, the last one he attended, Hatton's speech included a redoubtable attack on puritans and warned MPs against meddling in any 'matters or causes of religion except it be to bridle all those, whether papists or puritans, which are therewithal discontented'.[66]

Additionally, during 1589 and 1590, Hatton took the lead in preparing cases against presbyterian and separatist suspects. Together with Whitgift, he headed a legal team working to ensure the stiffest penalties were brought against 'subversives', and he proposed plans for a further campaign to bring radicals into line. By 1590, over eighty separatists were in jail. The next year, Hatton and Whitgift laboured hard to secure a conviction against nine puritan ministers in Star Chamber, despite insufficient evidence that the defendants were seditious in their denial of the Act of Supremacy.[67] No wonder, one contemporary protestant writer complained that during the years when Hatton held sway 'puritans were trounced and traduced as troublers of the state'.[68]

In his parliamentary addresses, Hatton always concentrated on the political dangers that puritan—and especially presbyterian and separatist—demands posed to the state. Theological matters, he claimed, were outside his compass. Even so, we can be reasonably sure that Hatton disliked Calvinist theology (especially its emphasis on predestination) and wholeheartedly approved of the set forms of ceremonial worship established in the prayer book. Hatton, for example, gave support to Everard Digby when this senior fellow at St John's College in Cambridge was threatened with dismissal on account of his anti-Calvinist theological stance. And Digby later dedicated his book attacking the puritan programme to Hatton, whom he called 'a most assured friend to the Church of Christ, a special benefactor to our universitie, and my most honorable & singuler good patron'.[69]

Although his hostility to puritans distinguished Hatton from privy councillors such as Walsingham, Mildmay, and Leicester, the vice-chamberlain came to be as hawkish as them in foreign policy, and more so than the queen. Hatton had in fact never been as pro-Spanish as Champigny chose to believe. In February 1576, the courtier had warned another of Philip II's agents that the king needed to respect Elizabeth's interests, since she had 'incredibly great forces' at her disposal.[70] At that time, though, Hatton hoped that the disagreements between the two monarchs could be resolved peacefully. Over the next few years, events persuaded him otherwise. Hatton became increasingly convinced that Philip intended to crush the Dutch insurgency and afterwards overthrow England's protestant regime. In 1577, the king had rejected a settlement with the rebels, and launched a new military campaign in the Netherlands. Then, in 1579, Spanish troops participated in a papal-sponsored expedition designed to incite rebellion in Ireland. Spanish power and ambitions seemed boundless, especially when in 1580 Philip laid claim to the throne of Portugal after the death of the previous childless monarch. If he proved successful there, declared Hatton, England's security would be seriously at risk from invasion: 'he will then, no doubte, with conjunct force assist this develishe pope to bringe aboute their Romishe purpose.'[71] Recent personal grievances fuelled the intensity of Hatton's anti-Spanish sentiment. When Philip's army ran amok and sacked Antwerp in November 1576, a Spanish captain Johan Romero seized as loot valuable silks, hangings, and fustians that Hatton had recently purchased to furnish his house, presumably Ely House. Despite numerous petitions to the king, Hatton received no compensation for his losses.[72]

Growing hispanophobia and alarm about England's security led Hatton to cooperate with privy councillors seeking to push Elizabeth into a more aggressive foreign policy. In 1580, Hatton urged Walsingham to continue 'to putt her majestie in contynuall remembrance of these perills, and with importunacie stirre up her most earnest princely care over God's cause and her owne'.[73] Likewise, Walsingham—especially when absent from court on diplomatic missions abroad—used Hatton to reinforce his own advice to the queen about foreign policy. Hatton was considered a useful ally in such causes because of his emollient tongue as well as his easy access to the queen. When in 1578 Walsingham felt frustrated that Elizabeth would not take his advice and provide the Dutch rebels with military aid, he appealed to Hatton: 'knowinge howe carefull you ar of her majestie's honor and safetie', he was sure that 'you will take the matter in suche sorte to hart as the cause importeth'.[74] Similarly, Walsingham turned to Hatton in the early summer of 1578 when he was desperate for 'a strayter knott of amitie' to be tied with the protestant Scottish regent but found 'her majestie in that poyncte, to rest uppon some nyce termes'. Hatton, he knew, was equally anxious to 'safely shutt up the posterne gate' to England, and Walsingham hoped 'by your good perswatione' that Elizabeth's objections would die away.[75]

The anti-Spanish Hatton had no compunction about sponsoring and investing in Francis Drake's 1577 voyage of exploration and plunder to the Americas that resulted unexpectedly in the first English circumnavigation of the globe. It may even have been through Hatton's influence that Elizabeth gave her blessing to Drake's project.[76] Although Walsingham, Leicester, and the lord admiral were among the investors, Drake chose to honour Hatton by renaming his flagship (the *Pelican*) as the *Golden Hind* when he reached the Strait of Magellan in August 1579, after Hatton's personal crest (a hind *trippant or*).[77] Hatton, moreover, was the first to learn of Drake's return home in September 1580 by means of his servant, John Brewer, who had accompanied the voyage as a trumpeter and now brought letters announcing the admiral's safe arrival. It was Hatton who then told the queen.

From the start, it was understood that Drake's convoy would raid Iberian shipping and settlements en route, so that the voyage would bring financial returns for its backers as well as strike a blow at the power of Spain. And Drake did indeed come back with ships laden with Spanish booty. Unsurprisingly, Philip branded Drake a pirate and demanded redress. Whereas some privy councillors—including Burghley—wanted the loot returned in order to avoid a rupture with Spain, Hatton, and the other shareholders were determined to protect Drake and their investment.[78] The queen agreed with them. After Drake had taken his cut, the remaining treasure was stashed in the Tower. Elizabeth then distributed some of the silver bullion to the investors, and, in the case of Hatton, she stated that his gains were to recompense him for his losses at the hands of the Spaniards, some six years previously.[79]

By 1581 Hatton was clearly associated with the anti-Spanish lobby at court. So, when Dom Antonio, the pretender to the throne of Portugal, arrived in England, the Spanish ambassador Bernardino de Mendoza believed Hatton to be one of the privy councillors protecting him. Philip II—king of Portugal since his conquest in August 1580—tried to demand Dom Antonio's expulsion from the realm or, better still, delivery into Spanish hands. But, according to Mendoza, Leicester and Hatton consistently stifled his request for an audience: 'I am every day getting further proofs that the queen's refusal to receive me as formerly is owing to the bad offices of Leicester and Hatton,' he complained. As vice-chamberlain, Hatton had some power over access to the queen, and he could—and sometimes did—use it for political purposes.[80]

Hatton was likewise at one with Leicester and Walsingham in their joint hostility to the Anjou marriage scheme. Negotiations for a marriage between Elizabeth and Duke Francis of Anjou, the Catholic heir to the French throne, had opened in the late summer of 1578 and continued intermittently until 1581. Initially, neither Hatton nor Leicester spoke out against the match; indeed, Mendoza even believed that they supported it. Far more likely, though, they kept their grave doubts to themselves, since they had no reason as yet to believe that this marriage project would fare any better than previous ones.[81] However, with the arrival in England of first Jean de Simier in January 1579 and then Anjou himself in the summer, their outward attitude changed. The familiarity Elizabeth allowed both Frenchmen signalled the seriousness of her intent to marry. Consequently, when the proposed match was discussed in council meetings, Hatton and Leicester—together with other opponents of the match—refused to express approval of Anjou's suit as the queen wanted.[82] Hatton's objections to Anjou are not recorded, but we can guess he disliked the marriage on both personal and political grounds, alarmed that it would loosen Elizabeth's ties to her English male courtiers and endanger political stability at home.

Elizabeth did not face only conciliar hostility to the match. Her subjects' deep opposition to it was expressed in libels (malicious writings), sermons, and pamphlets. For this reason, the queen put the marriage on hold. After all, her cousin Mary had been deposed when she made an unpopular marriage, and Elizabeth sensibly would not take the same risk. But, keen to sign an Anglo-French alliance against Spain, she resurrected the match again in the autumn of 1580. At this stage, Hatton seemed ready to give the marriage his support. Away from court, he wrote to Elizabeth:

> Agaynst love and ambityson your highness hathe holden a longe warre; they are the violent affections that incumber the harts of men: but now (my most dere Sovereyne) it is more then tyme to yeld, or els thys love will leve you in ware and disquetnes of yourself and estate, and the ambysion of the world wilbe most malycioslye bent too incumber your sweete quiett, and the happie peace of this most blessed realme.[83]

Yet, at heart, Hatton still disliked the match. All he wanted was for Elizabeth to reach a final resolution, one way or the other. As he disclosed to Walsingham, his real concern was that she was dangling marriage before the French but 'will leave it at the last' and 'what may we look for then, but that the pope, with Spain and France, will yoke themselves in all ireful revenge, according to their solemn combination so long ago concluded on against us?'[84] Marriage to Anjou—though undesirable—he thought better than risking the creation of a united Catholic crusade against England. Elizabeth, however, was paralysed. She would not end the marriage negotiations, because Henry III refused to sign an alliance unless she married his brother. At the same time, she was unwilling to venture on a marriage that so many of her subjects opposed and her privy council would not back.

Then suddenly in November 1581 it appeared that Elizabeth had decided to wed Anjou. The duke was on a second visit to the English court, and the French ambassador was pressing her to agree to a marriage as a precondition for an alliance. Elizabeth gave her answer on the 22nd. She kissed Anjou in public, announced that 'she wished to marry him', and gave him a ring 'as a sign for marriage'. In return she demanded a military alliance with France against Spain.[85] When Hatton heard of this, he revealed his true feelings. According to Mendoza, he spoke to the queen with 'great boldness and many tears about it'. Even if she wanted to marry, Hatton said, 'she ought to consider the grief she would bring upon the country by doing so, not to mention what might happen to her personally if she married against the wish of her people, upon whose affection the security of her throne depended'. Perhaps to everyone's surprise, Elizabeth did not fly into a rage at this impertinence; we do not know exactly what she said, but it was reported that she 'suffered him to speak thus and answered him very tenderly'.[86] Afterwards, she listened to Leicester's counsel along the same lines and agreed to back out of the match. Hatton was selected to stand alongside Elizabeth in an interview with the duke, where she explained that the objections to their marital union were insuperable. Once the marriage had been ruled out, Hatton was as keen as Leicester to support Anjou's independent military adventure against Spain in Flanders; indeed, Hatton supplied the funds for twelve of his servants to accompany his nephew in serving the duke at Cambrai.[87]

Possibly to mark the cessation of the match, Hatton commissioned a portrait of the queen from the workshop of Quentin Metsys, a painter based at Antwerp (Plate 10). It is one of a series of paintings, produced around the time of the Anjou match, in which Elizabeth holds in her hand a sieve—a symbol of virginity through its association with the Roman vestal virgin, Tuccia. In this particular one, behind the queen on her right is a pillar decorated with medallions, while behind her left arm is a globe on which ships sail westwards towards the Americas. The story depicted on the medallions tells how the Trojan hero Aeneas abandoned his Carthaginian lover Dido so that he could fulfil his destiny and found the Roman Empire. The message is clear: with her hand on the globe Elizabeth is the new Aeneas, sacrificing marriage in order to fulfil her nation's imperial destiny. That Hatton was the patron is indicated by the crest of the white hind on the cloak of one of the men in the background.[88]

The last area of policy where Hatton diverged from the queen concerned Mary Queen of Scots. Like all other privy councillors, Hatton had reached the conclusion by at least 1586 that Elizabeth's security depended upon Mary's execution. In the parliament of that year he listed her 'so detestable crimes' and then called for her death with the words *Ne periat Israell, periat Absolon* ('Absolom must perish, lest Israel perish'), referring to the case of King David and his rebellious son.[89] Then, in February 1587, when his close friend William Davison leaked to him the news that Elizabeth had at last signed the warrant for Mary's execution, Hatton went with the secretary straight to Burghley. Together they agreed to call a secret council meeting at which all who attended would take collective responsibility for dispatching the signed warrant to Fotheringhay, without telling the queen.[90] Despite his involvement, Hatton was one of the few who escaped the force of Elizabeth's wrath after the execution; indeed, he acted as an intermediary for Burghley when the queen denied the lord treasurer access.[91]

Despite his heavy duties as a councillor, Hatton did not abandon the role of courtier or give up the conventions of courtly love. He claimed a special intimacy with Elizabeth, writing to her in the guise of a faithful lover during his rare absences from court and proffering gifts that carried a special meaning.[92] In October 1582, distressed—possibly annoyed—about the growing prominence of the witty and handsome Sir Walter Ralegh, Hatton sent the queen three tokens to signify his pain: a diminutive bucket, a bodkin, and a book. While the meaning of the latter two emblems eludes us, the bucket was an obvious pun on Ralegh's first name, especially as Hatton in an accompanying letter warned that water was 'an unstable element' that would 'breed confusion'. Elizabeth read the letter 'with blusshinge cheekes', and playfully sent Hatton a token in return. Her gift was a jewel fashioned as a dove, a symbol of the receding flood in Genesis: Walter, she was telling Hatton, was no threat to his place in her affections.[93]

In May 1587, Hatton received a promotion that led him away from courtly pursuits. Despite a lack of legal experience, he was appointed lord chancellor of England, and 'left his hat and feather' (the mark of a courtier) for a 'flatt cap', as worn by Lord Treasurer Burghley.[94] According to one account, Whitgift, not Hatton, had been Elizabeth's first choice, but the archbishop had declined the office on the grounds that he 'had the burthen of all ecclesiastical businesses laid upon his back' and 'besought her highness' to select his ally for the office.[95] The same source claims that Whitgift, likewise, used his influence to have Hatton elected as chancellor of the University of Oxford when Leicester died in 1588, thereby trumping the candidacy of Robert Devereux, second earl of Essex.[96] Whatever the truth, by this time Hatton had become one of the most powerful figures at court. Although never ennobled, on St George's Day 1588 he was admitted to the order of the garter alongside English peers and foreign princes (Plate 11).[97]

Lord chancellors were sometimes described as 'the mouth, as it were, of the prince' because they heard cases in the prerogative court of chancery, commanded the great seal of the crown, and spoke for the monarch in the House of Lords.[98] After Hatton's death, some scoffed that he had no qualifications for this important and prestigious post.[99] Yet, when Leicester heard the news of Hatton's appointment, he exclaimed: 'Suerly he wylbe the fittest for yt.' Likewise, James VI politely commented that Hatton's 'worthines and wisdome' made him suitable for the office.[100] They judged correctly. The new lord chancellor had the intelligence, energy, and dedication to do a good job.

During term time Hatton heard cases from 8.00 till 11.00 a.m. every day in chancery and from 2.00 till 5.00 p.m. every Monday, Tuesday, and Friday at Ely House.[101] Lacking proficiency in the law, he could 'command other men's knowledge to as good purpose as his own' and 'did nothing without two lawyers'.[102] In his application of equity, Hatton took the view that the chancellor was not just the monarch's mouthpiece but 'the holy conscience of the queen', one who used her authority to mitigate the law when it seemed too severe and supply redress when the legal processes were inadequate.[103] This view was also propounded in a short treatise, bearing his name as author, which explained the relationship between statute, common law, and equity.[104] The significance of Hatton's approach to equity is that it elevated the royal prerogative and envisioned the monarch as a conduit for divine justice.[105] This emphasis on the royal prerogative was entirely consistent with his defence of the royal supremacy, and these were arguably the two main planks of his political principles. If a seventeenth-century biographer is to be trusted, Hatton said so himself, claiming to have been 'jealous' (fiercely protective) of just two things: 'his mistresse's the queen's prerogatives, and his mother the Churche's discipline'.[106]

As lord chancellor, Hatton's tasks were wide-ranging. In addition to judicial responsibilities, he had to keep abreast of correspondence, appoint commissions under the great seal, and ensure records of grants were in order. Again, these administrative tasks were carried out efficiently. When it came to his duties in parliament, Hatton prepared well. Never too arrogant to request guidance, he commissioned a long paper of 'advice' from the clerk of parliament about the 'manner of proceeding' in the Lords, especially at the opening and close of a session when he would deliver a speech in the queen's name.[107] A fine orator, Hatton still worked on his speeches carefully and sought advice whenever he thought it necessary: in his set pieces against presbyterians, he would draw on information and arguments produced by his chaplain Richard Bancroft;[108] and on at least one occasion he showed his intended closing speech to Burghley for approval.[109]

With the deaths of Leicester in September 1588, Mildmay in May 1589, and Walsingham in April 1590, the workload on Hatton—as on Burghley—grew correspondingly. It was evident that the privy council needed replenishing and new men groomed to take their share of the burden of government. Hatton, therefore, wisely ceased to worry about rivals at court and tried to bring on younger men. He put his weight behind the appointment to the privy council of Burghley's son—Robert Cecil—that took place in August 1591, and also backed him taking on the role of principal secretary, a promotion Hatton did not live to see. At the same time, Hatton protected Robert Devereux, the second earl of Essex, whenever his rash behaviour alienated the queen.[110]

Under the strain of the unrelenting pressure of work, Hatton's health—never strong—began to fail, and in September 1591 he told an absent friend that he had been stricken 'of late with some distemperature of body'. Yet, despite his illness, Hatton remained 'bussied' with the queen's service both in London and at court; only in mid-November was he too sick to work.[111] Hearing the news, Elizabeth made the trip from Richmond to Hatton's house, lodging there all night: 'I knowe no better remedie' for his health, wrote a friend Richard Broughton on 12 November with more hope than accuracy, for Hatton expired eight days later.[112] According to later gossip, he died of a broken heart because Elizabeth had demanded the repayment of his debts, but this seems most unlikely.[113] During his last illness, he was reported as 'very sicke of some disease that he often doth mak extraordinarie quantitie of water', an infirmity that sounds far more like cystitis or diabetes than a broken heart.[114] Very soon after his death, his friends learned of, and were astounded by, the 'huge somme' of his debts.[115] Nonetheless, Hatton was buried with great pomp in St Paul's Cathedral on 16 December 1591, and soon afterwards his nephew and heir erected in the choir a 'magnificent monument, ornamented with pyramids' in his uncle's memory.[116]

Hatton is an elusive figure and there is much about him that is still not fully understood: at the personal level, for example, we do not know why he never married; at the political, his views on the succession have not survived. His character is also difficult to pin down. During his lifetime and after his death he was described as gentle, sweet-tempered, charitable, and devoid of malice. And his correspondence suggests he was just that, containing as it does letters of thanks from widely differing men and women within the political elite: the rabidly anti-Catholic Thomas Norton; the Catholic William Tresham; the presbyterian Thomas Cartwright; the anti-puritan John Aylmer.[117] But did political motives lie behind his generosity? Did he lack the confidence and standing to risk causing offence? Or was he just a nice guy? My impression is that he was confident in his views, sometimes bold, but clever and temperate in the way he expressed them; however, not all historians agree.[118]

Unquestionably, Hatton's prominence at Elizabeth's court resulted from his personal intimacy with the queen. Their relationship during his years as a courtier was often flirtatious and even semi-erotic, but we can be pretty sure that Hatton was never the queen's lover, despite a number of accusations to the contrary.[119] Nor did Elizabeth seem as emotionally attached to him as she was to Leicester, but we cannot be certain, as no personal letters from her to him are extant; lack of a direct heir has resulted in the loss of his archive. Nevertheless, indirect evidence suggests that she valued the loyalty and capability Hatton consistently displayed in defending her person and prerogative. It was surely this rather than his fine legs and courtly manners that explain his place in her affections and his position in government. His steadfastness was first revealed during the crisis of 1569 to 1572 and contrasted with the secret intrigues of Norfolk and other lords. Later on, his single state distinguished him from courtiers such as Leicester who married behind the queen's back. Furthermore, Hatton was one of the few men close to her that Elizabeth could count on for support in the anti-puritan drive that began with the suppression of prophesyings and continued throughout the 1580s with Whitgift's policy of imposing conformity to the church settlement and crushing presbyterian cells. Other councillors, similarly, disliked presbyterianism, but, unlike Hatton, they shared some of the aspirations of moderate puritans who were also caught in Whitgift's net.[120] Historians have rightly complained that Elizabeth and William Cecil were too often treated in the past as if they were the front and hind legs of a pantomime horse.[121] It is Hatton who would be better cast as the rear legs; sometimes he pranced more quickly than his monarch, but they were usually in step and he never took off in an entirely different direction.

7

Her 'moste humble vassall': Robert Devereux, Second Earl of Essex

At 8.00 a.m. on Wednesday, 25 February 1601, the 35-year-old Robert Devereux, second earl of Essex, left a chamber in the Tower and, accompanied by three divines, walked to the scaffold within its walls. Dressed in black, he stood before the block and delivered a last speech. After confessing the sins of his youth, he begged forgiveness of 'her majestie and the state and ministers thereof', prayed for the queen's prosperity, and beseeched the world to hold a charitable opinion of him. He next removed his ruff and gown, and knelt in private prayer, which he said aloud. Then he took off his doublet to reveal a scarlet waistcoat, the colour of martyrdom, and lay down on the block, while reciting the beginning of the fifty-first psalm and awaiting the fall of the axe.[1] It was a fine performance before some hundred spectators. In death as well as in life, Essex knew how to develop a reputation for heroism. But what had brought England's premier nobleman to this lamentable end?

Robert Devereux was born on 10 November 1565, the elder son of Lettice Knollys, the queen's cousin, and Walter Devereux, Viscount Hereford, who was created earl of Essex in 1572 after inheriting the ancestral lands of the earliest Essex earls. Father and son took great pride in this lineage, counting themselves members of England's ancient nobility, superior to the 'new men' who held high positions at Elizabeth's court. However, when his father died in September 1576, the 10-year-old's inheritance was burdened with huge debts. Walter had borrowed heavily from the queen and mortgaged his estates to fund his ambitious project to establish an English colony in Ireland.[2]

Walter's death left Essex a ward of the crown, and very soon afterwards he entered the household of Burghley, who was one of his guardians. He did not stay there long; aged 11½, he left to study at Cambridge. There he struggled to live within his means—perhaps revealing a sign of his later extravagance—but he did not fritter away his time. Unusually for a nobleman, he received an MA degree in 1581 at the precocious age of 16. During short breaks from Cambridge, the earl visited the court, but, as he was little more than a child, his appearance went unnoticed.[3] On leaving university, still a minor, he lived briefly at York in the household of a second guardian, the earl of Huntingdon. Once again, Essex showed signs of extravagance, admitting somewhat shamefacedly to Burghley that he might have 'through wante of experience, in some sorte passed the bondes of frugality'.[4]

While Essex was at Cambridge, his widowed mother married Leicester and gave birth to a son. The boy died in July 1584, and it was then that Lettice and her husband showed a strong interest in promoting Essex's political career. With no legitimate child alive, Leicester now looked upon his stepson as a protégé and, in early September 1585, took him to court. But, despite his good looks, the queen paid the youth scant attention. Very likely, she had no wish to favour the son of Leicester's wife, whom she had barred from court and allegedly called 'a she-wolf'.[5] Nor did Essex make attempts to endear himself to the queen, even objecting to her written order that he should lodge Mary Queen of Scots at his 'poore and only house' at Chartley.[6]

Essex's stay at court was mercifully brief. To his great joy, he was given leave to serve with Leicester against Spain in the Netherlands, and both men sailed out in December 1585. Thanks to his stepfather's patronage, the inexperienced young aristocrat was immediately appointed a colonel-general in the cavalry, but he saw little military action until his participation in a reckless cavalry charge at the battle of Zutphen on 22 September 1586. In reward for his gallantry, Essex was awarded a knighthood banneret (the highest rank of knighthood to be received on the battlefield).[7]

Zutphen, though, had still greater significance for the earl. Leicester's nephew Sir Philip Sidney was mortally wounded during the fighting, and the dying soldier bequeathed Essex his 'best sword'. This legacy signified that Sidney had marked out the young nobleman as his spiritual heir, the chivalric knight who would replace him as the champion of international protestantism. From now on, Essex fashioned himself as the 'new Sidney', endorsing the chivalric values associated with the soldier-poet and seeking the fame that gave the dead hero a mythic status.[8] Essex's New Year's gift to Elizabeth in January 1587 displayed his new self-image: it was a jewel of rubies, diamonds, and opals, fashioned as a rainbow over twin pillars, 'one broken' to represent Sidney and the other sound, symbolizing himself.[9]

In October 1586, Essex returned to court. A war hero, he now made a powerful impression on the queen, helped no doubt by his dashing performance in the accession day tilts of November 1586. Within a few months, the earl was recognized as Elizabeth's main companion at court. There was 'no boddy neere her', bragged one of his servants in May 1587, 'but my Lord of Essex and at night my lord is at cardes or one game or an other with her that he commeth not to his owne lodginge tyll birdes singe in the morninge'.[10] With Leicester less often at court and Hatton busy with his new-found responsibilities as lord chancellor, a space had opened up in courtly circles that Essex filled admirably.

To assist his protégé's rise, Leicester resigned his office as master of the horse in May 1587, on condition that Essex could take up the position. Worth £1,500 a year, the office improved the earl's precarious financial position but was still more valuable in guaranteeing him easy access to the queen.[11] To reduce his debts and support his lifestyle, Elizabeth bestowed upon Essex additional material rewards. His New Year's gift to his sovereign in 1588 of a jewel fashioned as a naked man inside a flower of gold said it all, referencing as it did his utter dependency on the queen.[12]

Yet Essex was never Elizabeth's sole male companion, and this he found difficult to stomach. When during the late 1580s Sir Charles Blount wore a token of royal favour (a gold queen from a chess set) tied to his arm, Essex's jealousy was aroused. He taunted Blount, who bravely challenged him to a duel and expertly wounded him lightly on the thigh. Reconciled afterwards by the queen, the two men became friends for life; Blount also became the lover of Essex's married sister, Penelope.[13] Similarly, in the early 1590s, Essex grew unhappy when Elizabeth paid attention to the strikingly attractive and debonair Henry Wriothesley, third earl of Southampton. To express his dismay, Essex wrote a plaintive sonnet 'to be sung before the queene' by a musician whose voice she appreciated. The only surviving lines give a clue to its theme:

> And if thou shouldst by her be now forsaken,
> She made thy heart too strong for to be shaken.[14]

Elizabeth response was evidently satisfactory, as Essex's concerns 'quickly vanished, and there was, a good while after, fair weather over-head'.[15] Soon afterwards, the two earls also became firm friends.

A more bitter and long-lasting rivalry developed with Sir Walter Ralegh, a soldier who had served in Ireland but settled at court after 1582, as a groom of the privy chamber. Judging from his portraits, Ralegh was another man who was exceedingly handsome and stylish; he was also a talented poet and wit. But Essex despised the Devonshire gentleman as a parvenu and additionally considered him devoid of virtue because of his ill treatment of Leicester. Although Leicester had once been his patron, Ralegh joined critics of the earl's service in the Netherlands, much to Essex's disgust.[16] During 1587 and 1588, Essex's and Ralegh's competition for Elizabeth's favour was fought out in courtly exchanges, but they always threatened to turn into something altogether more unsettling and nasty.

Ralegh's insecurity in relation to Essex is evident in his poem entitled 'Fortune hath taken thee away my love'. Addressed to the queen, the verses expressed the courtier's fear that the earl's arrival at court left him out in the cold. Personified as 'Fortune', Essex was labelled Ralegh's 'mortal foe' and presented as someone with little merit other than the good fortune of his birth. Elizabeth reacted to the poem with verses of her own that were designed to brush aside Ralegh's anxieties and reassure him of her continuing favour:

> Ah, silly pug, wert thou so sore afraid?
> Mourn not, my Wat, nor be thou so dismayed.
> It passeth fickle Fortune's power and skill
> To force my heart to think thee any ill.[17]

For his part, Essex addressed a poem to the queen that mocked his rival as a 'cursed cockowe' (cuckoo) who 'could never cease to prate' (prattle) and was 'unhappie hatched' (ill-born). As Hatton had earlier, Essex exploited the pun on Walter's name to declare maliciously: 'That filthy water makes unholsome broth' and:

> But oh, no more, it is to much to thinke.
> So pure a mouth should puddle water drinke.[18]

The courtiers' rivalry also came across in two self-portraits, both presents to the queen. Roy Strong has convincingly attributed the subject of the 'Young Man among Roses' to Essex (Plate 12), a miniature that depicts a handsome lovelorn courtier leaning against a tree of constancy, entangled in eglantine roses (the queen's flower), and wearing her personal colours of black and white. The Latin legend at the top (translated as 'my praised loyalty brings my suffering') expressed Essex's anxieties as a courtier in competition for the queen's affections. But the motto also cast him as a soldier and heroic figure, since it was associated with the Roman general Pompey, who had won military renown at Essex's age.[19] Ralegh's self-portrait of 1588, likewise, depicts a devoted royal courtier. Dressed in the queen's colours, he is her man. A crescent moon in the top left-hand corner represents Elizabeth as Cynthia, the moon goddess, who commands the seas (water/Walter), while the white stripes on his black cloak shimmer like silver rays reflected from her glory (Plate 13).[20]

This court rivalry, however, was not confined to these harmless expressions of courtly love. Jealousy could sometimes prove disruptive. In July 1587, the queen refused to receive one of Essex's sisters, then residing at the house where the court intended to stay. Dorothy had annoyed Elizabeth by marrying without permission four years earlier, but Essex blamed Ralegh for the slight. The queen, complained Essex, had disparaged him and his sister 'only to please that knave Raleigh'. The earl's sulky remonstrance led to a full-blown quarrel with Elizabeth, and during their heated exchanges she spoke 'bitterly' against Essex's mother, an insult that led the earl to storm off in a fury, 'because I could not endure to see me and my house disgraced'. He then rode to the coast in search of a ship to take him to the wars in the Netherlands, but reached no further than the Kent coast before he was 'steyed' and brought back to court on the queen's orders.[21] Mirroring his stepfather's angry departures from court in the 1560s, Essex's behaviour was similarly forgiven, even though he had conspicuously failed to show the queen the respect she was due.

It soon became obvious that Essex was the victor in his competition with Ralegh. On 23 April 1588, he was elected a knight of the garter, and that June was granted the confiscated lands of a traitor. During the Armada crisis of 1588, Elizabeth appointed him overall commander of the horse in Leicester's army after the cavalry officers had already been named, because, he said, 'she wold not have me discontented'.[22] When the queen famously reviewed her troops at Tilbury, Essex attended upon her; and it was noticed that she 'much graced him openly in view of the souldiers and people, even above my Lord of Leicester'.[23] After the emergency had passed and Leicester retired to the country for a rest, Elizabeth allowed Essex to move into his stepfather's lodgings at court.

His stepfather's death in September 1588 lost Essex his chief patron but brought him benefits too. In January 1589, Elizabeth granted him Leicester's lucrative farm of sweet wines, an income that became the mainstay of Essex's finances, and he later negotiated leases for his stepfather's estate at Wanstead in Essex and took possession of Leicester House on the Strand, to be renamed Essex House by 1593.[24] Yet, despite these material advantages and further signs of royal favour, the earl's rivalry with Ralegh persisted. During December 1588, he challenged Ralegh to a duel, a fact that 'trobleth her majesty' and 'had to be bureed in silence' for her sake.[25] Once she learned of it, she travelled from Greenwich to Richmond to pacify them.[26] Far from encouraging factions, Elizabeth tried to preside over a harmonious court.

As much as Essex needed success at court, he nonetheless chafed at the role he was expected to play there. Rather than dancing attendance on the queen, he desired to serve her as a warrior and yearned for martial honour. He was consequently bitterly disappointed when Elizabeth ordered that none of her 'prime nobility' could 'hazzard themselves' in a new expedition planned for the spring of 1589 that would take the war to Spain and Portugal.[27] Indeed, Essex refused to accept this decision. On 3 April he slipped away from court to join the English fleet, successfully eluding his grandfather Sir Francis Knollys and ex-guardian Huntingdon, whom the queen dispatched to bring him back. Absolutely livid, Elizabeth vented her 'just wrath and indignation' somewhat unjustly on one of Essex's accomplices.[28] As far as she was concerned, 'these be no chyldish actions' but an affront to her authority: 'for as we have autoritie to rule, so we looke to be obeyed, and to have obedience directly and suerly continued unto us.'[29] For Essex too, his escape to the wars was no childish matter: he had planned the adventure for months and was prepared to risk Elizabeth's anger in order to fulfil what he saw as his martial destiny.[30] At the same time, the debt-ridden earl hoped that the expedition would bring him material rewards in the form of loot and thus end his humiliating dependence on the queen: 'Her majesty's goodness hath been so great, as I could not ask more of her,' he told his grandfather, therefore 'I will adventure to be rich' rather than sue for further grants.[31]

The commanders of the expedition did not send Essex home, as ordered, and so he came to participate in the 1589 campaign, which historians judge a disaster, given that it not only failed in its objectives but also resulted in the loss of over 10,000 soldiers. At the time, though, the official line was more upbeat, and Essex was applauded in print for his heroic performance. Despite some criticisms, 'most of the English thought themselves abundantly satisfied both for revenge and glory'.[32] But Elizabeth did not share the prevailing mood, since the cost in men and money was dreadful and to little or no effect. Nevertheless, she did not blame Essex for the debacle, and her anger at his insubordination had subsided by July when he was back at court. The intercession of family members (like Knollys) and supporters (like Hatton) aided his rehabilitation. These councillors spoke up for him in the belief that the young man, though hot-headed, was basically loyal and, anyway, a necessary balance to the influence of the unpopular Ralegh.

Once at court, Essex again jeopardized his hold on the queen's affections when in 1591 he secretly wed Walsingham's daughter and Sidney's widow, Frances, who soon became pregnant. Elizabeth initially railed at him for marrying without her permission and choosing a bride who lacked noble descent, but she actually took the news 'mor temperatly' than expected, and within a month the earl was again 'in good favor'. His recovery was no doubt helped by his decision to leave the countess 'very retyred' in her mother's house in London 'for her majestie's better satisfactyon'.[33] Luckily for Essex, Elizabeth did not discover that he was also the father of Elizabeth Southwell's illegitimate son, born in late 1591, for Thomas Vavasour initially took the blame. It was only when Essex acknowledged the child in 1595 that he incurred the queen's anger. And by then he had built up quite a reputation as a philanderer.[34]

After the excitement of the Portugal expedition, Essex found it difficult to settle down to a courtier's life and soon hankered after another military adventure. Although his friends advised him 'rather to seke a domesticall greatnesse like to his father in law', Essex was 'impatient of so slow a progresse as it must nedes have, during the life and greatnesse' of Hatton and Burghley.[35] Besides, he was a soldier at heart and preferred to go to war. A major opportunity arose in mid-1591 when Elizabeth decided to send an army of 4,000 men under an English nobleman to help the French protestant king, Henry IV, besiege Rouen, a strategically important town held by the French Catholic League. Essex was 'bent' on securing this military command, but Elizabeth thrice refused him, even after he begged her on his knees for two hours.[36] Only thanks to the good offices of Burghley and Hatton, as well as the lack of any other obvious candidate, did the queen relent and give him a two-month commission to be the general.[37] That Elizabeth remained concerned about Essex's youth and inexperience can be seen in her sending advisers to accompany him. One of these was Sir Thomas Leighton, a 'speciall person of wisdom, gravite, and knoledg in the warrs', whom she instructed to 'attend upon the sayd erle to serve us with gyvyng your advise and consell to hym in all martiall actions to be by hym taken in hand or intended', since the general was 'but yong in yeares, though otherwise very forward and well disposed to such a service'. So that there could be no misunderstanding, she told Essex herself that 'he should gyve hearyng to your [Leighton's] advise and not neglect the same'.[38]

It did not take long for Elizabeth to question the wisdom of selecting Essex for the post. One concern was that he failed to write as often as she demanded or to answer her points in full. Four days after his arrival in Normandy on 2 August 1591, she was aggrieved that her general 'forgott to answere some pointes' in her last letter, especially as the note had been written in her own hand and contained 'a divine prayer and [was] full of all princely favor'.[39] Essex immediately wrote back with the latest news, expressing his devotion to the queen and beseeching her 'to be constant to him who will, for your majestie's favour, forsake himself and all the world besides'.[40] This barely satisfied her, and she continued to grumble that his letters were in short supply and she was left without news.

Soon Elizabeth had more substantial cause for complaint. About ten days after his arrival, Essex decided to take a dangerous journey through enemy territory to meet Henry IV at his camp, instead of the king coming to see him at Dieppe, as originally arranged. Still worse, Essex agreed to commence the siege of Rouen without the king, who would be fighting elsewhere. Elizabeth was very angry. Henry had slighted her honour and, she suspected, duped Essex into taking on a greater burden of the campaign than had been negotiated. At this stage, however, her displeasure was 'not so permanent as sharpe in the beginning'.[41] Over the next weeks, however, it intensified. She grew impatient with the delay in commencing the siege of Rouen, suspicious that Henry had still not appeared, and annoyed at further French demands for supplies. Her troops and money, she feared, were being wasted, and she blamed Essex for 'being more plyable to a strange king's demaunds then to his soveraigne's instructions'.[42] Appalled by the earl's inertia and worried about her finances, she decided not to extend his two-month commission, which expired in mid-September, planning to pull out of Normandy altogether.[43]

Meanwhile Essex was having a hideous time. On 8 September, his 'deerest and only' brother Walter was killed in an ambush. He went sick with a violent fever and grew agitated by the queen's criticisms of his conduct, which were all too reminiscent of her treatment of his stepfather in the Netherlands and in his view equally unjust. After all, he had 'spent a greatt part of his substance, ventured his owne lyfe and many of his frends' in her service.[44] All these difficult circumstances plunged Essex into depression, and his colleagues noted 'a greate alteration' in him.[45] The royal revocation of his commission came as another devastating blow: 'to come home without doing any thing wold utterly overthrow my poore reputation,' he told the queen. It would also have dire political consequences, for, if Elizabeth withdrew her aid, 'this king looseth his hope and his state'.[46]

Essex was fortunate in that all the queen's privy councillors favoured the Normandy front. Their cause was helped when Henry offered to contribute to the cost of the English army and Essex made his case to her in person. But it took considerable persuasion for Elizabeth to agree to Essex remaining as her general. Hatton explained to him why:

> The chief reason, that maketh her stick in it, is for that she doubteth your lordship doth not sufficiently consider the dishonour, that ariseth unto her by the king's either dalliance, or want of regard, having not used the forces sent so friendly to his aid from so great a prince.[47]

Furthermore, continued Hatton, the queen—like all Essex's well-wishers—was concerned that, in pursuit of valour, the general would abandon good sense and hazard his own life. Fully aware of his impetuosity, everyone heartily wished that Essex could control his passionate nature. In the end, his commission was prolonged for a month, but again Elizabeth commanded her general to carry through no martial action without 'the assent' of Leighton and his captains 'of most discretion and understanding'.[48]

The siege of Rouen, which began on 11 November 1591, opened with Essex playing the chivalric knight by offering to meet the town's governor in single combat in order to determine that 'the king's quarrel is juster than the League's, that I am better than you, and my mistress is fairer than yours'.[49] If we consider that Elizabeth thought it 'very unmete' for her lieutenant to challenge 'a mere rebell' to a duel, it was fortunate that Villars declined Essex's dramatic gesture.[50] Once the fighting had started, Essex was in his element. He seemed tireless, displaying a courage that inspired his men. To no avail; the town's inhabitants resisted heroically, while the besiegers' troops diminished through death or injury. By the end of the year, Spanish reinforcements were expected any day, and Elizabeth called off the siege. Too many men, she wrote to Essex, had been 'consumed so litle to the purpose they were sent for'.[51]

Despite the failure, Essex returned to England with his status considerably enhanced. By commanding a royal army so valiantly, he had earned the respect and devotion of military men; and, by putting his weight behind the Normandy campaign, he came to be acknowledged by privy councillors as a significant political player. Nonetheless, Elizabeth was displeased with his military service and chose not to reward him for it—quite the contrary, for he was denied the chancellorship of Oxford University, which he had pursued on Hatton's death. At the same time, men who had not participated in the war received office and honours: Lord Buckhurst took the university post, a decision Essex bemoaned as a 'wrong' and an act of 'unkindness';[52] Sir Robert Cecil entered the privy council during the summer of 1591; and Ralegh succeeded Hatton as captain of the guard. Furthermore, Elizabeth made it clear that she now mistrusted Essex's judgement on international affairs; whenever he tried to promote Henry IV, Elizabeth said he was 'too partiall and doth not beleeve me'.[53]

Fortunately for Essex, Hatton's death opened up another possibility for political advancement. The late lord chancellor's place on the privy council urgently needed filling, preferably with a younger man, given that the average age of councillors was then about 60. Throughout 1592, Essex undertook to make himself the obvious choice for the position, aiming to demonstrate that he could exercise self-control and had matured into a responsible and valuable royal servant. As well as repairing his relationship with Ralegh, attempting to clear his debts, and cultivating a friendship with Archbishop Whitgift, he now extended his international contacts and became a leading patron of spies.[54] Essex's main competitor to fill the vacancy on the council was probably Ralegh, but in June 1592 the captain of the guard was banished from court after he was caught lying about his secret marriage.[55]

Essex won considerable ground. In the New Year's gift exchange of 1593, he received 510 ounces of plate from the queen, more than ten times as much as the next earl.[56] But the great reward came on 25 February that year, when he was sworn a privy councillor. Acknowledging his new responsibilities, Essex sat on parliamentary committees and helped steer government legislation through the

Upper House in the parliament then sitting.[57] He presented himself as 'a newe man, cleane forsakinge all hys former youthfull trickes, carriinge hym sealf with very honorable gravity'. In the same vein, he attended to his own finances, working to clear all his debts.[58]

Essex's main political objective as a privy councillor was to persuade Elizabeth to prosecute the war against Spain more aggressively. For this, he had to counter the influence of Burghley, who shared Elizabeth's preferences for defensive strategies, relatively inexpensive warfare, and a readiness to put out feelers for peace. To help impress his own viewpoint upon the queen, Essex utilized his intelligence network and diplomatic contacts abroad. Through them he was kept well informed about foreign affairs, while the need to brief the queen about his extensive correspondence offered him opportunities to see her in private audiences when he could impart his own opinions.

At the same time, the normally impatient Essex was playing a longish game. Anticipating prematurely the death of Burghley who was plagued with ill health, Essex was both grooming himself to become Elizabeth's next chief minister and paving the way to continue in that role after the queen's death by developing his communications with James VI of Scotland, whom he thought her most likely successor. The earl's aspirations were entirely realistic: not only was he England's premier nobleman, but also his international reputation was second to none as a result of hosting overseas emissaries and of employing agents to represent his interests abroad. He was fast becoming seen as a key expert in England's security and foreign affairs. He was also attracting into his following men who spanned the religious divide; Catholics and puritans sought him as a patron. However, his naked ambition made him an object of suspicion in some quarters.[59] Burghley, who had great hopes for his son Robert, in particular disliked Essex's attempts to upstage them both.

In early 1594, Essex exploited a chance to advance both his foreign policy and political career when his secret agents claimed that one of Elizabeth's personal physicians, Dr Roderigo Lopez, was involved in a most dangerous treason. Initially, the Cecils ridiculed the idea, and Elizabeth would hear none of it, calling Essex a 'rasshe and temerarious youthe to enter into a matter agaynst the poore man that he coulde not prove, whose innocencye she knewe well ynowghe'.[60] First furious then depressed by her mortifying rebuke, Essex soon came back fighting and denounced the Portuguese–Jewish doctor as a Spanish agent plotting to poison the queen. He pursued the matter tenaciously until Lopez admitted on the rack that he had accepted

50,000 crowns from the Spanish intelligence services to carry out the murder. Although the prisoner later retracted his confession, he was convicted in February and executed in June 1594. Whether or not he was guilty as charged is uncertain, but Essex undeniably benefited hugely from the doctor's downfall.[61] By all accounts he was Lopez's personal enemy, possibly because the doctor had revealed some shameful 'secrecies' about the earl's medical history.[62] Additionally, Essex had much to gain politically from bringing the doctor down. The revelation of an assassination attempt scuppered inchoate peace talks with Spain that the earl so intensely opposed. Equally important, Essex's successful hounding of Lopez exposed flaws in the Cecils' spy network and demonstrated both his own first-class intelligence system and his sound personal judgement. Essex won credentials as a grave and responsible councillor, and Elizabeth could no longer dismiss him as a callow youth. Nonetheless, the queen retained her doubts about Lopez's guilt, and ordered the lieutenant of the Tower to ignore the execution warrants. But, by then, the 'vile Jew' (as Robert Cecil called him) had so many powerful enemies that means were found to bypass her order and carry through the execution some months later.[63]

In addition to his activities as a councillor, Essex continued in his role as a favoured courtier. Internationally renowned and a charismatic physical presence, he enhanced the glamour of the court and was consequently a valuable asset to the queen. When Elizabeth was entertaining foreign ambassadors on twelfth night 1594, she placed him next to the 'highe throne' and, during the play and dancing 'she often devised' with him 'in swete and favourable maner'.[64] On other occasions, Essex—a fine horseman—jousted before Elizabeth, wrote her sonnets, which were set to music, and sponsored masques at court. But the entertainments he arranged were not concocted simply for the queen's amusement: those that have survived were evidently designed to advertise his political worth and advance his policy objectives by appealing to a wider audience.

One famous example was a 'device', written by members of Essex's entourage and performed by experienced university actors on the queen's accession day in 1595. It was in two parts: a dumb show, watched by a crowd of 10,000–12,000 in the tiltyard at Whitehall; and a masque, staged after supper in the palace. The mime showed the earl being greeted and offered gifts by a soldier, statesman, and hermit, who were messengers of Philautia or Self-Love. The masque contained exchanges between Essex's squire and Philautia's envoys, who urged the earl to forsake his mistress and follow instead their own course of life—namely, war, matters of state, and learning. The squire, however, affirmed his master's determination to renounce Philautia, explaining that for the 'defence & honor' of his mistress Essex would

> sacrifice his life in the warres, hoping to be embalmed in the sweete odours of her remembrance. To her service will he consecrate all his watchfull endevours, and will ever beare in his heart the picture of her bewty, in his actions of her will, and in his fortune of her grace and favour.[65]

The masque's meaning was that Essex's promotion of war was not for self-interested ends but for the welfare of the realm and good of the queen. To publicize this message further, manuscript copies were distributed around the court.[66]

Elizabeth, however, was not amused by this particular device: 'the queen sayd', wrote one observer, 'that if she had thought their had bene so moch said of her, she wold not have bene their that night, and soe went to bed'. She evidently disliked the self-aggrandizing quality of the earl, who was posing unconvincingly as her altruistic servant and courting popular acclaim. Possibly too, like many other spectators, she read the entertainment as an unflattering satire on Burghley and Cecil, because the former had posed as a hermit in his own recent entertainment held at Theobalds, while the latter was known to be seeking the principal secretaryship.[67] Additionally, Elizabeth would have disliked the entertainment because of its political purport. Not only was Essex bringing his martial agenda into the public arena, but she also disagreed with it. The strategic case for keeping troops on the Continent had diminished after Henry IV had converted to Catholicism in 1593, been crowned in February 1594, and was winning victories against Spain in Normandy. What was more, Elizabeth needed to bring back her veteran soldiers to Ireland, where a serious rebellion was brewing.

During late 1594 and 1595 Elizabeth remained unconvinced that an aggressive continental war would have any value. She preferred naval operations against Spanish shipping, enticed as she was by the prospect of lucrative plunder and provoked by faulty intelligence that a new armada was underway. Only when Spanish troops assaulted Calais in March 1596 did she reconsider her priorities and order Essex to organize a relief expedition. Yet, she remained uncommitted to the venture, postponed authorizing the army's dispatch, and charged the earl in his final orders: 'doe in no wise perill so faire an armye for an other prince's towne.'[68] Essex found the delay both frustrating and dishonourable: in fact, he took it personally, since he had given his word that 'succour' would arrive: 'I protest, before God I wold redeeme the infamy of yt with many onces of my blood, if the bargayn cold be made,' he told Cecil.[69]

To the earl's intense frustration, Calais fell on 15 April, before he set sail. He now turned his attention to securing from Elizabeth the go-ahead for an amphibious expedition to strike directly at Spain that he had long planned. He was only partially successful. A strategy was already in place for a joint Anglo-Dutch attack on the Spanish fleet to prevent the launch of a second armada, but Essex was pushing for a more ambitious project that involved the capture and garrisoning of the Spanish port where the fleet was harboured. This, he calculated, would provide a more permanent solution to the threat of a Spanish invasion, since it would act as 'a thorne' in Philip II's foot and divert him from assaulting England or Ireland. Elizabeth, however, rejected this proposal outright as far too dangerous. She even began to have doubts about the more limited venture. Fearing the consequences of leaving the English coastline under-protected, she delayed approving the fleet's departure for several weeks. Essex found this 'want of direction' infuriating: it cost him financially, since he was funding the army out of his own pocket, while the queen was wavering; but he was also temperamentally unsuited to waiting patiently for her decision, complaining to Cecil of 'this hellish torment I am in while we dwell in this uncertaynty'.[70] As a result, the epistolary exchanges between queen and general became tense and tetchy. At last, on 23 May, Elizabeth permitted the fleet of 100 English and 18 Dutch ships to sail under the dual command of Essex (general of the army) and Charles Lord Howard of Effingham (admiral of the fleet). The two men were ordered to destroy the Spanish fleet moored at Cadiz in Andalusia and seize as much plunder as possible, without endangering the English vessels or troops on board.

Essex had grudgingly agreed to what he saw as the expedition's inadequate military goals because he had 'raked [racked] my witt to gett this comission' and feared that Elizabeth would dismiss him or cancel the whole enterprise if he protested too strongly. Besides, he was secretly planning to drive through his own agenda once the voyage was underway. As he confessed to one of his secretaries: 'I know I shall never do her service, but against her will.'[71] Just before the fleet's departure, he arranged delivery of a letter to the privy council, timing it to arrive too late for his recall. Pressing his alternative strategy on the councillors, he argued that the capture of a base in Spain would make the queen 'both secured from his [Philip's] invasions, and become mistresse of the sea, which is the greatness that the queen of an iland should most aspire unto'.[72]

The attack on Cadiz in June 1596 turned out a startling success. Philip II's 'great fleet' was destroyed, and the port was captured with negligible English casualties. Throughout the action, Essex behaved with typical theatrical gallantry, famously throwing his hat into the sea and shouting 'Entramos, entramos' (we enter, we enter) when the order to attack was given. He was also the first to land, directing the army through the town's streets, and, once victory had been assured, he put his colours in the town hall.[73] But, despite his heroic conduct, Essex failed to achieve his political ends. Howard and the expedition's council of war rejected his proposal to hold onto the port as too dangerous and, moreover, against the queen's instructions.

Widely admired abroad, the Cadiz expedition had a mixed reception at home. A preacher at Paul's Cross in London praised Essex to the hilt, reportedly extolling his 'worthy fame, your justice, wisedome, valour and noble cariage in this action, making many comparisons of your lordship with the cheifest generalls'.[74] Later that year, Edmund Spenser lauded Essex as 'Great England's glory and the world's wide wonder', while Thomas Churchyard—hedging his bets—wrote in praise of Essex and the lord admiral.[75] Elizabeth, however, viewed Essex's efforts very differently. She had expected to offset the expedition's enormous cost with plunder, but most of the rich spoil had ended up in private hands. On top of this, because Essex had focused his efforts on storming the town, Spanish sailors found time to destroy the heavily laden Indies fleet, harboured nearby, rather than let so great a prize be captured.[76] Other matters niggled the queen. One was that Essex and Howard had knighted almost sixty men—an unprecedented number—flouting her express instructions; another was that Essex attempted to take full credit for the expedition's success and publicize his own account of the victory under an assumed name.[77] Most important of all, Essex had endeavoured to leave soldiers in Cadiz, when she badly needed them to serve in Ireland.

Elizabeth initially showed her disapproval by appointing Robert Cecil as her new secretary during Essex's absence in July, even though 'att his going from court the queene had given him a faithfull promise not to doe it'. When the news was broken to the earl on his return in

August, he could not conceal his discontent and was 'exceedinglie dejected in countenance and bitterly passionate in speech'.[78] Although Essex had previously displayed no personal animus towards Cecil, he wanted to prevent Burghley's able younger son from succeeding to his father's dominant position in the state. Elizabeth's indignation was also evident when she ordered an investigation into the disappearance of the plunder from Cadiz. Again Essex was disheartened by her decision, for the inquiry implied that he and his soldiers had embezzled goods owed to the crown, whereas he considered his soldiers had earned the prizes honourably as rewards for their martial valour.

These experiences convinced Essex that he was the victim of malice and faction. Through his reading of history, he was well aware of the subterfuges and treachery that had brought down worthy men in Classical Rome, and he now began to frame his own career in such terms. Learning from friends that Ralegh (who had participated in the expedition) and Henry Brooke (the son of the tenth Lord Cobham) had 'allso playd their parte' in turning the queen against him, Essex imagined a similar scenario of intrigue: the Cecils had conspired against him while abroad, and on his return Howard, Ralegh, and Brooke had joined with the new secretary to traduce him with the queen.[79] Essex's reading of the political situation was only partially correct. Ralegh and Howard had indeed provided the queen with alternative accounts of the Cadiz voyage, while Cecil backed the commission of inquiry. Nonetheless, Cecil's appointment owed nothing to faction. He had been fulfilling the secretarial functions with his father since Walsingham's death in 1590, and his appointment by 1596 was almost inevitable. Its timing in July, though, was probably prompted by Essex's own action in arrogantly seeking to subvert Elizabeth's orders.

From Essex's perspective, he deserved better from the queen. After all, he had sunk his own resources into the Cadiz venture, displayed great bravery in her service, and delivered a major blow to Spain. Both for the sake of his own honour and to publicize his opinion that the best way to 'annoy' the king of Spain was 'troublinge him at home', Essex was determined that the victory should be commemorated in style.[80] Shortly after his arrival home, he arranged for 'a publicke thanksgeving for this great victory' to take place in London and would have encouraged festivities elsewhere had Elizabeth not prohibited them outside the capital.[81] Because the queen also banned the printing of all the rival accounts of the campaign, he circulated his own version—the 'True Relacion'—in manuscript and sponsored the production of a map of Cadiz with illustrations depicting the battle. Then, to answer his critics, he composed a manuscript defence, known as 'The omissions of the Cadiz voyage', which was similarly widely disseminated. Finally, the earl commissioned a full-length self-portrait that showed him standing before the burning city of Cadiz (Plate 14); and, as a permanent visual reminder of his success, Essex kept the spade-shaped beard that he had grown during the voyage and that would make his image distinctive.[82]

Essex became a disaffected presence at court for months after his return from Cadiz. His relationship with the queen suffered as a result, so much so that a friend urged him to show her less formality and greater familiarity.[83] Essex's petulance when crossed now wearied Elizabeth. Once, after he had moodily withdrawn to his chamber for a fortnight, she was heard to say that she was 'resolved to breake hym of his will'.[84] But Essex's fits of temper were not always uncontrolled tantrums. Very often, his difficult behaviour was a deliberate ploy to get his own way with the queen. As he himself explained, his tactics were first to demand forthrightly a favour or recommend an action, then to attempt to 'sweten her withe all the arte I have', and finally, as a last resort, to absent himself so that he might be 'more gractiously harde [heard]'. The effect he likened to *saepe cadendo*, the slow drip of water hollowing out a stone.[85]

Essex's technique had considerable success when he chased suits for himself. He might initially be refused, but ultimately Elizabeth granted him an extraordinary number of offices, honours, and material rewards. At his trial, it was said he had received more than £300,000 in money terms from the queen.[86] Although Elizabeth preferred him not to take her munificence for granted, she undoubtedly valued his service and wished to recompense him for the financial costs of his endeavours. But Essex was far less successful when he applied his *modus operandi* on behalf of his friends. To his chagrin, he conspicuously failed in two high-profile suits during the 1590s: his attempts to obtain an important legal office for Francis Bacon (in 1593 and 1594) and the wardenship of the Cinque Ports for Sir Robert Sidney (in 1597). On both occasions, Essex's *saepe cadendo* irritated and at times enraged the queen. Nevertheless, she hoped to avoid alienating him and would go 'from a denial to a delay', deferring a decision for several months before finally appointing another.[87] Sometimes, too, she would offer the earl a consolation prize, as when she denied Sidney the wardenship but awarded Essex the mastership of the ordnance (the highest military office after the earl marshal, which was then left vacant) in April 1597. Despite her sensitivity to his feelings, Essex took the rejections very hard and blamed them on his so-called enemies. Yet, in truth, Bacon was too inexperienced to fill the post of attorney-general and missed out on the solicitor-generalship largely because he had offended the queen during the parliament of 1593.[88] The wardenship was always out of Sidney's reach, since it was well known that that the previous holder, Lord Cobham, 'did, before he died, get the promis of most of the counsel for his son' to replace him.[89]

Despite personal rivalries and grievances, the court did not descend into factionalism on Essex's return from Cadiz. Encouraged by the queen, Essex, Cecil, and Ralegh patched up their quarrels in early 1597, and by the spring reached an accord designed to settle their differences, satisfy their private ambitions, and safeguard the realm. Cecil and his father agreed to put their weight behind a new naval expedition commanded by Essex, and in return the earl promised to forward both the appointment of Cecil as chancellor of the duchy of Lancaster and the restoration of Ralegh as captain of the guard.[90] All that was needed was for the queen to approve the expedition. This she did, but only after 'much a doe'.[91] Despite deep reservations, she succumbed to the privy council's argument that Philip II had to be stopped from launching another armada, and she instructed Essex to 'employ all your power to assayle' the enemy's army and navy based at Ferrol on Spain's Atlantic coast. After that, he was to intercept the treasure fleet arriving from the Indies, and could leave a garrison on the island of Terceira in the Azores, even though she was 'not perswaded yet that it can be safe for us' to divert the Spanish fleet in this way from further invasions.[92] She concluded:

> And now that we have directed all these thinges in our power as your souverayn on earth, and can not but consider that all thinges else are in God's hands which belong to lyfe or death...altho we hope Almighty God will blesse both you and us in your all with safety to return for our contentment, yet must we not forbeare according to lyke custom in lyke cases, heerby also to give you commandement and autoritie, yf by sickness or death...you should doo otherwise than well to our no small greefe and losse, that that then our right trusty and welbeloved the Lord Thomas Howard shall be acknowledged our admiral.[93]

This time round, Essex faced few frustrations while preparing for the voyage. Elizabeth seemed fully behind the venture and sent him good-will messages and tokens, including a watch, a thorn (perhaps a reference to his determination to cause a thorn in Philip's foot?), and a 'fayre angel' (perhaps a medallion) to guard him.[94] In return, Essex penned frequent letters to the queen, full of sweet words and compliments: she was his 'deere lady' and 'most deere and most excellent soverayn'; he was her 'humblest and most affectionate vassall'.[95]

From July 1597 onwards, however, Essex had a run of bad luck, which began with unseasonable storms preventing the fleet's successful departure. At this point, Elizabeth seemed almost philosophical at the setback: 'I see as in a christall the right figure of my follye' for putting faith in the weather, she wrote Essex, but she still held the earl at least partially responsible. Her political experience should have warned her against accepting his plan:

> Eyes of youth have sharpe sightes, but commonlye not soe deepe, as those of elder age which makes me marvayle lesse at rashe attempts and hedstronge counsayles, which give not leisure to judgment's war-ninge, nor heds advise, but makes a laughter at the one, and despise with skorne the laste.[96]

After setting off again, the fleet ran into severe gales and could not risk an attack on Ferrol. Then in the Azores the English ships missed the Spanish silver convoy by three hours. Finally, Essex's dash to the Atlantic islands allowed the Spanish fleet to sail out of its harbour and travel towards an undefended England. Indeed, only violent storms prevented a Spanish assault on Falmouth in late October. Quite rightly Elizabeth viewed the whole enterprise, 'which hath styrred so great expectacon in the world and charged us so deeply', as a total disaster.[97] The fault, she felt, lay with Essex. His 'zeale and diligence' could not be doubted, but he had failed to follow 'the rules of advised deliberation' and had thereby exposed the realm to the threat of invasion.[98]

Physically and emotionally shattered by his exertions and failures, Essex was in no shape to accept any further setbacks. He therefore fell into a state of melancholy and anger on learning that during his absence Elizabeth had ennobled Lord Admiral Howard. For Essex, 'this was a double blowe', since the new earl of Nottingham had ceremonial precedence over him and was also credited in the patent of creation with 'the whole honour' of Cadiz. The latter, Essex thought, was 'so false a contestation' and 'injurious' to his own honour that he demanded the wording be amended.[99] Until this was done, he refused to attend parliament or council meetings, where Nottingham would take precedence over him. Playing his usual card, Essex retired to Wanstead in early November and, after a fortnight there, retreated to his London home, demanding some concession or compensation. Friends and colleagues begged him to return to work. By staying away, wrote one, 'the queene, well acquainted with the usuall course of thy absence', might feed him a small favour, but 'thy enemies are therby made stronge and thow becomest weake'.[100] Burghley too urged him to 'com hir, without yielding, without dysparagment of your honor, and [to] plead your own cause with your presence'.[101] As the council's main expert on martial and foreign affairs, Essex's presence in the privy council was vital during the last months of 1597, when a French envoy had arrived to discuss the war and possibilities of a peace. Nonetheless, it was not until 21 December that a deal was brokered. By it, Nottingham's letter patent remained unchanged, but Essex was appointed earl marshal, the highest military honour in the realm, which allowed him pre-eminence and precedence over his rival. Unsurprisingly, Nottingham was not best pleased.

Over the next months all appeared calm, and Essex's relations with the queen seemed repaired. Elizabeth even greeted his mother at court during the spring of 1598, albeit reluctantly and only once. However, disagreements about the direction of England's foreign policy had already begun to surface. While the Cecils and Nottingham favoured opening peace negotiations with the Habsburgs, Essex clung to his conviction that the 71-year-old Philip II was a tyrant who could not be trusted to make a lasting settlement. 'By treaty with us,' Essex maintained, 'he hopes to sever us from the Low Countries' and his ultimate aim was 'the extirpation of religion'.[102] To defend his bellicose stance towards Spain and the case against a negotiated peace, Essex wrote a well-reasoned paper (known as *An Apologie of the Earl of Essex...*), which was probably intended originally as an aide-memoire for a debate at council. However, the following year a manuscript version was widely disseminated, much to the annoyance of the queen, who abhorred state policy being given a public airing without her say-so.[103]

The advantages and disadvantages of a peace with Spain were argued in council before going into the public arena. At times the debates at the council table were personal and bitter. According to Camden, on one occasion Burghley accused Essex of warmongering, calling the earl a man of blood and claiming that he was 'the onely hinderer of the peace and quiet of his countrey'.[104] In June 1598, conciliar tensions ultimately exploded in a terrible quarrel between Essex and the queen, but not over foreign policy. Because he was increasingly viewing politics in factional terms, Essex objected to the nomination of Sir William Knollys, his key ally on the council, as lord deputy of Ireland. Instead he proposed one of Cecil's friends, 'so hee might ridde him from the court'. When Elizabeth scornfully dismissed Essex's choice, the earl contemptuously and 'uncivilly' turned his back on her, an insult that led the queen to box his ear. Instinctively Essex reached for his sword, only to be restrained by Nottingham from committing what would have been an act of treason. Storming out, Essex swore 'a great oath that hee neither could nor would swallow so great an indignity, nor would have borne it at King Henry the 8th his hands'.[105] In truth, no one would have dared such behaviour before Elizabeth's father.

Essex immediately retired 'his sick body and troubled mind into some place of rest', awaiting apologies from the queen and enticements to return.[106] They did not come. Nor, this time, did he enjoy any sympathy from friends or colleagues: 'you forsake your cuntrye, when it hath most neede of your counsel and helpe,' wrote Lord Keeper Thomas Egerton, '[and] you fayle in your indissoluble dutye, which you owe unto your most gracious soveraigne'.[107] Essex, however, was unrepentant; in his view, he was the innocent party, one 'who might expect a harvist of all theire painefull and carefull labors' but was, instead, the object of envy and spite. Far from forsaking his country, he had been 'dismised or misliked' by the queen. Nor did he fail in his duty of allegiance to her, for the 'duty of attendance is no indissoluble dutye', he declared proudly to Egerton, and he was not her 'villaine or slave'. Somewhat ominously, he then came close to accusing his mistress of tyranny: 'why, can not princes err and cannot subjects receive wronge? Is an earthlye power or authoritie infinite?' he asked rhetorically.[108]

In letters directed to Elizabeth personally, Essex was also unapologetic. Critical of her behaviour, he complained of the 'intollerable wrong' she had done him in breaking 'all lawes of affection' and acting 'against the honor of your sex' by resorting to violence against him. Nonetheless, he continued to retain the language of 'courtly love', calling himself 'your majestie's servaunte' and describing himself as 'wounded but not altered' by her 'unkindness'.[109] The two modes of speech were not incompatible.

Essex was the first to retreat. When the Irish rebels routed an English army on 14 August 1598, he seized the moment to resume his responsibilities with his honour intact: 'dutie', he claimed, 'was stronge enough to rouse me out of the deadest melancholie'. Elizabeth, however, was not yet ready to forgive him and rejected 'both me and my letter'.[110] The deadlock was broken only when the earl fell sick and the queen signified concern by enquiring after his health. Satisfied with this ritualized mark of royal affection, Essex attended a council meeting on 10 September 1598, his first for more than two months. Two days later the queen received him. Within four weeks, gossip relayed that Essex was 'in as goode termes (they say) as ever he was', and that he would obtain the prestigious and powerful office of master of the court of wards, which had become vacant on Burghley's death the previous August.[111]

The rumour mill was ill informed. Elizabeth 'denyed' Essex the mastership, apparently preferring to leave the office unfilled or even to abolish it rather than grant it to him.[112] Humiliated, Essex now considered taking on the role of lord deputy of Ireland himself in an effort 'to quiet that countrie'.[113] Military service there would give him the chance to restore his reputation, prove his indispensability to the queen, and 'be valued by her above them that are of no value'.[114] Criticizing the service of all previous deputies, he promised to prosecute the war in Ulster energetically and defeat the rebel leader, Hugh O'Neill, earl of Tyrone. However, as Essex well knew, great risks were involved in the Irish posting. Success was hardly guaranteed, as he would be fighting on difficult terrain against a determined foe. Furthermore, as friends warned him, 'enemyes' at home would take advantage of his absence 'to detracte both meanes and reputacon' from him. Steeped in Roman history, Essex and his circle fully expected to see 'a Hanno at Carthage or a Cato at Rome, barking at him that is every day venturing his life for his country'. But, despite these concerns, Essex felt honour-bound to proceed: 'I am tyed in myne own reputacon to use no tergiversacon [tergiversation]', he admitted after his appointment.[115]

On 27 March 1599, Essex left London with an army over 17,000 strong. Within a few months, all his fears seemed fulfilled. At home, his 'enemies' prospered, as the rich pickings on offer with Burghley's death were redistributed: in May, Cecil was granted the coveted mastership of the court of wards and Lord Buckhurst was made lord treasurer. Then, in August, Cecil's elder brother, the new Lord Burghley, was appointed president of the council of the north in preference to Essex's friend Lord Willoughby. By this time, Essex was convinced that his enemies were poisoning the queen's mind against him. He also blamed them for his logistical difficulties in Ireland, certain that they were deliberately starving him of resources. Cecil, Buckhurst, Nottingham, and others, he believed, sought to destroy his career so that they could sell England out to Spain by signing a peace treaty that would name the new king's sister as Elizabeth's heir. Beleaguered by these nightmarish thoughts, Essex contemplated bringing his army back to England to confront his enemies at court. Only the strong advice of his friend Southampton and stepfather Sir Christopher Blount dissuaded him from this act of treason.[116]

If enemies at court were indeed machinating against him, Essex played into their hands, for he contravened Elizabeth's express orders by appointing Southampton general of the horse and dubbing sixteen new knights 'upon so little service'.[117] For over three months, Essex avoided attacking Tyrone in Ulster but instead journeyed in Leinster and Munster, restoring order to the south. Elizabeth was displeased, complaining that he had failed to put 'the axe to the roote of that tree', as he had promised, and was spending 'excessive charges' for 'lytle publycke benefytt'. In her opinion, Essex had proved himself a foolish and arrogant councillor:

> you have nowe learned, uppon our expences, by knowledg of the contry, that those thinges are true, which wee have heretofore told you, if you would have believed us, howe farre dyfferent thinges would prove there from your expectacon.[118]

Stung into action by this censure, Essex marched towards Ulster in August. However, over the summer, his large army had greatly diminished in size and was now too demoralized to fight Tyrone. Consequently, in a flagrant disregard of his orders, Essex settled for a truce with the Irish chieftain on 7 September. Then, disobeying a royal command to stay put, he immediately embarked for the court to explain his action to Elizabeth in person.

About 10 a.m. on 28 September, Essex arrived at Nonsuch Palace, 'soe full of dirt and mire that his very face was full of yt'. Without waiting to be announced, he rushed into Elizabeth's bedchamber, 'where he found the queen newly up, the heare [hair] about her face'. Regaining her self-composure in very difficult circumstances, she graciously asked Essex to return in an hour, 'which seemed to give hym great contentment'. In their second interview, Elizabeth listened to his explanations calmly, but after lunch Essex 'found her much chaunged'.

Accusing him of grave insubordination, she called for her privy councillors to interrogate him. The queen and the earl never met again.[119]

The next day the privy council charged Essex with six offences, and on 1 October he was placed in the lord keeper's custody at York House. Friends and kin, including his wife, mother, sisters, and aunts tried to intercede for him, but Elizabeth was unmoved by their reports of the prisoner's submissiveness and sickness. 'For our honour's sake, we can do no less than in some measure to chastise him,' she stated publicly.[120] Only on hearing in December 1599 that he was close to death did she briefly soften, sending him her physician with some broth and the comforting message that she 'meant to correct and not to ruyne' him. But, on his recovery, she again hardened.[121] No doubt, Tyrone's breach of the truce did not help Essex's cause. During these autumn and winter months, the regime's chief concern was the stability of the realm, given that Essex had many supporters in the army, court, and London who might incite factionalism, sedition, and unrest. Subject to 'backebyters and libellers' who attacked their treatment of the earl, the queen and council were in no hurry to put Essex on trial and possibly provoke a disturbance.[122]

At Easter 1600, the earl returned to Essex House, and over the following weeks most of the remaining restrictions on his freedom were eased. Meanwhile, some of his friends misguidedly tried to keep Essex in the public eye through the media of manuscript publication and print. A 'private' letter, written to the queen by Penelope Lady Rich in her brother's defence, was first circulated in manuscript and then printed in May 1600 alongside the earl's own *Apologie* (composed originally in 1598).[123] Predictably, the queen and her councillors were incensed by this appeal to a wider public, especially as the hispanophobic *Apologie* was printed just when peace talks were underway at Boulogne. Essex denied responsibility, and no one was punished.

At last, on 5 June 1600, a specially appointed royal commission heard Essex's case. The earl refuted the charge of disloyalty, but humbly confessed his errors and calmly accepted the verdict that he was guilty of gross disobedience. As punishment, he was suspended from public office and banished from court. Nonetheless, Essex remained hopeful that Elizabeth's anger would abate, since in August she lifted all restraints on his liberty, though she still banned him from court.[124] Furthermore, Essex felt confident that his career would fully resume once the queen had died and James VI (her most likely successor) had taken the throne. Unlike Cecil, Essex had been in direct personal communication with the Scottish king over many years. Then suddenly ruin stared Essex in the face. On 30 October 1600, Elizabeth refused to renew his valuable monopoly on sweet wines, leaving him on the brink of bankruptcy. Concurrently, Essex became convinced that Cecil and his 'faction' intended to hand the realm over to the Spanish infanta on Elizabeth's death and so prevent the accession of his friend King James.[125]

Whatever the case earlier, Essex really did have enemies in 1600. Cecil, Nottingham, Buckhurst, Cobham, and Ralegh all believed that the earl's malice towards them was 'fixt', and they feared a future with James as king of England and Essex as his chief minister. Although not plotting a Spanish succession, as Essex feared, these men were looking to be rid of the earl by finding evidence that might incriminate him in treason.[126] They did not have to wait long. Since his disgrace, Essex had discussed with his partisans the possibility of ousting his enemies by force. Now he began to plan political action that would fall under the category of treason.

The council struck first.[127] On Saturday, 7 February 1601, Essex was summoned to appear before it and explain why so many men were gathering at his house. Sensing this was a pretext for the earl's arrest, the Essex group was panicked into a premature rising. That night, Essex House was fortified. The following morning, when four lords arrived to persuade Essex to come before the council, they were held hostage. The earl then departed for the City, accompanied by two dozen or so knights and gentlemen, including Southampton. Given entry when they called out 'they were for the queene', the troupe marched down Cheapside, shouting that Cobham, Cecil, and Ralegh intended to murder the earl. In Fenchurch Street, Essex appealed 'for ayde to defend the queene, religion, and his life' as 'the crowne of England was offred to be sould to the infanta'. Some 300 joined him, but the civic authorities would not. Small in number, Essex's company, when challenged, retreated by river, to his house, where they found the hostages had been released. Soon afterwards, they were besieged. Essex and Southampton swore they would never surrender, but later that evening they delivered themselves into the hands of Nottingham. Eleven days later the two men were put on trial in Westminster. Predictably found guilty, Essex did not plead for pardon, since 'to live was a continuall death and torment unto him'. By contrast, Southampton begged for mercy, 'alledging that his life might doo her majestie service, but his death noe honor'.[128] Essex was, of course, executed, but Southampton reprieved.

What was Essex up to in 1601? According to the government, the conspirators intended 'to deprive and depose the queen's majestie from her royall state and dignitie' and 'to sett the crowne upon his [Essex's] owne head'. The earl, it alleged, had modelled himself on the usurper Henry Bolingbroke, crowned as Henry IV, while Elizabeth was due for the same fate as Richard II. As clear evidence of their intentions, claimed the government, the conspirators had on the afternoon before their rising commissioned the lord chamberlain's men (Shakespeare's company) to stage a play 'of the deposing and killing of Richard II'.[129] The prisoners, however, presented their conduct differently. Essex swore he was 'a true hearted subject' and his purpose was only to remove the queen's 'evil councillors' who were threatening his life and aiming to overturn James VI's succession. Southampton agreed, declaring that they planned 'onely to cast themselves at her majestie's feet' and present their grievances to her.[130]

Some historians today are inclined to accept Essex's version of events. A number view him not as the instigator of a botched rebellion but as a loyal petitioner, intending to expound his case before Elizabeth.[131] Yet, even if Essex's rhetoric and agenda were indeed loyalist, his action in 1601 was illegitimate. He attempted to raise armed men from the City, aimed to force his way into the queen's private apartments, and intended to mount a coup against her chosen advisers. Thereafter he would impose his own policies on the queen, including settling the succession on James. It is hard to see how all this could have been achieved without bloody violence or without events escalating into the queen's deposition.[132] As Francis Bacon, a prosecutor, said at the trial, 'their peticons [petitions] bee armed peticons which always portend losse of libertie to the prince'.[133]

Too often Essex's relationship with Elizabeth has been portrayed as a romantic drama: an elderly, powerful, woman flattered by and half in love with a young, fascinating, but immature nobleman who resented her attempts to keep him in thrall and eventually resorted to rebellion. A recent biographer of the queen, for example, described Essex as 'a self-obsessed boy' who exploited the vulnerabilities and emotional needs of the 'susceptible old lady' until she eventually saw sense.[134] In such accounts, both monarch and courtier are presented as emotional, even irrational, in their behaviour towards each other.

Certainly Elizabeth showed Essex great favour and affection, initially because he was an attractive, talented, and cultured man, later because he was a celebrated figure who brought lustre to her court. But she was never infatuated or in love with him: her anger at his marriage was short-lived; he had no monopoly over her attention at court; and she did not hesitate in 1601 to issue his death warrant. In actual fact, Elizabeth did not really trust Essex: she disliked his recklessness, was suspicious of his bid for popularity, and became increasingly intolerant of his insubordination. The public offices and material rewards she gave him were recompense for his service, and she was careful not to allow him all he demanded. Perhaps she forgave his disobedience and difficult moods too readily, but she was usually induced to do so by councillors who recognized his worth to the state and mediated on his behalf.

Nor was Essex involved in an emotional relationship with Elizabeth. Whether he wrote to her of 'his matchless affection to your deerest person' or the 'misery' he endured during his absences abroad, he was always fashioning himself as a devoted knight making sacrifices in his lady's service, according to the conventions of 'courtly love'.[135] Similarly, he would reference Elizabeth as the distant mistress of romance literature when writing how he was 'afflicted' by her 'unkindness' and had no wish to be 'one of those that looke upon you afar of'.[136] But, behind courtly rhetoric, there lay a more problematic gender stereotyping. Like many of his contemporaries, Essex believed that Elizabeth lacked the 'masculine' virtues of decisiveness, fortitude, generosity, and constancy, displaying instead the 'feminine' characteristics of hesitancy, timidity, parsimony, and mutability—qualities that weakened governance and endangered the state.[137] As he told a French envoy in 1597, the council 'laboured under two things at this court, delay and inconstancy, which proceeded chiefly from the sex of the queen'.[138] But, unlike other contemporaries, Essex believed that his male 'will' had 'to conquerr' Elizabeth's female 'irresolution' and timidity, and the result was the disobedience and conflict described here.[139] Not a romantic drama then, the story of Elizabeth and Essex tells rather of a power struggle.

This power struggle was set against a wider power struggle at court. The smooth running of Elizabeth's government always depended upon servants working in harmony. Essex, however, despised most of the men who had taken office after the deaths of Elizabeth's first generation of councillors. Viewing them not as colleagues but unworthy rivals who were inferior to him in birth and virtue, Essex blamed their influence whenever Elizabeth rejected his advice, turned down his candidates for office, or showed him dishonour. For him, they were the narrow cabal, evil councillors, and corrupt politicians he (and his intellectual circle) encountered in history and literature.

What Essex failed to understand was that he needed Cecil, Nottingham, and the rest to be on his side. Early on, influential councillors had interceded with the queen on his behalf; by 1599 he had to rely on female courtiers to present his case, and their voices were simply not strong enough. The collapse of Essex's career had as much to do with his political isolation at the heart of government as with the breakdown of his relationship with the queen.

8

....

The Women who Served

Both men and women staffed Elizabeth's private apartments in the court. The men comprised two gentlemen, eight grooms, and a small number of ushers who guarded the doors of the rooms. But, because of the queen's gender, female servants attended to her personal needs and consequently dominated the inner sanctum of the court. Who were these women and what were their duties? Did they have a role to play in political life, as did their male counterparts, or did their gender and the queen's demands exclude them entirely from policy-making, court politics, and patronage networks? Was Elizabeth a tyrannical mistress, who forced her ladies to sacrifice their lives in her service? Was she—as so often portrayed in film—prone to sexual jealousy of her maids, taking cruel revenge when they married or pursued affairs of the heart?

All Elizabeth's female servants were from noble or gentry families, and many were the wives, sisters, or daughters of the queen's male courtiers. Like Elizabeth herself, most of her women were generally well educated—though not necessarily in Latin—were serious readers of 'worthie writers', and shared their mistress's love of music, dancing, hunting, and needlework.[1] Unfortunately, most of the women are all but invisible to modern historians. We know most of their names, but very little about their lives. Their correspondence is minimal, and, unless they caused a scandal, they are rarely mentioned in surviving documents, other than obliquely.

Although official records do not specify the exact number and titles of the privy chamber staff, we do have some information about their positions and functions.[2] The most prestigious posts were the three or four ladies of the bedchamber and the seven or eight ladies (sometimes called gentlewomen) of the privy chamber, each of whom received a salary of 50 marks (£33 6s. 8d.) a year as well as board, lodging, and various allowances.[3] One of these ladies—the chief gentlewoman—was in charge of the queen's most intimate bodily functions such as going to the toilet, while a second tasted her food and drink to ensure it had not been poisoned. At least one lady had custody of the queen's jewels, and another took responsibility for her wardrobe, although there existed no official office of 'mistress of the robes'.[4]

Of lesser standing were three or four chamberers, whose tasks were to supervise the washing and dressing of the queen, clean the bedchamber every morning, take care of the bed linen, and serve the midday meal. In the evening they saw to her toiletry again, undressing her, removing her make-up, and preparing her for bed. Despite wearing liveried uniform, earning the more modest wage of £20 a year in addition to their board, lodging, and wardrobe, and carrying out what today we would consider menial tasks, the chamberers were not menial servants but high-status gentlewomen, who received valuable rewards for their good service.[5]

The majority of Elizabeth's women in the privy chamber earned no wage. Six unpaid maids of honour performed minor domestic duties, accompanied the queen on informal occasions (such as morning walks), and carried her train on more formal ones (such as entries into a town or public building for an official reception).[6] Like the ladies, they were expected to entertain the queen with lively conversation, music-making, and playing cards. As unmarried girls from elite families, they had to be chaperoned by a mother of the maids, responsible for securing their good behaviour and honourable conduct. Their expenses were few, since they had board and lodging at court—usually sleeping in a dormitory known as the 'coffer-chamber'—and were provided with sumptuous gowns of rich materials and bright colours.[7] They did not always wear white, as sometimes stated.

Also 'without wage' were six or seven ladies of high rank, who attended the privy chamber regularly, and about a dozen 'extraordinary' gentlewomen of the privy chamber, who needed to reside at court only when 'the quene's majestie calleth for them'. These occasions could be to deputize for a regular attendant who was sick or absent, or when a prestigious guest arrived from abroad; in October 1600, for example, to greet the ambassador of the tsar: 'the court is by commandment full of great lords and ladies'.[8] These unwaged women had to fork out for their own servants, horses, and lodgings, all of which led to quite considerable expense. During the few months that the Sidney family was at court in 1575, Lady Sidney spent over £250 on apparel, horses, and 'charges when the queen was with her'.[9]

In addition to administering to the queen's everyday needs, all her women acted as chaperones and a decorative backdrop. To safeguard her sexual reputation, Elizabeth always had at least one of them present in her company and sleeping in her bedchamber. As ornaments that displayed Elizabeth's royal power and splendour, they were at all times part of the retinue accompanying the monarch, whether in her London palaces or on progress in the country. All were expected to attend formal events—such as grand suppers or tournaments—when the queen was on show.

On her accession, Elizabeth chose to fill her privy chamber with women who had either served previously in her household or else were her kin. Isabell (sometimes called Elizabeth) Markham and Margaret Willoughby, who had been part of the princess's staff at Hatfield, were now appointed gentlewomen of the privy chamber. Another gentlewoman was Elizabeth's cousin Katherine Carey, the eldest daughter of Lord Hunsdon, who had probably been in Elizabeth's household at Hatfield since 1556.[10] The chamberer Dorothy Broadbelt (or Broadbent) had entered Elizabeth's service in the 1550s and was almost definitely the daughter of one of the princess's chamberers of the 1530s. Elizabeth St Loe (known to history as Bess of Hardwick) owed her position as a gentlewoman to her husband William, who had been a servant at Ashridge and arrested at the time of Wyatt's rebellion. Among the first cohort of maids of honour were two other cousins on the Boleyn side, the 15-year-old Lettice Knollys and her sister, the 9-year-old Elizabeth, who was promoted to become a gentlewoman in 1566.[11]

All four ladies of the bedchamber named on Elizabeth's accession were likewise long-term servants and/or kin of the queen. Katherine Astley (née Champernowne)—or Kat as she was known—had attended upon the 3-year-old princess as a nurse and was later appointed her governess.[12] What is more, Kat became a member of Elizabeth's extended family, when she married Anne Boleyn's first cousin, John Astley, in 1544 or 1545. The bond between princess and governess was always deep. For years, Kat had insisted on sleeping alone with her charge, and the two evidently exchanged confidences, including unwise talk in the late 1540s about a possible match between the young princess and Thomas Seymour, the king's uncle. For such foolishness, Kat and her husband were briefly imprisoned in the Tower in January 1549, causing Elizabeth great distress.[13] Like their charge, Kat and John embraced religious reform under Edward VI and, subsequently, found themselves in trouble once Mary had taken the throne. Possibly because of some connection with Wyatt's rebellion, John slipped away to Italy in early 1554 to elude arrest, leaving behind his wife, who ended up in the Fleet prison. Kat, consequently, did not accompany Elizabeth to the Tower or Woodstock, but the two were reunited at Hatfield in the autumn of 1555, only to be parted again when Kat was jailed the following May, this time for possessing seditious books. Although released some months later, she was prohibited from re-entering Elizabeth's household.[14] Yet, despite these enforced absences, Kat was the most constant, loyal, and loving figure of Elizabeth's early life. It therefore came as no surprise to observers when, on Elizabeth's accession, Mistress Astley was appointed the chief gentlewoman of the privy chamber and her husband was made master of the jewel house. Her death, in July 1565, 'greatly grieved' Elizabeth, and two decades afterwards Kat was still remembered as one of the queen's 'most beloved and intimate ladies'.[15]

Blanche Parry—a second lady of the bedchamber—had also served Elizabeth in infancy. The niece of the princess's first nurse, Lady Troy, Mistress Blanche (as she was commonly called) was made a 'rocker' of the cradle soon after the baby's birth and continued in her service, as an attendant, probably continuously until November 1558. On Kat's death, Blanche became chief gentlewoman of the privy chamber, and she held this position until her own death in February 1590, even though she was by then blind and in her early eighties. Her special duties included taking charge of the books, jewels, sable skins, and fine cambric and Holland cloths presented as gifts to the queen. As well as a shared past, Blanche and Elizabeth had much in common: they were both of Welsh descent and 'never no man's wife'; they loved riding and reading, and were both attached to conservative religious practices denounced by godly protestants.[16] Elizabeth was so fond of her servant that she often treated her as a noblewoman. In breach of the sumptuary laws, she gave 'Mistress Blanche' (along with four baronesses) two sables in 1569; and after her death, Blanche 'was buried as a baroness', way above her rank as a gentlewoman.[17] Although her New Year's gifts to the queen tended to be modest, Blanche bequeathed her best diamonds to her mistress in her will.[18]

Lady Katherine Knollys (née Carey)—a third lady of the bedchamber—was Elizabeth's closest kin, the older child of Mary Boleyn. Definitely a first cousin, Katherine may also have been the queen's half-sister, as she was conceived around 1523 when her mother was Henry VIII's mistress, but she was officially recognized as the offspring of William Carey, who was then Mary's husband.[19] Married in 1540 to Sir Francis Knollys and thereafter pregnant almost every year, Katherine was rarely at court while Elizabeth was growing up. Nonetheless, the two developed a very close relationship and spent some time together at Hatfield.[20] When most of the Knollys family left England in the spring of 1556 to escape the Marian persecutions, Elizabeth pledged her continuing friendship to her cousin and declared herself broken-hearted at their separation:

> Relive [relieve] your sorow for your far jorney with joy of your shorte retorne, and thinke this pilgrimage rather a profe [proof, meaning test] of your frendes than a leving of your contrye, the lengthe of time and distance of place seperates not the love of frendes not deprives not the shewe of good will...And to conclude a worde that hardly I can say, I am driven by nede to write farewell, it is wiche in the sence one way I wische, the other waye I grive.

And she signed the letter 'cor rotto' (broken hearted).[21]

Delighted with her cousin's return, the new queen not only brought Katherine into the bedchamber but also appointed her husband a privy councillor, captain of the guard, vice chamberlain (and later treasurer) of the household. When Lady Knollys died in January 1569, the queen covered the expenses of the lavish funeral and arranged for her burial in St Edmund's Chapel in Westminster Abbey. A broadside eulogy commemorated the queen's special affection for her deceased cousin, whom the author described as 'in favoure with our noble queene/above the common sorte'. The verse went on sentimentally:

> There seemde between our queene and death
> Contencion for to be
> Which of them both more entier love
> To her could testifie.[22]

Almost nothing is known about Elizabeth Norwich, the fourth lady of the bedchamber appointed on Elizabeth's accession. She may have been originally in Queen Katherine Parr's household, attending afterwards upon the princess during the 1540s and again after 1554, but we cannot be sure.[23] Very early in the reign, she married the widower Sir Gawain Carew but, even so, continued with her duties in the bedchamber. For many years, she was in charge of the production of the queen's hoods, and she appears on the New Year's gift roll until 1594. That year, Elizabeth's gave her 30 ounces of plate, a weight matched only by the plate presented to Lady Hunsdon; these were gifts that marked out both women as recipients of particular favour.[24]

The unsalaried ladies and gentlewomen of the privy chamber were usually wives of important men at court, and most of them had also enjoyed a close relationship with Elizabeth before she was queen. One example is Elizabeth Lady Clinton (née Fitzgerald). A daughter of the ninth earl of Kildare, she had—at the age of about 11—entered the service of the 5-year-old princess. Despite marrying, Lady Elizabeth remained in the princess's household until November 1558, and it was probably through her influence that her second husband (the considerably older Edward Fiennes de Clinton, ninth Baron Clinton and Saye) retained his office as lord high admiral and was appointed to the new queen's first privy council. The baron had previously been a loyal servant of Queen Mary without any strong relationship with Elizabeth. As the reign progressed, he gave Elizabeth good service— directing the fleet during the 1560 Scottish campaign and helping to suppress the 1569 rebellion in the north. In reward, he was created earl of Lincoln in 1572, and so his wife became a countess. Lady Lincoln remained in the queen's service until her death in March 1589, when she was buried alongside her husband in St George's Chapel at Windsor Castle.[25]

Only two of the women 'without wage' who entered the privy chamber before the queen's coronation seem to have had no previous intimate relationship or kinship ties with the queen. They were the two sisters of Robert and Ambrose Dudley, Lady Mary Sidney and Katherine Lady Hastings. Mary, wife of Sir Henry Sidney, soon became close to Elizabeth. In October 1562, she nursed the queen when she fell ill with smallpox, but unfortunately caught a more virulent strain of the disease as a result of her 'contynuall attendance' in the sickroom. It left her so disfigured that her husband was horrified on seeing her again after his return from royal service in France. According to his later account, he 'lefte her a full faire ladie, in myne eye at least the fayerest, and when I retorned I found her as fowle a ladie as the smale poxe coulde make her'.[26] Despite the scarring, Mary did not withdraw from public life. She remained at court during the periods when she was not travelling with her husband to Ireland (for he spent many years there as lord deputy), but she usually wore a veil or mask 'to hide herself from the curious eyes of a delicate time'.[27] She was present at Kenilworth in 1575, when her brother entertained the court, and the queen then paid her a private visit in her chamber, a mark of great honour to the family.[28] Lady Sidney retired permanently from court in the summer of 1579. Although she was then suffering from ill health, her departure was more likely caused by Leicester's secret marriage, which put her own relationship with Elizabeth under strain.[29] Anyway, by then, Mary was thoroughly embittered by what she saw as the queen's ingratitude towards her and her husband. Although the Sidneys possessed fine clothes, expensive jewels, a well-furnished house at Penshurst, and lodgings at court when in London, she felt their devoted service had been inadequately rewarded. Sir Henry had not received an earldom, as expected, and she frequently complained that the queen was 'no more carefull of' her and that her family was driven into penury.[30] In 1573, her gift to the queen was a jewel shaped as a pelican (a bird that symbolized self-sacrifice), perhaps as a reminder of her own personal sacrifice and in expectation of some recompense.[31]

Mary Sidney's younger sister Katherine also frequented the privy chamber, although she had no official title. Married in her early teens to Henry Hastings, the son of the second earl of Huntingdon, she became a countess in June 1560. Eventually she was to be one of Elizabeth's closest companions, but her initial relationship with the queen could sometimes be tense, because her husband—as one of the very few surviving male descendants of Edward III—was attracting attention in the 1560s as a possible heir presumptive. 'At my wife's last being at court to doo her dutye, as became her,' complained the earl, 'it pleased her majestie to give her a privy nipp [a mocking remark], especially concerning my self, whereby I perceive she hath some jealous conceipt of mee'.[32] In reality, Huntingdon had no ambitions to be a king, as Elizabeth quickly realized. Knowing him to be an utterly loyal servant, she entrusted him with the custody of Mary Queen of Scots during the 1569 crisis, and appointed him lord president of the council in the north in 1572.[33]

Despite the countess's duties with her husband in York, she continued to attend court, albeit irregularly.[34] She was in the northern city when her brother Leicester died, but came down to London soon afterwards, and it seems very likely that her shared grief with the queen bound the two closely together.[35] At any rate, they were noticeably more intimate from then on. When Huntingdon died in December 1595, Elizabeth was so concerned about how his widow would react to this second bereavement that she insisted upon returning to Whitehall in order to break the news to her personally. As she suspected, Katherine was terribly distressed, and Elizabeth decided to return the next day to give comfort.[36] Thereafter, whenever Lady Huntingdon was at court, she was said to be 'every day private' with the queen or 'very long with her majesty'.[37] She outlived Elizabeth, dying in 1620 in her eighties.

The women who replenished the privy chamber over the reign differed little from these earliest entrants. Most of them were members of Elizabeth's family or relatives of existing royal servants, both female and male. Mary Shelton, who entered as a chamberer in 1567 when she was about 17 years old, was the queen's second cousin on the Boleyn side. A more distant cousin of the queen, Dorothy Lady Stafford, served as a gentlewoman of the privy chamber from about 1562, and her daughter was appointed a chamberer in 1568.[38] One daughter of Katherine Carey—now Lady Howard and afterwards countess of Nottingham—became a maid of honour sometime around 1578; another had been appointed a gentlewoman 'without wages' by 1578.[39] Then, in September 1599, Katherine's granddaughter—also confusingly called Katherine—became a maid. The sisters, Anne and Elizabeth Russell—both granddaughters of the one-time privy councillor, the second earl of Bedford—served as maids of honour from around 1594 until 1600.[40] Likewise, Burghley's daughter Anne attended upon the queen, as did his granddaughter Elizabeth de Vere, who was a maid of honour from mid-1589 until her disastrous marriage to the sixth earl of Derby in 1595. Burghley's much younger granddaughter Susan (born in 1587) was a maid by 1602. All these examples—and there are many more—demonstrate the family connectedness of these elite women, a pattern that is equally evident when tracing the family networks of the male office-holders at court. Today we might disapprovingly brand this narrow inner circle as a nepotistic clique, but that would be anachronistic. All Renaissance courts functioned in this way.

Few opportunities actually arose for the queen's elite band of female servants to be refreshed with new blood. Over the forty-four years of the reign, only twenty-eight women ever held paid positions and fifty-four were maids of honour; what is more, few newcomers appear on the lists of extraordinary unpaid female members.[41] So, whenever a rare vacancy arose in the privy chamber, there was intense competition to fill the post. After all, the holders enjoyed high status at court, usually married well, received valuable gifts, and had considerable influence with the queen when promoting their family's interests. Considerable lobbying, therefore, went on from family members or friends at court on behalf of different young women. When, in April

1597, rumours circulated that Lady Leighton might quit her position as a lady of the bedchamber, it was said that 'already a whole dozen of ladies' were jockeying to succeed her.[42] Somewhat earlier, the dowager countess of Bedford had paraded the talents of her two daughters before the queen in a bid to promote their entry into the privy chamber: during the queen's visit to Bisham Abbey in 1592, Elizabeth and Anne Russell participated in a masque (probably written by their mother) that showcased their skills in embroidery, eloquence, and wit.[43]

The queen made it clear at the very beginning of the reign that her women should stay out of politics, supposedly 'commanding them never to speak to her on business affairs'.[44] And, indeed, she punished those who became involved in political activity without her sanction. Despite their closeness to the queen, Kat Astley and Dorothy Broadbelt fell into deep water when they meddled in promoting a Swedish marriage for their mistress in 1562: the former was 'commaunded to kepe her chamber', while the latter was 'commytted to the custody of the secretary'.[45] Both women survived the queen's displeasure and returned to their posts within a month, but they learned their lesson. More seriously, Lady Cobham found herself in trouble when the queen suspected that her friendship with Norfolk might have lured her into questionable political activity in October 1571. During the investigations into the Ridolfi plot, her husband was detained, and she had to retire briefly from the court. Lady Cobham was again under investigation in 1575 when her name came up as a 'good frend' of the Scottish queen.[46] But she returned once more to Elizabeth's good books, receiving a crimson 'French kyrtle' (a satin gown) as a personal gift in August 1577.[47]

Nonetheless, when it suited her, the queen did permit—even encourage—her women to gossip about political matters. One permitted topic for discussion was Elizabeth's marriage prospects, and the women chattered in the privy apartments about the merits or otherwise of the different suitors for the queen's hand, both among themselves and with their sovereign.[48] This was not just merry, idle conversation, but rather a route for Elizabeth to discover the opinions of the wider court. The privy chamber women also acted as the queen's informants about significant goings-on at court or in their own families. According to Leicester, it was 'some bablinge weomen' who first leaked Norfolk's scheme to marry Mary Queen of Scots to the queen, and erroneously (he told the duke) 'made her highnes beleeve that you and wee should seeme to enterprise to goe through without makeinge her majestie privie, and that the matter was alreadie concluded'.[49]

Because of the exchange of gossip that was known to take place within the intimate confines of the privy chamber, Elizabeth's women were thought well placed to help promote the suits of their family, friends, or even casual acquaintances. Speaking well of a particular individual to the queen in an informal setting when she was in a good mood, it was believed, could result in a favourable royal response to a request from someone with less easy access to the privy chamber. In a treatise of 1592, Robert Beale, a clerk of the council, advised his readers: 'learne, before your accesse, her majestie's disposicon by some in the privie chamber with whom you must keepe creditt.'[50] The queen's women, he explained, were in the best position to judge when and how it might be best to broach a suit. For these reasons, men and women outside the privy apartments sought out Elizabeth's favourite female servants as intermediaries. One of the many who used the women in this way was the earl of Hertford, whose own relationship with his sovereign was almost always edgy. Seeking an answer to his petition about some lands in 1571, Hertford solicited Lady Stafford to remind the queen about his 'cause'. She was a wise choice. The gentlewoman proved successful not only in jogging the queen's memory about his suit, which 'she had partly forgotten', but also in offering advice when Elizabeth admitted that 'she could not tell what she might do'.[51]

The assistance of the queen's women was especially useful to petitioners who could not come to court themselves. In 1560, the bishop of Coventry and Lichfield, 'beyng absent' from London, recognized that he had 'great ned' of Kat Astley's help in supporting his 'rud suppication' to the queen, and he begged her to 'speak a good word to prosper yt', either when his request was delivered or else 'when you see best occasion'.[52] Elizabeth, countess of Shrewsbury, who was unable to leave Derbyshire where she was a custodian of Mary Queen of Scots, contacted Frances, countess of Sussex (then a lady of the bedchamber), to request help with a suit. Although Lady Sussex felt powerless to intervene personally, she recommended that her friend should seek out Blanche Parry, Lady Scudamore (previously Mary Shelton), Dorothy Abingdon, and Sir Francis Walsingham as the best people to speak up for her.[53] Towards the end of the reign, Sir Robert Sidney (who as governor of Flushing was absent from court) relied on his aunts—the countesses of Warwick and Huntingdon—to promote his interests with the queen. On one occasion, when Sidney was seeking a lease to the crown's estate at Otford Park in Kent, Lady Huntingdon told him 'how to proceed': she would attend court to help his wife gain 'private access to the queen's presence' and then Lady Sidney could herself present her husband's petition. The countess would stay in the background and not deliver her nephew's letter to the queen 'till there be cawse'.[54]

It was not only the powerful who used the privy chamber women in this way. Robert Beale's widow, who was struggling to provide for six children, enlisted the support of Lady Scudamore and Sir Robert Cecil, after getting nowhere with the queen in an earlier petition: 'I finde all willingness to doe me anye good that she [Scudamore] maye,' Edith Beale told Cecil, but 'if it maye please yor honor that with yor good lyking she maye remember me unto her majestie at some convenient time, when yor honor shalbe present'.[55] Although Mistress Beale implied that Cecil would be a more heavyweight intercessor, she did not underestimate the value of the gentlewoman's interventions.

Their role as intermediaries was so highly prized that those women most intimate with the queen became recipients of costly gifts from persons pursuing a particular suit. At the beginning of the reign, the elderly earl of Arundel was said to have given jewels worth 2,000 crowns to the women who surrounded the queen so that they would speak well of him as a potential husband and royal consort.[56] Similarly, the French envoy Jean de Simier distributed jewels to Lady Stafford and other gentlewomen to encourage them to talk in favour of the matrimonial proposal of the duke of Anjou. Rewards were also given for services rendered. John Manners, fourth earl of Rutland, had already prepared the gift of a cup for Lady Stafford in December 1587, but was told that Mary Ratcliffe 'was worthy to be presented with something', since 'she daily doth good offices for you'.[57] His son Roger, the fifth earl, used Lady Howard as an intermediary, though there is no record of any gift to her.[58] Nevertheless, like other women, she may well have supplemented her meagre salary in this way. Certainly, another gentlewoman—Lady Dorothy Edmondes—demanded a high fee for making 'expres sute' with the queen to obtain a pardon for a prisoner who had been condemned to pay a fine and lose his ears. Likewise, Lady Stafford haggled for a £200 fee for carrying out a favour; she also made it very clear to the petitioner that the queen knew her price.[59]

Men who encountered the queen's displeasure immediately sought out her women to present their case, since they were without direct access to the privy chamber themselves. One man out of favour was Thomas Wilkes (a one-time clerk of the council and diplomat), who had lost his positions as a result of his quarrel with Leicester during the late 1580s. Ostracized by his one-time friends at court, Wilkes turned first to 'an old acquaintance' Bridget Carre (a lady of the privy chamber), begging her to deliver a letter to the queen. When this had little effect, he took Bridget's advice to 'fynd frendes more than I'.[60] So, the following year, he turned to the more influential countess of Lincoln for help, imploring her to speak to the queen 'as occasion may be offered'.[61] It was perhaps due to Lady Lincoln's intercession that Wilkes resumed his role as clerk in August 1589.

The privy chamber women could also act as two-way conduits between the queen and more prominent men when they fell into temporary disgrace. In these cases, the men often used their female friends in the privy chamber to find out how the land lay with the queen, while Elizabeth used her ladies to convey messages that she did not wish to deliver personally. After Leicester had quarrelled with Elizabeth and left court in March 1566, he sent his kinsman to discover from Blanche Parry (a good friend of the earl) how the queen was reacting. Calling him to the privy chamber door, Mistress Blanche passed on that 'her majestie dothe muche marvell' that she had heard nothing from the earl and 'wylled me any wyse to advyse yor lordship' to get in touch.[62] A few days later, another good friend, Lady Stafford, warned that Leicester needed to return with speed to court if he hoped to retain favour with Elizabeth.[63] On two occasions when Burghley enraged the queen, it was Lady Cobham who acted as his intermediary. In June 1584, the queen 'wylled' her gentlewoman to thank him for the gift of gloves he had sent to mollify her; Lady Cobham then took the opportunity to divulge that, though Elizabeth was still distressed with Burghley, 'thank God she ys quieter then she was and spak not one bitter worde'.[64] In April 1587, when Burghley was in still greater disgrace for his part in the execution of Mary Queen of Scots, Lady Cobham urged him 'to hasten your commynge hether' to offer excuses to the queen but warned that 'her magesti continewes disscontented'.[65]

There were other kinds of circumstances when Elizabeth used her women as her mouthpiece. One evening in September 1559 she instructed Lady Sidney to begin discussions with the Spanish ambassador about the matrimonial suit of the Austrian archduke Charles. Elizabeth did not wish to commit herself to the marriage by issuing a personal invitation for him to visit her, a *sine qua non* for any serious candidate for her hand. Nevertheless, she wanted the Habsburgs to take the negotiations for the dynastic marriage seriously. Accordingly, Mary Sidney told Quadra 'with the queen's consent' that he should speak to Elizabeth about the marriage and urge Emperor Ferdinand to send his son at once to the English court. When, later, Elizabeth tried to back out of the courtship, the exasperated ambassador wrote that he had 'complained of Lady Sidney only, although in good truth she is no more to blame than I am'. Quadra correctly understood that it was Elizabeth who had misled him, and not Mary Sidney operating independently.[66]

The gentlewomen's function as intermediaries was embedded into courtly culture as well as politics. Courtiers who could not attend the ceremony of gift giving at the New Year delivered their presents to one of the queen's gentlewomen. Similarly, spontaneous gifts for the queen went through the hands of those women known to be her most intimate attendants. In early July 1583, Sir Thomas Heneage sent letters and a special jewel to the queen via Mary Scudamore; and Elizabeth communicated her delighted response through the same gentlewoman. A few weeks later, Heneage's man 'was yesternyght with Mistress Skidmore to knowe howe her majestie dyd', and Mary Scudamore then 'delyveryd me a token from her majestie to my master'.[67] The privy chamber women operated as surrogates for the queen in this—and other—ways not only because it was convenient. There was a symbolism attached to the practice: first, in accordance with the conventions of courtly love, courtiers wanted Elizabeth to perform on some occasions as their distant, untouchable, and adored mistress; second, because a monarch's body servants were believed to take on the charisma of royal authority, the gentlewomen could effectively stand in for the queen and undertake royal responsibilities and rituals.[68]

Elizabeth's women often remained in her service following their marriages. The queen's favourite cousin Katherine (née Carey) kept her place in the privy chamber after she wed Charles Howard of Effingham in 1563, and was later promoted to the position of lady carver, with responsibility for receiving the queen's food, laying it out on plates, and presiding over the table.[69] Isabell Markham, who married John Harington in 1559 and gave birth to their first son in 1560, continued as a gentlewoman of the privy chamber until her death in 1579, as did Brigit Skipworth (sometimes spelled Bridget Skipwith)—who married Brian Cave around 1566—until her death in 1588. Dorothy Broadbelt kept her position as a chamberer after her marriage to John Abingdon in 1567 (a clerk of the kitchen). Elizabeth Knollys remained at court as a gentlewoman, even while her husband (Sir Thomas Leighton) served as governor of Jersey and Guernsey in the Channel Islands. Women who married noblemen could even be promoted after their marriages to suit their new status: Frances Newton—who wed William Brooke, tenth Baron Cobham, in 1560—was advanced from a chamberer to a lady of the bedchamber and was subsequently given responsibility for caring for the queen's clothes. Anne Russell, a maid of honour in 1559, was made an extraordinary lady of the bedchamber after her marriage in 1565 to Ambrose, earl of Warwick.[70]

Nonetheless, all Elizabeth's married servants—male and female—were expected to prioritize their service to the queen over their family responsibilities. Lady Katherine Knollys, therefore, did not accompany her husband when he was posted on short-term assignments to Portsmouth, the Channel Islands, and Ireland. Nor was she allowed to join Francis at Bolton Castle where he was placed as custodian to Mary Queen of Scots in 1568. This greatly distressed Francis, who implored the queen to permit his wife to come north or else to relieve him of his post. Katherine, he explained, was sick and needed 'moderate travayle and qwyatnes of mynde' and 'untyll hyr bodie be stronger I dowte howe dayly attendance may increase hyr healthe'. But his requests went unheeded. With the excuse that the journey's length 'myghte be to hyr danger or discomoditie', Elizabeth refused permission for her cousin to leave court, and Francis's leave was promised but postponed.[71] As a result, Katherine died without seeing her husband.

Lady Knollys's situation was not exceptional. After her marriage to Sir Thomas Scrope, Philadelphia Carey, an 'extraordinary woman', was frequently required at court 'to yield her neccessary services' to the queen.[72] Another 'extraordinary woman'—Lady Anne Heneage (the wife of Sir Thomas)—was said to be 'so seldome' at home because of her duties at court; but at least her husband was there too.[73] Married women were also expected to continue their service throughout their pregnancies. In the summer of 1565, Cobham bitterly complained to Cecil that his six-month pregnant wife had to travel down to Dover on the queen's behalf to welcome a Swedish princess (who was herself heavily pregnant).[74]

Despite keeping on married women in her service, Elizabeth has been regularly misrepresented as implacably hostile to the marriages of her gentlewomen and maids. And indeed there are plenty of examples of the queen flying into a rage when she discovered one of them had wed secretly. Eleanor Brydges, a maid of honour, famously reported how the queen had badly maltreated Mary Shelton, after discovering her secret marriage to the gentleman pensioner John Scudamore: 'she hath telt liberall bothe with bloes and yevell words and hath not yet graunted her consent.' According to the unreliable testimony of the imprisoned Mary Queen of Scots, Elizabeth in her fury had broken one of Mary's fingers and tried to conceal the accident by claiming the injury had been done by a falling candlestick.[75] A worse punishment was in store for the maid of honour Bess (Elizabeth) Throckmorton. After her secret marriage to Sir Walter Ralegh and the birth of their child were disclosed in August 1592, she and her husband ended up in the Tower. He was released in mid-September in order to carry out an important administrative task for the queen, but she stayed there until 22 December. Both were then banished from court. It took some five years before Ralegh was granted access to court, but his wife was never readmitted.[76] Although many spoke up for her in 1597, wrote Lord Henry Howard, 'sed canunt surde' (they sing to a deaf woman).[77]

Two years after the Ralegh scandal, Bridget Manners (daughter of the fourth earl and countess of Rutland) was also imprisoned for marrying secretly. Said to be very beautiful and a fine lute-player, Bridget had been at court for about five years and promoted to the position of carver of the queen's meat, so she was something of a favourite with the queen. But, in July 1594, she slipped away to marry Robert Tyrwhit in secret. Elizabeth had given her a month's leave from court because the girl was said to have caught the measles and needed to recuperate at home. Bridget, though, did not return, preferring life with her husband. When the queen learned the truth, she was furious with the married couple and 'highly offended' with Bridget's mother, who had connived at the deception. Tyrwhit was sent to the Tower, and his bride placed in the keeping of the countess of Bedford. But they were released in November after friends mediated on their behalf.[78]

The explanation for Elizabeth's conduct in these cases is too often given as sexual jealousy or her desire that her maids 'remaine in virgin state as muche as may be'.[79] Yet, given her acceptance of so many of her women's marriages, such accusations do not hold water. In fact, what Elizabeth particularly objected to were secret marriages, those where her permission *in loco parentis* had not been granted and she had been kept in the dark, even lied to. In all the above situations, the women involved had practised deceit. In the case of Bess Throckmorton, not only had the maid violated the queen's trust by living a lie in her household for months, but also her husband had brazenly denied that they were wed when questioned about it by Sir Robert Cecil, the acting principal secretary.[80] In the case of Bridget Manners, her mother had pretended that her daughter was ill so that she could leave court.

It is true that maids who did ask permission to marry were sometimes refused, but the queen usually had a sound reason for withholding her consent. This could be a belief that her maid would be marrying beneath her, or the youth of the maid, or (perhaps less justifiably) a personal dislike of the male suitor. Elizabeth held back from approving a marriage between Frances Vavasour and Leicester's illegitimate son because she considered them both too young and made them promise to wait a few years.[81] Elizabeth objected to her cousin Frances Howard's wish to wed the earl of Hertford, partly because she did not trust him. Only after 'finding her resolute', did the queen eventually tell Frances that 'she would not be against my desire'.[82] The marriage took place in December 1585, and afterwards the new countess retained her position in the privy chamber and her place in the queen's affections. Elizabeth's fondness for her was on public display during a royal visit to the Hertfords' country house at Elvetham in 1591. There, the queen responded warmly to her hostess's words of welcome; she first embraced the countess, then 'tooke hir up, and kissed hir, using manie comfortable and princely speeches'.[83]

Elizabeth claimed that she always furthered 'any honest or honorable purposes of mariage or preferment to any of hers, when without scandall and infamye they have bene orderly broken unto her'.[84] And, to a large extent, this was true. When permission to marry had been requested and obtained, Elizabeth gave generous gifts to the brides and happily attended their weddings. She ordered a black satin gown as a wedding gift for Dorothy Broadbelt; Lady Elizabeth Manners received a jewel as a wedding present; and Margaret Edgecombe was given a pair of richly embroidered gloves.[85] Anne Russell's wedding to the earl of Warwick was held in the chapel royal at Whitehall Palace in November 1565 and afterwards celebrated with a great banquet and a tournament at court. In May 1571, Elizabeth permitted her 22-year-old maid of honour Helena Snakenborg to wed the 57-year old William Parr, marquess of Northampton, in the queen's closet at Whitehall Palace.[86] When Frances Radcliffe (the sister of the earl of Sussex and maid of honour to the queen) married the son of Sir Walter Mildmay, Elizabeth attended the nuptial supper, masques, and dances.[87] Elizabeth de Vere was given such a splendid send-off at Greenwich Palace when she wed William Stanley, earl of Derby, that her grandfather Lord Burghley expressed his delight with the queen's 'favorable disposition to do such honor to her mayd, for the old man's sake'.[88] On 16 June 1600, Elizabeth was a guest at the wedding of Anne Russell and Henry Somerset, Lord Herbert (son of the fourth earl of Worcester), which took place at the bride's mother's home in Blackfriars. During the festivities, the queen's eight maids of honour and other gentlewomen participated in a masque 'in the name of the muses that came to secke one of theyr fellowes'.[89]

Elizabeth's anger at the women who married without her permission soon abated if she was especially fond of them and their fault was judged not too great. Before long, Mary Scudamore was forgiven for her clandestine marriage, welcomed back into the privy chamber, and given a gift of expensive cloth to be sewn into the front part of a gown.[90] But, as with all her women, the queen expected the Scudamores to put their service to her before their married life. Consequently, Mary rarely left the court to go to her husband's house; and, when away in October 1576, she was summoned back. The ladies Scudamore and Stafford were Elizabeth's two favourite sleeping companions, but that October Dorothy Stafford broke her leg and so Mary had to return, for it was feared that 'untill you come her majestie shall not in the night have so good rest as she wyll take after your comyng'.[91] There were compensations for such dedication, however. On 7 June 1577, Mary was granted Cranbourne Park in Dorset, 'in consideration of her good, nice and faithful and acceptable services as a gentlewoman of the queen's private chambers'. Later, on 3 October 1584, Elizabeth awarded her an annuity of £100 (to be paid after the death of William Worthington), another £400 in April 1591, and still another 'free gift' of £300 in May 1594. As for John, he was knighted in 1592 and appointed the standard-bearer of gentlemen pensioners in 1599.[92]

Likewise received back in the queen's privy chamber were Helena, marchioness of Northampton, and her second husband, Sir Thomas Gorges (a gentleman of the privy chamber), who had both been banished from court after their secret marriage. This too was an unequal union, as Helena had retained her title of 'Lady Marques' after her first husband's death, while Gorges was merely a gentleman. But, once Elizabeth had become reconciled to the new arrangement, she showed great favour to the married couple. She was godmother to their first child, born in June 1578, and Gorges's subsequent career thrived. Elizabeth also granted them joint ownership of the site of the Carthusian monastery adjoining Richmond Palace and several manors in Huntingdonshire and Wiltshire.[93] She even took a hand in trying to arrange a marriage between one of their daughters and the son of a Mr Edward Griffin of Dingley. One consideration that Griffin should bear in mind, the queen wrote in 1596, was the parents' 'neereness of service to us':

> not that we intende hereby to sway your disposition as with authori-tie, although that yf we shall perceive that for our sake you shall satisfie the gent.'s desire, we shall have cause to take it as a great signe of the respect you beare to what may be pleasing to us.[94]

The combination of persuasion and veiled threat was sufficient to ensure the wedding took place.[95]

By contrast, Elizabeth was always unforgiving when her maids engaged in sex outside marriage. She seldom employed a double standard, and would punish male and female transgressors alike. On learning in March 1581 that Burghley's son-in-law (Edward de Vere, seventeenth earl of Oxford) had impregnated the 15-year-old Anne Vavasour, who was both a gentlewoman of the bedchamber and maid of honour, Elizabeth was said to be 'greatly grieved with the acci-dent'. On the very night that Anne gave birth to a son in the 'maidens' chamber', she was turfed out of court and, the following morning, committed to the Tower. Oxford, who tried to flee the country, was waylaid and also sent to the Tower, where he remained for three months. Barred from court for many years afterwards, the earl was 'punished as far or farther than any like crime hath been', despite the protests of Burghley, who was hoping for the rehabilitation of his son-in-law.[96]

As for Anne Vavasour, she re-emerged in 1590 as the wife of a John Finch and mistress of Sir Henry Lee, the queen's champion at the tilts. It is thought that the married Lee paid Finch a small annuity to wed Anne and give her some respectability. After the death of Lee's own wife, the couple lived together openly. What the queen knew or thought about these arrangements is unrecorded; all we know is that they did not stop her continuing to show Lee favour, including a visit to his estate at Ditchley in Oxfordshire during her 1592 progress, but she would not see Anne then or at any other time.[97]

Anne could not wed the father of her child, but, whenever it was possible, the best solution for an extramarital pregnancy was thought to be marriage. 'Shotgun weddings' salvaged the reputation of the gentlewomen, but they did not usually win back royal favour. Sir Francis Darcy secretly and belatedly married a maid of honour, a Mistress Legh, who 'was brought abed in the court' with a daughter in 1591, but this did not protect him, or his new wife, from the queen's wrath. Indeed the mother of the maid ended up in the Tower alongside Darcy for failing to supervise her charge properly.[98] When Elizabeth Vernon learned that she was pregnant by Henry Wriothesley, third earl of Southampton, in 1598, they too were secretly married. Nevertheless, the queen was 'grevousely offended' and considered that Southampton had behaved 'very contemptuousely'. He therefore spent several months in the Fleet prison, and the queen never forgave him or received his wife at court, despite her elevated status as a countess.[99]

In some cases, these pregnancies may have occurred after the informal exchange of vows between the lovers. The maid of honour Mary Fitton, who 'proved with chyld' in early February 1601, swore that she had been promised marriage by her 20-year-old lover William Herbert, third earl of Pembroke. He, however, refuted the claim and 'utterly renounceth all marriage'.[100] The queen was inclined to believe her maid. After ordering Pembroke to the Fleet, where he stayed for about a month, she exiled him from court and denied him any preferment. Still the earl could not be persuaded to marry Fitton. Feeling the queen had treated him badly, he begged 'to get leave to goe into some other land that the change of climate maye purge one of melancholie' and 'lessen if not wipe out the memory of my disgraces'.[101] Notwithstanding his many begging letters to Sir Robert Cecil, the earl had to wait until the next reign before he could return to court. As for Mary Fitton, she was first committed to the care of Lady Hawkins, in whose home she gave birth to a stillborn boy, and then left court to stay with her family in the country. Some say that soon after her disgrace she became the mistress of her distant cousin, Sir Richard Leveson, whose wife was insane, but there is no concrete evidence for this much-repeated allegation. After Leveson's death, however, Mary again brought 'a great deal of sorrow and grief' to her mother and 'such shame' to herself 'as never had Cheshire woman, worse now than ever' when she bore a bastard son to a certain Captain Polewhele—thought by her family to be a 'knave'. They eventually married in 1607.[102]

Once again sexual jealousy is a totally inadequate explanation for the queen's anger in these instances. Nor was she enraged simply because her maids had shown themselves disobedient and untrustworthy. Though that was certainly a factor, considerably more was at stake. The queen could not afford to let illicit sex go unpunished. She had already failed to protect and regulate her maids *in loco parentis*, so neglecting afterwards to deal severely with their indiscipline could raise doubts about her ability to govern the realm; in the sixteenth century, the household was generally viewed as a microcosm of the state. Additionally, the repercussions of non-marital sex within noble families could be politically and socially disruptive, resulting in duels and intense bad feelings. Anne Vavasour's brother Thomas issued threats against Oxford, and Sir Thomas Knyvet actually fought the earl in a duel, presumably over Anne, who was his kinswoman. The earl of Derby, in 1597, challenged, to 'the combat of lyff', anyone who declared that his wife (Burghley's granddaughter) was impure, even though—as he well knew—she was then having an affair with Essex.[103]

Another consideration for Elizabeth was that these court scandals reflected badly on her own reputation. What might malicious gossips say about the queen if her chaperones were found to be engaging in illicit sex? In such a climate, the carefully constructed idealization of the queen as a virgin goddess served by virtuous 'vestall maydens' looked somewhat hollow—even risible—for those in the know.[104] And many did know; as one observer wittily reported in October 1591, 'the talke nowe hear in London is all of the quene's maids that were'.[105] In 1598, English Catholics abroad were informed and took great delight in the fact that 'maids of the court goe scarce 20 wekes with child after they are maryed, and everie man hath lybertie of conscience to play the knave'.[106]

With the exception of the Vavasour affair, the major court scandals occurred during the 1590s. In 1591 alone, the queen lost half her complement of maids to illicit pregnancies and shotgun weddings.[107] During that decade, sexual liaisons with court ladies outside the privy chamber also came to light. Elizabeth Southwell bore Essex's child; the countess of Derby had her adulterous affair with Essex; and Elizabeth Brydges's name was also linked with the earl as well as Ralegh. Essex's married sister Penelope Lady Rich—a regular attendee at court—was openly the mistress of Sir Charles Blount, unashamedly naming their son Mountjoy after his baronetcy in 1597.[108]

We can only guess at an explanation for what seems to have been a breakdown in court discipline and a flagrant disregard of sexual

PLATE 1 A sixteenth-century portrait of Anne Boleyn.

PLATE 2 The Family of Henry VIII, c.1544 (oil on canvas), English School, (16th century).

PLATE 3
Elizabeth I when Princess, at the age of about 13, *c.*1546 (oil on panel), Guillaume Scrots (fl.1537-53) (attr. to) The Royal Collection.

PLATE 4
Portrait miniature of Lady Katherine Seymour, née Grey (c.1538–68) Countess of Hertford, holding her infant son and wearing her husband's miniature, *c.*1562, Lievine Teerlink (b.1510–20, d.1576) (attr. to).

PLATE 5 Double portrait of Mary Queen of Scots and James VI, dated 1583, when 'an association' was being promoted for their joint rule of Scotland.

PLATE 6 'The most ancient and famouse pedygrye' of the earl of Leicester.

PLATE 7
Robert Dudley, earl of
Leicester.

PLATE 8
Elizabeth I, 1575.

PLATE 9 Preparatory sketches of Elizabeth and Leicester by Federigo Zuccaro.

PLATE 10 Portrait of Queen Elizabeth I (1533–1603) in Ceremonial Costume (oil on canvas),
Zuccari, Federico Zuccaro, Federico (1540-1609).

PLATE 11 Portrait of Sir Christopher Hatton, probably commissioned in 1588 to commemorate his entry into the order of the garter and appointment as chancellor of the University of Oxford. In his right hand, Hatton holds the St George medallion, above which are the insignia and motto of the order; in his left hand is the crest of the University of Oxford, above which is 'an oxe in foorde'. Centred beneath Hatton is his emblem of the golden hind.

PLATE 12 'Young Man among Roses', a miniature by Nicholas Hilliard.

PLATE 13 Portrait of Sir Walter Raleigh (1554–1618) 1588 (oil on panel), English School, (16th century).

PLATE 14 Robert Devereux, 2nd Earl of Essex, *c.* 1596,
Marcus Gheeraerts, Marcus, the Younger (*c.*1561–1635).

PLATE 15 A lady called 'Countess of Nottingham' by John de Critz the elder.

PLATE 16
William Cecil, Lord Burghley, on his mule.

NON SINE SOLE
IRIS.

PLATE 19 Queen Elizabeth I, 'The Rainbow Portrait', c.1600 (oil on panel), Isaac Oliver (c.1565–1617).

probity. Did the flirtations associated with courtly love get
hand as time went by? Was the court more stifling during Eliz
later years, resulting in young people wanting to break free? W
young martial men at court—like Essex and Ralegh—more da
than previous courtiers, because of their greater independer
experience of the wars? Did the presence of these gallant w
prove exciting and irresistible to some young women? Did th
no longer command the same devotion, respect, and awe amo
younger generation of men and women who seemed disincl
meet her exacting standards, sexual or otherwise, and more p
to risk her anger? Perhaps all these factors came into play. C
porary gossip suggested that some maids did not take their d
service to the elderly queen as seriously as they should and ha
past. Lady Mary Howard, for example, was said to be negl
her duties in the spring of 1597: not only did she run off to s
young nobleman, but she failed to attend on the queen at t
she was accustomed 'to air in the garden', did not appear 'to c
cup of grace during the dinner', and was absent 'at the hou
majestie's going to prayer'.[109]

It was not easy serving the queen at any time. As Bridget I
was warned on her appointment as maid of honour, she was
to apply herself 'hollye' to the queen's service: 'with all m
love, and obediens; wherein you must be dyligent, secret, ar
full.' Some of the privy chamber women found the 'watchi
sittinges up' with the queen to be 'very tedious', but that wa
their necessary tasks.[110] Far worse was the abuse that the
sometimes had to tolerate. Any one of the queen's wom
become the target of her bad temper, especially when she
fering from emotional stress or physical pain (usually to
Even the most favoured women could suffer in this way
Knollys told his wife that, 'for the outward love that her
bears you, she makes you often weep for unkindness to
danger of your health'.[111] A foreign envoy commented in Ma
that Elizabeth swore at the countess of Warwick, when told
band was ill and could not attend upon her, and was so bad
one evening that she beat one or two of her women.[112] Eliz
humour, moreover, was thought to have grown consisten
during the 1590s, because of her disquiet about 'the Irish a
her last decade, it was said, she was 'more froward than co
she used to bear herself toward her women', now chiding
small neglects' so 'as to make these fair maids often cry and

piteous sort'.[113] Given the queen's conduct, we should not be surprised that some young women chose to break free.

At the same time, Elizabeth was also capable of many acts of kindness and generosity towards her women. When the earl of Hertford was briefly imprisoned in 1595, she wrote reassuringly to her 'good Francke', to stop her worrying unduly: 'we do well understand your disposition to be troubled with sudden impressions even in matters of little moment as wee would not nowe forget you in this accident of your lorde's misfortune.'[114] Whenever one of her women suffered a bereavement, Elizabeth tried to break the news to her personally and gently. She was particularly sensitive when the brother of Mary Ratcliffe died on active service in Ireland: 'by the queen's command' it was kept from the maid until Elizabeth could tell her in person. Once informed, Mary was relieved of her duties and permitted to keep to her chamber. But nothing could comfort the distraught woman, who apparently went about 'to starve her selfe' to death. She was then 'buried as a nobleman's daughter by the queen's command' and all her erstwhile companions 'have gone in blacke' for at least a week afterwards.[115]

Many of the ladies of the privy chamber were the queen's intimates, but can they be considered her friends? In early modern literary culture, inequality in status between two individuals did not preclude friendship, as long as mutuality and reciprocity were integral to the relationship. Ideally, however, reciprocity was not to be based on material or political gain. As Cicero explained in his seminal *De amicitia*—the text that provided the theoretical model for perfect friendship in this period—'freendship is to be desired of men, not ledde thereto with hope of rewarde, but because all the fruicte thereof resteth in very love itselfe'.[116] Or, as Francis Bacon later declared more succinctly: 'it is friendship when a man can say to himself, I love this man without respect of utility.'[117]

Elizabeth herself gave some consideration to the nature of friendship, and thought in those terms. When asked can a friend's request ever be denied, her answer was that, if a friend asked too much, then he or she was no friend:

What friendship is, what I deem to be one uniform consent of two minds such as virtue links and nought but death can break. Therefore I conclude that the house that shrinketh from his [its] foundation shall down for me, for friend leaves he to be that doth demand more than the giver's grant, with reason's leave, may yield. And if so then,

PLATES 17 (*above*) The Family of Henry VIII: An Allegory of the Tudor Succession, *c.*1570–75 (panel), Lucas de Heere (1534–84).

PLATES 18
Portrait of Sir Robert Cecil (1563–1612) 1st Viscount Cranborne and 1st Earl of Salisbury (oil on panel), John de Critz (*c.*1555–*c.*1641) (studio of).

my friend no more, [but] my foe...For where minds differ and opinions swerve, there is scant a friend in that company.[118]

This attitude may help to explain why Elizabeth seems to have been most attached to those ladies—such as the countesses of Huntingdon and Nottingham—who depended least upon her goodwill and requested little in the way of favours. If they knew her attitude, it might also account for their reticence in pushing forward suits directly.

The relationship between Elizabeth and her female courtiers obviously did not conform to the perfect *amicitia* countenanced in much classical and humanist discourse. Furthermore, Cicero identified adulation and flattery as repugnant to friendship, declaring that the exchange of honest advice was an essential component. Yet, it is hard to believe that any of her intimates—male or female—spoke frankly to the queen without any element of flattery.

Nonetheless, friendship in real life very rarely came close to the classical ideal. Rather, friends in early modern England were those individuals who were valued for providing opportunities for sociability and mutual advantage.[119] And Elizabeth's women did fulfil these two practical functions. They offered her companionship and social intercourse; they gave her service, gifts, and an outlet to the wider world of the court. In this sense they were her friends. What is more, although Elizabeth could never be entirely private, subject as she was to observation and comment, it was with her women that she could be most relaxed. Some of them—Kat Astley, Lady Knollys, and the countesses of Huntingdon and Nottingham—also provided deep affective relationships. Elizabeth genuinely and deeply mourned the loss of the three who predeceased her. On the death of Katherine, countess of Nottingham, one observer wrote that Elizabeth took the loss 'muche more heavyly' than did the earl, Katherine's husband; and, according to another report, the queen became so melancholic that she wasted away to die just a month later.[120] If true, their friendship was very close indeed.

Part 3

Councillors

9

'Sir Spirit': Sir William Cecil, Lord Burghley

Three days after her accession, Elizabeth held her first privy council meeting in the hall of her residence at Hatfield. There she formally installed Sir William Cecil as her principal secretary, an appointment that came as no surprise. Towards the end of Queen Mary's last illness, the Spanish ambassador Feria had been told 'for certain' that Cecil would be given the post, and immediately after news of her death reached Hatfield Cecil began work in earnest, setting out a 'memoriall' of things to be done and receiving official correspondence 'accordinge unto the quene's majestie's commandment'.[1] Why was Cecil selected for this key position in the realm? Two reasons stand out: he had both the necessary experience and the new queen's trust.

Cecil acquired his administrative and political experience in Edward VI's reign. Born into a family of minor royal servants in 1520, he had enjoyed a first-class classical education at St John's College, Cambridge, and obtained a legal training at Gray's Inn, London, but it was his second marriage to Mildred Cooke (the daughter of the scholar–courtier Sir Anthony Cooke) that launched his political career. Thanks to Cooke's influence, Cecil was appointed as first the factotum and then the private secretary of Lord Protector Somerset, positions he held from 1547 until the duke lost power in October 1549. With Somerset's fall, Cecil was briefly incarcerated in the Tower, but he survived in government thanks to his exceptional political acumen and administrative abilities. Soon he became the right-hand man of John Dudley, earl of Warwick (created duke of Northumberland in 1552), who was effectively ruling England. In September 1550, Cecil was made a privy councillor and junior secretary of the king; in October the following year, he was knighted. Although, during the succession crisis of 1553, Cecil initially signed the bond promising support for Lady Jane Grey, he swiftly switched sides to recognize Mary. While religious scruples kept him out of office, he nonetheless carried out two diplomatic missions for Mary's government.[2]

Cecil's relationship with Elizabeth was forged during these years. The princess's first known contact with him was about 1548, when, in an undated letter addressed to him from Kat Astley, Elizabeth added a postscript asking him to help 'a poor man's sute' on her behalf.[3] Elizabeth usually communicated with Cecil through Sir Thomas Parry (her cofferer and his distant relative). Parry wrote to Cecil sometimes as Somerset's secretary, passing on the letters the princess wanted to be directed to the lord protector.[4] At other times, Cecil and Elizabeth corresponded, again mainly through Parry, on matters related to her father's inheritance of landed property that she received in May 1548. Cecil's family had been the stewards of the lands before they were assigned to her, and he gradually assumed responsibility for managing them. By the time that Elizabeth had received the final instalment of her estates in February 1550, she trusted Cecil sufficiently to employ him as the 'surveyor' or manager of the lands.[5]

During Mary's reign Cecil also operated as constable and steward of Elizabeth's estates in Lincolnshire, which were near to his own property in the county. As her business manager, he evidently behaved with integrity; and, when appointing him her principal secretary in November 1558, the new queen expressed total confidence in his incorruptibility, exclaiming: 'this judgement I have of yow that yow will not bee corrupted with any maner of guift [gift] and that you wilbee faithfull to the state.'[6] During the Marian years, Elizabeth had also begun to rely upon Cecil for more general advice: in an undated letter sometime late in Mary's reign, Parry was told to ask Cecil how she should style herself in future. Her title 'Lady Elizabeth' was thought inadequate, as it denied her royal status and consequently her right to the throne. Unfortunately Cecil's reply has not survived, but one historian has suggested that she adopted the style 'Elizabeth, King's Edward's sister' at his suggestion.[7]

Although they communicated largely through intermediaries before her accession, Elizabeth had at least two personal meetings with Cecil in Mary's reign. He visited her at Somerset House in February 1558, when Elizabeth came to London, and he was also at Hatfield later that year.[8] We can be fairly sure that, on both occasions, the two discussed plans for ensuring the smooth transition of power to Elizabeth on Mary's death as well as the immediate policies the new queen would pursue.

Throughout his first stint as principal secretary from late 1558 until mid-1572, Cecil met Elizabeth almost every day in her private chambers to discuss and carry out state business. In these sessions, they talked over problems and policies, and Cecil took the opportunity to present and press hard his advice. There, he would also open letters, sometimes reading sections out aloud, sometimes letting her peruse them herself. According to his own account, he never opened correspondence addressed to the queen, 'without hir presence and assent'.[9] Elizabeth would afterwards dictate the text of documents going out in her name, or else give Cecil instructions for drafting them.[10] It was expected that all official correspondence would go through him; indeed, when one of the queen's ambassadors attempted to sidestep the secretary, Elizabeth was both astonished and annoyed that the individual should send her letters 'by this indirect and extraordinary meanes'.[11]

The many important letters directed to the secretary personally, Cecil did open in private. He would then act as a filter, choosing which ones deserved the queen's attention and deciding how best to present their contents to her, sometimes on a 'need-to-know' basis. In August 1561, for example, he downplayed the English losses in a disastrous skirmish against Shane O'Neill in Ulster in order to protect his friend, the lord lieutenant of Ireland: 'I made of the matter a little byckeryng wherin, as it was trew, Shane had the greatest loss,' he reassured the earl of Sussex.[12] Knowing this, Cecil's correspondents often preferred to write to him directly with sensitive information, so that he could 'insinuate' it to the queen in the best way possible to serve their interests.[13]

As principal secretary, Cecil was Elizabeth's key man on the privy council. After opening letters directed to the collective body himself, he would 'assemble' its members as soon 'as the causes require'.[14] At council meetings, he directed the agenda, discussed correspondence, and supervised the routine governmental business raised there. But he did not see his duties as clerical: 'I am no clerk to write your resolutions, nor letters for you or the councell. There be clerks for that purpose,' he told Lord Keeper Nicholas Bacon in July 1563.[15] Instead, Cecil rightly viewed himself as Elizabeth's pre-eminent privy councillor, advising and developing policies with his colleagues on all aspects of royal government, including foreign affairs, domestic security, royal finance, economic issues, and public relations. When she had appointed him secretary, Elizabeth had said: 'I give you this chardge that yow shalbee of my privy counsel and content yourself to take paynes for me and my realme' and 'to give me that counsaill that yow thinke best'.[16] And Cecil used his access to the queen and his role in the privy council to do just that.

Because Elizabeth usually saw no need to intervene directly in routine matters of governance, she left her secretary considerable scope for directing policy. She had relatively little interest in commonwealth issues (such as food supply, poverty, usury), and on these sorts of subjects Cecil's views very often prevailed in council, as can be seen by comparing the recommendations in his memoranda with the policies finally adopted. On policies related to the royal prerogative (religion, foreign affairs, dynastic marriage, and the succession), however, Cecil gave his advice, but Elizabeth had her own strong opinions, and, as we shall see, they did not always accord with her secretary's. Even so, her dependence upon Cecil for counsel can be detected in a Latin note she scribbled to him when he was sick at home. There she described herself as placed 'in such a manner of labyrinth' about Scottish matters that she urgently needed his views about what instructions to send to her ambassador in Edinburgh.[17]

Cecil relinquished the office of principal secretary on 13 July 1572, when he replaced the late William Paulet, marquess of Winchester, as lord high treasurer. Recently ennobled as baron of Burghley on 25 February 1571, he now sat in the House of Lords not the Commons. At the same time, Elizabeth showed her appreciation of Cecil's service by bestowing upon him the order of the garter. Later on, she thought about elevating him to the peerage, but Burghley was content to remain a baron. As he told his friend the sixth earl of Shrewsbury in January 1589:

> Hir majesty had some speche with me to call me to some other degre, but I have shewed hir majesty just cause to leave me as I am, havyng cause to diminish my lyvlihood by provydyng for my younger son; and besyde that, I am meter to be lett down into my grave then to be sett up any higher.[18]

But, even without an earldom, Burghley's prestige and influence were immense. In addition to his offices at the centre of power, he was chancellor of the University of Cambridge, and lord lieutenant of Essex and Lincolnshire.

As lord treasurer, Burghley's prime responsibility was the royal finances, an onerous task that entailed supervising the taxation system, managing crown estates, authorizing expenditure, and presiding over the court of the exchequer, which had jurisdiction over all revenues owed to the crown. During his tenure Burghley was diligent enough, but proved to be somewhat short-sighted and unadventurous. As a result, Elizabeth's income from land and customs failed to keep abreast of inflation. For all his love of maps, Burghley did not order a proper survey of crown lands that would reveal their true extent and worth. At the same time, he failed to act as a hard-headed land-lord on the queen's behalf. His paternalistic outlook and fear of incit-ing social unrest held him back from raising entry fines, imposing market rents, or drawing up new leases that would be more favourable to the crown. Good housekeeping, however, masked this problem. Because the costs of running the royal estates were kept in check or dropped significantly under his management, the net income coming to the crown from land was 40 per cent greater towards the end of the reign than at its start, even though the gross income was falling in real terms.[19]

Burghley could also have done far more to improve the queen's income from customs. During his lord treasuryship, the 1558 book of rates (a handbook setting down the official valuations of imported and exported goods) was not thoroughly updated, despite inflation and the expansion in the value of trade. What was more, Burghley did little to curb the rampant corruption within the customs service. It is estimated that his failure to act on both these fronts cost the queen some half a million pounds of lost revenue.[20] Nor did Burghley overhaul the system of direct taxation (especially the valuation of tax assessment), and as a result cash receipts fell in real terms. During the years of peace, these structural defects in the fiscal and taxation sys-tems did not materially damage the crown, for the queen cut back heavily on expenditure to balance the books and even build up a cash reserve: for example, she spent less than a tenth of her father's budget on royal palaces, while her household costs were limited to £40,000 a year. However, during the war years, the problem of a near static income hit hard, and Elizabeth was forced to run up debts and sell crown lands. Even so, the monarchy ran at a deficit, and the queen's successor had to pick up the tab.

Burghley was also responsible for overseeing the crown's feudal revenues, not as lord treasurer but in his role as master of the court of wards and liveries, an office he held from January 1561 until his death. Although a deputy carried out the day-to-day work, Burghley still presided over the court several times a week and took a personal interest in the supervision of royal wards.[21] Here too, Elizabeth's rev-enues did not benefit from his oversight. Under his watch, the monies coming into the court fell sharply. When Burghley became master, the net annual income had risen over the previous few years to stand at about £29,000, but it dropped to around £11,700 in 1570–1 and was £16,500 at the end of his mastership. The main reason was that most of the profits were siphoned off into private hands, including Burghley's own.[22] He would be offered large 'gifts' in return for lucrative wardships, which would then be sold to the suitor well below the market value. From a confidential paper that was endorsed 'This note to be burned', we learn that, in the last two and a half years of his life, Burghley received £3,016 from eleven individuals who were granted wardships, a sum that was well over three times as much as the profits obtained by the queen from the sale of the very same wardships.[23] So, for all Elizabeth's faith in Burghley's incorruptibility and devotion to her service, the baron lined his and his family's pockets at the queen's expense. Today we would call such practices corruption, but they were standard features of early modern governments.

Despite the major administrative burdens from his two financial offices, Burghley continued to dominate policy-making after stepping down as secretary.[24] His successors relied upon him for assistance and advice, even on relatively minor matters. For example, when preparing a royal proclamation prohibiting the carrying of small arms, Secretary Smith informed Burghley that he had drafted it 'acordyng as I take was yor meanyng', with 'a proviso which some of my lords thought necessary, to th'entent, that yor lordship perusing' it 'may correct and amend it, as yow shall thynk good'.[25] And, indeed, Burghley did compose, correct, or amend many of the council's letters and papers throughout the 1570s and 1580s.[26]

Elizabeth remained equally dependent on Burghley. When, in August 1583, he was laid up with gout at Theobalds and news arrived that Antwerp was under siege, he was immediately summoned back to court.[27] On 7 June 1586, desperate to discuss with her lord treasurer the costs of the campaign in the Netherlands, she came to visit him in his chamber because he was in too much pain to come to her rooms.[28] The following week, Burghley had recovered from illness, so she demanded his attendance at court, even though his presence was required for other business in Westminster.[29] Then, in 1589, Walsingham fell sick, dying in April the following year, and the queen requested that Burghley fill the gap to 'remedy the loss by applying of our selves'.[30] Despite his age and infirmities, Burghley continued until 1596 carrying out some of the secretarial work on top of all his other duties, initially with the intention of keeping the office warm for his younger son, Robert, whom he enlisted as a helpmate, and later because the queen would not let him go.

Burghley seemed irreplaceable because of his wide experience, excellent memory, extraordinary grasp of detail, and calm, reassuring temperament. He made lists of what needed to be done, consulted experts whom he trusted, and wrote 'thought-pieces' that he called 'memoranda', setting down the arguments for and against a particular proposition or policy. His massive archives in Hatfield House and the British Library, as well as the state papers housed at Kew, are filled with the tens of thousands of documents that he composed, read, and commented upon. Burghley's unrivalled expertise on almost every aspect of governing the realms of England, Wales, and Ireland gave him the edge in council meetings. Similarly, whenever he attempted to persuade Elizabeth into following a policy direction that she initially resisted, he used his wide knowledge and unruffled reasoning to present his arguments. He avoided nagging her, like Walsingham, and never stormed off in a temper, as Leicester and Essex were wont to do.

On top of policy-making, Burghley took responsibility for directing Elizabeth's propaganda efforts by both employing polemicists and writing pieces himself. The queen would present the rationale behind governmental policies in preambles to statutes and proclamations, which were often drafted by Burghley, but it was considered unseemly for apologia to go out in her name. As she explained:

> kinges and princes soverains...owe noe service nor tribute to any in the erth but onelie to God Almightie the king of kings [and] are not bownd to mak accompt of theire actions or defences of supposed crimes to anie earthlie persone, being onele answerable to the judgement seate of God ...[31]

So it was left to Burghley and his anonymous team to do the work of defending controversial royal policies.[32] His most important piece here was *The Execution of Justice in England* (1583), which was translated into French, Dutch, and Latin for foreign consumption. There, Burghley defended the crown's imprisonment and hanging of Roman Catholic missionary priests in the voice of a loyal English Catholic. Labelling Jesuits and Catholic seminary priests 'seedmen and sowers of rebellion', Burghley declared they were 'justly condemned as traitors', a view he shared with his queen but one that was naturally disputed by contemporary Catholics.[33] Burghley was also crucial in directing the campaign to discredit Mary Queen of Scots:

he ensured that the 'casket letters' went into print and was behind the pamphlets that made public Mary's involvement in the Norfolk marriage scheme and Catholic conspiracies. His purpose in this particular propaganda effort, however, was not only to act as a spin-doctor for the regime but also to apply pressure on Elizabeth to proceed more energetically against her cousin.

Undoubtedly Burghley had a tremendous capacity for work. But it came at a cost: 'I might wish my body or my fete war of iron or stele, for, with flesh and blood, I can not long endure,' he ruefully complained in June 1586.[34] The following year, he informed Shrewsbury that he had 'late been so oppressed with busynes' and 'therwith joyning my late extreme anguishes in my whole body' that 'I am weary to lyve'.[35] To his son in 1594, he declared: 'I live in pain, and yet spare not to occupie my self for hir majestie's cawses'; and indeed the schedule he outlined bore out his words.[36] Burghley's ill health was a great trial. As he entered his fifties, he frequently complained of pain in his legs and fingers from gout, or in his back from a stone. When in severe pain, he worked in his house on the Strand or retired to Theobalds, close enough to London to receive dispatches quickly; only on a couple of occasions could he slip away to Buxton to undergo the spa's medicinal regime.[37] During absences, he was always ready to return to court if his presence 'war ether nedefull or required'—which it often was—even when he feared further damage to his health by attending upon the queen.[38]

Burghley chose to be the queen's workhorse, for it put him at the centre of power, and, besides, he had little interest in recreational pursuits. Unlike Elizabeth, he had no passion for hunting, riding, dancing, or gambling: for companions on these fronts, she turned to Leicester, Hatton, or other courtiers. Burghley did occasionally hunt deer, but, as he was incapacitated by gout, his main exercise was walking or riding a little mule around his grounds, as depicted in his portrait (Plate 16).[39] In his 'time off' from public affairs, he was busy with private business. Apart from routine household matters, he put much time and thought into designing and managing the extensive and complicated building projects carried through at his three great houses: Cecil House on the Strand in London, Burghley House in Northamptonshire, and Theobalds in Hertfordshire.[40] 'If he had no business, which was very seldom,' wrote Burghley's long-term personal secretary and biographer, 'he was reading or collecting'.[41] A workaholic himself, Burghley disapproved of what he saw as idleness and frivolity in others. The letters he directed to his older son's tutor and chaperone in the autumn of 1561 are revealing in this respect. There he sounds dismayed and disgusted with the behaviour of the 19-year-old Thomas, who was supposedly studying in France but had to be warned by his father against falling into sloth, 'lewdness', extravagance, and self-indulgence.[42]

It is tempting, therefore, to think of Burghley as a very dull stick. Yet, it would be a mistake. He was certainly serious-minded and self-disciplined, but he well understood the value of courtly activities such as archery, hunting, and music-making.[43] He also enjoyed convivial society and lively conversation. His servants described him as liking 'to be merry' in company and 'a man free from all care and business' when hosting a dinner.[44] Burghley himself recommended that heavyweight matters should not be discussed over social meals, for 'meat and drink requireth meaner talk' and 'honest, merry talk'.[45] Indeed, the dedicated royal servant and genial host were two sides of the public persona that Burghley liked to project. In formal portraits, he was painted as the grave and wise statesman, usually dressed in black and carrying the staff of office; in letters he would often refer to the sacrifices he was making in the queen's service and proclaim that the sole purpose of his life was her well-being. Yet, knowing the value that Elizabethan society placed on hospitality and lively conversation, he generously and charmingly entertained scholars, colleagues, foreign visitors, and the queen.[46] All his houses were self-consciously designed not for private living but for entertaining Elizabeth, courtiers, and foreign ambassadors in the magnificent style recommended in classical texts.

However, Elizabeth never stayed at Cecil's principal seat at Burghley House. During her progress to Northamptonshire in 1564, she dined at his mother's home in the town of Stamford, presumably because the building works at Burghley were still underway. The queen's intended visit to the new prodigy house in the summer of 1566 had to be cancelled when Cecil's daughter Anne fell ill with what was thought to be smallpox. Nevertheless, since Burghley House was situated on the main arterial road from London to the north and within striking distance of Norwich, its owner had realistic, if unfulfilled, hopes that the queen might one day venture there. In anticipation of a visit from the court, Burghley continued lavishing huge sums on improving the house and gardens, but it was not to be.[47]

By contrast, Elizabeth visited Theobalds on progress on at least twelve occasions. The first was on 27 July 1564, the year that Cecil purchased the estate. It is unlikely that Elizabeth actually lodged there then, as the small manor house on the site was too modest and old-fashioned to meet her needs. The next time the queen stopped there was on her progress in September 1571, and by then the place had been transformed into a palatial mansion, matching Burghley's own transformation into a peer of the realm. Nonetheless, Elizabeth found fault 'with the small mesure of hir chamber', so Burghley continued to pour money into enlarging and embellishing the building until it reached the status of 'a princely seate' some fifteen years later.[48] He also paid attention to creating formal gardens, a variety of orchards, and ornamental water features that would provide an ideal setting for the house.

Very much to the queen's taste, Theobalds—only twenty miles from London—became a favourite haunt for Elizabeth. 'She was never in any place better pleased, and sure the howse, garden and walks may compare with any delicat place in Italy.' She sometimes invited 'strangers and ambassadors' to the house: 'where she hath been seen in as great royalty and served as bountifully and magnificently as at any other time or place'.[49] As part of the magnificence, Burghley set up a vessel in the form of a bunch of grapes just inside the gate-house so that 'when the queen is present they draw white wine from one part of it and red wine from another'.[50] No doubt, these royal visits were more relaxing for Elizabeth than for Burghley, who organized the living arrangements and counted the substantial cost of his hospitality.[51]

According to one contemporary, Burghley put on 'rich shows, pleasant devices, and all manner of sports' during royal visits to Theobalds.[52] However, only two fragmentary manuscript texts of 'shows'—those devised for the queen's stays in 1591 and 1594—are extant. It is possible that the dramatic interludes commissioned to entertain the court at other visits have not survived, but it could be that Burghley preferred in general not to stage masques and 'shows' for his royal mistress. The repose he offered at Theobalds would then make an effective contrast with the ostentatious courtier entertainments produced at other prodigy houses, such as Kenilworth; and the splendour of his house and gardens could also be admired without distractions.[53] When in 1591 and 1594 Burghley did put on a 'show' for the queen, he had a particular purpose in mind, intending to convey a particular message: the presentation of Robert as his political heir and potentially Elizabeth's new principal secretary.[54]

On the court's arrival at Theobalds on the afternoon of 10 May 1591, Elizabeth was greeted by an actor, dressed as a hermit, who delivered a speech of welcome in verse. Reminding the queen of

Burghley's recent bereavements—the deaths of his mother (in 1588), favourite daughter Anne (also in 1588), and wife Mildred (in 1589)—the hermit explained that Burghley, overtaken with 'excessyve greefe', had retired from the grand house and 'betooke hym to my sylly hermytage'. His sons and grandchildren, who were all present, stood ready—'deteyfull & dyllygent'—to fill in for Burghley and greet the queen in his place. The lord chancellor, Christopher Hatton, was then handed a mock charter to read out, the wording of which suggested assent to the hermit's oration. Burghley would be the new 'hermit of Theobalds', partially disengaged from public life.

Somewhat later—we do not know when—two players cast as a gardener and a mole-catcher embarked on a dialogue in prose, which combined flattery of the queen with the presentation of the 27-year-old Robert Cecil as Burghley's replacement. Robert, 'the yongest son of this honourable ould man', declared the gardener, had commanded the planting of an arbour of eglantine rose (a symbol for Elizabeth) in his garden at nearby Pymmes. Though this was superficially an infertile site, the plant would flourish: 'the deeper yt is rooted in the grounde, the sweeter it smelleth in the flower makinge it ever so greene, that the son of Spaine att the hottest cannot parche itt'. In other words, despite Robert's disadvantages (his youth and the deformity of a hunchback), the queen would thrive when he came to exercise political power, as secure from the threat of Spain as she was now with his father in control. The mole-catcher took up the theme. Pronouncing that Robert would uncover and destroy 'the moles in fildes', which 'were like ill subjectes in commonwelthes', the actor implied that Robert, like his father, would maintain the domestic security of the realm against dissidents.

Initially Elizabeth seemed to concur with the sentiment of the entertainment. On the morning of her departure from Theobalds, she knighted Robert, and that August she appointed him a privy councillor. But Burghley's hopes that he might be relieved of his duties as secretary in favour of his son were not immediately realized. For that reason, at Elizabeth's next visit to the house in June 1594, Burghley reprised the hermit's speech with an added note of urgency.[55] Reminding the queen of the passing of time, which 'leaves only yow untouched', the hermit told her that, since her last visit Burghley had been 'laden with yeares, oppressed with sicknes, having spent his strength for publick service', and now desired 'to be ridd of wordly cares, by ending his dayes', yet 'your majestie, with a band of princlie, kindnes even when he is most greviosly sicke, and lowest brought, holdes him back'. Robert, meanwhile, had done her good service, concluded the hermit: 'although his experience and judgment, be noe waie comparable, yett as the report goeth, he hath something in him like the child of such a parent.' Yet again Burghley's hope was foiled; it took another two years before his son was appointed principal secretary, thereby allowing the baron to retire from his duties.

Elizabeth dubbed Burghley her 'spirit'.[56] The nickname signified that he understood and carried through her wishes; it also implied that the two had much in common and saw eye to eye on most matters. To a certain extent this was true.[57] As far as their religious beliefs were concerned, both were committed and pious protestants who had reluctantly attended mass under Mary and were equally determined in November 1558 to dismantle the Roman Catholic Church in England and reintroduce a protestant form of worship. Intellectually they shared a strong interest in astrology and alchemy. Elizabeth famously consulted John Dee to predict a propitious day for her coronation and, less famously, defended his alchemical *Monas hieroglyphica* in 1564; Burghley had astrological charts drawn up and put his trust in alchemists' schemes to improve the royal finances.[58] As products of a humanist education, monarch and minister were lovers of the classics, valuing scholarship, and taking inspiration from the works of ancient writers. While queen, Elizabeth continued to read Latin and Greek texts with her Latin secretary, Roger Ascham, and her favourite author was said to be Seneca; for his part, Burghley's secular bible was Cicero's *De officiis* (*On Duties*), a three-volume essay that he reportedly carried around with him. Both valued the classical virtues of prudence, moderation, and temperance—qualities they tried to live up to. Elizabeth's caution is legendary; Burghley's memoranda reveal how he always weighed up arguments before committing himself to a line of action. Furthermore, after the disastrous Newhaven adventure of 1562–3, he—like the queen—became increasingly wary of military interventions abroad on behalf of protestant internationalism. The queen was renowned for her frugality, while Burghley kept tight control over her expenditure. In their personal lives, they each had a streak of temperance, being moderate in their eating habits, a characteristic that helps explain their long lives.

Yet, despite their shared values and outlook, Burghley and the queen diverged in their thinking over some crucial aspects of policy. At times they would pull in different directions, although their disagreements very seldom led to direct confrontations or estrangement.

Throughout his Elizabethan political career, Burghley wrestled with the dilemma of what to do when the queen rejected his advice and how to reconcile his conscience with his duty of obedience to her. Ultimately, his obedience to Elizabeth took priority: if he failed to convince her into his way of thinking after plainly and strongly stating his opinions, he outwardly accepted her decision because of his respect for the royal prerogative. As he told his son Robert: 'I will not change my opinion by affirming the contrary, for that were to offend God, to whom I am sworn first, but as a servant I will obey her majestie's commandment.'[59] However, on two occasions at least, Burghley came close to disobedience; and on many others, he worked behind the scenes in attempts to manipulate the queen and effect a change in policy.

Monarch and minister were generally in step when it came to continental politics. Both recognized the limitations of England's finances and defences that precluded a direct, full-scale war against Spain, yet neither was an appeaser. Burghley would sometimes march more decisively towards a particular foreign-policy objective—such as the treaties of Nonsuch with the Netherlands in 1585. Yet sometimes he would lag behind the queen: he was less keen than her on a dynastic marriage alliance with France in 1579 and 1581, and downright opposed to the confiscation of the Spanish treasure seized by Francis Drake during the sea captain's circumnavigation of the globe. During the war years, Burghley was less gung-ho than Essex; he had doubts about the Cadiz voyage, for example, and was always ready to extend peace overtures to Spain.[60] The areas of serious policy differences concerned religion, Mary Queen of Scots, and the succession.

Taking religion first, circumstantial evidence suggests that the principal secretary would have preferred a more radical protestant programme than the settlement that emerged in 1559.[61] Despite this, he accepted the prayer book as protestant enough, but evidently hoped for further reform and approved the moderate changes proposed by bishops and MPs in the mid-1560s and beyond. By contrast, Elizabeth considered the work of reform complete in 1559 and vetoed the religious changes put forward in the convocation (church assembly) of 1563 and parliament of 1566. Among the ecclesiastical reforms Cecil later backed—and Elizabeth rejected—were those designed to eliminate pluralism (clerics holding more than one living), so that parishes could be served with well-educated ministers.[62] Whereas Elizabeth had developed a deep suspicion of preaching owing to her fear of radicals dominating the pulpits, Burghley wanted the protestant Church to be a dynamic institution that evangelized and edified the laity through preaching. If sermons were absent or inadequate, he argued, popery could not be eradicated and the 'state of religion [would be] many weis weakned by coldness in the trew service of God'.[63] What was more, if the English Church continued to lack proper preaching and education, the Catholic missionaries who started to enter the realm in 1574—and especially the Jesuits who first arrived in 1580—would prosper. In order to counteract their message, reasoned Burghley, people needed to learn the errors of Catholic teaching and be instructed in true religion.[64]

Following on from this, Elizabeth and Burghley were at odds over the episcopal clampdown on protestant nonconformity. The queen believed that 'puritans' and presbyterians were at least as great a threat as papists to her monarchical authority, the royal supremacy, and the stability of the state.[65] Like Archbishop Whitgift, she was convinced that their sermons, pamphlets, and disobedience encouraged popular contempt not just for the prayer book and episcopacy but also for lawful and hierarchical authority in general.[66] Burghley strongly disagreed. He saw popery as the far greater peril, and he questioned whether those protestants, whose consciences held them back from wearing full clerical dress or performing all the rites in the prayer book, endangered the Church and State at all. Nor was he convinced that all presbyterians were seditious, as Elizabeth and the bishops claimed. To his mind, presbyterians (such as Thomas Cartwright and Walter Travers) had been driven into radical positions by the bishops' failure to reform the Church and policy of repression. Only extremists who utterly condemned the doctrine, discipline, prayer book, and governance of the Church did he brand subversives who should be prosecuted.[67]

Despite their different emphasis and outlook on this matter, Burghley's conscience did not lead him into a confrontation with Elizabeth until the mid-1580s. Before then, he accepted that the drive for conformity was within the queen's powers as supreme governor of the Church. Consequently, he had had no problem in upholding the royal supremacy in the mid-1560s by enforcing orders that demanded a uniformity of rites, ceremonies, and clerical dress as laid down by the prayer book.[68] For the same reason, in the mid-1570s, Burghley could not defend Archbishop Grindal's refusal to implement Elizabeth's directive to suppress prophesyings, 'wherby he [Grindal] did shew him self disobedient to hir majesty and hir supreme authoritie ecclesiasticall and for that purpose hir majesty cold do no less than to restrayne hym as she hath done'.[69] Although Burghley sought a compromise that would allow Grindal to stay in post, he saw the need for the archbishop to admit his fault and seek pardon.[70]

After Grindal's death and Whitgift's promotion to Canterbury in 1583, Burghley's conscience did play up. In particular he questioned the legality of the instruments used in the archbishop's anti-puritan campaign. Whitgift was demanding clerical subscription to twenty-four articles (later reduced to three) on pain of suspension or deprivation, and applying an *ex officio* oath to godly ministers who were suspected of subversive activities.[71] As this oath required a defendant to promise to answer questions truthfully before knowing what the questions actually were, it allowed self-incrimination, and was consequently an affront to common-law principles. Common lawyers—and Burghley—therefore vigorously contested its legitimacy, believing the bishops were overstepping their authority. In June 1584, Burghley protested to Whitgift that his methods smacked of the Spanish Inquisition: 'I think the inquisitors of Spain use not so many questions to comprehend and to trap their preyes.' Besides, thought Burghley, the timing of the anti-puritan drive was dangerous and absurd, for the episcopal authorities were provoking divisions and dissent within the Church just when protestant unity was needed against the major Catholic threat from recusants, Jesuits, and Spain.[72] Elizabeth, however, stood firmly behind Whitgift, as Burghley and the archbishop well knew she would.[73] As a result, for the first time in his career, Burghley found himself out of favour with the queen. It was in the summer of 1584 that Lady Cobham referred to the queen's displeasure towards him for raising a 'grievous' topic in a letter; and probably that topic concerned his dislike of the archbishop's proceedings.[74]

Because of royal support for Whitgift, Burghley's protests carried little weight. The queen brought the archbishop onto the privy council in February 1586, and thereafter (wrote the archbishop's secretary and later biographer) his 'courses...were not so much crossed nor impeded as heretofore'.[75] After the deaths of Leicester, Walsingham, and Mildmay—all protectors of moderate puritans—Burghley grew ever more isolated on the privy council, and proved unable in 1589 and 1590 to slow down the process of Whitgift's prosecution of Cartwright and other presbyterians in, first, the ecclesiastical court of High Commission and then Star Chamber.[76] Burghley's attempts to shield those he considered godly moderates also received a setback when the extremist fringe of the puritan movement gave the bishops a justification for renewing their allegation that all presbyterians were

'seditious'. The publication in 1588 and 1589 of comic and scurrilous pamphlets lampooning the bishops (under the pseudonym
'Martin Marprelate') created a furore, incensed Whitgift and his episcopal colleagues, and encouraged them to root out and prosecute
presbyterian leaders. Two years later, the bishops also exploited the
case of the mentally unhinged William Hacket to present puritans as
subversives; Hacket claimed to be the messiah and predicted the
deaths of several privy councillors if the presbyterian ministers under
arrest were not released.[77]

Given all these circumstances, Burghley decided against taking on
Whitgift directly. Instead, he aimed to deflect attention away from the
prosecution of moderate puritans and towards the persecution of
Catholics and 'turbulent' protestants 'who do violently seke to chang
the externall government of the Church'.[78] In November 1591, this
strategy had some success when he persuaded Elizabeth to issue a
royal proclamation establishing commissions to search out seminary
priests, Jesuits, and their lay Catholic supporters in England. That
Elizabeth agreed to the draconian measure is somewhat surprising,
for she usually worked to mitigate the severity of anti-Catholic laws,
but Burghley may have panicked her into action through his warnings that Philip II was planning a second invasion in 1592 and that
John Dee had predicted its success. The illness and death of Hatton
on 20 November, moreover, removed the influence of the most effective
spokesman against the draft proclamation.[79]

Over time, the 1591 proclamation did result in the government
and Church devoting more of its energies to punishing Catholics
rather than puritans, just as Burghley had wanted, but this was not
immediately apparent. In April 1593, Whitgift saw to it that the protestant sectarians Henry Barrow and John Greenwood were hanged,
despite two previous reprieves. Burghley spoke very peremptorily
about their executions to Whitgift and the bishop of Worcester, whom
he held responsible, 'and used some speache to the queen'. His protest had no effect, however, as another radical—John Penry—was
executed at Tyburn six weeks later.[80] After this, Whitgift's drive
against nonconformists lost momentum, but this was largely because
of the archbishop's success in breaking the organization of the presbyterian movement.

The second major area of Burghley's disagreement with the queen
arose over the twin problems of Mary Queen of Scots and the succession. Right from the beginning of the reign, Cecil was out of step with
his monarch about these vital areas of policy. Living in constant and

acute fear that the Roman Catholic Scottish queen might one day take Elizabeth's crown, either by usurpation or by natural succession, he long pressed Elizabeth to take pro-active policies: the English queen should name a protestant heir presumptive until she married and bore a child; and she should intervene aggressively in Scotland to the disadvantage of Mary. Elizabeth, however, did not accept his advice. She was adamant about refusing to name an heir, tried to reach a political settlement with Mary, and needed convincing that military intervention over the border would not prove perilous. As for marriage, although she declared herself ready to oblige, she found difficulties with each of the candidates on offer.

The differences between monarch and minister first emerged in 1559, when the Scottish protestant Lords of the Congregation re-belled against Mary of Guise, the French-born regent ruling Scotland in her daughter's name. From the very outset, for both ideological and strategic reasons, Cecil wanted the rebels to receive financial and military aid from England. As he told their leaders in July:

> rather than that realme [Scotland] shulde be with a forren nation and power oppressed and deprived of the aunciente liberties therto belonging, and the nobilitie, and specially suche as at this presente seeke to mayntayne the trueth of Christian religion, be expelled, the authoritie of Inglande wold adventure with power and force to ayde them.[81]

By 'foreign nation' Cecil meant, of course, France. The Scottish queen was then married to the dauphin, very soon to be the king of France, and Cecil expected French troops to arrive any day to suppress the protestant rising. His main fear was that, once Scotland had been conquered, the French army would turn its army towards England with the intention of deposing Elizabeth, crowning Mary, and restoring Catholicism. In the summer of 1559, Cecil judged that the Scots should be aided, first 'with all fair promises first, next with money, and last with armes'; by October that year he was certain that arms were necessary, for it had become evident that the rebels on their own could not avoid defeat.[82]

Elizabeth saw things differently. She detested John Knox, a prime mover of the rebellion, had no wish to encourage protestant rebellion in other countries, and feared international repercussions if she inter-vened militarily in Scotland. To be persuaded otherwise, she needed subtle handling. Cecil, therefore, bypassed her completely in the initial negotiations with the Scots, when he was assuring them of

English support and articulating his vision of a protestant Britain. After he had eventually brought the queen into the deliberations, he made sure that the arguments for military intervention were framed to play down ideological considerations and focus instead on the strategic threat to England if the Scottish lords were suppressed. Cecil also ensured that the representative of the lords, who arrived at court late in November 1559 in search of military aid, spoke to the queen about French tyranny in Scotland, not the rebels' religious aspirations, and emphasized the dire danger that France posed to England.[83]

On 15 December 1559, the question of military intervention was brought before the privy council. There, Cecil found as much difficulty in persuading some of his colleagues about the immediacy of the French threat and the wisdom of sending an army to Scotland as he had previously experienced with the queen. He could get them to agree only to fortify garrisons close to the border and take naval action to stop French reinforcements landing in Scotland.[84] The next day, the queen concurred with these limited measures: she instructed Admiral William Winter to sail north with a fleet of fourteen ships of war primarily to provision Berwick, Tynemouth, and Holy Island with munitions, but also, if necessary, 'to doo some effectuall enterprise upon the French navye...which otherwise shall tend to the grete danger of this our realm'. At the same time, Elizabeth ordered the levying of troops to defend the border.[85]

Still Cecil was not satisfied. He was certain that the French would 'within a moneth have there wills in Scotland', and feared that England was insufficiently strong to withstand the military invasion that would immediately follow. In his opinion, Elizabeth needed to send the duke of Norfolk to the borders 'reddy both to defend, and to invade or offend if cause be gyven';[86] and he put this recommendation before the council a week later. Learning that a convoy of troops had indeed left France for Scotland, all but one privy councillor agreed that a French invasion of England now appeared imminent. The whole body consequently endorsed Cecil's proposal for an immediate military response on the ground. But, perhaps because fighting in midwinter was far from ideal, a few councillors still preferred to defer outright hostilities. In any event, Cecil's plan of action was 'not allowed by the queen', even though she did dispatch Norfolk to Newcastle to help organize England's defences.[87]

At some point during December, Cecil became so disillusioned with the queen's refusal to launch an immediate assault into Scotland that he prepared in desperation a letter of resignation.[88] 'With a sorrowfull harte and watery eies,' he begged to 'be spared to entermedle' in the execution of Elizabeth's policy towards Scotland, since she misliked his advice and he could not 'with my conscience gyve any contrary advise'. He was 'sworne to be a minister of your majestie's determinations and not of myne owne', he wrote, but could not 'serve your majesty in any thing that my self can not allow'.[89] We cannot be sure that Cecil delivered his letter to the queen, but he wrote it in a fair hand and presumably intended it for her eyes. All we know for certain is that he remained in post, continuing his responsibilities towards Scotland. But then he had little reason to resign, because Elizabeth's aid to the rebels accelerated incrementally from December onwards, until, on 27 February 1560, she agreed to the treaty of Berwick, which committed her to open military intervention on their behalf.[90]

The ensuing campaign in Scotland was hardly a roaring success in military terms: an English attack on Leith in May 1560 was repulsed with some 500 casualties. Nonetheless, England won the peace. The treaty of Edinburgh, which had been negotiated by Cecil and other diplomats, secured almost everything the secretary wanted: the evacuation of the French from Scotland; Mary's renunciation of her immediate title to Elizabeth's crown; and Scotland to be governed by lords appointed by the Scottish monarch and her parliament. The religious question was to be postponed until a parliament was held in August 1560, and in that month a protestant Kirk was established. Despite these considerable achievements, Cecil initially earned little thanks from his mistress, who was dissatisfied at the expense of the campaign and disappointed that he had not secured the restoration of Calais in the peace terms, as 'a recompence for the great and dishonorable injuries that the sayd Frenche king and queene have offered unto us by using our armes and the tytles of our realmes'.[91] In fact, Elizabeth's instructions about Calais arrived after the treaty had been signed on 6 July 1560, much to Cecil's relief. As he bluntly told the queen, her demand was unrealistic and, if implemented, would have been counter-productive.[92]

Cecil's disagreements with Elizabeth over Scotland in 1559 were, therefore, satisfactorily resolved without incurring any damage to their personal or political relationship. Over the next few years, their approaches to the problem of the Scottish queen also significantly diverged, and for the most part Cecil similarly avoided any major confrontation with his mistress. After Mary's return to Scotland in May 1561, Cecil did not trust the Scottish queen one iota, believing that her continuing ambition to seize the English throne was evidenced by her refusal to ratify the treaty of Edinburgh.[93] Yet, although he would have much preferred Mary to be diplomatically isolated and excised from the succession, he ostensibly—if unenthusiastically—followed his sovereign's lead in her quest 'to kepe amytie' with the Scottish queen.[94] In consequence, Mary's protestant ministers, who had earlier been Cecil's allies, found him half-hearted, even withdrawn, when dealing with Anglo-Scottish matters: 'as in your letters yow always wrote obscurely, in privat communication yow seldom utered your owne judgement,' complained William Maitland of Lethington in 1564.[95] While keeping quiet, Cecil worked behind the scenes to unearth evidence of Mary plotting against Elizabeth in an effort to end the 'amity'.[96]

When it came to persuading Elizabeth to marry and settle the succession, Cecil was equally discreet and devious during the 1560s. He used all his powers of persuasion and diplomacy to promote the queen's marriage with a foreign prince, but not to the point of quarrelling with her. With regard to the succession, he favoured a parliamentary settlement and the title of Lady Katherine Grey, but, well aware of Elizabeth's opposition to this solution, he held his tongue on this issue as well, leaving others to take the initiative in presenting the case. Nowhere was this more obvious than in the parliaments held in 1563 and 1566.

Before the 1563 parliamentary session, Cecil admitted: 'I thynke somewhat will be attempted to acertayne the realme of a successor to this crowne but I feare the unwillyngnes of hir majesty to have such a person knowen will stey that matter.' His fear was justified. The Commons petitioned the queen to introduce a succession bill, but she blunted their initiative by promising to marry, so that, in her words, 'the realme shall not remayne destitute of an heire that may be a fit governor'.[97] Welcome as her change of heart was on that front, the danger remained that Elizabeth might still die childless, leaving a power vacuum at the centre and opening up the possibility of civil war. In desperation, Cecil drafted an emergency piece of legislation that provided for the establishment of an interregnum council on the queen's death with responsibility for summoning a parliament to elect a new monarch. Since Roman Catholics had just been barred from sitting in the Commons, Cecil could be confident that the parliamentary choice would fall on a protestant claimant and not Mary. But the draft bill got nowhere. Cecil may not even have presented it to the House, for he knew the queen would anyway veto it.

When parliament met again in September 1566, the queen was still unmarried and the problem of the succession more urgent than ever, since Mary had just given birth to a son. Again, Cecil realistically recognized that Elizabeth would not agree to establish an heir by statute: 'to require the succession is hardest to be obteyned, both for the difficulte to discuss the right and for the lothsomness in the queen majesty to consent therto.'[98] He was proved correct. After a tussle with MPs, Elizabeth was forced to admit that 'consideration' of the succession 'belongeth properly to hir majesty and the three estates of the realme', but she rejected any such parliamentary discussion on the grounds that it was too perilous 'to enter at this tyme into the decision therof'.[99] She again promised to consider marriage, but, when an attempt was made to include her promise within the preamble of the subsidy bill, she was furious: 'I know no reason why any my private answers to the realm should be made for prologue to a subsidies,' she scrawled at the foot of the bill, which was drafted by Cecil. The preamble had to be rewritten.[100]

During both these parliamentary sessions, Cecil kept his involvement in the drive to secure a succession bill under wraps. Not only did he allow others to take centre stage in presenting petitions, but in 1566 he also acted as Elizabeth's spokesman in the Commons, warning MPs in her name against continuing their petitions about marriage and succession.[101] Cecil would not risk a major dispute with the queen over an issue that he knew was impossible to win. As a result, Elizabeth's anger at the parliamentary lobbying was directed elsewhere: in 1566, Norfolk, Leicester, Northampton, and Pembroke bore the brunt of her rage.

After Mary's loss of power in Scotland, Elizabeth and Cecil again held different views. Unlike Elizabeth, Cecil quietly approved of Mary's deposition and wanted her to be put on trial for the murder of her husband. Norfolk's conspiracies, the northern rising of 1569, and the Ridolfi plot of 1571 gave him the opportunities to press home his standpoint. He now became more outspoken, and was 'bold to shew' his opinion to Elizabeth and give recommendations.[102] But Elizabeth held back from carrying through all his advice. In early 1572, for example, she postponed signing the warrant for Norfolk's execution, avoided putting Mary on trial, and offered only limited aid to the protestant regency in Scotland. At the same time, the 39-year-old Elizabeth was still unmarried, and the English succession continued to be unsettled.

Thoroughly exasperated, Burghley released his frustrations in writing a paper in April 1572, entitled 'Certen matters wherein the queen's majesty's forbearing and delayes hath produced not only inconveniences and incress of expences, but also dangers'. Three of his five points concerned Elizabeth's policy towards Mary, Scotland, and the succession: 'her coldness and forbearing...to proceed in marriage', her 'doubtful dealing' with the Queen of Scots, and her unwillingness 'to aid directly' the king of Scotland, 'whose party is wholly for the queen's majesty'.[103] Another concerned Elizabeth's failure to be tough on Catholics, while the final point criticized her unwillingness to create more peers to strengthen the realm.

A few months afterwards, Burghley took heart—albeit briefly—from events in parliament. Although Elizabeth continued to protect her cousin, the calls for Mary's and Norfolk's executions in both houses led her to sign the duke's death warrant, and on 2 June he was executed. Elizabeth also permitted a bill to exclude Mary from the succession to proceed through the Commons. Disappointment soon ensued. As Burghley disconsolately told Walsingham, then based in France: 'all that we laboured for, and had with full consent brought to fashion' in the parliamentary bill, 'was by her majestie neither assented to nor rejected, but deferred'.[104] By the end of the year Burghley was again thoroughly alarmed with what he saw as his monarch's lack of leadership qualities:

> If hir majesty will contnew hir delayes for provyding for hir own surety by just meanes given to hir by God, she and we all shall vaynely call upon God when the calamitie shall fall upon us. God send hir majesty strength of spirit to preserve God's cause, hir own lyf, and lyves of millyens of good subjects, all which ar most manifestly in danger, and that only by hir delayes, and so consequently she will be the cause of the overthrow of a noble crown and realm.[105]

Over the next few years Burghley's disillusionment with Elizabeth was to die down over, as the dangers from Scotland and Mary receded or at least looked less acute. With Mary in secure confinement, a protestant regent successful against her party in Scotland, and her Guise cousins embroiled in renewed civil war in France, there seemed little chance of the Catholic claimant taking the English throne by force in the event of Elizabeth's sudden death. The most likely successor now looked to be James VI of Scotland, who was in the care of Calvinist tutors. During this period, Burghley may not always have been comfortable with Elizabeth's decisions—or what he saw as a lack of decisions—but he did not think that she was seriously endangering the realm, perhaps because, on questions related to internal security, they were at one: Elizabeth gave him free range to clamp down on recusancy, sniff out conspiracies, and bring to trial Catholic priests.

However, the political crises of the early 1580s changed Burghley's mind. He again felt deeply troubled that Elizabeth did not appear to be taking purposeful action against the fresh dangers confronting the realm. Jesuits were pouring into England (or so he thought); James VI no longer looked a sure-fire anglophile protestant who would make a satisfactory heir or safeguard the northern border from invasion; Spanish power had grown alarmingly with Philip II's conquest of Portugal in 1580; and in 1583 the Throckmorton plot to murder the queen was revealed, implicating the Spanish ambassador, English Catholics, and the Guises. Then, in 1584, William of Orange was assassinated, intensifying fears for the queen's safety and leaving his cause in the Netherlands on the brink of disaster. Burghley and his fellow privy councillors now demanded drastic remedies: English military support for the Dutch rebels against Spain and further action against Mary. It was over the latter that Elizabeth and Burghley fell out.

The queen had no objection to the 'instrument' or bond of association that Burghley devised with the support of Walsingham and Leicester.[106] With Mary and James as its targets, the bond obliged all signatories individually to hunt down and kill anyone who made an attempt on Elizabeth's life or claimed the throne on her assassination. However, to reinforce the bond, Burghley and his colleagues planned that the parliament, called for November 1584, would introduce a bill for the Queen's Surety, which would protect Elizabeth against an assassination attempt. At around the same time, Burghley resurrected his earlier scheme to provide for an interim council to govern England on Elizabeth's death until parliament elected a new monarch. Elizabeth disliked both measures. Probably because of her intervention, the wording of the Act for the Queen's Surety that passed in March 1585 was amended so as to exclude James from its provision; the second scheme was never discussed in parliament.

Elizabeth was evidently very cross with Burghley's activities in this parliament. Although the year is not certain, it was very likely on 14 March 1585 that the lord treasurer wrote: 'I am so wounded with the late sharp and most heavy speeches of hir majesty to my self in the hearing of my Lord of Lecester and Mr Secretary Walsyngham.'

The queen's reprimand, Burghley explained, came after she had called him into her presence to discuss the Netherlands but then brought up the issue of Mary. After that interview, Elizabeth's 'displesor' and 'indignation' had grown to such an extent that Burghley suspected 'some secret enemyes' were stoking it. He even considered withdrawing from those public affairs in which he was 'not expressly by her majesty commanded' until her displeasure abated.[107]

As usual Elizabeth's anger did subside. But, two years later, Burghley's determination to bring Mary to the scaffold resulted in a longer-lasting rift with the queen. With the exposures of the Throckmorton, Parry, and Babington plots, the lord treasurer—along with other councillors—was urging Elizabeth to impose the death penalty on Mary. Although she eventually agreed to a trial, Elizabeth would not commit to an execution. She had told Burghley 'to forbear' pronouncing Mary's conviction before the tribunal sat in October, and she postponed publishing the death sentence until 4 December. Even then, she avoided signing a death warrant drawn up shortly afterwards.[108] So, when Elizabeth unexpectedly signed a new warrant on 1 February, Burghley summoned the privy council to meet secretly in his chambers, where all the ten councillors who attended agreed to send the document to Fotheringhay immediately without informing the queen.[109]

When told that Mary's execution had taken place, Elizabeth flew into a terrible rage, so much so that Burghley expressed alarm that 'therby your helth, the maintenance of your liff, must nedes be hyndred'.[110] The queen 'charged all her counsellors, which weare privie theareunto, most bitterlie', but 'her indignation lighteth most upon my lord treasurer and Mr Davison'. For months afterwards, Elizabeth refused to allow Burghley into her presence. Only in late June 1587 was the breach between them mended when she marked her readiness to forgive and forget by declaring her intention to come to Theobalds and 'abyde ther, as she sayth, a fortnight or three wekes'.[111] By then, Elizabeth could afford to let Burghley return to his usual place in her confidences, since she had successfully signalled to the world—especially James VI and the French—that she should not be held responsible for Mary's death; and she had also communicated to her privy councillors that they should not act independently. With Mary out of the way, Elizabeth and Burghley had little cause for further disagreement over Anglo-Scottish relations, or even the succession. As seen, religion still divided them, but their energies went into managing the continental war and suppressing rebellion in Ireland, neither of which caused any major disagreements between them.

It is sometimes said that Burghley's disputes with Elizabeth arose from a fundamental difference in their understanding of the nature of monarchy and royal service. Whereas Elizabeth believed in sacral monarchy, Burghley was prepared to countenance the deposition of Mary and regicide. While Elizabeth viewed her councillors as her personal servants, Burghley conceived of himself as a public servant as well as a royal one. Influenced by his religion and humanist–classical education, he thought his duty lay not only to the person of his monarch but to the interests of the protestant state.[112] There is a kernel of truth in this, but it should not be misunderstood or overstated. As shown by his statements and actions, Burghley did not challenge Elizabeth's royal prerogative nor flirt with positions that nowadays would be called 'republican'. Like many other Elizabethans, he saw the English constitution as a 'mixed polity', with the queen obviously providing the monarchical element, the privy council the aristocratic, and parliament the democratic. According to this vision, the ideal was that the three bodies worked together in harmony, but ultimate authority resided with the monarch.

During Burghley's last years, his relationship with Elizabeth subtly changed. As the first generation of Elizabethans died off, sentimentality as well as affection and respect bound them together. Burghley was the last man standing of Elizabeth's early privy councillors, and he was only just standing, for his last years were marked by frequent illnesses and absences from court. In messages sent through his son Robert, Elizabeth teased him gracefully: she hoped to see him dance at his granddaughter's wedding and she would do 'battle' with his gouty fingers. Despite failing health, Burghley worked on government business until late July 1598, and Elizabeth would not allow him to resign. The last surviving letter in his own hand was dated 10 July and written to his son Robert. In a postscript, he added: 'Serve God by serving of the queen.'[113]

Burghley died at Cecil House early on 4 August 1598, a few weeks before his seventy-eighth birthday. His funeral was conducted with elaborate splendour in Westminster Abbey, and his body was transported for burial in St Martin's church in Stamford. Elizabeth was devastated. She not only wept on hearing the news, but two years afterwards it was noticed that 'Burleigh's death doth often draw tears from her goodly cheeks'.[114] One month after the funeral Elizabeth visited Theobalds, perhaps as an act of commemoration, but she found her stay too distressing to be repeated and never went there again.[115]

Perceived to be the most powerful man in England, Burghley unsurprisingly generated considerable envy and dislike. Edmund Spenser famously satirized the lord treasurer in his 1591 beast fable *Mother Hubberd's Tale*, portraying him as a Machiavellian fox, who stole the crown of his sovereign for his private benefit and to aid the prospects of his 'cubs'.[116] During the 1590s, men in the earl of Essex's circle blamed Burghley for their lack of advancement, and spoke of him disparagingly as 'olde Saturnus', 'a melancholy and wayward planett, but yett predominant here'.[117] Relying on these men's reports, James VI wrote to Essex: 'I am…glad that he who rules all there is begun to be loathed at by the best and greatest sort there.'[118] Although the earl himself treated his former guardian with respect and without malice, Burghley's determination to make Robert his political heir took a toll on their relationship.

For a long time, historians assumed that Leicester was Cecil's 'reputed enemy' or 'very jealous of the Lord Burghley', and even that Elizabeth encouraged their mutual dislike as 'she ruled much by faction'.[119] But, although their relationship could be marred by moments of coldness, there is no evidence of any deep-seated or permanent political rivalry; certainly neither one sought to oust the other from power.[120] On the contrary, their correspondence reveals a high degree of cooperation in both private and public affairs. Furthermore, when Leicester was in disgrace with the queen over taking up the title of governor-general in the Netherlands, Burghley attempted to speak up for him, and Leicester likewise offered Burghley words of support during his period of disgrace in 1587.[121]

The most open and venomous attacks on Burghley came from members of the English Catholic community, living in exile abroad. Impugning him for the queen's religious policy, they made him the target of their propaganda. The anonymous *A Treatise of Treasons* (1572) attacked the lord treasurer (and his brother-in-law Sir Nicholas Bacon) for putting their private interests before those of the state, alleging that their heresy, anti-Catholicism, and attempts to exclude Mary were not the result of genuine religious convictions but their materialistic ambitions to dominate and milk the state. Richard Verstegan's *A Declaration of the True Causes of the Great Troubles* (1592) revamped these accusations, indicting Burghley for instigating heresy and destroying the ancient nobility of the realm. According to Verstegan, Elizabeth was totally manipulated by the baron, and

England had become a '*regnum Cecilianum*', 'Burghley's common-wealth'.[122] In a similar vein, Robert Persons's *Philopater* (1592) called Burghley the '*auctor et actor*' of the recently issued anti-recusancy proclamation and persecution of Catholic priests.[123]

Burghley was always sensitive to such criticisms. As Elizabeth wrote to and of him in May 1583: 'I have late seen an *ecce signum* [proof], that if an ass kicke you, you feele it too soone.'[124] And, indeed, the allegations that he manipulated the queen and had created a *regnum Cecilianum* cut the lord treasurer to the quick. He strenuously denied the accusations that he was guilty 'of falsehood, of injustyce, of bribery, of dissimulation, of dooble dealing in advise in counsell ether with hir majesty or with the counsellors'. Similarly, he swept aside the notion of a *regnum Cecilianum*: 'if my actions be considered, if ther be any cause gyven by me of such a nycknam, ther may be found owt in many others juster causes to attribut other names than myne.' He went on: 'I cold not omitt to answer a notable, absurd, manifest lye, which is that counsellors ar forced to seke at my handes meanes for ther sutes.' Unlike other persons, he protested, he did not promote his friends or kinsmen to offices or place, not least because he did not have the power to do so: 'in very truth I know my credit in such cases so meane' while 'others I fynd so ernest'.[125] Throughout his career, Burghley made strenuous efforts to suppress all such defamations against him: in September 1573, for example, a royal proclamation was issued condemning libellous attacks upon privy councillors.[126] Later on, Spenser's book was 'by superior awthoritie called in'.[127]

Burghley eventually won the war of words. By censoring his own archive and handing over the papers to his protegé William Camden with the recommendation that he should write a history of Elizabeth's reign, he ensured that posterity would receive a favourable account of his service. In Camden's *Annales*, Burghley is the hero, while Leicester the villain. Later accounts followed Camden, with the result that Catholic critiques of Burghley slid away without influence, while the portrait of Leicester in *Leicester's Commonwealth* lived on. The publication of a biographical sketch of Burghley in the mid-eighteenth century by an admirer who worked in the lord treasurer's household further enhanced the statesman's reputation.[128] As a result, in so far as historians have accepted the notion of a *regnum Cecilium*, they have believed his predominance worked to the advantage of the realm. For centuries, the Cecil who appeared in most English histories was:

the most vigilant, active, and prudent minister ever known in England: and as he was governed by no views but the interests of his sovereign, which he inflexibly pursued, his authority over her became every day more predominant. Ever cool himself, and uninfluenced by prejudice or affection, he checked those sallies of passion, and sometimes of caprice to which she was subject.[129]

Today, however, the portrait has been substantially modified. Whereas few historians would doubt Cecil's diligence or his commitment to serving the interests of his queen and country, they recognize the depths of his passionate anti-Catholic prejudices, the self-interest that lay behind some of his political actions, and the limitations of his vigilance over the royal finances.[130] Many—though not all—of us would also question the extent of his dominance over the queen, whether for good or evil. The relationship of queen and minister is far more complex than was once supposed.

10

The 'Moor': Sir Francis Walsingham

Thanks to Shekhar Kapur's two films *Elizabeth* (1998) and *Elizabeth: The Golden Years* (2007), Sir Francis Walsingham has emerged as one of the best-known—if most misunderstood—of Elizabeth's councillors. On screen he is depicted absurdly as a gay paedophile and ruthless murderer, and somewhat more credibly as the queen's Machiavellian spymaster and spin doctor. In contrast to the colourful Dudley and Ralegh, he is always dressed in black to signify his dour seriousness and murderous intent as the queen's *éminence grise*. Although little in this portrayal comes close to the reality, it does reflect—aside from the gay paedophilia—a version of Walsingham that has its roots both in Elizabethan Catholic polemic and some serious historical writing of the twentieth century.

For Catholics, Walsingham was a dangerous fanatic who used his 'subtile [and] sifting wit' to hatch conspiracies and entrap innocents like Mary Queen of Scots.[1] 'This Walsingham is of all heretics the worst,' wrote a resident Spanish agent, and 'any evil may be expected from him and his friends in the council'.[2] Considering him 'a most violent persecutor', English Catholics put Walsingham on a par with Burghley and greeted his death in 1590 with deep satisfaction, one of them describing his corpse in providential terms, his putrefied body exposing to the world the poison of his soul: 'in the end, his uryne came foorth at his mouth, and nose, with so odious a stench, that none could endure to come neere him.'[3] For a long time, historians too described Walsingham as a protestant extremist, even a fanatic—one calling him 'the one wholehearted ideologue in the council' and another 'the embodiment of the crusading spirit'.[4]

Walsingham was indubitably a persecutor of Catholics, as was Burghley. He can also justifiably be identified as one of the godly protestants. During Mary's reign he chose exile abroad rather than Nicodemism at home.[5] Under Elizabeth, he was regarded as 'a patrone of godliness and a maintainer of true religion', like Leicester and

247

Burghley providing protection to puritan ministers who fell foul of the episcopal authorities because of their refusal to conform to all prayer-book ceremonies or subscribe to Whitgift's 1583 articles. In 1586, he endowed a lectureship in divinity at Oxford University, and recommended John Rainolds, a 'godly' academic (not popular with the queen), to fill the position.[6] Walsingham was equally committed to advancing the godly cause abroad, consistently urging the queen to give financial help to, or take up arms on behalf of, protestants in the Netherlands, France, and Scotland. His closest friends and colleagues were those who, likewise, promoted the 'godly' cause in England and elsewhere. The secretaries he employed included the puritan Nicholas Faunt and presbyterian Laurence Tomson; and among his close family connections were Robert Beale and Peter Wentworth, puritans who fell into trouble with the queen as a result of their outspokenness on religious and political issues.[7]

Yet, Walsingham's religious zeal went only so far. Again like Leicester and Burghley, he was no precisionist, determined at all costs to follow the literal mandates of the Bible. On the contrary, he advised fellow protestants to abide by the rule of law, even in religious matters where their consciences were touched. When he learned that English merchants abroad were intending to follow religious services that were not in accordance with the Elizabethan prayer book, he warned them against it: 'I do not wryte this as one that myslykethe of soche a foorme and exercyse of prayer; only I woold have all reformatyons don by publycke awthoryte.' A pragmatist by temperament, Walsingham also saw no point in pushing for further reformation that the queen was bound to reject. In 1578, for example, he advised his friend William Davison that 'the seeking of more might hazard (according to man's understanding) that which we already have'. Instead of pushing against the boundaries set by the queen, Davison should

> deale warely in this tyme when pollecye carryethe more swaye than zeale. And yet have we great cause to thank God for that we at presently enjoye, having God's woorde syncerely preached, and the sacraments truly mynistered. The rest we lacke, we are to beg by prayers and attend with patyence.[8]

Perhaps for this reason—unlike Burghley, Leicester, Knollys, and Beale—Walsingham never openly took on Archbishop Whitgift in defence of puritan ministers during the 1580s.

It would, moreover, be wrong to portray Walsingham as the stereotypical or stage puritan who despised fun, hated secular music, rejected art as 'graven images', and condemned the 'vanity' and moral corruption of plays. Of course, not many real-life puritans conformed to this characterization. Nonetheless, unlike so many of the godly, Walsingham was a patron of the theatre. Indeed, he was a co-founder of the Queen's Men theatre company formed in 1583, and he even insisted that they should give regular weekday performances, thereby challenging the puritan city authorities of London who were trying to limit the new company's playing time.[9] Also during the 1580s Walsingham employed John de Critz the elder, who painted his patron's portrait and acquired for him works of art from abroad, including a painting of St John and another of Neptune ravishing the virgin Coenis—neither subject, we would expect, to appeal to a puritan.[10] While he certainly was a staunch advocate for reforming 'the enormities of the saobathe', devising means to clamp down on dancing, hunting, and music-making on Sundays, Walsingham's drive was supported by men who were far from godly protestants but simply wanted to suppress disorderliness.[11] In his personal life, moreover, the sabbath was not set aside for spiritual edification. According to John Harington's reminiscences, 'when my lord treasurer did come in from prayers, Sir Francis Walsingham did in merrie sorte say, that he wished himself so goode a servant of God as Lord Burleigh, but that he had not been at churche for a weeke past'.[12]

Although it is impossible to get close to the man, since his personal archive has not survived, there is considerable evidence that Walsingham pursued wide intellectual interests, loved music, was the patron of painters, and enjoyed falconry (though presumably not on the sabbath).[13] He was no killjoy nor out of place in the cultured Elizabethan court. In *The Faerie Queene* Edmund Spencer hailed him as 'the great Maecenas of this age', referring to the great Roman patron of the poet Virgil, although quite possibly the compliment was based more on hope than experience. Apart from the drama, there is little evidence that Walsingham was much of a patron of the literary arts.

Like most royal servants, Walsingham owed the start of his political career to court connections. His mother was a Denny (kin to Kat Astley), his stepfather a Carey (the paternal uncle of Lord Hunsdon), and his brothers-in-law included Sir Walter Mildmay (Elizabeth's first chancellor of the exchequer) and, after 1562, John Tamworth (a groom of the privy chamber and keeper of the privy purse from 1559 to 1569). Walsingham's main patrons seem, however, to have been fellow Marian exiles, men with whom he had started an acquaintance in Padua and Basle between 1555 until the end of 1558. It was the second earl of Bedford who found Walsingham, aged about 26, a seat in Elizabeth's first parliament of 1559, where he represented a Cornish borough under the earl's control as lord warden of the stannaries (the tin mines of the West Country). Sir Nicholas Throckmorton took Walsingham under his wing during the 1560s.[14] Also counted among his friends from the years in exile were Sir Henry Killigrew and Thomas Randolph, both employed as diplomats under Elizabeth.

Walsingham made no mark on the 1559 parliament; according to the admittedly defective Commons' journal, he did not even deliver a speech there. Nonetheless, Cecil wanted him returned to the next session, noting in a memorandum on forthcoming parliamentary business: 'Mr Walsingham to be of the House'. Presumably, Walsingham had already begun working for the secretary, who may have been introduced to the younger man through Throckmorton, Mildmay, or Killigrew.[15] Despite this promising start, the new MP for Lyme Regis (he had changed constituencies) played no prominent role in political life during the 1560s; he certainly did not shine in the parliament of 1563 nor did he attend that of 1566.[16] No papers survive, moreover, that record his involvement in governmental matters before late 1568.

In fact, we know very little about Walsingham's activities before then. The likelihood is that he was caught up in family affairs as a result of his two marriages. His second—to the widow Ursula St Barbe in the autumn of 1566—took him away from London for a couple of years and involved him in a time-consuming legal case over the inheritance of two stepsons who had been killed in a terrible accident.[17] It was only after Walsingham had returned to London that he built up a working relationship with Cecil and Leicester, both of whom enlisted his help in intelligence-gathering. Useful in this respect because of the continental contacts he had first forged during the later 1550s, Walsingham relayed information and rumours about Catholic activities and intentions that he learned from sources in Scotland, Italy, and France, as well as from London merchants.[18] He proved remarkably assiduous in making enquiries about suspicious characters, then coining the aphorism that was later to be his hallmark when dealing with security operations: 'there is lesse daynger in fearinge to myche [too much] then to lyttle.'[19]

It was through the recommendations of Cecil and Leicester that Elizabeth gave Walsingham his first significant assignment. In early October 1569, he was told to detain and interrogate the Florentine merchant Roberto di Ridolfi, who was suspected of plotting with Mary Queen of Scots and the pope. For a month, Ridolfi was kept in custody at Walsingham's house, during which time the prisoner partially admitted his associations with Mary's agent, John Leslie, and his knowledge about the Norfolk marriage scheme. Yet, despite his evident involvement in these dangerous matters of state, Elizabeth decided in November 1569—on the basis of Walsingham's intelligence—that the Florentine was safe to be set free.[20] What Walsingham passed on, we do not know, but historians suspect that he reported that Ridolfi had been 'turned' and was prepared to act as a double agent, even an *agent provocateur*, for the Elizabethan regime.[21] Otherwise, it is difficult to explain the extraordinary leniency shown towards the merchant in November, as well as the freedom of movement he was permitted after his release. After all, plots and a major rebellion were unsettling the regime at that time, while England's relations with Spain were perilously tense.

If Walsingham and his masters (and mistress) were attempting to use Ridolfi as a 'mole', they were playing a very dangerous game. Not only did the Florentine continue his intrigues with Mary, the duke of Norfolk, and the Spanish and French ambassadors, but he also went to Rome and Spain, where he convinced the pope and Philip II that a grand enterprise against England was feasible as well as desirable. Had it not been for the caution of the duke of Alva (the Spanish governor-general in the Netherlands), Philip might well have launched an armada against Elizabeth in 1571, for the king embraced the project with a religious fervour.[22] In the event, Walsingham and Cecil were on top of the conspiracy and exposed it easily during the summer, but the Ridolfi plot could easily have ended less happily for the queen.

Before the plot eventually broke, Walsingham was given a new responsibility that went beyond intelligence-gathering. In August 1570, he was appointed a special ambassador to France with instructions to help the Huguenots secure favourable terms in a peace treaty that was then being negotiated with their king. At the same time he was told to convey Elizabeth's version of the recent rising in the north to both Charles IX and his powerful mother, Catherine de' Medici. But, since the peace of St Germain was actually concluded before Walsingham left England, he was given the new charge of congratulating the king on his accord with his protestant subjects.[23] Almost certainly, Walsingham's appointment was intended as a try-out for the more important role as resident ambassador to France. Sir Henry Norris, who had been in post since January 1567, was very keen to leave, and Walsingham seemed a good replacement. University educated and an experienced traveller, he had excellent Latin, French, and Italian. He was also a proven intelligencer, with far-flung connections on the Continent, an important consideration as he was expected to send home information from the French court about 'all manner of their doings there, aswell private as publick', and especially anything that might be 'prejudiciall' to the queen and realm. Since Walsingham was living off the income from his landed estates, he was thought to have sufficient financial resources to maintain a grand household in the notoriously expensive embassy without making too many demands on the public purse, but this advantage he strongly denied, and his daily allowance was consequently raised to slightly more than Norris had received. It was, of course, Cecil who proposed Walsingham; Elizabeth had had very little interaction with her new ambassador before his appointment.[24]

Walsingham—now aged about 38—landed in France on 3 January 1571. While there, he communicated almost exclusively with Burghley and Leicester, not Elizabeth. The secretary usually sent Walsingham the queen's instructions, and the ambassador's dispatches were mainly addressed to the secretary. During his first year as ambassador, Walsingham wrote only one letter directly to the queen and that was co-written with his departing predecessor.[25] When writing to Burghley, Walsingham normally sent two letters at a time; one was intended for the queen, 'to the end you may advertise her majestie'; the other was a 'pryvate letter', containing Walsingham's personal views about the political situation directed to Burghley alone.[26] Otherwise, Leicester was the most common recipient of private letters in which Walsingham would unburden himself.

The diplomatic task that dominated Walsingham's embassy during 1571 and early 1572 comprised the negotiations for some kind of Anglo-French alliance. Walsingham had his own strong views on the subject, and consequently did not always stick to his official instructions but followed his own independent judgement. In late 1570, the 37-year-old Elizabeth had decided to pursue a marriage alliance with Charles IX's brother, the 19-year-old Henry, duke of Anjou. Despite the age difference, the match had some clear advantages. If achieved, it might resolve the English succession problem, cut off the Scottish queen from her chief ally France, and offer England protection against Spain. Initially, though, Walsingham was not entrusted with the delicate negotiations, as Elizabeth preferred to keep her overture to Anjou informal and secret. Consequently, she dispatched her kinsman Thomas Sackville, Lord Buckhurst, to Paris at the head of a special embassy whose outward purpose was to congratulate the king on his recent marriage but whose secret objective was to elicit a matrimonial proposal from Catherine de' Medici.[27] Walsingham's role was simply to introduce Buckhurst to the French court and to bolster the envoy's position by speaking generally to the court of the queen's recent resolution to marry someone from 'the family of a prince'. To keep the talks off the record, Elizabeth did not inform Walsingham about them directly; instead her instructions to him were, as usual, transmitted via Burghley.[28]

Without clearing it with the queen, Walsingham decided to prepare the way for Buckhurst. Because he saw 'so great necessity' for the marriage', he broached the matter with Catherine, talking to her as 'a pryvat person, not having commyssion as a publycke person', concerning the value of a 'good amytie betwene the two crownes'. If this intervention was an error, he confided to Burghley, the secretary should tell him so, since an admonishment would make him 'the better able to serve hir majestie with the more skyll' in the future.[29] In fact Walsingham did well. Catherine spoke positively to both the resident ambassador and the special envoy about the Anjou match. She talked privately to Buckhurst, meeting him as if by chance in the Tuileries gardens on 12 March; and, twelve days later, Walsingham was brought into the negotiations. Catherine insisted upon it. If Elizabeth was really serious about a marriage, said the queen mother to Walsingham, then 'none might deal there in the same, betwixt them and us, but you as our ambassador'.[30]

To facilitate the negotiations in France, Elizabeth outlined for Walsingham the main terms for any matrimonial treaty. Her most important condition was that Anjou would be denied Catholic rites in England and expected to attend protestant services on public occasions.[31] At one level, Walsingham was pleased with the queen's firmness on this point: 'above all things, I wysshe God's glorye and next the queen's savetye; yf this matche may advaunce them bothe then I wysshe yt to proceade, otherwyse not.'[32] However, he feared the time was not yet right to communicate Elizabeth's bald message to Catherine, since she might immediately withdraw from the negotiations. He explained his dilemma to Burghley:

> I was very myche parplexed what coorse to take, but when I beheld her majestye fyrst howe in her judgement she fyndethe yt more

exspedyent for her to marrye. Secondarylly that yf her majestye meane to marrye abrode this only gentleman remayneth fyt for her to marrye. Thirdly the dyscontentement of her subjects at home for not marryenge. Fowerthelye howe presently abrode she is beset with a numbre of foreyn practises the exequutyon wherof stayethe only uppon the event of this matche I then resolved that yt was most fyt for me to forget my selfe and to thinke only of her majestye and of her savetye wheruppon I tooke this coorse.[33]

The course Walsingham took was to keep quiet about Elizabeth's uncompromising stance on religion. In swerving from his sovereign's instructions, he compared himself to the Roman who, in order to repel an enemy assault, disobeyed a law not to loiter on a town wall.

As a result of Walsingham's disobedient discretion, the negotiations continued, but it soon became evident that religion was the sticking point. In April, Elizabeth again made her position clear. She would proceed no further, until the French accepted her condition that Anjou would have to forgo the mass in England: 'you shall give them no other comfort in this behalf,' she ordered Walsingham.[34] This time, Burghley encouraged Walsingham to soften the message. Unless he should 'moderate the matter better', the secretary warned, the French would imagine that religion was merely a pretext for getting out of the marriage: 'I know your wisdome sufficient to invent sufficient answers to mollifie their hard conceits. Thus you see how inwardly I deale with you, and trust you will so use it.'[35]

Walsingham complied with Burghley's secret instructions in order to give the negotiations every chance to succeed. This, he believed, was vital, because, as far as 'my poore eyesight can discern', the marriage was essential for 'God's glory and her majesty's safety'. The need for it was evident in that the Huguenots 'ernestly' desired it, and equally earnestly the 'papists' sought 'to impeach the same'. Besides, Walsingham was inclined to think that the French royal family was taking a tough stance on religion purely for form's sake and would retreat if the queen stayed firm. It was also likely, he reflected, that the young Anjou would convert once in England.[36]

However, during the summer, Walsingham changed his mind. Catherine had stiffened her position on the religious condition, and Anjou had become so 'alyenated' from the marriage through 'the practyces' of his Catholic friends that he would not go through with it, even were Elizabeth to offer him toleration.[37] The project seemed to him dead in the water. The talk now in France was of a league without marriage, and this strategy Walsingham could back whole-heartedly: 'I thincke wee have cause to thanck God that offereth us soe good an occasion both to advance his glorie and also her majesty's safety,' he told Leicester. It was true that England had traditionally allied with the rulers of the Netherlands against France, he explained, but now the Spanish Habsburgs were ruling those territories and they had 'become the pope's champion and professed enimy unto the ghospell'. An alliance with France 'yeeldeth not soe much temporall proffit, yett in respect of the spirituall fruite that thereby may ensue I think it worthie the embraceng', he went on, for it would not only result in 'an advancement of the ghospell [there] but also else where'.[38] At the same time, an Anglo-French alliance would bring one immensely valuable political advantage—namely, 'an inward remedye of a very daungerouse sore, I meane the Queen of Scottes'—as it would break the 'auld alliance' with Scotland and end French agitation for Mary's restoration to the Scottish throne.[39] On all counts, then, Walsingham believed, an Anglo-French alliance was the way forward.

But would a league with France result in a war against Spain? In a letter to Burghley, dated 3 August, Walsingham said not. If, as seemed likely, Charles IX—confident in his alliance with England—took on Philip II, Elizabeth would be left 'a peaceable looker on'.[40] However, a week later Walsingham suddenly presented a much bolder proposition. He had just held talks with Louis of Nassau (William of Orange's brother, who was an exile in France after his failed rebellion in the Netherlands), and the count had proposed that Elizabeth should join an offensive league against Spain, with France and the German Lutheran princes as allies. If successful, the participants would partition the Netherlands among themselves.[41]

The project of an international league against Spain greatly appealed to Walsingham. Although he acknowledged that giving his opinion on such a matter was 'folly' and outside the 'compasse of my calling', he could not resist telling Leicester what he thought. Essentially he favoured fighting against Spain in the Netherlands. Certainly, the outcome of any war was always 'doubtfull', and entering a war 'for increase of dominion' was always unjust. Nevertheless, wars 'for safetye's sake' were 'most necessarie', and England could not ultimately stay out of one against the Spanish king, who held such 'malice' towards the queen. Victory was a real possibility too, if France and the German princes were England's allies. Finally, Nassau's proposal for the partitioning of the Netherlands (with England acquiring Holland and Zeeland) would prevent the French from taking over the whole territory. Despite all these considerations, Walsingham suspected that Elizabeth would reject the road to war, warning Leicester: 'if her majestie will not be a partie, then nether can their growe unto her that honor, proffit and surety that otherwise weare to be wished.'[42]

Walsingham had good reason for his unease, since the queen had, several months earlier, rebuffed his advice that she should send money to Nassau for an enterprise in the Netherlands.[43] Actually, Elizabeth did not reject this new proposal out of hand but waited to see what the French would do: would they pull out of the marriage and offer her a league instead? All was, therefore, in abeyance, and Walsingham grew impatient. In mid-September he complained to Burghley: 'yt [is] feared that the matter wilbe so longe protracted as the oportunitye for the enterprise wilbe lett slippe, which yf yt so fall out the unkindness betwixt the French king and king of Spain wilbe reconciled.'[44] But Burghley disagreed. He did not consider that a league was possible without marriage and (unlike Leicester) would not press it upon the queen.[45]

At this crucial moment, Walsingham was taken ill and had to leave the French court to 'attende on phisicke'. This was the first indication of the ill health (caused by a urinary infection) that was to plague him for the rest of his life. As it was wrongly expected that he would be incapacitated for just a month, the experienced Killigrew was sent to France in October as a temporary substitute.[46] Then, in late December, Killigrew was joined by another diplomat, Sir Thomas Smith, who was instructed to make one last push for the marriage and, if that failed, to discuss a treaty of friendship. It was not to be the offensive league Walsingham preferred, but a defensive alliance, reflecting the preferences of Elizabeth and Burghley, neither of whom wanted war against Spain.

During his illness, Walsingham had continued to work from home, but it was only in mid-February 1572 that he was fit enough for Killigrew to be sent home. Smith remained to work on the final stages of the treaty with Walsingham. Together they ironed out the last disputed details, and on 19 April a treaty of mutual defence was signed at Blois. The diplomatic coup for England was that the French agreed not to intervene in Scotland on Mary's behalf and promised to aid Elizabeth even if attacked by Catholic Spain. In thanks for Walsingham's hard work in preparing the way and negotiating the treaty, Elizabeth presented her resident ambassador with a large painting to commemorate its conclusion (Plate 17). The subject was an allegory of the family of Henry VIII: in the centre sits the enthroned king, looking towards his protestant heirs on the right: a kneeling Edward VI and the dominant Elizabeth, who is holding hands with a figure representing peace and attended by another representing prosperity. On the left stand the smaller figures of Mary and Philip, followed by Mars, the god of war. The message was clear. In contrast to her sister's Habsburg alliance, Elizabeth's French alliance—albeit with a Catholic power—would bring peace and prosperity to the realm without sacrificing 'true' religion. Along the bottom are the words: 'The quene to Walsingham this tablet sente | marke of her people's and her own contente.'

Walsingham, however, was far less satisfied with the outcome of Blois than was his mistress. In early August 1572, he confided to Leicester his disappointment that the queen had not committed herself to an offensive alliance, and he urged the earl to use his influence to promote a combined Anglo-French campaign in the Netherlands.[47] Just two weeks later Walsingham realized his error. From the eve of St Bartholomew's Day on 23 August until the 29th, Catholics in Paris fell prey to a frenzy of fanaticism and massacred nearly 3,000 Huguenots; and, when the slaughter spread to the provinces, perhaps another 7,000 met their deaths. This traumatic event laid bare for Walsingham the power of Catholic forces at the French court and demonstrated his foolishness in trusting the French royal family: his only excuse, he said, was that his 'error in that behalfe was common with a great many wiser then my selfe'.[48]

Despite her horror at the massacre and against the advice of Burghley, Elizabeth did not recall her ambassador. To avoid isolation in Europe, she hoped to prevent a diplomatic rupture with France and keep the hard-won amity in place. Walsingham, however, considered the treaty of Blois a dead letter. Notwithstanding French talk of continuing friendship, he decided, 'we have cause to suspect the contrary'. He added that the queen would do far better to seek safety by allying with protestants in Scotland and Germany.[49] Scotland was now the focus of Walsingham's attention; England's rear door had to be made secure from the French and Scottish Catholics; and ideally Mary should be executed, so that she could not be used as their instrument.

Walsingham and his wife were understandably eager to return to England. Paris was now an uncongenial residence and, besides, his debts had been mounting during the staggeringly expensive embassy, much of which Walsingham had had to pay for himself. Although Elizabeth would have liked him to continue in his diplomatic post, for she appreciated his 'wisdom and discretion', she agreed to a replacement, and in April 1573 he returned home.[50] At the English court, it was rumoured that she intended to appoint him her junior secretary, but it took eight months before Walsingham received the office and a seat on the privy council. As always, there were reasons for Elizabeth's hesitation. It was, after all, a novelty to install a second principal secretary—and she disliked novelties; additionally, from her point of view, Walsingham was not an ideal choice. His letters in Paris marked him out as an anti-Spanish hawk, and she was now ready to restore diplomatic and commercial relations with Philip II.[51] Nonetheless, Walsingham had proven abilities, and Burghley and Leicester both forwarded his advancement.

Walsingham initially shared the secretarial duties with the capable Sir Thomas Smith, but the senior man retired in April 1576 because of ill health. Walsingham then assumed sole responsibility, preparing papers for council meetings, handling Elizabeth's correspondence, and meeting her in regular audience. It was after this promotion that the queen came to know the man, showing an appreciation for his dry sense of humour and developing the intimacy that eventually led her to call him by a nickname, the 'moor' (presumably a reference to his dark complexion). For his part, Walsingham entered into the rituals of court life, joining the queen on progress and participating (with his wife) in the New Year's gift exchange. He would host the queen at his house in Barn Elms on three separate occasions in the 1580s, ensuring she was well entertained.[52] In portraits of 1587 and 1589, he wears a cameo of the queen at his waist.

As principal secretary with no junior, Walsingham found the office punishing. He was overburdened with work, laid low with his recurring illness, and in disagreement with the queen on major issues of policy. In September 1576, he told Burghley that he was ready to quit, as his service was 'subject unto so many thwartes and harde speeches'.[53] The 'thwartes' encompassed Elizabeth's unwillingness to send troops to co-religionists abroad, forge an alliance with the protestant regent in Scotland, and spend large sums on the defences of the realm. The 'harde speeches' were the queen's reprimands whenever she suspected her secretary was ignoring her wishes or making policy by the back door.

It was soon evident that queen and secretary had a different approach to England's security. To Walsingham's mind, Elizabeth was far too complaisant about the international situation, and he warned

Burghley that 'yt behovethe her majesty to looke into her estate and not to slumber as she doothe in a weake security'. Her 'great neighbours' were arrayed against her and their friendship 'hollowe'.[54] Walsingham also thought the queen overly lax about security at home, lamenting her 'loose kind of dealing' where 'faults are judged no faults' and complaining that she was too lenient with potential plotters, such as the men he discovered communicating with the Queen of Scots.[55] It was absurd, he wrote, that she refused to send such conspirators to the Tower, because she 'thinkethe yt an abasement of the place to have so meane personages comytted thither'; in his view, these people were traitors, and the state prison was therefore the right place for them.[56]

In letters to the queen (let alone unrecorded interviews) Walsingham repeatedly sounded so like a Jeremiah that it is surprising that she did not give him that nickname instead of the 'moor'.[57] Typical were the alarmist warnings he sent the queen in January 1575 while absent from court because of sickness. Sending her papers related to recently uncovered 'plots', he emphasized 'howe hardly they [sic] twoe great princes your neighbors are affected towards you, as also what unsownd subjectes you have at home'. Mixing his metaphors, Walsingham then predicted a dire outcome if she did not take immediate action:

> the maladie in tyme will growe uncurable, and the hidden sparkes of treason that nowe lye covered will (no doubt of it) breake owt into an unquenchable fyer. For the love of Gode, Madame, let not the cure of your diseased estate hange any longer in delyberation. Diseased states are no more cured by consultation, when nothing resolved on is present in execution than...diseased bodies by only conference with physitians withowte receaving the remedies by them prescribed.[58]

Elizabeth, however, consistently ignored Walsingham's advice. She held back from openly aiding the Huguenots during the renewed civil wars in France, from forging a league with Regent Morton of Scotland, and from allying with Orange, who was heading the protestant rebellion raging in Holland and Zeeland. At the same time, she would not confine Mary Stewart in a more secure prison and so restrain her from seditious 'practise', as her secretary counselled.[59] Walsingham was highly critical of these decisions—or rather what he saw as procrastinations—calling them 'dyshonourable' and dangerous; and he expressed his views 'bothe playnely and dutyfully' to the queen as well as to Burghley and Leicester.[60]

But Elizabeth recognized the limitations of England's military power and therefore wanted to avoid provoking the Catholic monarchs by openly supporting rebels in their territories, treating the Scottish queen as if she were an obvious prisoner, and concluding a league with Mary's protestant adversary in Scotland. Warned off from intervening in Scotland by the French ambassador, Elizabeth declared her goodwill to Morton but offered him nothing concrete in the form of pensions or a bilateral treaty. In France and the Netherlands, her preference was to work for a peace settlement that would guarantee the rebels their liberties, including liberty of conscience. Guided by Burghley, she was especially anxious to avoid a diplomatic breach with Philip II that would endanger England's valuable commercial activities both in the Netherlands and in Spain.[61]

At times, Walsingham found his conscience baulked at carrying out the queen's orders because he feared they put England's security at risk, but he never flouted her will, or at least not openly. Two incidents illustrate this point. The first was when a quarrel erupted between Elizabeth and Morton over the regent's handling of violence on the borders in the summer of 1575. Walsingham and the privy council wanted the matter to be handled sensitively so as not to jeopardize the amity between the two protestant regimes, but Elizabeth considered the regent had so affronted her honour that she reacted without moderation or finesse. She insisted that Walsingham tear up the council's original letter complaining about the episode, because it was 'tempered with too much fleame' [phlegm] and told him to draw up instead a message full of 'choler' (the opposite humour). Walsingham confessed: 'I never wrote a letter with worse wyll'; but he did write it.[62] In fact, a diplomatic crisis was averted only because the English envoy (Killigrew) orally watered down the reprimand so that Morton would not take offence.[63] The second occasion was in the spring of 1576, when a serious quarrel erupted between Elizabeth and William of Orange. Elizabeth was incensed at the ongoing piracies of the Dutch protestants that had resulted in the seizure of English ships passing to and from Antwerp and London. In a flash of rage she even threatened to join the Spanish king in suppressing their rebellion. Walsingham reluctantly signed the queen's angry letters, but he secretly let Orange know what he needed to do 'for the satisfaction of her majestie' to prevent this catastrophe.[64]

For the most part, all Walsingham could do to save the queen from herself (as he saw it) was to bombard her with his opinions and encourage like-minded councillors and agents to do the same. In July

1577, for example, he told one of his regular correspondents that he would do 'us a most useful service', if he were to write frequently of the evils and 'impending danger' from the Catholic powers and 'arouse us who are in a deep sleep and heedlessly secure'; by 'us', of course, Walsingham meant the queen.[65] On the whole, Elizabeth was patient under the barrage, although we do learn of a few occasions when she lost her temper at his vocal support for military intervention in the Netherlands. However, since the recorded incidents were in front of a Spanish envoy, it is quite possible that she was engaging in a piece of diplomatic theatre.[66] Nonetheless, Elizabeth was genuinely irate whenever she suspected that her secretary was promoting the interests of his protestant friends abroad rather than her own— though, of course, he could not see the difference. Told that Walsingham was intriguing with Orange, she confronted him with an accusation of disloyalty; but, when he self-righteously denied that he had been acting against her welfare, she chose to believe him.[67]

Despite his frustrations, overwork, and bouts of serious illness, Walsingham did not resign in 1576. The following year, matters improved for him. His duties as secretary eased when the experienced diplomat Dr Thomas Wilson was sworn in as his junior partner in September 1577.[68] That year, too, Elizabeth seemed to be moving inexorably, albeit reluctantly, towards the interventionist policy in the Netherlands that Walsingham and his friends had long pursued. She was not worn down by their arguments, however. Her change of tack was prompted by external factors: an escalation of the Dutch rebellion in late 1576; ambassadorial reports from France that the Catholic powers were conspiring against her; and evidence that the French king's brother—Francis, duke of Anjou—was all set to intervene militarily in the Netherlands, though, whether as an ally of Spain, a supporter of the rebels, or an instrument of the French crown with ambitions to annex the provinces, no one was quite sure.

The event that sparked off the new developments in the Netherlands was the so-called Spanish fury. Over three days in early November 1576, the unpaid Spanish army in Antwerp rioted, sacking property and murdering some 8,000 civilians. As a direct result, the loyalist Catholic south signed a pact with the Calvinist rebels of Holland and Zeeland, uniting for the first time all seventeen provinces against Spain. Still seeking a mediated peace, Elizabeth instantly sent envoys to Brussels and Spain for this purpose. Simultaneously, however, she began the process of intervention by promising the Dutch rebels' representative that she would lend them £100,000 if Philip II's governor-general in the Netherlands, Don John of Austria, refused their terms for a settlement. In February 1577, she dispatched the staunchly protestant Philip Sidney to the Empire to test the water for a trans-European protestant league that would include both German Lutheran and Calvinist princes. In June she followed up this initiative by sending further envoys to Germany with instructions to forge the league with the leading princes. If this diplomacy proved successful, it would mean that England would not stand alone in any confrontation with Spain in the Netherlands. A protestant alliance, moreover, would act as a counterweight to a Catholic league, then thought to be in the making. Although Walsingham was irritated at the slow pace of action, he was at least content that the queen was finally taking the 'correct' course.[69]

In the Netherlands itself, Don John signed a 'perpetual edict' with the newly formed states-general in February 1577, but it lasted a mere five months. That July, he broke its terms by seizing Namur Castle, and a renewal of war looked imminent. With the possibility of German allies at hand and in order to undercut the French, Elizabeth agreed to help the states-general. In the summer she pledged to guarantee a substantial loan and to contribute over 5,000 foot soldiers and 1,000 horsemen under the command of an English nobleman, whom everyone expected to be Leicester. Walsingham and the earl were delighted, but their joy was short-lived, as it soon became obvious that Elizabeth's promise of intervention was partly designed to put further pressure on Philip II. Still hankering after a compromise settlement, Elizabeth sent off embassies to the Spanish king and Don John, even while she was still negotiating with the Dutch. According to Burghley, she had three main reasons for her reluctance to be drawn directly into the conflict. First, 'to ayde the Low-Countrees is to deale with people that lack a head, and also to encorradg subjectes ageynst ther soverayn lord'. Second, her aid would 'justly irritat' the Catholic princes. Third, she did not think it good 'to aventure ye blood of hir naturall subjectes for ye savety of strangers' but to reserve them for the defence of England.[70] Walsingham, of course, disagreed fervently. However, the events of late 1577 and early 1578 confirmed the queen in her caution.

By the autumn of 1577, it was evident that the proposed Anglo-German league would come to nothing. A disappointed Walsingham rightly blamed the confessional divisions among the German protestants for the failure, and admitted: 'for myn owne parte, if I had thought the succes wold have prooved no better, I wold not have bene so foreward in advisinge her majestie to send, as I was.'[71] During the same season, he had to acknowledge that the rebel provinces in the Netherlands showed 'so great iresolutenesss in all their doings as they make all their friends desperate of any good success'.[72] Even worse, in January 1578, a rebel army was routed at the battle of Gembloux, and Don John went on to capture several towns in the south. As a result of these events, whatever 'taste' Elizabeth might have had for military intervention daily dissipated; as one commentator correctly noted, 'from this, the queen has taken to defend her tardiness in executing her designs, against Leicester, Walsingham and others, who had persuaded her to a more active course'.[73] She was prepared to lend the rebels £20,000 to pay for a mercenary army, but the focus of her policy was again to attempt a negotiated settlement. Like his mistress, Burghley considered this the better option in order to avoid a direct war against Spain alongside allies who were politically divided and militarily weak.[74] But Walsingham disagreed, as did Leicester, Hatton, and William Davison (who was then Elizabeth's agent in the Netherlands). The secretary argued that the Dutch towns could, with adequate assistance, hold out against the Spanish army, and he dismissed Philip II's terms for a settlement as 'an offer of abuse to wyn tyme'.[75]

Let down by England, the rebel leaders began negotiations for a military alliance with Anjou in the spring of 1578. Although the duke offered Elizabeth friendship, she and her advisers were understandably far from convinced of his goodwill. Consequently, she decided to send a high-profile embassy to the Netherlands to make one last-ditch attempt at peace. If Don John would not agree to her mediation, her representatives could then offer the rebels aid, but only on the condition that they broke off talks with the duke. At the same time, the embassy was to operate as a fact-finding mission. The queen had started to distrust Davison's observations about the situation, fearing his dispatches were incomplete and one-sided, and she wanted more detailed and balanced views about 'the state of the country and the force therof'.[76] Elizabeth alighted upon Walsingham (known to be a friend of Orange) and Lord Cobham (thought to be more sympathetic to Spain) as her representatives, despite Leicester's willingness to go, and her secretary's preference to stay behind 'upon very privat cause'.[77]

The English embassy arrived in Antwerp on 28 June. Over the next few months, Walsingham reviewed the rebel army outside the city, and spoke to diplomats from all sides. These experiences on the ground confirmed, rather than changed, his earlier attitude. He remained pessimistic about the prospects of peace, sanguine about the rebels' strength, deeply impressed with Orange, profoundly suspicious of Anjou, and unwaveringly convinced that supplying the states-general with immediate loans was the best course for Elizabeth's honour and safety. 'Her majestie shall never have the like occasion offered to do them good, as she might by yielding the relief they demanded,' he told Hatton.[78] Elizabeth ignored this advice, even though it was reinforced by most of her privy councillors.

By September 1578, Walsingham felt desperate in the face of what he saw as the queen's blind obstinacy:

> When the advise of grave and faithfull counsellors cannot prevaile with a prynce of her majestie's rare judgment, it is a signe that God hath closed up her heart from seeing and executing that which may be for her safety, which we, that love her and depende of her fortune, cannot but with griefe think of.[79]

As for Elizabeth, she increasingly suspected that Walsingham was not giving peace a chance nor providing her with a full and fair assessment of Anjou: 'we se not that yow did follow that course which yow did know befor your departure was our speciall meaning,' she complained in early August. Walsingham and Cobham had failed to interview the duke in person, as she had commanded, and the secretary was consequently 'too hard' in his assessment of the Frenchman; if peace were indeed impossible, as Walsingham asserted, she needed to know whether or not Anjou could be trusted to help the Dutch rebels without endangering her interests.[80] Anjou's ambassadors kept assuring Elizabeth that he was at her devotion, so could he be used as her agent?

Elizabeth had even more to think about concerning Anjou. In July, his ambassador unexpectedly proposed a marriage alliance between the 25-year-old duke and 45-year-old queen. This needed serious thought. While the age discrepancy was a major disadvantage, the match might bring—or so it was argued—the best prospect for international peace and a means of neutralizing the French in the Netherlands. Ideally Elizabeth and Anjou, bound together in marriage, would be able to force Philip II into a peaceful settlement with his rebellious provinces; failing that, Anjou could take up arms against Spain, but as Elizabeth's husband not an independent player nor the instrument of the king of France. Because of these considerations, Elizabeth thought it imperative that Walsingham discovered whatever he could about the duke's motives and trustworthiness. Until then, she kept her thoughts about the matrimonial proposal close to her chest: a perturbed Leicester told Walsingham in August that the queen would discuss the match with no one: 'at least not with me, nor for aught I can lern with none other.'[81]

After Elizabeth's rebuke, Walsingham and Cobham went to see Anjou and found him 'very wyse, well spoken, and not so deformed as he was'—the duke had been scarred by smallpox. In Walsingham's view, however, the suggested match was an unwelcome distraction. The age difference did not seem to bother him, nor did he mention Anjou's religion as an obstacle. Instead the secretary focused upon the problem that the duke would inherit the French throne after the death of his childless brother; the 'dyffycultye' as 'yt is to lyve under a vyceroye' made the match, in his view, unthinkable. But, in fact, Walsingham did not believe Anjou was serious about wedding the queen; although she was 'the best maryage in her paryshe', the duke was simply raising the prospect of their union 'as a means to render her majestie more inclynable to allowe of his proceadyngs here'.[82]

For the remainder of the year, the Anjou match crept up the political agenda, just as the possibility of England's armed intervention in the Netherlands slipped down it. Walsingham and Cobham could not prevent the states-general from signing an alliance with Anjou on 13 August, much to Elizabeth's disgust. However, without the backing of his brother or England, the duke lacked the resources to start a campaign in the Netherlands, and Henry III had no intention of starting a war against Spain. Consequently, early in January 1579, Anjou's special envoy, Jean de Simier, arrived in London to start proper matrimonial negotiations.

After a couple of months of wooing by Simier, the queen referred the marriage question to her inner ring of councillors (Burghley, Leicester, Walsingham, Wilson, Sussex, and Hunsdon).[83] For several days they met together from 8.00 a.m. until dinner, after which they conferred with the queen and then reconvened for further deliberations. In May, Elizabeth asked for their individual views, and called upon the whole council to discuss the match.[84] No one at the meetings doubted that the international situation was intensely dangerous. As far as they were concerned, the Catholic powers were bent on Elizabeth's destruction; the Queen of Scots was an implacable foe; her son, James VI, was an unknown entity; Elizabeth had no strong or certain allies; and the defences of the realm were weak. But very few of the councillors were convinced that a French Catholic marriage was the best remedy. In his own individual assessment, Walsingham presented a range of arguments against the match: he doubted Anjou's sincerity; the life of the queen would be at risk were she to fall pregnant; if Anjou inherited the French throne, England would lose its independence; and in the meantime English Catholics would be encouraged in their conspiracies. At this point, he also stated his religious objections: a Catholic king-consort would be an affront to God and a threat to the English Church. Instead of marriage, he believed, the queen should put her faith in God, whose goodness had so far frustrated the evil designs of the Catholic powers. If she looked to her defences and supported her allies, all would ultimately be well. His recommended strategy of subsidizing the Scottish, French, and Dutch protestants would cost money but was, he believed, affordable.[85]

Elizabeth did not listen to Walsingham or the others who spoke against the match. During 1579, she enjoyed the courtship rites with Simier, and for two weeks in August she appeared entranced with Anjou, who came over 'in secreat manner' to woo her.[86] Walsingham was scathing about the entertainments that Elizabeth was putting on for her suitor. Apart from their expense, he considered them to be a dangerous diversion from far more important matters taking place within Britain. After all, Regent Morton's fall from power had led to Francophile Catholics gaining influence in Scotland, while in Ireland a papal-funded army had landed, intent upon inciting rebellion to restore the Catholic Church.[87]

Walsingham did not attend the meetings in early October 1579 when privy councillors debated the marriage again. The most likely explanation is that he was sick at home, but his absence may have been enforced. In France the rumour circulated that the queen 'had dismissed him from the court', an observation probably communicated by Mendoza to his counterpart in Paris.[88] Mendoza had previously reported that Elizabeth had blamed her secretary for at least one pamphlet that was written against the match. On Walsingham's return to court at the end of the year, Elizabeth certainly treated him as a *persona non grata*. He complained ruefully that he had 'no accesse of speache unto hir majestie sithens my repaire to the court, beyng as yet interteined as a man not throughly restored to her hyness' favour'. Only in February 1580 were comments made about his 'restitucon in favour'.[89]

The general lack of enthusiasm for—even downright hostility towards—the Anjou marriage stayed Elizabeth's hand. Nonetheless, her retreat was not obvious at the time. She shed 'manny teares' in October when her privy councillors refused to give the marriage their blessing and afterwards showed 'hir great mislykyng' of anyone she thought 'wold not prefer hir mariadg before any other devise of suerty'. Abashed, her councillors then agreed to promise the queen their 'services in furderance of this mariadg', and they afterwards hammered out a draft matrimonial treaty, which Simier took back to France.[90] But the treaty contained an escape cause: Elizabeth could withdraw within two months if she failed to win over her country to the match. This she effectively did in June 1580.

This apparent end of the Anjou match brought Walsingham only small comfort, for events at home and abroad during 1580 and 1581 disturbed his peace of mind on an almost daily basis. A new domestic threat arose from the arrival of a tiny band of Jesuits from Rome in 1580, hard on the heels of seminarians from Douai. Although they claimed their mission was purely pastoral, the government believed that the priests were instigating conspiracy and unrest. Meanwhile, within Ireland, a serious Catholic rebellion had broken out in 1579, attracting foreign intervention in the form of a small army of 600 men under a Spanish commander that captured the fortress at Smerwick in county Kerry in September 1580. Then, throughout that year, the instability in Scotland was a cause of great concern. When in December Morton was arrested and sentenced to death, Walsingham and his agents were convinced that the newly created earl of Lennox fully intended 'to overthrowe religion', procure a foreign marriage for the king, and advance the Queen of Scots' 'title and partye'.[91] And, as if that was not enough, Philip II's power was growing ominously: in August 1580, he successfully invaded and annexed Portugal, while in the Netherlands his army and government were revitalized under the effective governorship of Alexander Farnese, prince of Parma, appointed on Don John's death in October 1579.

As always, Walsingham believed the queen was complaisant and supine in confronting all these enormous perils. He pushed for her to take a much tougher line towards the English Catholics and missionary priests: 'for nothing hathe don more harme then the over myche lenyte that hathe ben used in that behalfe.'[92] In foreign matters, he continued to urge that Elizabeth should aid Orange, but Scotland, he insisted, ought to be her priority. She needed to be proactive in dealing with the 'brocken state of things' there, by rescuing Morton by force, dragging James from the clutches of Lennox, and distributing pensions among the protestant lords who would then put aside their factional squabbles and be at her command.[93] As the secretary had observed earlier, Scotland was something of an obsession with him: 'though the countrie bee coulde, I can neither thynke nor speake of it, butt in heate.'[94]

Elizabeth disregarded Walsingham's advice yet again. She was reluctant to pay out pensions to the Scots because of the heavy expenses incurred in suppressing the Irish rebellion. Furthermore, as already seen, she recognized that her intervention in the northern kingdom would alienate Henry III, just when she believed a French alliance was essential for her security. To her mind, only a French alliance could give the realm sufficient protection against Spain, keep in check Catholic conspiracy on behalf of Mary, and possibly help resolve the problem of the Netherlands. But, in Walsingham's judgement, a French alliance was a chimera, since it was built on 'a hope of their sincerity', which was flimsy at best. By pursuing it exclusively, he believed, Elizabeth was putting the realm at risk: 'yf yt fall out otherwise, our danger wilbe the greater since we have neglected other helps.' Given the queen's intransigence on this matter, all he could do (or so he said) was pray: 'when I consider howe deere His owne glorye is unto Him I doubt nothing but that He wyll consume in the end both the conspyracyes and conspyrers.'[95] In reality, he was in close communication with Scottish protestants, ready to give them underhand assistance whenever possible.

Elizabeth's hopes for a French alliance looked realistic in 1581. During much of the previous year France had been engulfed in another phase of civil war, but soon after the cessation of hostilities the king turned his thoughts to an English alliance. Alarmed by Philip's absorption of Portugal and the resurgence of Habsburg power on his north-eastern border, Henry III decided to reignite the Anjou match as a preliminary to an alliance with protestant England. In April 1581, he sent a huge embassy to London for the purposes of concluding and ratifying the draft matrimonial treaty. However, to the queen's disappointment, the delegation had no instructions to negotiate an alliance without marriage. Elizabeth was now in a bind. The English opposition to the match had not abated, but the embassy was too high profile to be dismissed empty-handed. Henry would be insulted, and her hopes for an alliance probably smashed. The queen, therefore, appointed some of her privy councillors—including Walsingham—to conclude the marriage treaty. They solemnly set to work, even though they knew very well that it would never be implemented.[96] Shortly after the embassy's return home in May, Elizabeth sent word that she could not marry Anjou, and her ambassador in France proposed an anti-Spanish alliance instead. Henry III, however, insisted the marriage had to come first.

In one last effort to change the king's mind, Elizabeth arranged for Walsingham to head an embassy to France in the summer. Undoubtedly, he was chosen because of his diplomatic skills and previous experience, but Elizabeth also recognized that he would push hard for an alliance without marriage. As she told Leicester jokingly: 'she doth know her moore can not change his culor.'[97] Unsurprisingly, Walsingham had no wish to go. Remembering 'howe hardely I was used in my last voyage [to the Netherlands] and as this is a matter of more danger then that, so have I cause to feare to be served with harder measure then I was'. A major cause of Walsingham's concern was the confused—even contradictory—set of instructions he received from the queen. Nonetheless, he had to obey the royal command, fatalistically 'leaving the successe of my negotiations to the good pleasure of God'.[98]

Elizabeth's ideal outcome was an alliance with France without marriage. She was now ready to go beyond a mutual defence treaty, as signed at Blois, and to participate in a joint enterprise against Spain on land and sea. All this pleased Walsingham, but during the negotiations he was troubled about two matters: first, that the French would find the queen's offer of military help insufficient as she quibbled about details; second, that she continued to hold onto the marriage as a last resort, thereby weakening her bargaining position. His disquiet proved justified. Henry III suspected that Elizabeth intended to leave the French to bear the lion's share of the financial burden of a campaign in the Netherlands; and, because she continued to talk of marriage to the French ambassador in England, Walsingham found 'all hope of league withowt is nowe taken awaye'.[99]

Walsingham's failure to conclude the French alliance was a severe blow, and he put the blame squarely on the queen's shoulders. From France he bluntly criticized her for her irresolution concerning the marriage and for failing to accept the costs of war. If she continued to take the same course, he concluded that 'no one that serveth in place of a councellor that ether wayeth his owne creditt or carrieth that sound affection to your majestie...wold not wishe him selfe rather in the farthest part of thiopia [Ethiopia] then enjoy the fairest palace in England'.[100] By playfully alluding to his nickname (in his reference to 'Ethiopia'), Walsingham presumably hoped to remove the sting from his damning message. If so, he judged it well, for (as far as we know)

Elizabeth did not take offence. It is even possible that she may have taken the criticism to heart. Within a few months of Walsingham's return, she was preparing to subsidize Anjou's campaign in the Netherlands, and it went ahead early the next year under her sponsorship and without the open backing of his brother.

Once back in England, Walsingham found his workload had substantially increased. Wilson had died the previous May, and Walsingham had to soldier along alone as secretary until the end of September 1586, when Davison was appointed his junior partner. Furthermore, the information-gathering and analysis that were part of the secretary's duties were growing ever more extensive and burdensome. Walsingham and Burghley had been running networks of intelligencers for more than a decade, employing respectable diplomats, merchants, artists, poets, and musicians, who travelled widely or were based in foreign cities, and they often paid for their information out of their own pockets.[101] However, during the early and mid-1580s, Walsingham built on this base to expand the surveillance network and set up a secretarial team in his own London household to decipher, analyse, and assess the news pouring in. With the Catholic threat greatly exaggerated in his mind, he was desperate to uncover the whereabouts and activities of seminary priests and Jesuits from the Continent and to detect the conspiracies they supposedly hatched. During these years, Walsingham had some notable successes in suborning Catholics to enter his service. Most usefully, a secretary of the French ambassador became a spy in 1583, passing over to Walsingham correspondence that included packets of ciphered letters to and from Mary Queen of Scots. As we shall see, it was thanks to this source that the government obtained knowledge of the Throckmorton plot.[102]

In the midst of all this activity in defence of the realm, Walsingham was selected in August 1583 for a new diplomatic task. This time he had to go to Scotland. The queen's relationship with the young king was in trouble, and Walsingham's instructions were to upbraid her cousin for his lack of friendship towards her and advise him how to retrieve her goodwill. At best, Elizabeth hoped James could be induced to accept a pension and renew the amity; at worst, he would be warned against undertaking policies that were against her interests.[103] Walsingham thought the journey a complete waste of effort: 'as I fearre me I shalbe hable to do litte good ther, and therefore I would most willingly avoyd the journey yf by anye meanes I might do yt without her majesty's extreame displeasure.'[104] From his agents, he had learned of James's nefarious intrigues with his mother, France, and Spain. What was now needed, thought Walsingham, was military action to separate James from his present 'evil' advisers and to place the anglophile protestant lords in power.

Well before his interviews with James, Walsingham had decided to be tough and dismissive. In his view the young king needed to be reminded that the queen had not 'her sworde glewed in the scabbard, yf any wronge or dishonor be offred unto her'.[105] When he did come into the royal presence, he delivered a robust critique of the king's past conduct and lectured him about the nature of good kingship. Going well beyond his brief, Walsingham told the young king 'howe farr fourth his regalitye stretched' and challenged James's statement that his power was absolute with the words:

> yong princes were many tymes carryed into great errours uppon an opinion of the absolutnes of ther royall authoritye, and do not consider that when they transgresse the bounds and limitts of the lawe they leave to be kings and become tyrants.

The histories of England, continued Walsingham, provided 'sufficient presidents' of kings deposed because they had not put aside their evil councillors who advised them to go along the path of absolute rule and 'make will stand for lawe'. James should not forget, Walsingham concluded, that, 'as subjects are bound to obey dutifully, so were princes bound to command justlyie'.[106] As to be expected, such temerity went down badly with James, who was also insulted when Walsingham refused to parley with his ministers. The ambassador's remarks, moreover, mounted a challenge to monarchical authority in general, one that could just as easily be applied to England. Realizing he had gone too far and fearing a complaint might be lodged against him, Walsingham asked for Burghley's support. He justified his behaviour to the queen by relaying his genuine opinion that James had moved into his mother's camp and intended to be 'an instrument' of foreign powers against Elizabeth.

To counter the threat he perceived, Walsingham decided—on his own initiative—to hold secret talks with representatives of 'well affected' Scottish lords 'to lay som such plot as he [James] may be bridled and forced, whether he will or not, to depend upon your majesty's favor'.[107] At their covert meeting, the Scottish lords made an offer 'to remove the yll affected from abowt the king', provided that the queen gave them aid. To Walsingham's dismay—but surely not surprise—Elizabeth vetoed this proposal and chose instead to continue the path of negotiation.[108]

Walsingham's return to London in October 1583 coincided with the uncovering of the Throckmorton plot. In his absence, Burghley had been keeping watch over the correspondence passing through the French ambassador's house, and, a fortnight after the secretary's return, it was decided to arrest a young recusant gentleman Francis Throckmorton, who was a letter carrier for Mary. Under torture, Throckmorton confessed to the existence of an international conspiracy to invade England and place Mary on the throne. The ensuing wave of arrests and interrogations incriminated several Catholic noblemen, Henry duke of Guise, the Jesuit Robert Persons, and Mendoza, who was expelled from England in January 1584. However, nothing concrete could be pinned on Mary or her son James.

The following summer, Scottish involvement in conspiracy against Elizabeth did come to light. After a Scottish Jesuit, William Crichton, had been extradited to England, he was found to be carrying papers that revealed Lennox's involvement in planning a 'great enterprise' against England in 1582. Walsingham interrogated the Jesuit and was satisfied that Mary had approved the plan and that it would again be put into operation after a Spanish victory in the Netherlands.[109] With this knowledge to hand, the privy council took two significant decisions in October 1584. First, it agreed that Elizabeth had to prevent the collapse of the Dutch revolt; second, it approved the bond of association, which Walsingham drafted with Burghley and helped administer.[110]

Mary's destruction in 1586 is often blamed on Walsingham and his spy network, as if the Scottish queen bore no responsibility for her role in the Babington plot. At her trial, she formally accused the secretary of falsifying the evidence against her, which he publicly, calmly, and convincingly denied. As already seen, he and his code-breaker Thomas Phelippes did forge a postscript to her incriminating letter to Anthony Babington, but the letter itself was genuine.[111]

Any joy that Walsingham experienced in exposing Mary's guilt did not last long. Two days after her trial was over, he learned of the death of his son-in-law Sir Philip Sidney at Zutphen in October, a cause of great grief to him and his daughter. Apart from the personal loss, it left Walsingham with a huge financial burden. Sidney's debts amounted to £6,000, and Walsingham took on the responsibility—which he could ill afford—of paying all them off, since Sidney's uncle Leicester would not help out. In dire financial need, Walsingham appealed to the queen for some assistance, and on 10 December Burghley spoke up in this 'particular cause', reminding Elizabeth of the extraordinary service rendered by her secretary, 'as one under God she ought to acknowledge the preservacon of her life'. Her answer 'in general was good' and Burghley 'had good hope therof', but feared that—as ever—she would make no sudden resolution.[112] Additionally, it is possible that Elizabeth saw no need to act swiftly. The previous year, she had awarded Walsingham the farm of the customs of the outports, which would bring him a lucrative income from overseas trade, so perhaps she thought he had income enough: after all, he had no son to provide for and his daughter might marry again. Whatever the cause of her lack of immediate generosity, Walsingham thought it most unjust and left the court in mid-December in offence: 'her majesty's unkynd dealyng towards me hath so wounded me as I cold take no comfort to staye there.' He transferred the signet and the privy seal into Davison's custody, and intended to withdraw from active public life: 'I howld them happyest in this governement that may be rather lookers on then actors.'[113]

Physically and mentally broken, Walsingham remained away from court over the winter. When Elizabeth signed Mary's death warrant on 1 February 1587, she told Davison to take it to Walsingham, who was still at home, and quipped that 'the grief thereof would go near (as she merrily said) to kill him outright'. Walsingham did not attend the meeting held in Burghley's room when all the privy councillors agreed to send off the warrant, but he approved the decision and made arrangements for the dispatch of the executioner to Fotheringhay.[114] Elizabeth either did not know about, or else chose to ignore, his involvement. Dismissing Davison, she summoned Walsingham back to court on 14 February to resume his duties. That year, he also received rewards for his good service: several royal manors in fee farm (a grant of the right to retain land in return for a fixed rent) in April; and the chancellorship of the duchy of Lancaster on 15 June.[115]

Back at court, Walsingham resumed the administrative responsibilities for the war against Spain. He had approved Elizabeth's decision to send an army under Leicester to the Netherlands, certain that otherwise the Dutch would be defeated and England would have to face a future Spanish invasion without any allies. Consequently, he disapproved strongly of the peace feelers that Elizabeth was extending to Philip and his representatives before the armada set sail in 1588. The secretary exchanged harsh words with the queen about the direction of policy, and—if information brought to Mendoza (now based in Paris) was accurate—Elizabeth even threw a slipper in his face, because she believed he was keeping information from her that might lead her to withdraw from the perilous and increasingly expensive campaign in the Netherlands.[116]

The strain of the war not only affected Elizabeth's temper; it also took its toll on Walsingham's health. As secretary he took charge of mustering troops, organizing coastal defences, securing the Scottish border, dealing with diplomatic exchanges, all on top of the routine and heavy secretarial duties. Illness kept him away from court for a short time in late 1587, and he had nearly four months' leave from council meetings during 1589. Rallying in the latter half of the year, he attended again until a week before his death. The queen expected him to work despite his sicknesses: during the night of 2 April 1590 he had a fit, and the next day Elizabeth told him to make arrangements for a meeting between an Italian visitor and Burghley, and reminded him to carry out 'the spedy dispatche' of all Irish matters.[117] Four days later Walsingham was dead. There is no evidence that Elizabeth visited him on his sickbed or mourned his death. She showed her appreciation of his long service only by excusing the debts he left her.[118] Walsingham had no state funeral but was buried in the same tomb as Sidney at St Paul's in a simple ceremony that accorded with his wishes.

Walsingham's temperament was very different from that of the queen. He was impetuous in his policy recommendations, whereas she was generally cautious. He lacked patience, dreading the consequences of delays; she thrived on delays and preferred to postpone making decisions until events forced her hand. He feared the consequences of God's displeasure; she took comfort in her firm belief that God would protect her from present dangers as He had in the past. At the same time, they did not share the same vision of international politics: for Walsingham, England's security could not be separated from transnational protestantism; for Elizabeth, there was a clear distinction between the two, and her priority was always the former.

Of course Walsingham was not alone in advising Elizabeth to take a more proactive course against the Catholic threat at home and abroad. But, unlike Burghley, he was not a reassuring presence when offering counsel; and, unlike Leicester, he did not provide light relief by entertaining or flattering the queen when proposing policy. From the surviving evidence, Walsingham appears in the persona of a doctor offering unpalatable medicine for a serious disease without adopting a soothing bedside manner. Given these circumstances, the queen's and secretary's ability to work closely together for over two decades is remarkable. It was possible only because Elizabeth valued

Walsingham's abilities and capacity for hard work; she trusted his loyalty and recognized that on some occasions his observations were correct. For his part, the secretary respected her royal authority, even though he sometimes came dangerously close to challenging it. Although he feared Elizabeth was not always wise, he did not view her as a tyrant, for he believed that she had the welfare of the state at heart. Their collaboration is testimony to the queen's readiness to listen to (though not necessarily to follow) wide-ranging views and to have about her councillors who were not 'yes-men'. This was the great strength of her rule.

II

The 'Pygmy': Sir Robert Cecil

The younger son of Lord Burghley, Robert Cecil did not initially seem marked out for high political office. Born on 1 June 1563, he was 21 years younger than his half-brother Thomas, sickly from birth, and very short of stature, with a curved spine that was almost certainly the result of hereditary scoliosis.[1] His unprepossessing appearance made him the butt of jokes, his enemies in the 1590s, for example, thinking it very funny when a visitor failed to notice him in the privy chamber, because he was 'so litle'.[2] But Robert Cecil had a strong intellect and serious frame of mind that led his father to select him—rather than Thomas—as his political heir.

Schooled at home, under the supervision of his mother, Mildred, Cecil received a first-class education in the classics and modern languages (French and Italian), subjects that would prepare him well for public life. Aged 17, he entered Gray's Inn to study the basics of common law—also useful for a royal servant—but he continued living at Burghley House on the Strand, probably because of his weak constitution. The next year (1581) he moved on to study at St John's College Cambridge, Burghley's *alma mater*, but he returned to Theobalds in the autumn of 1582 to be tutored by the Cambridge scholar William Wilkinson, who was recommended for his 'good knowledge in the Latin and Greke toungues' and 'good sight in the mathmaticke sciences, especiallie cosmographie'.[3] The breadth of the young man's education was not exceptional for gentlemen in later Elizabethan England, but in his case it was designed to equip him for a distinguished life in royal service. Residing at home, moreover, gave him the opportunity to mingle with the queen's councillors and officers, as well as Elizabeth herself.

During the summers of 1583 and 1584, Cecil was physically fit enough to travel to France for educational purposes. On the first occasion he stayed with Edward Stafford, the newly appointed English ambassador, on the second with the sieur de Marchaumont, a

member of the late duke of Anjou's household. We know little about
Cecil's activities during the first trip, but letters home in 1584 reveal
that he was regularly attending lectures at the Sorbonne, the theological college of the University of Paris. That September and October,
the 21-year-old also wrote out several papers in French that related
observations of the country, its nobility, and the political situation
there. Sent to Walsingham, the reports were based on existing texts
and probably contained information that was already known to the
secretary. But, since intelligence-gathering was a valuable skill for an
aspiring royal servant, Burghley had most likely set his son the exercise as part of his political training.[4]

On his return to England, Cecil entered the House of Commons.
Inevitably, he obtained his place through the influence of his father:
in 1584 and 1586 he represented Westminster, where Burghley was
high steward; from 1589 onwards he was elected as the senior knight
for Hertfordshire, a county where the baron had recently been
appointed lord lieutenant. In the 1586 session, Cecil sat on a committee
to discuss Mary Queen of Scots, and was caught up in the clamour
for her execution. Soon afterwards his name—or rather his initials—
first appeared in print. As part of his father's campaign against Mary,
Cecil contributed the preface to *The Copie of a Letter to the Right
Honourable the Earle of Leycester*, a pamphlet that printed the
queen's responses to parliamentary petitions calling for Mary's death.
Ostensibly written to bring Leicester up to date with events that had
occurred during his absence in the Netherlands, *The Copie* was in
reality a public relations exercise. Soon to be translated into Latin
and French, it was published to impart Elizabeth's unwillingness to
sign Mary's death warrant, and consequently to minimize her role in
the execution when—and if—it took place. Elizabeth fully collabor-
ated in the project. Although Cecil apologized in the text for his
'slender maner of report, so to have blemished the excellencie of her
majestie's speaches', the truth was that the queen had heavily cor-
rected the original drafts before they went to the printers.[5]

By this time, Cecil was already on cordial terms with the queen.
They had met many times at his father's houses, and she had received
him in the presence chamber at court in 1584. That year he wrote to
her from France, detailing the 'honorable reception' he had received
there.[6] In 1587, they had a misunderstanding, when Cecil requested
the reversion of all his father's offices in Hertfordshire (meaning that
he would hold them after his father's death or retirement). As Cecil
told Burghley: 'I am sory she did mistrost so much my naturall duty

to your lordship, as to think that...I cold have the thought to dreame of the use of it during your lordship's time, otherwise then by your permission'. Thanks to the earl of Essex's mediation, the queen saw her mistake and agreed to the grant.[7] In 1588, Cecil's name appears for the first time on the New Year's gift roll, when he presented the queen with a green porcelain cup with an ornamental silver cover.[8] By then, Elizabeth was showing Cecil another mark of favour: she was addressing him by a nickname, albeit one he despised, 'her sporting name of pigmy'.[9]

Cecil's first semi-official mission on the queen's behalf came in February 1588. The 24-year-old was granted permission to accompany the earl of Derby to Bourbourg near Ostend on a peace mission to the duke of Parma. Even though Cecil doubted that the talks would end Anglo-Spanish hostilities, he was very keen to go 'in order to see and heare something that may make me wiser and yeld me the satisfaction that the being present at such a matter sow ever it succed may afford my yong yeares'.[10] But, fearing for his son's health, Burghley was reluctant for him to travel, and only gave way when his wife weighed in on Cecil's side. Elizabeth also approved the young man's participation in the embassy, telling him to write directly to her while he was away.[11]

While waiting for the colloquy at Bourbourg to convene, Cecil set off to view the Netherlands. Despite his disability, he survived the rigours of poor accommodation, freezing cold, and dangerous travel in the war-torn towns and countryside, without any mishap and in good humour. Every minute of his time was filled with worthwhile activities: he read up on treaties, discussed civil law with two of his companions, wrote a daily journal, and sent long, detailed observations of the country to his father. At Ghent, he had an audience with Parma; in the Hague, he met Maurice of Nassau, the son of William of Orange, who had assumed leadership of the revolt against Spain. While at Antwerp and Sluys, Cecil took note of the Spanish fortifications and shipping, deciding then—if not before—that the prospects for peace were poor. Perhaps for this reason he decided to leave the embassy early and return home in April.[12]

Over the next year or so, Cecil's main focus was family matters. His adored sister Anne died in June 1588 and his mother the following April. Both bereavements hit him and Burghley hard. But Cecil's loss was alleviated by the new happiness he found through a marriage to Elizabeth (Bess), the daughter of the tenth Lord Cobham and one of the queen's favourite goddaughters, who was often in the privy chamber. They had been betrothed shortly before Lady Burghley's death and wed quietly at Cobham's house on 31 August 1589. It was a love match—unusual for early modern couples—but it was also a desirable political alliance for both sets of parents. Robert's and Bess's first child (named William after his paternal grandfather) was born in March 1591; a second (Frances) followed in 1593.[13]

Soon after his marriage Cecil began to assist his father in carrying the administrative load of the principal secretary. Instead of appointing someone new to the office after Walsingham's death in April 1590, Elizabeth let the burden of work fall on her trusted Burghley. Nearly 70 and in almost constant pain, he nearly broke under the strain, but the arrangement allowed Cecil to work under his father's tutelage, learning the craft of governance and acquiring much-needed political experience. Burghley tried to have the young man awarded the vacant post, but the queen resisted and in the early 1590s there was no guarantee that the secretaryship would eventually be his. Other candidates included seasoned governmental servants such as Thomas Wilkes, Edward Wotten, Sir Edward Dyer, and Henry Killigrew. Unlike them, Cecil was young and had not yet filled any diplomatic posting or held public office. His appointment to this crucial and powerful position could therefore smell of nepotism and provide Catholics with further ammunition against a regime they already claimed was narrowly based and a *regnum Cecilianum*. Fortunately for the Cecils, Robert's potential rivals lacked any significant patrons, whereas he could rely on support from Hatton and Buckhurst, and not just his father. Although Essex strongly opposed Cecil's appointment, the earl unrealistically put his weight behind the disgraced William Davison, whose rehabilitation Elizabeth had no intention of considering.[14]

Elizabeth's knighting of Cecil in May 1591 and—more importantly—his entry into the privy council a few months later were marks of the queen's growing confidence in him. As a privy councillor, Cecil became a regular at court with access to the privy chamber. He grew accustomed to the queen's moods and learned to work around them. So, for example, when he found her 'owt of quiet with her forraine fowes [foes] and her home broyls [disorders]', he would hold back letters requesting special favours or containing bad news until better 'occasion may serve'.[15] Equally important, Cecil began assuming a more public profile and taking on greater responsibilities.

In 1592, the queen gave Cecil two major assignments. In April he sat on the commission that found Sir John Perrot guilty of treason, pretty much a foregone conclusion; and in September he was ordered to supervise the unloading of rich cargo from the captured Iberian carrack the *Madre de Dios*, which had been towed into Dartmouth, Devon. This was a far more difficult task. Private looting was already underway and needed to be stopped so that the queen could obtain her due return. But the Cecils had hardly any influence in the West Country, which limited Robert's personal authority there. Wisely he and his father persuaded the queen to release Sir Walter Ralegh from the Tower (where he had been languishing since the summer) so that the Devonshire sea captain could assist him in salvaging what remained of the cargo. Ralegh proved his worth, but Cecil bore the brunt of the administrative burden, supervising investigations into the thievery, ordering searches of 'everye bagg or male [mail] cominge from the west', demanding the arrest of suspicious characters, and attending when their depositions were taken. In this way he arranged 'a patorne' (pattern) that, if followed after his departure, would result in the recovery of 'muche pillage'.[16]

Perhaps fearing that his tough actions might result in malicious complaints, Cecil wrote to Elizabeth from Dartmouth. The language he employed followed the conventions of courtly love we more readily associate with Hatton or Essex but were widespread in the late-Elizabethan court:

> Herein I am most blessed that I am a vassall to His celestiall creature, who pleasethe out of angellyke grace, to pardone and allowe my carefull and zealous desires. My services are attended with envie, I must be offensive to the multitude, and to others that may be revenge-full, who also have many and great friends. I can please none because I thirst only to please one.[17]

Cecil had no need to fear. Elizabeth was delighted with his service, and, as far as we can ascertain, no voices were raised maligning him.

Cecil's growing prominence was plain to see in the 1593 parliament. Up till then he had never delivered a speech in the Commons, but on 26 February that year he took a lead in presenting the government's case for the subsidy bill. However, he did not acquit himself well. Normally a single subsidy was collected over a two-year period, but this time Burghley in the Lords demanded three subsidies to be paid in as many years, and the bill ran into trouble. Instead of wooing the Commons—as Hatton might have done—Cecil was inclined to be tetchy and, worse still, was caught out in two untruths that lost him the confidence of the House. The first was when he tried to deflect criticisms from the queen by making the absurd statement that she 'never demaunded three nor yet one' subsidy. The second was his denial that Elizabeth had been told the names of those MPs who had taken the lead in objecting to the measure. As many in the Commons were aware, Elizabeth knew very well who the troublemakers were, and indeed they paid for their outspokenness afterwards.[18] In the event, the government obtained most of the supply it required. So, although Cecil's parliamentary performance had been far from sure-footed, he impressed Elizabeth with his loyalty and ultimate success.[19]

Over the next few years, Cecil increasingly took over the day-to-day secretarial work, as his father was frequently sick and absent from court. Burghley would pass on to Cecil letters that needed the queen's urgent response, and her instructions often went out in Cecil's name.[20] As Cecil lived in an annexe of Burghley House in the Strand, communication between father and son was usually quick and easy; and, even when Burghley retired to Theobalds, Cecil had only a short distance to travel or dispatch his posts. Burghley, however, still clung on to power: 'I looke before I slepe to heare from you, how far her majesty do allow of my simple opinion for the Irland causes,' he wrote from Theobalds to his son on 7 December 1593. Later that night he wrote again, this time with his opinions about the English campaign in Brittany and sums of money for Ireland.[21] A few months into 1594, Burghley was either concerned that Cecil was failing to keep on top of the paperwork or irritated that he was being sidelined; towards the end of one day he complained to his son: 'I marvell that I heare not from you concerning the letters to be sent to Ireland, whyther I also I have in readiness some from myself.'[22]

In truth, power was slowly slipping away from the old man into the hands of his son. In April 1594, Robert Bowes (the then English ambassador in Scotland) explained that he would no longer send dispatches for the queen via Burghley, since 'it hathe pleased her majestie to imploy and use the services of Sir Robert Cicill in th'advertisements of her majestie's pleasures and derreccons [directions] latelye geven for negociacion of the causes here'.[23] By the end of that year, moreover, Burghley was not always able to follow through his close attention to detail. When posting Cecil two packets of letters from Ireland, he explained: 'I minde not to write unto you the particulars therof, for that they be verie many, and therefore to be more diligently perused. My healthe serveth me not to enter into any finall consideration therof.'[24] Nonetheless, the lord treasurer's mind remained focused on matters of state: he continued to receive many of the letters directed to the privy council, and he met his son regularly to discuss a wide range of governmental business.

From necessity, Elizabeth had to rely more heavily on Cecil's counsel during the 1590s. His father was simply not always available for meetings. Sometimes, Elizabeth would wait for Burghley's opinions to come through to her by means of his son; but, as time passed and Burghley's health deteriorated, Cecil's presence and advice were the ones required. In October 1594, for example, the queen would 'mak no answer' to the Scottish ambassador until her acting secretary came to the court at Nonsuch.[25]

Eventually in July 1596 Cecil received his prize: the secretaryship. His promotion, however, threatened to disrupt the smooth running of the privy council, since Essex found it hard to accept the decision gracefully, especially as the queen had broken a promise to him in making the appointment. Equally galling for the earl was the leading role that Cecil played immediately afterwards in the commission set up to investigate the cost of the Cadiz campaign and the extent of the booty seized by English soldiers and sailors.[26] Even today it is unclear as to whether Cecil was spurred on primarily by political ambition or public service in his drive to dig out financial irregularities. But, Essex and his friends were in no doubt that Cecil was seeking to discredit the earl in order to forward his own career.

Harmony began to be restored only when the commissioners ended their work in mid-September without any formal charges being brought against Essex or his followers. Burghley also helped to pacify the earl by recommending strongly that the victorious general should be granted the profits of the prisoners' ransoms from Cadiz, counsel that provoked the queen's anger and led the lord treasurer to moan that he was caught between the Scylla of the queen's fury and the Charybdis of the earl's displeasure.[27] Whatever Essex's true feelings were towards Cecil, he had to put them aside that autumn, when Philip II unexpectedly launched a new armada against England as a reprisal for the attack on Cadiz. The invasion threat forced Elizabeth's privy councillors to work together to withstand the challenge. What is more, during the crisis, Essex proved unusually conciliatory; when the queen wanted a temporary council of war established on 2 November, he nominated his long-standing rival Ralegh and Cecil's friend Sir George Carew as members, and moved that the meetings should take place at Burghley's house under the lord treasurer's presidency.[28]

In the end, the invasion scare came to nothing, as an autumn gale scattered the Spanish navy off Cape Finisterre in Brittany. But it was quite clear that poor intelligence had contributed to the panic at the English court. Until then, there had been a high (if misplaced) degree of confidence in the informants operating on the Continent and reporting separately to Essex or the Cecils. Although these men were adept at uncovering assassination plots against Elizabeth (whether real or imagined), the armada of October 1596 had come totally out of the blue and revealed the need for more reliable knowledge about Habsburg wartime strategy. To improve matters, Cecil instantly set to work on improving and enlarging the intelligence service, and, by early 1598, he had more than twenty agents in the field who were based in Portugal, Italy, Brussels, Spain, Flanders, Sweden, and Scotland. To finance this expansion, Cecil was able to draw upon monies in the privy purse, a coffer that the principal secretary might access for intelligence work as well as other unspecified purposes. Without this resource, Essex simply could not compete with Cecil's level of recruitment and spending, even though he kept up his own agents.[29] Recognition of this fact, no doubt, fostered the earl's insecurities and fuelled his resentment towards Cecil, who was increasingly proving indispensable to the queen.

Shortly after the invasion scare of 1596, the court settled down for Christmas. The workload on Cecil did not cease, despite the court festivities, and additionally he and his pregnant wife had to entertain the queen at his lodgings in the Strand for a day in December. A month later, Cecil's wife miscarried her third child and died, a personal tragedy for the widower, who was by all accounts broken-hearted. His friends rallied round: Ralegh wrote him a beautiful letter of condolence, and the lord admiral expressed similar sentiments in his blunt style. Sir Edward Hoby offered Cecil the use of his house: 'for the nearenes thereof to the courte, it mought any waies be agreable unto your honour to remove your self thither from the place I know yow can take no greate delight in.'[30] If the queen wrote, her letter has not survived.[31] But she showed her respect for her secretary and affection for his late wife by allowing her the rank of a baroness at her burial in Westminster Abbey.[32] Six months afterwards, the widower was still grieving for his loss, leading one of his aunts to advise that he leave behind the melancholy that threatened to make him 'a sullen, sharp, sowre plumme' and 'a miseanthropos hateful to God and man'.[33] Others proposed that he took another wife, but Cecil never remarried.

Notwithstanding his bereavement, Cecil was back at his desk within days of Bess's death. The queen expected no less, as his services were needed. Top of the agenda for discussion in early 1597 was Essex's project for a new assault on Spain, and from April the secretary joined the earl, Lord Admiral Howard, and Ralegh (who was not yet restored to royal favour) to prepare a campaign to attack the Spanish fleet at Ferrol and intercept the treasure at the Azores. All the councillors were behind the venture, which became known as the 'Islands' voyage'. 'I lyk so well to attempt some thing against our Spanish popish proven enemy, as I hope God will prosper your purpose,' declared Burghley in approval.[34] During July, while Essex and the fleet were stalled at port awaiting better weather, Burghley and Cecil were both supportive of the earl. Burghley sent him some verses of the 107th psalm for comfort; Cecil passed on court news, taking especial delight in relating how the queen had wrong-footed the Polish ambassador when she responded to his rudeness in perfect *ex tempore* Latin.[35] He also let Essex know that 'the queen is so disposed now to have us all love you, as she and I do evry night talk like angells of yow'.[36] In other words, Cecil made clear that he was not exploiting the earl's absence from court and difficulties in setting sail to speak ill of him to the queen.

Unanimity and goodwill disintegrated, however, as the expedition failed in all its objectives. Essex and Ralegh quarrelled irreconcilably on the voyage; Cecil's new appointment as chancellor of the duchy of Lancaster rankled with Essex, who thought the secretary had honours enough; Howard and Essex almost came to blows over the lord admiral's elevation to an earldom. The queen tried unsuccessfully to contain these spats, while Cecil stayed out of them. Throughout Essex's period of withdrawal from court in late 1597, the secretary's attention was focused on the parliament summoned for October and the preparations for a diplomatic mission to France.

Thanks to his new office, Cecil could influence the selection of MPs for the boroughs within the duchy of Lancaster, and he utilized this patronage energetically to secure a compliant Commons. During the session, the Cecils' political dominance was on show when a conference was held between the two Houses in January 1598, for Burghley then led the Lords and Cecil the Commons. Cecil's private memoranda reveal that he was better prepared for this parliament, and he had no difficulty in obtaining a grant of three subsidies. Nevertheless, he was unable to withstand the Commons' protests about monopolies (royal patents to protect the manufacture and trade of new commodities). Since these patents touched the royal prerogative, Elizabeth thought them outside the competence of parliamentary debate, but

MPs argued that monopolies were affecting the country adversely by causing prices to rise. Only Elizabeth's promise to reform abuses in the system prevented a major disturbance—at least until the next parliament in 1601.[37]

No sooner was the parliament over than Cecil set off on his first official diplomatic mission. Elizabeth ordered him to lead an embassy to the king of France to discuss prospects for an international peace. Although on the quiet Henry IV had already decided to sign an agreement with Spain, the terms of the triple alliance of 1596 he had signed with England and the United Provinces stated that none of the parties could make a separate peace. Consequently, Henry now invited his two allies to join him in a comprehensive treaty to end the European war. Like the French king, Elizabeth was war-weary, but she would not engage in peace negotiations unless the security of the Dutch protestants was assured; and Cecil and his fellow envoys were instructed to convey this message to the French as well as to prevent them from acting alone.[38] Their task demanded considerable finesse, as Elizabeth wanted them 'to deale with the king in formalitie and generalitie' rather than 'openlie and roundlie'.[39]

Cecil had been initially loath to take on the assignment, fearing that a journey abroad might endanger his political position at home. Without daily access to the queen, he would be vulnerable to malicious attack from rivals. For that reason, he held 'many privat conferences, many consultacions' with Essex, who had returned to court. Before leaving, Cecil wanted assurances that 'nothing shuld pass here in his absence that might be a prejudice or offensive unto hym'. To show his own goodwill towards the earl, Cecil 'delt very earnestly...to favour Sir Edward Wotten to be a baron' and promised to do what he could to further Robert Sidney's suit—neither of which actually came to pass. More successfully, Cecil persuaded the queen to make Essex a free gift of £7,000 from the cargo of cochineal captured in the 1597 Islands voyage. As a result of his endeavours, a truce between the two councillors was agreed, and Essex 'did assure hym [Cecil] that in his absence, nothing should be done here that might be disagreeable unto him'.[40] The earl kept his word.

To retain Essex's favour while abroad, Cecil wrote to him regularly, keeping the earl (who was acting as temporary secretary) abreast of his proceedings in France. In one letter, moreover, he emphasized just how important it was for the two men to treat each other with love and respect, and so dispel rumours of factional conflict:

> I do not only conceave inward contentment in the knowledge of your
> care and affection, but am apt to let it appeare externally, here to my
> company, how much I am valued by yow ... I hope we shall overcome
> all pety doubts what the world can judg of our correspondency.

After all, Cecil continued, 'nothing is so deare unto us as her majesty's
service which heretofore hath prospered the worse by our misfor-
tunes of pleasing our followers'.[41] To sustain the show of friendliness
between them, Cecil contacted Essex immediately upon his homecoming; he was writing first to the earl, explained the principal secretary, 'as him to whom I have professed entirely love and service'.[42]

As it turned out, Cecil needed Essex's goodwill while abroad, for
the embassy to France began badly and ended in failure. Lengthy
storms and the death of one of the three English envoys (Thomas
Wilkes) had delayed the delegation, so that by the time it arrived in
Paris the French king had moved on to Angers. On his own initiative,
Cecil agreed to meet Henry there, and had to convince the queen
(who was not best pleased) that he really had no choice but to leave
Paris and go towards Brittany. After he gained access to the king on
24 February, all seemed well for a short time, but their interviews
became cold and acrimonious once it became apparent that Henry
was on the point of signing a separate peace with Spain.[43] Without
further ado, the English diplomats left France on 15 April. The French
and their king, Cecil complained to Elizabeth, had no sense of honour,
for they stated openly 'that necessity hath no law; that every man
ought to provide first for himself'. Not wanting to insult a monarch
to another monarch, Cecil blamed French national characteristics for
what he saw as Henry's betrayal: 'France will be France, and leave his
best friends.'[44] Elizabeth agreed. As she told Cecil:

> wee had that princelie opinion of the king himselfe that in no wise he
> would ever sever himselfe from us, and other his allies ... neither that
> anie particular respect to his present private commoditie or ease,
> though percase not durable, should drawe him a prince of honor
> against manie his solemne promises to endanger his friends that had in
> his adversities and great lacke succoured him with monie and men.[45]

But what ought she do next? Should England follow France and
make peace with Spain? The treaty of Vervins (published in May
1598) allowed the queen a six-month window to join the Anglo-French
settlement. On this issue Elizabeth, Cecil, and his father were at one.
Queen, secretary, and lord treasurer wanted the United Provinces to

join England in negotiations with Spain. If the Dutch refused to parley with the enemy, Elizabeth would not abandon them, but she and the Cecils all agreed that the Dutch should then contribute more to the costs of war. Essex, however, found this approach pusillanimous. Spain was in his view a dangerous and untrustworthy foe, as could be seen by Philip II's support for Irish rebel leaders and attempted naval assaults in 1596 and 1597. The earl, consequently, argued in council for the continuation of all-out war against Spain. The disputes between him and the Cecils became personal and bitter.[46]

Unexpectedly, Cecil and Essex soon crossed swords about another matter: who should be the new lord deputy of Ireland. The previous one—Thomas third Baron Burgh—had died from typhus in October 1597, but as yet no one had been appointed to replace him, although the earl of Ormond had been made lieutenant general of the army. By the summer of 1598, the position clearly had to be filled, given the escalating rebellion in Ulster. No agreement could be reached, however. Elizabeth supported Cecil's nominee, Sir William Knollys, but Essex viewed this proposal as a factional device to deprive him of a key supporter in the privy council. The result—as we have seen in Chapter 7—was Essex's withdrawal from court on 1 July 1598.

During the earl's absence, Cecil tried to pour some oil on troubled waters. He would not, for example, support the earl of Pembroke, who asked him to bring a complaint against Essex before the privy council. Pembroke had heard that Essex had greeted the news of his candidate for an office 'with scoffinge laughter', but Cecil assured Pembroke that nothing had occurred 'tendinge to your disgrace' and urged him to drop the charge.[47] At the same time, Cecil (and Burghley) would not back down from promoting the peace policy that Essex so fervently opposed, and their arguments were difficult to counter while he remained away from council meetings.

Suffering from an economic recession, high inflation, and repeated bad harvests between 1594 and 1598, the realm was in no shape to provide the resources for the new continental campaign that Essex advocated. The failure of the Islands' voyage, as well as disappointing profits from privateering ventures, gave rise to doubts about whether booty seized from Iberian (or even neutral) vessels could help finance a new offensive against Spain.[48] Furthermore, all sums of money and manpower that could be raised were needed for Ireland. So it was no wonder that privy councillors—as well as the queen—rejected the aggressive wartime strategy, backed by Essex, and also favoured cutting back on England's existing expenditure in the Netherlands.

Consequently, when Dutch envoys arrived in England in the summer of 1598 to renew their alliance with England—necessary now that the French king had withdrawn from their struggle—they confronted a privy council united in demanding tough terms. Signed on 6 August, the new treaty reduced England's military and financial costs in the Netherlands and promised Dutch repayment of English loans on a yearly basis. Although Elizabeth promised not to abandon her allies, her commitment to them was not open-ended, as she did not rule out starting peace negotiations with Spain in the future. Nonetheless she realized that England's security was entwined with that of the United Provinces, and accepted that any peace terms reached with Spain had to safeguard Dutch independence.[49]

Three days before the Anglo-Dutch treaty was signed, Burghley died. Though his death was hardly unexpected, Cecil was bereft of his closest family member, mentor, and confidant. It seems that as a result he became emotionally isolated, for he was distant from his children and had few friends whom he could trust entirely. The queen was always his 'gracious sovereign', and Cecil could not share confidences with her as he had with his father. Indeed, as we will see, his letters to his one close friend—Sir George Carew—suggest that he was rather frightened of Elizabeth, uncertain of her good opinion or continuing favour.[50]

Burghley's death also left his younger son politically and financially vulnerable. While Cecil's political position was secure enough thanks to Essex's difficult behaviour, his own administrative competence, and Elizabeth's dislike of change, it was far from certain that he would advance any further and receive the offices left vacant by his father's death. The Cambridge dons immediately elected Essex as their new chancellor, although Cecil had been high steward of the university since 1591; many people expected that the queen would appoint the earl as master of the court of wards; and Lord Buckhurst was correctly identified as the most likely future lord treasurer. Yet, without additional public office—and ideally the mastership of the court of wards—Cecil would struggle to maintain a prestigious position in the state. As the older brother, Thomas had inherited the barony, Burghley House, the house on the Strand, and Burghley's midland estates, whereas Robert had received only Theobalds and the Hertfordshire landholdings, which brought him an income of no more than £1,800 a year. The secretary was therefore in need of the lucrative mastership and further royal grants in order to maintain Theobalds, a large household, and his family commitments, let alone to display the magnificence expected of a prominent public figure.[51] But Cecil had to wait nearly nine months before securing the mastership.

Even without the mastership, Cecil had a huge workload. At one point he described himself as labouring 'like a pack horse', and he was not exaggerating.[52] The paperwork involved became too much for one man to read, assess, and answer, and consequently in 1600 his personal secretary Sir John Herbert was appointed a second secretary for the state, earning the jibe 'Mr Secondary Secretary'. Herbert seems to have concentrated on economic affairs, leaving Cecil freer to focus on foreign policy and Ireland.[53] But Herbert was also weighed down with his service to the crown, and the burdens on Cecil were not reduced as much as he would have liked. Indeed, all active councillors were clearly overstretched, as indeed they had been for many years. Cecil continued to attend council meetings assiduously and, like his father beforehand, acted as the interface between the privy council and the queen. However, unlike his father, Cecil sometimes suffered from stress. After 'some indisposition' that kept him from court, the secretary admitted that 'cares and payns (which are annexed to our dutyes) bringe with them anxietyes of mynde and decaye of health (even in the best constitutions)'.[54] And of course, his constitution was not the strongest.

One of the duties facing Cecil and the privy council in 1599 was to provide Essex (who had taken over the Irish command after his return to court in September 1598) with the military supplies needed for defeating Tyrone in Ulster. After Essex's departure in March 1599, Cecil drew up lists of what was required, and the council sent off directives for provisioning the army, transporting troops, and defending Irish towns. Given the secretary's responsibilities, it is easy to see why he came into the firing line when the supplies—especially munitions and means of transport—proved to be too few and too slow in arriving. But there is no evidence that Cecil did other than his best in trying to ensure the success of Essex's campaign. The logistical difficulties of sending war materials to Ireland were formidable.[55] Furthermore, other administrative matters were also demanding the attention of Cecil and the council in the summer of 1599, not least the defence of the English coast, as there was another armada scare, and the 'very lewd and dangerous practizes of certaine Jesuits' and seminary priests.[56]

Despite the threat of another Spanish invasion attempt, Cecil was also occupied in this period with tentative peace negotiations. The previous year, Archduke Albert of Austria and his wife Isabella (the infanta of Castile) had become rulers of the Netherlands, and in late August 1599 they sent their envoy Jerome Cooman to London to raise informally the possibility of a peace treaty.[57] Cecil's response was positive but cautious. His position was that 'peace would be wellcome' provided that 'yt com accompaigned with safe circumstances'.[58] The queen, Cecil believed, shared this view. She was ready 'to treat for the good of her people', he revealed, but at the same time it 'behoveth her majestie to do all she can to bring the states [United Provinces] to good conditions or, if she cannot draw them into the treaty, then to foresee by som good means how theire state may be kept from danger'.[59]

Campaigning in Ireland, Essex could not counteract this move, but it filled him and his friends with dread. They blamed Cecil for the peace initiative and spread rumours about the secretary's malign influence over the queen. A foreign informant based in London learned that the queen was 'wholye directed in all busynes by Mr Secretary, who now rules all as his father did' and that Cecil was 'in heart' Essex's greatest enemy 'albeit he pretend love and frendshipp' to him.[60] Then, after the earl's impulsive return to court and subsequent arrest in the autumn of 1599, a flood of libels attacked Cecil and his relationship with the queen, giving public expression to the private aspersions long made against him within the earl's circle.[61] In one poem—'Where Medwaye greets old Thamesis silver streames'—Cecil was allegorized as a 'camel', because of his 'crookbackt', and accused of deceiving the sleeping 'lion' (the queen) into destroying 'a stately hart' (Essex). Unlike the hart, the 'cammell for burthen is...And not for kingdom's stern and scepter's swaye.' The 'noble lion' should therefore wake up 'and this cammell scorne', declared the anonymous poet.[62] In another libel, Cecil was called a 'cub', a name that alluded to his nepotistic rise as the son of Burghley. Referencing his 'crooked waies', the poet also implied a connection between Cecil's devious political methods and his physical disability.[63]

Cecil was not the only politician to be libelled in these verses; Nottingham, Ralegh, and Cobham were satirized too, but at least one 'libell' addressed the secretary alone and is worth reciting in full:

> Proude and ambitious wretch that feedest on naught but faction
> Prevaile and fill thy selfe, and burst with vile detraction[64]
> Detraction is thy game, and hathe bene since thie youthe
> And wilbe to thie dyinge daie, he lies that speakes the truthe

But well I knowe thy bosome is fraught, with naught but scorne
Dissemblinge smothfac'd dwarfe, wold god thad'st ne're bene borne
First did thy Sire and now thy selfe by Machivillian skill
Prevaile, and curbe the peeres as well befittes your will
Secreat-are I knowe your crookebacke spider shapen
Poison to the state and comons, foe to vertue frend to rapine
Soe farewell I post to hell
To bringe more newes
Good gentlemen let this bill stand
Ill some good bodie have put to his hande
God save the queene.[65]

Here can be seen the literary tropes engendered by Cecil's enemies that were to besmirch his reputation for the remainder of his life: his twisted back that reflected a twisted mind (like that of Richard III); his proud ambition and factious villainy that resulted in the destruction of the martial hero, Essex; and the creation of a new *regnum Cecilianum*.[66] Understandably, Cecil, complained that such libellers were 'vipers' and 'the children of the divell, for he ys the author of all lyes and there ys no truth in their papers'.[67] In his support, the privy council attempted to crackdown on the publication of such smears, but it failed to prevent them circulating in manuscript and being copied into gentlemen's commonplace books.[68]

Essex's imprisonment not only exposed Cecil and the rest of Elizabeth's government to venom; it also left open the question of what to do now in Ireland: would the truce the earl had negotiated with Tyrone still stand? Elizabeth decided it had to, although she admitted 'wee cannot hyde that wee are displeased that our kingedome hath ben so ill ordred, as that wee must accept of such proceedinges, before the rebell had tasted somewhat of our power'.[69] As a longer-term solution, Elizabeth was prepared to receive the rebel 'into our grace and mercy' provided that he submitted to her authority. However, Tyrone presented her with political demands that were utterly unacceptable, including as they did the restoration of the Roman Catholic Church, the exclusion of Englishmen from all Irish offices, and the retention by Irish chieftains of their ancient rights and lands. Tyrone's propositions, pronounced Elizabeth, were 'both full of scandal to our realm and future peril in that state'. Cecil concurred, simply writing 'Ewtopia' on his copy of Tyrone's articles.[70] With the unanimous agreement of her privy councillors, the queen therefore decided to keep her army in the field under a new lord deputy, Charles

Lord Mountjoy, who was instructed to plant garrisons in the lands of the rebel chieftains.[71] Over the next year, he campaigned successfully in Ulster, while Sir George Carew—the new lord president of Munster— restored order to that province.

The responsibility for policy-making about Irish affairs often weighed Cecil down. His greatest fear was that a wrong decision could harm his political relationship with the queen: 'I know that if success be nought it wilbe scorn to me,' he confided to Carew; 'my zeale to the queen's service, and my assurance that all evill success shalbe layd on me, thogh I be inocent,' he continued, 'make me handle these points to and fro'.[72] Cecil's anxiety could be especially acute when he persuaded the queen to take an action that conflicted with her own judgement. Following the advice of Carew and other Irish specialists (including Ralegh and Mountjoy), Cecil 'made a great adventure to presse and importune' the queen to grant James fitz Gerald Fitzgerald (the son of the fourteenth earl of Desmond) his father's title and lands before sending him to Munster to help quell the rising in the province.[73] Since Fitzgerald had been a prisoner in the Tower for sixteen years, there was no guarantee of his loyalty, and Elizabeth was therefore unwilling to grant him a title and lands until he had proved himself in her service. When she eventually gave way— signing the patent of creation on 1 October 1600—Cecil was full of misgivings, admitting that 'every peril now objects it self to my sence' and 'I do never shutt myne eyes but with feare at my waking to heare some ill newes of him'.[74]

At the same time as Cecil and the queen were preoccupied with Ireland, they were pursuing—admittedly without much optimism— peace with the Habsburgs. Even though her Dutch allies declined to join her, Elizabeth entered into official peace talks with the archdukes in early 1600. Their ambassador was received openly in February and formally met all the privy councillors and lords (bar, of course, Essex, who was still in custody).[75] In May, English and Spanish representatives convened at Boulogne to discuss peace terms. Cecil and other senior privy councillors, however, did not attend, perhaps because they were needed to hear the Star Chamber proceedings against Essex that began in June. Maybe, too, the queen chose not to send her senior men because she believed that the conference had little chance of success. The February talks had certainly revealed that the initial demands of the two sides were irreconcilable, since—in contrast to the archdukes—Philip III (king of Spain since September 1598) was assuming a hard-line negotiating position, refusing, for example, to guarantee Dutch independence or allow Englishmen to trade in the New World.[76]

The conference was indeed a failure. The representatives never discussed serious matters, as they became bogged down in squabbles over diplomatic minutiae. In June, Elizabeth decided to withdraw her commissioners. No progress had yet been made, and she was banking on the Habsburgs becoming more accommodating in the future.[77] However, her calculation proved incorrect. By the end of August, the Spaniards were even less ready to hammer out a peace that would meet England's demands. Cecil suspected this was because 'ether that they should thinke that her majesty is sufficiently intangled with Ireland, or that they are in hope to prevayle over the Low Countryes, whoe indeed (to tell you trew) doe everie day grow worse and worse'.[78]

In December 1600, Cecil became a little more hopeful. Once again, Spain looked to be on the brink of war with France, this time over disputed lands in Savoy, and Philip III seemed ready to give way on some issues of precedence.[79] Yet, the prospects of a peace with Spain were actually pretty slim. The archdukes needed a truce with England, but Philip had resolved on an enterprise in Ireland, while some of his counsellors suggested that he should also back the infanta's claim to the English succession on the grounds that she had the best title as a direct descendant of John of Gaunt and hence Edward III.[80] However, Essex must have heard false rumours of an impending peace, for he wrote to James VI in December about the menacing danger arising from the Elizabethan government's 'juggling with our enemies', and he intimated that Cecil would be prepared to recognize the infanta's title to the English succession in return for a treaty with her brother.[81] In reality, Cecil had no thought of making such a deal with Spain on those terms, nor would Elizabeth have allowed it.[82] But, partly to prevent such an occurrence, Essex attempted his coup in February 1601.[83]

As the man in charge of collecting the evidence against Essex and his followers, Cecil fashioned his own official version of the earl's aims and motives in the London rising. In Star Chamber, the secretary accused 'this popular traytor' (popular was a pejorative word in this period) of nourishing a hope for five or six years 'to become king of England'. The earl's ambition, alleged Cecil, could be detected in a recently published book on Henry Bolingbroke's deposition of Richard II, 'wherein many thinges were inserted to mak this tyme seeme like the tyme of King Richard II, and that they were to be reformed by him as like by Henry IV'.[84] That Elizabeth bought into this interpretation can be seen from her somewhat later quip: 'I am Richard II, know ye not that?'[85]

Essex's trial soon turned into a personal duel between the earl and Cecil. Denying the charges of treason against him, the defendant accused Cecil of plotting 'to sell the kingdom of England to the infante of Spayne' and saying that she 'had the best title' to succeed Elizabeth.[86] Cecil's honour was now at stake, and he went down on his knees to beg a hearing against such 'malicious slaunders'. Granted this concession, he demanded that Essex reveal the source for his false allegation, but the earl refused, saying that his co-defendant Southampton had been a witness and neither of them would lie. Southampton, however, named Sir William Knollys as their informant. Demanding to hear Knollys's testimony, Cecil declared that, if his name was not cleared, 'I doe publiquely vowe upon my salvacon...that I will never more serve her in place of a counsellor; while I live, I will dye her subiect and servant but will never serve her as a counsellor or secreatorie'. When Knollys was brought in, he refuted the slander and explained how it had arisen. According to his testimony, he and the secretary had been discussing the infanta's title, as promoted in Robert Doleman's notorious book about the succession, and the secretary had asked if it were not 'a strange impudencie' that the author had given the right of the succession of England to the infanta. Hearing this, Essex immediately backtracked and told the court that the story had been told to him in a very different tenor. Cecil then addressed Essex directly. The earl's malice towards him, he said, stemmed from their differences over the question of peace with Spain. For Essex, 'it hath beene a maxim to prefer war before peace', whereas he laboured for peace for the good and quiet of his country, even though he hated the Spaniard as much as any man and found the infanta's title to the English throne to be anathema.[87]

Before his execution, Essex entreated the queen to allow him to see Cecil, Lord Keeper Egerton, Buckhurst, and Nottingham in the Tower so that he could seek their pardon. She agreed. At their meeting, Essex 'dyd freely acquite' Cecil from the charge he had made against him during the trial, declaring that he 'was ashamed to have spoken it, having no better ground'.[88] Nonetheless, Essex's accusation against Cecil did not die with the earl and had even continued into the twentieth century.[89]

How far Essex's execution affected Cecil's own immediate standing in England is debatable. Contemporaries had long believed that the secretary 'rules both court and crowne', and nothing much changed there. Similarly Cecil continued to be libelled, as the 'cankred' man responsible for Essex's downfall.[90] Cecil expected no less: 'bitter imput-ations', he told an associate, 'are often throwne uppon those whoe by their place and service are every day subject to the calumniacions of all sorts of men.'[91] While Essex's friends were no longer an obvious danger to him—those who had not been imprisoned or executed were generally seeking his favour—Cecil sensed that new enemies and political rivals had emerged. He did not specify who these 'vypars' were, but oblique references in his letters suggest that he was thinking of his one-time allies Cobham and Ralegh.[92] On one occasion, he told Carew how greatly he was hurt by 'the mutinys of those whom I do love and will (howsoever they do me)'; on others, he informed Carew that he was 'left to seek new freends' and that 'two old freends use me unkindly, but I have covenanted with my hart not to know it, for in shew we are great, and all my revenge shalbe to heape coals on their hedds'.[93] His brother-in-law Cobham may have seemed to Cecil the more serious danger. Ralegh was less often at court after his appointment as governor of Jersey in August 1600, but Cobham had access to the queen, who found him a charming courtier. The baron's influence grew, moreover, in May 1601, when he married her Boleyn cousin, Frances, dowager countess of Kildare, a gentlewoman 'without wages' in the privy chamber who also had easy access to the queen.[94]

The contemporary libel that the secretary totally ruled Elizabeth and the privy council was wide off the mark. Cecil often worked in a triumvirate with Buckhurst and Nottingham especially in dealing with continental affairs and national security.[95] When decisions had to be made about the Irish war—the dominant issue of the day—the queen generally took the advice of Mountjoy before that of Cecil.[96] Sometimes, moreover, Elizabeth would go her own way, and make decisions that conflicted with the advice of Cecil and other leading figures. On those occasions, Cecil fell back on the same tactics that his predecessors as secretary had used: working surreptitiously with people on the ground and controlling her correspondence. To take one example: after Mountjoy's army had defeated the Irish rebels at the battle of Kinsale in January 1602, Elizabeth rejected Cecil's advice that she grant Tyrone a pardon and allow him to keep his lands and English title.[97] Instead, she demanded the rebel's unconditional surrender and would agree to spare his life only if that was proved necessary; permitting him to retain his lands and title was out of the question: 'this is her owne, and neither our proposition nor conceipt', Cecil told Carew in frustration. However, he could see no point in continuing the argument, as the queen was beginning to treat objections to her position as an affront to her authority. The better tactic, Cecil thought, was for everyone to comply with her orders *pro tempore*, for she would undoubtedly drop them once she became 'satisfied from you that we have obeyed her and that you find the impossibility of these things which she would be glad of'. To ensure that this happened, Carew was told to send two sets of letters from Ireland: one that 'is fytt to be showed her majesty', the other for Cecil alone.[98] However, it was not until a year later that Elizabeth agreed to a compromise. On 17 February 1603, she reluctantly offered Tyrone his liberty, though not the retention of his title, and, once again, Cecil attempted to evade the queen's instructions, telling Mountjoy: 'all honest servants must strain a little when they will serve princes.'[99]

Cecil showed a similar tendency to 'strain a little' when it came to the succession. For practically the whole of the reign, the prospect of a disputed succession on Elizabeth's death was a major source of political anxiety. In the later 1590s it had taken a new turn with fears that Philip III might invade in support of the infanta. But, even if the transition to a new dynasty proved to be untroubled and peaceful, some of Elizabeth's councillors had reason to worry that their new monarch—whoever it might be—would dispense with their services. If the successor were to be James VI, Cecil would be especially vulnerable to dismissal, as the Scottish king had long viewed the Cecils as hostile to his present interests and future prospects. Probably for this reason, the secretary started to buy up crown property (then flooding the market to finance the Irish wars); if forced to retire, he could at least retain comfort and prestige as a substantial landowner.[100] After Essex's execution, however, an opportunity arose for Cecil to build up a personal relationship with James VI. But he had to keep his communications with the king secret from Elizabeth.

During the 1590s James had courted Essex to counteract the influence of the Cecils, and consequently the earl's execution filled him with alarm, as he believed (erroneously) that it left the secretary 'king there in effect'. To remedy the situation, James sent two envoys to London in April 1601 with instructions to build up a party of powerful English supporters for the Scottish title. Those to be targeted were the queen's privy councillors, and especially Cecil. If 'Mr Secretary and his followers' did not respond positively, they were to be warned that, 'since now, when they are in their kingdom, they will thus misknow me, when the chance shall turn, I shall cast a deaf ear to their requests'.[101]

James's overture was obviously welcome to Cecil. He knew all too well that Essex had traduced him in Scotland, repeating the false assertion that the infanta was the secretary's preferred successor. With Essex dead and James in need of another ally on the council, Cecil could repair the damage. Forging a warm relationship with the Scottish king would allow him to stay in power were James to take the throne on Elizabeth's death, as seemed most likely; otherwise, his political future looked bleak. Personal concerns as much as public interest were at stake for Cecil.

Towards the end of April 1601, Cecil met James's ambassadors and assured them of his 'innocency from being Spanishly affected or ever to have practised maliciously against the king'. A few weeks afterwards, James wrote the first letter to Cecil in what was to be a secret correspondence between them. It had to be secret, because sharing confidential information with a foreign monarch could at best 'prejudice' Cecil 'in her majestie's judgment' and at worst be construed as treason.[102] In these letters, Cecil made it clear that his first loyalty was to the queen, his 'deare and precious souverayne', his 'individuall center', 'whose creature I am'.[103] Yet, at the same time, he did what he could to support the king's interests, perhaps convincing himself that they were equally the queen's. Not only did Cecil encourage Elizabeth to pay James a regular pension of £5,000 a year, but he shifted from being a keen proponent of peace with Spain to 'earnest opposition'. James told him that 'suche a peace at this tyme must be greatlie præjudiciall' to the 'state of religion in generall', to the 'religion and policie of this yle in speciall', and 'most perrelouse for my just claime in particulaire'.[104] Accordingly, when at a privy council meeting on 24 May 1602 Lord Treasurer Buckhurst spoke out in favour of resuming peace negotiations, Cecil—alongside Nottingham and Sir William Knollys—advised against it, and one of the arguments they produced was that there was 'no safetie to have peace with Spaine, for that the enfanta makes title of succession'. It is true they voiced other considerations, not least Philip III's recent aid to Tyrone and the possibility of continuing Spanish intervention in Ireland.[105] What is more, Cecil may have also had a private interest in wanting to continue the state of warfare, for both he and the lord admiral had recently amassed a fortune from successful privateering voyages.[106] Nonetheless, according to Cecil's and Nottingham's own accounts, James's wishes played a large part in their rethinking of the advisability of peace at that time.[107]

In his letters to James, Cecil promised to ease the king onto the English throne after the queen's death, provided that he made no further moves during her remaining years. Out of respect for the queen, explained Cecil, James had to cease pressing her to declare his right in parliament: it would be far better for the king, he wrote, to put his trust in 'a choyce election of a feaw in the present' (namely, a few nobles and privy councillors) rather than 'any generall acclamation of many' (in parliament).[108] This advice can be credited with improving relations between James and Elizabeth during her last years. With Cecil on his side, James grew in confidence that the English throne would be his, a confidence that expanded when he received pledges of support from Nottingham and other prominent figures at Elizabeth's court.[109]

The day of Elizabeth's passing seemed close. For much of 1601 the 69-year-old queen looked to be fading. Onlookers referred to her suffering periods of melancholy and losing her appetite, which even at the best of times was small. Her memory also was not what it was. It was noticed too that she appeared to tire more easily and was less steady on her feet. On at least one occasion she needed a staff when walking up stairs, and at the opening ceremony of parliament in October 1601 she would have fallen 'if some gentlemen had not suddenly cast themselves under that side that tottered, and supported her'.[110] Yet, despite these frailties, it was during this parliament that Elizabeth delivered her second most celebrated speech, the one known to history as the 'Golden Speech'.[111]

The 1601 parliament—the last of the reign—was disorderly and difficult to manage. On the floor of the House Cecil complained that the MPs' unruly conduct was 'more fitt for a grammer schoole' than a parliament, and he proved unable to head off a frontal attack on royal monopolies and their holders. When the Speaker was ready to accept a bill curbing the practice, Cecil sounded appalled: 'I am servante unto the queene and before I would speake or give consent to a case that should debase her prerogatyve or abridge it, I would wishe my tounge cutt out of my head.' Instead of drafting a bill, he went on, the MPs should petition the queen to reform the abuses in the system, for 'her majestie's eares be open to all our greivancees, and her handes stretched out to everye man's peticions'.[112] In the end, it was Elizabeth who saved the day by taking her cue from Cecil's speech and issuing a proclamation that addressed the Commons' grievances. In gratitude, a delegation of 140 MPs came to Whitehall Palace, to express their appreciation. And it was there that the queen delivered the 'Golden Speech', in which she thanked her listeners for drawing her attention to the abuses of monopolists and assured them of her care for their welfare and commitment to impartial justice:

> I do assure you there is no prince that loveth his subjects better or whose love can countervail [match] our love. There is no jewel, be it of never so rich a price, which I set before this jewel, I mean your love. For I do more esteem of it than of any treasure or riches, for that we know how to prize, but love and thanks I count unvaluable [invaluable].

And she ended with the words: 'though you have had, and may have, many mightier and wiser princes sitting in this seat, yet you never had, nor shall have, any that will love you better.'[113] Presumably her address went down well with those present—for it was printed soon afterwards—but we have no record of its reception among MPs.

The following year, Elizabeth's health and confidence seemed to recover somewhat. She went on a short progress in the vicinity of London, and determinedly rode, hunted, even danced, though her joints ached. To the outside world she appeared 'frolicky and merry', trying to disguise her age with puffing out her cheeks with cloth and much make-up.[114] On 6 December, she visited Cecil at his newly built house on the Strand in London. The gossip of the day was that he had prepared a 'greate varietie of entertainment' and 'many rich jewells and presents' for her.[115]

The queen's entrance into Cecil's house was greeted with 'a pretty dialogue' (written by the poet Sir John Davies) between a maid, a widow, and a wife, who disputed among themselves which one should take precedence in presenting gifts to Astraea, the virgin goddess of justice, in the guise of the queen. Naturally the virgin won the contest. Later in the proceedings, a second dialogue was performed, this one 'a conference' between a 'post' (messenger) and a gentleman usher. Here the two actors discussed the nature of royal service. The queen, said the usher, made use of royal service as the mind uses the senses: 'manye thinges shee sees and heares through them but the judgment and election is her owne.' How then, asked the post, were 'the rewards of their service soe greate', if the value of it to the queen was 'soe smaule'? The usher replied by comparing the queen to the sun whose beams lit up 'darke and grosse boodies' and 'clear and transparent boodies' that were without light themselves. He concluded his speech with further compliments to the queen. The evening ended with Cecil presenting the queen with a golden mantle.[116] Unfortunately, when departing by barge, the queen slipped and strained her foot—another sign of her advancing age.

Almost certainly, Cecil commissioned the 'Rainbow Portrait' (Plate 19) to commemorate the queen's visit to his new town house. The iconography of the painting closely mirrors the entertainments in which the queen was depicted as a virgin, Astraea, and the sun. In the portrait, Elizabeth wears a headdress that we can be pretty sure was part of the costume of the 'wife' in the first 'dialogue'. Decorated with a crown (the symbol of her majesty) and a jewelled crescent (a symbol of virginity), the headdress visually represents virginity trumping marriage. In the portrait Elizabeth can also be identified as Astraea, for the flowers on her bodice have an association with the eternal springtime that the goddess was said to create. That Elizabeth is the sun can be seen from the motto—'nil sine sole Iris' (nought without the sun)—and the golden mantle wrapped around her, an image that echoes Cecil's parting gift as well. The remaining symbols in the portrait all draw attention to Cecil's faithful and attentive service to his monarch, as referenced in the usher's speech. The eyes and ears on the mantle illustrate the 'senses' of royal servants, and especially those of her chief intelligencer and principal secretary; the serpent symbolizes wise council. As for the rainbow, it probably stands for the policy of peace that was identified with the Cecils as well as the period of concord that followed the turmoil of the Essex years.[117]

During the queen's visit, Cecil played the courtier as well as the councillor. It was a role he could rarely fulfil, busy as he was in managing matters of state and drowning in a mass of paperwork. However, he understood the importance of relating to the queen in informal, light-hearted ways, such as participating with her in card games and hawking.[118] Likewise, Cecil did not stand aloof from the culture of courtly love. Like other courtiers, he sometimes wore a miniature of the queen.[119] In September 1595, his gift to her was probably a poem (possibly a panegyric); at any rate, her reply via an intermediary was:

> To use the queen's frase, she yeldeth you a myllyon of thanks for your present, the which she lyketh and commendeth exceedynglye, only she fereth she shall never fytte yt with any future wourke of her owne.[120]

Cecil composed at least one other poem for the queen, and its circumstance reveals a playful exchange between queen and secretary that may have been more typical than the surviving documentation allows us to appreciate. In the summer of 1602, Elizabeth 'espied' the countess of Derby, Cecil's niece, wearing a jewelled miniature 'in her bosom'. The queen wanted to see who was the countess's *amour*, especially when Lady Derby tried to avoid showing it to her. Elizabeth then 'snatched it away', only to be surprised to find that inside the case was a portrait of the countess's uncle. In jest, Elizabeth pinned the miniature first to her shoe and then attached it to her elbow sleeve. When Cecil learned of this, he wrote some verses and had a musician sing the ditty in his chamber and afterwards to the queen. According to the courtier, who recounted the incident, 'some of the verses argue that he repines not, though her majesty please to grace others, contents himself with the favour he hath'.[121] This affectation of modesty was typical of Cecil's self-presentation and designed to please the queen.

Elizabeth's last sickness began in late February or early March 1603, when she lost her appetite and suffered from insomnia. Her symptoms grew significantly worse on 18 March. According to one—admittedly not very trustworthy account—Cecil then told her to go to bed:

> To which she smiled wonderfully contemning him saing that the word 'must' was not to be used to princes, thereupon said little man, little man yf your father had lived ye durst not have said so much: but thou knowest I must die and that maketh thee so presumtious.[122]

Only three days before her death, which occurred in the early hours of the 24th, did she consent to retire to bed. By then she was speechless and ate nothing.

Well before the end, Cecil and his fellow councillors put in place preparations for the smooth accession of James: noblemen were summoned to the court at Richmond Palace; extra guards were placed around important London buildings such as the Tower; and a watch was kept on Lord Beauchamp and Arbella Stuart. With the help of the council—and probably the nobility—Cecil drafted the proclamation that would announce James's accession and had it sent to Scotland for his approval.[123] Several contemporary accounts describe Elizabeth on her deathbed indicating her endorsement of James's succession; Sir Robert Carey, for example, maintained that, on 23 March, 'by signes she called for her councill, and putting her hand to her head, when the king of Scottes was named to succeed her, they all knew hee was the man she desired should reigne after her'.[124] But it is possible that Cecil and Nottingham encouraged such stories to be circulated in order to legitimize the Scot taking the throne. Some other extant texts contain no mention of Elizabeth denoting her heir.[125]

Cecil did well under the new regime. He acquired an earldom in 1605, became a knight of the garter in 1606, and added the lord treasuryship to his portfolio of offices in 1608. His death in May 1612, shortly before his forty-ninth birthday, was greeted with another outpouring of malicious libels. But both Elizabeth and James recognized and respected his administrative competence, political pragmatism, and dedication to their service.[126] Whether or not they felt deep affection for him is another matter. Despite the queen's dependence on her secretary during her last years, she preferred to have Nottingham and Buckhurst about her in the privy chamber. The comment of the Venetian ambassador in May 1606 that Cecil's power was 'based not so much on the grace of his majesty, as on an excellent prudence and ability' could have applied equally well to his service under Elizabeth.[127] Like his father, Cecil was appreciated as a great principal secretary; unlike his father, he could not command anything like the same warmth and favour from his mistress.

Epilogue

No sooner had Elizabeth died than her subjects began the work of creating their own judgements and constructing their own image of the queen and her reign. Within a few weeks, printers and booksellers were selling ditties, poems, and pamphlets that praised her life and mourned her death. In them Elizabeth was idealized as a beloved prince, rare phoenix, 'queene of vertue', 'peace-preserving queene', and a ruler blessed by God.[1] Of course, we cannot know if these elegies reflected a sincere grief, but, given the political instabilities and economic hardships of the late 1590s, it seems unlikely that all her subjects experienced deep sorrow at her passing. Relief that the succession had passed onto James without any discord or disturbance was probably the dominant emotion of most writers and readers. Certainly this sentiment can be detected in the title of the broadsheet elegy 'Weepe with joy, a lamentation for the losse of our late soveraigne lady Queene Elizabeth, with joy and exultation for our high and mightie prince, King James, her lineall and lawful successor'. Moreover, the immediate epitaphs for Elizabeth were usually accompanied by protestations of loyalty to the new king.[2]

The idealization of Elizabeth did not stop with James I's coronation. On the contrary, it continued throughout the early Stuart period in a variety of genres, including drama, verse, histories, and political discourse.[3] Some of these works were little more than hagiographies, treating Elizabeth's reign as 'a patterne for governement to all the princes in Christendome'.[4] But others attempted a more balanced approach, preferring to follow the model of the Roman historian Tacitus—very much in vogue—by writing 'plainly and truly...void of fear, partiality, and all private respects', and reporting honestly the vices as well as virtues of men and women in public life.[5] But, whichever form they took, early seventeenth-century writings hailed Elizabeth as both the founder of the Anglican Church and a national hero, who had brought internal stability to the state and victory over Spain.

A significant number focused, too, on her style of leadership, the nature of her court, and the qualities of the men who inhabited it. Here, there was less consensus, some authors being full of praise, while others (those who followed the model of Tacitus) proving more critical. Among the hagiographies was Francis Bacon's eulogistic essay, *In felicem memoriam Elizabethae*, composed in 1608.[6] For Bacon, Elizabeth's key characteristic was her moderation, which could be seen in her management of people as well as her religious and foreign policies. 'Yea, he pronounced, 'those who she advanced to highest honours, she kept in such a ballance and restraint, that every one laboured most to please her will, whilst she remained mistris of her self'.[7] John Speed in his 1611 *History of Great Britaine* (1611) agreed:

> Yea what is more admirable in her sex, so reserved was shee from giving any man too-much interest, or being lead and overswaied by any of her great-ones about her, that they al stood in a reverent awe of her very presence and aspect, but much more of her leaste frown or checke...[8]

Both Bacon and Speed also thought that Elizabeth had chosen her servants well; in the words of the former: 'she was not onely happy in her own, but also in the abilities of her servants; for she had such gifted men about her as perhaps this Island had rarely brought forth before.'[9] Why Bacon and Speed wrote in this vein is not entirely clear. One suggestion has been that their celebration of Elizabeth's rule provided a way of praising James I, making the Scottish king appear as her true heir not only lineally but also in his policies and lifestyle.[10] But, it is just as likely that their celebrations of Elizabeth's reign—as indeed those of many other Jacobean writers—arose from disillusionment and disaffection with her successor, since offering Elizabeth as a political model could operate as a stick with which to beat the king, who was widely criticized for pursuing a pacific foreign policy, presiding over a corrupt court, and succumbing to favourites.[11]

Bacon also contributed to Elizabeth's posthumous reputation by including her sayings in a set of 'apophthegms' (aphorisms) delivered by historical and current figures. His illustrations of Elizabeth's dry wit have been much repeated, and seem to offer an insight into both her character and relationships. To take two examples: according to Bacon, when she heard that the earl of Essex had knighted twenty-four men at Rouen and that many of these gentlemen were 'of weak and small means', she retorted: 'My lord may have done well to have built his alms-houses before he made his knights.' And, when Lord

Burghley asked the queen to make seven knights at her departure from Theobalds, she chose to knight them in reverse order from that he had intended. Burghley had placed them in line according to their rank, but she knighted the lowest first and so upwards, commenting: 'I have but fulfilled the scripture; "the first shall be last, and the last first".'[12] Bacon also related pithy sayings of her courtiers, bishops, and ministers that illustrated the playful interactions and honest talk between Elizabeth and members of her circle. One example was the rejoinder that his father, Sir Nicholas Bacon, had made to Elizabeth after she had visited him while on progress and complained about the small size of his house: 'Madam, my house is well, but it is you who have made me too great for my house.'[13]

Another occurrence of a eulogistic approach to the late queen can be found in the English versions of William Camden's *Annales rerum Anglicarum et Hibernicum regnante Elizabetha*. Camden's Latin texts—published in two parts in 1615 and 1625—had held back from encomia and preferred to follow Tacitus' precepts for history writing. Indeed Camden's treatment of Elizabeth in her dealings with Mary Queen of Scots and James VI was especially unflattering, as he portrayed her as bullying, mendacious, and cunning. However, two of Camden's early Stuart translators (Abraham Darcie and Robert Norton) departed from the tone of the original text and were uninhibited in their praise of the queen in their English versions.[14] Their books had new titles that reflected their more eulogistic intent. Darcie's was called *The True and Royall History of the Famous Empresse Elizabeth...of...Happy Memory* and had as its stated purpose 'to make vulgar [popularize] the heroicke acts and divine vertues of Albion's best queen and the most religious, learned and prudent empresse that ever lived on earth'.[15] Norton's 1630 work was entitled *The Historie of the Life and Reigne of the Most Renowmed [sic] and Victorious Princesse Elizabeth, Late Queene of England*; and he explained in his preface that he had 'admired her vertues while shee be lived, and honour her memory being dead'. What Norton found most remarkable about the queen was that she was

> a woman, and (if that not be enough) an unmarried virgin, destitute of all helpe of parents, brethren, husband, beset with divers nations her mortall enemies...held the most stout and warlike nation of the English foure and forty yeares and upwards, not onely in awe and duty, but even in peace also, and (which is most of all) in the true worship of God.[16]

Both translators did not stop there but explicitly, or implicitly, praised most of Elizabeth's courtiers and councillors. Darcie portrayed Burghley as a prudent councillor, and called Hatton 'a noble personage, excellently endued [endowed] with rare vertues...one whose merit had purchased him the honour to be dearely affectionate and intimate to her majestie'.[17] Norton—a military engineer—much admired Essex, Ralegh, and 'many others whose valour and vertues deserved to have their names and memories recorded to all posterity'. According to his account, Essex had 'an innate goodnesse', but was led astray by 'sinister counsellors'; the earl's action in 1601 was no revolt, he wrote, but simply intended 'to secure his accesse to the queene, to complaine in her presence of the injuries done unto him'. Recognizing this, went on Norton, Elizabeth had been in two minds as to whether to order his execution.[18] Only Leicester came off badly in these translations. As in the original Latin text, the authors presented the earl as a malign influence at Elizabeth's court.

Try as they might, Camden's English translators could not entirely avoid the original's sympathy for Mary Queen of Scots and consequent critique of Elizabeth's conduct towards her. Darcie's translation left open the possibility that Elizabeth was insincere in her compassion towards her 'unfortunate' cousin in May 1568.[19] In Norton's translation, Mary was 'utterly ignorant' of the Babington plot; Elizabeth's councillors were 'not all of one and the same minde' about what to do with Mary after its discovery; and some impartial observers 'thought she was somewhat sharpely dealt withall'. Ultimately Elizabeth was let off the hook in Norton's account, as he held Davison responsible for acting against her will.[20]

At face value, Sir Robert Naunton's *Fragmenta regalia* was hagiographic too. Composed in 1635, his lively set of sketches of the queen and her circle was not printed until 1641, but the book then became immensely popular, running into five editions in twelve years. Like Bacon's and Camden's translators, Naunton expressed admiration for the queen, praising her virtues, 'intellectuals and abilities', and her handling of her great men:

> Her ministers and instruments of state, such as were *participes curarum* [partners of cares] and bare a great part of the burthen, were many, and those memorable, but they were onely favorites, not minions; such as acted more by her own princely rules and judgements, then by their own wills and appetites, which she observed to the last.

This success in preventing the dominance of her government by one man, explained Naunton, was because 'she ruled much by faction and parties, which her self, both made, upheld, and weakned, as her own great judgement advised'.[21]

Yet, for all Naunton's words of approval, his verdicts on the queen and her circle were not devoid of criticisms; like Camden, he followed Tacitus' precept of writing plainly and honestly. Consequently, so 'that truth may appear without retraction from the honour of so great a princesse', Naunton pointed to a number of governmental ills, notably the financial burdens the queen imposed on her subjects, many of which were extra-parliamentary exactions, and the lack of financial probity to be found in some of her councillors. Elizabeth could be hypocritical, and the execution of Mary was a 'taint' on her reign. Most important of all, Naunton saw the Elizabethan court as 'academies of art and cunning', a site of deceit, obsequiousness, decadence, and corruption; and he had harsh things to say about many of Elizabeth's courtiers.[22] Repeating the libels of *Leicester's Commonwealth*, Naunton called the earl a Machiavellian, accused him of poisoning the first earl of Essex, and described him as a courtier of 'cunning and dexterity', the 'inheritor of the genius and craft of his father' (the infamous Northumberland).[23] Hatton, Naunton dismissed as a man of no merit who had been advanced simply on account of his attractive looks, grace in dancing, and subtle ability to 'learn the discipline and garb both of the times and court'.[24] As for Essex, Elizabeth ruined whatever good qualities he had. Because of 'the violent indulgency of the queen (which is incident to old age, where it encounters with a pleasing and suitable object)', Essex

> drew in too fast, like a childe sucking on an over-uberous nurse, and had there been a more decent decorum observed in both, or either of those, without doubt, the unity of their affections had been more permanent, and not so in and out as they were, like an instrument ill-tuned, and lapsing to discord.[25]

As in Camden, Burghley was one of the few who were above deceits, and he is admired as a statesman of great stature, while Robert Cecil was 'the inheritor of his wisdome' and 'proficient in all disciplines of state'.[26]

Naunton's jaundiced observations were based less on his own knowledge of the Elizabethan court than on the tropes about the corruption of court life and duplicity of courtiers to be found in Tacitus' history of the imperial court of Rome. His Tacitean view of the court, moreover, repeated many of the observations of John Clapham, a one-time clerk in Burghley's household, who wrote his own commentary a few months after Elizabeth's death with the intention of revising it later for publication.[27] Clapham's Elizabeth may have had 'many princely virtues' and 'commendable qualities', but (like imperial emperors) she was capricious, susceptible to flattery, and had a number of 'favourites'.[28] The worst of them—in Clapham's prose—was, of course, Leicester, who was 'a cunning dissembler', dissolute in his lifestyle, 'desirous of his own glory', and eager to enact revenge 'where he had once conceived offence'—a portrait that not only reflected earlier Catholic views of the earl but also Tacitus' depiction of Sejanus, the evil favourite of Emperor Tiberius.[29] Hatton, thought Clapham, was 'very passionate and being provoked, a violent and implacable enemy'.[30] Ralegh and Essex were more worthy 'favourites', but still had 'vices': the former was intellectually gifted and a valiant soldier, but 'insolent in prosperity', 'ungrateful' to his friends, and 'seemed to take a pride in being hated of the people'.[31] Essex, to his credit, was 'no flatterer nor dissembler', but his vice was that 'to fleshly wantonness he was much inclined and overmuch swayed by the bent of his will'.[32] Were it not for the queen's reliance on the worthy Burghley, implied Clapham, the realm would not have been so well governed, for 'nothing was thought well done, whereof he was not the contriver and director'.[33]

Though the product of their own cultural and political times, all these early seventeenth-century opinions fed into later interpretations and representations of the queen and her circle. Some of them are still with us. Although revisionist histories have punctured the myth of Gloriana by contesting the extent of the queen's popularity and achievements, many academic and popular accounts still describe Elizabeth, her court, and her relationships in terms that are recognizably drawn from Camden, Naunton, and Clapham. Elizabeth is often portrayed as capricious, vain, desperate for flattery, and susceptible to comely young men of little talent, while her court is populated with sycophantic, self-interested, and duplicitous figures.[34] The portrayals of the queen and her courtiers on film have often conformed to this type.[35] Furthermore, many writers continue to criticize her conduct towards her cousin Mary and other members of her family. More nuanced views of some courtiers and councillors are emerging in the historiography, but Elizabeth's complex relationships with them and with her family—especially Mary Queen of Scots—still need reassessment and a wider understanding. I hope this book aids the process.

ABBREVIATIONS

APC	*Acts of the Privy Council of England*
BL	British Library
Camden	William Camden, *Annales rerum gestarum Angliae et Hiberniae regnante Elizabetha* (the year of the entry is indicated in parentheses)
CP	Cecil Papers, Hatfield
CPREliz	*Calendar of Patent Rolls, Elizabeth*
CSPDom	*Calendar of State Papers, Domestic*
CSPDomAdd	*Calendar of State Papers Domestic Series, Addenda*
CSPForEliz	*Calendar of State Papers, Foreign, in the Reign of Elizabeth*
CSPScot	*Calendar of State Papers, Relating to Scotland and Mary Queen of Scots*
CSPSp	*Calendar of State Papers, Spanish*
CSPSpEliz	*Calendar of Letters, Despatches, and State Papers Relating to English Affairs Preserved Principally in the Archives of Simancas*
CSPVen	*Calendar of State Papers, Venetian*
CUL	Cambridge University Library
CWE	*Elizabeth I: Collected Works*, ed. Leah S. Marcus, Janel Mueller, and Mary Beth Rose (Chicago, 2000)
FSL	Folger Shakespeare Library
Haynes	Samuel Haynes (ed.), *A Collection of State Papers: Relating to Affairs in the Reigns of King Henry VIII, King Edward VI, Queen Mary and Queen Elizabeth: from the Year 1542 to 1570 Transcribed from Original Letters and other Authentick Memorials, Never before Publish'd, Left by William Cecill, Lord Burghley, and now Remaining at Hatfield House* (London, 1740)
HL	Huntington Library, San Marino, CA
HMC	Historical Manuscripts Commission
LP	*Letters and Papers, Foreign and Domestic, Henry VIII*, British History Online, ed. J. S. Brewer, James Gairdner, and R. H. Brodie, 21 vols (London, 1864–1920) <www.british-history.ac.uk> (accessed March 2014)
LPL	Lambeth Palace Library
Machyn	Henry Machyn, *A London Provisioner's Chronicle, 1550–1563* <http://quod.lib.umich.edu/m/machyn/(accessed 2014)
Murdin	William Murdin (ed.), *A Collection of State Papers, Relating to Affairs in the Reign of Queen Elizabeth, from the Year 1571 to*

	1596 Transcribed from Original Papers and Other Authentic Memorials Never Before Published, Left by William Cecill, Reposited in the Library of Hatfield House (London, 1759)
Nichols	John Nichols, *Progresses and Public Processions of Queen Elizabeth I: A New Edition of the Early Modern Sources*, ed. Elizabeth Goldring, Faith Eales, Elizabeth Clarke, and Jayne Elisabeth Archer, 5 vols (Oxford, 2014)
ODNB	*Oxford Dictionary of National Biography*
SP	State Papers in The National Archives, Kew

NOTES

INTRODUCTION

1. For this model of Tudor politics, see Natalie Mears, 'Courts, Courtiers and Culture in Tudor England', *Historical Journal*, 46 (2003), 703–22.
2. Most recently, Anna Whitelock, *Elizabeth's Bedfellows: An Intimate History of the Queen's Court* (London, 2012). One exception is Christopher Haigh, *Elizabeth I* (Harlow, 1988), but his organizational structure is based on institutions: court, council, parliament, *inter alia*.
3. Kristin Bundesen, '"No other faction but my own": Dynastic Politics and Elizabeth I's Carey Cousins', Ph.D., University of Nottingham (2008), 81, 85.
4. For examples, see *CWE* 6, 126, 294–7; SP 52/9, fo. 35; SP 52/10, fo. 132; Nichols, iv. 214. For Lettice Knollys, see Chs 5 and 7.
5. Bundesin, '"No other faction but my own"', 62 and appendix 1. Elizabeth could count some 190 English relatives (including their spouses) during her reign, many of whom were descended from Edward III on her father's side and Thomas Howard, first duke of Norfolk, on her mother's.
6. I have discussed Ralegh's role in 'Elizabeth I and her Favourites: The Case of Sir Walter Ralegh', in Donald Stump, Linda Schenk, and Carole Levin (eds), *Elizabeth I and the 'Sovereign Arts': Essays in Literature, History, and Culture* (Tucson, 2011), 157–74.
7. Doran, 'Elizabeth I and her Favourites', 157–74.
8. Mary Hill Cole, *The Portable Queen: Elizabeth I and the Politics of Ceremony* (Amherst, 1999).
9. Paul Hentzner, *Travels in England, during the Reign of Queen Elizabeth*, ed. and trans. Horace, late earl of Orford (London, 1797), 36–7.
10. Penry Williams, 'Court and Polity under Elizabeth I', *John Rylands University Library*, 65 (1983), 259–86.
11. Hentzner, *Travels*, 57.
12. 7 January 1574, *CSPSpEliz*, ii, no. 389.
13. G. W. Groos (ed.), *The Diary of Baron Waldstein: A Traveller in Elizabethan England* (London, 1981); Hentzner, *Travels*, 21–2.
14. 1597, HMC, *De L'Isle*, ii. 245–6; G. Waller, *Edmund Spenser, a Literary Life* (London 1994), 43.
15. For courtly love in Elizabethan England, see Jennifer G. Wollock, *Rethinking Chivalry and Courtly Love* (Santa Barbara, CA, 2011), 2, 221–4.
16. Nichols, ii. 185.
17. For its functions, see 'A treatise of the office of…principall secretarie, 1592', in Conyers Read, *Mr Secretary Walsingham and the Policy of Queen Elizabeth* (Cambridge and Oxford, 1925), 1, app.
18. For up-to-date work on the Elizabethan privy council, see Norman Jones, 'Governing Elizabethan England', in Susan Doran and Norman Jones (eds), *The Elizabethan World* (London, 2011), 19–34; David J. Crankshaw, 'The Tudor Privy Council, c.1540–1603', *State Papers Online, 1509–1714*, Cengage

Learning EMEA Ltd (Reading, 2009); and Natalie Mears, *Queenship and Polit-ical Discourse in the Elizabethan Realms* (Cambridge, 2005).

19. Cited in David Dean, 'Elizabethan Government and Politics', in Robert Tittler and Norman Jones (eds), *A Companion to Tudor England* (Oxford, 2004), 48.

20. 8 March 1573, *APC* viii. 203–5.

21. John Guy, *The Court of Star Chamber and its Records to the Reign of Elizabeth I* (London, 1985).

22. Crankshaw, 'The Tudor Privy Council'.

23. Michael Barraclough Pulman, *The Elizabethan Privy Council in the Fifteen-Seventies* (Berkeley and Los Angeles, 1971), 39, 41.

24. Note too Sir Robert Cecil's comment when Hatton was appointed lord chan-cellor: 'he hath left his hat and feather, and now wears a flatt velvet cap, not different from your lordship's' (Murdin, 588). For a critique of distinguishing courtiers from councillors, see Mary Partridge, 'Lord Burghley and *Il Corte-giano*: Civil and Martial Models of Courtliness in Elizabethan England', *Trans-actions of the Royal Historical Society*, 6th ser., 19 (2009), 95–116.

25. CWE 194.

CHAPTER I

1. Edward Hall, *The Union of the Two Noble and Illustre Famelies of Lancastre [and] Yorke…*(London, 1550), fo. 218ʳ.

2. *LP* 7, no. 464.

3. *LP* 13i, no. 1057.

4. *LP* 10, no. 913; William Loke, *An Account of the Materials Furnished for the Use of Queen Anne Boleyn, and the Princess Elizabeth*, ed. J. B. Heath (London, 1862–3), 10–13.

5. *LP* 10, no. 141.

6. 1 September 1559, *CSPForEliz*, i. 524–34 (p. 527).

7. For the historiography, see Retha M. Warnicke, *Wicked Women of Tudor England: Queens, Aristocrats, Commoners, Queenship and Power* (Basingstoke, 2012), ch. 2.

8. See Ch. 8.

9. *LP* 10, no. 909.

10. *LP* 14ii, no. 238; *LP* 17, no. 267; *LP* 20ii, no. 909; *LP* 21i, no. 963.

11. *LP* 16, no. 1389.

12. *LP* 18i, nos 364, 509; *LP*, 18ii, nos 9, 111.

13. Eric. W. Ives, 'Tudor Dynastic Problems Revisited', *Historical Research*, 81 (2008), 255–79.

14. SP 1/182, fo. 150; *LP* 19i, no. 78; HMC, *Rutland*, i. 30.

15. CWE 5; John Gough Nichols (ed.), *Literary Remains of King Edward the Sixth*, 2 vols (London, 1857), i, p. xxxviii. For interpretations of this letter, see David Starkey, *Elizabeth: Apprenticeship* (London, 2000), 35–6.

16. *LP* 19ii, nos 41, 726; Susan E. James, *Kateryn Parr: The Making of a Queen* (Aldershot, 1999), 185.

17. 13 May 1557, *CSPVen*, vi, no. 884.

18. Anon., *The Passage of our Most Drad Soueraigne Lady Quene Elyzabeth through the Citie of London to Westminster the Daye before her Coronacion* (London, 1559), sig. Eiiiʳ.

19. e.g. Starkey, *Elizabeth*, 49, 51, 53, 54–5, 56.

20. Jonathan Gibson, 'Katherine Parr, Princess Elizabeth and the Crucified Christ', in Victoria E. Burke and Jonathan Gibson (eds), *Early Modern Women's Manuscript Writing: Selected Papers from the Trinity/Trent Colloquium* (Aldershot, 2004), 34.

21. For the text, see Marc Shell (ed.), *Elizabeth's Glass* (Lincoln, NB, 1993). For some interpretations, see Starkey, *Elizabeth*, 47–9, 51–3, 88–9; Lisa M. Klein, 'Your Humble Handmaid: Elizabethan Gifts of Needlework', *Renaissance Quarterly*, 50 (1997), 476–83; Frances Teague, 'Princess Elizabeth's Hand in *The Glass of the Sinful Soul*', *English Manuscript Studies 1100–1700*, 9 (2000), 33–48.

22. For this view, see Anne Lake Prescott, 'The Pearl of the Valois and Elizabeth I: Marguerite de Navarre's *Miroir* and Tudor England', in Margaret P. Hannay (ed.), *Silent but for the Word: Tudor Women as Patrons, Translators, and Writers of Religious Works* (Kent, OH, 1985), 66, 68–71, and Susan Snyder, 'Guilty Sisters: Marguerite de Navarre, Elizabeth of England, and the *Miroir de l'ame pecheresse*', *Renaissance Quarterly*, 50 (1997), 443–58. Maria Perry believes the errors were natural for a child struggling to complete a difficult task to time: *The Word of a Prince: A Life of Elizabeth I* (Woodbridge, 1990), 32.

23. Probably, Elizabeth's French tutor Jean Bellemain gave her the chapter. Significantly, she did not credit the work to Calvin by name but referred just to 'my author'.

24. Janel Mueller and Joshua Scodel (eds), *Elizabeth I: Translations 1544–1589* (Chicago, 2009), 203–14; Roger Ellis, 'Elizabeth Tudor's Juvenile Translations', *Translation and Literature*, 18 (2009), 160–1, 167–71.

25. Mueller and Scodel (eds), *Elizabeth I: Translations*, i. 139.

26. Feria had remarked that she was on 'good terms' with Paget; see M. J. Rodriguez-Salgado and Simon Adams (eds), 'The Count of Feria's Dispatch to Philip II of 14 November 1558', *Camden Miscellany*, 28, fourth series, 29 (London, 1984), 331.

27. Paget to Sir Thomas Parry, in Haynes, 210.

28. For all of the following, see *ODNB*.

29. Walsingham to Davison, 12 July 1584, SP 52/35, fo. 54ʳ.

30. See Ch. 8.

31. John Bruce and Thomas Perowne (eds), *Correspondence of Matthew Parker* (Cambridge, 1853), 391; see also pp. 59, 400.

32. R. Warwick Bond (ed.), *The Nobility of Women by William Bercher 1559*, Roxburghe Club (London, 1904), 87–9.

33. Maria Dowling (ed.), 'William Latymer's Chronickille of Anne Bulleyn', *Camden Fourth Series*, 39 (London, 1990). For another example, see address to Elizabeth at Windsor in 1563: Nichols, i. 317.

34. Brett Dolman, 'Wishful Thinking: Reading the Portraits of Henry VIII's Queens', in Thomas Betteridge and Suzannah Lipscomb (eds), *Henry VIII and the Court* (Farnham, 2013), 119.

35. 1 Mary *c*.1, *Statutes of the Realm*, iva. 200.

36. For Anne's grave, see Hentzner, *Travels*, 27. In her will Mary requested that her mother be reburied with her in Westminster Abbey: Anne McLaren, 'Memorializing Mary and Elizabeth', in Alice Hunt and Anna Whitelock (eds), *Tudor Queenship: The Reigns of Mary and Elizabeth* (Basingstoke, 2010), 15.

37. 1 Eliz. *c* 2, *Statutes of the Realm*, iva. 358.

38. 1 Eliz. *c*.23, *Statutes of the Realm*, iva. 397.

39. Anon., *The Passage of . . . Lady Quene Elyzabeth*, sig. Aiiiiᵛ.

40. e.g. Christopher Ocland, *The Valiant Actes and Victorious Battailes of the English Nation: Elizabeth Queene* (London, 1585), 4, 1.

41. John Aylmer, *An Harborowe for Faithfull and Trewe Subjectes, Agaynst the Late Blowne Blaste, Concerninge the Government of Women* (London, 1559), sig. B4ᵛ.

42. John Foxe, *The Unabridged Acts and Monuments Online or TAMO* (1576 edn) (HRI Online Publications, Sheffield, 2011) <http//www.johnfoxe.org> (accessed 2012) (1563), 564–5, 581.

43. Ulpan Fulwell, *The Flower of Fame* (London 1575), sigs Miiii–Niii.

44. HL, HM 3135. The manuscript dedicated to Elizabeth is incomplete. It ends with John of Gaunt, before moving onto Elizabeth's parents.

45. John Daus, *A Famous Cronicle of Oure Time, Called Sleidanes Commentaries* (London, 1560), fo. 140.

46. John Stow, *The Chronicles of England* (London, 1580), 1006–7.

47. Foxe, *Acts and Monuments* (1570), 1399, 1272.

48. Andy Wood, 'The Queen is "a goggyll eyed hoore"': Gender and Seditious Speech in Early Modern England', in Nicholas Tyacke (ed.), *The English Revolution c.1590–1720* (Manchester, 2007), 89.

49. 11 August 1561, SP 70/29, fo. 39.

50. For an English version, see Nicholas Sander, *The Rise and Growth of the Anglican Schism*, ed. and trans. David Lewis (London, 1877). For one commentary, see Christopher Highley, 'A "pestilent and seditious book": Nicholas Sander's *Schismatis Anglicani* and Catholic Histories of the Reformation', in Paulina Kewes (ed.) *The Uses of History in Early Modern England* (San Marino, CA, 2006), 147–65.

51. William Allen, *An Admonition to the Nobility* (n.p., 1588), sig. A.5ʳ.

52. This was reported by a Catholic priest late in Elizabeth's reign: HMC, *Rutland*, i. 310.

53. *LP* 6, no. 1528.

54. *LP* 7, nos 373, 530, 662, 939.

55. *LP* 9, no. 219.

56. *LP* 11, no. 132.

57. 13 August 1543, *CSPSp*, vi, pt 2, no. 205; Frank Mumby, *The Girlhood of Queen Elizabeth: A Narrative in Contemporary Letters* (London, 1909), 26.

58. 8 February 1548: Nichols (ed.) *Literary Remains*, i. 40; for translation, see Mumby, *Girlhood*, 29.

59. Elizabeth's letters are undated, though internal evidence provides clues. Eight of them from the Smith MS in the Bodleian Library have been translated by Mary Anne Everett Wood; see *Letters of Royal and Illustrious Ladies of Great Britain*, 3 vols (London, 1846), iii. 221–35.

60. *CWE* 13, 14.

61. Mueller and Scodel (eds), *Elizabeth I: Translations*, i. 292–302; *CWE* 16.

62. A letter to this effect comes from Leti's *Vita di Elisabeta* but cannot be trusted. Many of Leti's originals have disappeared, and those that remain are inaccurate translations.

63. Best on the Seymour affair is Alan Bryson, '"The speciall men in every sphere": The Edwardian Regime, 1547–1553', Ph.D., University of St Andrew's (2001), 85–9, 104–5.

64. Haynes, 90.

65. *CWE* 35. For a possible significance in the change of language from Latin to English, see Ted W. Booth, 'A Switch of Language: Elizabeth I's Use of the

Vernacular as a Key to her Early Protestantism', *Journal of Anglican Studies*, 11 (2013), 100–13.

66. John Aylmer, in Hastings Robinson (ed.), *Original Letters Relative to the English Reformation; Written during the Reigns of King Henry VIII, King Edward VI, and Queen Mary: Chiefly from the Archives of Zurich* (Cambridge, 1846), i. 278–9.

67. Camden, Introduction.

68. Susan Brigden (ed.), 'The Letters of Richard Scudamore to Sir Philip Hoby...', *Camden Miscellany*, 30, fourth series, 39 (London, 1990), 101–2.

69. 19 December 1549, *CSPSp*, ix. 489.

70. 21 and (?) January 1551, *CSPSp*, x. 203, 215–16.

71. Wood, *Letters*, 222–3.

72. Machyn, fo. 7v.

73. *CWE* 38–9.

74. Diarmaid MacCulloch (ed. and trans.), 'The *Vita Mariae Angliae Reginae* of Robert Wingfield of Brantham', *Camden Miscellany*, 28, fourth series, 29 (London, 1984), 247.

75. Eric Ives, *Lady Jane Grey: A Tudor Mystery* (Oxford, 2009), 140, 142–3, 167.

76. Diana Scarisbrick, *Tudor and Jacobean Jewellery* (London, 1995), 47.

77. Ives, *Lady Jane Grey*.

78. 6 August 1553, *CSPSp*, xi. 151; MacCulloch, '*Vita Maria*', 271; Machyn, fos 19ᵛ, 20ʳ.

79. Mumby, *Girlhood*, 82–4.

80. Mumby, *Girlhood*, 85–6.

81. 18 August 1554, *CSPVen*, v, no. 934; Mumby, *Girlhood*, 92.

82. 28 November 1553, *CSPSp*, xi. 393–4.

83. 1, 28, and 29 November 1553, *CSPSp*, xi. 334–5, 400, 401; Mumby, *Girlhood*, 92.

84. Mumby, *Girlhood*, 95–7; 8 and 20 December 1553, *CSPSp*, xi. 418, 446.

85. For the evidence against Elizabeth, see Starkey, *Elizabeth*, esp. 137–8, 143–4.

86. 29 January 1554, *CSPSp*, xii. 56.

87. Mumby, *Girlhood*, 102–3, 108–9.

88. Mumby, *Girlhood*, 105.

89. Patrick Fraser Tytler, *England under the Reigns of Edward VI and Mary*, 2 vols (London 1839), ii. 313.

90. The modernized version in *CWE* 41–2 mistakenly gives the date as 16 March. Machyn and the Tower chronicler date Elizabeth's removal to the Tower as 18 March, which was the day after the letter was written. Another transcription is in *Queen Elizabeth I: Selected Works*, ed. Steven W. May (New York, 2004), 126–8.

91. *Queen Elizabeth I: Selected Works*, ed. May, 126–8.

92. Mumby, *Girlhood*, 113.

93. John Gough Nichols (ed.), 'The Chronicle of Queen Jane and of Two Years of Queen Mary...', *Camden Society*, 48 (1849), 71.

94. Nichols (ed.), 'Chronicle', 73–4, note a.

95. Tytler, *England under Edward and Mary*, ii. 375.

96. C. R. Manning (ed.), 'State Papers Relating to the Custody of the Princess Elizabeth at Woodstock, in 1554; Being Letters between Queen Mary and her Privy Council, and Sir Henry Bedingfield, Knight, of Oxburgh', *Norfolk Archaeology*, 4 (1855), 141.

97. Manning (ed.), 'State Papers', 158, 141.

98. Manning (ed.), 'State Papers', 166–7.
99. Manning (ed.), 'State Papers', 170.
100. Manning (ed.), 'State Papers', 182–3.
101. Manning (ed.), 'State Papers', 192–3, 202.
102. Manning (ed.), 'State Papers', 203–4. The council's response—if any—is not extant.
103. Manning (ed.), 'State Papers', 208–9.
104. Manning (ed.), 'State Papers', 214–15, 218–19.
105. Mumby, *Girlhood*, 191–2, 189–90.
106. John Guy, *The Children of Henry VIII* (Oxford, 2013), 163.
107. John Strype, *Ecclesiastical Memorials…*, 3 vols (London, 1822), 3i. 360.
108. 21 October 1555, *CSPVen*, vi, no. 251.
109. 2 and 9 June 1556, *CSPVen*, vi, nos 505, 510.
110. 16 June 1556, *CSPVen*, vi, no. 514.
111. *CWE* 43–4.
112. 1 December 1556, *CSPVen*, vi, no. 743.
113. 7 December 1556, *CSPVen*, vi, no.752.
114. Susan Doran, *Monarchy and Matrimony: The Courtships of Elizabeth I* (London, 1996), 17–20.
115. BL, Cotton Vitellius CXVI, fo. 334ᵛ.
116. Machyn, fo. 88ʳ.
117. 13 May 1557, *CSPVen*, vi, no. 884.
118. In the codicil to her will dated 18 October 1558, Mary did not mention Elizabeth by name, just referring to 'her next heir and successor by the laws and statutes of this realme' (FSL, X. d.471, printed in Robert Tittler, *The Reign of Mary I* (London, 1983), 100–299).
119. 7 November 1558, *CSPSp*, xiii, no. 498.
120. Henry Clifford (ed.), *The Life of Lady Jane Dormer, Duchess of Feria* (London, 1887), 90, 72.
121. Edwin Sandys to Henry Bullinger, in Hastings Robinson (ed.), *The Zurich Letters Comprising the Correspondence of Several English Bishops and Others, with Some of the Helvetian Reformers, during the Early Part of the Reign of Queen Elizabeth 1558–1602* (Cambridge, 1843), 3–4.
122. Rodriguez-Salgado and Adams, 'The Count of Feria's Dispatch', 331.
123. Elizabeth's interview with William Maitland of Lethington in 1561, quoted in *CWE* 66.
124. Judith Richards, 'Examples and Admonitions: What Mary Demonstrated for Elizabeth', in Hunt and Whitelock, *Tudor Queenship*, 34.
125. Paulina Kewes, 'Godly Queens: The Royal Iconographies of Mary and Elizabeth', in Hunt and Whitelock, *Tudor Queenship*, 56. See also Paulina Kewes, 'Two Queens, One Inventory: The Lives of Mary and Elizabeth Tudor', in Kevin Sharpe and Steven N. Zwicker (eds), *Writing Lives: Biography and Textuality, Identity and Representation in Early Modern England* (Oxford, 2008), 187–207.
126. Carole Levin, '"Would I give you help and succour": Elizabeth I and the Politics of Touch', *Albion*, 21 (1989), 195.
127. *CWE* 46–7.
128. Thomas Churchyarde, *A Handeful of Gladsome Verses Given to the Queenes Maiesty at Woodstocke this Prograce* (Oxford 1592), sig. C1.

CHAPTER 2

1. After Elizabeth, the crown was bequeathed: 'In default, to the heirs of the body of Lady Frances' (the elder daughter of Mary, countess of Suffolk) (*LP* 21ii, no. 634).
2. Ives, 'Tudor Dynastic Problems Revisited', 255–79.
3. In the *ODNB* entry for 'Henry Stanley, Fourth Earl of Derby', by Louis A. Knafla, Margaret's date of birth is given as 1540, but in a deposition of 3 February 1562 Margaret gave her age as 24: HL, HM 68350.
4. See Ch. 1.
5. BL, Cotton Julius FVI, fo. 203.
6. Leanda de Lisle, *The Sisters who would be Queen* (London, 2008), 161.
7. Although she is not recorded as being a maid of honour, other evidence suggests otherwise: 13 May 1557, *CSPVen*, vi, no. 884; 24 March 1559, *CSPSpEliz*, i, no. 21.
8. This information comes from a newspaper item filed in the Huntington Library along with HM 68350.
9. Henry Ellis, *Original Letters, Illustrative of English History*, 2nd ser., 4 vols (London, 1827), ii. 218; 13 May 1557, *CSPVen*, vi, no. 884.
10. For one example of negative comments about Elizabeth's treatment of Margaret Clifford, see Barry Coward, *The Stanleys, Lord Stanley and Earls of Derby 1385–1672* (Manchester, 1983), 144.
11. Nichols, i. 402, 445; SP 12/66, fo. 109ʳ. Lady Strange also headed the New Year's roll of gift giving, a position reserved for Elizabeth's relations of royal blood: Jane A. Lawson (ed.), *The Elizabethan New Year's Gift Exchanges 1559–1603* (Oxford, 2013), 35, 55, 64, 91, 111, 134, 161, 170, 183.
12. HL, Ellesmere 1287, 1288.
13. SP 15/13, fo. 223ᵛ.
14. 18 February 1570, SP 12/66, fo. 111.
15. SP 12/66, fo. 109ʳ.
16. Nichols, ii. 46, 523; iii. 1.
17. Charlotte Isabelle Merton, 'The Women who Served Queen Mary and Queen Elizabeth: Ladies, Gentlewomen and Maids of the Privy Chamber, 1553–1603', Ph.D., University of Cambridge (1992), 37; 24 March 1559, *CSPSpEliz*, i, no. 21.
18. John Middleton to Cecil, 24 March 1560, CP 201/133ᵛ. See also 29 December 1559, CP 2/19, fo. 25ʳ.
19. This and the account of their courtship and marriage come from BL, Harley 6286, a copy of the proceedings of the commission of inquiry that was presented to their elder son Lord Beauchamp. Other manuscript copies exist.
20. Nicholas Harris Nicolas (ed.), *The Literary Remains of Lady Jane Grey* (London, 1825), pp. cxvi–vii.
21. The 1536 Act of Treason made it high treason for a member of the royal family to marry without the monarch's written permission, but the statute was abolished in 1547.
22. For the role of privy chamber ladies as intermediaries, see Ch. 8.
23. BL, Cotton Titus BXIII, fo. 50ᵛ.
24. Philip Lord Hardwicke (ed.), *Miscellaneous State Papers*, 2 vols (London, 1778), i. 174; Haynes, 368. For Elizabeth's relationship with Dudley, see Ch. 5; for the problems with Mary, see Ch. 3.

25. Bruce and Perowne, *Correspondence of Matthew Parker*, 148.
26. Cecil to Throckmorton, 26 August 1561, Hardwicke, *State Papers*, i. 177.
27. 13 September 1561, *CSPSpEliz*, i, no. 139.
28. 17 August 1561, Haynes, 369–70.
29. BL, Harley 6286, p. 87. Katherine and Hertford's testimonies of 22 August and 12 September are pp. 78–90.
30. SP 12/19, fo. 66ʳ&ᵛ.
31. 10 February 1562, Haynes, 378. The commission was dated 31 January 1562: SP 12/21, fo. 76.
32. BL, Harley 6286, pp. 32–57, 91–3.
33. For further discrepancies, see HMC, *Salisbury*, xiii. 61.
34. The few contemporary accounts comment that the lack of witnesses was a significant weakness in their case: SP 12/21 fo. 105.
35. Bodleian Library, Tanner 84, fos 191, 196ᵛ.
36. Ian W. Archer, Simon Adams, G. W. Bernard et al. (eds), 'Religion, Politics, and Society in Sixteenth Century England', *Camden Fifth Series*, 22 (Cambridge, 2003), 82; Camden (1562); Haynes, 396; 21 September 1561, SP 70/30, fo. 76.
37. Thomas Wright (ed.), *Queen Elizabeth and her Times: A Series of Original Letters...*, 2 vols (London, 1838), i. 129.
38. John H. Baker (ed.), *Reports from the Lost Notebooks of Sir James Dyer*, Selden Society, 2 vols (London, 1994), i. 81–3.
39. Haynes, 396.
40. Ellis, *Original Letters*, ii. 273.
41. CWE 67.
42. For Elizabeth's relationship with Mary, see Ch. 3.
43. Haynes, 405.
44. Haynes, 405; 21 August 1563, SP 12/29, fo. 124.
45. Ellis, *Original Letters*, ii. 281–2.
46. Among those who spoke in their favour were Sir Nicholas Throckmorton, Lord Robert Dudley, Sir William Cecil, and Anne, duchess of Somerset: *CSPForEliz*, vi. 378; SP 12/33, fo. 68; Ellis, *Original Letters*, ii. 276, 286–8.
47. 22 March and 1 April 1564, SP 12/33, fos 68, 88.
48. BL, Additional 8878, fos 30, 32; Wright, *Queen Elizabeth*, i. 173; and 'Interrogatories and their Answers', April 1564, in Haynes, 412, 413, 414, 416, 417; BL, Harley 6990, fo. 62. For Beale, see CUL, MS Dd.3. 85(2) and Ii.5.3.
49. HMC, *Bath*, iv. 374.
50. BL, Additional 8878, fos 32ᵛ–33; Baker, *Dyer's Lost Notebooks*, i. 95–7.
51. Mortimer Levine, *The Early Elizabethan Succession Question, 1558–1568* (Stanford, CA, 1966), 62–85.
52. Wright, *Queen Elizabeth*, i. 179.
53. 'Sir Nicholas Bacon', by Robert Tittler, *ODNB*.
54. Levine, *Succession Question*, 75.
55. Haynes, 414.
56. For Hales, Grey, and Bacon, see *ODNB*. For Bacon, see also HL, HM 1340, fo. 83ʳ&ᵛ.
57. See Levine, *Succession Question*, *passim*.
58. 4 June 1565, SP 52/10, fo. 124.
59. Wright, *Queen Elizabeth*, i. 184.
60. Keyes had also been appointed Dudley's deputy as master of the horse in August 1562: *APC* vii. 127.

61. BL, Lansdowne 102, fo. 115.
62. SP 12/37, fo. 32.
63. 1 September 1565, SP 12/37, fo. 52.
64. 2 October 1567, SP 12/44, fo. 54.
65. 2 February 1568, *CSPSpEliz*, ii, no. 5.
66. SP 12/46, fos 52, 53, 110. Eventually, her remains were transferred to the Seymour tomb in Salisbury Cathedral.
67. 2 February 1568, *CSPSpEliz*, ii, no. 5. Circulating in manuscript was a narrative of Katherine's last hours, which was designed to establish her protestant credentials and possibly rehabilitate her with the queen; see BL, Additional 35237. In the early 1570s, Thomas Churchyard wrote a poem on the subject of her death, which was printed in 1575: William M. Schutte, 'Thomas Churchyard's "Dollfull discourse" and the Death of Lady Katherine Grey', *Sixteenth Century Journal*, 15 (1984), 477–8.
68. HMC, *Bath*, iv. 135.
69. Matthew Parker to Burghley, 9 March 1574, CP 159/85.
70. See Ch. 4.
71. Ellis, *Original Letters*, ii. 308–10; SP 12/39, fo. 174.
72. SP 12/73, fo. 166.
73. SP 12/46, fo. 163; BL, Lansdowne 94, fo. 42.
74. 10 June 1571, SP 12/78, fo. 247.
75. Nichols, ii. 298, n. 477.
76. HMC, *Bath*, iv. 197.
77. 7 October 1571, SP 12/81, fo. 103.
78. SP 12/85 fo. 216.
79. An undated letter from Mary to Hertford was sent from 'my house': HMC, *Bath*, iv. 138–9.
80. Nichols, ii. 523.
81. De Lisle, *Sisters who would be Queen*, 290.
82. BL, Harley 787, fo. 16^v; 25 August 1579, *CSPSpEliz*, ii, no. 593; 10 September 1579, *CSPVen*, vii, no. 774.
83. BL, Harley 787, fo. 16^v.
84. *APC* xi. 316–17; xii. 102, 317; xiii. 89, 289, 434.
85. Letters from Margaret to Hatton, BL, Additional 15891, fos 35^r, 76$^{r\&v}$, 88^v; her letter to the queen, fo. 76^r. The last time Margaret appeared on the New Year's gift roll was 1579.
86. Anne Clifford wrote that the countess died 'in her house then newly built in Clerkenwell', see A. G. Dickens (ed.), *Clifford Letters of the Sixteenth Century*, Surtees Society, 172 (Durham and London, 1957), 145.
87. Notarial instruments affirming Thomas Seymour to be the legitimate son of Hertford and Lady Katherine, 23 October 1588, SP 12/217, fo. 91$^{r\&v}$; 30 October 1589, SP 12/227, fo. 60; 21 October 1590, SP 12/233, fo. 199.
88. 5 November 1595, SP 12/254, fo. 118. He was released in early January 1596, SP 12/256, fo. 6.
89. HMC, *Bath*, iv. 148–9, 155, 190–6.
90. For Beauchamp's concern that he had offended the queen, see 28 September 1582, SP 12/155, fo. 95. For the queen's attitude, see BL, Lansdowne 103, fos 58, 59.
91. *CSPDom, 1595–97*, pp. 236–7, 242, 244–5, 250, 251–2.

92. Confined since 1588 in her grandmother's house, Arbella was probably making a desperate bid for freedom. For details of the affair, see E. T. Bradley, *Life of the Lady Arabella Stuart*, 2 vols (London, 1889), ii. 99–145; HMC, *Salisbury*, xii. 593–7, 627–30, 681; University of Glasgow, ID: 142 <http://www.bessofhardwick.org/letter.jsp?letter=142> (accessed 2014).

93. 'Ferdinando Stanley, Fifth Earl of Derby', by David Kathman, *ODNB*; Lawrence Manley, 'From Strange's Men to Pembroke's Men: 2 Henry VI and the First Part of the Contention', *Shakespeare Quarterly*, 54 (2003), 253–87.

94. 21 May 1591, SP 12/238, fos 243ᵛ, 246ʳ; 3 July 1592, SP 15/32, fo. 72; 13 June 1594, SP 12/249, fo. 20ʳ. Stanley, fighting in the Netherlands, had deserted with his Irish troops to the Spanish in 1587.

95. CP 170/68ʳ; CP 170/17. See also 4, 5, 7, November 1593, HMC, *Salisbury*, iv. 408–11; xiii. 491.

96. Countess of Derby to Robert Cecil [November 1593], CP 170/16.

97. HMC, *Salisbury*, iv. 517. For a description of Derby's symptoms and the belief that the earl was bewitched, see Edmund Lodge (ed.), *Illustrations of British History, Biography and Manners in the Reigns of Henry VIII…[to] James I, in Papers from the MSS. of the Families of Howard, Talbot and Cecil …*, 3 vols, 2nd edn (London, 1838), ii. 459–62.

98. See, e.g. Coward, *The Stanleys*, 144; Judith Richards, *Elizabeth I* (Abingdon, 2012), 63–4; Schutte, 'Churchyard's "Dollfull discourse"', 474; and Bundesin, '"No other faction but my own"', 64.

99. *CWE* 65.

CHAPTER 3

1. This has been standard fare in film, opera, and popular histories such as Jane Dunn, *Elizabeth and Mary: Cousins, Rivals, Queens* (New York, 2004). For an alternative perspective, see John Guy, *My Heart is My Own* (London, 2004), *passim*.

2. *CSPForEliz*, i. 91, 145, 314, 348; ii. 108; *CSPScot*, i. 271; BL, Cotton Caligula BV, fo. 325; Hardwicke, *State Papers*, i. 131.

3. SP 70/5, fo. 76ʳ.

4. For further details, see Ch. 9.

5. SP 52/4, fo. 88. For other terms, see Ch. 9.

6. Haynes, 376–8. Mary repeated this point when negotiations resumed in 1561 and 1562. Robert Keith, *History of the Affairs of Church and State in Scotland, from the Beginning of the Reformation to the Year 1568*, ed. John Parker Lawson and C. J. Lyon, 3 vols (Edinburgh, 1844–50), ii. 134.

7. 13 April 1561, SP 70/25, fo. 46; 16 August 1561, SP 52/6, fo. 123.

8. This was expressed to Mary in personal letters and through Elizabeth's envoy in January 1561: SP 52/6, fo. 19ʳ&ᵛ.

9. *CSPForEliz*, iv. 108; 1 July 1561, SP 52/6, fo. 103ᵛ.

10. These fears were also expressed by Scottish protestants: BL, Cotton Caligula BX, fo. 152ʳ&ᵛ; *CSPScot*, i. 542.

11. SP 59/5, fos 148ᵛ, 149; Keith, *History*, ii. 69, 96–7.

12. Keith, *History*, ii. 13, 134–5.

13. e.g. SP 12/23, fo. 121; SP 52/6, fo. 176; SP 52/7, fo. 7; BL, Cotton Caligula BX, fos 146ᵛ–147, 209; Haynes, 388; Keith, *History*, ii. 136.

14. *CSPForEliz*, v. 162; SP 12/23, fo. 121.
15. Keith, *History*, ii. 116–17.
16. 15 July 1562, *CSPScot*, i. 183.
17. Instructions to Sir Henry Sidney, in Keith, *History*, ii. 148–50.
18. Keith, *History*, ii. 152 (n. 2); SP 52/7, fo. 65.
19. Keith, *History*, ii. 227–8.
20. Lord James Stewart to Elizabeth, 6 August 1561, *CSPScot*, i. 540–1; Cecil to Throckmorton, 14 July 1561, Hardwicke, *State Papers*, i. 174.
21. 7 October 1561, Haynes, 373.
22. 1561, *CWE* 62–3.
23. *CWE* 58–70.
24. Keith, *History*, ii. 176–7, 185, 191–2; Sir James Melville, *Memoirs of his Own Life*, ed. Thomas Thomson (Edinburgh, 1827), 114–15.
25. Keith, *History*, ii. 206–8, 211, 216–17.
26. Randolph to Cecil, 8 March 1564, referring to a conference with Mary on 27 February, SP 52/9, fo. 41^r.
27. Keith, *History*, ii. 219, 225; SP 52/9, fos 51, 53–4^v.
28. Keith, *History*, ii. 109, 112–13. The issue was over the earl of Lennox's return to Scotland.
29. Melville, *Memoirs*, 109, 116–17.
30. Melville, *Memoirs*, 120–5, 128.
31. Melville, *Memoirs*, 129.
32. Keith, *History*, ii. 244–5, 250–6; *CSPScot*, ii. 102–4, 105–9; Katherine P. Frescoln, 'A Letter from Thomas Randolph to the Earl of Leicester', *Huntington Library Quarterly*, 37 (1973), 83–8.
33. Keith, *History*, ii. 276–83, 299–300, 336–7. Elizabeth responded by imprisoning Darnley's mother and confiscating his father's English estates.
34. Keith, *History*, ii. 298.
35. June 1565, Keith, *History*, ii. 291–2. For Mary's letters, see SP 52/10, fo. 131.
36. Conference by the privy council, 4 June 1565: *CSPForEliz*, vii. 384–7; Wright, *Queen Elizabeth*, i. 201.
37. Wright, *Queen Elizabeth*, i. 201.
38. 13 August 1565, SP52/11, fo. 25$^{r\&v}$.
39. Guy, *My Heart is My Own*, 245–7, 288.
40. 30 March, 11 and 29 April 1566, *CSPSpEliz*, i, nos 347, 349, 354.
41. 4 June 1566, *CSPSpEliz*, i, no. 360; 31 October 1566, SP 52/12, fo. 110. For Elizabeth's gift, see Ch. 4.
42. 7 November 1566, BL, Cotton Caligula BX, fos 399^v–401. Elizabeth had discussed such terms in June, with Robert Melville, Mary's ambassador to her court: 15 June 1566, *CSPSpEliz*, i, no. 362.
43. The 1544 Act of Succession had stipulated that the king's determination on the succession had to be signed by him.
44. BL, Cotton Caligula BX, fos 400^v–401; SP 52/13, fo. 1.
45. Keith, *History*, ii. 490–2; 3 January 1567, SP 52/13, fo. 1.
46. 24 February 1567, *CWE* 116–18.
47. April 1567, SP 52/13, fos 39–40^v.
48. *CWE* 118.
49. Elizabeth to the lords of Scotland, 30 June, SP 52/13, fo. 82.
50. *CWE* 118–19; *CSPScot*, ii. 336.
51. 5 July 1567, *CSPSpEliz*, i, no. 430.

52. Instructions to Throckmorton, 20 and 27 July 1567, SP 52/14, fos 40$^{r\&v}$, 71.
53. 26 July 1567, BL, Cotton Caligula CI, fos 36–7^v; 27 July, SP 52/14, fo. 73^r.
54. 27 July 1567, SP 52/14, fo. 72^r.
55. 14 August 1567, SP 52/14, fo. 130.
56. 17 May 1568, CSPScot, ii. 407.
57. 8 June 1568, SP 53/1, fo. 16^r.
58. A memorial of the consultation touching the Queen of Scots, 20 June 1568, BL, Cotton Caligula CI, fo. 137$^{r\&v}$.
59. For the disagreements between Elizabeth and Cecil over Mary, see Ch. 9.
60. For these conferences, see Gordon Donaldson, *The First Trial of Mary Queen of Scots* (London, 1969). For transcriptions of the eight 'casket letters', see A. E. MacRobert, *Mary Queen of Scots and the Casket Letters* (London and New York, 2002), 163–93.
61. SP 52/16, fo. 4.
62. Leslie to Mary, 2 May 1569, SP 53/3/77.
63. 8 and 14 May 1569, SP 53/3/78–9; SP 52/16, fo. 112; Haynes, 535, 541–2.
64. Stephen Alford, *The Early Elizabethan Polity: William Cecil and the British Succession Crisis, 1558–1569* (Cambridge, 2002), 199–203.
65. SP 52/16, fo. 91; Haynes, 535–45.
66. It was published in England in May.
67. Articles to be performed by the Q of Scottes, 7 May 1570, CSPScot, iii. 162–4.
68. Anon., *Cabala sive scrinia sacra: Mysteries of State and Government...*(London, 1663), 177.
69. CSPScot, iii. 210–11, 320; BL, Cotton Caligula CII, fo. 31.
70. The pamphlets were printed together in one volume at Rheims: CSPScot, iii. 114–15, 160.
71. Anon., *Cabala sive scrinia sacra*, 179.
72. BL, Additional 34216, fos 4^{r+v}, 7.
73. BL, Additional 34216, fos 4$^{r\&v}$, 7.
74. For the articles and Mary's responses, see Haynes, 609–14.
75. BL, Additional 34216, fo. 7.
76. For the Scots' delays, Haynes, 624.
77. For more on the Ridolfi plot, see Ch. 10. For Mary's role, see Retha M. Warnicke, *Mary Queen of Scots* (Abingdon, 2006), 194–8.
78. HL, HM 41954, fos 210–11.
79. Shrewsbury to Elizabeth, 9 September 1571, Wright, *Queen Elizabeth*, i. 396.
80. D. M. Lockie, 'The Political Career of the Bishop of Ross, 1568–80', *University of Birmingham Historical Journal*, 4 (1954), 109–11; Gerald Bowler, '"An axe or an acte": The Parliament of 1572 and Resistance Theory in Early Elizabethan England', *Canadian Journal of History*, 19 (1984), 349–59.
81. CWE 133–4. In some versions, 'poll' was used instead of 'pull', the word transcribed in CWE. The poem circulated widely in manuscript before being printed in 1589. Scholars disagree as to whether Elizabeth intended the poem to be made public or not. See Peter C. Herman, *Royal Poetrie: Monarchic Verse and the Political Imaginary of Early Modern England* (Ithaca, NY, 2010), 101–14. For Elizabeth's poetry, see Jennifer Summit, '"The arte of a ladies penne": Elizabeth I and the Poetics of Queenship', *English Literary Renaissance*, 26 (1996), 395–422.
82. 10 September 1572, Murdin, 224. These secret instructions are in Burghley's hand.

83. HL, HM 41954, pp. 211, 213. Similar precautions had been put in place in November 1569, HL, HA 4138.

84. Rayne Allinson, *Monarchy of Letters* (Basingstoke, 2012), 87–8.

85. HL, HM 41954, pp. 233, 243.

86. Antonia Fraser, *Mary Queen of Scots* (London, 1969), 480–1, 482–3; Allan J. Crosby and John Bruce (eds), 'Accounts and Papers Relating to Mary Queen of Scots', *Camden Society*, 93 (1867), 1–27.

87. Alexandre Labanoff (ed.), *Lettres, instructions et mémoires de Marie Stuart, reine d'Écosse*, 7 vols (London, 1844), v, 266–7.

88. SP 53/11, fo. 198ᵛ.

89. SP 53/11, fos 183ʳ&ᵛ, 185ʳ&ᵛ.

90. 17 March 1583, *CSPSpEliz*, iii, no. 321; BL, Cotton Caligula CVI, fo. 189; SP 53/12, no. 48 (fo. 97).

91. 6 April 1583, SP 53/12, nos 49 &51, esp. fos 113, 124ʳ&ᵛ.

92. Conyers Read (ed.), 'The Bardon Papers: Documents Relating to the Imprisonment and Trial of Mary Queen of Scots', *Camden Third Series*, 17 (1909), 17–19.

93. William Waad to Walsingham, and instructions for Robert Beale, *CSPScot*, vii. 69–70, 108–9.

94. *CWE* 183–5. The bond was called the 'Instrument of association' or just 'the Association', but it is known to history as 'the bond'.

95. *The Harleian Miscellany; or a Collection of Scarce, Curious, and Entertaining Pamphlets*, ed. William Oldys, viii (London, 1810), 207–10.

96. Labanoff, *Lettres*, vi. 124–5.

97. See Ch. 10.

98. John Hungerford Pollen SJ, *Mary Queen of Scots and the Babington Plot* (Edinburgh, 1922), 20–2.

99. For the letter, see Pollen, *Mary Queen of Scots*, 38–46, and BL, Cotton Caligula CVIII, fos 375–8ᵛ.

100. Warnicke, *Mary Queen of Scots*, 237–8.

101. 20 May 1586 to Charles Paget, in Labanoff, *Lettres*, vi. 313–14.

102. *CWE* 288.

103. 1 February 1586, John Morris (ed.), *The Letter-Books of Sir Amias Poulet; Keeper of Mary Queen of Scots* (London, 1874), 359–60. Paulet refused outright.

104. Sir Nicholas Harris Nicolas, *Life of William Davison, Secretary of State and Privy Counsellor to Queen Elizabeth* (London, 1823), 240, 264.

105. BL, Cotton Caligula CVIII, fo. 650ʳ.

106. *CWE* 201.

107. 19 December 1586, Labanoff, *Lettres*, vi. 475–80.

CHAPTER 4

1. Gordon Donaldson (ed.), *The Memoirs of Sir James Melville of Halhill* (London, 1969), 56.

2. This was certainly the view expressed by the Venetian ambassador in France: 23 January 1567, *CSPVen*, vii, no. 378. See also Keith, *History*, ii. 477–9.

3. 7 November 1566, BL, Cotton Caligula BX, fos 399ʳ&ᵛ.

4. *CSPVen*, vii, no. 378.

5. Rayne Allinson, 'Queen Elizabeth I and the "nomination" of the Young Prince of Scotland', *Notes and Queries*, 53 (2006), 425–7.
6. See Ch. 3.
7. *CSPScot*, v. 379; vi. 573; SP 52/28, fo. 146; 52/34, fo. 36; SP 52/58, fo. 108; BL, Cotton Caligula CVIII, fo. 127; *CWE* 366.
8. James P. R. Lyell, 'A Tract on James VI's Succession to the English Throne', *English Historical Review*, 51 (1936), 289–301.
9. 5 October and 7 November 1579, and 22 February 1580, *CSPScot*, v. 352, 358, 379.
10. Communication of Thomas Pounde, 18 September 1580, SP 52/30, fo. 62ᵛ.
11. Jean Teulet, *Relations politiques de la France et de l'Espagne avec l'Écosse au XVIe siècle*, 5 vols (Paris, 1862), iii. 95, 99.
12. Michel de Castelnau, sieur de Mauvissière—the French ambassador—warned Elizabeth that her intervention in Scotland would be 'désagréable' to the French king: Teulet, *Relations politiques*, 101.
13. 16 April 1580, SP 52/28, fo.19ᵛ.
14. 19 April 1580, BL, Cotton Caligula CV, fo. 13; 31 August 1580, SP 52/28, fo. 147.
15. 7 February 1581, SP 52/29, fo. 239; 10 May 1580, SP 52/28, fo. 186.
16. See Ch. 3.
17. Mauvissière's report, '[Elle] le [Jacques VI] hait plus qu'elle ne feist jamais la royne d'Escosse sa mère et estime un jour sa ruyne de ce côté-la' in Teulet, *Relations politiques*, iii. 128.
18. 1 September 1582, *CSPSpEliz*, iii, no. 283.
19. 30 August 1582, SP 52/30, fo. 395.
20. 1 February and 12 September 1583, SP 52/33, fo. 40.
21. Sir George Carey to Elizabeth, 14 September 1582, SP 52/30, fo. 517ʳ.
22. 7 February 1583, BL, Cotton Caligula CVII, fo. 126; Joseph Stevenson (ed.), *The Correspondence of Robert Bowes* (Edinburgh, 1842), 365; 1 March 1583, SP 52/31, no. 47.
23. 2 July 1583, SP 52/32, fo. 87.
24. September 1583, David Calderwood, *The True History of the Church of Scotland, from the Beginning of the Reformation, unto the End of the Reigne of King James VI...*, ed. T. Thomson, 8 vols (Edinburgh, 1842–9), iii. 726; see also pp.724, 759, and *CSPScot*, vi. 560.
25. Robert Bowes to Walsingham, 13 July 1583, SP 52/32, fo. 100ᵛ.
26. Walsingham brought these demands to Scotland in August 1583: *CSPScot*, vi. 572–4.
27. *CSPScot*, vi. 618.
28. *CSPScot*, vi. 644; 4 and 19 September 1583, SP 52/33, fos 29, 46.
29. See Ch. 11 for Walsingham's attitude towards James.
30. *CSPScot*, vii. 68–9.
31. [25 April], BL, Cotton Caligula CVII, fo. 20.
32. 'Instructions for A.B. to be presently sent into Scotland', [25 April], SP 52/34, pp. 83–90; Elizabeth's instructions to William Davison, 29 April, BL, Cotton Caligula CVIII, fos 127–9ʳ.
33. Bowes to Walsingham, 8 May 1584, *CSPScot*, vii. 118–19.
34. For these events, see Calderwood, *History*, iv. 21–38.
35. 4 May 1584, *CSPScot*, vii. 111–12.
36. May 1584, SP 52/34, no. 79.
37. Teulet, *Relations politiques*, iii. 269–70. Despite its name, the bodyguard was mainly constituted of Frenchmen.

38. See Ch. 3.
39. [19 May] 1584, SP 52/34, fo. 72^{r&v}; BL, Cotton Caligula CVII, no. 37.
40. Francis, duke of Anjou, heir to the French throne, died in June 1584, leaving the protestant Henry, king of Navarre, next in line. Another phase of the religious wars looked imminent.
41. 2 June 1584, SP 52/35, fo. 1, refers to a letter of May from the ambassador William Davison.
42. 2 August 1584, SP 52/36, fo. 6.
43. 7 August 1584, SP 52/36, fo. 12; Wright, *Queen Elizabeth*, ii. 236; 3 October 1584, BL, Cotton Caligula CVIII, fo. 150.
44. The proposal was conveyed privately to Hunsdon, who passed it on to Elizabeth and Burghley: Patrick Gray (ed.), *Letters and Papers Relating to Patrick, Master of Gray, afterwards Seventh Lord Gray* (Edinburgh, 1835), 13.
45. Burghley to Hunsdon, 20 August 1584, SP 52/36, fo. 38^{v}.
46. SP 52/36, fo. 83^{r&v}.
47. 1 November 1584, BL, Cotton Caligula CVIII, fos 172–3.
48. The 'instrument' or 'bond of association' was drawn up on 19 October 1584. No names were mentioned in it, but the meaning was clear. I must thank Paulina Kewes for drawing my attention to the relationship between the bond and Anglo-Scottish relations. See also Ch. 3.
49. Gray (ed.), *Master of Gray*, 26, 28.
50. Jane Rickard, *Authorship and Authority: The Writings of James VI and I* (Manchester, 2007), 78; Daniel Fischlin, '"To eate the flesh of kings": James VI and I, Apocalypse, Nation and Sovereignty', in Daniel Fischlin and Mark Fortier (eds), *Royal Subjects: Essays on the Writings of James VI and I* (Detroit, 2002), 388–420.
51. 22 January 1585, SP 52/37, fo. 5^{v}.
52. *CSPScot*, vii. 611–14.
53. John Bruce (ed.), 'Letters of Queen Elizabeth and King James VI', *Camden Society*, 46 (1849), 19.
54. 11 September 1585, *CSPSpEliz*, iii, no. 406; Bruce, 'Letters of Queen Elizabeth and King James', 22–4.
55. Printed in Peter C. Herman, 'Authorship and the Royal "I" King James VI/I and the Politics of Monarchic Verse', *Renaissance Quarterly*, 54 (2001), 1498.
56. June 1586, SP 52/40, no. 62.
57. 2 June 1586, SP 52/40, no. 1.
58. 'George Gordon, First Marquess of Huntly', by J. R. M. Sizer, *ODNB*; Thomas M. McCoog SJ, *The Society of Jesus in Ireland, Scotland, and England 1541–1588: 'Our Way of Proceeding?'* (Leiden, 1996), 242.
59. CWE 286, 289. The quotations come from Elizabeth's replies.
60. 29 September 1586, Murdin, 569.
61. Murdin, 572–3, 568.
62. November 1586, HMC, *Salisbury*, iii. 199 (no. 409). See also *CSPScot*, ix. 120–2, and Susan Doran, 'Revenge her Foul and Most Unnatural Murder: The Impact of Mary Stewart's Execution on Anglo-Scottish Relations', *History*, 85 (2000), 589–607.
63. Robert Rait and Anne I. Cameron, *King James's Secret: Negotiations between Elizabeth and James VI, Relating to the Execution of Mary Queen of Scots, from the Warrender Papers* (London, 1927), 60–1.
64. Rait and Cameron, *King James's Secret*, 65, 989.
65. CWE 291–3. See Rait and Cameron, *King James's Secret*, 179–82, for original spelling.

66. 14 February 1587, Rait and Cameron, *King James's Secret*, 296.
67. Doran, 'Revenge', 600–7.
68. Annie I. Cameron (ed.). *The Warrender Papers*, 2 vols (Edinburgh, 1931–2), ii. 13.
69. His grandmother Margaret, countess of Lennox, had died in 1578.
70. 7 April 1587, SP 52/42, fo. 29. See also 16 July 1588, *CSPScot*, ix. 580–2.
71. Asheby to Walsingham, 25 July 1588, BL, Cotton Caligula DI, fo. 344ʳ.
72. 3, 6 and 10 August 1588, *CSPScot*, ix. 589–91, 594–5.
73. 22 August 1588, *CSPScot*, ix. 598–9, 600.
74. For more on the Marprelate tracts, see Ch. 9.
75. *CSPScot*, x. 528.
76. 6 July 1590, Bruce, 'Letters of Queen Elizabeth and King James', 63–4.
77. *CSPScot*, x. 363–4.
78. This was despite the fact that they had taken up arms against James in a bid to do their own version of the Ruthven raid, and separate him from the rival faction then in power.
79. 16 March 1589, Cameron (ed.), *Warrender Papers*, ii. 102–4 (p. 103); SRO, GD 406/1/43.
80. McCoog, *The Society of Jesus*, 80–1; Cameron (ed.), *Warrender Papers*, ii. 192–202.
81. Calderwood, *History*, v. 238.
82. 22 December 1593: CWE 372–4; Bruce, 'Letters of Queen Elizabeth and King James', 72.
83. National Library of Scotland, Advocates MS 35.5.3 (iii), fo. 257; *CSPScot*, x. 45–8, 69–70; 20 December 1593, SP 52/52, fo. 17.
84. CWE 375–7; Bruce, 'Letters of Queen Elizabeth and King James', 72. See also Susan Doran, 'Loving and Affectionate Cousins? The Relationship between Elizabeth I and James VI of Scotland', in Susan Doran and Glenn Richardson (eds), *Tudor England and its Neighbours* (Basingstoke, 2005), 203–34.
85. *CSPScot*, xi. 410; Cameron, *Warrender Papers*, ii. 266.
86. 5 January 1597, Edinburgh University Library, Laing MS, 3, pp. 45–6.
87. Bruce, 'Letters of Queen Elizabeth and King James', 68–9.
88. 27 April 1598, *CSPScot*, xiii(i). 196–7.
89. See Chs 7 and 11.
90. *A Conference about the Next Succession to the Crowne of Ingland* (1594). For the wider significance of this work, see Susan Doran and Paulina Kewes (eds), *Doubtful and Dangerous: The Question of Succession in Late Elizabethan England* (Manchester, 2014).
91. Doran, 'Loving and Affectionate Cousins?', 220.
92. 1 July 1598, Bruce, 'Letters of Queen Elizabeth and King James', 125–6.
93. September 1600, Bruce, 'Letters of Queen Elizabeth and King James', 132–3.
94. See Ch. 11.
95. Queen Elizabeth to George Nicolson, 31 December 1598, SP 52/52, fo. 234.

CHAPTER 5

1. This work was probably a collaborative project produced by a group of Catholic laymen. See D. C. Peck, 'Introduction', in Peck (ed.), *Leicester's Commonwealth: The Copy of a Letter Written by a Master of Art of Cambridge (1584) and Related Documents* (Athens, OH, and London, 1985); online edn <http://www.

dpeck.info/write/leic-comm.pdf> (accessed 2012). The wording differs in the various extant manuscripts of the work, but I have gone with Peck.

2. In the French ambassador's dispatch, translated and printed in Simon Adams, *Leicester and the Court* (Manchester, 2002), 139.

3. Dudley's year of birth was either 1532 or 1533. For his early life, see 'Robert Dudley, Earl of Leicester', by Simon Adams, *ODNB*, and Chris Skidmore, *Death and the Virgin* (London, 2011), 11–61.

4. Camden (1560).

5. Examination of John Dymock, 6 August 1562, SP 70/40, fo. 72ʳ.

6. Rodríguez-Salgado and Adams, 'The Count of Feria's Dispatch', 332.

7. The patent was not issued until 11 January 1559.

8. *CPREliz*, i. 60, 61.

9. Adams, *Leicester*, 162–3.

10. Camden (1560); 28 March 1563, *CSPSpEliz*, i, no. 216.

11. Simon Adams (ed.), 'Household Accounts and Disbursement Books of Robert Dudley, Earl of Leicester, 1558–1561, 1584–1586', *Camden Fifth Series*, 6 (Cambridge, 1995), 72, 80; 9 April 1560, Kervyn de Lettenhove (ed.), *Relations politiques des Pay-Bas et de l'Angleterre, sous le règne de Philippe II*, 11 vols (Brussels, 1882–1900), ii. 304.

12. 18 and 29 April 1559, *CSPSpEliz*, i, nos 27, 29; 4 and 10 May 1559, *CSPVen*, vii, nos 69, 71.

13. Many of these letters can be found in HMC, *Bath*, v. 137–48, 152–60.

14. 1 October 1559, SP 70/8, fo. 8ʳ. See also 10 May 1559, *CSPSpEliz*, i, no. 31; Doran, *Monarchy and Matrimony*, 21–39.

15. 30 June 1559, SP 70/5, fo. 70ʳ.

16. 8 November 1559, SP 70/8, fo. 112ᵛ.

17. 13 November 1559, *CSPSpEliz*, i, no. 74.

18. 6 August 1559, Victor von Klarwill (ed.), *Queen Elizabeth and Some Foreigners: Being a Series of Hitherto Unpublished Letters from the Archives of the Habsburg Family*, trans. T. H. Nash (London, 1928), 113–14.

19. 17 February 1560, HMC, *Salisbury*, i. 257.

20. 13 August 1560, SP 12/13, fo. 55.

21. 15 June 1560, SP 12/12, fo. 107.

22. Lettenhove, *Relations politiques*, ii. 52, 123.

23. Klarwill, *Queen Elizabeth*, 114–15.

24. *CPREliz*, i. 288, 321, 324.

25. Archer et al., 'Religion, Politics, and Society', 67; Adams, 'Household Accounts', 15, 74, 116; 11 September 1560, *CSPSpEliz*, i, no. 19.

26. 11 September 1560, *CSPSpEliz*, i, no. 74.

27. Norfolk told Quadra this, though he said he did not believe it: Lettenhove, *Relations politiques*, ii. 527.

28. 18 April 1559 and 28 March 1560, *CSPSpEliz*, i, nos 27, 95; 4 May 1559, *CSPVen*, vii, no. 69.

29. 13 November 1559, *CSPSpEliz*, i, no. 74; 12 November and 5 December 1559, Klarwill, *Queen Elizabeth*, 152, 157.

30. 11 September 1560, *CSPSpEliz*, i, no. 119.

31. Adams, 'Household Accounts', 377–8.

32. George Adlard, *Amye Robsart and the Earl of Leycester: A Critical Inquiry into the Authenticity…of Amye Robsart, and of the Libels on the Earl of Leycester, with a Vindication of the Earl by his Nephew Sir Philip Sydney* (London, 1870), 32.

33. Haynes, 362.

34. Archer et al., 'Religion, Politics, and Society', 66.
35. 23 September and 10 October 1560, SP 52/5, fo. 32; SP 70/19, fo. 39.
36. Skidmore, *Death and the Virgin*, 377–8.
37. Derek Wilson suggests Cecil was as plausible a candidate for a murderer as Dudley: *The Uncrowned Kings of England* (London, 2005), 275.
38. Adlard, *Amye Robsart*, 33–6.
39. The evidence is laid out brilliantly by Skidmore. However, I disagree with his tentative conclusion that Dudley's retainers were responsible. Also needing consideration is the fact that the selection of a favourable jury was not particularly unusual for a man of influence. See FSL, L.a.461.
40. 20 November 1560, *CSPSpEliz*, i, no. 121; Hardwicke, *State Papers*, i. 164; 17 November 1560, SP 70/20, fo. 38ᵛ; Haynes, 364–5.
41. 30 November 1560, Hardwicke, *State Papers*, i. 167–8.
42. 30 December 1560, SP 70/21, fo. 117.
43. For details, see Doran, *Monarchy and Matrimony*, 46–51.
44. Bedford to Throckmorton, 16 March 1561, SP 70/24, fo. 42ᵛ.
45. *CPREliz*, ii. 189–90; Lodge, *Illustrations*, i. 424.
46. BL, Additional 35831, no. 18.
47. *CPREliz*, ii. 244–5, 270–1, 310, 361.
48. 30 June 1561, *CSPSpEliz*, i, no. 134.
49. SP 70/40, fo. 67ᵛ.
50. For the French campaign, Wallace T. MacCaffrey, 'The Newhaven Expedition, 1562–1563', *Historical Journal*, 40 (1997), 1–21.
51. Nichols, i. 362.
52. 2 July and 7 August 1564, *CSPSpEliz*, i, nos 255, 261.
53. 28 March 1563, *CSPSpEliz*, i, no. 216; Wright, *Queen Elizabeth*, i. 177, 183. For details of the marriage plan, see Ch. 4.
54. HL, HM 68350.
55. 23 July 1565, *CSPSpEliz*, i, no. 310.
56. Wright, *Queen Elizabeth*, i. 206–7.
57. Wright, *Queen Elizabeth*, i. 198.
58. 5 May and 20 August 1565, *CSPSpEliz*, i, nos 298, 315.
59. 4 February 1566, *CSPSpEliz*, i, no. 336. See also SP 12/39, fo. 105.
60. Anne McLaren uses the term 'king-figure' in 'The Quest for a King: Gender, Marriage, and Succession in Elizabethan England', *Journal of British Studies*, 41 (2002), 259–90.
61. Elizabeth to Sir Thomas Smith, 9 October 1564, SP 70/74, fos 154ᵛ–5ᵛ; October 1565, Wright, *Queen Elizabeth*, i. 211
62. Robert Naunton, *Fragmenta regalia* (London, 1650), 7–8.
63. 23 July and 2 September 1565, *CSPSpEliz*, i, nos 310, 318. Cecil noted in August 1565 that Elizabeth, 'semed to be much offended' with Leicester (CP 229, fo. 31ʳ).
64. 'Sir Thomas Heneage', by Michael Hicks, *ODNB*.
65. 'Thomas Butler, Tenth Earl of Ormond', by David Edward, *ODNB*.
66. 29 March 1566, SP 15/13, fo. 8ᵛ; 11, 18, and 30 March 1566, *CSPSpEliz*, i, nos 342–3, 347.
67. 11 May, 15 June, and 6 July 1566, *CSPSpEliz*, i, nos 356, 362, 367.
68. SP 59/9, fo. 166; *CSPDom, 1547–80*, p. 273.
69. e.g. *CSPDomAdd, 1566–1579*, pp. 2–3.
70. Nichols, i. 380, 385–6, 389.

71. For marriage proposals with the brothers of the French king, see Doran, *Monarchy and Matrimony*, 99–144.

72. *Leicester's Commonwealth* accused him of 'carnality' and 'licentiousness'.

73. Gilbert Talbot to his father, earl of Shrewsbury, 10 May 1573, HL, HM 41954, p. 237 (Lodge, *Illustrations*, ii. 17–18, and Nichols, ii. 49–50).

74. Details of the affair came out in 1580 and in a Star Chamber case of 1605, when their son unsuccessfully claimed his father's inheritance. See Skidmore, *Death and the Virgin*, 310–12, 328.

75. Conyers Read, 'A Letter from Robert, Earl of Leicester to a Lady', *Huntington Library Bulletin*, 9 (1936), 19, 20, 25.

76. Richard Morris, '"I was never more in love with an olde howse nor never newe worke coulde be better bestowed": The Earl of Leicester's Remodelling of Kenilworth Castle for Queen Elizabeth I', *Antiquaries Journal*, 89 (2009), 241–305.

77. The garden is described in *Robert Laneham's Letter: Describing a Part of the Entertainment unto the Queen's Majesty at Kenilworth*, ed. F. J. Furnivall (New York and London, 1907). This was published anonymously but was probably written by Robert Langham (aka Laneham). For the garden's symbolism, see Elisabeth Woodhouse, 'Propaganda in Paradise: The Symbolic Garden Created by the Earl of Leicester at Kenilworth, Warwickshire', *Garden History*, 36 (2008), 94–113.

78. Two versions of the entertainments are extant: Laneham's *Letter* and George Gascoigne's *The Princely Pleasures of Kenilworth Castle 1575*. The latter, printed anonymously in 1576, records the text of the unperformed entertainments. Although Gascoigne claims it was cancelled because of the unseasonable weather, historians think this unlikely. The descriptions of the entertainments come from both texts.

79. The analysis of the portraits is based on Elizabeth Goldring, 'Portraits of Queen Elizabeth I and the Earl of Leicester for Kenilworth Castle', *Burlington Magazine*, 147 (2005), 654–60, and 'Portraiture, Patronage and the Progresses: Robert Dudley, Earl of Leicester and the Kenilworth Festivities of 1575', in Jayne Elizabeth Archer, Elizabeth Goldring, and Sarah Knight (eds), *The Progresses, Pageants, & Entertainments of Queen Elizabeth I* (Oxford, 2007), 163–88.

80. The earl's portrait was cut down to three-quarter length and now hangs in the National Portrait Gallery. Goldring convincingly argues that the queen's portrait was also cut down and is the one now hanging in the Reading Museum. For the New Year's gift, see Nichols, ii. 226.

81. Nichols, ii. 245.

82. 19 February 1576, Lettenhove, *Relations politiques*, viii. 194, an ambassador from the Netherlands (Champigny) commented on Elizabeth dancing with Leicester. 17 October 1578, SP 12/126, fo. 20, refers to him keeping Elizabeth company day and night, when she had a severe 'payne in her cheke' from toothache. See also September 1585, SP 12/182, fo. 41; for an earlier instance (1572), see Wright, *Queen Elizabeth*, i. 445.

83. See 4 September 1575, SP 12/105, fo. 88.

84. Lettenhove, *Relations politiques*, x. 15.

85. 5 December 1575, *CSPSpEliz*, ii, no. 431.

86. HMC, *Bath*, v. 205–6; Warnicke, *Wicked Women*, 118.

87. Nichols, iii. 4.

88. Leicester to Walsingham, 10 September 1578, SP 83/9, fo. 19. For details, see Ch. 10.
89. Camden (1578). In 'Leicester', *ODNB*, Adams questions Camden's account, and it is certainly exaggerated.
90. 12 November 1579, BL, Harley 6992, fo. 114$^{r\&v}$, printed in Wright, *Queen Elizabeth*, ii. 103–5. In some of his earlier letters to the queen, Leicester also called himself her bondman.
91. For the loan repayment, see 'Leicester', by Adams, *ODNB*. For the lands, SP 12/140, fo. 46$^{r\&v}$, and BL, Lansdowne 31, no. 39.
92. 20 February 1580, BL, Cotton Caligula CIII, fo. 582.
93. 'Douglas Lady Sheffield', by Simon Adams, *ODNB*. Douglas had just married Edward Stafford.
94. 20 July 1580, SP 12/140, fo. 46.
95. BL, Additional 15891, fo. 129^r.
96. Patrick Collinson, *Godly People: Essays on English Protestantism and Puritanism* (London, 1983), 50–3, 58–92.
97. 17 April 1580, *CSPSpEliz*, iii. 19.
98. SP 12/161, fos 120–1.
99. For further details, see Ch. 4. Camden attributes the bond of association to Leicester.
100. Simon Adams, 'Elizabeth I and the Sovereignty of the Netherlands 1576–1585', *Transactions of the Royal Historical Society*, 6th ser., 14 (2004), 309–19.
101. SP 84/3, fo. 106; SP 12/182, fo. 1.
102. Calendared under [21?] September, SP 12/182, fo. 41.
103. John Bruce (ed.), 'Correspondence of Robert Dudley, Earl of Leicester, during his Government of the Low Countries', *Camden Society*, 27 (1844), 12, 57–63, 112.
104. Wallace T. MacCaffrey, *Queen Elizabeth and the Making of Policy, 1572–1588* (Princeton, 1981), 355–6; 'Leicester', by Adams, *ODNB*.
105. Bruce, 'Correspondence of Robert Dudley', 112. Many biographers suggest Elizabeth's anger arose from her personal jealousy of the countess.
106. SP 84/6, fos 71, 122, 124.
107. Bruce, 'Correspondence of Robert Dudley', 110, 105–7.
108. Bruce, 'Correspondence of Robert Dudley', 194; *CWE* 277.
109. 'Leicester', by Adams, *ODNB*.
110. Bruce, 'Correspondence of Robert Dudley', 451; Sidney was his heir after the death of his 3-year-old son Denbigh in 1584.
111. David Trim, 'Fighting "Jacob's warres": English and Welsh Mercenaries in the European Wars of Religion: France and the Netherlands', Ph.D., University of London (2002), 210, 211–12.
112. 16 April 1587, SP 84/14, fo. 77.
113. BL, Additional 12520, fos 9^r–14^r (transcript).
114. 13 January 1588, SP 12/208, fo. 15 $^{r\&v}$. 'Sacred majesty' is a marked difference from his usual styles of address: 'my most dere lady' in SP 12/29, fo. 122, or 'my moost gracious lady' in SP 12/105, fo. 88.
115. 17 September, *CSPSpEliz*, iv, no. 432.
116. HMC, *Bath*, v. 94.
117. David Cressy, *Dangerous Talk: Scandalous, Seditious, and Treasonable Speech in Pre-Modern England* (Oxford 2010), 69–73.
118. by Adams, *ODN*. 'Leicester' by Adams, *ODNB*.

CHAPTER 6

1. Naunton, *Fragmenta regalia*, 44.
2. Camden (1591).
3. 'Sir Christopher Hatton', by Wallace T. MacCaffrey, *ODNB*. It is worth noting that, in their visitation of 1564, heralds recorded Hatton as an esquire, not a gentleman, and that he then bore no coat of arms. Eric St John Brooks, *Sir Christopher Hatton* (London, 1946), 73.
4. For tropes employed about favourites, see Curtis Perry, *Literature and Favouritism in Early Modern England* (Cambridge, 2006), 2.
5. He read Italian and was to build up a library of Italian books over his lifetime. See W. O. Hassall, 'The Books of Sir Christopher Hatton at Holkham', *Library*, 5th ser., 5 (1950), 1–13.
6. Hatton's later parliamentary orations followed rhetorical principles recommended in Cicero and Quintillian, works that were part of the university curriculum; see Peter Mack, 'Elizabethan Parliamentary Oratory', *Huntington Library Quarterly*, 64 (2001), 36–7. Hatton also possessed an Italian translation of Aristotle's *Rhetoric*: Hassall, 'The Books of Hatton', 6.
7. Wilfrid R. Prest, *The Inns of Court under Elizabeth I and the Early Stuarts* (Totowa, NJ, 1972), 153.
8. Roger Ascham, *The Scholemaster* (London, 1570), 117; James P. Cunningham, *Dancing in the Inns of Court* (London, 1965); Margaret M. McGowan, *Dance in the Renaissance* (New Haven and London, 2008), 17.
9. Gerard Legh, *The Accedens of Armory* (London, 1566), fo. 124ʳ. The play was Act 4 of *The Tragedie of Tancred and Gismund Compiled by the Gentlemen of the Inner Temple*...(London, 1592). For details, see Brooks, *Hatton*, 33.
10. For these men, see *ODNB*. Richard Onslow and Roger Manwood were also at the Inn during Hatton's time there.
11. Legh, *The Accedens of Armory*, fo. 124ʳ. The 'Christmas prince' was elected annually and acted as a lord of misrule during the Christmas revels; the 'master of the game' was an elected officer in the prince's Christmas court.
12. 30 June 1564, SP 12/34, fo. 2, warrant of the queen to provide full armour for her 'welbeloved servant Christopher Hatton', but he had to pay the 'just value'.
13. Henry Brackenbury, *The History of his Majesty's Body Guard of the Honourable Corps of Gentlemen-at-Arms* (London, 1905), 78–9; Samuel Pegge, *Curialia: Or an Historical Account of Some Branches of the Royal Household*, 3 vols (London, 1784), ii. 47–57.
14. 14 May 1571, HMC, *Rutland*, i. 92.
15. Brackenbury, *History*, 87–91.
16. *CPREliz*, iv. 157, 252–3, 386; v. 207, 273, 304, 305. Holdenby was a hereditary manor, which Hatton exchanged with the queen for the site of the abbey at Sulby.
17. *CPREliz*, iv. 228; v. 15–16.
18. Murdin, 204.
19. Bruce and Perowne, *Correspondence of Matthew Parker*, 400–1.
20. October 1572, SP 12/89, fo. 142ᵛ (printed in Nicholas Harris Nicolas, *Memoirs of the Life and Times of Sir Christopher Hatton* (London, 1847), 21).
21. *History of Parliament* <http://www.historyofparliamentonline.org/volume/1558–1603/member/hatton-christopher-i-1540-91> (accessed July 2014); T. E. Hartley (ed.), *Proceedings in the Parliaments of Elizabeth I*, 3 vols (Leicester, 1981), i. 333–4.

22. Norfolk told his son that 'Mr Hatton is a marvellous constant friend' but this was just after his condemnation in January and before the parliament that met in May: Nicolas, *Hatton*, 9.
23. See Ch. 3.
24. The yeomen themselves were excluded from entry in the privy chamber. For the yeomen of the guard, see Pegge, *Curialia*, 3. Knollys was promoted to treasurer of the household in 1570. There were over 100 yeomen and, among their functions, they served dishes to the sovereign in the presence chamber and kept order there during dinner.
25. SP 12/89, fo. 142^{r&v} (printed in Nicolas, *Hatton*, 20–2).
26. Lodge, *Illustrations*, ii. 18; Nicolas, *Hatton*, 17.
27. Nicolas, *Hatton*, 17–18.
28. Lodge, *Illustrations*, ii. 18.
29. Nicolas, *Hatton*, 24.
30. [7] and 17 June 1573, SP 12/91, fos 100, 116; [July] 1573, 12/92, fo. 42 (printed in Nicolas, *Hatton*, 25–30).
31. The letter ended up in Burghley's archive: Murdin, 256. See also B. M. Ward, 'Further Research on *A hundreth sundrie flowres*', *Review of English Studies*, 13 (1928), 35–48.
32. Nicolas, *Hatton*, 31–2.
33. BL, Lansdowne 16, fos 196^{v}–98^{v}.
34. Ellis, *Original Letters*, iii. 26–7.
35. Of the seven books in his theological library, none was 'popish', one was a book against the mass, and another (in a fine armorial binding) was Beza's *Confession of faith*.
36. Anon., *An Advertisement Written to a Secretarie* (n.p., 1592), 13.
37. *CPREliz*, vii. 2, 203–4, 328–9.
38. BL, Lansdowne 20, fo. 144^{v}; 18, fo. 204; Brooks, *Hatton*, 221.
39. 13 September 1577, BL, Harley 6992, fo. 79. Hatton complained to Walsingham about a financial arrangement the queen offered him. See also BL, Lansdowne 18, fo. 204.
40. Such as the 'splendid' musical entertainments he put on for Champigny at Eltham in late February 1576: Lettenhove, *Relations politiques*, viii. 221. In his absence, Mildmay and Burghley were sumptuously entertained at Holdenby.
41. Malcolm Deacon, 'Sir Christopher Hatton', *Northamptonshire Past and Present*, 64 (2011), 28; Nikolaus Pevsner, *The Buildings of England: Northamptonshire*, 2nd edn (New Haven, 2002), 280–3.
42. BL, Lansdowne 28, fo. 140.
43. Emily Sophia Harthorne, *Memorials of Holdenby* (London, 1868), 18.
44. *CPREliz*, vii. 403–4.
45. Cited in E. Williams, *Early Holborn and the Legal Quarter of London* (London, 1927), nos 361, 429.
46. Hartley, *Proceedings*, i. 435. For Hatton's role in 1576 Parliament, see *History of Parliament* <http://www.historyofparliamentonline.org/volume/1558–1603/member/> (accessed 12 March 2014); 11 February 1576, *CSPSpEliz*, ii, no. 442.
47. Nicolas, *Hatton*, 37.
48. It arrived in January 1576. See Adams, 'Elizabeth I and the Sovereignty of the Netherlands', 309–19.
49. 28 February 1576, *CSPSpEliz*, ii, no. 444; 28 February, 3 and 20 March 1576, Lettenhove, *Relations politiques*, viii. 157, 162, 205, 221–2, 289.

50. Lettenhove, *Relations politiques*, viii. 221–2: 'toute ceste court en has esté bransle, pour le grand crédit qu'ils sçavent que cestuy-cy a avec la Royne, et qu'elle luy deffère autant et plus que à nul de son conseil, encoires qu'il n'en soit point.'

51. Lettenhove, *Relations politiques*, viii. 288–9.

52. William Nicholson (ed.), *The Remains of Edmund Grindal: Successively Bishop of London and Archbishop of York and Canterbury*, Parker Society (Cambridge, 1843), 467.

53. This allegation appears on a copy of Archbishop Grindal's letter to the queen objecting to the order: HMC, *Hastings*, i. 433; SP 52/26/1, fos 60–1ᵛ. It may not, of course, be true.

54. Nicolas, *Hatton*, 52–3, 119; Patrick Collinson, *Archbishop Grindal, 1519–1583: The Struggle for a Reformed Church* (London, 1979), 263–4.

55. APC x. 85. According to Nicolas, Hatton received the knighthood in late November: Nicolas, *Hatton*, 38–9.

56. Bruce and Perowne, *Correspondence of Matthew Parker*, 477–8. See also Brett Usher, *William Cecil and Episcopacy, 1559–1577* (Aldershot, 2003), 132–3, 135.

57. MacCaffrey, *Queen Elizabeth and the Making of Policy*, 450, 452–3.

58. BL, Additional 15891, fo. 41ʳ.

59. Aylmer to Hatton, 8 and 17 June 1578, BL, Additional 15891, fos 41ᵛ–2ʳ, 35ᵛ–36ʳ.

60. 5 September 1578, FSL, L.a.707; 9 March 1590, FSL, L.a.724.

61. 2 May 1585, BL, Additional 15891, fo. 155ᵛ.

62. 17 July 1584, BL, Additional 15891, fo. 128ᵛ.

63. George Paule, *The Life of the Most Reverend and Religious Prelate John Whitgift, Lord Archbishop of Canterbury* (London, 1612), 48.

64. *History of Parliament* <http://www.historyofparliamentonline.org/volume/1558-1603/member/> (accessed 12 March 2014); *The Journal of Sir Simond D'Ewes* <http://www.british-history.ac.uk/report.aspx?compid=43705> (accessed 12 March 2014), 339.

65. The prepared speech is in SP 12/199/1, fos 1–4ᵛ. For his arguments, Hatton depended heavily on Bancroft's notes, and the prepared text is actually endorsed as Dr Bancroft's discourse. See Patrick Collinson, *The Elizabethan Puritan Movement* (London, 1967), 313–14.

66. Patrick Collinson, *Richard Bancroft and Elizabethan Anti-Puritanism* (Cambridge, 2013), 58.

67. Collinson, *Bancroft*, 58–9; William Richardson, 'The Religious Policies of the Cecils, 1588–1598', D.Phil., University of Oxford (1993), 30–2, 38, 54–7.

68. William Bradshaw and Thomas Digges, *Humble Motives for Association to Maintaine Religion Established…* (n.p., 1601), 25.

69. Everard Digby, *Everard Digbie, his Dissuasive, from Taking away the Lyvings and Goods of the Church* (London, 1590), sig. A5.

70. 28 February 1576, *CSPSpEliz*, ii, no. 444.

71. 26 September 1580, BL, Additional 15891, fo. 21ʳ, printed in Wright, *Queen Elizabeth*, ii. 106–9, where the letter is dated 26 April.

72. HL, Ellesmere 6236.

73. 26 September 1580, BL, Additional 15891, fo. 21ʳ.

74. 23 June 1578, BL, Additional 15891, fo. 48ᵛ.

75. 16 and 27 June 1578, BL, Additional 15891, fos 46ᵛ, 48ʳ. See Ch. 10.

76. For Drake's voyage and his return, see Helen Wallis (ed.), *Sir Francis Drake: An Exhibition to Commemorate Francis Drake's Voyage around the World 1577–80* (London, 1977); Derek Wilson, *The World Encompassed: Drake's Great Voyage 1577–1580* (London, 1977, 1998).

77. It has been suggested the change of name arose to keep Hatton's support, after his man Thomas Doughty had been executed on a charge of mutiny on 2 July 1578.

78. 23 October 1580 and 4 July 1581, *CSPSpEliz*, iii, nos 47, 110.

79. HL, Ellesmere 6236. How much Hatton received is unknown. The total treasure brought to the Tower was registered as over ten tons of silver bullion, 512lb of coarse silver, and nearly 102lb of gold bullion.

80. 1 October 1581, *CSPSpEliz*, iii, no. 138. See also 20 October, no. 148.

81. 31 March 1579, *CSPSpEliz*, ii, no. 563.

82. CP 148, fos 42–3ᵛ. See Ch. 10.

83. 19 September 1580, SP 12/142, fo. 73 (Nicolas, *Hatton*, 157–8).

84. 26 September 1580, BL, Additional 15891, fo. 21ʳ&ᵛ.

85. Marnix to the council of state, 22 November 1581, P. L. Muller and A. Diegerick (eds), *Documents concernant les relations entre le duc d'Anjou et Les Pay-Bas* (Gravenhage, 1898), iv. 258–9.

86. 4 December 1581, *CSPSpEliz*, iii, no. 174.

87. HMC, *Salisbury*, xiii. 207.

88. The imperial theme is in line with his patronage of Drake and John Dee, an enthusiastic advocate of exploration and maritime enterprise.

89. His speech is printed in Hartley, *Proceedings*, ii. 214–17; notes for the speech are ii. pp, 219–21.

90. The objections against Mr Davison, BL, Cotton Caligula CVIII, fo. 648ᵛ.

91. One of the letters that Burghley sent to the queen was delivered by Hatton; see BL, Lansdowne 102, fo. 7ᵛ.

92. The 1578 New Year's gift was a jewel fashioned as a dog leading a man over a bridge, and it had verses on the back that presumably explained its meaning: Nichols, ii. 532.

93. BL, Additional 15801, fos 101ᵛ–102ʳ.

94. Murdin, 588.

95. Paule, *The Life of John Whitgift*, 49–50. Hatton seemed to think he owed the promotion to Burghley: Murdin, 588.

96. Murdin, 50–1; Thomas Birch, *Memoirs of the Reign of Queen Elizabeth, from the Year 1581 till her Death…From the Original Papers of…Anthony Bacon*, 2 vols (London, 1754), i. 74–5. Hatton was elected 23 September 1588: Northamptonshire Record Office, FH 2733.

97. HMC. *Rutland*, i. 248.

98. William Lambarde, *Archeion* (London, 1635), 63, 47. It was first written in October 1591.

99. Camden (1587).

100. SP/14, fo. 77; 22 May 1587, CP 15/116.

101. Williams, *Holborn*, i. 363.

102. David Lloyd, *The Statesmen and Favourites of England since the Reformation* (London, 1665; reissued in 1670), 522.

103. Quoted in the preface by Samuel Thorne in Edward Hake, *Epieikeia: A Dialogue on Equity in Three Parts*, ed. D. E. C. Yale (New Haven, 1953). Further discussion is in Dennis Klinck, *Conscience, Equity and the Court of Chancery*

in Early Modern England (Farnham, 2010), 89, 91 and nn. 78, 89. Hatton was described as 'keeper of the queen's conscience' (Nichols, iii. 597).

104. *A Treatise Concerning Statutes, or Acts of Parliament, and the Exposition thereof Written by Sir Christopher Hatton* (London, 1677).

105. This view was contested by common lawyers and may explain their hostility to his appointment as expressed in Camden (1587).

106. Lloyd, *Statesmen*, 522.

107. FSL, V.b.303, fos 145–6, cited in G. R. Elton, *The Parliament of England 1559–81* (Cambridge, 1989), 323.

108. Collinson, *Bancroft*, 57.

109. 27 March 1589, SP 12/223, fo. 51. Burghley praised it highly.

110. Archer et al., 'Religion, Politics, and Society', 222–3, 225, 228. See Ch. 8.

111. Joseph Stevenson (ed.), *Correspondence of Sir Henry Unton, Ambassador from Queen Elizabeth to Henry IV. King of France, in the Years MDXCI. and MDXCII* (London, 1847), 58, 84.

112. 12 November 1591, Richard Broughton (Richard Bagot's son-in-law) to Richard Bagot, FSL, L.a.265.

113. Camden (1591); Nichols, iii. 597.

114. FSL, L.a.265.

115. Letters from Robert Cecil and Mr Fortescue, in Stevenson, *Correspondence of Sir Henry Unton*, 174, 177.

116. For a drawing of his elaborate funeral procession, see FSL, Z.e.3, and BL, Additional 35324. For the monument, see Hentzner, *Travels*, 7.

117. Nicolas, *Hatton*, 234–5, 242–3, 301–42, 351–3.

118. See, e.g. MacCaffrey, *Queen Elizabeth and the Making of Policy*, 450.

119. For examples of such rumours, see Gottfried von Bülow, 'Journey through England and Scotland Made by Lupold von Wedel in the Years 1584 and 1585', *Transactions of the Royal Historical Society*, NS 9 (1895), 263, 265. Hatton's letters printed in Nicolas give a flavour of their erotic nature.

120. See Ch. 9.

121. Patrick Collinson was the first to say this; see 'The Monarchical Republic of Queen Elizabeth', *John Rylands University Library of Manchester*, 69 (1987), 402.

CHAPTER 7

1. William Barlow, *A Sermon Preached at Paules Crosse, on the First Sunday in Lent: Martij 1. 1600* (London, 1603).

2. All of Paul E. J. Hammer's work is indispensable for this chapter. See Bibliography for a full list.

3. FSL, L.a.37.

4. BL, Lansdowne 36, fo. 37.

5. 11 June 1583, *CSPSpEliz*, iii, no. 343.

6. *CSPScot*, viii. 113; 28 September 1585, Bodleian Library, Tanner 78, fo. 7.

7. 'Robert Devereux, Second Earl of Essex', by Paul E. J. Hammer, *ODNB*.

8. Gavin Alexander, *Writing after Sidney: The Literary Response to Sir Philip Sidney 1586–1640* (Oxford, 2006), 56–61.

9. Nichols, iii. 349. For other representations of Essex as the new Sidney, see Richard Wood, "Cleverly playing the stoic": The Earl of Essex, Sir Philip

Sidney and Surviving Elizabeth's Court', in Annaliese Connolly and Lisa Hopkins (eds), *Essex* (Manchester and New York, 2013), 29–30.

10. FSL, L.a.39.
11. FSL, L.a.39.
12. Lawson, *Elizabethan New Year's Gift Exchanges*, 367–8.
13. W. B. Devereux (ed.), *Lives and Letters of the Devereux, Earls of Essex...
1540–1646*, 2 vols (London, 1853), i. 193–4.
14. S. W. May, 'The Poems of Edward de Vere, Seventeenth Earl of Oxford and of
Robert Devereux, Second Earl of Essex', *Studies in Philology*, 77 (1980), 44, 88.
15. Sir Henry Wotton, *Reliquiae Wottonianae* (London, 1672), 165–6.
16. William Herle to Leicester, BL, Cotton Galba DII, fo. 27ᵛ.
17. CWE 307–8. For a commentary, see Peter Herman, who explains that Elizabeth
'does more than reassure a jittery courtier of her continued favour; the poem
also serves to reinforce the queen's place at the top of the hierarchy' (*Royal
Poetrie: Monarchic Verse*, 147–89).
18. May, 'Poems', 43–4, 85–7. May convincingly dates the poem at 1590 or 1591.
19. Roy Strong, *The Cult of Elizabeth: Elizabethan Portraiture and Pageantry*
(London, 1999), 74–8.
20. Strong, *The Cult of Elizabeth*, 74–8.
21. Bodleian Library, Tanner 76, fo. 29ʳ&ᵛ. See also Tanner 7, fo. 178ʳ; HMC, *Ancaster*, 49; F. H. Mares (ed.), *The Memoirs of Robert Carey* (Oxford, 1972), 5.
22. 'Essex', by Paul Hammer, *ODNB*.
23. Wotton, *Reliquiae*, 178.
24. Paul E. J. Hammer, *The Polarisation of Elizabethan Politics* (Cambridge, 1999),
130 (nn. 98, 100).
25. 19 December 1589, SP 12/219, fo. 115.
26. 12 January 1589, *CSPSpEliz*, iv, no. 499.
27. Camden (1589).
28. Anthony Bagot to Richard Bagot, 8 April 8 1589, FSL, L.a.40.
29. Elizabeth to Sir John Norris and Sir Francis Drake, 4 May 1589, SP 12/224,
fo.14 (printed in Devereux, *Lives and Letters*, 200–1).
30. On Essex's military vocation, see Hammer, *Polarisation*, esp. 226.
31. Murdin, 634–5.
32. Camden (1589); Hugh Gazzard, '"Many a *Herdsman* more disposde to morne":
Peele, Campion, and the Portugal Expedition of 1589', *Review of English
Studies*, 57 (2006), 16–42.
33. Nichols, iii. 516; Lodge, *Illustrations*, iii. 14, 16.
34. Johanna Rickman, *Love, Lust, and License in Early Modern England: Illicit Sex
and the Nobility* (London, 2008), 30–1. See Ch. 11.
35. SP 12/239, fo. 93.
36. Lodge, *Illustrations*, iii. 31–2.
37. SP 78/25, fo. 68.
38. Elizabeth to Leighton, 13 July 1591, SP 15/32, fo. 29ʳ&ᵛ. For other advisers, see
Hammer, *Polarisation*, 103 (nn. 161–2).
39. Archer et al., 'Religion, Politics, and Society', 227.
40. 7 August 1591, SP 78/25, fo. 182ʳ&ᵛ.
41. Archer et al., 'Religion, Politics, and Society', 231.
42. Archer et al., 'Religion, Politics, and Society', 244–5.
43. Elizabeth to Essex (21 and 23 September) 1591, SP 78/25, fos 344, 348.
44. BL, Additional 74286, fos 19ʳ, 20, 25. Indeed Essex had recruited his clients and
possibly his tenants for the army: Trim, 'Fighting "Jacob's warres"', 252.

45. Stevenson, *Correspondence of Sir Henry Unton*, 77.
46. BL, Additional 74286, fo. 25.
47. Murdin, 646.
48. Murdin, 644–5.
49. G. B. Harrison, *The Life and Death of Robert Devereux, Earl of Essex* (London, 1937), 62.
50. SP 78/26, fo. 194$^{r\&v}$.
51. SP 78/26, fo. 321^{v}.
52. Essex learned this while in Rouen, December 1591: Murdin, 650.
53. BL, Cotton Caligula EVIII, fo. 176. See also Hammer, *Polarisation*, 112.
54. Hammer, *Polarisation*, 116–18; Stephen Alford, *The Watchers: A Secret History of the Reign of Elizabeth I* (London, 2012), 267–8.
55. See Ch. 8.
56. Lawson, *Elizabethan New Year's Gift Exchanges*, 417.
57. FSL, L.a.269.
58. FSL, L.a.45.
59. Hammer, *Polarisation*, 128–32, 137–44.
60. LPL 650, fo. 26^{r}.
61. David S. Katz thinks Lopez was probably guilty as charged: *The Jews in the History of England 1485–1850* (Oxford, 1994), ch. 2. Alford thinks it 'very unlikely'; see *The Watchers*, 304–6.
62. Dominic Green, *The Double Life of Doctor Lopez: Spies, Shakespeare and the Plot to Poison Elizabeth I* (London 2003), 199.
63. SP 12/247, fo. 158; John Guy, *Imagining and Detecting Conspiracy, 1571–1605* <http://www.tudors.org/public-lectures/imagining-and-detecting-conspiracy-1571-1605> (accessed 31 October 2013).
64. LPL 649, fo. 10^{r}.
65. Nichols, iv. 870–7.
66. Paul E. J. Hammer, 'Upstaging the Queen: The Earl of Essex, Francis Bacon and the Accession Day Celebrations of 1595', in David Bevington and Peter Holbrook (eds), *The Politics of the Stuart Court Masque* (Cambridge, 1998), 41–66.
67. Nichols, iv. 865–7. See Ch. 9.
68. Elizabeth to Essex, 14 April 1596, SP 12/257, fo. 46. Elizabeth had wanted to keep the town as her price for aid, but Henry IV refused.
69. 14 April 1596, SP 12/257, fo. 45.
70. CP 40/75; CP 40/193.
71. LPL 657, fo. 140.
72. SP 12/259, fo. 30^{r}.
73. Logan Pearsall Smith, *The Life and Letters of Sir Henry Wotton* (Oxford, 1907), i. 31; Paul E. J. Hammer, 'New Light on the Cadiz Expedition of 1596', *Historical Research*, 70 (1997), 193, 196.
74. LPL 658, fo. 260$^{r\&v}$.
75. *Works of Spenser: A Variorum Edition*, ed. E. Greenlaw et al., 10 vols (Baltimore, 1932–57), ix. 428–9; Alexandra Gajda, *The Earl of Essex and Late Elizabethan Political Culture* (Oxford, 2012), 172 (n. 156).
76. LPL 658, fos 259^{v}–60^{r}; HMC, *Salisbury*, vi. 329.
77. For details, see Paul Hammer, 'Myth-Making: Politics, Propaganda and the Capture of Cadiz in 1596', *Historical Journal*, 40 (1997), 621–42.
78. BL, Egerton 2026, fo. 32^{r}.
79. LPL 658, fo. 260^{r}.
80. CP 44/55.

81. LPL 658, fos 135, 260ʳ.
82. Hammer, 'Myth-Making', 632–7.
83. Devereux, *Lives and Letters*, 397.
84. Arthur Collins (ed.), *Letters and Memorials of State...Written and Collected by Sir Henry Sydney...Sir Philip Sydney, and his Brother Sir Robert Sydney...Robert, the Second Earl of Leicester...Philip Lord Viscount Lisle...*, 2 vols (London, 1746), ii. 17, 18, 19.
85. Full quotation: '*Gutta cavat lapidem non vi, sed saepe cadendo*' (LPL 650, fos 147, 148; 649, fo. 253ʳ); Stevenson, *Correspondence of Sir Henry Unton*, 317; Hammer, *Polarisation*, 327–9.
86. HL, HM 41952, fo. 38ᵛ.
87. Birch, *Memoirs*, i. 172.
88. For Bacon and the parliament, see Ch. 11.
89. CP 39/6.
90. Collins (ed.), *Letters and Memorials*, ii. 25, 42, 44, 49, 54.
91. Collins (ed.), *Letters and Memorials*, ii. 52.
92. 15 June 1597, SP 12/263, fos 147ʳ–150ᵛ.
93. SP 12/263, fo. 150ᵛ.
94. BL, Additional 74286, fos 60, 69.
95. BL, Additional 74286, fos 60–83.
96. SP 12/264, fo. 19ʳ.
97. CP 133/172.
98. CP 56/60.
99. BL, Egerton 2026, fo. 32ᵛ; CP 58/1.
100. 'A true servant' to Essex, 16 November 1597, SP 12/265, fo. 16ʳ&ᵛ.
101. SP 12/265, fo. 36.
102. 17 May 1598, CP 61/25. For Burghley's views, see SP 12/266, fos 3–4; for Cecil's, see Ch. 11.
103. Alexandra Gajda, 'Debating War and Peace in Late Elizabethan England', *Historical Journal*, 52 (2009), 851–78, and 'Essex and the Popish Plot', in Doran and Kewes, *Doubtful and Dangerous*, 115–33; Hugh Gazzard dates the first draft of Essex's paper in January 1598 and the finished version by late April; see '"Idle Papers": An Apology of the Earl of Essex', in Connolly and Hopkins, *Essex*, 184, 186–7. See also Ch. 11.
104. Camden (1598); Robert Devereux, earl of Essex, *An Apologie of the Earle of Essex against those which Falsly and Maliciously Taxe him to be the Onely Hinderer of the Peace and Quiet of his Country* (London, 1600?).
105. Camden (1598). For Essex seeking to promote Sir George Carew to 'remove him from cowrte', see also Nichols, iii. 734.
106. BL, Additional 74286, fo. 101.
107. SP 12/268, fo. 70.
108. SP 12/268, fos 73–4ʳ. Essex's exchange with Egerton soon moved from the private to the public arena. A number of manuscript copies exist and they were obviously circulated widely and deliberately.
109. BL, Additional 74286, fos 101, 113. This language also dominated his letters to Elizabeth in 1600 after his fall from power.
110. BL, Additional 6177, fo. 32ʳ; CP 63/75.
111. SP 12/268, fo. 114ʳ.
112. CP 65/29.
113. SP 12/268, fo. 141ʳ&ᵛ; Camden (1598).

114. HMC, *Salisbury*, ix. 4.
115. CP 199/57; CP 58/9.
116. CP 83/82; Gajda, 'Essex and the Popish Plot'. See also Ch. 11.
117. For Elizabeth's anger towards Southampton, see Ch. 8.
118. 19 July 1599, SP 63/204, fos 178ᵛ–9ᵛ. For Essex's campaign in Ireland, see Wallace T. MacCaffrey, *Elizabeth I, War and Politics, 1588–1603* (Princeton, 1992), ch. 21.
119. HMC. De L'Isle, ii. 395–6; Camden (1599).
120. *Calendar of the Carew Manuscripts, Preserved in the Archiepiscopal Library at Lambeth*, ed. J. S. Brewer and William Bullen, 6 vols (London, 1867–73), iii. 342.
121. HMC, *De L'Isle*, ii. 398–9, 407, 410, 422, 423, 424; Essex to Elizabeth, 12 May 1600, SP 12/274, fo. 232.
122. FSL, V.b.142, fos 49ʳ&ᵛ, 50ʳ; SP 12/274, fos 1, 34; HMC, *De L'Isle*, ii. 398, 405, 406, 420.
123. HMC, *De L'Isle*, ii. 435, 459.
124. HMC, *De L'Isle*, ii. 470; SP 12/275, fos 63, 131, 136, 143ʳ; *Cal. Carew MSS*, iii. 436–7; SP 12/275, fo. 81ᵛ.
125. Cuffe's confession, BL, Additional 6177, fos 75–6.
126. CP 90/150; SP 12/275, fos 53, 56ʳ–7ʳ, 58.
127. The narrative of the rising is based on HL, HM 41952, fos 23ʳ–30; CP 76/91; BL, Additional 6177, fo. 83.
128. BL, Additional 6177, fo. 62ᵛ.
129. Paul E. J. Hammer disagrees; see 'Shakespeare's *Richard II*: The Play of 7 February 1601, and the Essex Rising', *Shakespeare Quarterly*, 59 (2008), 1–35.
130. HL, HM 41952, fos 34ʳ–6ʳ. For the different constructions of the rising, see Alexandra Gajda, 'Essex and "Politic History"', in Connolly and Hopkins, *Essex*, 246–52.
131. Hammer, 'Shakespeare's *Richard II*'; Janet Dickinson, *Court Politics and the Earl of Essex, 1589–1601* (London, 2012), ch.3.
132. Gajda, *Essex and Late Elizabethan Political Culture*, ch. 1.
133. HL, HM 41952, fo. 59ʳ.
134. David Loades, *Elizabeth I* (London, 2003), 277, 280.
135. BL, Additional 74286, fos 13, 95ᵛ.
136. BL, Additional 74286, fos 20ʳ, 101ʳ.
137. LPL 650, fos 25ᵛ, 147; 657, fo. 140.
138. A. H. de Maisse, *A Journal*, trans. and ed. G. B. Harrison and R. A. Jones (London, 1931), 115.
139. LPL 657, fo. 140; BL, Additional 74286, fos 95ᵛ, 49.

CHAPTER 8

1. For quotation, see Lancelot-Voisin, sieur de La Popelinière, *The Historie of France the Foure First Books* (London, 1595).
2. Pam Wright, 'A Change in Direction: The Ramifications of a Female Household, 1558–1603', in David Starkey (ed.), *The English Court: From the Wars of the Roses to the Civil War* (Harlow, 1987), 158; Merton, 'Women who Served', 5.
3. This salary was obviously high compared to the wage of ordinary male labourers and female servants, who might earn about £2 a year. It was also higher than the wages of many other royal servants: the queen's laundress, for instance, was

paid £4 a year; grooms of the privy chamber received £20 a year, and the gentlemen ushers £30 a year. The gentlemen of the privy chamber were paid the same as the gentlewomen. See William Tighe, 'Familia reginae: The Privy Court', in Doran and Jones, *The Elizabethan World*, 81.

4. Merton, 'Women who Served', 247.

5. Merton, 'Women who Served', 190–1.

6. References to maids of honour carrying the royal train are sprinkled in a variety of texts.

7. Catherine Louise Howey, 'Busy Bodies: Women, Power and Politics at the Court of Elizabeth I, 1558–1603', Ph.D., University of Rutgers (2007), 90, 93–4.

8. HMC, *De L'Isle*, ii. 488.

9. HMC, *De L'Isle*, i. 426.

10. Merton dates her entry into the privy chamber in November 1558, but Simon Adams ('Katherine Howard [*née* Carey]'), in the *ODNB*, states that, 'no older than fifteen, she was appointed a gentlewoman of the privy chamber on 30 January 1560'.

11. Merton, 'Women who Served', app. 1; Bundesen, '"No other faction but my own"', 26. William St Loe was also rewarded at the beginning of the reign with an appointment as captain of the guard.

12. 'Katherine Astley [*née* Champernowne]', by Charlotte Merton, *ODNB*.

13. SP 10/6, fos 16–17, 51; Haynes, 70. See Ch. 1.

14. Christina Hallowell Garrett, *The Marian Exiles: A Study in the Origins of Elizabethan Puritanism* (Cambridge, 1938), 73; Starkey, *Elizabeth*, 185, 196–7.

15. 23 July 1565, *CSPSpEliz*, i, no. 310; 17 June 1587, *CSPSpEliz*, iv, no.105.

16. 'Blanche Parry', by Peter R. Roberts, *ODNB*; Ruth E. Richardson, *Mistress Blanche, Queen Elizabeth I's Confidante* (Woonton, 2007).

17. Janet Arnold, '*Lost from her Majesties Back*': Items of Clothing and Jewels Lost or Given away by Queen Elizabeth (London, 1980), 39; HMC, *Salisbury*, vii. 41.

18. Charles Angell Bradford, *Blanche Parry. Queen Elizabeth's Gentlewoman* (London, 1935), 80.

19. 'Katherine Knollys [*née* Carey]', by Sally Varlow, *ODNB*; Sally Varlow, 'Sir Francis Knollys's Latin Dictionary: New Evidence for Katherine Carey', *Historical Research*, 80 (2007), 315–23.

20. Elizabeth's household accounts for April 1552 refer to Mistress Carey's departure from Hatfield; see Percy Clinton Sydney Smythe, 6th Viscount Strangford (ed.), 'Household Expenses of the Princess Elizabeth 1551–2', *Camden Society*, 55 (1853), 39.

21. BL, Lansdowne 94, fo. 21.

22. Thomas Newton, *An Epitaphe upon the Worthy and Honorable Lady, the Lady Knowles* (London, 1569).

23. SP 10/6, fo. 17. Merton identifies her as the daughter of Susan Norwich, a gentlewoman of the privy chamber to Queen Katherine: 'Women who served', 32. John Harington praised Norwich in verse as one of the women serving Elizabeth at Hatfield: Henry Harrington (ed.), *Nugae antiquae: A Miscellaneous Collection of Original Papers in Prose and in Verse*, 2 vols (London, 1769–75), i. 89.

24. BL, Lansdowne 34, fo. 76ʳ; Lawson, *Elizabethan New Year's Gift Exchanges*, 418–19; Wright, 'A Change in Direction', 150.

25. 'Elizabeth de Fiennes, Countess of Lincoln', by Susan Brigden, *ODNB*; CP 203/53.

26. 1 March 1583, SP 12/159/38ᵛ, also quoted in 'Mary, Lady Sidney [*née* Dudley]', by Simon Adams, *ODNB*.
27. Michael G. Brennan, *The Sidneys of Penshurst and the Monarchy, 1500–1700* (Burlington, VT, 2006), 39. For Lady Sidney with the court on progress, Nichols, ii. 187.
28. HMC, *De L'Isle*, i. 259.
29. See Ch. 5.
30. SP 63/30, fo. 108; SP 63/36, fo. 30.
31. Howey, 'Busy Bodies', 131.
32. BL, Harley 787, fo. 15ʳ.
33. HL, HA 2536, 2537. Huntingdon's ardent protestantism made him a safe pair of hands.
34. HL, HA 13057, 13064.
35. HL, HA,1020.
36. HMC, *De L' Isle*, ii. 203, 204, 474.
37. HMC, *De L' Isle*, ii. 314, 317, 472, 474.
38. Elizabeth (later Lady Drury).
39. Elizabeth Howard, later married to Sir Richard Southwell, and Frances Howard, married in 1589 to the twelfth earl of Kildare.
40. All these women can be traced through Nichols, the *ODNB*, and Bundesen, '"No other faction but my own"'.
41. Wright, 'A Change in Direction', 157–8; Charlotte Merton, 'Women, Friendship and Memory', in Whitelock and Hunt, *Tudor Queenship*, 244.
42. Collins, *Letters and Memorials*, ii. 271.
43. Nichols, iii. 602–9.
44. 29 December 1558, *CSPSpEliz*, i, no. 6.
45. Archer et al., 'Religion, Politics, and Society', 110.
46. SP 53/10, fo. 61. Under investigation, Henry Cockyn (a letter carrier for Mary Stewart) also mentioned Lady Cobham; see SP 53/10, fo. 11. Ten years later, Mary tried to renew communication with Frances but without success; see *CSP-Scot*, viii. 268.
47. Arnold, *'Lost from her Majesties Back'*, 57.
48. 30 May 1559, *CSPSpEliz*, i, no. 36; Klarwill, *Queen Elizabeth*, 226–7; David McKeen, *A Memory of Honour: The Life of William Brooke, Lord Cobham*, 2 vols (Salzburg, 1986), i. 182–3, 212.
49. Duke of Norfolk's confession, *CSPScot*, iv. 36.
50. Robert Beale, 'A Treatise of the Office of a Councellor and Principall Secretarie', reproduced in Read, *Mr Secretary Walsingham*, i. 423–43.
51. HMC, *Bath*, iv. 186.
52. Rosemary O'Day (ed.), 'The Letter-Book of Thomas Bentham, Bishop of Coventry and Lichfield. 1560–1561', *Camden Miscellany*, 27, fourth series, 22 (1979), 136.
53. FSL, X.d.428 (128).
54. HMC, *De L'Isle*, ii. 411–12.
55. 29 July 1601, CP 87/29; 11 January 1602 CP 84/57.
56. 29 December 1558, *CSPSpEliz*, i, no. 6.
57. HMC, *Rutland*, i. 232.
58. 17 March 1603, CP 92/46.
59. LPL 652, fos 312–3; Merton, 'Women who Served', 177–8.
60. 16 January 1588, SP 12/208, fo. 17.

61. 8 February 1589, SP 12/222, fo. 98ʳ.
62. SP 12/13, fo. 8ʳ&ᵛ.
63. 31 March 1566, SP 15/13, fo. 11ᵛ.
64. SP 12/17, fo. 43.
65. SP 12/200, fo. 38.
66. 7 September and 13 November 1559, *CSPSpEliz*, i, nos 60, 74. See Natalie Mears, 'Politics in the Elizabethan Privy Chamber: Lady Mary Sidney and Kat Ashley', in James Daybell (ed.), *Women and Politics in Early Modern England, 1450–1700* (Aldershot, 2004), 69–70.
67. HMC, *Finch*, i. 24–5.
68. David Starkey, 'Representation through Intimacy: A Study in the Symbolism of Monarchy', in I. Lewis (ed.), *Symbols and Sentiments: Cross-Cultural Studies in Symbolism* (London, 1977), 187–224.
69. 11 March 1579, *CSPSpEliz*, ii, no. 564; Merton, 'Women who Served', 18.
70. For these women, see *ODNB*; Howey, 'Busy Bodies'; McKeen, *A Memory of Honour*, i. 144.
71. William Knollys, 'Papers Relating to Mary Queen of Scots Communicated by General Sir William Knollys', *Philobiblon Society Miscellanies*, 14 (1872–6), 14–15.
72. SP 12/32, fo.168. Sir Thomas was to become tenth Baron Scrope of Bolton.
73. HMC, *Finch*, i. 29; see also pp. 26, 28.
74. HMC, *Finch*, i. 145, 155.
75. HMC, *Rutland*, i. 107; Warren Skidmore, *Lady Mary Scudamore (c.1550–1603)*, Occasional Papers, no. 29 <http://www.skidmoregenealogy.com/.../OccPap_no._29_revised_pdf> (accessed August 2014). The marriage took place sometime before January 1574.
76. HMC, *Finch*, ii. 33–4; Rickman, *Love, Lust, and License*, 31–2.
77. Sir David Dalrymple (ed.), *The Secret Correspondence of Sir Robert Cecil with James VI King of Scotland* (Edinburgh, 1766), 68.
78. HMC, *Salisbury*, v. 596–7; HMC, *Rutland*, i. 322, 324.
79. Henry Harington (ed.), *Nugae antiquae: Being a Miscellaneous Collection of Original Papers, in Prose and Verse*; ed. Thomas Park, 2 vols (London, 1804), i. 233. For secondary sources, see Violet A. Wilson, *Queen Elizabeth's Maids of Honour and Ladies of the Privy Chamber* (London, 1922), 4; Haigh, *Elizabeth I*, 95–6; Rickman, *Love, Lust, and License*, 68.
80. Anna Beer, *Bess: The Life of Lady Ralegh, Wife to Sir Walter* (London, 2004), 71.
81. Frances did not wait, but ran off with Thomas Sherley; see 21 September 1591, *CSPDom, 1591–94*, p. 105.
82. 30 January 1585, in HMC *Bath*, iv. 158–9.
83. Nichols, iii. 580.
84. Robert Cecil to Sir Thomas Sherley, 21 September 1592, SP 12/240, fo. 31ʳ.
85. Howey, 'Busy Bodies', 98.
86. Charles Angell Bradford, *Helena, Marchioness of Northampton* (London, 1936), 57.
87. For the masque, see Bodleian Library, Rawlinson Poetry 108, fo. 30.
88. Wright, *Queen Elizabeth*, ii. 440.
89. HMC, *De L'Isle*, ii. 468; SP 12/275, fo. 20ᵛ.
90. Arnold, '*Lost from her Majesties Back*', 179.
91. Skidmore, *Lady Mary Scudamore*.

92. Skidmore, *Lady Mary Scudamore.*
93. Bradford, *Helena*, 60–7, 86–7, 111. Bradford surmised that the marriage took place in the autumn of 1576.
94. SP 12/260, fo. 34$^{r&v}$. For another surviving letter where Elizabeth also tried to arrange a match for a servant (this time Sir Robert Stapleton), see BL, Additional 15891, fos 91^v–2^r.
95. Merton, 'Women who Served', 129–30.
96. 12 March 1583, Nicolas, *Hatton*, 323; Walsingham to Huntingdon, 23 March 1581, HL, HA13066; 'Anne Vavasour', by Steven W. May, *ODNB.*
97. HMC, *Hastings*, iii. 29; Nichols, iii. 691 n. 309. On Lee's death in 1611, Anne was bequeathed a jointure worth £700.
98. 29 October 1591, CP 20/65.
99. Cecil to Southampton, 3 September 1598, and John Chamberlain to Dudley Carleton, 22 November 1598, SP 12/268, fos 76, 186^v.
100. 5 February 1601, John Maclean (ed.), 'Letters from Sir Robert Cecil to Sir George Carew', *Camden Society*, 88 (1864), 65; 18 May 1601, CP 86/50.
101. 19 June 1601, CP 86/108; 13 August 1601, CP 87/95; 26 August 1601, CP 87/141; 2 September 1601, CP 87/161.
102. Lady Newdigate-Newdegate (ed.), *Gosssip from a Muniment-Room, Being Passages in the Lives of Anne and Mary Fytton 1574–1618* (London, 1898), 42–50, 77–84.
103. 20 August 1597, CP 179/140. The Derby affair could have added a personal dimension to the worsening relations between Essex and the Cecils. See Ch. 7.
104. See the dedication by Anthony Gibson to Elizabeth's women, including Mary Fitton: Alexandre de Pontaymeri, *A Womans Woorth* (London, 1599), sig. A2; Nichols, iii. 522, 524.
105. 24 October 1591, CP 168/55; 27 October 1591, CP 20/65.
106. 19 November 1598, SP 12/268, fo. 181^v.
107. Paul E. J. Hammer, 'Sex and the Virgin Queen: Aristocratic Concupiscence and the Court of Elizabeth I', *Sixteenth Century Journal*, 31 (2000), 90.
108. Hammer, *Polarisation*, 319, 385; Sally Varlow, *The Lady Penelope: The Lost Tale of Love and Politics in the Court of Elizabeth I* (London, 2007).
109. Harington, *Nugae antiquae*, ed Park, i. 232–3.
110. HMC, *Rutland*, i. 275, 278.
111. Knollys, 'Papers Communicated by General Sir William Knollys', 14–15.
112. Champigny to the council of state, 20 March 1576, Lettenhove, *Relations politiques*, viii. 289. See also p. 265.
113. Harington, *Nugae antiquae*, ed Park, i. 235.
114. SP 12/254, fo. 118.
115. August 1599, HMC, *De L'Isle*, ii. 384, 387, 417; 16 November, Isaac Herbert Jeayes (ed.), *Letters of Philip Gawdy of West Harling Norfolk and of London to Various Members of his Family 1579–1616* (London, 1906), 103.
116. *Fowre Severall Treatises of M. Tullius Cicero…* (London, 1577), fo. 15^r. This translation was the most widely read in early modern England. Cicero also argued that superiors could have friendship with inferiors.
117. Cited in Keith Thomas, *The Ends of Life: Roads to Fulfilment in Early Modern England* (Oxford, 2009), 193. See also David Wootton, 'Francis Bacon: Your Flexible Friend', in J. H. Elliott and W. B. Brockliss (eds), *The World of the Favourite* (London and New Haven, 1999), 188–202.
118. 'Essay', in *Queen Elizabeth I: Selected Works*, ed. May, 265.

119. Thomas, *The Ends of Life*, 187–92, 198–9.
120. Katherine died on 24 February 1603. Jeayes, *Letters of Philip Gawdy*, 126; Henry Foley (ed.), *Records of the English Province of the Society of Jesus*, 7 vols (London, 1877–83), i. 52.

CHAPTER 9

1. BL, Cotton Titus CX, no. 21; SP 12/1, fos 3, 4–5ʳ, 8.
2. Stephen Alford, 'Politicians and Statesmen II: William Cecil, Lord Burghley (1520–98)', *State Papers Online, 1509–1714*, Thomson Learning EMEA Lt (Reading, 2007). See also his *Burghley: William Cecil at the Court of Elizabeth I* (London and New Haven, 2008).
3. Bryson, '"The speciall men in every sphere"', 184.
4. e.g. September 1549, SP 10/8, fo. 117.
5. Conyers Read, *Mr Secretary Cecil and Queen Elizabeth* (London, 1955; paperback edn, 1965), 63–6; Starkey, *Elizabeth*, 236–8; Bryson, '"The speciall men in every sphere"', 183–4.
6. 20 November 1558, SP 12/1, fo. 12.
7. Guy, *Children of Henry VIII*, 166.
8. Alford, *Burghley*, 80–1.
9. 23 December 1565, SP 63/15, fo. 189ʳ.
10. Mark Taviner, 'Robert Beale and the Elizabethan Polity', Ph.D., University of St Andrews (2000), 207–10.
11. SP 70/86, fo. 44, cited in Taviner, 'Robert Beale', 112.
12. Cecil to Sussex, 12 August 1561, BL, Cotton Titus BXIII, fo. 50ʳ.
13. For other examples, see Walsingham's letters while ambassador in France in Ch. 10.
14. SP 63/15, fo. 189ʳ.
15. BL, Lansdowne 102, fo. 70ᵛ. These clerks would include the clerks of the council and the clerks of the signet, as well as his own secretariat.
16. SP 12/1, fo. 12.
17. 'In ejusmodi labarintho posita sum…Invenias igitur aliquid boni quod in mandatis scriptis Randoll dare possem, et in hac causa tuam opinionem mihi indica' (23 September 1564, SP 52/9, fo. 113). English translation: *CWE* 115.
18. HMC, *Bath*, v. 97.
19. Richard Hoyle, *The Estates of the English Crown 1558–1640* (Cambridge, 1992), 9–44, 58–87.
20. N. S. B. Gras, 'Tudor "Books of Rates": A Chapter in the History of the English Customs', *Quarterly Journal of Economics* (1912), 766–75; T. S. Willan, *A Tudor Book of Rates* (London, 1962).
21. The wards were the under-age children of the queen's tenants in chief. Most of the wardships were sold, but Burghley personally brought up in his household eight noble wards, including the earls of Oxford, Rutland, Essex, and Southampton.
22. Joel Hurstfield, *The Queen's Wards* (London, 1958), 262–3, 274–6, 282.
23. Hurstfield, *The Queen's Wards*, 264–8; Joel Hurstfield, 'Lord Burghley as Master of the Court of Wards, 1561–98', *Transactions of the Royal Historical Society*, 31 (1949), 108–9.
24. For later secretaries, see Ch. 10.

25. BL, Harley 6992, fos 33–4, quoted in Taviner, 'Robert Beale', 115.
26. For example, Burghley drew up a letter signed by the council for Henry Killigrew as envoy to Scotland in August 1575, which in the event had to be discarded because of the queen's disapproval: BL, Harley 6992, fo. 13.
27. HMC, *Bath*, v. 45.
28. 8 June 1586, SP 12/190, fo. 26.
29. 16 June 1586, SP 12/190, fo. 82.
30. BL, Lansdowne 103, fo. 194$^{r\&v}$.
31. 1585, BL, Lansdowne 94, fo. 73^r.
32. Conyers Read, 'William Cecil and Elizabethan Public Relations', in S. T. Bindoff et al. (eds), *Elizabethan Government and Society* (London, 1961), 21–55.
33. William Cecil, *'The Execution of Justice in England' by William Cecil...*, ed. Robert M. Kingdon (Ithaca, NY, 1965), 7.
34. SP 12/190, fo. 82.
35. HMC, *Bath*, v. 85.
36. 29 April 1594, SP 12/248, fo. 194^r.
37. SP 63/94, fo. 47^r; Lodge, *Illustrations*, ii. 84; BL, Lansdowne 20, fo. 20^r.
38. 25 October 1575, SP 12/126, fo. 29.
39. In 1580, he thanked Leicester for the gift of an excellent hunting hound: SP 12/141, fo. 94.
40. Burghley House is now within Cambridgeshire, and near Stamford in Lincolnshire but was then within 'the soke of Peterborough', considered part of Northamptonshire.
41. Anon., *The Anonymous Life of William Cecil, Lord Burghley*, ed. Alan J. Smith (Lewiston, NY, 1990), 70.
42. SP 12/19, fos 48, 73; SP 12/20, fos 1, 55.
43. He practised archery with his son, and recommended dancing in the 'exercises' he devised for his ward, the earl of Oxford, and hunting for the earl of Rutland.
44. Anon, *Anonymous Life*, 120–2; John Clapham, *Elizabeth of England: Certain Observations Concerning the Life and Reign of Queen Elizabeth*, ed. Evelyn Plummer Read and Conyers Read (Philadelphia, 1951), 71; Ascham, *The Scholemaster*, sig. Bi. See also Mary Partridge, 'Images of the Courtier in Elizabethan England', Ph.D., University of Birmingham (2008), 127–31.
45. Jacob Zeitlin, 'Commonplaces in Elizabethan Life and Letters', *Journal of English and German Philology*, 19 (1920), 57.
46. Nichols, i. 374, 375, 706; BL, Harley 6992, fo. 104. See also Conyers Read, 'Lord Burghley's Household Accounts', *Economic History Review*, 9 (1956), 347–8.
47. Jill Husselby, 'The Politics of Pleasure: William Cecil and Burghley House', in Pauline Croft (ed.), *Patronage, Culture and Power: The Early Cecils* (New Haven and London, 2002), 21–45, and her 'Architecture at Burghley House: The Patronage of William Cecil, 1553–1598', Ph.D., University of Warwick (1996), 78–9, 82, 83–4, 101, 150–1, 211–12, 216–24.
48. Malcolm Airs, '"Pomp or Glory": The Influence of Theobalds', in Croft, *Patronage*, 3–7; James M. Sutton, *Materializing Space at an Early Modern Prodigy House: The Cecils at Theobalds, 1564–1607* (Aldershot, 2004), 80–1, 88; SP 12/181, fo. 159^r.
49. HMC, *Rutland*, i. 150–1; Anon., *Anonymous Life*, 92–3.
50. Groos, *The Diary of Baron Waldstein*, 83.

51. CP 140/18-27, 140/33-36; 143/66-8; SP 12/238, fos 157–8.
52. Anon., *Anonymous Life*, 93.
53. For this view, see Sutton, *Materializing Space*, 89–95.
54. Sutton, *Materializing Space*, 99–119; for text, see Nichols, iii. 530–9. See Ch. 11.
55. Nichols, iii. 735–8; Sutton, *Materializing Space*, 120–5.
56. See, e.g. her letters: Wright, *Queen Elizabeth*, ii. 201, and *Queen Elizabeth I: Selected Works*, ed. May, 179.
57. For further discussion, see Michael A. R. Graves, *Burghley: William Cecil, Lord Burghley* (London and New York, 1998), ch.5.
58. For the importance of Cecil's interest in natural magic, see Glyn Parry, *The Arch-Conjuror of England: John Dee* (New Haven and London, 2011), and 'Occult Philosophy and Politics: Why John Dee Wrote his *Compendious rehearsal* in November 1592', *Studies in History and Philosophy of Science Part A*, 43 (2012), 480–8.
59. 23 March 1595, Wright, *Queen Elizabeth*, ii. 457.
60. MacCaffrey, *Elizabeth I, War and Politics*, 555–7.
61. Usher, *Cecil*, 11–13, 29–32.
62. 28 November 1585, SP 12/184, fos 135ᵛ-6ʳ. For more details, Conyers Read, *Lord Burghley and Queen Elizabeth* (London, 1961; paperback edn, 1965), 119–20.
63. 'A short memoryall of the state of the realme', Haynes, 579, 585–6.
64. BL, Lansdowne 104, fo. 128ʳ&ᵛ.
65. Knollys to Burghley, 9 January 1592, in Wright, *Queen Elizabeth*, ii. 417.
66. Peter Lake, 'Puritanism, (Monarchical) Republicanism and Monarchy: Or John Whitgift, Antipuritanism and the "Invention" of Popularity', *Journal of Medieval and Early Modern Studies*, 40 (2010), 463–95.
67. Richardson, 'The Religious Policies of the Cecils'; SP 12/223, fos 48–9; BL, Lansdowne 103, fo. 206. Travers was for a time chaplain in Burghley's household.
68. Collinson, *Godly People*, 331.
69. 29 November 1577, BL, Lansdowne 103, fo. 14ʳ&ᵛ. For more on prophesyings (the exercises designed to encourage a better standard of preaching), see Ch. 6.
70. 'These procedyngs can not but irritat our mercifull God', Burghley told Walsingham, 31 May 1577, when Elizabeth was planning Grindal's deprivation: BL, Additional 5935, fo. 68.
71. See also Ch. 6.
72. 1 July 1584, SP 12/172, fo. 2ʳ&ᵛ, printed in John Strype, *The Life and Acts of John Whitgift*, 3 vols (Oxford, 1822), iii. 105–7.
73. See Whitgift's reply, BL, Lansdowne 42, fo. 115ᵛ. For further examples of Elizabeth's support for Whitgift, see J. E. Neale, *Elizabeth I and her Parliaments*, 2 vols (London, 1953–7), ii. 65–71.
74. 15 June 1584, SP 12/171, fo. 43. See Ch. 8.
75. Paule, *The Life of John Whitgift*, 37.
76. Collinson, *Elizabethan Puritan Movement*, 411–20.
77. Collinson, *Bancroft*, 138–47.
78. SP 12/231, fo. 181ʳ; Archer et al., 'Religion, Politics, and Society', 226–7.
79. Parry, 'Occult Philosophy and Politics'. For Elizabeth's earlier mitigation, see Neale, *Elizabeth I and her Parliaments*, i. 386–9.
80. Thomas Phelippes to William Sterell, SP 12/244, fo. 219ʳ; Collinson, *Elizabethan Puritan Movement*, 428.

81. 4 July 1559, SP 52/1, fo. 99. On 10 July, Mary's husband, Francis, inherited the French throne.
82. SP 52/1, fo. 105ʳ.
83. Alford, *Early Elizabethan Polity*, 6–8, 43, 53–5, 64–5; Clare Kellar, *Scotland, England and the Reformation 1534–61* (Oxford, 2003), 193–4, 201; Alford, *Burghley*, 105–8; *CSPForEliz*, ii. 174–7.
84. Lord Keeper Bacon, Lord Treasurer Winchester, Sir William Petre, Sir John Mason and Dr Nicholas Wotten.
85. BL, Cotton Caligula BX, fo. 65; SP 12/7, fo. 169ʳ&ᵛ; *CSPForEliz*, ii. 195–6, 199–201.
86. BL, Lansdowne 103, fo. 3ʳ&ᵛ.
87. *CSPForEliz*, ii. 220–2, 254, 255.
88. He was resigning not as secretary but from carrying out responsibilities towards Scotland.
89. BL, Lansdowne 102, fo. 1. The letter is undated.
90. Haynes, 223, 224, 229.
91. Haynes, 342
92. SP 52/4, fos 167–8.
93. See Ch. 3.
94. Wright, *Queen Elizabeth*, i. 98.
95. Maitland of Lethington to Cecil, 6 June 1564, SP 52/9, fo. 84ᵛ.
96. Parry, *The Arch-Conjuror*, 60–4.
97. Hartley, *Proceedings*, i. 45; Doran, *Monarchy and Matrimony*, 73–98.
98. SP 12/40, fo. 195.
99. Hartley, *Proceedings*, i. 163, 151.
100. *CWE* 103.
101. For the 1563 and 1566 parliaments, see Read, *Mr Secretary Cecil*, 268–9, 355–69; Alford, *Early Elizabethan Polity*, 105–15, 142–57.
102. 6 October 1569, BL, Cotton Caligula CI, fo. 456ʳ; Cotton Caligula CII, fo. 82ʳ&ᵛ.
103. BL, Cotton Caligula CIII, fo. 457. See also HMC, *Salisbury*, ii. 15.
104. Dudley Digges, *The Compleat Ambassador* (London, 1655), 219.
105. Burghley to Leicester, 8 November 1572, BL, Cotton Caligula CIII, fo. 408.
106. See Chs 3 and 4.
107. 14 March 1585, BL, Lansdowne 115, fo. 48ʳ&ᵛ. The year of this document is under dispute. Graves dates it 1586. A clean copy with slightly different wording is in Lansdowne 102, fo. 10. Conyers Read and Stephen Alford date them 1587. But, if Burghley were indeed banished from the queen's presence for several months (*ODNB*), it would be better placed in 1585 (the date given in the catalogue for the Lansdowne 115 manuscript).
108. *CWE* 288–9. The death warrant was drawn up on 10 December: Murdin, 574–5.
109. Nicolas, *William Davison*, 240, 264.
110. CP 164/15.
111. 3 April 1587, SP 52/42, no. 34; Wright, *Queen Elizabeth*, ii. 332, 335; 7 April, HMC, *Salisbury*, iii, no. 512; BL, Lansdowne 102, fo. 8ʳ&ᵛ; HMC, *Bath*, v. 80.
112. Stephen Alford, 'The Political Creed of William Cecil', in John F. McDiarmid (ed.), *The Monarchical Republic of Early Modern England* (Aldershot, 2007), 75–90; John Guy, 'The Rhetoric of Counsel in Early-Modern England', in Dale Hoak (ed.), *Tudor Political Culture* (Cambridge, 1995), 292–310, esp. 302.

113. Read, *Burghley*, 545.
114. Harington, *Nugae antiquae*, ed. Park, i. 121.
115. Sutton, *Materializing Space*, 130.
116. Louis Montrose, 'Spenser and the Elizabethan Political Imaginary', *English Literary History*, 69 (2002), 915–16.
117. HMC, *De L'Isle*, ii. 123; Collins, *Letters and Memorials*, i. 331.
118. G. P. V. Akrigg (ed.), *Letters of King James VI and I* (Berkeley and Los Angeles, 1984), 143. Akrigg thinks that James is referring to Robert Cecil rather than Burghley, but I am not convinced.
119. Edward Nares, *Memoirs of the Life and Administration of…William Cecil, Lord Burghley*, 3 vols (London, 1828–31), iii. 355–6; Naunton, *Fragmenta regalia*, 6; J. E. Neale, 'The Elizabethan Political Scene', *Proceedings of the British Academy*, 34 (1948).
120. For an example of Leicester's 'misliking' of Burghley', see 11 August 1585, BL, Lansdowne 102, fo. 230$^{r\&v}$. For further discussion, see Adams, *Leicester*, ch. 3.
121. 7 February 1586, BL, Cotton Galba CIX, fo. 71; Murdin, 586. For further discussion, see Adams, *Leicester*, ch. 3, and 'The Patronage of the Crown in Elizabethan Politics: The 1590s in Perspective', in John Guy (ed.), *The Reign of Elizabeth I: Court and Culture in the Last Decade* (Cambridge, 1995), 38.
122. Victor Houlistan, 'The Lord Treasurer and the Jesuit: Robert Persons's Satirical *Responsio* to the 1591 Proclamation', *Sixteenth Century Journal*, 32 (2001), 383–401.
123. Andreas Philopater [*vere* Robert Persons], *Elizabethae Angliae Reginae haeresim Calvinianum propugnantis* (Antwerp, 1592). Catholic exiles generally preferred to attack the queen's advisers rather than Elizabeth herself in order to preserve their claim to be loyal; see Jan Machielsen, 'The Lion, the Witch, and the King: Thomas Stapleton's *Apologia pro Rege Catholico Philippo II* (1592)', *English Historical Review*, 129 (2014), 19–46.
124. Wright, *Queen Elizabeth*, ii. 201.
125. Burghley to William Herle, 14 August 1585, SP 12/181, fos 158^v–60^r.
126. Paul L. Hughes and James F. Larkin (eds), *Tudor Royal Proclamations*, 3 vols (New York and London, 1969), ii. 376–9.
127. Letter of Sir Thomas Tresham; see Bruce Danner, *Edmund Spenser's War on Lord Burghley* (New York, 2011), 6.
128. John Clapham's memoir, in Francis Peck, *Desiderata curiosa* (1732–5).
129. David Hume, *The History of England: Under the House of Tudor* (London, 1759), ii. 511.
130. John Guy, <www.tudors.org> (accessed March 2014).

CHAPTER 10

1. Anon., *An Humble Supplication to her Majestie* (n.p., 1600), 32.
2. 7 November 1574, *CSPSpEliz*, ii, no. 404.
3. Richard Verstegan, *A Declaration of the True Causes of the Great Troubles* (Antwerp, 1592), 54.
4. MacCaffrey, *Queen Elizabeth and the Making of Policy*, 441; John Guy, *Tudor England* (Oxford and New York, 1990), 252, 280.
5. Nicodemus was a Pharisee who visited Christ secretly at night, and so outward conformity to the established religion to escape detection is called Nicodemism.

6. Quotation from John Cosyn, *Musike of Six, and Five Partes* (London, 1585), sig. A2ᵛ; 'Sir Francis Walsingham', by Simon Adams and Alan Bryson, rev. Mitchell Leimon, *ODNB*.

7. Read, *Mr Secretary Walsingham*, ii. 261.

8. 8 May 1578, SP 83/6, fo. 106ʳ&ᵛ.

9. M. O'Connell, *The Idolatrous Eye* (Oxford, 2000), 14–15; Scott McMillan and Sally-Beth MacLean, *The Queen's Men and their Plays* (Cambridge, 1998), 23–4.

10. 21 April and 14 October 1582, SP 15/27, fos 109, 193.

11. Lancashire Record Office, DDKE/acc. 7840 HMC/fo. 63d [n.d.] <www.nationalarchives.gov.uk> (accessed 1 December 2013).

12. Nichols, iv. 66.

13. Warwick Edwards, 'The Walsingham Consort Books', *Music and Letters*, 55 (1974), 209–14; SP 63/53, fo. 102; SP 63/68, fo. 113; 'John de Critz the Elder', by Mary Edmond, *ODNB*.

14. Peter Hasler claims it was Cecil who arranged Walsingham's election in 1559: *History of Parliament* <http://www.historyofparliamentonline.org/volume/1558-1603/member/walsingham-francis-1532-90> (accessed 1 December 2013). In 1571 Leicester referred to Throckmorton as 'our good friend' (Digges, *Compleat Ambassador*, 51). See also SP 12/47, fo. 84, where Walsingham wrote to Cecil on behalf of Throckmorton, 'whos strengthe woolde not serve hym to wryte'.

15. Killigrew was Cecil's brother-in-law. It is also possible that Cecil originally met Walsingham at Cambridge, as Sir John Cheke, Cecil's father-in-law, was the provost at King's College, where Walsingham studied from 1548 until 1550.

16. *History of Parliament* <http://www.historyofparliamentonline.org/volume/1558-1603/member/walsingham-francis-1532-90> (accessed 1 December 2013).

17. 'Walsingham, Sir Francis', by Simon Adams and Alan Bryson, rev. Mitchell Leimon, *ODNB*.

18. 18 August, 7, 15, 24 September, 21 October, 20 December 1568, SP 12/47, fos 84, 115, 148–9; SP 70/102, fo. 86; SP 12/48, fos 50, 165.

19. 20 December 1568, SP 12/48, fo. 165.

20. SP 12/59, fos 11, 81, 84. He was released in January.

21. John Cooper, *The Queen's Agent: Francis Walsingham at the Court of Elizabeth I* (London, 2011), 57–9.

22. Geoffrey Parker, 'The Place of Tudor England in the Messianic Vision of Philip II of Spain', *Transactions of the Royal Historical Society*, 6th ser., 12 (2002), 192–205.

23. 11 August 1570, SP 70/113, fos 91–5ʳ. Digges, *Compleat Ambassador*, 5–6. Drafted by Cecil, SP 70/113, fo. 115.

24. Walsingham was appointed resident ambassador on 7 September 1570. Digges, *Compleat Ambassador*, 6–7, 9, 19; Read, *Mr Secretary Walsingham*, i. 94–5.

25. 29 January 1571, SP 70/116, fos 49–53; Taviner, 'Robert Beale', 100.

26. For the queen's eyes, see Taviner, 'Robert Beale', 5, 9, 10, 11, 27, 36, 43, 50; SP 70/117, fo. 6. For Burghley only, see SP 70/116, fos 74–5, and SP 70/119, fos 45–6.

27. Digges, *Compleat Ambassador*, 18, 20. For the embassy and marriage negotiations, see Doran, *Monarchy and Matrimony*, 105–29; Rifka Zim, 'Dialogue and Discretion: Thomas Sackville, Catherine de Medici and the Anjou Marriage Proposal 1571', *Historical Journal*, 40 (1997), 287–310.

28. 3 March 1571, Digges, *Compleat Ambassador*, 54–5.

29. 9 February 1571, SP 70/116, fos 74ʳ, 75ʳ.
30. Digges, *Compleat Ambas*sador, 62.
31. Digges, *Compleat Ambas*sador, 62–6 (religion is mentioned on p. 65).
32. Walsingham to Leicester, 28 April 1571, SP 70/117, fo. 156ᵛ.
33. 1 February 1571, SP 70/117, fo. 64ʳ&ᵛ.
34. 16 April, SP 70/117, fo. 130ʳ&ᵛ.
35. 19 April 1571, Digges, *Compleat Ambassador*, 188.
36. Walsingham to Leicester, 3 August 1571, BL, Harley 260, fo. 96ᵛ.
37. 27 July 1571, SP 70/119, fo. 45ʳ.
38. 3 August, BL, Harley 260, fos 126ʳ–7ᵛ.
39. Walsingham to Burghley, 3 August 1571, SP 70/119, fo. 75ᵛ.
40. SP 70/119, fo. 75ᵛ.
41. BL, Harley 260, fos 129ʳ–35ʳ.
42. BL, Harley 260, fos 135ᵛ–6ᵛ.
43. Read, *Mr Secretary Walsingham*, i. 148–51.
44. SP 70/120, fo. 48ʳ.
45. Digges, *Compleat Ambassador*, 139.
46. 15 September and 8 October 1571, SP 70/120, fos 45, 71ʳ.
47. Digges, *Compleat Ambassador*, 225–6, 233–4.
48. 24 September 1572, BL, Harley 260, fo. 324ᵛ.
49. Digges, *Compleat Ambassador*, 276.
50. Digges, *Compleat Ambassador*, 310; 7 January 1573, Wright, *Queen Elizabeth*, i. 449.
51. On 11 May it was 'thought he shall be made secretary' (Nichols, ii. 52).
52. Nichols, ii. 297–8, 350, 478, 531, 533; iii. 8, 10, 26, 100, 191.
53. 12 September 1578, SP 12/109, fo. 11ʳ.
54. 13 January 1574, BL, Harley 6991, fo. 110ʳ.
55. Copy of a letter from 11 March 1574, BL, Harley 6991, fo. 128.
56. 30 April 1575, BL, Cotton Caligula CIII, fo. 523; 9 May, SP 53/10, fo. 49. On this particular matter at least, Walsingham persuaded Elizabeth to change her mind.
57. The soubriquet that may have been his before entering royal service. In July 1570, Bedford thanked Cecil for his 'greate good will in thinking upon the Moore' (CP 157/46). This is obviously oblique, but may refer to Walsingham.
58. 15 January 1575, BL, Cotton Caligula CIV, fo. 310ʳ.
59. SP 12/45, fo. 23ʳ&ᵛ; BL, Cotton Caligula CIX, fo. 4ʳ.
60. BL, Harley 6991, fo. 92ʳ. For similar sentiments, see SP 53/10, fo. 13.
61. Lettenhove, *Relations politiques*, viii. 127–9, 263–5. For Scotland, see Read, *Mr Secretary Walsingham*, ii. 131–9.
62. 3 August 1575, BL, Harley 6992, fo. 170.
63. Amos C. Miller, *Sir Henry Killigrew* (Leicester, 1963), 176.
64. Lettenhove, *Relations politiques*, viii. 372–3. Adams suggests Elizabeth's decision to reject the sovereignty of Holland in 1576 may be attributed as much to her anger over Dutch piracies as to a fear of Spanish reprisals: Adams, 'Elizabeth I and the Sovereignty of the Netherlands', 316; 16 April 1576, SP 70/138, fo. 423; 30 August, SP 70/139, fos 119–20; Walsingham to Sir Nicholas Bacon, 17 September 1576, FSL, L.d.612, printed in A. Hassell Smith, Gillian Baker, and R. W. Kenny (eds), *Papers of Nathaniel Bacon of Stiffkey*, 3 vols (Norwich, 1979), i. 223.
65. *Zurich Letters (Second Series)*, 287–8.

66. Lettenhove, *Relations politiques,* viii. 265–8.
67. SP 70/140, fo. 258^{r&v}; Lettenhove, *Relations politiques,* viii. 372–3; 16 April 1576, SP 70/138, fos 42–3; 30 August, SP 70/139, fo. 119–20; FSL, L.d.612, printed in Hassell Smith et al., *Papers,* i. 223; 16 October 1576, BL, Harley 6992 fo. 56^{r&v}; Read, *Mr Secretary Walsingham,* i. 33–5.
68. 18 September 1577, SP 12/115, fo. 66.
69. David Scott Gehring, *Anglo-German Relations and the Protestant Cause* (London, 2013), 55–79; MacCaffrey, *Queen Elizabeth and the Making of Policy,* 225; Read, *Mr Secretary Walsingham,* i. 299, 343.
70. Lettenhove, *Relations politiques,* x. 153–4.
71. 2 November 1577, SP 81/1, fo. 103^r.
72. Leicester to Beale, 30 October 1577, BL, Additional 48149, fo. 39^v.
73. Walsingham to Davison, 20 March 1578, SP 83/5, fo. 87; Philip Sidney to Hubert Languet, 10 March 1578, in *Zurich Letters (Second Series),* 300.
74. 22 March 1577, SP 83/5, fos 93^r–4^r. The earl of Sussex was of the same mind as Burghley: W. J. Tighe, 'The Counsel of Thomas Radcliffe, Earl of Sussex, to Queen Elizabeth I Concerning the Revolt of the Netherlands, September 1578', *Sixteenth Century Journal,* 18 (1987), 323–31.
75. They were put forward by Philip II's new ambassador, Bernardino de Mendoza, 17 March 1578, SP 94/1, fo. 13.
76. Instructions, 2 June 1578, Lettenhove, *Relations politiques,* x. 506–8; Instructions, 12 June, BL, Cotton Galba CVI, fos 169^r–70^v.
77. 11, 2 and 16 May 1578, SP 83/6, fos 110^v, 84^v, 131^v.
78. Walsingham to Hatton, 9 September 1578, in Wright, *Queen Elizabeth,* ii. 93–4.
79. Wright, *Queen Elizabeth,* ii. 94.
80. Lettenhove, *Relations politiques,* x. 678–80; SP 83/8, fos 16^r–17^v.
81. 7 August 1578, SP 83/8, no. 14. On the other hand, the French ambassador reported to Henry III that she talked of it all the time: Natalie Mears, 'Love-Making and Diplomacy: Elizabeth I and the Anjou Marriage Negotiations, *c.*1578–1582', *History,* 86 (2001), 456.
82. Walsingham to Leicester, 18 August 1578, Lettenhove, *Relations politiques,* x. 743–5.
83. Natalie Mears does not consider the series of meetings starting on 27 March to be actual council meetings: 'Love-Making', 454.
84. 4 April 1579, Lodge, *Illustrations,* ii. 149; 14 May 1579, *CSPSpEliz,* ii, no. 576.
85. BL, Cotton Galba CVI, fo. 94^{r&v}; BL, Harley 1582, fo. 49^v; SP 12/133/23, fo. 50^v.
86. SP 12/131, fo. 169.
87. 10 August 1579, SP 63/68, fo. 41^r.
88. 27 October 1579, *CSPVen,* vii, no. 783. Mendoza reported that Elizabeth told Walsingham to 'be gone' (16 October 1579, *CSPSpEliz,* ii, no. 607).
89. 9 November 1579, APC xi. 304; Walsingham to Cobham, 30 December 1579, SP 78/3, fo. 60^r; Mitchell MacDonald Leimon, 'Sir Francis Walsingham and the Anjou Marriage Plan, 1574–1581', Ph.D., University of Cambridge (1989), 194–6.
90. CP 148/64.
91. 1 June 1580, SP 52/28, fo. 54^r; 28 January and 3 February 1581, HL, HA 13056, 13058. For Lennox and events in Scotland, see Ch. 4.
92. Walsingham to Burghley, 11 August 1581, SP 78/6, fo. 20^v (no. 7).
93. 1 June 1580, SP 52/28, fo. 54^r; 24 and 28 January and 3 February 1581, HL, HA 13055, 13056, 13058.

94. 27 June 1578, BL, Additional 15891, fo. 48ʳ (Nicolas, *Hatton*, 67).
95. [Walsingham] to [Henry Cobham], late October 1580, SP 78/4, B art. 171 (*CSPForEliz*, xiv. 473).
96. Doran, *Monarchy and Matrimony*, 179–82.
97. 30 July 1581, CP 11/97.
98. 19 July 1581, SP 78/5/121.
99. Walsingham to Burghley, 17 August 1581, SP 78/6, fo. 14.
100. 12 September 1581, CP 12/3.
101. Stephen Alford, 'Some Elizabethan Spies in the Office of Sir Francis Walsingham', in Robyn Adams and Rosanna Cox (eds), *Diplomacy and Early Modern Culture* (Basingstoke, 2011), 46–60, and *The Watchers*, 81–8.
102. Alford, *The Watchers*. John Bossy, *Under the Molehill: An Elizabethan Spy Story* (New Haven and London, 2001), 31–3.
103. 13 August 1583, SP 52/33/9, and BL, Cotton Caligula CIV, fos 312–13.
104. 6 August 1583, SP 52/33, fo. 5.
105. 5, 11 and 12 September 1583, SP 52/33, nos 58, 35, and 39.
106. Conference between James and Walsingham, SP 52/33, fo. 43ʳ.
107. 15 September 1583, SP 52/33, fo. 161ʳ.
108. 22 September 1583, SP 52/33, fo. 50. See Ch. 4.
109. Read, *Mr Secretary Walsingham*, ii. 374–5; 'William Crichton', by Mark Dilworth, *ODNB*.
110. For the bond, see Ch. 3.
111. Read, *Mr Secretary Walsingham*, iii. 53. See also Ch. 3.
112. Davison to Walsingham, 10 December 1586, SP 12/195, fo. 99ʳ. For the draft of Walsingham's petition for £200 a year on 14 December 1586, see HMC, *Salisbury*, iii. 202.
113. 16 December 1586, SP 12/195, fo. 111ʳ. (It is mistakenly calendared on 6 December.) Warrant to Davison, 12 December 1586, BL, Cotton Vespasian CXIV, fo. 256.
114. Nicolas, *Life of William Davison*, 236–7.
115. Walsingham had to surrender his chancellorship of the garter to his main competitor, Sir Amias Paulet.
116. 30 March 1586, *CSPSpEliz*, iii, no. 431.
117. Thomas Windebank to Walsingham, 2 April 1590, SP 12/231, fo. 116.
118. Read, *Mr Secretary Walsingham*, iii. 442–8.

CHAPTER 11

1. He seems to have inherited scoliosis from his mother and passed it on to his daughter: Pauline Croft, 'Can a Bureaucrat be a Favourite? Robert Cecil and the Strategies of Power', in J. H. Elliott and L. W. B. Brockliss (eds), *The World of the Favourite* (New Haven and London (1999), 94 (n. 9). For Frances's, problems, see HMC, *Salisbury*, x. 335.
2. Anthony Bacon to Essex, 29 January 1595, CP 24/105.
3. 8 October 1582, CP 12/73.
4. SP 12/172, fo. 176; SP 78/12, fos 221–33ᵛ, 237–42ᵛ, 244–9, 286ᵛ. Archer et al., 'Religion, Politics, and Society', 4–8.
5. R.C., *The Copie of a Letter* (London, 1586), 3; Neale, *Elizabeth I and her Parliaments*, ii. 129–31.

6. Letter addressed from court, 28 February 1584, SP 12/168, fo. 71; endorsed from France, [1585], BL, Cotton Galba EVI, fos 282–3ᵛ.
7. 25 August 1587, CP 165/94.
8. Nichols, iii. 392. His gifts in 1594 and 1597 were expensive pieces of jewellery: Lawson, *Elizabethan New Year's Gift Exchanges*, 412, 430, 450, 469, 488. The gift list was for accounting not for public purposes.
9. 16 February 1588, SP 15/30, fo. 156.
10. SP 12/208, fo. 108ᵛ.
11. SP 12/208, fo. 108ʳ&ᵛ; P. M. Handover, *The Second Cecil: The Rise to Power 1563–1604 of Sir Robert Cecil, Later First Earl of Salisbury* (London, 1959), 56–7.
12. SP 12/208, 57–62; *CSPForEliz*, xxi. 161–2, 184–5, 191–2, 225–6, 233; Wright, *Queen Elizabeth*, ii. 367.
13. Handover, *Cecil*, 66.
14. Nicolas, *Life of William Davison*, 169, 171, 173–5. See also Chs 7 and 10.
15. Cecil to Sir Thomas Heneage, 25 May 1592, SP 12/242, fo. 57.
16. 19 September 1592, SP 12/243, fo. 26; BL, Lansdowne 70, fo. 151; HMC, *Salisbury*, iv. 226, 232–3.
17. 29 September [1592], CP 98/62.
18. The careers of both Sir Henry Unton and Francis Bacon were stymied as a result of their conduct in this parliament: CP 19/54; CP 19/65; CP 26/58.
19. Hartley, *Proceedings*, iii. 71–3, 99–100, 102.
20. Cecil to Lord Zouche, 23 January 1594, SP 52/52, fo. 25ʳ&ᵛ.
21. Wright, *Queen Elizabeth*, ii. 428.
22. Wright, *Queen Elizabeth*, ii. 433.
23. Bowes to Burghley, 13 April 1594, SP 52/53, fo. 30.
24. Wright, *Queen Elizabeth*, ii. 440.
25. James Hudson to Cecil, 18 October 1594, SP 52/54, fo. 67.
26. The papers reside mainly in the Cecil archive at Hatfield. See also BL, Lansdowne 115, fo. 76; letter from Christopher Blount to Cecil, SP 12/260, fo. 44, which lists 'the commodytyes gotten by me in Cales'. For Essex's view of the Cecils' actions, see Birch, *Memoirs*, ii. 131.
27. Birch, *Memoirs*, ii. 146–7.
28. HMC, *Salisbury*, vi. 469; Hammer, *Polarisation*, 376–8.
29. Alford, *The Watchers*, ch. 20; Hammer, *Polarisation*, 197–8.
30. Sir Edward Hoby to Cecil, 25 January 1597, CP/37/103; CP 37/97/2; CP 37/102.
31. As Elizabeth often wrote letters of condolence to her courtiers, it seems unlikely that she would not have written to Cecil.
32. 'Robert Cecil, First Earl of Salisbury', by Pauline Croft, *ODNB*.
33. CP 175/92.
34. May 1597, SP 12/263, fo. 104. For the voyage and the queen's attitude to it, see Ch. 7.
35. 23 and 27 July, SP 12/264, fos 66, 81; *CSPDom, 1595–1597*, p. 474.
36. 26 July, SP 12/264, fo. 81.
37. *History of Parliament* <http://www.historyofparliamentonline.org/volume/1558-1603/parliament/1597> (accessed September 2014).
38. R. B. Wernham, *The Return of the Armadas: The Last Years of the Elizabethan War against Spain, 1595–1603* (Oxford, 1994), 210–15.
39. Elizabeth to the envoys, 17 March 1598, BL, Cotton Caligula EIX (2), fo. 147ʳ. Only in mid-March did she want a more direct approach.

40. Roland Whyte to Sir Robert Sidney, 1, 4, 11, and 12 February 1598, in Collins, *Letters and Memorials*, ii. 87, 88, 89, 90.

41. 19 February 1598, SP 12/266, fo. 98.

42. 29 April 1598, SP 78/41, fo. 167. See also SP 78/41, fo. 135.

43. Thomas Birch, *An Historical View of the Negotiations between England, France, and Brussels 1592–1617* (London, 1749), 105–39, 141–57.

44. Birch, *Historical View*, 151, 152. In fact Henry IV promised the Dutch a generous subsidy over the next four years.

45. BL, Cotton Caligula EIX (2), fo. 147^v.

46. Essex was not alone in these views. Manuscript treatises and printed tracts echo his arguments; see Gajda, 'Debating War and Peace', 851–78.

47. 7 July 1598, CP 62/29; 26 June 1598, CP 61/105.

48. For the earl of Cumberland's privateering venture, see Wernham, *Return of the Armadas*, 256.

49. Wernham, *Return of the Armadas*, 241–2.

50. 29 September 1600, Maclean, 'Letters from Cecil to Carew', 26, 27.

51. Cecil had probably received an annuity from his father during Burghley's lifetime. For Cecil's income from land, see Lawrence Stone, 'The Fruits of Office: The Case of Robert Cecil, First Earl of Salisbury', in F. J. Fisher (ed.), *Essays in the Economic and Social History of Tudor and Stuart England* (Cambridge, 1961), 90.

52. Maclean, 'Letters from Cecil to Carew', 26.

53. 'Sir John Herbert', by T. G. Watkin, *ODNB*; Florence M. G. Evans, *The Principal Secretary of State* (Manchester, 1923), 57.

54. 29 November 1602, CP 213/120.

55. Richard W. Stewart, 'The "Irish Road": Military Supply and Arms for Elizabeth's Army during the O'Neill Rebellion in Ireland, 1598–1601', in Mark Charles Fissel (ed.), *War and Government in Britain, 1598–1650* (Manchester, 1991), 16–29, 31–2. For a different viewpoint, see L.W. Henry, 'The Earl of Essex and Ireland, 1599', *Bulletin of the Institute of Historical Research*, 85 (1959), 8–9, and Chris Butler and Willy Maley, '"Bringing Rebellion Broached on his Sword": Essex and Ireland', in Connolly and Hopkins, *Essex*, 139–40.

56. *APC* xxix. 402; BL, Harley 168, fos 144^v–56^r.

57. Two days after the treaty of Vervins had been signed, Philip II ceded the Netherlands to his daughter and her husband-to-be Albert. Their wedding took place in April 1599.

58. Edmund Sawyer (ed.), *Memorials in the Reigns of Q. Elizabeth and K. James I Collected (Chiefly) from the Original Papers of the Right Honourable Sir Ralph Winwood*, 3 vols (London, 1725), i. 56.

59. Sawyer, *Winwood Memorials*, i. 96.

60. SP 12/271, fo. 171^r.

61. The animal imagery used against Cecil can be found in the private correspondence of Anthony and Francis Bacon, Antonio Pérez, and Henry Howard for several years before 1599; see Gajda, *Essex and Late Elizabethan Political Culture*, 148.

62. Bodleian, MS Don. *c*.54, fos 19^r–20^r, printed in Alastair Bellany and Andrew McCrae, *Early Stuart Libels: An Edition of Poetry from Manuscript Sources* <http://www.earlystuartlibels.net/htdocs/pdf/esl.pdf> (accessed August 2014).

63. Bodleian, MS Rawlinson Poet. 26, fo. 20^v, printed in Bellany and McCrae, *Early Stuart Libels*.

64. Detraction here is the device of presenting the qualities of virtuous men as vices.
65. Richard Roberts's commonplace book, Bodleian MS Don. c.54, fo. 20ʳ, printed in Bellany and McCrae, *Early Stuart Libels*.
66. Harold Spencer Scott (ed.), *The Journal of Sir Roger Wilbraham, Solicitor-General in Ireland and Master of Requests, for the Years 1593–1616*…(London 1902), 30; Pauline Croft, 'The Reputation of Robert Cecil: Libels, Political Opinion and Popular Awareness in the Early Seventeenth Century', *Transactions of the Royal Historical Society*, 6th ser., 1 (1991), 47–8.
67. FSL, V.b.142, fos 49ʳ⁻ᵛ, 50ʳ.
68. Croft, 'Reputation', 47–8.
69. Elizabeth to Irish council, 6 October 1599, SP 63/204, fo. 190ᵛ.
70. 5 and 6 November 1599, *Cal. Carew MSS*, iii. 344–5, 356–7. See also Sawyer, *Winwood Memorials*, i. 119.
71. Mountjoy arrived in Ireland on 24 February 1600.
72. 9 September 1600, Maclean, 'Letters from Cecil to Carew', 26, 27.
73. Maclean, 'Letters from Cecil to Carew', 29.
74. Maclean, 'Letters from Cecil to Carew', 60. See also 'James fitz Gerald Fitzgerald, Fifteenth Earl of Desmond', by Anthony M. McCormack, *ODNB*. Fitzgerald proved loyal but ineffective.
75. *CSPDom, 1598–1601*, p. 397.
76. Pauline Croft, 'Rex Pacificus, Robert Cecil and the 1604 Peace with Spain', in Glenn Burgess, Rowland Wymer, and Jason Lawrence (eds), *The Accession of James I: Historical and Cultural Consequences* (Basingstoke, 2006), 144; Paul C. Allen, *Philip III and the Pax Hispanica, 1598–1621* (New Haven and London), 42, 47–9.
77. Sawyer, *Winwood Memorials*, i. 137, 215–26; Wernham, *Return of the Armadas*, ch. 20.
78. Maclean, 'Letters from Cecil to Carew', 21.
79. Maclean, 'Letters from Cecil to Carew', 62.
80. Croft, 'Rex Pacificus', 146; Allen, *Philip III*, 35, 100–101
81. BL, Additional 31022, fo. 107.
82. Joel Hurstfield, 'The Succession Struggle in Late Elizabethan England', in Joel Hurstfield, *Freedom, Corruption and Government in Elizabethan England* (London, 1973), 104–36.
83. For the coup, see Ch. 7.
84. SP 12/278, fos 79ᵛ–80ʳ. Cecil was presumably referring to the first part of John Hayward's book *The First Part of the Life and Raigne of King Henrie the IIII*, which was dedicated to Essex and reprinted in January 1601. The government considered it seditious, since its story told of a childless monarch who was unable to suppress revolt in Ireland, imposed unpopular exactions on his subjects, and was ultimately deposed. Hayward remained in the Tower until the end of the reign. There is no evidence that Essex was behind the publication of the book.
85. Jason Scott-Warren, 'Was Elizabeth I Richard II? The Authenticity of Lambarde's "Conversation"', *Review of English Studies*, 64 (2012), 208–30. For more details of the insurrection and trial, see Ch. 7.
86. Maclean, 'Letters from Cecil to Carew', 68–70.
87. Proceedings of the trial of Essex and Southampton, HL, HM 41952, fos 49ᵛ–54ᵛ; Maclean, 'Letters from Cecil to Carew', 70.
88. Maclean, 'Letters from Cecil to Carew', 69–72.

89. Leo Hicks, 'Sir Robert Cecil, Father Parsons, and the Succession, 1600–1', *Archivum Historicum Societatis Iesu*, 24 (1955), 95–139.
90. Satirical ballad, SP 12/278, fo. 31; CUL, Add. MS 4138, fo. 49ʳ, printed in Bellany and McCrae, *Early Stuart Libels*.
91. Cecil to Sir Henry Poole, [January 1603], CP 130/165.
92. Maclean, 'Letters from Cecil to Carew', 108.
93. Maclean, 'Letters from Cecil to Carew', 84–5, 89, 116. 'Coals on their head' is a reference to Romans 12:20 and Proverbs 25:17–21, which enjoined men and women to treat unkindness with kindness and leave revenge to God. In fact, Cecil took his revenge in speaking against their entry into the privy council.
94. Nichols, iv. 124, 125. 'Henry Brooke, eleventh Baron Cobham', by Mark Nicholls, and 'Sir Walter Ralegh', by Mark Nicholls and Penry Williams, *ODNB*. Frances was the daughter of the earl and countess of Nottingham.
95. Carew sought the opinions of all of them: *CSP Ireland*, xi. 366, 368, 501. In October 1601, Harrington commented that Buckhurst was much with the queen 'and few else': *Nugae antiquae*, ed. Park, i. 318.
96. Maclean, 'Letters from Cecil to Carew', 98. But she refused leave for Mountjoy to come home in October 1602: p.138.
97. For Kinsale, see Hiram Morgan (ed.), *The Battle of Kinsale* (Bray, 2004).
98. Morgan, *Battle of Kinsale*, 105.
99. *Cal. Carew MSS*, iv. 417–18. The two men got their way but only because Elizabeth died on 24 March, six days before Tyrone met the lord deputy and agreed terms.
100. Stone, 'Fruits of Office', 105–8.
101. Dalrymple, *Secret Correspondence*, 6, 9. For a full account of the correspondence and its background, see Alexander Courtney, 'The Scottish King and the English Court: The Secret Correspondence of James VI, 1601–1603', in Doran and Kewes, *Doubtful and Dangerous*, 134–51, and Courtney, 'The Accession of James VI to the English Throne, 1601–1603', M. Phil., University of Cambridge (2004).
102. John Bruce (ed.), 'Correspondence of King James VI of Scotland with Sir Robert Cecil and Others in England during the Reign of Queen Elizabeth: With an Appendix Containing Papers Illustrative of Transactions between King James and Robert Earl of Essex, Principally Published for the First Time from Manuscripts Preserved at Hatfield', *Camden Society*, 78 (1861), 5.
103. Bruce, 'Correspondence of King James VI', 4, 5.
104. The letter is undated: Bruce, 'Correspondence of King James VI', 30–1; Dalrymple, *Secret Correspondence*, 60.
105. Scott, *The Journal of Sir Roger Wilbraham*, 49–50.
106. Stone estimates that in 1601–2 'his share of captures must have brought him a net profit of about £7,000' ('Fruits of Office', 93–4).
107. Courtney, 'The Scottish King and the English Court'.
108. Bruce, 'Correspondence of King James VI', 7–8.
109. Courtney, 'The Scottish King and the English Court'.
110. Harington, *Nugae antiquae*, ed. Park, 315, 317, 320, 323; Henry Howard to the earl of Mar, Dalrymple, *Secret Correspondence*, 26.
111. One MP said of the speech: 'it was worthy to be written in gold', and, when reprinted in 1659, it was entitled 'the Golden Speech'. For later versions of the

speech, see John Watkins, '"Old Bess in the Ruff": Remembering Elizabeth I, 1625–1660', *English Literary Renaissance*, 30 (2000), 108–10. The Tilbury speech is arguably the most celebrated, although it was not printed at the time.

112. Hartley, *Proceedings*, iii. 385–6, 392.
113. Donald Stump and Susan M. Felch (eds), *Elizabeth I and her Age* (New York, 2009), 502–7. See also *CWE* 340–2. The version printed in 1601 differed from manuscript versions and 'is better described as a summary than transcription' (*CWE* 343 (n. 1)).
114. Foley, *Records of the English Province of the Society of Jesus*, i. 24, 43, 46, 47.
115. Norman Egbert McClure (ed.), *The Letters of John Chamberlain*, i (Philadelphia, 1939), 176, 177; R. P. Sorlien (ed.), *The Diary of John Manningham of the Middle Temple 1602–1603* (Hanover, NH, 1976), 150.
116. Nichols, iv. 205–8.
117. Mary C. Erler, 'Sir John Davies and the Rainbow Portrait of Queen Elizabeth', *Modern Philology*, 84 (1987), 359–71; Roy Strong, *Gloriana: The Portraits of Queen Elizabeth I* (New York, 1987; London, 2003), 157–61.
118. HMC, *De L'Isle*, ii. 425.
119. HMC, *Salisbury*, xxiii. 41.
120. 9 September 1595, CP 34/111.
121. Lodge, *Illustrations*, ii. 576.
122. Catherine Loomis, 'Elizabeth Southwell's Manuscript Account of the Death of Queen Elizabeth [with Text]', in Kirby Farrell and Kathleen M. Swain (eds), *The Mysteries of Elizabeth I: Selections from English Literary Renaissance* (Amherst, *c*.2003), 220.
123. Courtney, 'The Scottish King and the English Court', 144–6. Letters to noblemen were issued on 19 March; James received the draft proclamation on the 23rd, and it was probably sent on the 21st.
124. Nichols, iv. 213–17. For other accounts, see Nichols, iv. 218–20, 224–7.
125. Nichols, iv. 212–13, 217.
126. Outside the scope of this book are the social reforms and commercial enterprises he encouraged. For them, see Handover, *Cecil*.
127. 31 May 1606, *CSPVen*, x, no. 527. Cited in 'Robert Cecil, First Earl of Salisbury', by Pauline Croft, *ODNB*.

EPILOGUE

1. e.g. Samuel Rowlands, *An Epitaph upon the Death of her Majestie our Late Queen* (London, 1603).
2. For further details and examples, see Catherine Loomis, *The Death of Elizabeth I: Remembering and Reconstructing the Virgin Queen* (Basingstoke, 2010), ch. 2.
3. For another—Fulke Greville—see Lisa Richardson, 'Elizabeth in Arcadia: Fulke Greville and John Hayward's Construction of Elizabeth 1610–12', in Susan Doran and Thomas S. Freeman (eds), *The Myth of Elizabeth* (Basingstoke, 2003), 100–1.
4. John Speed, *The History of Great Britaine*... 2nd edn (London, 1623), 1056.
5. Clapham, *Elizabeth of England*, 67, 97. Clapham's phrasing was lifted directly from Tacitus.

6. Bacon's Latin essay was published in English in 1651. For a recent commentary, see Brandie R. Siegfried, '*Bonum theatrale*: The Matter of Elizabeth I in Francis Bacon's *Of Tribute* and Margaret Cavendish's *Blazing World*', in Elizabeth H. Hageman and Katherine Conway (eds), *Resurrecting Elizabeth I in Seventeenth-Century England* (Cranbury, NJ, 2007), 185–6, 192–4.

7. Nichols, iv. 804.

8. Speed, *History*, 1235.

9. Nichols, iv. 804, 806.

10. For this view, see Curtis Perry, *The Making of Jacobean Culture* (Cambridge, 1997), 159–60. See also Watkins, '"Old Bess in the Ruff"', 101.

11. Anne Barton, 'Harking back to Elizabeth: Ben Jonson and Caroline Nostalgia', *English Literary History*, 48 (1981), 706–31; Elizabeth Pentland, '"Elizian Fields": Elizabeth, Essex, and the Politics of Dissent', in Hageman and Conway, *Resurrecting Elizabeth*, 149–67.

12. Francis Bacon, 'Apophthegms, New and Old', in James Spedding and Douglas Denon Heath (eds), *The Literary and Professional Works of Francis Bacon*, 14 vols (London, 1861–79), ii. 125, 157–8.

13. Bacon, 'Apophthegms, New and Old', 144.

14. A third translator was Thomas Browne, but he worked only on book 4 of the *Annales*, which began at 1587, and his version disappeared without trace. For a discussion of Camden and the English translations, see Patrick Collinson, 'One of Us? William Camden and the Making of History', *Transactions of the Royal Historical Society*, 6th ser., 8 (1998), 151–7, 159, and 'William Camden and the Anti-Myth of Elizabeth: Setting the Mould?', in Doran and Freeman, *The Myth of Elizabeth I*, 79–98.

15. Published in 1625, Darcie's translation was from a French version not Camden's Latin text and covered Camden's first three books.

16. William Camden, *The Historie of the Life and Reigne of the most Renowmed [sic] and Victorious Princesse Elizabeth Late Queene of England Contayning the Most Important and Remarkeable Passages of State, during Her Happy, Long and Prosperous Raigne*, trans. Robert Norton (London, 1630), sigs A1ᵛ, A2ᵛ–A3ʳ.

17. William Camden , *Annales, the True and Royall History of the Famous Empresse Elizabeth Queene of England France and Ireland &c. True Faith's Defendresse of Diuine Renowne and Happy Memory. Wherein All Such Memorable Things as Happened During hir Blessed Raigne…are Exactly Described*, trans. Abraham Darcie (London, 1625), 230–1.

18. Camden, *The Historie of the Life and Reigne*, sigs A1ᵛ, pp. 170, 172, 182, 188.

19. Camden, *Annales, the True and Royall History*, 178.

20. Camden, *The Historie of the Life and Reigne*, 79, 81, 104, 109.

21. Naunton, *Fragmenta regalia*, 4–6.

22. Naunton, *Fragmenta regalia*, 79.

23. Naunton, *Fragmenta regalia*, 19–24.

24. Naunton, *Fragmenta regalia*, 51.

25. Naunton, *Fragmenta regalia*, 64.

26. Naunton, *Fragmenta regalia*, 78.

27. It remained in manuscript until the mid-eighteenth century. In 1827, Henry Ellis printed long extracts in *Original Letters*, iii. 189–96. See Clapham, *Elizabeth of England*, 1–2, 18, 30.

28. Clapham, *Elizabeth of England*, 67, 68, 69, 85–6, 88–90, 96–7. Like Bacon, Clapham included 'moderation' among her princely virtues.
29. Clapham, *Elizabeth of England*, 90–1, 61.
30. Clapham, *Elizabeth of England*, 91–2.
31. Clapham, *Elizabeth of England*, 92–4.
32. Clapham, *Elizabeth of England*, 94–6.
33. Clapham, *Elizabeth of England*, 79.
34. Most notably, but not uniquely, Haigh, *Elizabeth I*, especially ch. 5.
35. For representations of Elizabeth on film, see Susan Doran and Thomas S. Freeman (eds), *The Tudors and Stuarts on Film* (Basingstoke, 2009), chs 6–9, 11–13.

SELECT BIBLIOGRAPHY

MANUSCRIPTS

Bodleian Library, Oxford

Arundel 35
Rawinson Poetry 108
Tanner 7, 76, 78, 79, 84

British Library

Additional 5935, 6177; 8878; 12520; 15891 (letter book of Sir Christopher Hatton); 34216, 35237; 48149; 74286 (Microfilm 2275)
Cotton: Caligula BV, BX, CI, CII, CIII, CIV, CV, CVI, CVIII, CIX, DI, EVIII, EIX; Galba CVI, CIX, DII, EVI; Julius FVI; Titus BXIII, CX; Vespasian CXIV, Vitellius CXVI
Egerton 2026
Harley 168, 260, 787, 1582, 6286, 6991, 6992
Lansdowne 16, 18, 20, 28, 34, 36, 42, 94, 102, 103, 115
Royal 7C 16
Stowe 167

Cambridge University Library

Dd.3. 85(2) and Ii.5.3

Edinburgh University Library

Laing MS

Folger Shakespeare Library

L.a. 37, 39, 40, 45, 265, 267, 269, 461, 707, 724
L.d.612
V.b. 142, 303
X.d.428
Z.e.3

Hatfield House

Cecil Papers

Huntington Library, San Marino, CA

Ellesmere
Hastings
Miscellaneous, 102, 267, 1340, 3135, 30881, 41952, 41954, 41955, 68350

Lambeth Palace Library

649, 650, 651, 657, 658, 664

Lancashire Record Office

The Manuscripts of Lord Kenyon, DDKE/acc. 7840 HMC/fo. 63d

The National Archives, Kew

State Papers 12 (Domestic), 15 (Domestic Addenda), 52 (Scotland), 53 (Mary Queen of Scots), 59 (Borders), 63 (Ireland), 70 (Foreign), 78 (France), 83 (Holland, Flanders), 84 (Holland, Flanders)

National Library of Scotland

Advocates MS 1.2, 35

Northamptonshire Record Office

FH2733

Scottish Record Office

GD

University of Glasgow

ID: 142 <http://www.bessofhardwick.org/letter.jsp?letter=142> (accessed 2014)

PRINTED PRIMARY SOURCES

Acts of the Privy Council of England: AD 1542–June 1631, ed. John Roche Dasent (London, 1890–1907).

Adams, Simon (ed.), 'Household Accounts, and Disbursement Books of Robert Dudley, Earl of Leicester, 1558–1561, 1584–1586', *Camden Fifth Series*, 6 (Cambridge, 1995).

Adlard, George, *Amye Robsart and the Earl of Leycester: A Critical Inquiry into the Authenticity…of Amye Robsart, and of the Libels on the Earl of Leycester, with a Vindication of the Earl by his Nephew Sir Philip Sydney* (London, 1870).

Akrigg, G. P. V. (ed.), *Letters of King James VI and I* (Berkeley and Los Angeles, 1984).

Allen, William, *An Admonition to the Nobility* (n.p., 1588).

Anon., *The Passage of our Most Drad Soueraigne Lady Quene Elyzabeth through the Citie of London to Westminster the Daye before her Coronacion* (London, 1559).

Anon., *An Advertisement Written to a Secretarie* (n.p., 1592).

Anon., *An Humble Supplication to her Majestie* (n.p., 1600).

Anon., *A Lamentable Dittie Composed upon the Death of Robert Lord Devereux Late Earle of Essex who was Beheaded in the Tower of London, upon Ashwednesday in the Morning, 1601* (n.p., 1603).

Anon., *Cabala, sive, scrinia sacra: Mysteries of State and Government…*(London, 1663).

Anon., *The Anonymous Life of William Cecil, Lord Burghley*, ed. Alan J. Smith (Lewiston, NY, 1990).

Archer, Ian W., Adams, Simon, Bernard, G. W., et al. (eds), 'Religion, Politics, and Society in Sixteenth Century England', *Camden Fifth Series*, 22 (Cambridge, 2003).

Arnold, Janet, *'Lost from her Majesties Back': Items of Clothing and Jewels Lost or Given away by Queen Elizabeth I* (London, 1980).

Arnold, Janet, *Queen Elizabeth's Wardrobe Unlock'd: The Inventories of the Wardrobe of Robes Prepared in July 1600* (Leeds, 1988).

Ascham, Roger, *The Scholemaster* (London, 1570).

Aylmer, John, *An Harborowe for Faithfull and Trewe Subjectes, agaynst the Late Blowne Blaste, Concerninge the Government of Women* (London, 1559).

Bacon, Francis, 'Apophthegms, New and Old', in James Spedding and Douglas Denon Heath (eds), *The Literary and Professional Works of Francis Bacon*, 14 vols (London, 1861–79).

Baker, John H. (ed.), *Reports from the Lost Notebooks of Sir James Dyer*, Selden Society, 2 vols (London, 1994).

Barlow, William, *A Sermon Preached at Paules Crosse, on the First Sunday in Lent: Martij 1. 1600* (London, 1603).

Bellany, Alastair, and McCrae, Andrew, *Early Stuart Libels: An Edition of Poetry from Manuscript Sources* <http://www.earlystuartlibels.net/htdocs/pdf/esl.pdf> (accessed August 2014).

Birch, Thomas, *An Historical View of the Negotiations between England, France, and Brussels, 1592–1617* (London, 1749).

Birch, Thomas, *Memoirs of the Reign of Queen Elizabeth, from the Year 1581 till her Death...From the Original Papers of...Anthony Bacon*, 2 vols (London, 1754).

Bradshaw, William, and Digges, Thomas, *Humble Motives for Association to Maintaine Religion Established...* (n.p., 1601).

Brigden, Susan (ed.), 'The Letters of Richard Scudamore to Sir Philip Hoby...', *Camden Miscellany*, 30, fourth series, 39 (London, 1990), 67–148.

Bruce, John (ed.), 'Correspondence of Robert Dudley, Earl of Leicester, during his Government of the Low Countries', *Camden Society*, 27 (1844).

Bruce, John (ed.), 'Letters of Queen Elizabeth and King James VI', *Camden Society*, 46 (1849).

Bruce, John (ed.), 'Correspondence of King James VI of Scotland with Sir Robert Cecil and Others in England during the Reign of Queen Elizabeth: With an Appendix Containing Papers Illustrative of Transactions between King James and Robert Earl of Essex, Principally Published for the First Time from Manuscripts Preserved at Hatfield', *Camden Society*, 78 (1861).

Bruce, John, and Perowne, Thomas (eds), *Correspondence of Matthew Parker* (Cambridge, 1853).

Bülow, Gottfried von, 'Journey through England and Scotland Made by Lupold von Wedel in the Years 1584 and 1585', *Transactions of the Royal Historical Society*, NS 9 (1895), 223–70.

Calderwood, David, *The True History of the Church of Scotland, from the Beginning of the Reformation, unto the End of the Reigne of King James VI...*, ed. T. Thomson, 8 vols (Edinburgh, 1842–9).

Calendar of the Carew Manuscripts, Preserved in the Archiepiscopal Library at Lambeth, ed. J. S. Brewer and William Bullen, 6 vols (London, 1867–73).

Calendar of Patent Rolls Elizabeth I, 36 vols (London, 1939–2005).

Calendar of State Papers, Domestic, ed. Robert Lemon and Mary Anne Everett Green, 6 vols (London, 1856–70).

Calendar of State Papers, Domestic Addenda, ed. Mary Anne Everett Green, 2 vols (London, 1871–2).

Calendar of State Papers, Foreign Series, of the Reign of Elizabeth..., ed. Joseph Stevenson, Allan James Crosby, Arthur John Butler, S. C. Lomas, A. B. Hinds, and R. B. Wernham, 23 vols (London, 1863–1950).

Calendar of State Papers Relating to Ireland..., ed. Hans Claude Hamilton, 11 vols (London, 1871–1943).

Calendar of State Papers, Scotland, ed. Joseph Bain and William K. Boyd, 9 vols (London, 1898–1915).

Calendar of State Papers, Spain, British History Online, ed. G. A. Bergenroth, Royall Tyler, Pascual de Gayangos, and Martin A.S. Hume, 13 vols (London, 1862–1954) <www.british-history.ac.uk> (accessed March 2014).

Calendar of State Papers Relating to English Affairs Preserved Principally in the Archives of Simancas, British History Online, ed. Martin A. S. Hume, 4 vols (London, 1892–9) <www.british-history.ac.uk> (accessed March 2014).

Calendar of State Papers, Venice, British History Online, ed. Rawdon Brown, G. Cavendish Bentinck, and Horatio F. Brown, vols 5–9 (London, 1873–97) <www.british-history.ac.uk> (accessed March 2014).

Camden, William, *Annales, the True and Royall History of the Famous Empresse Elizabeth Queene of England France and Ireland &c. True Faith's Defendresse of Diuine Fenowne and Happy Memory. Wherein all such Memorable Things as Happened during hir Blessed Raigne...are Exactly Described*, trans. Abraham Darcie (London, 1625).

Camden, William, *The Historie of the Life and Reigne of the most Renowmed [sic] and Victorious Princesse Elizabeth Late Queene of England Contayning the Most Important and Remarkeable Passages of State, during Her Happy, Long and Prosperous Raigne*, trans. Robert Norton (London, 1630).

Camden, William, *Annales rerum gestarum Angliae et Hiberniae regnante Elizabetha* (1615, 1625), ed. and trans. Dana F. Sutton <http://www.philological.bham.ac.uk/camden> (accessed March 2014).

Cameron, Annie I. (ed.), *The Warrender Papers*, 2 vols (Edinburgh, 1931–2).

Castelnau, Michel de, *Mémoires*, ed. Jacques Castelnau (Paris, c.1621).

Cecil, William, *The Execution of Justice in England by William Cecil...*, ed. Robert M. Kingdon (Ithaca, NY, 1965).

Churchyarde, Thomas, *A Handeful of Gladsome Verses Given to the Queenes Maiesty at Woodstocke this Prograce* (Oxford, 1592).

Clapham, John, *Elizabeth of England, Certain Observations Concerning the Life and Reign of Queen Elizabeth*, ed. Evelyn Plummer Read and Conyers Read (Philadelphia, 1951).

Clifford, Henry (ed.), *The Life of Lady Jane Dormer, Duchess of Feria* (London, 1887).

Collins, Arthur (ed.), *Letters and Memorials of State...Written and Collected by Sir Henry Sydney...Sir Philip Sydney, and his Brother Sir Robert Sydney...Robert, the Second Earl of Leicester...Philip Lord Viscount Lisle...*, 2 vols (London, 1746).

Cosyn, John, *Musike of Six, and Five Partes* (London, 1585).

Crosby, Allan J., and Bruce, John (eds), 'Accounts and Papers Relating to Mary Queen of Scots', *Camden Society*, 93 (1867).

Dalrymple, Sir David (ed.), *The Secret Correspondence of Sir Robert Cecil with James VI, King of Scotland* (Edinburgh, 1766).

Daus, John, *A Famous Cronicle of Oure Time, Called Sleidanes Commentaries* (London, 1560).

Devereux, Robert, earl of Essex, *An Apologie of the Earle of Essex Against Those which Falsly and Maliciously Taxe Him to be the Onely Hinderer of the Peace and Quiet of his Country* (London, 1600?).

Devereux, Walter Bourchier (ed.), *Lives and Letters of the Devereux, Earls of Essex...1540–1646*, 2 vols (London, 1853).

Dickens, A. G. (ed.), *Clifford Letters of the Sixteenth Century*, Surtees Society, 172 (Durham and London, 1957).

Digby, Everard, *Everard Digbie, his Dissuasive, from Taking away the Lyvings and Goods of the Church* (London, 1590).

Digges, Dudley, *The Compleat Ambassador…*(London, 1655).

Donaldson, Gordon (ed.), *The Memoirs of Sir James Melville of Halhill* (London, 1969).

Dowling, Maria (ed.), 'William Latymer's Chronickille of Anne Bulleyn', *Camden Fourth Series*, 39 (London, 1990).

Elizabeth I: Collected Works, ed. Leah S. Marcus, Janel Mueller, and Mary Beth Rose (Chicago, 2000).

Ellis, Henry, *Original Letters, Illustrative of English History with Notes and Illustrations*, 2nd ser., 4 vols (London, 1827).

Foley, Henry (ed.), *Records of the English Province of the Society of Jesus*, 7 vols (London, 1877–83).

Foxe, John, *The Unabridged Acts and Monuments Online or TAMO* (1576 edn) (HRI Online Publications, Sheffield, 2011) <http//www.johnfoxe.org> (accessed 2012).

Fulwell, Ulpan, *The Flower of Fame* (London, 1575).

[Gascoigne, George], *The Princely Pleasures of Kenilworth Castle 1575* (London, 1576).

Gray, Patrick (ed.), *Letters and Papers Relating to Patrick, Master of Gray, afterwards Seventh Lord Gray* (Edinburgh, 1835).

Groos, G. W. (ed.), *The Diary of Baron Waldstein: A Traveller in Elizabethan England* (London, 1981).

Hall, Edward, *The Union of the Two Noble and Illustre Famelies of Lancastre [and] Yorke…*(London, 1550).

Hardwicke, Philip Lord (ed.), *Miscellaneous State Papers*, 2 vols (London, 1778).

The Harleian Miscellany; or a Collection of Scarce, Curious, and Entertaining Pamphlets, ed. William Oldys, viii (London, 1810).

Harington, Henry (ed.), *Nugae antiquae: A Miscellaneous Collection of Original Papers in Prose and in Verse*, 2 vols (London, 1769–75).

Harington, Henry (ed.), *Nugae antiquae: Being a Miscellaneous Collection of Original Papers, in Prose and Verse…*, newly arranged by Thomas Park, 2 vols (London, 1804).

Harrison, G. B. (ed.), *The Letters of Queen Elizabeth* (London, 1935).

Hartley, T. E. (ed.), *Proceedings in the Parliaments of Elizabeth I*, 3 vols (Leicester, 1981).

Hassell Smith, A., Baker, Gillian, and Kenny, R. W. (eds), *Papers of Nathaniel Bacon of Stiffkey*, 3 vols (Norwich, 1979).

Hatton, Sir Christopher, *A Treatise Concerning Statutes, or Acts of Parliament, and the Exposition Thereof Written by Sir Christopher Hatton* (London, 1677).

Haynes, Samuel (ed.), *A Collection of State Papers: Relating to Affairs in the Reigns of King Henry VIII, King Edward VI, Queen Mary and Queen Elizabeth: from the Year 1542 to 1570 Transcribed from Original Letters and other Authentick Memorials, Never before Publish'd, Left by William Cecill, Lord Burghley, and now Remaining at Hatfield House* (London, 1740).

Hentzner, Paul, *Travels in England, during the Reign of Queen Elizabeth*, ed. and trans. Horace, late earl of Orford (London, 1797).

Historical Manuscripts Commission, 9, *The Manuscripts of the Marquis of Salisbury…*, 24 vols (London, 1883–1976).

Historical Manuscripts Commission, 24, *The Manuscripts of the Duke of Rutland*..., 4 vols (London, 1888–1905).

Historical Manuscripts Commission, 58, *The Manuscripts of the Marquis of Bath*..., 5 vols (London, 1904–80).

Historical Manuscripts Commission, 66, *The Manuscripts of the Earl of Ancaster*... (London, 1907).

Historical Manuscripts Commission, 71, *The Manuscripts of Allan George Finch*, 5 vols (London, 1913–2004).

Historical Manuscripts Commission, 77, *The Manuscripts of Lord de L'Isle and Dudley*..., 6 vols (London, 1933).

Historical Manuscripts Commission, 78, *Report on the Manuscripts of the Late Reginald Rawdon Hastings, Esq, of the Manor House, Ashby de la Zouche*, 4 vols (London, 1928–47).

Hughes, Charles (ed.), 'Nicholas Faunt's Discourse Touching the Office of Principal Secretary of Estate, &c. 1592', *English Historical Review*, 20 (1905), 499–508.

Hughes, Paul L., and Larkin, James F. (eds), *Tudor Royal Proclamations*, 3 vols (New York and London, 1969).

Jeayes, Isaac Herbert (ed.), *Letters of Philip Gawdy of West Harling Norfolk and of London to Various Members of his Family 1579–1616* (London, 1906).

Keith, Robert, *History of the Affairs of Church and State in Scotland, from the Beginning of the Reformation to the Year 1568*, ed. John Parker Lawson and C. J. Lyon, 3 vols (Edinburgh, 1844–50).

Klarwill, Victor von (ed.), *Queen Elizabeth and Some Foreigners: Being a Series of Hitherto Unpublished Letters from the Archives of the Habsburg Family*, trans. T. H. Nash (London, 1928).

Knollys, William. 'Papers Relating to Mary Queen of Scots Communicated by General Sir William Knollys', *Philobiblon Society Miscellanies*, 14 (1872–6), 14–69.

Labanoff, Alexandre (ed.), *Lettres, instructions et mémoires de Marie Stuart, reine d'Écosse*, 7 vols (London, 1844).

Lambarde, William, *Archeion* (London, 1635).

Laneham, Robert, *Robert Laneham's Letter: Describing a Part of the Entertainment unto Queen Elizabeth at the Castel of Kenilworth in 1575*, ed. F. J. Furnivall (New York and London, 1907).

Lawson, Jane A. (ed.), *The Elizabethan New Year's Gift Exchanges 1559–1603* (Oxford, 2013).

Legh, Gerard, *The Accedens of Armory* (London, 1566).

Lettenhove, Kervyn de, *Relations politiques des Pay-Bas et de l'Angleterre, sous le règne de Philippe II* (ed.), 11 vols (Brussels, 1882–1900).

Letters and Papers, Foreign and Domestic, Henry VIII, British History Online, ed. J. S. Brewer, James Gairdner, and R. H. Brodie, 21 vols (London, 1864–1920) <www.british-history.ac.uk> (accessed March 2014).

Lloyd, David, *The Statesmen and Favourites of England since the Reformation* (London, 1665; reissued 1670).

Lodge, Edmund (ed.), *Illustrations of British History, Biography and Manners in the Reigns of Henry VIII...[to] James I, in Papers from the MSS. of the Families of Howard, Talbot and Cecil*..., 3 vols, 2nd edn (London, 1838).

Loke, William, *An Account of the Materials Furnished for the Use of Queen Anne Boleyn, and the Princess Elizabeth*, ed. J. B. Heath (London, 1862–3).

Loomis, Catherine, 'Elizabeth Southwell's Manuscript Account of the Death of Queen Elizabeth [with Text]' in Kirby Farrell and Kathleen M. Swain (eds), *The Mysteries of Elizabeth I: Selections from English Literary Renaissance* (Amherst, c.2003).

Lyell, James P. R., 'A Tract on James VI's Succession to the English Throne', *English Historical* Review, 51 (1936), 289–301.

McClure, Norman Egbert (ed.), *The Letters of John Chamberlain*, i (Philadelphia, 1939).

MacCulloch, Diarmaid (ed. and trans.), 'The *Vita Mariae Angliae Reginae* of Robert Wingfield of Brantham', *Camden Miscelleny*, 28, fourth series, 29 (1984).

Machyn, Henry, *A London Provisioner's Chronicle, 1550–1563* <http://quod.lib. umich.edu/m/machyn/ (accessed 2014).

Maclean, John (ed.), 'Letters from Sir Robert Cecil to Sir George Carew', *Camden Society*, 88 (1864).

MacRobert, A. E., *Mary Queen of Scots and the Casket Letters* (London and New York, 2002).

Maisse de, A. H., *A Journal*, trans. and ed. G. B. Harrison and R. A. Jones (London, 1931).

Manning, C. R. (ed.), 'State Papers Relating to the Custody of the Princess Elizabeth at Woodstock, in 1554; Being Letters between Queen Mary and her Privy Council, and Sir Henry Bedingfield, Knight, of Oxburgh', *Norfolk Archaeology*, 4 (1855).

Mares, F. H. (ed.), *The Memoirs of Robert Carey* (Oxford, 1972).

May, S. W., 'The Poems of Edward de Vere, Seventeenth Earl of Oxford and of Robert Devereux, Second Earl of Essex', *Studies in Philology*, 77 (1980), 5–132.

Melville, Sir James, *Memoirs of his Own Life*, ed. Thomas Thomson (Edinburgh, 1827).

Morris, John (ed.), *The Letter-Books of Sir Amias Poulet: Keeper of Mary Queen of Scots* (London, 1874).

Mueller, Janel, and Scodel, Joshua (eds), *Elizabeth I: Translations 1544–1589* (Chicago, 2009).

Muller, P. L., and Diegerick, A. (eds), *Documents concernant les relations entre le duc d'Anjou et Les Pay-Bas*, (Gravenhage, 1898), iv.

Mumby, Frank, *The Girlhood of Queen Elizabeth: A Narrative in Contemporary Letters* (London, 1909).

Murdin, William (ed.), *A Collection of State Papers, Relating to Affairs in the Reign of Queen Elizabeth, from the Year 1571 to 1596. Transcribed from Original Papers and Other Authentic Memorials Never Before Published, Left by William Cecill, Reposited in the Library of Hatfield House (London, 1759)*.

Naunton, Robert, *Fragmenta regalia* (London, 1650).

Newdigate-Newdegate, Lady (ed.), *Gosssip from a Muniment-Room, Being Passages in the Lives of Anne and Mary Fytton 1574–1618* (London, 1898).

Newton, Thomas, *An Epitaphe upon the Worthy and Honorable Lady, the Lady Knowles* (London, 1569).

Nichols, John, *The Progresses and Public Processions of Queen Elizabeth I: A New Edition of the Early Modern Sources*, ed. Elizabeth Goldring, Faith Eales, Elizabeth Clarke, and Jayne Elisabeth Archer, 5 vols (Oxford, 2014).

Nichols, John Gough (ed.), 'The Chronicle of Queen Jane and of Two Years of Queen Mary...', *Camden Society*, 48 (1849).

Nichols, John Gough (ed.), *Literary Remains of King Edward the Sixth*, 2 vols (London, 1857).

Nicholson, William (ed.), *The Remains of Edmund Grindal: Successively Bishop of London and Archbishop of York and Canterbury*, Parker Society (Cambridge, 1843).

Nicolas, Sir Nicholas Harris, *Life of William Davison, Secretary of State and Privy Counsellor to Queen Elizabeth* (London, 1823).

Nicolas, Sir Nicholas Harris, *The Literary Remains of Lady Jane Grey* (London, 1825).

Nicolas, Sir Nicholas Harris, *Memoirs of the Life and Times of Sir Christopher Hatton* (London, 1847).

Ocland, Christopher, *The Valiant Actes and Victorious Battailes of the English Nation: Elizabeth Queene* (London, 1585).

O'Day, Rosemary (ed.), 'The Letter-Book of Thomas Bentham, Bishop of Coventry and Lichfield. 1560–1561', *Camden Miscellany*, 27, fourth series, 22 (1979), 113–238.

Paule, George, *The Life of the Most Reverend and Religious Prelate John Whitgift, Lord Archbishop of Canterbury* (London, 1612).

Peck, Dwight (ed.), *Leicester's Commonwealth: The Copy of a Letter Written by a Master of Art of Cambridge (1584) and Related Documents* (Athens, OH, and London, 1985) <http://www.dpeck.info/write/leic-comm.pdf> (accessed March 2014).

Pegge, Samuel, *Curialia: Or an Historical Account of Some Branches of the Royal Household*, 3 vols (London, 1782–91).

Philopater, Andreas [*vere* Robert Persons], *Elizabethae Angliae Reginae haeresim Calvinianum propugnantis* (Antwerp, 1592).

Pollen, John Hungerford SJ, *Mary Queen of Scots and the Babington Plot* (Edinburgh, 1922).

Pontaymeri, Alexandre de, *A Womans Woorth* (London, 1599).

Queen Elizabeth I: Selected Works, ed. Steven W. May (New York, 2004).

Rait, Robert, and Cameron, Anne I., *King James's Secret: Negotiations between Elizabeth and James VI, Relating to the Execution of Mary Queen of Scots, from the Warrender Papers* (London, 1927).

R.C., *The Copie of a Letter* (London, 1586).

Read, Conyers (ed.), 'The Bardon Papers: Documents Relating to the Imprisonment and Trial of Mary Queen of Scots', *Camden Third Series*, 17 (1909).

Read, Conyers, 'A Letter from Robert, Earl of Leicester to a Lady', *Huntington Library Bulletin*, 9 (1936), 15–26.

Read, Conyers, 'Lord Burghley's Household Accounts', *Economic History Review*, 9 (1956), 343–8.

Robinson, Hastings (ed.), *The Zurich Letters Comprising the Correspondence of Several English Bishops and Others, with Some of the Helvetian Reformers, during the Early Part of the Reign of Queen Elizabeth 1558–1602* (Cambridge, 1843).

Robinson, Hastings (ed.), *The Zurich Letters (Second Series) Comprising the Correspondence of Several English Bishops and Others, with Some of the Helvetian Reformers, during the Early Part of the Reign of Queen Elizabeth 1558–1602* (Cambridge, 1845).

Robinson, Hastings (ed.), *Original Letters Relative to the English Reformation: Written during the Reigns of King Henry VIII, King Edward VI, and Queen Mary: Chiefly from the Archives of Zurich*, 2 vols (Cambridge, 1846–7).

Rodriguez-Salgado, M. J., and Adams, Simon (eds), 'The Count of Feria's Dispatch to Philip II of 14 November 1558', *Camden Miscellany*, 28, fourth series, 29 (1984).

Rowlands, Samuel, *An Epitaph upon the Death of her Majestie our Late Queen* (London, 1603).

Sander, Nicholas, *The Rise and Growth of the Anglican Schism*, ed. and trans. David Lewis (London, 1877).

Sawyer, Edmund (ed.), *Memorials in the Reigns of Q. Elizabeth and K. James I Collected (Chiefly) from the Original Papers of the Right Honourable Sir Ralph Winwood*, 3 vols (London, 1725).

Scott, Harold Spencer (ed.), *The Journal of Sir Roger Wilbraham, Solicitor-General in Ireland and Master of Requests, for the Years 1593–1616…*(London, 1902).

Shell, Marc (ed.), *Elizabeth's Glass* (Lincoln, NB, 1993).

Smythe, Percy Clinton Sydney, 6th Viscount Strangford (ed.), 'Household Expenses of the Princess Elizabeth 1551–2', *Camden Society*, 55 (1853).

Sorlien, R. P. (ed.), *The Diary of John Manningham of the Middle Temple 1602–1603* (Hanover, NH, 1976).

Speed, John, *The History of Great Britain…* 2nd edn (London, 1623).

Spenser, Edmund, *Works of Spenser: A Variorum Edition*, ed. E. Greenlaw et al., 10 vols (Baltimore, 1932–57).

Statutes of the Realm, ed. A Luders et al., 11 vols (London, 1810–28).

Stevenson, Joseph (ed.), *The Correspondence of Robert Bowes* (Edinburgh, 1842).

Stevenson, Joseph (ed.), *Correspondence of Sir Henry Unton, Ambassador from Queen Elizabeth to Henry IV. King of France, in the Years MDXCI. and MDXCII* (London, 1847).

Stow, John, *The Chronicles of England* (London, 1580).

Strype, John, *Ecclesiastical Memorials…*, 3 vols (Oxford, 1822).

Strype, John, *The Life and Acts of John Whitgift*, 3 vols (Oxford, 1822).

Stump, Donald, and Felch, Susan M. (eds), *Elizabeth I and her Age* (New York, 2009).

Teulet, Jean, *Relations politiques de la France et de l'Espagne avec l'Écosse au XVIe siècle…*, 5 vols (Paris, 1862).

Tytler, Patrick Fraser, *England under the Reigns of Edward VI and Mary*, 2 vols (London, 1839).

Verstegan, Richard, *A Declaration of the True Causes of the Great Troubles* (Antwerp, 1592).

Warwick Bond, R. (ed.), *The Nobility of Women by William Bercher 1559*, Roxburghe Club (London, 1904).

Wingfield, Anthony, *A True Coppie of a Discourse Written by a Gentleman, Employed in the Late Voyage of Spaine and Portingale* (London, 1589).

Wood, Mary Anne Everett (ed.), *Letters of Royal and Illustrious Ladies of Great Britain*, 3 vols (London, 1846).

Wotton, Sir Henry (ed.), *Reliquiae Wottonianae* (London, 1672).

Wright, Thomas, *Queen Elizabeth and her Times: A Series of Original Letters…*, 2 vols (London, 1838).

SECONDARY SOURCES

Adams, Simon, 'The Patronage of the Crown in Elizabethan Politics: The 1590s in Perspective', in John Guy (ed.), *The Reign of Elizabeth I: Court and Culture in the Last Decade* (Cambridge, 1995), 20–45.

Adams, Simon, *Leicester and the Court* (Manchester, 2002).

Adams, Simon, 'Elizabeth I and the Sovereignty of the Netherlands 1576–1585', *Transactions of the Royal Historical Society*, 6th ser., 14 (2004), 309–19.

Alexander, Gavin, *Writing after Sidney: The Literary Response to Sir Philip Sidney 1586–1640* (Oxford, 2006).

Alford, Stephen, *The Early Elizabethan Polity: William Cecil and the British Succession Crisis, 1558–1569* (Cambridge, 2002).

Alford, Stephen, 'The Political Creed of William Cecil', in John F. McDiarmid (ed.), *The Monarchical Republic of Early Modern England* (Aldershot, 2007), 75–90.

Alford, Stephen, 'Politicians and Statesmen II: William Cecil, Lord Burghley (1520–98)', *State Papers Online, 1509–1714*, Thomson Learning EMEA Lt (Reading, 2007).

Alford, Stephen, *Burghley: William Cecil at the Court of Elizabeth I* (New Haven and London, 2008).

Alford, Stephen, 'Some Elizabethan Spies in the Office of Sir Francis Walsingham', in Robyn Adams and Rosanna Cox (eds), *Diplomacy and Early Modern Culture* (Basingstoke, 2011), 46–62.

Alford, Stephen, *The Watchers: A Secret History of the Reign of Elizabeth I* (London, 2012).

Airs, Malcolm, ' "Pomp or Glory": The Influence of Theobalds', in Pauline Croft (ed.), *Patronage, Culture and Power: The Early Cecils* (New Haven and London, 2002), 3–19.

Allen, Paul C., *Philip III and the Pax Hispanica, 1598–1621* (New Haven and London).

Allinson, Rayne, 'Queen Elizabeth I and the 'Nomination' of the Young Prince of Scotland', *Notes and Queries*, 53 (2006), 425–7.

Allinson, Rayne, *Monarchy of Letters* (Basingstoke, 2012).

Barton, Anne, 'Harking Back to Elizabeth: Ben Jonson and Caroline Nostalgia', *English Literary History*, 48 (1981), 706–31.

Beer, Anna, *Bess: The Life of Lady Ralegh, Wife to Sir Walter* (London, 2004).

Booth, Ted W., 'A Switch of Language: Elizabeth I's Use of the Vernacular as a Key to her Early Protestantism', *Journal of Anglican Studies*, 11 (2013), 100–13.

Bossy, John, *Under the Molehill: An Elizabethan Spy Story* (New Haven and London, 2001).

Bowler, Gerald, ' "An axe or an acte": The Parliament of 1572 and Resistance Theory in Early Elizabethan England', *Canadian Journal of History*, 19 (1984), 349–59.

Brackenbury, Henry, *The History of His Majesty's Body Guard of the Honourable Corps of Gentlemen-at-Arms* (London, 1905).

Bradford, Charles Angell, *Blanche Parry: Queen Elizabeth's Gentlewoman* (London, 1935).

Bradford, Charles Angell, *Helena, Marchioness of Northampton* (London, 1936).

Bradley, E. T., *Life of the Lady Arabella Stuart*, 2 vols (London, 1889).

Brennan, Michael G., *The Sidneys of Penshurst and the Monarchy, 1500–1700* (Burlington, VT, 2006).

Brooks, Eric St John, *Sir Christopher Hatton* (London, 1946).

Bundesen, Kristin, 'Lousy with Cousins: Elizabeth I's Family at Court', in Liz Oakley-Brown and Louise J. Wilkinson (eds), *The Rituals and Rhetoric of Queenship: Medieval to Early Modern* (Dublin, 2009), 74–89.

Butler, Chris, and Maley, Willy, '"Bringing Rebellion Broached on his Sword": Essex and Ireland', in Annaliese Connolly and Lisa Hopkins (eds), *Essex* (Manchester, 2013), 133–50.

Cavanagh, Sheila, 'The Bad Seed: Princess Elizabeth and the Seymour Incident', in Julia M. Walker (ed.), *Dissing Elizabeth: Negative Representations of Gloriana* (Durham, NC, 1998), 9–29.

Cole, Mary Hill, *The Portable Queen: Elizabeth I and the Politics of Ceremony* (Amherst, 1999).

Collinson, Patrick, *The Elizabethan Puritan Movement* (London, 1967).

Collinson, Patrick, *Archbishop Grindal, 1519–1583: The Struggle for a Reformed Church* (London, 1979).

Collinson, Patrick, *Godly People: Essays on English Protestantism and Puritanism* (London, 1983).

Collinson, Patrick, 'The Monarchical Republic of Queen Elizabeth', *John Rylands University Library of Manchester*, 69 (1987), 394–424.

Collinson, Patrick, 'One of Us? William Camden and the Making of History', *Transactions of the Royal Historical Society*, 6th ser., 8 (1998), 139–63.

Collinson, Patrick, 'William Camden and the Anti-Myth of Elizabeth: Setting the Mould?', in Susan Doran and Thomas S. Freeman (eds), *The Myth of Elizabeth I* (Basingstoke, 2003), 79–98.

Collinson, Patrick, *Richard Bancroft and Elizabethan Anti-Puritanism* (Cambridge, 2013).

Cooper, John, *The Queen's Agent: Francis Walsingham at the Court of Elizabeth I* (London, 2011).

Courtney, Alexander, 'The Scottish King and the English Court: The Secret Correspondence of James VI, 1601–3', in Susan Doran and Paulina Kewes (eds), *Doubtful and Dangerous: The Question of Succession in Late Elizabethan England* (Manchester, 2014), 134–51.

Coward, Barry, *The Stanleys, Lord Stanley and Earls of Derby 1385–1672* (Manchester, 1983).

Crankshaw, David J., 'The Tudor Privy Council, c.1540–1603', *State Papers Online, 1509–1714*, Cengage Learning EMEA Ltd (Reading, 2009).

Cressy, David, *Dangerous Talk: Scandalous, Seditious, and Treasonable Speech in Pre-Modern England* (Oxford 2010).

Croft, Pauline, 'The Reputation of Robert Cecil: Libels, Political Opinion and Popular Awareness in the Early Seventeenth Century', *Transactions of the Royal Historical Society*, 6th ser., 1 (1991), 43–69.

Croft, Pauline, 'Can a Bureaucrat be a Favourite? Robert Cecil and the Strategies of Power', in J. H. Elliott and L. W. B. Brockliss (eds), *The World of the Favourite* (New Haven and London, 1999), 81–95.

Croft, Pauline, 'Rex Pacificus, Robert Cecil and the 1604 Peace with Spain', in Glenn Burgess, Rowland Wymer, and Jason Lawrence (eds), *The Accession of James I: Historical and Cultural Consequences* (Basingstoke, 2006), 140–54.

Cunningham, James P., *Dancing in the Inns of Court* (London, 1965).

Danner, Bruce, *Edmund Spenser's War on Lord Burghley* (New York, 2011).

Daybell, James, 'Women, Politics, and Domesticity: The Scribal Presentation of Lady Rich's Letter to Elizabeth I', in Anne Lawrence-Mathers and Phillipa Hardman (eds), *Women and Writing, c.1340–c.1650: The Domestication of Print Culture* (York, 2010), 111–30.

Deacon, Malcolm, 'Sir Christopher Hatton', *Northamptonshire Past and Present*, 64 (2011), 22–33.

Dean, David, 'Elizabethan Government and Politics', in Robert Tittler and Norman Jones (eds), *A Companion to Tudor England* (Oxford, 2004).

De Lisle, Leanda, *The Sisters who would be Queen* (London, 2008).

Dickinson, Janet, *Court Politics and the Earl of Essex, 1589–1601* (London, 2012).

Dolman, Brett, 'Wishful Thinking: Reading the Portraits of Henry VIII's Queens', in Thomas Betteridge and Suzannah Lipscomb (eds), *Henry VIII and the Court* (Farnham, 2013).

Donaldson, Gordon, *The First Trial of Mary Queen of Scots* (London, 1969).

Doran, Susan, *Monarchy and Matrimony: The Courtships of Elizabeth I* (London, 1996).

Doran, Susan, 'Revenge her Foul and Most Unnatural Murder: The Impact of Mary Stewart's Execution on Anglo-Scottish Relations', *History*, 85 (2000), 589–607.

Doran, Susan, 'Loving and Affectionate Cousins? The Relationship between Elizabeth I and James VI of Scotland', in Susan Doran and Glenn Richardson (eds), *Tudor England and its Neighbours* (Basingstoke, 2005), 203–34.

Doran, Susan, 'Elizabeth I and her Favourites: The Case of Sir Walter Ralegh', in Donald Stump, Linda Schenk, and Carole Levin (eds), *Elizabeth I and the 'Sovereign Arts': Essays in Literature, History, and Culture* (Tucson, 2011), 157–74.

Doran, Susan, and Freeman, Thomas S. (eds), *The Myth of Elizabeth I* (Basingstoke, 2003).

Doran, Susan, and Jones, Norman (eds), *The Elizabethan World* (London, 2011).

Doran, Susan, and Kewes, Paulina (eds), *Doubtful and Dangerous: The Question of Succession in Late Elizabethan England* (Manchester, 2014).

Dunn, Jane, *Elizabeth and Mary: Cousins, Rivals, Queens* (New York, 2004).

Edwards, Warwick, 'The Walsingham Consort Books', *Music and Letters*, 55 (1974), 209–14.

Ellis, Roger, 'Elizabeth Tudor's Juvenile Translations', *Translation and Literature*, 18 (2009), 157–80.

Elton, G. R., *The Parliament of England 1559–81* (Cambridge, 1989).

Erler, Mary C., 'Sir John Davies and the Rainbow Portrait of Queen Elizabeth', *Modern Philology*, 84 (1987), 359–71.

Evans, Florence M. G., *The Principal Secretary of State* (Manchester, 1923).

Fischlin, Daniel, '"To eate the flesh of kings": James VI and I, Apocalypse, Nation and Sovereignty', in Daniel Fischlin and Mark Fortier (eds), *Royal Subjects: Essays on the Writings of James VI and I* (Detroit, 2002), 388–420.

Fraser, Antonia, *Mary Queen of Scots* (London, 1969).

Frescoln, Katherine P., 'A Letter from Thomas Randolph to the Earl of Leicester', *Huntington Library Quarterly*, 37 (1973), 83–8.

Frye, Susan, and Robertson, Karen (eds), *Maids and Mistresses, Cousins and Queens* (Oxford, 1999).

Gajda, Alexandra, 'Debating War and Peace in Late Elizabethan England', *Historical Journal*, 52 (2009), 851–78.

Gajda, Alexandra, *The Earl of Essex and Late Elizabethan Political Culture* (Oxford, 2012).

Gajda, Alexandra, 'Essex and "Politic History"', in Annaliese Connolly and Lisa Hopkins (eds), *Essex* (Manchester, 2013), 237–62.

Gajda, Alexandra, 'Essex and the Popish Plot', in Susan Doran and Paulina Kewes (eds), *Doubtful and Dangerous: The Question of Succession in Late Elizabethan England* (Manchester, 2014), 115–33.

Garrett, Christina Hallowell, *The Marian Exiles: A Study in the Origins of Eliza-bethan Puritanism* (Cambridge, 1938).

Gazzard, Hugh, '"Many a *herdsman* more disposde to morne": Peele, Campion, and the Portugal Expedition of 1589', *Review of English Studies*, 57 (2006), 16–42.

Gazzard, Hugh, '"Idle papers": An Apology of the Earl of Essex', in Annaliese Connolly and Lisa Hopkins (eds), *Essex* (Manchester, 2013), 179–200.

Gehring, David Scott, *Anglo-German Relations and the Protestant Cause* (London, 2013).

Gibson, Jonathan, 'Katherine Parr, Princess Elizabeth and the Crucified Christ', in Victoria E. Burke and Jonathan Gibson (eds), *Early Modern Women's Manuscript Writing: Selected Papers from the Trinity/Trent Colloquium* (Aldershot, 2004), 33–50.

Goldring, Elizabeth, 'Portraits of Queen Elizabeth I and the Earl of Leicester for Kenilworth Castle', *Burlington Magazine*, 147 (2005), 654–60.

Goldring, Elizabeth, 'Portraiture, Patronage and the Progresses: Robert Dudley, Earl of Leicester and the Kenilworth Festivities of 1575', in Jayne Elizabeth Archer, Elizabeth Goldring, and Sarah Knight (eds), *The Progresses, Pageants, & Entertainments of Queen Elizabeth I* (Oxford, 2007), 163–88.

Gras, N. S. B., 'Tudor "Books of Rates": A Chapter in the History of the English Customs', *Quarterly Journal of Economics* (1912), 766–75.

Graves, Michael A. R., *Burghley: William Cecil, Lord Burghley* (London and New York, 1998).

Green, Dominic, *The Double Life of Doctor Lopez: Spies, Shakespeare and the Plot to Poison Elizabeth I* (London 2003).

Gristwood, Sarah, *Elizabeth and Leicester: Power, Passion, Politics* (London, 2007).

Guy, John, *The Court of Star Chamber and its Records to the Reign of Elizabeth I* (London, 1985).

Guy, John, *Tudor England* (Oxford and New York, 1990).

Guy, John, 'The Rhetoric of Counsel in Early-Modern England', in Dale Hoak (ed.), *Tudor Political Culture* (Cambridge, 1995), 292–310.

Guy, John (ed.), *The Reign of Elizabeth I: Court and Culture in the Last Decade* (Cambridge, 1995).

Guy, John, *My Heart is My Own* (London, 2004).

Guy, John, *The Children of Henry VIII* (Oxford, 2013).

Guy, John, *Imagining and Detecting Conspiracy, 1571–1605* <http://www.tudors.org/public-lectures/imagining-and-detecting-conspiracy-1571-1605> (accessed 31 October 2013).

Hageman, Elizabeth H., and Conway, Katherine (eds), *Resurrecting Elizabeth I in Seventeenth-Century England* (Cranbury, NJ, 2007).

Haigh, Christopher, *Elizabeth I* (Harlow, 1988).

Hammer, Paul E. J., 'Myth-Making: Politics, Propaganda and the Capture of Cadiz in 1596', *Historical Journal*, 40 (1997), 621–42.

Hammer, Paul E. J., 'New Light on the Cadiz Expedition of 1596', *Historical Research*, 70 (1997), 182–202.

Hammer, Paul E. J., 'Upstaging the Queen: The Earl of Essex, Francis Bacon and the Accession Day Celebrations of 1595', in David Bevington and Peter Holbrook (eds), *The Politics of the Stuart Court Masque* (Cambridge, 1998), 41–66.

Hammer, Paul E. J., *The Polarisation of Elizabethan Politics* (Cambridge, 1999).

Hammer, Paul E. J., 'Sex and the Virgin Queen: Aristocratic Concupiscence and the Court of Elizabeth I', *Sixteenth Century Journal*, 31 (2000), 77–97.

Hammer, Paul E. J., 'The Smiling Crocodile: The Earl of Essex and Late-Elizabethan Popularity', in Peter Lake and Steven Pincus (eds), *The Politics of the Public Sphere in Early Modern England* (Manchester, 2008), 95–115.

Hammer, Paul E. J., 'Shakespeare's *Richard II*: The Play of 7 February 1601, and the Essex Rising', *Shakespeare Quarterly*, 59 (2008), 1–35.

Handover, P. M., *The Second Cecil: The Rise to Power 1563–1604 of Sir Robert Cecil, Later First Earl of Salisbury* (London, 1959).

Harrison, G. B., *The Life and Death of Robert Devereux, Earl of Essex* (London, 1937).

Harthorne, Emily Sophia, *Memorials of Holdenby* (London, 1868).

Hassall, W. O., 'The Books of Sir Christopher Hatton at Holkham', *Library*, 5th ser., 5 (1950), 1–13.

Henry, L. W., 'The Earl of Essex and Ireland, 1599', *Bulletin of the Institute of Historical Research*, 85 (1959), 1–23.

Herman, Peter C., 'Authorship and the Royal "I" King James VI/I and the Politics of Monarchic Verse', *Renaissance Quarterly*, 54 (2001), 1495–1530.

Herman, Peter C., *Royal Poetrie: Monarchic Verse and the Political Imaginary of Early Modern England* (Ithaca, NY, 2010).

Hicks, Leo, 'Sir Robert Cecil, Father Parsons, and the Succession, 1600–1', *Archivum Historicum Societatis Iesu*, 24 (1955), 95–139.

Highley, Christopher, 'A "pestilent and seditious book": Nicholas Sander's *Schismatis Anglicani* and Catholic Histories of the Reformation', in Paulina Kewes (ed.), *The Uses of History in Early Modern England* (San Marino, CA, 2006), 147–65.

History of Parliament <historyofparliamentonline.org/volume/1558–1603/member/> (accessed 12 March 2014).

Houlistan, Victor, 'The Lord Treasurer and the Jesuit: Robert Persons's Satirical *Responsio* to the 1591 Proclamation', *Sixteenth Century Journal*, 32 (2001), 383–401.

Hoyle, Richard, *The Estates of the English Crown 1558–1640* (Cambridge, 1992).

Hume, David, *The History of England: Under the House of Tudor*, 2 vols (London, 1759).

Hurstfield, Joel, 'Lord Burghley as Master of the Court of Wards, 1561–98', *Transactions of the Royal Historical Society*, 31 (1949), 95–114.

Hurstfield, Joel, *The Queen's Wards* (London, 1958).

Hurstfield, Joel, 'The Succession Struggle in Late Elizabethan England', in Joel Hurstfield, *Freedom, Corruption and Government in Elizabethan England* (London, 1973), 104–36.

Husselby, Jill, 'The Politics of Pleasure: William Cecil and Burghley House', in Pauline Croft (ed.), *Patronage, Culture and Power: The Early Cecils* (New Haven and London, 2002), 21–45.

Ives, Eric, *Lady Jane Grey: A Tudor Mystery* (Oxford, 2009).

Ives, Eric W., 'Tudor Dynastic Problems Revisited', *Historical Research*, 81 (2008), 255–79.

James, Susan E., *Kateryn Parr: The Making of a Queen* (Aldershot, 1999).

Katz, David S., *The Jews in the History of England 1485–1850* (Oxford, 1994).

Kellar, Clare, *Scotland, England and the Reformation 1534–61* (Oxford, 2003).

Kewes, Paulina, 'Two Queens, One Inventory: The Lives of Mary and Elizabeth Tudor', in Kevin Sharpe and Steven N. Zwicker (eds), *Writing Lives: Biography and Textuality, Identity and Representation in Early Modern England* (Oxford, 2008), 187–207.

Kewes, Paulina, 'Godly Queens: The Royal Iconographies of Mary and Elizabeth', in Alice Hunt and Anna Whitelock (eds), *Tudor Queenship: The Reigns of Mary and Elizabeth* (Basingstoke, 2010), 47–62.

Klein, Lisa M., 'Your Humble Handmaid: Elizabethan Gifts of Needlework', *Renaissance Quarterly*, 50 (1997), 476–83.

Klinck, Dennis, *Conscience, Equity and the Court of Chancery in Early Modern England* (Farnham, 2010).

Lake, Peter, 'Puritanism, (Monarchical) Republicanism and Monarchy: Or John Whitgift, Antipuritanism and the "Invention" of Popularity', *Journal of Medieval and Early Modern Studies*, 40 (2010), 463–95.

Lawson, Jane A., 'This Remembrance of the New Year: Books Given to Queen Elizabeth as New Year's Gifts', in Peter Beal and Grace Ioppolo (eds), *Elizabeth I and the Culture of Writing* (London, 2007), 133–71.

Levin, Carole, '"Would I give you help and succour": Elizabeth I and the Politics of Touch', *Albion*, 21 (1989), 191–205.

Levin, Carole, *The Heart and Stomach of a King: Elizabeth and the Politics of Sex and Power* (Philadelphia, 1994).

Levin, Carole, '"We shall never have a merry world while the queene lyveth": Gender, Monarchy and the Power of Seditious Words', in Julia M. Walker (ed.), *Dissing Elizabeth: Negative Representations of Gloriana* (Durham, NC, 1998), 77–95.

Levine, Mortimer, *The Early Elizabethan Succession Question, 1558–1568* (Stanford, CA, 1966).

Loades, David, *Elizabeth I* (London, 2003).

Lockie, D. M., 'The Political Career of the Bishop of Ross, 1568–80', *University of Birmingham Historical Journal*, 4 (1954), 109–11.

Loomis, Catherine, *The Death of Elizabeth I: Remembering and Reconstructing the Virgin Queen* (Basingstoke, 2010).

MacCaffrey, Wallace T. *The Shaping of the Elizabethan Regime* (London, 1969).

MacCaffrey, Wallace T., *Queen Elizabeth and the Making of Policy, 1572–1588* (Princeton, 1981).

MacCaffrey, Wallace T., *Elizabeth I, War and Politics, 1588–1603* (Princeton, 1992).

MacCaffrey, Wallace T., 'The Newhaven Expedition, 1562–1563', *Historical Journal*, 40 (1997), 1–21.

McCoog, Thomas M. SJ, *The Society of Jesus in Ireland, Scotland, and England 1541–1588: 'Our Way of Proceeding?'* (Leiden, 1996).

McCoy, Richard, *The Rites of Knighthood: The Literature and Politics of Elizabethan Chivalry* (Berkeley, 1989).

McGowan, Margaret M., *Dance in the Renaissance* (New Haven and London, 2008).

Machielsen, Jan, 'The Lion, the Witch, and the King: Thomas Stapleton's *Apologia pro Rege Catholico Philippo II* (1592)', *English Historical Review*, 129 (2014), 19–46.

Mack, Peter, 'Elizabethan Parliamentary Oratory', *Huntington Library Quarterly*, 64 (2001), 23–61.

McKeen, David, *A Memory of Honour: The Life of William Brooke, Lord Cobham*, 2 vols (Salzburg, 1986).

McLaren, Anne, 'The Quest for a King: Gender, Marriage, and Succession in Elizabethan England', *Journal of British Studies*, 41 (2002), 259–90.

McLaren, Anne, 'Memorializing Mary and Elizabeth', in Alice Hunt and Anna Whitelock (eds), *Tudor Queenship: The Reigns of Mary and Elizabeth* (Basingstoke, 2010).

McManus, Caroline, 'Reading the Margins: Female Courtiers in the Portraits of Elizabeth I', *Ben Jonson Journal*, 2 (1995), 31–58.

McMillan, Scott, and MacLean, Sally-Beth, *The Queen's Men and their Plays* (Cambridge, 1998).

Maginn, Christopher, '"Behind every great woman…": William Cecil and the Elizabethan Conquest of Ireland', *History Ireland*, 20 (2012), 4–17.

Manley, Lawrence, 'From Strange's Men to Pembroke's Men: 2 Henry VI and the First Part of the Contention', *Shakespeare Quarterly*, 54 (2003), 253–87.

Mears, Natalie, 'Love-Making and Diplomacy: Elizabeth I and the Anjou Marriage Negotiations, *c.*1578–1582', *History*, 86 (2001), 442–66.

Mears, Natalie, 'Courts, Courtiers and Culture in Tudor England', *Historical Journal*, 46 (2003), 703–22.

Mears, Natalie, 'Politics in the Elizabethan Privy Chamber: Lady Mary Sidney and Kat Ashley', in James Daybell (ed.), *Women and Politics in Early Modern England, 1450–1700* (Aldershot, 2004), 67–82.

Mears, Natalie, *Queenship and Political Discourse in the Elizabethan Realms* (Cambridge, 2005).

Merton, Charlotte, 'Women, Friendship and Memory', in Alice Hunt and Anna Whitelock (eds), *Tudor Queenship: The Reigns of Mary and Elizabeth* (Basingstoke and New York, 2010), 239–50.

Miller, Amos C., *Sir Henry Killigrew* (Leicester, 1963).

Montrose, Louis, 'Spenser and the Elizabethan Political Imaginary', *English Literary History*, 69 (2002), 907–46.

Morgan, Hiram (ed.), *The Battle of Kinsale* (Bray, 2004).

Morris, Richard, '"I was never more in love with an olde howse nor never newe worke coulde be better bestowed": The Earl of Leicester's Remodelling of Kenilworth Castle for Queen Elizabeth I', *Antiquaries Journal*, 89 (2009), 241–305.

Nares, Edward, *Memoirs of the Life and Administration of…William Cecil, Lord Burghley*, 3 vols (London, 1828–31).

Neale, J. E., 'The Elizabethan Political Scene', *Proceedings of the British Academy*, 34 (1948).

Neale, J. E., *Elizabeth I and her Parliaments*, 2 vols (London, 1953–7).

Oxford Dictionary of National Biography, ed. Lawrence Goldman. Online edn. (Oxford, 2014).

Parker, Geoffrey, 'The Place of Tudor England in the Messianic Vision of Philip II of Spain', *Transactions of the Royal Historical Society*, 6th ser., 12 (2002), 167–221.

Parry, Glyn, *The Arch-Conjuror of England: John Dee* (New Haven and London, 2011).

Parry, Glyn, 'Occult Philosophy and Politics: Why John Dee Wrote his *Compendious rehearsal* in November 1592', *Studies in History and Philosophy of Science Part A*, 43 (2012), 480–8.

Partridge, Mary, 'Lord Burghley and *Il Cortegiano*: Civil and Martial Models of Courtliness in Elizabethan England', *Transactions of the Royal Historical Society*, 6th ser., 19 (2009), 95–116.

Payne, Helen, 'The Cecil Women at Court', in Pauline Croft (ed.), *Patronage, Culture and Power: The Early Cecils* (New Haven, 2002).

Perry, Curtis, *Literature and Favouritism in Early Modern England* (Cambridge, 2006).

Perry, Maria, *The Word of a Prince: A Life of Elizabeth I* (Woodbridge, 1990).

Pevsner, Nikolaus, *The Buildings of England: Northamptonshire*, 2nd edn (New Haven, 2002).

Prescott, Anne Lake, 'The Pearl of the Valois and Elizabeth I: Marguerite de Navarre's *Miroir* and Tudor England', in Margaret P. Hannay (ed.), *Silent but for the Word: Tudor Women as Patrons, Translators, and Writers of Religious Works* (Kent, OH , 1985), 61–76.

Prest, Wilfrid R., *The Inns of Court under Elizabeth I and the Early Stuarts* (Totawa, NJ, 1972).

Pulman, Michael Barraclough. *The Elizabethan Privy Council in the Fifteen-Seventies* (Berkeley and Los Angeles, 1971).

Read, Conyers, *Mr Secretary Walsingham and the Policy of Queen Elizabeth*, 3 vols (Cambridge and Oxford, 1925).

Read, Conyers, 'William Cecil and Elizabethan Public Relations', in S. T. Bindoff et al. (eds), *Elizabethan Government and Society* (London, 1961), 21–55.

Read, Conyers, *Mr Secretary Cecil and Queen Elizabeth* (London, 1955; paperback edn, 1965).

Read, Conyers, *Lord Burghley and Queen Elizabeth* (1961; paperback edn,1965).

Richards, Judith, 'Examples and Admonitions: What Mary Demonstrated for Elizabeth', in Alice Hunt and Anna Whitelock (eds), *Tudor Queenship: The Reigns of Mary and Elizabeth* (Basingstoke and New York, 2010), 31–46.

Richards, Judith, *Elizabeth I* (Abingdon, 2012).

Richardson, Ruth E., *Mistress Blanche, Queen Elizabeth I's Confidante* (Woonton, 2007).

Rickard, Jane, *Authorship and Authority: The Writings of James VI and I* (Manchester, 2007).

Rickman, Johanna, *Love, Lust, and License in Early Modern England: Illicit Sex and the Nobility* (London, 2008).

Scarisbrick, Diana, *Tudor and Jacobean Jewellery* (London, 1995).

Schutte, William M., 'Thomas Churchyard's "Dollfull discourse" and the Death of Lady Katherine Grey', *Sixteenth Century Journal*, 15 (1984), 471–87.

Scott-Warren, Jason, 'Was Elizabeth I Richard II? The Authenticity of Lambarde's "Conversation"', *Review of English Studies*, 64 (2012), 208–30.

Shephard, Robert, 'Sexual Rumours in English Politics: The Cases of Elizabeth I and James I', in Jacqueline Murray and Konrad Eisenbichler (eds), *Desire and Discipline* (Toronto and London, 1996), 101–22.

Skidmore, Chris, *Death and the Virgin* (London, 2011).

Skidmore, Warren, *Lady Mary Scudamore (c.1550–1603)*, Occasional Papers, no. 29 <http://www.skidmoregenealogy.com/.../OccPap_no._29_revised_pdf> (accessed August 2014).

Smith, Logan Pearsall, *The Life and Letters of Sir Henry Wotton*, 2 vols (Oxford, 1907).

Starkey, David, 'Representation through Intimacy: A Study in the Symbolism of Monarchy', in I. Lewis (ed.), *Symbols and Sentiments: Cross-Cultural Studies in Symbolism* (London, 1977), 187–224.

Starkey, David, *Elizabeth: Apprenticeship* (London, 2000).

Stewart, Richard W., 'The "Irish Road": Military Supply and Arms for Elizabeth's Army during the O'Neill Rebellion in Ireland, 1598–1601', in Mark Charles Fissel (ed.), *War and Government in Britain, 1598–1650* (Manchester, 1991), 16–37.

Stone, Lawrence, 'The Fruits of Office: The Case of Robert Cecil, First Earl of Salisbury', in F. J. Fisher (ed.), *Essays in the Economic and Social History of Tudor and Stuart England* (Cambridge, 1961), 89–116.

Strickland, Agnes, *Lives of the Tudor Princesses Including Lady Jane Gray and her Sisters* (London, 1868).

Strong, Roy, *The Tudor and Stuart Monarchy: Pageantry, Painting, Iconography*, 2 vols (Woodbridge, 1995).

Strong, Roy, *The Cult of Elizabeth: Elizabethan Portraiture and Pageantry* (London, 1999).

Strong, Roy, *Gloriana: The Portraits of Queen Elizabeth I* (New York, 1987; London, 2003).

Summit, Jennifer, '"The arte of a ladies penne": Elizabeth I and the Poetics of Queenship', *English Literary Renaissance*, 26 (1996), 395–422.

Sutton, James M., *Materializing Space at an Early Modern Prodigy House: The Cecils at Theobalds, 1564–1607* (Aldershot, 2004).

Teague, Frances, 'Princess Elizabeth's Hand in *The Glass of the Sinful Soul*', *English Manuscript Studies 1100–1700*, 9 (2000), 33–48.

Thomas, Keith, *The Ends of Life: Roads to Fulfilment in Early Modern England* (Oxford, 2009).

Tighe, W. J., 'The Counsel of Thomas Radcliffe, Earl of Sussex, to Queen Elizabeth I Concerning the Revolt of the Netherlands, September 1578', *Sixteenth Century Journal*, 18 (1987), 323–31.

Tittler, Robert, *The Reign of Mary I* (London, 1983).

Usher, Brett, *William Cecil and Episcopacy, 1559–1577* (Aldershot, 2003).

Varlow, Sally, ' Sir Francis Knollys's Latin Dictionary: New Evidence for Katherine Carey', *Historical Research*, 80 (2007), 315–23.

Varlow, Sally, *The Lady Penelope: The Lost Tale of Love and Politics in the Court of Elizabeth I* (London, 2007).

Waller, G., *Edmund Spenser, a Literary Life* (London, 1994).

Wallis, Helen (ed.), *Sir Francis Drake: An Exhibition to Commemorate Francis Drake's Voyage around the World 1577–80* (London, 1977).

Ward, B. M., 'Further Research on *A hundreth sundrie flowres*', *Review of English Studies*, 13 (1928), 35–48.

Warnicke, Retha M., 'Conflicting Rhetoric about Tudor Women: The Example of Queen Anne Boleyn', in Carole Levin and Patricia A. Sullivan (eds), *Political Rhetoric, Power, and Renaissance Women* (Albany, 1995), 39–55.

Warnicke, Retha M., *Mary Queen of Scots* (Abingdon, 2006).

Warnicke, Retha M., *Wicked Women of Tudor England: Queens, Aristocrats, Commoners, Queenship and Power* (Basingstoke, 2012).

Watkins, John, '"Old Bess in the Ruff": Remembering Elizabeth I, 1625–1660', *English Literary Renaissance*, 30 (2000), 95–116.

Wernham, R. B., *The Return of the Armadas: The Last Years of the Elizabethan War against Spain, 1595–1603* (Oxford, 1994).

Whitelock, Anna, *Elizabeth's Bedfellows: An Intimate History of the Queen's Court* (London, 2012).

Willan, T. S., *A Tudor Book of Rates* (London, 1962).

Williams, E., *Early Holborn and the Legal Quarter of London* (London, 1927).

Williams, Penry, 'Court and Polity under Elizabeth I', *John Rylands University Library*, 65 (1983), 259–86.

Wilson, Derek, *The World Encompassed: Drake's Great Voyage 1577–1580* (London, 1977, 1998).

Wilson, Derek, *The Uncrowned Kings of England* (London, 2005).

Wilson, Violet A., *Queen Elizabeth's Maids Of Honour and Ladies of the Privy Chamber* (London, 1922).

Wollock, Jennifer G., *Rethinking Chivalry and Courtly Love* (Santa Barbara, CA, 2011).

Wood, Andy, 'The Queen is "a goggyll eyed hoore": Gender and Seditious Speech in Early Modern England', in Nicholas Tyacke (ed.), *The English Revolution c.1590–1720* (Manchester, 2007), 81–94.

Wood, Richard, '"Cleverly playing the stoic": The Earl of Essex, Sir Philip Sidney and Surviving Elizabeth's Court', in Annaliese Connolly and Lisa Hopkins (eds), *Essex* (Manchester and New York, 2013), 25–46.

Woodhouse, Elisabeth, 'Propaganda in Paradise: The Symbolic Garden Created by the Earl of Leicester at Kenilworth, Warwickshire', *Garden History*, 36 (2008), 94–113.

Wootton, David, 'Francis Bacon: Your Flexible Friend', in J. H. Elliott and W. B. Brockliss (eds), *The World of the Favourite* (London and New Haven, 1999), 184–204.

Wright, Pam, 'A Change in Direction: The Ramifications of a Female Household, 1558–1603', in David Starkey (ed.), *The English Court: From the Wars of the Roses to the Civil War* (Harlow, 1987), 147–72.

Young, Alan, *Tudor and Jacobean Tournaments* (London, 1987).

Zeitlin, Jacob, 'Commonplaces in Elizabethan Life and Letters', *Journal of English and German Philology*, 19 (1920), 47–65.

Zim, Rifka, 'Dialogue and Discretion: Thomas Sackville, Catherine de Medici and the Anjou Marriage Proposal 1571', *Historical Journal*, 40 (1997), 287–310.

UNPUBLISHED THESES

Bryson, Alan, '"The speciall men in every sphere": The Edwardian Regime, 1547–1553', Ph.D., University of St Andrew's (2001).

Buchanan, Catherine, 'The Massacre of St Bartholomew's (24–27 August 1572) and the Sack of Antwerp (4–7 November 1576): Print and Political Responses in Elizabethan England', Ph.D., London School of Economics (2011).

Bundesen, Kristin, '"No other faction but my own": Dynastic Politics and Elizabeth I's Carey Cousins', Ph.D., University of Nottingham (2008).

Campbell, James Stuart, 'The Alchemical Patronage of Sir William Cecil, Lord Burghley', MA, Victoria University of Wellington (2009).

Courtney, Alexander, 'The Accession of James VI to the English Throne, 1601–1603', M. Phil., University of Cambridge (2004).

Husselby, Jillian, 'Architecture at Burghley House: The Patronage of William Cecil, 1553–1598', Ph.D., University of Warwick (1996).

Howey, Catherine Louise, 'Busy Bodies: Women, Power and Politics at the Court of Elizabeth I, 1558–1603', Ph.D., University of Rutgers (2007).

Leimon, Mitchell MacDonald, 'Sir Francis Walsingham and the Anjou Marriage Plan, 1574–1581', Ph.D., University of Cambridge (1989).

Mears, Natalie, 'The "Personal Rule' of Elizabeth I: Marriage, Succession and Catholic Conspiracy c.1578–1582', Ph.D., St Andrews (2000).

Merton, Charlotte Isabelle, 'The Women who Served Queen Mary and Queen Elizabeth: Ladies, Gentlewomen and Maids of the Privy Chamber, 1553–1603', Ph.D., University of Cambridge (1992).

Partridge, Mary, 'Images of the Courtier in Elizabethan England', Ph.D., University of Birmingham (2008).

Richardson, William, 'The Religious Policies of the Cecils, 1588–1598', D.Phil., University of Oxford (1993).

Taviner, Mark, 'Robert Beale and the Elizabethan Polity', Ph.D., University of St Andrews (2000).

Trim, David, 'Fighting "Jacob's warres": English and Welsh Mercenaries in the European Wars of Religion: France and the Netherlands', Ph.D., University of London (2002).

PICTURE ACKNOWLEDGEMENTS

INDEX

accession day 42
  tilts 167, 176
  see also tournaments
Adams, Simon 330 n. 89, 340 n. 10,
  350 n. 64
Albert, archduke of Austria (later
  archduke of the Netherlands)
  xvii, 290, 292
Alford, Stephen 337 n. 61, 347 n. 107
Allen, William, Cardinal 24
Alva, duke of, Fernando Álvarez de
  Toledo xv, 251
ambassadors 4, 14, 90, 95, 120, 151,
  176, 194, 213, 290,
  Austrian 120, 128
  English 46, 65, 70, 73, 80, 99, 106,
    113, 121, 124, 221, 222, 250–1,
    256, 260, 269, 270, 281, 345 n. 26
  French 33, 85, 159, 260, 269, 272,
    351 n. 81
  imperial 28, 31, 33
  Polish 284
  Scottish 63, 71, 90, 282, 296–7
  Spanish 50, 57, 74, 86, 120, 121,
    122, 124, 125, 127, 128, 129,
    157, 158, 159, 204, 205, 266,
    272, 351 n. 88
  Venetian 17, 38, 39, 45, 302
Anjou, Francis, duke of, previously
  duke of Alençon 277, 325 n. 40
  match xvi, 135, 136, 138, 158, 159,
    203, 264–5, 266, 267, 268, 269
  and Netherlands 261, 263, 264,
    265, 270
Anne Boleyn, queen of England xiii,
  2, 13, 14, 15, 18, 19–24, 25, 27,
  29, 31, 104, 19
Anne of Cleves 15, 122
Antwerp xvi, 138, 147, 151, 159,
  224, 260, 263, 278
  sack of 156, 261
Apologie of the Earl of Essex 184,
  188, 338 n. 103

armada, *see* Spain
Asheby, William 106
Ascham, Roger 144, 230
Ashridge, Hertfordshire 17, 33, 195
Astley, John 20, 195–6
Astley, Katherine (Kat), *née*
  Champernowne 20, 249
  before Elizabeth's accession 15, 25,
    38, 195–6, 220
  after Elizabeth's accession 195–6,
    201, 202, 215
astrology 59, 230
Aylmer, John, later bishop of
  London 22, 152, 153–4, 163
Azores 182, 183, 284, 304

Bacon, Sir Francis 181, 182, 190,
  304–5, 353 n. 18, 354 n. 61
Bacon, Sir Nicholas 55, 221,
  244, 305
Bancroft, Dr Richard, later bishop of
  London 182, 333 n. 65
Barn Elms 258
Barrow, Henry 234
Beale, Edith 203
Beale, Robert 54, 84, 85, 202, 248
Bedingfield, Sir Henry 35, 36
Bellemain, Jean 313 n. 23
Bentham, Thomas, bishop of
  Coventry and Lichfield 122, 202
Bercher, William 20
Berkshire 122
Berwick–on–Tweed 20, 72, 99, 236;
  see also treaty of Berwick
bishops 8, 82, 152, 231, 232, 233,
  234, 248
  episcopacy 98, 107, 232
Blackfriars 209
Blount, Sir Charles, later Lord
  Mountjoy 212
  courtier 167
  lord deputy in Ireland 291–2, 295,
    296, 355 n. 71, 356 n. 96

381

Blount, Sir Christopher 187
Blount, Thomas 122, 124
Boleyn, Anne, *see* Anne Boleyn, queen
    of England
Boleyn, Mary 2, 20, 196–7
Bolton Castle, Yorkshire 77, 206
bond of association xvi, 86–7, 88,
    101, 241, 272, 325 n. 94,
    325 n. 48, 330 n. 99
Boulogne, peace talks at xvii,
    188, 292
Bourbourg, peace talks at xvii, 278
Bowes, Robert 281
Brandon, Charles, duke of
    Suffolk 43, 122
Brittany 281, 282, 286
Brooke, Elizabeth, *see* Cecil,
    Elizabeth
Brooke, Frances *née* Newton, Lady
    Cobham 201, 204, 206, 233,
    341 n. 46
Brooke, Henry, eleventh Lord
    Cobham 154, 180, 182, 189,
    290, 295
Brooke, William, tenth Lord
    Cobham 180, 182, 201, 206,
    263, 264, 265, 278, 279
Broadbelt, Dorothy, later Abingdon
    195, 201, 202, 205–6, 208
Brussels 121, 151, 261, 283
Bryan, Lady Margaret 15, 25
Brydges, Eleanor 207, 212
Buchanan, George 91
Burchet, Peter 148–9
Butler, Thomas, tenth earl of Ormond
    129–30, 145, 147, 287
Buxton, Derbyshire 134, 141, 226

Cadiz expedition xi, xvii, 178–9,
    180, 181, 183, 231, 282
Calais xvii, 126, 177, 178, 237
Calvin, John 18, 313 n. 23
    Calvinist 91, 155, 240, 261, 262
Cambridge, University of 20, 117,
    130, 155, 166, 219, 222,
    276, 288
Camden, William 28, 118, 135–6,
    143, 184, 245, 305–6, 307, 308,
    330 n. 99
Carew, Sir Gawain 197

Carew, Sir George 282, 288, 292,
    295, 296, 338 n. 105
Carey, Anne, Lady Hunsdon 2, 198
Carey, Henry, Lord Hunsdon 2, 8,
    20, 96, 99, 100, 130, 195, 249,
    265, 325 n. 44
Carey, Katherine, *see* Howard,
    Katherine, Lady Howard of
    Effingham
Carey, Katherine, later Lady
    Knollys 2, 196–7, 213, 215
Carey, Mary, *see* Boleyn, Mary
Carey, Philadelphia, later Lady
    Scrope 206
Carey, Robert 2, 301
Carlisle, Westmorland 77
Carre, Bridget 204
Cartwright, Thomas 183, 233
Castiglione, Baldassare 143
Catherine de' Médici 251, 253
Catholics 82, 85, 233
    In England 22, 23, 61, 62, 64, 65,
        67, 69, 78, 79, 153–4, 163, 234,
        238, 240
    exiles 24, 62, 117, 212, 244,
        348 n. 123
    international Catholic league xvi,
        65, 73, 86, 95, 101, 102, 159,
        171, 262, 272
    priests xvi, 62, 154, 225, 232, 234,
        241, 267, 270
    proclamation against (1591) xvii,
        234, 245
    propagandists 3, 111, 117, 148,
        149, 244–5, 247, 279
    Scottish 98, 101, 103–4, 107–9,
        110, 266
    see also Jesuits
Cecil, Anne, *see* Vere, de, Anne,
    countess of Oxford
Cecil, Elizabeth *née* Brooke (wife of
    Sir Robert Cecil) 278–9, 283
Cecil, Mildred, *née* Cooke 219, 229,
    276, 278
Cecil, Sir Robert 176, 203, 208,
    356 n. 93
    abilities and workload 276, 278,
        280, 283, 289, 300, 302
    diplomatic assignments 178,
        285–6

early life 276–8
and Essex 178, 180, 182, 189, 192,
   278, 279, 282, 283, 284, 285,
   286, 287, 290, 291, 292, 293–4,
   297, 343 n. 103
family matters 278–9, 283
finances 288, 296, 297, 354 n. 51,
   356 n. 106
foreign policy 184, 286–7,
   292–3, 297
health and disability 229, 276,
   278, 289, 290–1, 352 n. 1
intelligence gathering 176, 283
intimacy with the queen 277–8,
   279, 280, 282, 288, 299,
   300–1, 302
and Ireland 289, 292, 295–6
lands and offices 182, 186, 282,
   284, 288, 289, 302
libels against 290–1, 295, 302
and parliament 277, 280–1,
   284–5, 298
privy councillor 162, 174,
   229, 279
relationship with father 243,
   276, 277–8, 279, 281, 273,
   282, 288
reputation and image 9, 244–6,
   307
secretary 6, 179, 282, 283, 295–6,
   302
secretaryship 162, 177, 180,
   228–30, 279
and succession 111, 112, 294,
   296–8, 301–2
Cecil, Thomas, later Lord Burghley 2,
   186, 227, 276, 288
Cecil, Sir William, Lord Burghley 7,
   48, 49, 50, 52, 54, 58, 59, 67, 72,
   82, 120, 148, 210
early relationship with
   Elizabeth 220
Edwardian career 219–20
character and interests 225, 226,
   227, 230
Elizabeth's dependence upon 222,
   224–5, 279
disagreements with the queen 77,
   160, 204, 222, 225, 230, 231–40,
   241–2, 243, 345 n. 26

and Essex 166, 171, 184–5, 244,
   282, 284
foreign policy and war strategy 68,
   75, 80, 157, 175, 182, 184–5,
   230, 231, 235–7, 254, 256, 260,
   263, 284, 286–7
houses 226, 227, 228, 276, 281,
   288 see also Theobalds
ill health 175, 224, 226, 229, 243,
   279, 281
image 227, 229
intelligence gathering 176, 250–1,
   270, 272
intimacy with the queen 141, 209,
   242, 243, 302
lord treasurer 222–3, 280
and Mary Queen of Scots 68, 69,
   73, 75, 77, 79, 80–1, 83, 88,
   160, 234–6, 237–8, 239–40,
   241, 242, 277
master of court of wards 223–4
political creed 243
political dominance 171, 180, 222,
   224, 229, 244–6, 284
principal secretary 6, 219, 220–2,
   250, 252, 347 n. 88
propaganda writings 225, 277
regnum Cecilianum 245, 279, 291
relationship with Robert Dudley
   121, 122, 123, 124, 126, 130,
   136, 244, 345 n. 39
religion 220, 230, 231–4, 249
reputation 164, 306, 307, 308
and sons 175, 182, 224, 226–7,
   228–9, 243, 244, 276, 277, 278,
   281, 282, 290
and succession 55, 56, 69, 73, 101,
   111, 235, 238–9
Challoner, Thomas 121
Champernowne, Katherine,
   see Astley, Katherine
Champigny, see Perrenot, Frédéric,
   baron de Champigny
Charles, archduke of Austria
   xv, 73, 120, 127, 128, 130,
   204–5
Charles V, emperor 13, 15, 37
Charles IX, king of France 82, 90,
   128, 251, 253, 255
Chartley Castle 87, 166

chivalry 5, 166–9, 173 *see also* order
    of the garter
chronicles 23, 42
Church of England 30
    under Elizabeth xv, 62, 81, 107,
        141, 146, 152, 154–5, 162, 232,
        233, 234, 266, 303
Churchyard, Thomas 42, 179,
    319 n. 67
Cicero 214, 215, 230, 331 n. 6,
    343 n. 116
Clapham, John 308
Clifford, Eleanor, *née* Brandon xiii,
    44, 45
Clifford, Henry, second earl of
    Cumberland 44, 46
Clifford, Margaret, *see* Stanley,
    Margaret
Clinton, Edward Fiennes de, Lord
    Clinton and Saye, lord admiral,
    later earl of Lincoln 156, 198
Clinton, Elizabeth Fiennes de, *née*
    Fitzgerald, later countess of
    Lincoln 49, 198, 204
Condé, Louis, prince of 68
Cooke, Anthony 219
Cooman, Jerome 290
court
    courtiers 2, 3, 4, 5, 6, 8–9, 14, 119,
        121, 124, 143, 144, 146, 160,
        161, 164, 193, 205, 213, 300,
        305, 307, 308, 310 n. 24
    courtly love 5–6, 9, 148, 160, 185,
        191, 205, 280, 300
    culture and ethos 5, 8, 9, 23, 131,
        142, 143, 307
    functions 3–5, 9
    offices 6, 19, 20, 56, 119, 129,
        140, 144–5, 153, 157, 332 n. 24
    presence chamber 2, 4, 28, 83
        (Mary's), 277, 332 n. 24
    rivalries 5, 6, 117, 128, 129, 145,
        148, 160, 162, 167–9, 170,
        284, 295
    royal household 3, 14, 15, 16, 18,
        25, 28, 62, 223
    see also favourites; privy chamber
Courtenay, Edward, earl of Devon
Cranmer, Thomas, archbishop of
    Canterbury 14

Crichton, William SJ 98, 272
customs 223

Darcy, Sir Francis 211
Davies, Sir John 299
Davison, William 248
    diplomat 263
    secretary 88, 160, 270, 273
    dismissal 8, 242, 279
Dee, John 230, 234, 334 n. 88
Devereux, Dorothy 169
Devereux, Penelope later Lady
    Rich 167, 188, 212
Devereux, Robert, second earl of
    Essex 3, 162
    character and moods 162, 171,
        173, 175, 178, 181, 183–4,
        186, 190
    correspondence with the queen
        172, 174, 178. 182, 183, 185,
        186, 187, 191
    as a courtier 167, 168–9, 170, 171,
        176, 181
    disgrace 188–9
    early life 165–7
    enemies and rivals 167–9, 174,
        180, 181, 182, 183–4, 186, 187,
        189, 191, 282, 290
    execution 8, 165, 189, 294
    finances 165, 166, 167, 170, 174,
        175, 179, 189, 190
    friends 167, 168, 171, 174, 180,
        181, 184, 186, 187, 188, 189,
        290, 295
    grants of lands and offices
        167, 169, 170, 181, 182,
        184, 191
    grievances 173, 174, 178, 179–80,
        181–2, 183–4, 185
    intelligence gathering 174, 175–6,
        283
    lineage 165
    military ambitions 166, 169, 170,
        171, 177
    patronage 175, 181
    poems by 167, 168, 176
    portraits 9, 168–9, 181
    privy councillor 174
    quarrels with Elizabeth 169, 170,
        171, 185–6

relationship with King James 111,
175, 293, 296
reputation 165, 171, 173, 174,
175, 186, 306, 307, 308
rising in 1601 xvii, 189–90, 293
royal favour towards 167, 169,
170, 176, 183, 186, 190–1, 285
self–promotion 176–7, 179, 180–1
sexual liaisons 171, 212
soldier and military commander
166, 171–3, 174, 177–9, 183,
186–7, 289
trial 181, 188, 189, 190, 293–4
war strategy and opposition to
peace 174, 175, 176, 177,
178–9, 180, 182, 184, 284,
287, 290
Devereux, Walter, Viscount Hereford,
first earl of Essex 129,
134–5, 165
Devon 7, 121, 168, 280
Digby, Everard 155
Doleman, Robert, see Persons,
Robert SJ
Don John of Austria xvi, 262,
263, 267
Dormer, Jane, later countess of
Feria 40
Douglas, Archibald, eighth earl of
Angus 95, 96, 97, 102
Douglas, James, fourth earl of
Morton (Scottish regent) xv, xvi,
84, 91, 92, 93, 95, 156, 259, 260,
266, 267
Douglas, Margaret, countess of
Lennox, see Stewart, Margaret
Douglas, William, tenth earl of
Angus 108
Drake, Sir Francis xvi, 157, 231, 334
drama, plays 4, 62, 142, 144, 176,
190, 249, 303 see also masques
dramatic companies 62, 119, 141,
190, 249
Drury, William 130
Dudley Ambrose, earl of Warwick 8,
119, 125, 126, 134, 136, 206, 208
Dudley, Amy née Robsart 118,
119–20, 121–24
Dudley, Anne née Russell, countess of
Warwick 202, 206, 208, 213

Dudley, Andrew 45
Dudley, Guildford 30, 44, 118, 127
Dudley, John, duke of
Northumberland 30, 44, 45,
117, 118, 125, 219, 307
Dudley, Robert, later earl of
Leicester 54, 78, 83, 101,
198, 201, 204, 241, 244, 248,
252, 277
abilities 119, 131, 133, 142
courtier 3, 9, 129
death 141, 161, 170, 199
early connections with
Elizabeth 118
foreign policy 126, 133, 135, 137,
140, 157, 255, 256, 263
grants to 119, 121, 125, 127,
137, 140
intimacy with queen 49, 58, 70,
71, 119–21, 124, 125, 126, 128,
129, 134, 136, 137, 138, 140,
141, 142, 145, 147, 329 n. 82,
330 n. 114
Leicester's Commonwealth 117,
135, 142, 307, 329 n. 72
lineage 117, 127, 131
marriages 118, 130–1, 134, 135,
136, 138, 139, 164, 199
military role in Netherlands xvi,
134, 138–40, 166, 168, 262
offices 119, 121, 125, 130, 137,
140, 141
political influence 49, 120, 125,
126, 128–9, 130, 135, 137, 138,
141–2, 233, 250, 257, 258
portraits 9, 133
possible marriage to the queen 49,
50, 72, 79, 121–2, 123, 124–5,
126–7, 130, 131–4
privy councillor 8, 126, 137
proposed marriage to Mary Queen
of Scots 53, 70, 71, 127
quarrels with the queen 129–30,
133–4, 136 , 139–40, 141, 146,
204, 225, 239, 328 n. 65
and queen's matrimonial
negotiations 128, 135, 158,
159, 265
reputation 117, 123, 130, 142,
306, 307, 308

Dudley, Robert, later earl of Leicester
(*cont.*)
  sexual liaisons 130–1, 134–5
  sons 130, 137, 166, 208, 329 n. 74,
    339 n. 110
  and stepson 166, 167, 169
  unpopularity 117–18, 121, 128,
    129, 142
  see also Dudley, Amy, and
    Kenilworth
Dyer, Edward 144, 147, 279

Edinburgh xvi, 67, 99, 108, 222
  see also treaty of Edinburgh
Edmondes, Lady Dorothy 203
Edward III, king of England 199,
  293, 309 n. 5
Edward VI, king of England
  as prince 15, 17, 25, 26, 43
  as king 26–30, 31, 41, 42, 44, 119
  will and death 29–30, 69
Egerton, Thomas, lord keeper 185,
  188, 294, 338 n. 108
Elizabeth I, queen of England
  birth and early life, 13, 14–17, 24,
    25–40, 44, 118, 195, 196, 197,
    198, 220
  accession and coronation xv, 2,
    17, 19, 22, 39, 42, 65, 196,
    220, 230
  character and temperament 5, 16,
    27, 40, 46, 124, 134–5, 142, 258,
    273, 274, 299, 301, 304, 305
  clemency 54, 59, 61, 104, 189, 191
  criticisms of 52, 111, 121, 169,
    185, 240, 258–9, 261, 264, 267,
    269–70, 280
  death xvii, 63, 298, 301, 303,
    356 n. 99
  foreign policy 39, 66, 68, 91, 92–3,
    96–7, 98, 99, 109, 112, 126, 134,
    135, 137, 139, 140, 151, 152,
    153, 157, 172, 177, 178, 230,
    231, 235–6, 250–1, 252, 256,
    257, 258–60, 261, 262. 263,
    268, 269, 287
  gender 6, 42, 89, 121, 129, 141,
    147, 185, 191, 193, 304, 305
  illnesses xv, 63, 69, 125, 134, 198
  interests 193, 194, 196, 230

marriage proposals and
  negotiations xv, xvi, 14, 15–16,
  37, 39, 49, 73, 120, 121–2, 123,
  124–5, 126–8, 129, 130, 131–3,
  135, 137, 153, 158–9, 201, 203,
  204–5, 235, 252–4, 264, 265–7,
  268–9
moods and anger 6, 18, 49, 50, 55,
  56, 58, 71, 76, 79, 88, 104, 107,
  109, 126, 129, 136, 139–40,
  141, 147, 149, 160, 170, 171,
  172, 180, 181, 185, 187, 188,
  201, 207, 209, 210, 211–12,
  213–14, 239, 242, 260, 261,
  273, 279, 282, 298, 330 n. 105
poems and verses by 42, 82, 168,
  322 n. 81, 336 n. 17
portraits 28, 67, 132, 159–60, 300
progresses 4, 42, 48, 49–50, 52,
  130, 131–2, 135, 137, 145, 153,
  195, 201, 208, 210, 227–8, 299
religion 18–19, 26, 28, 29, 30–1,
  32, 36, 37, 38, 39, 40, 41, 63,
  107, 149, 152, 153, 164, 196,
  231, 232, 234, 254–5
reputation 1, 24, 27, 65, 88, 89,
  121, 122, 123, 145, 195, 212,
  303, 306, 307, 308
self-presentation 1–2, 22, 28,
  41, 212
sexual jealousy 131, 193, 207–8,
  211–12
speeches 9, 141, 277, 284, 298,
  299, 356–7 n. 111
translations by 17–19, 26–7, 29
views on succession question
  40–1, 47, 52–3, 55, 56, 63, 68,
  69, 70, 72, 74–5, 81, 82, 103,
  105, 106, 112, 234–5, 238,
  293, 301
virginity 3, 53, 90, 120, 121, 142,
  159–60, 212, 299, 300, 305
wit 134, 273, 304–5
Eltham Palace 14, 48, 145, 151,
  332 n. 40
Ely House 150, 154, 156, 161, 162
Emmanuel Philibert, prince of
  Piedmont and duke of Savoy 39
Erasmus 17
Eric XIV, king of Sweden 49, 120

Erskine, John, second earl of Mar 95, 96, 97, 102
Essex 121
Essex, earls of, *see* Devereux, Robert and Walter
Eton school 126

faction
   in England 14, 124, 170, 180, 182, 185, 188, 189, 285–6, 287, 290, 307
   in Scotland 74, 93, 94, 104, 109, 110, 268, 326 n. 78
Falmouth 183
Farnese, Alexander, prince, later duke of Parma 267, 278
Faunt, Nicholas 248
favourites 3, 5, 71, 121, 143, 144, 145, 146, 202, 207, 209, 304, 308
Ferdinand I, Holy Roman Emperor 120, 127, 205
Feria, Gómez Suárez de Figueroa y Córdoba, fifth count of Feria 40, 46, 120, 219, 313 n. 26
Ferrol, Spain 182, 183, 284
Fitton, Mary 211, 343 n. 104
FitzAlan, Henry, twelfth earl of Arundel 78, 120, 203
Fitzgerald, James fitz Gerald 292, 355 n. 74
Fleet Prison 7, 55, 56, 58, 196, 211
Fotheringhay Castle 88, 160, 242, 273
Foxe, John 22, 23, 42
France, the French 37, 49, 50, 51, 65, 66, 67, 78, 95, 123
   civil wars xv, 68, 75, 107, 125, 240, 251
   England's wars in xv, xvii, 16, 17, 68, 125, 126, 171–4
   English alliance with xv, xvi, 82, 92, 135, 158, 159, 268, 269
   St Bartholomew's Day massacre xv, 257
   Rouen campaign (1591) xvii, 171–3, 304, 337 n. 52
   see also the individual kings of France; Scotland: 'auld alliance'
Francis I, king of France

Francis II, dauphin and afterwards king of France xv, 37, 66,
Fulwell, Ulpan 23

Gascoigne, George 132, 329 n. 78
Gazzard, Hugh 338 n. 103
German Lutherans 255, 257, 262
Gifford, Gilbert 87
gifts 45, 215, 220
   New Year's gifts 25, 26–7, 29, 41, 46, 59, 125, 132, 135, 146–7, 167, 174, 196, 197–8, 205, 258, 278, 317 n. 11, 319 n. 85, 334 n. 92
   from Elizabeth to her father and stepmother 17–19, 25
   to courtiers 6, 160, 201, 203, 205, 209, 257, 285
   to Elizabeth 15, 25, 32, 38, 40, 160, 196, 199, 204, 205, 299, 300, 301
   to foreign rulers 68, 89, 90, 102, 110, 113
Glamis, master of, *see* Lyon, Sir Thomas, of Auldbar, master of Glamis
Goldring, Elizabeth 329 n. 80
Gordon, George, sixth earl of Huntly 103–4, 108, 109, 110
Gorges, Sir Thomas 209–10
Gray, Patrick, master of 100, 101, 104
Greenwich Palace 14, 51, 144, 170, 209
Greenwood, John 234
Gresham, Sir Thomas 58
Grey, Frances *née* Brandon, duchess of Suffolk xiii, 31, 44–5, 47, 48, 51, 59
Grey, Henry, marquess of Dorset later duke of Suffolk 44
Grey, Lady Jane, later Dudley xiii, 30, 31, 34, 44, 45, 63, 69, 118, 127, 219
Grey, Lady Katherine xiii, 8, 44, 45, 46–52, 53–4, 55, 56–7, 58, 61, 63, 70, 238, 319 n. 67
Grey, Lady Mary, later Keyes xiii, 44, 45, 48, 56, 57–8, 58–9, 63
Grey, Lord John 52, 53, 54, 55, 56

Grindal, Edmund, bishop of London afterwards archbishop of Canterbury xvi, 51, 152, 153, 232–3, 333 n. 53, 346 n. 69
Guise family 73, 77, 92, 95, 96, 99, 240, 241
  Charles, cardinal of Lorraine 66
  Francis, duke of Guise 66, 68
  Henry, duke of Guise 86, 272
  Mary of Guise xiii, 66, 235

Hacket, William 234
Hales, John 54–5
Hamilton, James, second earl of Arran 16
Hammer, Paul 335 n. 2, 339 n. 129
Hampton Court 4, 15, 17, 37
  see also treaty of
Hanworth, Middlesex 26, 47
Hardwick Hall, Derbyshire 61, 112
Harington, John 205
Harington, John 249, 340 n. 23
Hastings, Henry, third earl of Huntingdon 166, 170, 199, 341 n. 33
Hastings, Katherine, née Dudley, countess of Huntingdon 199–200, 202, 203, 215
Hatfield, Hertfordshire 29, 30, 38, 39, 118, 195, 196, 197, 219, 220, 225, 340 n. 23
  see also Ashridge, Hertfordshire
Hatton, Sir Christopher 2, 3, 9, 60–1, 137, 171, 173
  abilities and character 143, 145, 153, 161, 162, 163–4, 280
  chancellor of University of Oxford 161
  dancer 143, 144
  descent 143, 150, 331 n. 3
  early life 143–4
  finances 147, 149, 150, 159, 163, 332 n. 39
  foreign policy 151, 152, 155–9, 263
  gentleman pensioner 144–5, 147, 331 n. 12
  grants of land and office 145, 146, 147, 149, 150, 153, 161
  health 147, 162–3
  intimacy with the queen 145–6, 147, 148, 149, 151–2, 153, 156, 159, 160–1, 162–4
  lord chancellor 161–2, 167, 229, 310 n. 24
  in parliament 144, 146, 150, 154, 155, 162, 280, 331 n. 6
  patronage 144, 150, 153, 155, 159, 160, 334 n. 88
  privy councillor 150, 153
  relationships with other councillors 144, 153, 156, 157, 158, 160, 162
  religion 148, 149, 152, 153–5, 164, 234, 332 n. 35
  reputation 143, 148, 150, 153, 306, 307, 308
Hay, Francis, ninth earl of Erroll 108
Hayward, John 355 n. 84
Heneage, Lady Anne 206
Heneage, Sir Thomas 3, 129, 145, 150, 205, 206
Henry II, king of France 65
Henry III, king of France (previously duke of Anjou) xvi, xvii, 92, 96, 97, 99, 138, 139, 151, 159, 252, 253, 254, 265, 268, 269
Henry IV, king of England 190, 293–4
Henry IV, king of France xvii, 171, 172, 173, 174, 177, 285, 286, 337 n. 68
Henry VII, king of England xiii, 48
Henry VIII, king of England 2, 7, 13, 14, 15, 16, 17, 19, 22, 23, 24, 25, 27, 29, 31, 36, 43, 44, 64, 72, 104, 185, 196
  will 16, 26, 43, 44, 54–5, 75, 317 n. 1
Hepburn, James, fourth earl of Bothwell 75, 76, 78, 79
Herbert, Henry, second earl of Pembroke 44, 287
Herbert, Sir John 289
Herbert, William, first earl of Pembroke 44, 78, 130, 239
Herbert, William, third earl of Pembroke 211
Hesketh, Richard 62, 63
High Commission, court of 233

Hoby, Sir Edward 283
Holdenby, Northamptonshire 145,
    150, 332 n. 40
Holland, *see* Netherlands
Holt, William SJ 98
Hopton, Owen 57
Howard, Charles, Lord Howard of
    Effingham, later earl of
    Nottingham 215, 290, 298,
    356 n. 94
  and earl of Essex 180, 183–4, 185,
    187, 189, 294, 284
  lord admiral 178, 179, 283, 284
  privy councillor 295, 297, 302
Howard, Frances, later countess of
    Hertford 58, 130, 208, 214
Howard, Frances, dowager countess
    of Kildare later Baroness
    Cobham 295
Howard, Lady Mary 213
Howard, Lord Henry 207,
    354 n. 61
Howard, Katherine, *née* Carey, Lady
    Howard of Effingham, later
    countess of Nottingham xi, 195,
    200, 205, 215, 340 n. 10, 344
    n. 120, 356 n. 94
Howard, Thomas, fourth duke of
    Norfolk 121, 129, 130, 239, 311
    n. 5, 327 n. 27, 332 n. 22
  execution 8, 82, 146, 240
  plans to marry Mary Queen of
    Scots 79, 81, 146, 163, 201,
    226, 251
  and Scotland 236
Howard, William, Lord Howard of
    Effingham 19, 33, 56, 130
Hunsdon, Henry, Lord, *see* Carey,
    Henry, Lord Hunsdon

Inns of Court 144
  Gray's Inn 219, 276
  Inner Temple 143–4
Ireland 7, 65, 66, 134, 165, 206, 214,
    281, 289, 296
  lord deputies and lieutenants 19,
    185, 186–7, 198, 221, 287
  rebels in xv, xvi, xvii, 67, 109, 111,
    177, 186, 187, 253, 267, 291–2,
    295–6

Spanish and papal troops in
    xvii, 156, 178, 266, 267, 287,
    293, 297
Isabella Clara Eugenia, infanta of
    Castile (later archduchess
    of the Netherlands) xvii, 111,
    187, 189, 290, 293, 294,
    296, 297
'Islands' voyage xvii, 182–3, 284,
    285, 287

James IV, king of Scotland 2
James VI, king of Scotland and I of
    England 21
  accession and rule in England 90,
    301–2, 303, 304, 357 n. 123
  birth, baptism, and coronation in
    Scotland 74, 76, 90–1
  heir to English throne 57, 61, 63,
    91, 100, 101, 102, 103, 104,
    105, 106, 111–12, 240, 241,
    296–8, 301
  marriage 102, 267
  minority 78, 80, 81, 83, 91,
    92, 95
  pension 95, 99, 102, 103, 106,
    108, 110–11, 113, 270, 297
  relationships with English
    councillors and courtiers 111,
    112, 175, 188–9
  relationship with mother 81, 83,
    86, 87, 93, 94, 99, 101, 104–5,
    111, 242, 270
  rule in Scotland 84, 85, 86,
    91–113, 270
  security threat to England 92, 93,
    95, 98, 108, 109, 137, 241, 267,
    270–1
  religion 91, 98, 107, 110
  writings 101, 103
Jesuits xv, 63, 98, 101, 104, 107,
    108, 111, 154, 225, 232, 233,
    234, 241, 267, 270, 272, 289
John of Gaunt 293, 314 n. 44

Kapur, Shekhar 247
Katherine of Aragon, queen of
    England xiii, 13, 14, 31, 89, 122
Katherine Howard, queen of
    England 15

Katherine Parr, queen of England 15, 16, 17, 18, 19, 25, 26, 27, 44, 197
Katz, David S. 337 n. 61
Kenilworth, Warwickshire 58, 127, 130, 131, 132
  entertainments 131–2, 133–4, 198, 228
Kewes, Paulina 325 n. 48
Keyes, Thomas xiii, 56, 58, 318 n. 60
Killigrew, Henry 250, 256, 260, 279, 345 n. 26, 349 n. 15
Knollys, Elizabeth, later Lady Leighton 195, 201, 206
Knollys, Lady Katherine, *see* Carey, Katherine
Knollys, Sir Francis 2, 8, 77, 135, 147, 170, 171, 197, 213, 248, 332 n. 24
Knollys, Sir William 135, 185, 287, 294, 297
Knollys, Lettice, later countess of Essex and countess of Leicester 2, 129, 130, 134, 135, 136, 139, 141, 165, 166, 169, 184, 195
Knox, John 235
Knyvet, Sir Thomas 212

Langham, Robert 329 n. 77
Latimer, William 20–1
law 60, 152, 153, 161, 248, 254, 271, 286
  canon 52
  civil 76, 278
  common 7, 16, 43, 54, 55, 144, 233, 276
  equity 161–2
  martial 149
  see also statute
Lee, Sir Henry 210, 343 n. 97
Leighton, Lady, *see* Knollys, Elizabeth
Leighton, Sir Thomas 172, 173, 206
Leslie, John, bishop of Ross 78, 79, 80, 81, 82, 251
libels 24, 158, 188, 245, 290–1, 302, 307
Lincolnshire 220, 222

Lindsay, David, eleventh earl of Crawford 108
Lochleven Castle 76, 77, 81, 89
London 22, 26, 29, 30, 33, 37, 38, 39, 53, 58, 59, 62, 68, 77, 78, 117, 118, 120, 121, 134, 180, 188, 189, 212, 226, 227, 228, 249, 260, 270, 299
Lopez, Dr Roderigo 175–6, 337 n. 61
Louis, prince of Nassau 255, 256
Lumley, John, Baron Lumley 78
Lyon, Sir Thomas, of Auldbar, master of Glamis 96, 97, 102

magic 46, 59, 64, 346 n. 58
Maitland, William, laird of Lethington 63, 67, 69, 238
Manners, Bridget 207, 208, 213
Manners, Elizabeth 208
Manners, John, fourth earl of Rutland 203, 207
Manners, Roger, fifth earl of Rutland 203
Margaret, queen of Scotland (elder sister of Henry VIII) xiii, 2, 43, 45, 61, 72, 122
Markham, Isabell 195, 205
Marprelate tracts xvii, 107, 234
Mary, duchess of Suffolk (younger sister of Henry VIII) xiii, 2, 43, 44, 48, 122
Mary I, queen of England xiii
  as princess 13, 14, 15, 16, 25, 27, 28, 29
  as queen 19, 21, 22, 30–40, 41, 42, 44–5, 69, 198
  burnings 37, 41, 197
  will 40, 313 n. 36, 316 n. 118
Mary Stewart, queen of Scotland, aka Mary Queen of Scots xiii, 37, 40, 47, 49, 55, 56, 63, 149, 240
  claim to English throne 65, 66, 67, 68–9, 73, 80, 81, 88, 92, 237, 267
  ruling queen of Scotland xv, 66–8, 69, 70, 71, 73, 74, 90–1
  imprisonment and deposition xv, 57, 76, 77, 81, 91, 158
  captive in England xv, 47, 65, 77–89, 199, 207

'casket letters' 78, 226
health 31, 33, 84
marriages xv, 43, 53, 68, 70, 71,
  72–3, 74, 75, 76, 77, 79, 84, 127,
  146, 201–2, 226
negotiations for restoration xv, xvi,
  77, 78, 79, 80, 81, 83–6, 87, 93,
  97, 99, 101, 137
relationship with son 81, 83, 85,
  87, 89, 98
reputation 78, 80, 81, 111,
  225–6, 306
trial and execution xvii, 8, 62,
  82–3, 88, 104–5, 146, 160, 242,
  272, 273, 277, 347 n. 108
tomb 21, 89
see also plots; Scotland; succession;
  and York tribunal
masques and shows 4, 5, 9, 45,
  131–2, 133, 176–7, 201, 209,
  228–9, 299–300
mass 14, 28, 29, 30, 31, 32, 36, 68, 73,
  104, 128, 148, 230, 254, 332 n. 35
Maxwell, John, seventh Lord
  Maxwell, earl of Morton 108
McLaren, Anne 328 n. 60
Mears, Natalie, 351 n. 83
Mendoza, Bernardino de 157, 158,
  159, 266, 272, 273, 351 n. 88
Melville, Sir James 71–2, 90
Metsys, Quentin 159
Michiel, Giovanni 38, 39, 45
Mildmay, Sir Walter 80, 81, 85,
  155, 162, 209, 233, 249, 250,
  332 n. 40
miniatures, see portraits
monopolies 189, 284–5, 298–9

Naunton, Sir Robert 129, 143,
  306–7, 308
Netherlands 37, 255–6, 260, 278
  revolt and rebels in xv, xvi, 75, 86,
    96, 133, 133, 135, 137, 151,
    153, 156, 241, 248, 255, 261–3,
    264, 267, 269, 272
  sovereignty of xvi, 133, 138, 139,
    151, 152, 354 n. 57
  'Spanish fury' in 156, 261
  states-general of 138, 139, 140,
    262, 265

war in xvii, 134, 138–9, 166, 169,
  140, 224, 255–6, 261, 265,
  273–4, 287–8, 293
see also United Provinces and
  treaty of Nonsuch
Newdigate, Francis 55
Noailles, Antoine de 32
Nonsuch Palace 137, 187, 282
  see also treaty of Nonsuch
Norris, Sir Henry 15
Norris, Sir Henry, later Baron Norris
  of Rycote 80, 251–2
Northern Rebellion xv, 79, 198, 199,
  239, 251
Northamptonshire 143, 146, 149,
  150, 226, 227, 345 n. 40
Norton, Thomas 7, 144, 163
Norwich. Elizabeth, later Lady
  Carew 197, 340 n. 23

O'Neill, Hugh, earl of Tyrone xvii,
  186, 187, 188, 289, 291, 295–6,
  297, 356 n. 99
O'Neill, Shane 221
Ochino, Bernardo 26
order of the garter 20, 113, 120, 161,
  169, 222, 302
order of St Michael 128–9
Oxford 122
  University of 143–4, 161, 174, 248
Oxfordshire 35, 123, 141, 161, 210

Paget, William, baron of Beaudesert
  19, 31, 32, 33, 313 n. 26
papacy and popes 13, 22, 37, 73, 82,
  86, 101, 156, 159, 251, 255
  bull of excommunication xv, 79
  see also Rome
Parker, Matthew, archbishop of
  Canterbury 20, 50, 51, 57,
  145, 153
parliament 9, 13, 14, 69, 72, 73, 82,
  111, 144, 162, 174–5, 184, 243,
  277, 298, 307, 331 n. 6
  1543–4 session 16
  Marian parliaments 30, 31, 32
  1559 session 21, 250
  1563 session xv, 55, 70, 238, 250
  1566 session xv, 55, 57, 74–5,
    231, 239

parliament (*cont.*)
  1572 session 146, 240
  1576 session 150–1
  1584–5 session xvi, 87, 102,
    154–5, 241
  1586 session 88, 155, 160
  1589 session 155
  1593 session 182, 280–1
  1597 session 284–5
  1601 session 298–9
  see also statutes
Parr, Elizabeth, marchioness of
  Northampton 49
Parr Helena *née* Snakenborg,
  marchioness of Northampton,
  later married to Sir Thomas
  Gorges 209–10
Parr, William, marquess of
  Northampton 208, 239
Parry, Blanche 196, 202, 204
Parry, Sir Thomas 220
patronage 2, 5, 20, 27, 62, 141, 142,
  144, 150, 153, 155, 160, 166,
  168, 170, 174, 175, 193, 202–3,
  204, 247–8, 249–50, 279, 284,
  334 n. 88
Paule, George 154
Paulet, Sir Amias 87, 88, 323 n. 103,
  352 n. 115
Paulet, William, second marquess of
  Winchester 34, 222, 347 n. 84
Penry, John 107, 234
Perrenot, Frédéric, baron de
  Champigny 151, 155, 329 n. 82,
  332 n. 40
Perrot, Sir John 143, 279
Perry, Maria 313 n. 22
Persons, Robert SJ (Robert Doleman)
  xvi, 111, 272, 294
  Philopater 245
Peterborough Cathedral 89
Petre, Sir William 51, 56, 347 n. 84
Phelippes, Thomas 87, 272
Philip, king of England and afterwards
  King Philip II of Spain xvii, 32,
  34, 37, 38, 39, 40, 45, 47, 50,
  73, 82, 86, 88, 92, 95, 101, 108,
  124, 125, 127, 137, 139, 156,
  234, 251, 255, 263, 354 n. 57
  see also Spain; Netherlands

Philip III, king of Spain xvii, 292,
  293, 296
Pickering, Sir William 120
plots and conspiracies 46, 50, 55, 61,
  62, 63, 65, 80, 85, 86, 89, 98,
  100, 102, 104, 108, 111, 175–6,
  226, 251, 259, 266, 270, 272
  under Queen Mary 32, 33, 34, 38,
    41, 46
  Babington xvii, 87–8, 104, 242,
    272, 306
  Parry xvi, 86, 242
  Ridolfi xv, 81–2, 83, 201, 239,
    250–1
  Spanish blanks xvii, 108–9
  Throckmorton xvi, 86, 100, 241,
    242, 270, 272
poems and verses 5, 6, 9, 18, 42, 62,
  82, 126, 167, 168, 197, 226,
  227, 249, 258, 290–1, 300–1,
  303, 319 n. 67, 322 n. 81, 336
  n. 17, 336 n. 18
Pole, Reginald, cardinal and
  archbishop of Canterbury 39
Pope, Sir Thomas 38
portraits xi, 5, 9, 21, 28, 67, 68, 71,
  74, 132–3, 159–60, 168–9, 181,
  258, 300, 301
Portugal xvii, 137, 156, 157, 241,
  268, 283
  1589 campaign xvii, 170–1
presbyterians
  English xvi, xvii, 107, 152,
    154–5, 162, 163, 164, 232,
    233–4, 248
  Scottish 97, 98, 107
privy chamber 4, 47, 48, 83 (Mary's),
  193–214
  access to 3, 5, 45, 145, 146, 147,
    153, 295, 306, 332 n. 24
  bedchamber 3, 4, 71, 187,
    194, 195
  chamberers 194, 195, 200,
    205, 206
  chief gentlewoman 193–4, 196
  'extraordinary' gentlewomen 130,
    206, 295
  gentlemen of the privy
    chamber 124, 129, 168, 193,
    209, 249

ladies or women of the
bedchamber 120, 193, 195–8,
201, 202, 206, 210
ladies of the privy chamber 5, 58
ladies or gentlewomen without
wage 119
maids of honour 45, 46, 48, 49,
194, 195, 200, 206, 207, 208,
209, 210, 211, 212, 213–14
marriages 205–10
mother of the maids 49, 211
political role of women 193, 201–5
sexual affairs 210–13
wages of staff, 193, 194, 339–40 n. 3
privy council 7, 243
clerks 7, 202, 204, 221, 344 n. 15
divisions in 236, 282
Elizabeth's council 6, 7, 8, 19, 20,
55, 59, 61, 69, 73, 78, 80, 82, 86,
88, 92, 99, 100, 106, 124, 135,
139, 150, 151, 152, 154, 159, 173,
174, 178–9, 182, 188, 191–2, 198,
221–2, 224, 233, 264, 267, 268,
272, 288, 289, 291, 301
Mary I's council 34, 36, 37, 38, 40
meetings 7–8, 158, 160, 184, 186,
189, 221, 225, 236, 242, 265,
266, 274, 287, 297
prophesyings xvi, 152, 164, 232,
346 n. 69
protestants 55, 57, 63, 69, 79, 155
abroad 77, 86, 248
clergy 49–50, 152
propagandists 22, 24, 41, 42
Puckering, Sir John 154
puritans 148, 152, 153, 154, 155,
164, 175, 232, 233, 234, 248–9
see also protestants;
presbyterians; separatists

Quadra, Alvaro de la, bishop of
Aquila 50, 120, 121, 122, 124,
125, 205, 327 n. 27

Radcliffe, Frances, later
Mildmay 208
Radcliffe, Frances, née Sidney,
countess of Sussex 202
Radcliffe, Henry, second earl of
Sussex 34

Radcliffe, Thomas, third earl of
Sussex 8, 19, 208, 221, 265,
351 n. 74
Rainolds, John 248
Ralegh, Sir Walter xi, 3, 160, 168,
169, 170, 171, 174, 180, 182,
189, 207, 208, 212, 213, 247,
280, 282, 283, 284, 290, 292,
295, 306, 308
Randolph, Thomas 70, 73, 250
Ratcliffe, Mary 203
Renard, Simon 31, 32, 33, 34
Richard II, king of England 190,
293, 294
Richmond Palace 35, 119, 162, 170,
210, 301
Riccio, David 74
Ridolfi, Roberto di 81, 251
Rishton, Edward 24
Rogers, Honora 60, 61
Rome
Roman Catholic Church 13,
22, 30, 73, 125, 291
see also papacy
Roman history 180, 186;
see also Tacitus
Russell, Anne, later Lady
Herbert 200, 201, 209
Russell, Elizabeth 200, 201
Russell, Elizabeth countess of
Bedford 201
Russell, Francis, second earl of
Bedford 74, 75, 102
Russell, Sir Francis 102
Ruthven raid xvi, 93–4, 95, 96, 97
Ruthven, William, fourth Lord
Ruthven and first earl of
Gowrie 93, 96, 97

Sackville, Sir Richard 19–20
Sackville, Thomas, Lord Buckhurst
154, 187, 189, 253, 279, 294,
295, 297
offices 20, 174, 186, 253, 288,
302, 356 n. 95
St Loe, Elizabeth, later countess of
Shrewsbury 49, 50, 195, 202
St Loe, William 195, 340 n. 11
Sander, Nicholas 24
Sandes, Elizabeth 35, 36

Scotland 16, 53, 78, 80, 81, 82, 84, 88, 105–6, 240
amity with England 67–8, 71, 75, 79, 97, 98, 101, 102–3, 252–7, 269
'auld alliance' with France 37, 66, 67, 73, 86, 91, 93, 99, 112, 235, 255
borders 67, 80, 99, 102, 105, 109, 260
civil war 80, 81, 91, 268
English campaign (1560) 66, 67, 198, 236–7
Kirk 67, 69, 98, 107, 110,
lords 66, 74, 75, 76, 77, 86, 91, 92, 93, 94, 95, 96, 97, 98, 99, 100, 101, 102, 108–9, 235, 236, 237, 267, 271
Scrope, Lord Henry 77
Scrope, Sir Thomas 206
Scudamore, Sir John 207, 209
Scudamore, Lady Mary née Shelton 200, 202, 203, 205, 207, 209
Seckford, Thomas 59, 60
secretary of state 6–7, 9
separatists 154, 155
sermons, preachers 26, 28, 42, 107, 152, 158, 179, 232
Seymour, Anne, duchess of Somerset 28, 47, 48, 53, 318 n. 46
Seymour, Edward, lord protector, duke of Somerset 27, 28, 51, 219, 220
Seymour, Edward, earl of Hertford xiii, 47–9, 50, 51, 52, 53, 54, 56, 57, 58, 60, 61, 112, 202, 208, 214
Seymour, Edward, Lord Beauchamp (son of Katherine Grey) xiii, 51, 53, 57, 60–1, 63, 70, 111, 112, 301, 317 n. 19
Seymour, Edward (son of Lord Beauchamp) 61
Seymour, Lady Jane (sister of the earl of Hertford) 47, 48, 51
Seymour, Thomas, Baron Sudeley 27, 28, 195
Seymour, Thomas (son of Katherine Grey) xiii, 52, 53, 57, 60, 61, 70, 112

Sheffield Castle 83, 84, 85
Sheffield, Lady Douglas, née Howard 130–1, 136, 330 n. 93
Shelton Mary, see Scudamore, Lady Mary
Sidney, Lady Barbara (wife of Robert) 203
Sidney, Lady Frances, see Walsingham, Frances
Sidney, Lady Mary, née Dudley, 119, 194, 198–9, 204–5
Sidney, Sir Henry 8, 198, 199
Sidney, Sir Philip 8, 140, 141, 166–7, 262, 272, 274
Sidney Sir Robert 181, 182, 202, 285
Silva, Diego Guzman de 127, 128, 129
Simier, Jean de xvi, 135–6, 158, 203, 265, 266, 267
Skidmore, Chris 328 n. 39
Skipworth, Brigit, later Cave 205
Smeaton, Mark 15
Smith, Sir Thomas (later secretary) 7, 55, 224, 256, 258
Somerset House and Place 30, 38, 118, 220
Southwell, Elizabeth 171, 212
Spain xvi, 7, 86, 92, 96, 151, 177, 178, 260
armada (1588) xvii, 106, 141, 169, 273
armada (1596) 183, 262, 263
plunder of Spanish shipping 157, 177, 178, 179, 180, 182, 280, 284, 297, 334 n. 79
talks of peace with xvii, 140, 176, 184–5, 187, 188, 231, 262, 273, 278, 285, 286–7, 289–90, 292, 293
war against 107, 110, 111, 182
see also Philip II; Philip III; plots; Netherlands
Spenser, Edmund 111, 141, 179, 244, 245
spies, spy network 86, 174, 176, 247, 270, 272, 283
Stafford, Dorothy, Lady 200, 202, 203, 204, 209
Stafford, Edward 276, 330 n. 93
Stanley, Edward, third earl of Derby 45

Stanley, Ferdinando, later fifth earl of
Derby xiii, 61–3
Stanley, Henry, Lord Strange, later
fourth earl of Derby xiii, 45, 46,
62, 278
Stanley, Margaret, *née* Clifford, Lady
Strange, later countess of
Derby xiii, 8, 44, 45–6, 59–60,
63–4, 317 n. 3, 317 n. 11, 319
n. 85, 319 n 86
Stanley, William, sixth earl of
Derby xiii, 63, 200, 209, 212
Stanley, William (renegade) 62,
320 n. 94
Star Chamber xvii, 7, 52, 155, 233,
292, 293
statute law 21, 29, 31, 54, 69, 70, 72,
73, 196, 234, 248, 316 n. 118
Act of Treason (1536) 14, 317 n. 21
Act of Succession (1544) 16, 17,
21, 29, 321 n. 43
Act of Recognition of the Queen's
Highness Title (1559) 21
Act for the Queen's Surety
(1585) xvi, 87, 101, 111, 137
Stewart, Francis, earl of
Bothwell 109, 110
Stewart, Henry, Lord Darnley xiii,
xv, 72, 73, 74, 75, 78, 80, 81, 83,
92, 127
Stewart, Prince Henry (son of
James VI) 110
Stewart, Captain James, later earl of
Arran xvi, 92, 93, 94, 95, 98, 99,
100, 102
Stewart, James, earl of Moray xv, 67,
74, 76, 78, 79, 80, 92
Stewart, Margaret, *née* Douglas,
countess of Lennox xiii, 31, 45,
72, 106, 321 n. 33, 326 n. 69
Stewart, Matthew, fourth earl of
Lennox 72, 74, 92, 321 n. 28
Stirling Castle 96, 97, 102
Stokes, Adrian 45, 47, 51, 58, 59
Strong, Roy 168
Stuart, Arbella xiii, 61, 111, 112,
301, 320 n. 92
Stuart, Esmé, the lord of Aubigny, earl
and later duke of Lennox 84, 92,
93, 94, 95, 267, 272

Stuart, Ludovick, second duke of
Lennox 95, 96
succession xv, 13, 16, 17, 19, 32, 37,
39–40, 43, 45, 46, 47, 50, 52–3,
54–5, 57, 59, 60, 61, 62, 63, 65,
66, 68–70, 72, 73, 74–5, 79, 81,
82, 84, 90, 91, 100, 103, 104,
105, 106, 125, 111–12, 137,
187, 190, 199, 235, 238–9, 240,
293, 294, 296
succession crisis (1553) 30, 41, 44,
53, 69, 118, 219
succession tracts 54–5, 57, 80
see also statutes

Tacitus 303, 304, 305, 307, 308
Talbot, Elizabeth, countess of, *see*
St Loe, Elizabeth
Talbot, George, sixth earl of
Shrewsbury 78, 141, 222, 226
Tamworth, John 249
taxation 307
subsidy 223, 239, 280, 284
see also customs
Theobalds, Hertfordshire 150, 177,
224, 226, 227, 228–9, 242,
243–4, 276, 281, 288, 305
Thomas, Valentine 111
Throcking, Hertfordshire 118
Throckmorton, Elizabeth, later Lady
Ralegh 207, 208
Throckmorton, Sir Nicholas 72, 76,
77, 123, 124, 250, 318 n. 46,
349 n. 14
Tilbury 141, 169
Tomson, Laurence 248
tournaments, jousts, and tilts 4, 45,
119, 130, 145, 167, 176, 195,
208, 210
Tower of London 7, 31, 34, 35, 36,
41, 50, 51, 53, 55, 59, 60, 79,
112, 118, 121, 136, 151, 195,
207, 210, 211, 219, 259, 292,
294, 315 n. 90
lieutenant of 50, 176
Travers, Walter 232, 346 n. 67
treason 7, 8, 27, 33, 37, 45, 48, 59,
64, 82, 87, 97, 104, 106, 108,
111, 117, 148, 175, 185, 187,
189, 259, 279, 294, 297

treaties of Nonsuch xvi, 138, 231
Treatise of Treasons 148, 244
treaty of Berwick
  (1560) xv, 237
  (1586) xvii, 103–4, 105, 106,
  109, 110
treaty of Blois xv, 256, 257, 269
treaty of Cateau–Cambrésis xv, 126
treaty of Edinburgh xv, 66, 67, 75,
  237, 238
treaty of Hampton Court xv, 126
treaty of Vervins xvii, 286
triple alliance (1596) xvii, 285
Tutbury Castle, Staffordshire 87
Tyrwhit, Robert 207

United Provinces 285, 286–7, 288,
  290, 292

Vavasour, Anne 210, 212, 343 n. 97
Vavasour, Frances 208, 342 n. 81
Vavasour, Thomas 171, 212
Vere de, Anne, *née* Cecil, countess of
  Oxford 147, 200, 227, 229, 278
Vere de, Edward, seventeenth earl of
  Oxford 147, 148, 210, 212,
  344 n. 21
Vere de, Elizabeth de, later countess
  of Derby 63, 200
Vernon, Elizabeth, later countess of
  Southampton 211
Verstegan, Richard
  *A Declaration of the True Causes
  of the Great Troubles* 244–5

wardship 166, 344 n. 21
  master of court of wards 186,
  223–4, 288, 289
Waldegrave, Robert 107
Walsingham, Frances, married to
  Philip Sidney and afterwards
  countess of Essex 8, 171,
  172, 173
Walsingham, Sir Francis 202,
  241, 247
  and Anjou match 265, 266,
  268, 269
  character and interests 249, 274
  diplomat 251–8, 263–5, 269,
  270–1

disagreements with queen 258–9,
  260–1, 262, 263, 264, 266, 267,
  268–70, 271, 273
  early life 249–50, 349 n. 15
  family 8, 249, 250
  finances 252, 257, 272–3
  foreign policy 96, 156–7, 158,
  255–6, 257, 261, 262, 264,
  267–8, 271, 273
  ill health and death 224, 256, 258,
  259, 274
  and Mary Queen of Scots 241,
  255, 257, 259, 270, 272, 273
  and queen's marriage 253–4
  nickname 258, 259, 269,
  350 n. 57
  and protestant league 248, 257,
  262, 266, 274
  relationships with privy
  councillors 138, 153, 156–7,
  158, 250, 252, 258, 259, 271,
  349 n. 15
  religion 233, 247–9, 253, 266
  reputation 247
  rewards 273, 274
  secretary 6, 7, 87, 258–61, 270,
  273, 274
  and security 87, 101, 167, 250–1,
  252, 259, 267, 268, 270, 272
  see also plots; spies
Wanstead, Essex 135, 170, 184
Warner, Sir Edward 50, 51
Warwick Castle and town 125
Wentworth, Peter 150, 248
Westminster 7, 31, 33, 48, 51
Westminster Abbey 21, 59, 89, 197,
  243, 283, 313 n. 36
Whitehall Palace 4, 17, 33, 39, 45,
  176, 208, 299
Whitgift, John, bishop of Worcester,
  later archbishop of Canterbury
  xvi, 8, 152, 154, 155, 161, 164,
  232, 233, 234, 248
  1583 articles xvi, 233, 248
Wilkes, Thomas
William of Orange xvi, 86, 138, 241,
  255, 259, 260, 261, 263, 264,
  267, 278
Wilson, Derek 328 no. 37
Wilson, Dr Thomas 261, 270

Windsor 121, 125, 126
Woodstock, Oxfordshire 35, 36, 37,
    41, 42, 118
Wotton, Sir Edward 102
Wriothesley, Henry, third earl of
    Southampton 167, 187, 189,
    211, 294, 344 n. 21
Wyatt, Sir Thomas 34
  rebellion (1554) 32–3, 34,
    41, 44

York 68, 166, 199
  archbishop of 8
  York House 188
  York tribunal 78
Young, Peter 91
Yoxford, Suffolk 57

Zeeland, *see* Netherlands
Zuccaro, Federigo 132
Zutphen, battle of xvii, 140, 166, 272